Essentials of Business Communication

Seventh Edition

Mary Ellen Guffey

Professor Emerita of Business
Los Angeles Pierce College

Richard Almonte

George Brown College

NELSON / EDUCATION

NELSON / EDUCATION

Essentials of Business Communication, **Seventh Canadian Edition**
by Mary Ellen Guffey and Richard Almonte

Vice President, Editorial Higher Education:
Anne Williams

Acquisitions Editor:
Anne-Marie Taylor

Marketing Manager:
Terry Fedorkiw

Developmental Editor:
Theresa Fitzgerald

Photo Researcher:
Carrie McGregor

Permissions Coordinator:
Carrie McGregor

Content Production Manager:
Claire Horsnell

Production Service:
MPS Limited, a Macmillan Company

Copy Editor:
Margaret Crammond

Proofreader:
Jennifer A. McIntyre

Indexer:
Sonya Dintaman

Senior Production Coordinator:
Ferial Suleman

Design Director:
Ken Phipps

Managing Designer:
Franca Amore

Interior Design:
Peter Papayanakis

Cover Design:
Johanna Liburd

Compositor:
MPS Limited, a Macmillan Company

Printer:
RR Donnelley

Library and Archives Canada Cataloguing in Publication

Guffey, Mary Ellen

Essentials of business communication / Mary Ellen Guffey, Richard Almonte. — 7th Canadian ed.

Includes bibliographical references and index.
ISBN 978-0-17-650357-4

1. Business writing—Textbooks. 2. English language—Business English—Textbooks. 3. Business communication—Textbooks. I. Almonte, Richard II. Title.

HF5718.3.G84 2012   808'.06665
C2011-904352-1

ISBN-13: 978-0-17-650357-4
ISBN-10: 0-17-650357-9

Essentials of Business Communication

Seventh Edition

From the emphasis on professionalism to new *Workplace in Focus* photo essays, Guffey has updated tools and created new ways to keep you interested and engaged. The following six pages describe features that will help students succeed in today's technologically enhanced workplace.

WORKPLACE IN FOCUS

With energy independence at the forefront of international concerns, many leaders have high expectations for Suncor Energy, a Canadian firm with a high-tech process for extracting oil from Alberta's bitumen-rich sands. The company recently rolled out "Oil Sands: The Next Generation," a communications blitz conveying Suncor's forward-looking vision, to more than 3,000 employees. The campaign included keynote speeches, newsletter inserts, off-site breakout meetings, and a *Star Trek* parody to motivate workers to double Suncor's oil sands production. Employee feedback surveys provided managers with a gauge of the campaign's effectiveness. *Why might organizations use multiple communication channels to transmit messages?*

conversation can be completed online without the time delay that can occur when sending and responding to e-mail.

A few years ago, *The Globe and Mail* reported that instant messaging would soon surpass e-mail as the primary way in which people interact electronically. While this prediction has not yet come true, experts like Tapscott signal that instant messaging is certainly a force to be reckoned with, especially because it is already so much a part of many young people's personal lives.[4]

New Workplace in Focus Photo Essays

Vivid photos with intriguing stories demonstrate real-world applicability of business communication concepts. Each photo essay concludes with a critical thinking question.

I think the text does a great job of covering topics that are relevant in today's business world.

— TRACEY FLEET, COLLEGE OF THE NORTH ATLANTIC

Essentials offers a four-in-one learning package that gets results:

- Authoritative textbook
- Practical workbook
- Self-teaching grammar/mechanics handbook
- Fully supported student support Web site – www.guffeyessentials7ce.com

Emphasis on Grammar

Throughout the text, you are encouraged to build on your basic grammar skills. Grammar/Mechanics Check-ups, Grammar/Mechanics Challenges, and Web-based grammar activities help you practise and sharpen your skills.

what to include. At first, you may rely on these plans considerably. As you progress, these plans will become less important. Later in the book, no plans are provided.

Writing Plan for Information and Procedure E-Mails and Memos

- **Subject line:** Summarize the content of the message.
- **Opening:** Expand the subject line by stating the main idea concisely in a full sentence.
- **Body:** Provide background data and explain the main idea. Consider using lists, bullets, or headings to improve readability. In describing a procedure or giving instructions, use command language (*do this, don't do that*).
- **Closing:** Request a specific action, summarize the message, or present a closing thought. If appropriate, include a deadline and a reason.

Emphasis on Writing Plans

Ample, step-by-step writing plans help you get started quickly on organizing and formatting messages.

Emphasis on Professionalism

The Seventh Canadian Edition increases its emphasis on professional workplace behaviors and illustrates the importance of professionalism. Businesses have a keen interest in a professional workforce that effectively works together to deliver positive results that ultimately boost profits and bolster a company's image. In this edition, you'll discover the professional characteristics most valued in today's competitive workplace.

Career Relevance

Because employers often rank communication skills among the most requested competencies, the Seventh Canadian Edition emphasizes the link between excellent communication skills and career success—helping you see for yourself the critical role business communication will play in your life.

Abundant Activities and Cases

Chapter concepts are translated into action as you try out your skills in activities designed to mirror "real-world" experiences.

© OLIVER ELTINGER, FANCY/JUPITER IMAGES

More Before-and-After Model Documents

Before-and-after sample documents and descriptive callouts create a road map to the writing process, demonstrating the effective use of the skills being taught, as well as the significance of the revision process.

Before — — — — — Transfer Special Tools Window Help

| E | E | E | A⁺ | A⁻ | ⁺E | •E | A | **Send** |

To: All TechTron Team Members
From: Rayford Williams <ray.williams@techtron.com>
Subject: Company Needs to Reduce Employee Driving Trips to Office
Cc:
Attached:

Our company faces harsh governmental penalties if we fail to comply with the Ministry of the Environment's program to reduce the number of automobile trips made by employees.

The aforementioned program stipulates that we offer incentives to entice employees to discontinue driving their vehicles as a means of transportation to and from this place of employment.

First, we are prepared to offer a full day off without penalty. However, the employee must not drive to work and must maintain a 75 percent vanpool participation rate for six months. Second, we offer a vanpool subsidy of $100 a month, and the vanpool driver will not be limited in the personal use he makes of the vehicle on his own time. Third, employees in the vanpool will not be forced to park in outlying lots.

Pertaining to our need to have you leave your cars at home, all employees are herewith instructed to communicate with Saul Salazar, who will be facilitating the above-referenced program.

After — — — — — Message Transfer Special Tools Window Help

| E | E | E | A⁺ | A⁻ | ⁺E | •E | A |

To: All TechTron Team Members
From: Rayford Williams <raywilliams@techtron.com>
Subject: Great Perks for Driving Less
Cc:
Attached:

Focuses on receiver's viewpoint and audience benefits *(day off, less driving stress, lower gas bill)*

Hi, Team,

Want to earn a full day off with pay, reduce the stress of your gas? You can enjoy these and other perks if you make fewer d

As part of the Ministry of the Environment's Trip Reduction Pl ing benefits by reducing the number of trips you make to wor.

Places options in bulleted list with "you" view

Full Day Off. If you maintain a 75 percent participation rate six-month period, you will receive one day off with pay.

Vanpool Subsidy. By joining a vanpool, you will receive ass with a monthly $100 subsidy. Even better, if you become a have unlimited personal use of the vehicle off company tim

Preferential Parking. By coming to work in vanpools, you ca reserved spaces.

Repeats audience benefits using conversational tone and familiar words

Why not help the environment, reduce your gas bill, and enjo program? For more information and to sign up, please contact @techtron.com before February 1.

Ray

Rayford Williams
Senior Coordinator, Human Resources
ray.williams@techtron.com

Communication Workshops

Communication Workshops develop critical thinking skills and provide insight into special business communication topics such as ethics, technology, career skills, and collaboration.

Communication Workshop

Sharpening Your Skills for Critical Thinking, Problem Solving, and Decision Making

Gone are the days when management expected workers to follow the leader blindly and do only what they were told. Today, you'll be expected to think critically. You'll be solving problems and making decisions. Much of this book is devoted to helping you solve problems and communicate those decisions to management, fellow workers, clients, governments, and the public. Faced with a problem or an issue, most of us do a lot of worrying before making a decision. All that worrying can become directed thinking by channelling it into the following procedure.

1. **Identify and clarify the problem.** Your first task is to recognize that a problem exists. Some problems are big and unmistakable, such as failure of a courier service to get packages to customers on time. Other problems may be continuing annoyances, such as regularly running out of toner for an office copy machine. The first step in reaching a solution is pinpointing the problem area.

2. **Gather information.** Learn more about the problem situation. Look for possible causes and solutions. This step may mean checking files, calling suppliers, or brainstorming with fellow workers. For example, the courier service would investigate the tracking systems of the airlines carrying its packages to determine what is going wrong.

3. **Evaluate the evidence.** Where did the information come from? Does it represent various points of view? What biases could be expected from each source? How accurate is the information gathered? Is it fact or opinion? For example, it is a fact that packages are missing; it is an opinion that they are merely lost and will turn up eventually.

4. **Consider alternatives and implications.** Draw conclusions from the gathered evidence and pose solutions. Then weigh the advantages and disadvantages of each alternative. What are the costs, benefits, and consequences? What are the obstacles, and how can they be handled? Most important, what solution best serves your goals and those of your organization? Here's where your creativity is especially important.

5. **Choose and implement the best alternative.** Select an alternative and put it into action. Then, follow through on your decision by monitoring the results of implementing your plan. The courier company decided to give its unhappy customers free delivery service to make up for the lost packages and downtime. Be sure to continue monitoring

---

I like the section on using technology to enhance the writing process. This is a critical dimension lacking in many books published earlier. Much has changed in only a few years and it is critical for students to understand the latest trends in business and in business communication.

— SUSAN BAUMAN, SENECA COLLEGE

supervisors may want to create buy-in when introducing a healthier cafeteria menu. In these instances, a persuasive memo using the indirect pattern may be most effective.

The goal is not to manipulate employees or to deceive them with trickery. Rather, the goal is to present a strong but honest argument, emphasizing points that are important to the receiver or the organization. In business, honesty is not just the best policy—it is the only policy. People see right through puffery and misrepresentation. For this reason, the indirect pattern is effective only when supported by accurate, honest evidence.

Persuading the Boss. Another form of persuasion within organizations centres on suggestions made by subordinates. Convincing management to adopt a procedure or invest in a product or new equipment generally requires skillful communication. Managers are just as resistant to change as others are. Providing evidence is critical when subordinates submit recommendations to their bosses. "The key to making a request of a superior," advises communication consultant Patricia Buhler, "is to know your needs and have documentation [facts, figures, evidence]." Another important factor is moderation. "Going in and asking for the world off the cuff is most likely going to elicit a negative response," she adds.[2] Equally important is focusing on the receiver's needs. How can you make your suggestion appealing to the receiver?

Obviously, when you set out to persuade someone at work who has more clout than you, do so carefully. Use words like *suggest* and *recommend*, and craft sentences to begin with these words: *It might be a good idea if....* That lets you offer suggestions without threatening the person's authority.

In Figure 6.3 you see a persuasive memo written by Marketing Assistant Monica Cho, who wants her boss to authorize the purchase of a multi-function colour laser copier. She has researched the prices, features, and maintenance costs of the machines. They often serve as copiers, faxes, scanners, and printers and can cost several thousand dollars. Monica has found an outstanding deal offered by a local office supplier. Because Monica knows that her boss, Samuel Neesen, favours "cold, hard facts," she lists current monthly costs for copying at Copy Quick to increase her chances of gaining approval. Finally, she calculates the amortization of the purchase price and monthly costs of running the new colour copier.

Notice that Monica's memo isn't short. A successful persuasive message will typically take more space than a direct message because proving a case requires evidence. In the end, Monica chose to send her memo as an e-mail attachment accompanied by a polite, short e-mail message because she wanted to keep the document format in Microsoft Word intact. She also felt that the message was too long to paste into her e-mail program. Monica's persuasive memo and her e-mail include a subject line that announces the purpose of the message without disclosing the actual

Office Insider
To accentuate how excellent communication skills translate into career success, the *Office Insider* demonstrates the importance of communication skills in real-world practice.

Writing Improvement Exercises

These exercises will develop your writing skills and allow you to practise the concepts explained in the chapter.

Writing Improvement Exercises

Selecting Communication Channels

Using Figure 2.2, suggest the best communication channels for the following messages. Assume that all channels shown are available. Be prepared to explain your choices.

1. As department manager, you wish to inform four members of a training session scheduled for three weeks from now.

2. As assistant to the vice president, you are to investigate the possibility of developing work placement programs with several nearby colleges and universities.

3. You wish to send price quotes for a number of your products in response to a request from a potential customer in Taiwan.

4. You must respond to a notice from the Canada Revenue Agency insisting that you did not pay the correct amount for last quarter's employee remittance.

5. As a manager, you must inform an employee that continued tardiness is jeopardizing her job.

6. Members of your task force must meet to discuss ways to improve communication among 500 employees at 12 branches of your company. Task force members are from Toronto, Winnipeg, Calgary, Regina, and Halifax.

7. You need to know whether Davinder in Printing can produce a special pamphlet for you within two days.

Audience Benefits and the "You" View

Revise the following sentences to emphasize the perspective of the audience and the "you" view.

8. To prevent us from possibly losing large sums of money, our bank now requires verification of any large cheque presented for immediate payment.

9. We take pride in announcing daily flights to Singapore.

10. So that we may comply with new federal privacy legislation, we are asking you to complete the enclosed waiver.

11. For just $1,195 (CDN) per person, we have arranged a seven-day trip to Las Vegas that includes deluxe accommodations, a Cirque du Soleil performance, and selected meals.

12. I give my permission for you to attend the two-day workshop.

Tips for Preparing Business Messages

Tips boxes summarize practical suggestions for creating effective business messages. Study them before completing your writing assignments.

1. Our starting salary for the position is in the range of $44,000 to $49,000. Given Gerry's experience with you, is this range reasonable?

2. Is Gerry responsible for managing accounts with your organization or writing copy?

3. Does Gerry have any experience in public relations campaigns with your organization?

Thanks for sending him to interview for our junior account coordinator job. His interview was very successful; and his résumé suggests that he has the education, background, and experience we need.

The interview committee agreed that Pyramid would benefit from adding him to our team. So that we can prepare an offer for Gerry, please let me know your answers to these questions by Wednesday, August 18.

All the best,

Brent Atkins, Director, Finance
Pyramid Financial
1890 boul Rene-Levesque O.
Montreal, QC H3Z 2V5
E batkins@pyramid.com
T (514) 555-2367
F (514) 555-2360

Double spaces between paragraphs

Lists questions to improve readability

Includes end date to motivate action

Closes politely

Tips for Formatting E-Mails

- After *To*, type the receiver's e-mail address.
- After *From*, type your name—your e-mail program should insert it automatically.
- After *Subject*, provide a specific description of your message.
- Insert the names of anyone receiving carbon or blind copies.
- Include a salutation (such as *Dear Pat, Hi Pat, Greetings*) or weave the receiver's name into the first line.
- Double-space between paragraphs.
- Do not type in all caps or in all lowercase letters.
- Include a complimentary close including your name (and contact information if an automatic signature block has not been enabled in your e-mail program).

Brief Contents

Contents

Today's graduates enter working environments with ever-increasing demands. As a result of growing emphasis on team management and employee empowerment, they will be expected to gather data, solve problems, and make decisions independently. They will be working with global trading partners and collaborating with work teams in an increasingly diverse workplace. And they will be using sophisticated technologies to communicate.

Surprisingly, writing skills are becoming more and more important. In the past, businesspeople may have written a couple of business letters a month, but now they receive and send hundreds of e-mails and texts weekly. Their writing skills are showcased in every message they send. To help students develop the skills they need to succeed in today's technologically enhanced workplace, we have responded with a thoroughly revised Seventh Canadian Edition.

Effective Features That Remain Unchanged

The Seventh Canadian Edition maintains the streamlined, efficient approach to communication that has equipped past learners with the skills needed to be successful in their work. It is most helpful to postsecondary and adult learners preparing themselves for new careers, planning a change in their current careers, or wishing to upgrade their writing and speaking skills. The aim of this edition is to incorporate more of the comments, suggestions, and insights provided by adopters and reviewers over the last few years. For those new to the book, some of the most popular features include the following:

- **Text/Workbook Format.** The convenient text/workbook format presents an all-in-one teaching–learning package that includes concepts, workbook application exercises, writing problems, and a combination handbook/reference manual. Students work with and purchase only one volume for efficient, economical instruction.
- **Comprehensive but Concise Coverage.** An important reason for the enormous success of *Essentials of Business Communication* is that it practises what it preaches. The Seventh Canadian Edition follows the same strategy, concentrating on essential concepts presented without wasted words.
- **Writing Plans and Writing Improvement Exercises.** Step-by-step writing plans structure the writing experience so that novice writers get started quickly—without struggling to provide unknown details to unfamiliar, hypothetical cases. Many revision exercises build confidence and skills.
- **Wide Coverage of Communication Technology.** All relevant chapters build technology skills by including discussions and applications involving e-mail, instant messaging, PDAs, cell phones, Web research, contemporary software, online employment searches, and electronic presentations.
- **Grammar/Mechanics Emphasis.** Each chapter features a systematic review of the Grammar/Mechanics Handbook. Readers take a short quiz to review specific concepts, and they also proofread business documents that provide a cumulative review of all concepts previously presented.
- **Challenging Cases.** The reality of the work world is that communication situations will not always easily fit the models provided in a business communication

textbook. As a result, we have threaded ambiguity and complexity into the tasks so that students have a chance to use their critical thinking skills as well as their business communication skills regularly.

Revision Highlights

The following new features update the Sixth Canadian Edition:

- **Workplace in Focus Feature.** Chapters now contain a Workplace in Focus feature that ties in the content being discussed in the chapter to a real-world example. These features make ideal starting points for in-class discussion.
- **Updated Communication Technology in the News Feature.** Units open with all-new "hot-off-the-press" articles from Canadian media outlets that bring home the relevance of business communication to today's technology-driven workplace. Topics covered range from texting lingo in the workplace to mastering anger when sending e-mail.
- **Updated Communication Workshops.** Chapters conclude with a number of new Communication Workshop features in which an enrichment activity is offered to students. These workshops cover topics that are related to but not gone into depth in the preceding chapter. They can be used as group activity assignments, in-class discussion prompts, or homework assignments.
- **Increased Analysis of New Communication Technologies.** Technology manufacturers' ability to innovate can seem to outstrip teachers' ability to contextualize the changes happening to communication. This edition stays ahead of the curve by contextualizing podcasts, LinkedIn, Facebook, wikis, blogs, and other of-the-moment technologies in more detail than any other business communication textbook.
- **Plagiarism.** An unfortunate reality of the Internet age is the difficulty today's students have in understanding the need for proper citation and documentation, as well as the difficulty in understanding the seriousness of plagiarism and its difficult repercussions. We have expanded our discussion of, and exercises on, plagiarism by offering concrete examples of the real world ramifications of this behaviour.
- **New Activities and Cases.** Each chapter has at least three new activities or cases. As with the last edition, these new cases recognize the pedagogical usefulness of scripting, role play, and performance as effective means of practising business communication skills. These new activities/cases are based on realistic Canadian business examples.

Other Features That Enhance Teaching and Learning

Although the Seventh Canadian Edition of *Essentials of Business Communication* packs considerable information into a small space, it covers all of the critical topics necessary in a comprehensive business communication course; it also features many teaching–learning devices to facilitate instruction, application, and retention.

- **Focus on Writing Skills.** Most students need a great deal of instruction and practice in developing basic and advanced writing techniques, particularly in view of today's increased emphasis on communication by e-mail. Writing skills have returned to the forefront since so much of today's business is transacted through written messages.
- **E-Mail Emphasis.** *Essentials* devotes a chapter to the writing of e-mail, which has become the most-used communication channel in the business world.

- **Listening, Speaking, and Nonverbal Skills.** Employers are increasingly seeking well-rounded individuals who can interact with fellow employees as well as represent the organization effectively. *Essentials* provides professional tips for managing nonverbal cues, overcoming listening barriers, developing speaking skills, planning and participating in meetings, and making productive telephone calls.

- **Coverage of Formal and Informal Reports.** Two chapters develop functional report-writing skills. Chapter 8 provides detailed instruction in the preparation of six types of informal reports, while Chapter 9 covers proposals and formal reports. For quick comprehension all reports contain marginal notes that pinpoint writing strategies.

- **Collection Letters.** Recognizing the importance of the small-business sector to the Canadian economy, and the fact that small-business owners often have to take the collections function into their own hands, we have a section on how to write collection letters.

- **Employment Communication Skills.** Successful résumés, cover letters, and other employment documents are among the most important topics in a good business communication course. *Essentials* provides the most realistic and up-to-date résumés in the field. The models show chronological, functional, combination, and computer-friendly résumés.

- **Focus on Oral Communication Skills.** Chapter 10 looks at oral interpersonal skills: person-to-person conversations, telephone communication (including cell phone etiquette), and business meeting skills, while Chapter 11 specifically discusses business presentation skills.

- **Employment Interviewing.** *Essentials* devotes an entire chapter to effective interviewing techniques, including a discussion of screening interviews and hiring interviews. Chapter 13 also teaches techniques for fighting fear, answering questions, and following up.

- **Models Comparing Effective and Ineffective Documents.** To facilitate speedy recognition of good and bad writing techniques and strategies, *Essentials* presents many before-and-after documents. Marginal notes spotlight targeted strategies and effective writing. We hope that instructors turn this before-and-after technique into effective pedagogy whereby all their students' written assignments undergo the scrutiny of an editing and revising process before being handed in as final products.

- **Variety in End-of-Chapter Activities.** An amazing array of review questions, critical-thinking questions, writing improvement exercises, revision exercises, activities, and realistic case problems holds student attention and helps them apply chapter concepts meaningfully.

- **Diagnostic Test.** An optional grammar/mechanics diagnostic test helps students and instructors systematically determine specific student writing weaknesses. Students may be directed to the Grammar/Mechanics Handbook for remediation.

- **Grammar/Mechanics Handbook.** A comprehensive Grammar/Mechanics Handbook supplies a thorough review of English grammar, punctuation, capitalization style, and number usage. Its self-teaching exercises may be used for classroom instruction or for supplementary assignments. The handbook also serves as a convenient reference throughout the course and afterwards.

- **CourseMate.** The more students study, the better the results. Students can make the most of their study time by accessing everything they need to succeed in one place. CourseMate includes
  - Interactive eBook with highlighting, note taking, and an interactive glossary
  - Interactive learning tool, including:
    - Quizzes
    - Flashcards
    - Activities
    - Videos
    - Cases

Unparallelled Instructor Support

The Seventh Canadian Edition of *Essentials* continues to set the standard for business communication support. Classroom success is easy to achieve with the many practical ancillary items that supplement Guffey textbooks. No other author matches Mary Ellen Guffey's level of support.

About NETA

The **Nelson Education Teaching Advantage (NETA)** program delivers research-based instructor resources that promote student engagement and higher-order thinking to enable the success of Canadian students and educators.

Instructors today face many challenges. Resources are limited, time is scarce, and a new kind of student has emerged: one who is juggling school with work, has gaps in his or her basic knowledge, and is immersed in technology in a way that has led to a completely new style of learning. In response, Nelson Education has gathered a group of dedicated instructors to advise us on the creation of richer and more flexible ancillaries that respond to the needs of today's teaching environments.

The members of our editorial advisory board have experience across a variety of disciplines and are recognized for their commitment to teaching. They include:

> **Norman Althouse**, Haskayne School of Business, University of Calgary
> **Brenda Chant-Smith**, Department of Psychology, Trent University
> **Scott Follows**, Manning School of Business Administration, Acadia University
> **Jon Houseman**, Department of Biology, University of Ottawa
> **Glen Loppnow**, Department of Chemistry, University of Alberta
> **Tanya Noel**, Department of Biology, York University
> **Gary Poole**, Director, Centre for Teaching and Academic Growth and School of Population and Public Health, University of British Columbia
> **Dan Pratt**, Department of Educational Studies, University of British Columbia
> **Mercedes Rowinsky-Geurts**, Department of Languages and Literatures, Wilfrid Laurier University
> **David DiBattista**, Department of Psychology, Brock University
> **Roger Fisher**, PhD

In consultation with the editorial advisory board, Nelson Education has completely rethought the structure, approaches, and formats of our key textbook ancillaries. We've also increased our investment in editorial support for our ancillary authors. The result is the Nelson Education Teaching Advantage and its key components: *NETA Engagement, NETA Assessment,* and *NETA Presentation.* Each component includes one or more ancillaries prepared according to our best practices, and a document explaining the theory behind the practices.

NETA Engagement presents materials that help instructors deliver engaging content and activities to their classes. Instead of Instructor's Manuals that regurgitate chapter outlines and key terms from the text, NETA Enriched Instructor's Manuals (EIMs) provide genuine assistance to teachers. The EIMs answer questions like *What should students learn?, Why should students care?,* and *What are some common student misconceptions and stumbling blocks?* EIMs not only identify the topics that cause students the most difficulty, but also describe techniques and resources to help students master these concepts. Dr. Roger Fisher's *Instructor's Guide to Classroom Engagement (IGCE)* accompanies every Enriched Instructor's Manual.

NETA Assessment relates to testing materials: not just Nelson's Test Banks and Computerized Test Banks, but also in-text self-tests, Study Guides, Web quizzes, and homework programs like CNOW. Under *NETA Assessment,* Nelson's authors create multiple-choice questions that reflect research-based best practices for constructing effective questions and testing not just recall but also higher-order thinking. Our guidelines were developed by David DiBattista, a 3M National Teaching Fellow whose recent research as a professor of psychology at Brock University has focused on multiple-choice testing. All Test Bank authors receive training at workshops conducted by Prof. DiBattista, as do the copy editors assigned to each Test Bank. A copy of *Multiple Choice Tests: Getting Beyond Remembering,* Prof. DiBattista's guide to writing effective tests, is included with every Nelson Test Bank/Computerized Test Bank package.

NETA Presentation has been developed to help instructors make the best use of PowerPoint® in their classrooms. With a clean and uncluttered design developed by Maureen Stone of StoneSoup Consulting, NETA Presentation features slides with improved readability, more multimedia and graphic materials, activities to use in class, and tips for instructors on the Notes page. A copy of *NETA Guidelines for Classroom Presentations* by Maureen Stone is included with each set of PowerPoint slides.

Instructor Ancillaries

Key instructor ancillaries are provided on the *Instructor's Resource CD* (ISBN 978-0-17-661672-4), giving instructors the ultimate tool for customizing lectures and presentations. The IRCD includes:

- NETA Engagement: The Enriched Instructor's Manual was written by Betty-Anne Schlender, NAIT. It is organized according to the textbook chapters and addresses eight key educational concerns, such as typical stumbling blocks student face and how to address them. It also includes elements of a traditional Instructor's Manual, including answers to problems, suggested answers to exercises and cases, and so on.
- **NETA Assessment**: The Test Bank was written by Betty-Anne Schlender, NAIT. It includes over 250 multiple-choice questions written according to NETA guidelines for effective construction and development of higher-order questions. Also included are 260 true/false questions and 130 completion questions. Test Bank files are provided in Word format for easy editing and in PDF format for convenient printing, whatever your system.

  The Computerized Test Bank by ExamView® includes all the questions from the Test Bank. The easy-to-use ExamView software is compatible with Microsoft Windows and Mac. Create tests by selecting questions from the question bank, modifying these questions as desired, and adding new questions you write yourself. You can administer quizzes online and export tests to WebCT, Blackboard, and other formats.
- **NETA Presentation**: Microsoft® PowerPoint® lecture slides for every chapter have been created by Cassandra Alexopoulos, Seneca College. There is an average of 25 slides per chapter, many featuring key figures, tables, and photographs from *Essentials of Business Communication*. NETA principles of clear design and engaging content have been incorporated throughout.
- **DayOne:** Day One—Prof InClass is a PowerPoint presentation that you can customize to orient your students to the class and their text at the beginning of the course.

Acknowledgments

The Seventh Canadian Edition of *Essentials of Business Communication* includes many of the constructive suggestions and timely advice provided by professional communicators, educators, and students who use the book across Canada. These dedicated reviewers include Susan Bauman, Seneca College; Marie Brodie, Nova Scotia Community College; Rhonda Dynes, Mohawk College; Tracey Fleet, College of the North Atlantic; Leslie Mannion, Algonquin College; and Kathryn Pallister, Red Deer College.

A new edition like this would not be possible without the development team at Nelson Education Ltd. Special thanks go to Anne-Marie Taylor, Terry Fedorkiw, Theresa Fitzgerald, and Claire Horsnell. I would also like to thank Anoop Chaturvedi and his team at MPS. Thanks also go to the copy editor, Margaret Crammond.

—Mary Ellen Guffey and
Richard Almonte

Communicating Today

Chapter 1
Career Success Begins With Communication Skills

COMMUNICATION TECHNOLOGY IN THE NEWS

Texting Lingo Shows Up at Office; Set Limits but Don't Discourage Young Employees

Source: Derek Sankey, "Texting lingo shows up at office." *National Post*, April 14, 2010, p. FP 12. Material reprinted with the express permission of POSTMEDIA NEWS, a division of Postmedia Network Inc.

CALGARY – While Maria Bakardjieva was conducting research about how people across the world integrate the Internet and technologies into their lives, she was astounded by stories she heard from teachers.

In one group of 11- and 12-year-olds in Britain, the teacher asked her students to recount how they spent their summers. One girl wrote a paper entirely in the lingo of texting.

"It was hilarious. It was impossible. Not simply abbreviated words in the way they are spelled, but also abbreviated thoughts," recalls Ms. Bakardjieva, a professor of communication at the University of Calgary.

Now, texting shortcuts are creeping into everyday communication, even in the workplace.

"There are these discreet, almost distinct speech genres appropriate for different situations, at the same time they always overlap and influence one another and there is overflow from one into the other," Ms. Bakardjieva says.

Some academic researchers examine different speech genres and how we recognize how to communicate in different situations specific to that culture or situation. It can be a fine line for some people when deciding what's appropriate—even decipherable—in the workplace.

Technology gadgets also appear to be hampering workplace etiquette.

About 42 percent of more than 270 chief information officers across Canada with 100 or more employees stated the number of breaches in workplace etiquette have increased as a result of mobile electronic gadgets, a study by Robert Half Technology found.

"Electronic gadgets have facilitated increased productivity amongst employees, but they may also cause interruptions," says Megan Slabinski, president of Robert Half's Canadian operations.

The report identifies several examples, such as the "misguided multi-tasker," referring to somebody who thinks e-mailing or texting during a meeting demonstrates efficiency; the "broadcaster" who has no shame about when and where these mobile devices are used, such as the washroom; and the "distractor," who has good intentions by setting the device to vibrate, but a constant flow of buzzing on a desk can be a huge distraction.

It's not that proper grammar has been erased or obliterated either, but there clearly is a new genre of communication resulting from technology. Deciding on appropriate language in the workplace is common sense for many, but there is still a need for employers to be clear about it by setting guidelines, Ms. Bakardjieva says.

"People who are socialized in this culture, educated in this culture, they know how to switch from one to the other."

"[Employers] have to set clear limits. They have to engage with this problem head on and show clearly to their employees where the boundaries are drawn," she says.

At the same time, they cannot ignore the fact these technologies are ubiquitous and workers—in particular, younger generations—rely on them to carry out their tasks.

"I don't think they should be completely fascist and limiting about these things," she says. "This is the way this generation breathes. You want to have an engaged, happy employee."

© PHOTOS.COM

Summarize the article you've just read in a two- to three-sentence paragraph. Answer the following questions, either on your own or in a small group. Be prepared to give your answers in a short presentation or in an e-mail to your instructor.

QUESTIONS:

1. How does what you've learned in this article change your perception of business communication?

2. How might what you've learned in this article change your own communication style?

3. Come up with pro and con arguments for the following debate/discussion topic: Employers need to accommodate their young employees' communication styles, instead of expecting new employees to communicate in old-fashioned ways.

Career Success Begins With Communication Skills

Employers... have two options. They can refuse to adapt to the Net Gen, stick to their old hierarchies, and reinforce the generational firewall that separates the managers from the newly hired minions.... In this complex business environment, that would be a bad choice. Instead... the winners will be those companies... who choose... to embrace the Net Geners' collaborative ways.

Don Tapscott,
Grown Up Digital: How the Net Generation Is Changing Your World[1]

LEARNING OBJECTIVES

1. Understand the importance of becoming an effective business communicator in today's changing workplace.

2. Identify ways in which technology helps improve business writing.

3. Discuss how to become an effective listener.

4. Analyze nonverbal communication and explain techniques for improving nonverbal communication skills.

5. Explain how culture affects communication and describe methods for improving cross-cultural communication.

6. Identify specific techniques that improve effective communication among diverse workplace audiences.

Becoming an Effective Business Communicator

People with different backgrounds bring varied views to decision making. As Don Tapscott shows in his influential recent book on new digital working styles, embracing new ways of doing things at work (in this case collaborative communication practices and technologies) is what will lead to business success in the knowledge economy of tomorrow. Businesses must rely on their employees' ability to work with a highly diverse group of people who are located across international borders. The more effectively employees work together, the more successful their company is. In this age of information, career success is directly related to good communication, a skill that is made more challenging by tremendous changes in technology, the workforce, work environments, and the globalization of business.

The information revolution has made communication skills extremely important.

Today's graduates are light-years ahead when it comes to computer know-how. However, the long hours they spend instant messaging and "twittering" could be hampering important career skills. Nearly two thirds of employers say that college students are not prepared to work in the global economy, and communication is the skill that professionals find most lacking among new recruits. Tech-savvy youth are certainly expert at sending cryptic text messages at rapid-fire speed; however, analysts spot a correlation between prolonged use of electronic communication and the erosion of solid writing and speaking abilities. *What specific communication skills are essential for career success?*

Because communication skills are learned, you control how well you communicate.

Through e-mail, instant messaging, and other technology-based communication channels, business communicators today are doing more writing than ever before. Their writing is also having a more immediate impact. This book focuses on developing business writing skills. But you will also learn to improve your listening, nonverbal, and speaking skills.

While you are born with the ability to acquire language and to listen, effective business communication skills are learned. Good communicators are not born; they are made. Your ability to thrive in the dynamic and demanding contemporary world of work will depend on many factors, some of which you cannot control. One factor that you do control, however, is how well you communicate.

The goals of this book are to teach you basic business communication skills, such as how to write an effective e-mail, memo, or letter and how to make a presentation. Anyone can learn these skills with the help of effective instructional materials and good model documents, all of which you'll find in this book. You also need practice—with meaningful feedback. You need someone such as your instructor to tell you how to modify your responses so that you can improve.

We've designed this book to provide you with everything necessary to make you a successful business communicator in today's dynamic workplace. Given the increasing emphasis on communication, Canadian corporations are paying millions of dollars to communication coaches and trainers to teach employees the very skills that you are learning in this course. For example, Ottawa-based Backdraft Corporation, a leading provider of corporate writing training, and the first writing services company in the world to be granted ISO 9000 registration, lists among its clients the Royal Bank of Canada, Siemens Canada, the National Gallery of Canada, and the Government of Alberta.[2] Your coach is your instructor. Get your money's worth! Pick his or her brains.

This book and this course might well be the most important in your postsecondary education.

Once you've had a couple of years of business experience, you will look back on this course and this textbook as the most important in your entire postsecondary education. To get started, this first chapter presents an overview. You'll take a look at (1) the changing workplace, (2) the communication process, (3) listening, (4) nonverbal communication, (5) culture and communication, and (6) workplace diversity. The remainder of the book is devoted to developing specific writing and speaking skills.

Succeeding in the Changing World of Work

The entire world of work is changing dramatically. The kind of work you'll do, the tools you'll use, the form of management you'll work under, the environment in which you'll work, the people with whom you'll interact—all are undergoing a pronounced transformation. Many of the changes revolve around processing and communicating information, as you can see in Figure 1.2 on page 8. As a result, the most successful players in this new world of work will be those with highly developed communication skills. The following business trends illustrate the importance of excellent communication skills.

Trends in the new world of work emphasize the importance of communication skills.

- **Innovative communication technologies.** E-mail, instant messaging, the Web, mobile technologies, audio- and videoconferencing—all of these technologies mean that you will be communicating more often and more rapidly than ever before. Your writing and speaking skills will be showcased and tested as never before.
- **Flattened management hierarchies.** To better compete and to reduce expenses, businesses have for years been trimming layers of management. This means that as a frontline employee, you will have fewer managers. You will be making decisions and communicating them to customers, to fellow employees, and to executives.
- **More participatory management.** Gone are the days of command-and-control management. Now, even new employees will be expected to understand and contribute to the success of the organization. Improving productivity and profitability will be everyone's job, not just management's.
- **Increased emphasis on self-directed work and project teams.** Businesses today are often run by cross-functional teams of peers. You can expect to work with a team in gathering information, finding and sharing solutions, implementing decisions, and managing conflict. Good communication skills are extremely important in working together successfully in a team environment.
- **Heightened global competition.** Because Canadian companies are required to move beyond local markets, you may be interacting with people from many different cultures. At the same time, because of increased immigration, you may be expected to interact with people from many cultures in your local market as well as in your organization.[3] As a successful business communicator, you will want to learn about other cultures. You'll also need to develop interpersonal skills including sensitivity, flexibility, patience, and tolerance.
- **New work environments.** Mobile technologies and the desire for better work/family balance have resulted in flexible working arrangements. You may become part of the 1.5 million Canadians engaged in full- or part-time telecommuting.[4] Working away from the office requires exchanging even more messages in order to stay connected.
- **The move to a knowledge economy.** As Statistics Canada researchers Desmond Beckstead and Tara Vinodrai show in their paper "Dimensions of Occupational Changes in Canada's Knowledge Economy, 1971–1996," the decrease in the importance of sectors such as manufacturing and agriculture has taken place at the same time as "the importance of knowledge occupations has continuously increased over the last three decades."[5] By definition, such "knowledge occupations," many of which are in business, require excellent communication skills.

How Technology Improves Business Writing

Another basic for beginning business communicators is learning to use technology to enhance their writing efforts. Although computers and software programs cannot actually do the writing for you, they provide powerful tools that make the entire process easier and the results more professional. Technology can help you improve written documents, oral presentations, and Web pages.

1. **Designing and producing professional-looking documents, presentations, and Web pages.** Most popular word processing programs include a large selection of scalable fonts (for different character sizes and styles), italics, boldface, symbols, and styling techniques to help you produce consistent formatting and professional-looking results. Moreover, today's presentation software, such as Microsoft's PowerPoint, enables you to incorporate animated slide effects, colour, sound, pictures, and even movies into your talks for management or customers. Web document builders also help you design and construct Web pages. Another widely used software is Adobe's Portable Document Format, or PDF for short. A PDF is a file format that creates a document that is more permanent, transferable, and difficult to make changes to. Businesses use PDFs regularly for important forms that shouldn't be changed by the receiver. These tools can be used effectively to help you reinforce your message and help your audience understand and remember your message.

2. **Using templates.** One of the most useful and time-saving features of today's word processing software for the business writer is templates. As Figure 1.1 illustrates, templates are pre-formatted documents; business writers simply add the content. Any time you open up a new document in Microsoft Word, for example, on the right-hand side of your document you will see the option to choose a template. Typical templates include memos, letters, résumés, and reports. For the purposes of your business communication course, you should always choose a "professional" template, such as Word's Professional Letter template. Templates save time for business writers because instead of memorizing the various parts of a letter (e.g., how many spaces from the top the date and address should be placed), they can now concentrate on the more important things, such as making sure grammar and style are perfected. This is not to say that knowing the parts of a letter is unimportant (see Appendix A), only that most of us don't have time to think about these features every time we sit down to write. In many large companies, templates have been customized for that company's needs, and few people write letters from "scratch" anymore. Similarly, doing an Internet search on "templates" will bring up thousands of other non-corporate and non-proprietary templates that you might use in your daily business writing.

> Powerful writing tools can help you fight writer's block, collect information, outline and organize ideas, improve correctness and precision, add graphics, and design professional-looking documents.

FIGURE 1.1 Microsoft Templates

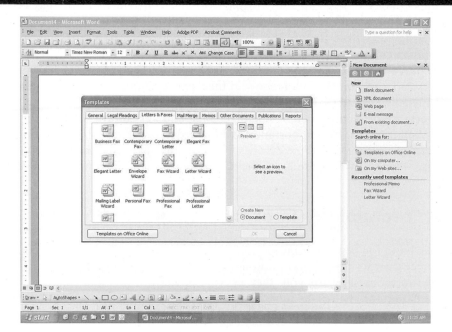

3. **Collecting information electronically.** Much of the world's information is now accessible by computer. Through a library's online databases you can locate many full-text articles from magazines, newspapers, and government publications. Massive amounts of information are available from the Internet and from online services. Through specialized library online databases such as ABI-INFORM and CBCA Reference you can have at your fingertips the latest business, legal, scientific, and scholarly information.

4. **Adding graphics for emphasis.** Your letters, memos, and reports may be improved by the addition of graphs and artwork to clarify and illustrate data. You can import charts, diagrams, and illustrations created in database, spreadsheet, and graphics programs, or from Internet sites such as Google Images. Moreover, ready-made pictures, called clip art, can be used to symbolize or illustrate ideas.

5. **Improving correctness and precision.** Word processing programs today provide features that catch and correct spelling and typographical errors. Poor spellers and weak typists universally bless their spell checkers for repeatedly saving them from humiliation. Most popular word processing programs today also provide grammar checkers that are markedly improved over earlier versions. They now detect many errors in capitalization, word use (such as *it's/its*), double negatives, verb use, subject–verb agreement, sentence structure, number agreement, number style, and other writing faults. However, grammar programs don't actually correct the errors they detect. You must know how to do that. Similarly, spell checkers don't catch all misspelled words. This is especially important in Canada because most spell checkers use American spelling. For example, if you have written the word *traveling* in your memo and your spell checker hasn't caught the mistake, this is because *traveling* is the correct American spelling, whereas *travelling* is the correct Canadian spelling. You must know how to correct your own spelling mistakes.

DILBERT   By Scott Adams

6. **Using software for team writing.** As part of today's team-based work environment, you can expect to work with others on projects. Word processing programs usually have an editing feature with commenting and strikeout that allows you to revise easily, to identify each team member's editing, and to track multiple edits. E-mail and instant messaging programs allow group members to share documents and information freely and work on the same document from several remote locations at the same time. Other computer-based communication systems such as wikis allow members of a team or community group or online group to collectively add information to an evolving site. Some wikis are free to access and create (if you Google "wiki" you'll see the variety of free sites) while others are proprietary software, such as Microsoft's SharePoint. While collaboration between team and group members is a positive aspect of computer-based writing, such collaboration also entails an extra responsibility. When a number of people are working on an assignment and using computers to piece together the various parts they've worked on, there is often a temptation not to revise the document sufficiently.

Remember to build in enough time to edit and proofread the document that has been created by pasting together the work of numerous people, so

FIGURE 1.2 Communication and Collaborative Technologies

Communication Technologies: Reshaping the World of Work

Today's workplace is changing dramatically as a result of innovative software, superfast wireless networks, and numerous technologies that allow workers to share information, work from remote locations, and be more productive in or away from the office. We are seeing a gradual progression from basic capabilities, such as e-mail, instant messaging, and calendaring, to deeper functionality, such as remote database access, multifunctional devices, and Web-based collaborative applications. Becoming familiar with modern office and collaboration technologies can help you be successful in today's digital workplace.

Telephony: VoIP

Savvy businesses are switching from traditional phone service to Voice over Internet Protocol (VoIP). This technology allows callers to communicate using a broadband Internet connection, thus eliminating long-distance and local telephone charges. Higher-end VoIP systems now support unified voice mail, e-mail, click-to-call capabilities, and softphones (phones using computer networking). Free or low-cost Internet telephony sites, such as the popular Skype, are also increasingly used by businesses.

Multifunctional Printers

Stand-alone copiers, fax machines, scanners, and printers have been replaced with multifunctional devices. Offices are transitioning from a "print and distribute" environment to a "distribute and print" environment. Security measures include pass codes and even biometric thumbprint scanning to make sure data streams are not captured, interrupted, or edited.

Open Offices

Widespread use of laptop computers, wireless technology, and VoIP have led to more fluid, flexible, and open workspaces. Smaller computers and flat-screen monitors enable designers to save space with boomerang-shaped workstations and cockpit-style work surfaces rather than space-hogging corner work areas. Smaller breakout areas for impromptu meetings are taking over some cubicle space, and digital databases are replacing file cabinets.

Handheld Wireless Devices

A new generation of lightweight, handheld smartphones provide phone, e-mail, Web browsing, and calendar options anywhere there is a wireless network. Devices such as the BlackBerry, the iPhone, and the Palm Treo now allow you to tap into corporate databases and intranets from remote locations. You can check customers' files, complete orders, and send out receipts without returning to the office.

Company Intranets

To share insider information, many companies provide their own protected Web sites called intranets. An intranet may handle company e-mail, announcements, an employee directory, a policy handbook, frequently asked questions, personnel forms and data, employee discussion forums, shared documents, and other employee information.

Voice Recognition

Computers equipped with voice recognition software enable users to dictate up to 160 words a minute with accurate transcription. Voice recognition is particularly helpful to disabled workers and to professionals with heavy dictation loads, such as physicians and attorneys. Users can create documents, enter data, compose and send e-mails, browse the Web, and control the desktop—all by voice.

Electronic Presentations

Business presentations in PowerPoint can be projected from a laptop or PDA or posted online. Sophisticated presentations may include animations, sound effects, digital photos, video clips, or hyperlinks to Internet sites. In some industries, PowerPoint slides ("decks") are replacing or supplementing traditional hard-copy reports.

Collaboration Technologies: Rethinking the Way We Work Together

Global competition, expanding markets, and the ever-increasing pace of business accelerate the development of exciting collaboration tools. New tools make it possible to work together without being together. Your colleagues may be down the hall, across the country, or around the world. With today's tools, you can exchange ideas, solve problems, develop products, forecast future performance, and complete team projects any time of the day or night and anywhere in the world. Blogs and wikis, part of the so-called Web 2.0 era, are social tools that create multidirectional conversations among customers and employees. Web 2.0 moves Web applications from "read only" to "read-write," thus enabling greater participation and collaboration.

Blogs, Podcasts, and Wikis

A *blog* is a Web site with journal entries usually written by one person and comments by others. Businesses use blogs to keep customers and employees informed and to receive feedback. Company developments can be posted, updated, and categorized for easy cross-referencing. *Podcasts* are usually short audio or video clips that users can either watch on a company Web site or download and view or listen to on their computers or MP3 players on the go. A *wiki* is a Web site that allows multiple users to collaboratively create and edit pages. Information gets lost in e-mails, but blogs and wikis provide an easy way to communicate and keep track of what is said. *RSS* (really simple syndication) *feeds* allow businesspeople and customers to receive updates automatically whenever podcasts, news stories, or blog entries become available on their favorite Web sites.

Voice Conferencing

Telephone "bridges" allow two or more callers from any location to share the same call. *Voice conferencing* (also called *audioconferencing*, *teleconferencing*, or just plain *conference calling*) enables people to collaborate by telephone. Communicators at both ends use enhanced speakerphones to talk and be heard simultaneously.

Videoconferencing

Videoconferencing allows participants to meet in special conference rooms equipped with cameras and television screens. Groups see each other and interact in real time although they may be continents apart. Faster computers, rapid Internet connections, and better cameras now enable 2 to 200 participants to sit at their own PCs and share applications, spreadsheets, presentations, and photos.

Web Conferencing

With services such as GoToMeeting, WebEx, Microsoft LiveMeeting, or the free Skype, all you need are a PC and an Internet connection to hold a meeting (*webinar*) with customers or colleagues in real time. Although the functions are constantly evolving, Web conferencing currently incorporates screen sharing, chats, slide presentations, text messaging, and applicationsharing.

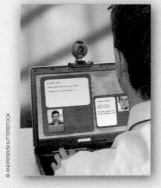

Presence Technology

Presence technology makes it possible to locate and identify a computing device as soon as users connect to the network. This technology is an integral part of communication devices including cell phones, laptop computers, PDAs, pagers, and GPS devices. Collaboration is possible wherever and whenever users are online.

Video Phones

Using advanced video compression technology, video phones transmit real-time audio and video so that communicators can see each other as they collaborate. With a video phone, people can videoconference anywhere in the world over a broadband IP (Internet Protocol) connection without a computer or a television screen.

that it reads as if it was written by one person. Another danger in collaborative writing is plagiarism. Plagiarism is the stealing of another writer's words or ideas by putting them in one's own assignment without crediting the original author. Plagiarism is the most serious of academic offences, usually leading to a failing grade on the assignment, if not the course. When proven in the work world, plagiarism may lead to the firing of the guilty person.[6] Plagiarism is discussed in greater detail in Chapter 9.

Examining the Communication Process

As you can see, in today's workplace you can expect to be communicating more rapidly, more often, and with greater numbers of people than ever before. Since good communication skills are essential to your success, we need to take a closer look at the communication process.

Communication is the transmission of information and meaning from one individual or group to another.

Just what is communication? For our purposes communication is the transmission of information and meaning from one individual or group (the sender) to another (the receiver). The crucial element in this definition is meaning. Communication has as its central objective the transmission of meaning. The process of communication is successful only when the receiver understands an idea as the sender intended it. This classic theory of communication was first articulated by theorist Harold Lasswell (1947) and later expanded upon by Claude E. Shannon and Warren Weaver (1949). This theoretical process generally involves five steps, discussed here and shown in Figure 1.3.

FIGURE 1.3 Communication Process

Communication barriers may cause the communication process to break down.

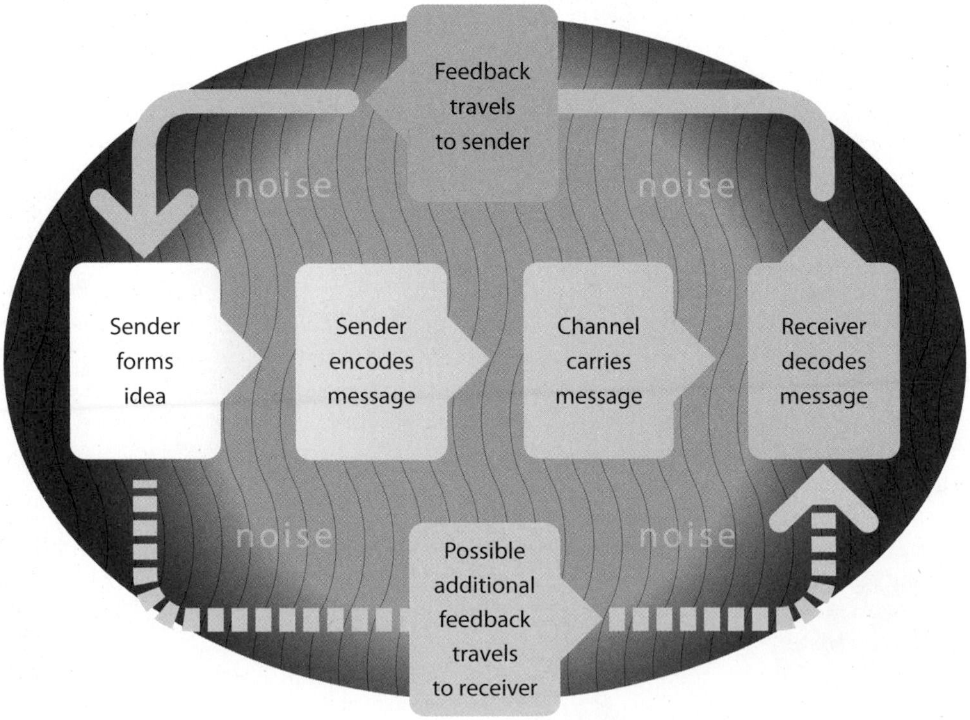

1. **Sender forms an idea.** The idea may be influenced by the sender's mood, frame of reference, background, and culture, as well as the context of the situation. (For example, an accountant realizes income tax season is about to begin.)

2. **Sender encodes the idea in a message.** *Encoding* means converting the idea into words or gestures that will convey meaning. A major problem in communicating any message is that words have different meanings for different people. That's why skilled communicators try to choose familiar words with concrete meanings on which both senders and receivers agree. (For example, the accountant writes an e-mail asking all her clients to begin scheduling income tax appointments.)

3. **Message travels over a channel.** The medium over which the message is transmitted is the channel. Messages may be sent by computer, telephone, fax, BlackBerry, traditional mail, Web site, or blog. Because both verbal and non-verbal messages are carried, senders must choose channels carefully. Any barrier that disrupts the transmission of a message in the communication process is called noise. Channel noise ranges from static that disrupts a telephone conversation to spelling and grammar errors in an e-mail message, to e-mails that are not sent because of firewalls. Such errors can damage the credibility of the sender. (For example, the accountant sends her e-mail to 125 clients in late December.)

4. **Receiver decodes message.** The person for whom a message is intended is the receiver. Translating the message into meaning involves decoding. Successful communication takes place only when a receiver understands the meaning intended by the sender. Such success is often hard to achieve because barriers and noise may disrupt the process. (For example, client reads accountant's e-mail, but decides to do his taxes himself this year.)

5. **Feedback travels to sender.** The response of the receiver creates feedback, a vital part of the entire communication process. Feedback helps the sender know that the message was received and understood. Senders can encourage feedback by including statements such as *Please let me know what you think as soon as possible.* Senders can further improve feedback by delivering the message at a time when receivers can respond. Senders should also provide only as much information as a receiver can handle. Receivers can improve the process by paraphrasing the sender's message. They might say, *Thanks for your e-mail explaining the new safe procedure.* (For example, client calls accountant, leaves voice mail thanking her for e-mail but letting her know he's going to do his taxes himself this year.)

The communication process has five steps: idea formation, message encoding, message transmission, message decoding, and feedback.

A good summary and critique of the work of the transmission theorists (Lasswell, Shannon, and Weaver) can be found on the Web site *Cultsock: Communication, Culture, Media* (**http://www.cultsock.org/**) by searching under "Shannon-Weaver model." For example, well-known Canadian communication theorist Marshall McLuhan (1911–1980) believed that communication couldn't be theorized in the straightforward, linear way that Lasswell, Shannon, and Weaver articulated. "McLuhan," it has been argued, "worked to disprove that communication moved in a singular line from transmitter to audience. Rather, he insisted communication was more like a field, creating an environment from which meanings were derived."[7] A good example of McLuhan's "field" is synchronous communication such as instant messaging. In instant messaging, there's hardly enough time for the traditional communication cycle, as described by Lasswell, to take place. Receivers decode messages and send feedback almost instantaneously on a screen in real time.

Marshall McLuhan

© CP ARCHIVE PHOTO PUBLIC

Chapter 1: Career Success Begins With Communication Skills

As another example, McLuhan might argue that the widespread use of e-mail and texting in today's society, both at home and at work, has changed the environment in which we live. He'd be less interested in theorizing a neat pattern about how an e-mail or a text message is sent, received, and understood than in claiming that, because we now routinely use e-mail and texting, we talk on the phone and in person much less, we work much more after hours and on weekends, and so on. Where the transmission theorists saw communication as a hermetically sealed process, McLuhan would argue that the process has repercussions beyond itself.

Developing Better Listening Skills

Most individuals listen at only 25 percent efficiency.

Due to the synchronous, interruption-prone nature of modern technology (e.g., you may have received three text messages while reading these words, whereas if you had been reading them 30 years ago you would be much less likely to be interrupted), an incredibly important part of the communication process is effective listening and attention-paying. By many accounts, however, most of us are not very good listeners. Do you ever pretend to be listening when you're not? Do you know how to look attentive in class when your mind wanders far away? How about losing interest in people's messages when their ideas are boring or complex? Do you find it hard to focus on ideas when a speaker's clothing or mannerisms are unusual?

You probably answered yes to one or more of these questions because many of us have developed poor listening habits. In fact, some researchers suggest that we listen at only 25 percent efficiency. Such poor listening habits are costly in business. Letters must be rewritten, shipments re-shipped, appointments rescheduled, contracts renegotiated, and directions restated.

To improve listening skills, we must first recognize barriers that prevent effective listening. Then we need to focus on specific techniques that are effective in improving listening skills.

Barriers to Effective Listening

As you learned earlier, barriers and noise can interfere with the communication process. Have any of the following barriers and distractions prevented you from hearing what's said?

Barriers to listening may be physical, personal, verbal, or nonverbal.

- **Physical barriers.** You cannot listen if you cannot hear what is being said. Physical impediments include hearing impairments, poor acoustics, and noisy surroundings. It's also difficult to listen if you're ill, tired, uncomfortable, or worried.
- **Personal barriers.** Everyone brings to the communication process a different set of cultural, ethical, and personal values. Each of us has an idea of what is right and what is important. If another person's ideas run counter to our preconceived thoughts, we tend to lose interest in his or her message and thus fail to hear.
- **Language problems.** Unfamiliar words can destroy the communication process because they lack meaning for the receiver. In addition, if a speaker's oral communication skills are compromised by a thick accent or pronunciation mistakes, listeners may be unable to understand what follows.
- **Nonverbal distractions.** Some of us find it hard to listen if a speaker is different from what we are expecting. Unusual clothing, speech mannerisms, body twitches, or a radical hairstyle or hair colour sometimes cause enough distraction to prevent us from hearing what the speaker has to say.
- **Thought speed.** Because we can process thoughts over three times faster than speakers can say them, we can become bored and allow our minds to wander.
- **Faking attention.** Most of us have learned to look as if we are listening even when we're not. Faked attention seriously threatens effective listening because it encourages the mind to engage in flights of unchecked fancy. Those who practise faked attention often find it hard to concentrate even when they want to.

OFFICE INSIDER

Listening is hard work. Unlike hearing, it demands total concentration. It is an active search for meaning, while hearing is passive.

- **Grandstanding.** Would you rather talk or listen? Naturally, many of us would rather talk. Since our own experiences and thoughts are most important to us, we want the attention in conversations. We sometimes fail to listen carefully because we're just waiting politely for the next pause so that we can have our turn to speak.
- **Technological barriers.** Sometimes your ability to listen attentively is undermined by your habitual need to check various devices such as your Blackberry or cell phone. Different workplaces will accommodate this lack of attention in different ways, from accepting it to banning it.

Tips for Becoming an Active Listener

You can reverse the harmful effects of poor listening habits by making a conscious effort to become an active listener. This means becoming involved and taking responsibility for understanding. The following techniques will help you become an active and effective listener.

- **Stop talking.** The first step to becoming a good listener is to stop talking. Let others explain their views. Learn to concentrate on what the speaker is saying, not on what your next comment will be.
- **Control your surroundings.** Whenever possible, remove competing sounds. Close windows or doors, turn off handheld devices such as cell phones and BlackBerrys, turn off radios and noisy appliances, and move away from loud people or engines. Choose a quiet time and place for listening.
- **Establish a receptive mindset.** Expect to learn something by listening. Strive for a positive and receptive frame of mind. If the message is complex, think of it as a mental challenge. It's hard work but good exercise to stretch and expand the limits of your mind.
- **Keep an open mind.** We all sift and filter information through our own biases and values. For improved listening, discipline yourself to listen objectively. Be fair to the speaker. Hear what is really being said, not what you want to hear.
- **Listen for main points.** Concentration is enhanced and satisfaction is heightened when you look for and recognize the speaker's central themes.
- **Capitalize on lag time.** Make use of the quickness of your mind by reviewing the speaker's points. Anticipate what's coming next. Evaluate evidence the speaker has presented. Don't allow yourself to daydream.
- **Listen between the lines.** Focus both on what is spoken and what is unspoken. Listen for feelings as well as for facts.
- **Judge ideas, not appearances.** Concentrate on the content of the message, not on its delivery. Avoid being distracted by the speaker's looks, voice, or mannerisms.
- **Be patient.** Force yourself to listen to the speaker's entire argument or message before reacting. Such restraint may enable you to understand the speaker's reasons and logic before you jump to false conclusions.
- **Take selective notes.** For some situations thoughtful note taking may be necessary to record important facts that must be recalled later. Select only the most important points so that the note-taking process does not interfere with your concentration on the speaker's total message.
- **Provide feedback.** Let the speaker know that you are listening. Nod your head and maintain eye contact. Ask relevant questions at appropriate times. Getting involved improves the communication process for both the speaker and the listener.

Most North Americans speak at about 125 words per minute. The human brain can process information at least three times as fast.

To become an active listener, stop talking, control your surroundings, develop a positive mindset, listen for main points, and capitalize on lag time.

Listening actively may mean taking notes and providing feedback.

Improving Your Nonverbal Communication Skills

Understanding messages often involves more than listening to spoken words. Nonverbal clues, in fact, can speak louder than words. These clues include eye contact, facial expression, body movements, space, time, distance, and appearance. All these nonverbal clues affect how a message is interpreted, or decoded, by the receiver.

Just what is nonverbal communication? It includes all unwritten and unspoken messages, whether intended or not. These silent signals have a strong effect on receivers. But understanding them is not simple. Does a downward glance indicate modesty? Fatigue? Does a constant stare reflect hostility? Dullness? Do crossed arms mean defensiveness? Withdrawal? Or do crossed arms just mean that a person is cold?

Messages are even harder to decipher when the verbal and nonverbal codes do not agree. What would you think if Scott says he's not angry, but he slams the door when he leaves? Or what if Fatimah assures her server that the meal is excellent, but she eats very little? The nonverbal messages in these situations speak more loudly than the words.

When verbal and nonverbal messages conflict, research shows that receivers put more faith in nonverbal cues. In one study speakers sent a positive message but averted their eyes as they spoke. Listeners perceived the total message to be negative. Moreover, they thought that averted eyes suggested lack of affection, superficiality, lack of trust, and nonreceptivity.[8]

Successful communicators recognize the power of nonverbal messages. Although it's unwise to attach specific meanings to gestures or actions, some cues broadcast by body language are helpful in understanding the feelings and attitudes of senders.

How the Eyes, Face, and Body Send Silent Messages

Words seldom tell the whole story. Indeed, some messages are sent with no words at all. The eyes, face, and body can convey a world of meaning without a single syllable being spoken.

Eye Contact. The eyes have been called the "windows of the soul." Even if they don't reveal the soul, the eyes are often the best indicator of a speaker's true feelings. Most of us cannot look another person straight in the eyes and lie. As a result, in Canada we tend to believe people who look directly at us. Sustained eye contact suggests trust and admiration; brief eye contact signals fear or stress. Good eye contact enables the message sender to see if a receiver is paying attention, showing respect, responding favourably, or feeling distress. From the receiver's viewpoint, good eye contact reveals the speaker's sincerity, confidence, and truthfulness.

Facial Expression. The expression on a person's face can be almost as revealing of emotion as the eyes. Experts estimate that the human face can display over 250,000 expressions.[9] To hide their feelings, some people can control these expressions and maintain "poker faces." Most of us, however, display our emotions openly. Raising or lowering the eyebrows, squinting the eyes, swallowing nervously, clenching the jaw, smiling broadly—these voluntary and involuntary facial expressions can add to or entirely replace verbal messages.

Posture and Gestures. A person's posture can convey anything from high status and self-confidence to shyness and submissiveness. Leaning toward a speaker suggests attraction and interest; pulling away or shrinking back denotes fear, distrust, anxiety, or disgust. Similarly, gestures can communicate entire thoughts via simple movements. However, the meanings of these movements differ in other cultures. Unless you know local customs, they can get you into trouble. In Canada, for example, forming the thumb and forefinger in a circle means everything's OK. But in Germany and parts of South America, the gesture is obscene.

Nonverbal communication includes all unwritten and unspoken messages, intended or not.

When verbal and nonverbal messages clash, listeners tend to believe the nonverbal message.

The eyes are thought to be the best indicator of a speaker's true feelings.

Nonverbal messages often have different meanings in different cultures.

Understanding body language, gestural literacy, and other nonverbal messages requires that you be aware that they exist and that you value their importance. To take stock of the kinds of messages being sent by your body, ask a classmate to critique your use of eye contact, facial expression, and body movements. Another way to analyze your nonverbal style is to videotape yourself making a presentation and study your performance. This way you can make sure your nonverbal cues send the same message as your words.

How Time, Space, and Territory Send Silent Messages

In addition to nonverbal messages transmitted by your body, three external elements convey information in the communication process: time, space, and distance.

Time. How we structure and use time tells observers about our personality and attitudes. For example, if a financial planner sets aside one-hour blocks of time for client meetings, he is signalling respect for, interest in, and approval of the visitor or the topic to be discussed. If, however, he schedules only a 15-minute meeting, the client may feel less important.

Space. How we order the space around us tells something about ourselves and our objectives. Whether the space is a bedroom, a classroom, an office, or a department, people reveal themselves in the design and grouping of their furniture. Generally, the more formal the arrangement, the more formal the communication. The way office furniture is arranged sends cues on how communication is to take place. An instructor who arranges chairs informally in a circle rather than in straight rows conveys her desire for a more open exchange of ideas. A manager who creates an open office space with few partitions separating workers' desks seeks to encourage an unrestricted flow of communication and work among areas.

Territory. Each of us has certain areas that we feel are our own territory, whether it's a specific spot or just the space around us. Family members may have a favourite living-room chair, students who sit in a chair during their first class may return to that chair throughout the term, a cook might not tolerate intruders in his or her kitchen, and veteran employees may feel that certain work areas and tools belong to them.

We all maintain zones of privacy in which we feel comfortable. Figure 1.4 categorizes the four classic zones of social interaction among North Americans, as formulated by anthropologist Edward T. Hall.[10] Notice that North Americans are a bit standoffish; only intimate friends and family may stand closer than about 45 cm (1.5 feet). If someone violates that territory, North Americans feel uncomfortable and defensive and may step back to re-establish their space.

People convey meaning in how they structure and organize time and how they order the space around themselves.

The distance required for comfortable social interaction is controlled by culture.

FIGURE 1.4 Four Space Zones for Social Interaction

Zone	Distance	Uses
Intimate	0 to 45 cm (1.5 feet)	Reserved for members of the family and other loved ones.
Personal	45 cm to 123 cm (1.5 to 4 feet)	For talking with friends privately. The outer limit enables you to keep someone at arm's length.
Social	123 cm to 360 cm (4 to 12 feet)	For acquaintances, fellow workers, and strangers. Close enough for eye contact yet far enough for comfort.
Public	360 cm and over (12 feet and over)	For use in the classroom and for speeches before groups. Nonverbal cues become important as aids to communication.

How Appearance Sends Silent Messages

The physical appearance of a business document, as well as the personal appearance of an individual, transmits immediate and important nonverbal messages.

Appearance of Business Documents. The way an e-mail, letter, memo, or report looks can have either a positive or a negative effect on the receiver. Sloppy e-mail messages send a nonverbal message that says you are in a terrific hurry or that the reader or message is not important enough for you to care. Envelopes— through their postage, stationery, and printing—can suggest routine, important, or junk mail. Letters and reports can look neat, professional, well organized, and attractive—or just the opposite. In succeeding chapters you'll learn how to create documents that send positive nonverbal messages through their appearance, format, organization, readability, and correctness.

Appearance of People. The way you look—your clothing, grooming, and posture—sends an instant nonverbal message about you. On the basis of what they see, viewers make quick judgments about your status, credibility, personality, and potential. Because appearance is such a powerful force in business, some aspiring professionals are turning for help to image consultants. For example, Kingston, Ontario-based image consultant Catherine Bell's company Prime Impressions offers corporate training in the areas of professional attire, dining protocol, and interview coaching among many others. Bell even offers a "telecoaching" service that provides training over the phone.[11]

"Here come the suits."

Tips for Improving Your Nonverbal Skills

Nonverbal communication can outweigh words in the way it influences how others perceive us. You can harness the power of silent messages by reviewing the following tips for improving nonverbal communication skills:

- **Establish and maintain eye contact.** Remember that in Canada appropriate eye contact signals interest, attentiveness, strength, and credibility.
- **Use posture to show interest.** Encourage communication interaction by leaning forward, sitting or standing erect, and looking alert.

> Because nonverbal clues can mean more than spoken words, learn to use nonverbal communication positively.

- **Improve your decoding skills.** Watch facial expressions and body language to understand the complete verbal and nonverbal message being communicated.
- **Probe for more information.** When you perceive nonverbal cues that contradict verbal meanings, politely seek additional clues (*I'm not sure I understand, Please tell me more about . . .*, or *Do you mean that . . .*).
- **Avoid assigning nonverbal meanings out of context.** Make nonverbal assessments only when you understand a situation or a culture.
- **Associate with people from diverse cultures.** Learn about other cultures to widen your knowledge and tolerance of intercultural nonverbal messages.
- **Appreciate the power of appearance.** Keep in mind that the appearance of you, your business documents, and your business space sends immediate positive or negative messages to receivers.
- **Observe yourself.** Ensure that your verbal and nonverbal messages agree by filming and evaluating yourself making a presentation.
- **Enlist friends and family.** Ask them to monitor your conscious and unconscious body movements and gestures to help you become a more effective communicator.

Understanding How Culture Affects Communication

Comprehending the verbal and nonverbal meanings of a message is difficult even when communicators are from the same culture. But when they are from different cultures, special sensitivity and skills are necessary.

Negotiators for a Canadian company learned this lesson when they were in Japan looking for a trading partner. The Canadians were pleased after their first meeting with representatives of a major Japanese firm. The Japanese had nodded assent throughout the meeting and had not objected to a single proposal. The next day, however, the Canadians were stunned to learn that the Japanese had rejected the entire plan. In interpreting the nonverbal behavioural messages, the Canadians made a typical mistake. They assumed the Japanese were nodding in agreement as fellow Canadians would. In this case, however, the nods of assent indicated comprehension—not approval.

> Verbal and nonverbal meanings are even more difficult to interpret when people are from different cultures.

Every country has a common heritage, joint experience, and shared learning that produce its culture. These elements give members of that culture a complex system of shared values and customs. The system teaches them how to behave; it conditions their reactions. Comparing Canadian values with those in other cultures will broaden your world view. This comparison should also help you recognize some of the values that shape your actions and judgments of others.

Comparing Key Cultural Values

While it may be difficult to define a typical Canadian, one poll found that Canadians are convinced that a unique national identity exists—even if they are unable to agree on what it is. When asked what makes Canadian individuals distinct, respondents highlighted the tendency toward nonviolence and tolerance of others. When asked what makes Canada as a country distinct, respondents cited social programs and a nonviolent tradition as the two leading factors that make Canada different from the United States and other countries.[12]

Research shows that Canadians tend to be more collective, conforming, and conservative than their U.S. neighbours. Canadians are more supportive of civil and political institutions and collective decision making. Americans, on the other hand, tend to be much more supportive of individual decision making and questioning of collective decisions.[13]

Despite the differences outlined above, most Canadians have habits and beliefs similar to those of other members of Western, technologically advanced societies.

With more than 1 billion people and a growing reputation as the second-largest English-speaking country, India has become a hot market for out-sourced call centre jobs. To accommodate the high demand for international customer support professionals in India, the city of Delhi offers more than 300,000 English and communication skills classes—and that is in addition to call centre training offered locally through multinational corporations such as IBM and Wipro. *What challenges do India's call centre professionals face when communicating with customers from across the globe?*

It's impossible to fully cover the many habits and beliefs of Western culture here, but we can look at four of the crucial ones that characterize the Canadian context.

Individualism versus Collectivism.

One of the most identifiable characteristics of Western culture is its built-in tension between individualism, an attitude of independence and freedom from control, and collectivism, the idea that the group or nation is more important than its individual citizens. Political scientist Seymour Martin Lipset has persuasively argued that Canadians are more collectivist than Americans (e.g., they support universal health care).[14] Today, however, regional tensions over oil revenues, for example, between some parts of Western Canada and Central Canada, demonstrate that Canadians' collectivist past may not be as assured in the future. Some non-Western cultures are even more collectivist than Canada. They encourage membership in organizations, groups, and teams and acceptance of group values, duties, and decisions. Members of these cultures sometimes resist independence because it fosters competition and confrontation instead of consensus.

> While Canadians value both individualism and collectivism, as well as personal responsibility, other cultures emphasize group- and team-oriented values.

Formality.

A second significant dimension of Canadian culture is its attitude toward formality. Canadians place less emphasis on tradition, ceremony, and social rules than do people in some other cultures. We dress casually and are soon on a first-name basis with others. Our lack of formality is often characterized by directness in our business dealings. Indirectness, we feel, wastes time, a valuable commodity.

Communication Style.

A third important dimension of our culture relates to communication style. We value straightforwardness, are suspicious of evasiveness, and distrust people who might have a "hidden agenda" or who "play their cards too close to the chest." Canadians also tend to be uncomfortable with silence and impatient with delays. Moreover, we tend to use and understand words literally. Another feature of our collective communication style is our well-known politeness. Academics, journalists, and bloggers continue to debate whether this extra-politeness is real or not: you can Google "politeness Canada" for a taste of the debate. Still, some recent informal research has proved that Canadians tend to communicate and act in a more polite and reserved way than people from other countries.[15]

> Canadians tend to be direct and to understand words literally.

Time Orientation. A fourth dimension of our culture relates to time orientation. Canadians consider time a precious commodity to be conserved. We equate time with productivity, efficiency, and money. Keeping people waiting for business appointments wastes time and is also rude. In other cultures, time may be perceived as an unlimited and never-ending resource to be enjoyed.

Canadians equate time with productivity, efficiency, and money.

Controlling Ethnocentrism and Stereotyping

The process of understanding and accepting people from other cultures is often hampered by two barriers: ethnocentrism and stereotyping. These two barriers, however, can be overcome by developing tolerance, a powerful and effective aid to communication.

Ethnocentrism. The belief in the superiority of one's own culture is known as ethnocentrism. This attitude is found in all cultures. If you were raised in Canada, the values just described probably seem "right" to you, and you may wonder why the rest of the world doesn't function in the same sensible fashion. A Canadian businessperson in a foreign country might be upset at time spent over coffee or other social rituals before any "real" business is transacted. In many cultures, however, personal relationships must be established and nurtured before earnest talks may proceed.

Ethnocentrism is the belief in the superiority of one's own culture and group.

Ethnocentrism causes us to judge others by our own values. We expect others to react as we would, and they expect us to behave as they would. Misunderstandings naturally result. A Canadian who wants to set a deadline for completion of a deal may be considered pushy overseas. Similarly, a foreign businessperson who prefers a handshake to a written contract is seen as naive and possibly untrustworthy by a Canadian. These ethnocentric reactions can be reduced through knowledge of other cultures and development of flexible, tolerant attitudes.

Stereotypes. Our perceptions of other cultures sometimes cause us to form stereotypes about groups of people. A stereotype is an oversimplified behavioural pattern applied to entire groups. For example, the Swiss are hard working, efficient, and neat; Germans are formal, reserved, and blunt; Americans are loud, friendly, and impatient; Canadians are polite, trusting, and tolerant; Asians are gracious, humble, and inscrutable. These attitudes may or may not accurately describe cultural norms. But when applied to individual business communicators, such stereotypes may create misconceptions and misunderstandings. Look beneath surface stereotypes and labels to discover individual personal qualities.

A stereotype is an oversimplified behavioural pattern applied to entire groups.

Tolerance. Working among people from other cultures demands tolerance and flexible attitudes. As global markets expand and as our multicultural society continues to develop, tolerance becomes critical. Tolerance does not mean "putting up with" or "enduring," which is one part of its definition. Instead, tolerance is used in a broader sense. It means having sympathy for and appreciating beliefs and practices that differ from our own.

One of the best ways to develop tolerance is by practising empathy. This means trying to see the world through another's eyes. It means being nonjudgmental, recognizing things as they are rather than as they "should be." It includes the ability to accept others' contributions in solving problems in a culturally appropriate manner. When a few Canadian companies began selling machinery in China, an Asian advisor suggested that the companies rely less on legal transaction and more on creating friendships. Why? In China, the notion of friendship implies a longer-term relationship of trust and loyalty where business obligations are transacted. Instead of insisting on what "should be" (contracts and binding agreements), these companies adopted successful approaches by looking at the challenge from another cultural point of view.[16]

Developing intercultural tolerance means practising empathy, being nonjudgmental, and being patient.

Making the effort to communicate with sensitivity across cultures can be very rewarding in both your work life and your personal life. The suggestions below provide specific tips for preventing miscommunication in oral and written transactions across cultures.

Tips for Minimizing Oral Miscommunication Among Cross-Cultural Audiences

You can improve cross-cultural oral communication by using simple English, speaking slowly, enunciating clearly, encouraging feedback, observing eye messages, accepting blame, and listening without interruption.

When you have a conversation with someone from another culture, you can reduce misunderstandings by following these tips:

- **Use simple English.** Speak in short sentences (under 15 words) with familiar, short words. Eliminate puns, specific cultural references, slang, and jargon (special business terms). Be especially alert to idiomatic expressions that can't be translated, such as burn the midnight oil and under the weather.
- **Speak slowly and enunciate clearly.** Avoid fast speech, but don't raise your voice. Over-punctuate with pauses. Always write numbers for all to see.
- **Encourage accurate feedback.** Ask probing questions, and encourage the listener to paraphrase what you say. Don't assume that a yes, a nod, or a smile indicates comprehension or assent.
- **Check frequently for comprehension.** Avoid waiting until you finish a long explanation to request feedback. Instead, make one point at a time, pausing to check for comprehension. Don't proceed to B until A has been grasped.
- **Observe eye messages.** Be alert to a glazed expression or wandering eyes. These tell you the listener is lost.
- **Accept blame.** If a misunderstanding results, graciously accept the blame for not making your meaning clear.
- **Listen without interrupting.** Curb your desire to finish sentences or to fill out ideas for the speaker. Keep in mind that Canadian listening and speaking habits may not be familiar to other cultures.
- **Remember to smile.** Roger Axtell, international behaviour expert, calls the smile the single most understood and most useful form of communication in either personal or business transactions.
- **Follow up in writing.** After conversations or oral negotiations, confirm the results and agreements with follow-up letters or e-mails. For proposals and contracts, engage a translator to prepare copies in the local language.

Tips for Minimizing Written Miscommunication Among Cross-Cultural Audiences

You can improve cross-cultural written communication by adopting local styles, using short sentences and short paragraphs, avoiding ambiguous wording, and citing numbers carefully.

When you write to someone from a different culture, you can improve your chances of being understood by following these tips:

- **Adopt local styles.** Learn how documents are formatted and how letters are addressed and developed in the intended reader's country. Use local formats and styles.
- **Consider hiring a translator.** Engage a translator if (1) your document is important, (2) your document will be distributed to many readers, or (3) you must be persuasive.
- **Use short sentences and short paragraphs.** Sentences with fewer than 15 words and paragraphs with fewer than 5 lines are most readable.
- **Avoid ambiguous wording.** Avoid idioms (*once in a blue moon*), slang (*my presentation really bombed*), acronyms (*ASAP* for *as soon as possible*), abbreviations (*DBA* for *doing business as*), and jargon (*input, output, bottom line*). Use action-specific verbs (*purchase a printer* rather than *get a printer*).
- **Cite numbers carefully.** Always convert dollar figures into local currency. Avoid using figures to express the month of the year. For clarity, always spell out the month so it doesn't get confused with the day (e.g., 03/05/06 can be read as March 5, 2006 or May 3, 2006).

Capitalizing on Workforce Diversity

As global competition opens world markets, Canadian businesspeople will increasingly interact with customers and colleagues from around the world. At the same time, the Canadian workforce is also becoming more diverse—in race, ethnicity, age, gender, national origin, physical ability, and countless other characteristics. For example, the latest Statistics Canada data shows that the Canadian labour force is made up of 8.4 million men and 7.5 million women, with the gap between the two genders closing quickly.[17]

No longer, say the experts, will the workplace be predominantly male or oriented toward Western cultural values alone. The majority of new entrants to the workforce are women, First Nations, new Canadians, and other visible-minority groups. The Canadian workforce is getting older as the baby-boom generation ages and mandatory retirement laws are abolished or changed in various parts of the country. By the year 2016 half of the Canadian population will be over 40 and 16 percent over 65. At the same time, the proportion of people under 15 will shrink to 19 percent from the current 25 percent.[18]

While the workforce is becoming more diverse, the structure of many businesses across Canada is also changing. As you learned earlier, workers are now organized by teams. Organizations are flatter, and employees are increasingly making decisions among themselves and being asked to manage relationships with customers, suppliers, and others along the supply chain. What does all this mean for you as a future business communicator? Simply put, your job may require you to interact with colleagues and customers from around the world. Your work environment will probably demand that you cooperate effectively with small groups of coworkers. And these coworkers may differ from you in race, ethnicity, gender, age, and other ways.

> You can expect to be interacting with customers and colleagues who may differ from you in race, ethnicity, age, gender, national origin, physical ability, and many other characteristics.

A diverse work environment has many benefits. Customers want to deal with companies that reflect their values and create products and services tailored to their needs. Organizations that hire employees with different experiences and backgrounds are better able to create the customized products these customers desire. In addition, businesses with diverse workforces suffer fewer human rights complaints, fewer union clashes, and less interpersonal conflict. That's why diversity is viewed by a growing number of companies as a critical bottom-line business strategy to improve employee relationships and to increase productivity. For some businesses, diversity also makes economic sense. As Virginia Galt reports in *The Globe and Mail*, "There is one token Canadian on Western Union's national marketing team in Canada. The rest come from China, India, Colombia, Poland, the Philippines." According to Galt, while "Western Union may be further along than most employers in diversifying its work force ... others are planning to follow suit, driven by a competitive need to expand into international markets and serve the increasingly diverse population at home."[19]

> Diversity programs have become an important business strategy because of the benefits to consumers, work teams, and organizations.

Tips for Effective Communication With Diverse Workplace Audiences

Capitalizing on workplace diversity is a challenge for most organizations and individuals. Harmony and acceptance do not happen automatically when people who are dissimilar work together. The following suggestions can help you become a more effective communicator as you enter a rapidly evolving workplace with diverse colleagues and clients.

- **Understand the value of differences.** Diversity makes an organization innovative and creative. Sameness fosters "groupthink," an absence of critical thinking sometimes found in homogeneous groups. Diversity in problem-solving groups encourages independent and creative thinking.

- **Don't expect conformity.** Gone are the days when businesses could demand that new employees or customers simply conform to the existing organization's culture. Today, the value of people who bring new perspectives and ideas is recognized. But with those new ideas comes the responsibility to listen and to allow those new ideas to grow.

- **Create zero tolerance for bias and stereotypes.** Cultural patterns exist in every identity group, but applying these patterns to individuals results in stereotyping. Assuming that Canadians of African descent are good athletes or that women are poor at math fails to admit the immense differences in people in each group. Check your own use of stereotypes and labels. Don't tell sexist or ethnic jokes. Avoid slang, abbreviations, and jargon that imply stereotypes. Challenge others' stereotypes politely but firmly.

- **Practise focused, thoughtful, and open-minded listening.** Much misunderstanding can be avoided by attentive listening. Listen for main points; take notes if necessary to remember important details. The most important part of listening, especially among diverse communicators, is judging ideas, not appearances or accents.

- **Invite, use, and give feedback.** As you learned earlier, a critical element in successful communication is feedback. You can encourage it by asking questions such as *Is there anything you don't understand?* When a listener or receiver responds, use that feedback to adjust your delivery of information. Does the receiver need more details? A different example? Slower delivery? As a good listener, you should also be prepared to give feedback. For example, summarize your understanding of what was said or agreed on.

- **Make fewer assumptions.** Be careful of seemingly insignificant, innocent workplace assumptions. For example, don't assume that everyone wants to observe the holidays with a Christmas party and a decorated tree. Celebrating only Christian holidays in December and January excludes those who honour Hanukkah, Chinese New Year, and Ramadan. Moreover, in workplace discussions, don't assume that everyone is married or wants to be, and don't assume people's sexual orientation. For invitations, avoid phrases such as "managers and their *wives.*" *Spouses* or *partners* is more inclusive.

- **Learn about your cultural self.** Knowing your own cultural biases helps you become more objective and adaptable. Begin to recognize the reactions and thought patterns that are automatic to you as a result of your upbringing. Become more aware of your own values and beliefs. That way you can see them at work when you are confronted by differing values.

- **Seek common ground.** Look for areas where you and others not like you can agree or share opinions. Be prepared to consider issues from many perspectives, all of which may be valid. Accept that there is room for different points of view to coexist peacefully. Although you can always find differences, it's much harder to find similarities. Look for common ground in shared experiences, mutual goals, and similar values. Professor Nancy Adler of McGill University offers three useful methods to help diverse individuals find their way through conflicts made more difficult by cultural differences: (1) Look at the problem from all participants' points of view, (2) uncover the interpretations each side is making on the basis of their cultural values, and (3) create cultural synergy by working together on a solution that works for both sides.[20] Looking for common ground and mutual goals can help each of you reach your objectives even though you may disagree on the approach you should take.

Summing Up and Looking Forward

This chapter described the importance of becoming an effective business communicator in the knowledge economy. Many of the changes in today's dynamic workplace revolve around processing and communicating information. Flattened management hierarchies, participatory management, increased emphasis on work teams, heightened global competition, and innovative communication technologies are all trends that increase the need for good communication skills. Today's computer software provides wonderful assistance for business communicators. Technological tools help you collect information, pour content into templates, improve correctness and precision, add graphics, design professional-looking documents and presentations, and collaborate on team writing projects. To improve your skills, you should understand the communication process. Communication doesn't take place unless senders encode meaningful messages that can be decoded by receivers.

One important part of the communication process is listening. You can become a more active listener by keeping an open mind, listening for main points, capitalizing on lag time, judging ideas and not appearances, taking selective notes, and providing feedback.

The chapter also described ways to help you improve your nonverbal communication skills.

You learned the powerful effect that culture has on communication, and you became more aware of key cultural values. Finally, the chapter discussed ways that businesses and individuals can capitalize on workforce diversity.

The following chapters present the writing process. You will learn specific techniques to help you improve your written expression. Remember, communication skills are not inherited. They are learned.

Critical Thinking

1. Why should students and business professionals bother to worry about communication? Aren't customer service, sales, and profit-making in general, the most important things in business?

2. If you were giving a presentation and you noticed that two of your colleagues weren't listening to you but were speaking to each other, and another colleague was typing on his BlackBerry under the table, what would you do about it?

3. How are listening skills important to employees, supervisors, and executives? Who should have the best listening skills?

4. When and how do we learn about body language? If you had to give a one-hour seminar on body language, what would be your five important take-away points?

5. Since English is becoming the preferred language in business globally, why should Canadians bother to learn about other cultures?

Chapter Review

1. Are communication skills acquired by *nature* or by *nurture*? Explain.

2. List seven trends in the workplace that affect business communicators. How might they affect you in your future career?

3. Name seven ways technology can help you improve written documents.

4. Give a brief definition of the following words:
   a. Encode
   b. Channel
   c. Decode

5. List and explain 11 techniques for improving your listening skills.

6. What is nonverbal communication? Give several examples.

7. Why is good eye contact important for communicators?

8. What is the difference between individualism and collectivism? Can you think of evidence to support the argument that Canadians are more collectivist than Americans?

9. What is ethnocentrism, and how can it be reduced?

10. List and explain seven suggestions for enhancing comprehension when you are talking with people for whom English is a second language.

11. List and explain eight suggestions for becoming a more effective communicator in a diverse workplace.

1.1 Getting to Know You

Your instructor wants to know more about you, your motivation for taking this course, your career goals, and your writing skills.

Your Task. Send an e-mail or write a memo of introduction to your instructor. See Chapter 4 for formats and tips on preparing e-mail messages. In your message include the following:

a. Your reasons for taking this class

b. Your career goals (both temporary and long-term)

c. A brief description of your employment, if any, and your favourite activities

d. An assessment and discussion of your current communication skills, including your strengths and weaknesses

For online classes, write a letter of introduction about yourself with the preceding information. Post your letter to your discussion board. Read and comment on the letters of other students. Think about how people in virtual teams must learn about each other through online messages.

1.2 Class Listening

Observe the listening habits of the students in one of your classes for a week. What barriers to effective listening did you observe? How many of the suggestions described in this chapter are being implemented by listeners in the class? Write a memo or an e-mail to your instructor describing your observations. (See Chapter 4 to learn more about memos and e-mails.)

1.3 Role Play: What Was That You Said?

Think of a recent situation in your life that matches one of these situations: someone wouldn't stop talking, so you stopped listening; there was so much noise around you that you stopped listening; you didn't agree with someone's opinions or didn't like the way he or she looked, so you stopped listening; or someone was talking and you didn't provide feedback. With a partner, write a three-minute skit that dramatizes one of the above "before" situations. Then, write another three-minute skit that dramatizes an "after" situation where the poor listening situation was improved so that you could listen actively. Perform the two skits for your class.

1.4 Listening to the News on TV

Experts say there are several ways to teach listening besides just teaching people when to be quiet and pay attention. One way is to learn how to take notes and another way is to predict what will come next. In order to practise these two listening skills, visit the CBC Digital Archives at **http://archives.cbc.ca/economy_business/business/clips/8727/**. Watch the TV clip from 2004 and

a. Stop the clip after the newsreader says "but as Michel Godbout reports." What do you predict she might say next?

b. Keep listening to the clip. Stop it again when you hear the reporter say "She says the merger is a sad event in the family's history." What do you predict Karen Molson might say next?

c. Watch the clip one more time all the way through, taking notes about important facts, statistics, names, dates, etc. Then, answer the following questions:

  i. What American company is part of this story?

  ii. How much is the merger between the two companies worth?

  iii. What reason does Eric Molson give for the merger?

  iv. What is Karen Molson's chief objection to the merger?

  v. Why has the merger not yet taken place?

d. Come up with two more listening questions you could ask to test how well someone has listened to this clip.

1.5 Video Research: Body Language in Business

YouTube is an amazing resource when searching for visual elements to add to a presentation. Imagine your boss has asked you, a manager, to improve the body language of your employees during presentations. Go to YouTube (**http://www.youtube.com**) and, using the search term "body language business," find three high-quality videos that you can use in a 15-minute presentation to your employees to teach them three separate body language skills or types. Either e-mail the presentation to your instructor (including YouTube links) or give the presentation in front of your class.

1.6 Role Play: You're in My Space

Working in groups of three or four, test the findings of anthropologist Edward T. Hall (see Figure 1.4 on p. 15) by writing a couple of short skits in which you turn his findings upside down. Begin by choosing a zone of social interaction (e.g., intimate), then write a one-minute skit where instead of standing at the correct distance (45 centimetres), a person communicating something intimate stands at an inappropriate distance (e.g., 4 metres) from his or her audience. Perform your skits for your class, and after each skit, ask the class what was wrong with the situation as you presented it. Can you or your classmates dramatize any situations where Hall's findings don't hold up?

1.7 Body Language

What attitudes do the following body movements suggest to you? Do these movements always mean the same thing? What part does context play in your interpretations?

a. Whistling, wringing hands

b. Bowed posture, twiddling thumbs

c. Steepled hands, sprawling sitting position

d. Rubbing hand through hair

e. Pacing back and forth, twisting fingers through hair

f. Wringing hands, tugging ears

1.8 The True Meaning of Diversity

WEB

You are the new human resources manager of a fast-growing sports apparel company, Proforme Ltée, headquartered in Laval, Quebec. The company manufactures T-shirts and baseball caps as well as more specialized clothing for soccer, tennis, and hockey players. Due to increased immigration to the Montreal area (see endnote 3), Proforme's CEO has asked you to propose a plan for diversifying the workforce. He says to you that this "should be easy as it's just a matter of hiring a few immigrants, right?" You want to please your new boss, but you quickly realize that his understanding of diversity issues needs to be updated. A good friend of yours works for the National Bank, a company that has an advanced diversity policy. You can learn some information from the company's Web site. Also research some other companies with strong diversity policies. Write your boss an e-mail that clears up his misconception about diversity (without offending him) and that proposes some positive steps Proforme can take.

Related Web site: **http://www.nbc.ca** On the home page, enter "diversity" into the Search box.

1.9 Analyzing Diversity at Reebok

Reebok grew from a $12-million-a-year sport shoe company into a $3 billion footwear and apparel powerhouse without giving much thought to the hiring of employees. "When we were growing very, very fast, all we did was bring another friend into work the next day," recalled Sharon Cohen, Reebok vice president. "Everybody hired nine of their friends. Well, it happened that nine white people hired nine of their friends, so guess what? They were white, all about the same age. And then we looked up and said, 'Wait a minute. We don't like the way it looks here.' That's the kind of thing that can happen when you are growing very fast and thoughtlessly."[21]

Your Task. In what ways would Reebok benefit by diversifying its staff? What competitive advantages might it gain? Outline your reasoning in an e-mail message to your instructor.

1.10 Translating Idioms

Explain in simple English what the following idiomatic expressions mean. Assume that you are explaining them to people for whom English is a second language.

a. let the cat out of the bag

b. take the bull by the horns

c. he is a tightwad

d. putting the cart before the horse

e. to be on the road

f. lend someone a hand

g. with flying colours

h. turn over a new leaf

1.11 Role Play: Walking a Fine Line With a New Client

You are an account manager at an up-and-coming advertising agency in Calgary named Crane & Kim. You've recently landed a new client, IPCO Petroleum, one of Canada's best-known oil and gas producers. IPCO has hired you to perk up its image, which hasn't changed much in the last 20 years. As part of your mandate, you are to design and produce a television commercial and a series of newspaper advertisements promoting IPCO as a progressive company. Your design and production staff has come up with an energetic new campaign that features people of various ethnicities and racial backgrounds. When Frank Pekar, director of marketing at IPCO, sees the campaign materials for the first time, he is anxious. He tells you that the blatant diversity in the materials is not really what he's looking for. Keeping in mind that you need to balance your personal belief in diversity and your belief in the strengths of diversity as a marketing tactic alongside Pekar's reservations and his importance as a client, script a five-minute skit between yourself and Pekar where you try to settle the issue. Perform your skit with a partner for your class.

1.12 Interview: The Changing World of Communication

A lot of workplaces are using new methods of communication, such as blogs, intranets, VOIP (Voice over Internet Protocol), and videoconferencing.

Your task. Interview a friend or family member who is working full-time. Ask him or her to explain the main changes in workplace communication over the past ten years. Next, ask him or her to tell you what a "day in the life" at the office is like, specifically concerning communication (for example, how many phone calls, e-mails, meetings, Web sites, blogs, instant messages, and so on he or she encounters). Then, ask him or her to offer a list of pros and cons about new communication technologies used in the workplace. Finally, ask one more communication technology-related question that you come up with by yourself. Once your interview is finished, analyze what your interviewee told you in order to summarize the information for your instructor and your class. Create a five-slide PowerPoint presentation in which you summarize your interview.

The following sentences contain a variety of inaccuracies, including grammar, punctuation, style, and spelling. Revise each sentence making the appropriate corrections. Then, learn about each type of error in the Grammar/Mechanics Handbook at the back of this book. More exercises are located in the handbook to help reinforce your ability to write accurately.

Example: Before eating sixteen members of the Committee met in the sabin centre.

Revision: Before eating, 16 members of the committee met in the Sabin Centre.

1. At last Sundays graduation ceremonys Jennifer Riddock who uses a wheelchair, was honoured because she was the only graduate who had never missed a day of classes.

2. If its not to late to register my brother and myself plan to take courses in History, Management, and English.

3. In just two hours time I was able to locate 9 excelent Web sites, containing relevant information for my report.

4. Mistakes are a fact of life, however it is the response to the error that really counts.

5. Complicating the problem is inefficent legislation, and lack of enforcement personel.

6. We cannot procede with the mailing, until the list of names and address are verified.

7. My new Sport Utility Vehicle came equiped with: antilock brakes, alloy wheels and a trip computer.

8. My bosses biggest computer worry is the possibility of us being hacked, and not knowing it.

9. Beside your résumé and cover letter you must submit a seperate employment application form.

10. Elizabeth was suprised that the Ingles who once owned 2 popular resterants were now her neighbour.

11. Although the manufacture promised excelent milage my wife and me get only fifteen miles to the gallon.

12. Your bill of two hundred dollars is now ninety days overdue, therefore we are submitting it to a agency for collection.

13. If you have all ready sent your payment please disregard this notice.

14. Of the 350 letters mailed only five were returned as reported by Ms. Sandhus assistant.

Document for Revision

The following document contains some writing accuracy issues, including grammar, spelling, punctuation, and style. Read the document and edit it as you go, identifying inaccuracies and fixing them. Your instructor will take up the correct answers with you.

Memo

To: Tran Nguyen
From: Rachel Stivers, Manager
CC:
Date: May 14, 2012
Re: WORK AT HOME GUIDELINES

Hello

Hi Tran,

please Since you will be completeing most of your work at home for the next 4 months. Follow these guidelines; :

board
1. Check your message bored daily and respond promptly, to those who are trying to reach you.
2. Call the office at least twice a day to pick up any voicemail, *and* return these calls promly.
3. Transmit any work you do, via e-mail to Jerry Jackson in our computer *Jerry* services department, he will analyze each weeks accounts, and send it to the proper Departments.
4. Provide me with monthly reports of your progress.

Staff meetings will be held once a week on Friday's at 10:00am our
We will continue to hold once a week staff meetings on Friday at 10 a.m. in the morning. Do you think it would be possible for you to attend 1 or 2 of these *one/two* meeting. The next one is Friday May 17th.

will
I know you will work satisfactory at home Tran. Following these basic guidelines should help you accomplish your work, and provide the office with adequate contact with you.

Cheers,

Rachel

What Employers Are Looking For

In this workshop, you will investigate the importance, prevalence, and relevance of communication skills in today's workplace.

WEB

Your Task

Go to **http://www.workopolis.ca,** the largest job-search site in Canada. Click on "Search Jobs." Choose three different job categories that interest you (for example, accounting, marketing, financial).

- For each job category, find five entry-level jobs you might apply for at the end of your college/university program.
- For each of the 15 jobs you locate, read carefully the qualifications for the position. Make a note of each time that communication skills are mentioned.
- Create three Excel spreadsheets, one for each job category. In each spreadsheet, list the company, position, and communication-related skills and qualifications required.
- Once you've filled in your three spreadsheets with the 15 jobs and their communication qualifications, analyze the results of your research in order to answer the following question: How important are communication skills to today's employers?

Related Web sites: You may also consider http://www.monster.ca for this workshop.

2

The Business Writing Process

COMMUNICATION TECHNOLOGY IN THE NEWS

Employers Slow to Embrace Web 2.0's Potential at Work

Source: Sarah Dobson, *Canadian HR Reporter*, May 17, 2010, Vol. 23, issue 10, p. 2. Reprinted with permission.

In June 2008, Canam Group decided to start a Facebook page in anticipation of its tri-annual managers' conference. About 200 employees at the Quebec construction company created profiles and were presented with different activities before the three-day event.

The first was a quiz assessing personality colours, which Canam used to sort people into "parties" for the opening night, as with an election (those who didn't respond to the survey were labeled "independent"). The managers were also encouraged to post pictures as part of a contest.

"Our goal was to present social media to this top management and, after that, develop our intranet the (Web) 2.0 way, using Facebook . . . to show them how easy it is to use, to publish pictures, publish videos, use a forum," said Nathalie Pilon, Canam's electronic communications manager. "We showed them what social media is and it was a real success."

Canam is now encouraging employees to use social media for business purposes. It resurrected a shelved intranet project and went on to launch other initiatives, including "CanamTube," for internal purposes such as training or CEO speeches, and a Flickr account to publish pictures of construction projects.

In May, the company hopes to publish a "Canampedia," similar to Wikipedia, providing a company lexicon that can be modified by employees. The content will be available in French and English and people can add more languages.

"Employees are asking for tools like that in the company," said Pilon. "People are asking to be able to publish content, they want to see the same thing that they see outside in the company."

Canam's attitude is a rarity, according to a recent survey from Aon Consulting Canada. Despite the proliferation of social networks, rich media outputs and online collaboration tools, organizations have been slow to adopt the power of Web 2.0. Only 12 per cent use Facebook, Twitter or similar social networks to communicate with employees or recruit potential employees while 71 per cent restrict Internet usage at work.

"A lot of employers are not really maximizing the power of this kind of communication, mostly because of fear and the fact that, on their side, they may perceive it as a high risk because it's unpredictable," said Diane McElroy, senior vice president and communications practice lead at Aon.

It's clear there's a giant gap between the workplace and people's personal lives, said Ron Shewchuk, a corporate communications consultant in Vancouver.

"These new ways of communicating have woven themselves into the very fabric of our social existence and yet they have been very slow to be adopted in the workplace," he said. "This is not something for geeks and teenagers. It really is time for the corporate world to start embracing these tools."

Many employees are not fully engaged and Web 2.0 provides access to powerful tools of engagement, said Shewchuk.

"All these social media tools are built from the ground up, to engage people, to improve collaboration, to create a sense of community, and all of these things are what drive employee engagement and drive retention."

If an employer limits or bans the use of these tools, most people will find another way.

"Why not actually sanction it and be able to control it, rather than just turning a blind eye to it?" he said.

That sentiment is backed up by a soon-to-be-released survey by Aon of 8,000 employees that found workers are already using Web 2.0 tools to get their jobs done, even if it's not directly approved by the employer. This can involve setting up networks to seek co-worker feedback around problems or informal chat pages used by global workers. They find that more efficient than what their employer has, said McElroy.

"Employers are still using the very traditional means of communication and missing a huge potential of using social media in the workplace. And it has many benefits, because it's more cost-effective, it reaches more people."

Employers Slow to Embrace Web 2.0's Potential at Work (*contd.*)

Those companies that are using these tools are largely using them for recruitment purposes, found Aon. Canam has learned, for recruitment purposes, 2.0 media are not only a good idea but necessary, said Pilon.

"New people coming in the company ask for that, they go directly to the intranet," she said.

But executive buy-in is the number-one barrier to social media implementation and rollout, according to a 2009 survey by Prescient Digital Media, which also found about one-half of organizations in the Western world have some form of Web 2.0 on the intranet, said Toby Ward, Toronto-based president and CEO of Prescient.

"Many executives don't have time to be messing around with social media and many don't understand it," he said.

Corporate reluctance can also be explained by perceived risks around giving workers the ability to comment on and rate a company or do potential damage to its reputation or trade secrets.

"That goes against traditional style of management, which is top-down: 'Why would we expose ourselves to public criticism inside the company?'" said Shewchuk.

But the risks are "far outweighed by the ability that it gives people to get information, to collaborate online, to have access to that world," he said.

There's also concern about employee productivity, but if someone is wasting time on these tools, it's a management or supervision problem, just as it is when someone goes for too many smoke breaks, said Pilon. If there is abuse of the media, Canam will treat it on a case-by-case basis, she said.

When it comes to rules and governance, fewer than one third (31 per cent) of employers have a social media policy, found Aon's survey. Canam recently published a policy to help workers understand the company's mindset and to encourage them to use the tools, she said.

Prescient's 2009 survey found about 58 per cent of companies have a governance policy and that appears to remain the same for 2010.

"It's a little disappointing that more organizations aren't doing their homework and their due diligence around this stuff," said Ward, because if people are using these tools externally, organizations are left quite vulnerable.

Summarize the article you've just read in a paragraph of two to three sentences. Answer the following questions, either on your own or in a small group. Be prepared to present your answers in a short presentation or in an e-mail to your instructor.

QUESTIONS:

1. How does what you've learned in this article change your perception of business communication?

2. How might what you've learned in this article change your own communication style?

3. Come up with pro and con arguments for the following debate/discussion topic: Social media is more of a personal communication trend than a workplace communication trend. Attempt to generate primary data for your discussion by canvassing everyone in your life who works and asking them one question: "Do you use social media at work?"

Before You Write

I write for a number of different business audiences and I always consider my audience before starting. The content, tone, and level of detail varies depending on whether I'm writing to clients, financial advisors, or other stakeholders.[1]

John DeGoey,
*Vice President, Burgeonvest
Securities Limited*

© CHRIS SCHMIDT/ISTOCKPHOTO.COM

LEARNING OBJECTIVES

1. Understand that business writing should be audience oriented, purposeful, and economical.

2. Identify and implement the three phases of the writing process.

3. Appreciate the importance of analyzing the task and profiling the audience for business messages.

4. Create messages that spotlight audience benefits and cultivate a "you" view.

5. Develop a conversational tone and use positive language.

6. Explain the need for inclusive language, plain expression, and familiar words.

Basics of Business Writing

An Ipsos Reid study conducted among Canadian CEOs indicated that CEOs devote half of their time (49 percent) to communicating with a variety of audiences including both external stakeholders, such as investors, government, the media, and customers, and internal audiences, such as employees and management.[2] All members of the organization, from the CEO to frontline staff, must concern themselves with their audience.

Audience awareness is one of the basics of business communication, as John DeGoey indicates above. This chapter focuses on writing for business audiences. Business writing may be different from other writing you have done. High-school or college compositions and term papers may have required you to describe your

Excellent communicators concentrate on the receivers of their messages.

feelings, display your knowledge, or prove a thesis or argument. Business writing, however, has different goals. In preparing business messages and oral presentations, you'll find that your writing needs to be

- **Audience-oriented.** You will concentrate on looking at a problem from the receiver's perspective instead of seeing it from your own. A recent ad campaign for Microsoft's Windows 7 phone with the tagline "Be here now" is a subtle hint that instead of getting sidetracked by our gadgets and social media, we should remember our real-time audiences. If you Google "Windows Phone 7 ads" you can find the less-subtle and very funny TV ads from this campaign that drive the point home.
- **Purposeful.** You will be writing to solve problems and convey information. You will have a definite purpose to fulfill in each message.
- **Professional.** You should fight the temptation to write e-mails and other messages at work that look and sound like the kind of informal messages you would send to friends.
- **Economical.** You should always try to present ideas clearly and concisely. Length, especially in this day of short-messaging, is not necessarily rewarded.

Business writing is audience-oriented, purposeful, and economical.

The ability to prepare concise, audience-centred, professional, and purposeful messages does not come naturally. Very few people, especially beginners, can sit down and compose an effective letter or report without training. But following a systematic process, studying model messages, and practising the craft can make nearly anyone a successful business writer or speaker.

Writing Process for Business Messages and Oral Presentations

Following a systematic process helps beginning writers create effective messages and presentations.

Whether you are preparing an e-mail, memo, letter, or oral presentation, the process will be easier if you follow a systematic plan. Our plan breaks the entire task into three phases: prewriting, writing, and revising, as shown in Figure 2.1.

The writing process has three parts: prewriting, writing, and revising.

As an example, let's say that you own a popular local fast-food restaurant franchise. At rush times, you've got a big problem. Customers complain about the chaotic multiple queues to approach the service counter. You once saw two customers nearly get into a fight over who was first in line. And customers often are so intent on looking for ways to improve their positions in line that they fail to look at the menu. Then they don't know what to order when their turn arrives. You want to convince other franchise owners that a single-line (serpentine) system would work better. You could telephone the owners, but you want to present a serious argument

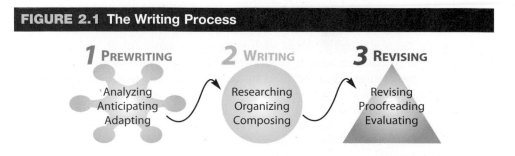

FIGURE 2.1 The Writing Process

1 PREWRITING — Analyzing Anticipating Adapting

2 WRITING — Researching Organizing Composing

3 REVISING — Revising Proofreading Evaluating

with good points that they will remember and be willing to act on when they gather for their next district meeting. You decide to write a letter that you hope will win their support.

Prewriting

The first phase of the writing process involves analyzing your purpose for writing. The audience for your letter will be other franchise owners who represent a diverse group of individuals with varying educational backgrounds. Your purpose in writing is to persuade fellow franchisees that a change in policy would improve customer service. You are convinced that a single-line system, such as that used in banks, would reduce wait times and make customers happier because they would not have to worry about where they are in line.

Prewriting also involves anticipating how your audience will react to your message. You're sure that some of the other owners will agree with you, but others might fear that customers seeing a long single line might go elsewhere. In adapting your message to the audience, you try to think of the right words and the right tone that will win approval.

> **The first phase of the writing process involves analyzing and anticipating the audience and then adapting to that audience.**

Writing

The second phase of the process involves researching, organizing, and then composing the message. In researching information for this letter, you would probably investigate other kinds of businesses that use single lines for customers. You might check out your competitors. What are other fast-food outlets doing? You might do some phoning around to see if other franchise owners are concerned about customer lines. Before writing to the entire group, you might generate ideas with a few owners to increase the number of potential solutions to the problem.

Once you have collected enough information, you would focus on organizing your letter. Should you start out by offering your solution? Or should you work up to it slowly, describing the problem, presenting your evidence, and then ending with the solution? The final step is actually composing the letter. Naturally, you'll do it at your computer so that you can make revisions easily.

> **The second phase of the writing process includes researching, organizing the message, and actually writing it.**

Revising

The third phase of the process involves revising, proofreading, and evaluating your letter. After writing the first draft, you'll spend time revising the message for clarity, conciseness, tone, and readability. Could parts of it be rearranged to make your point more effectively? This is the time when you look for ways to improve the organization and tone of your message. Next, you'll spend time proofreading carefully to ensure correct spelling, grammar, punctuation, and format. The final step involves evaluating your entire message to decide whether it accomplishes your goal.

> **The third phase of the writing process includes revising for clarity and readability, proofreading for errors, and evaluating for effectiveness.**

Scheduling the Writing Process

Although the business writing process described above shows the three phases equally, the time you spend on each varies depending on the complexity of the task, the purpose, the audience, and your schedule. Here are some rough estimates for scheduling a project:

- Prewriting—25 percent
- Writing—25 percent
- Revising—50 percent

These are rough guides, yet you can see that good writers spend most of their time on the final phase of revising and proofreading. What's critical to remember, though, is that revising is a major component of the writing process. It may appear that you complete one phase of the business writing process and progress to the next, always following the same order. Most business writing, however, is not that rigid. Although writers perform the tasks described, the steps may be rearranged, abbreviated, or repeated. Some writers revise every sentence and paragraph as they go. Many find that new ideas occur after they've begun to write, causing them to back up, alter the organization, and rethink their plan.

Analyzing the Purpose for Writing

We've just taken a look at the total writing process. As you develop your business writing skills, you should expect to follow this process closely. With experience, though, you'll become like other good writers and presenters who alter, compress, and rearrange the steps as needed. But following a plan is helpful at first. The remainder of this chapter covers the first phase of the writing process. You'll learn to analyze the purpose for writing, anticipate how your audience will react, and adapt your message to the audience.

Identifying Your Purpose

The primary purpose of most business messages is to inform or to persuade; the secondary purpose is to promote goodwill.

As you begin to write a message, ask yourself two important questions: (1) Why am I sending this message? and (2) What do I hope to achieve? Your responses will determine how you organize and present your information.

Your message may have primary and secondary purposes. For college work your primary purpose may be merely to complete the assignment; secondary purposes might be to make yourself look good and to get a good grade. The primary purposes for sending business messages are typically to inform and to persuade. A secondary purpose is to promote goodwill: you and your organization want to look good in the eyes of your audience.

Selecting the Best Channel

Choosing an appropriate channel depends on the importance of the message, the feedback required, the need for a permanent record, the cost, the formality needed, and best practices of your company.

After identifying the purpose of your message, you need to select the most appropriate communication channel. Some information is most efficiently and effectively delivered orally. Other messages should be written, and still others are best delivered electronically. Whether to set up a meeting, send a message by e-mail, or write a report depends on some of the following factors:

- Importance of the message
- Amount and speed of feedback required
- Necessity of a permanent record
- Cost of the channel
- Degree of formality desired
- Best practices in your company

An interesting theory, called media richness, describes the extent to which a channel or medium recreates or represents all the information available in the original message. A richer medium, such as face-to-face conversation, permits more interactivity and feedback. A leaner medium, such as a report or proposal, presents a flat, one-dimensional message. Richer media enable the sender to provide more verbal and visual cues, as well as allowing the sender to tailor the message to the audience.

FIGURE 2.2 Choosing Communication Channels

Channel	Best Use
Blog	When one person needs to present digital information easily so that it is available to others.
E-mail	When you need feedback but not immediately. Lack of security makes it problematic for personal, emotional, or private messages.
Face-to-face conversation	When you need a rich, interactive medium. Useful for persuasive, bad-news, and personal messages.
Face-to-face group meeting	When group decisions and consensus are important. Inefficient for merely distributing information.
Fax	When your message must cross time zones or international boundaries, when a written record is significant, or when speed is important.
Instant message	When you are online and need a quick response. Useful for learning whether someone is available for a phone conversation.
Letter	When a written record or formality is required, especially with customers, the government, suppliers, or others outside an organization.
Memo	When you want a written record to clearly explain policies, discuss procedures, or collect information within an organization.
Phone call	When you need to deliver or gather information quickly, when nonverbal cues are unimportant, and when you cannot meet in person.
Report or proposal	When you are delivering considerable data internally or externally.
Voice mail message	When you wish to leave important or routine information that the receiver can respond to when convenient.
Video- or teleconference	When group consensus and interaction are important but members are geographically dispersed.
Wiki	When digital information must be made available to others. Useful for collaboration because participants can easily add, remove, and edit content.

The six factors mentioned above will help you decide which of the channels shown in Figure 2.2 is most appropriate for delivering a message.

Switching to Faster Channels

Technology and competition continue to accelerate the pace of business today. As a result, communicators are switching to ever-faster means of exchanging information. In the past, business messages within organizations were delivered largely by hard-copy memos. Responses would typically take a couple of days. But that's too slow for today's communicators. Cell phones, faxes, Web sites, e-mail, and instant messaging can deliver that information much faster than traditional channels of communication.

In fact, according to business writer Don Tapscott, within some organizations and between colleagues at different organizations, instant messaging is being added to e-mail as a popular channel choice. Tapscott even names some large companies, like IBM, that have abandoned e-mail in favour of instant messaging.[3] Instant messaging software alerts colleagues in distant locations that a coworker is prepared to participate in an online exchange. Once signed in, individuals or entire groups can carry on and manage two-way discussions. Instant messaging resembles a conversation where a sender types a one- or two-sentence note, followed by the receiver who types his or her response to the note. Responses appear next to the original message for both sender and receiver to see. Through instant messaging, an entire

conversation can be completed online without the time delay that can occur when sending and responding to e-mail.

A few years ago, *The Globe and Mail* reported that instant messaging would soon surpass e-mail as the primary way in which people interact electronically. While this prediction has not yet come true, experts like Tapscott signal that instant messaging is certainly a force to be reckoned with, especially because it is already so much a part of many young people's personal lives.[4]

Within many organizations, hard-copy memos are still written, especially for messages that require persuasion, permanence, or formality. But the channel of choice for corporate communicators today is clearly e-mail. It's fast, cheap, and easy. Thus, fewer hard-copy memos are being written. Fewer letters are also being written. That's because many customer service functions are now being served through Web-based customer relationship management tools or by e-mail. Interestingly, the fact that fewer memos and letters are being written does not make knowing how to write one less important. In fact, it makes it more important. This is because novice business communicators often assume business e-mails can be as informal as their personal e-mails. The reality is that business e-mails should be nearly as structured as memos and letters have always been.

Whether your channel choice is e-mail, a hard-copy memo, or a report, you'll be a more effective writer if you spend sufficient time in the prewriting phase.

Anticipating the Audience

A good writer anticipates the audience for each message: What is the reader like? How will the reader react to the message? Although you can't always know exactly who the reader is, you can imagine some characteristics of the reader. Picturing a typical reader is important in guiding what you write. By profiling your audience and shaping a message to respond to that profile, you are more likely to achieve your communication goals.

Profiling the Audience

Visualizing your audience is a pivotal step in the writing process. The questions in Figure 2.3 will help you profile your audience. How much time you devote to

FIGURE 2.3 Asking the Right Questions to Profile Your Audience

Primary Audience	Secondary Audience
Who is my primary reader or listener?	Who might see or hear this message in addition to the primary audience?
What are my personal and professional relationships with that person?	How do these people differ from the primary audience?
What position does the person hold in the organization?	Do I need to include more background information?
How much does that person know about the subject?	How must I reshape my message to make it understandable and acceptable to others to whom it might be forwarded?
What do I know about that person's education, beliefs, culture, and attitudes?	
Should I expect a neutral, positive, or negative response to my message?	

answering these questions depends on your message and its context. An analytical report that you compose for management or an oral presentation before a big group would, of course, demand considerable audience anticipation. On the other hand, an e-mail message to a coworker or a letter to a familiar supplier might require only a few moments of planning. No matter how short your message, spend some time thinking about the audience so that you can adjust your words appropriately for your readers or listeners. "The most often unasked question in business and professional communication," claims a writing expert, "is as simple as it is important: *Have I thought enough about my audience?*"[5]

> By profiling your audience before you write, you can identify the appropriate tone, language, and channel.

Responding to the Profile

Profiling your audience helps you make decisions about shaping the message. You'll discover what kind of language is appropriate, whether you're free to use specialized technical terms, whether you should explain everything, and so on. You'll decide whether your tone should be formal or informal, and you'll select the most desirable channel. Imagining whether the receiver is likely to be neutral, positive, or negative will help you determine how to organize your message.

> After profiling the audience, you can decide whether the receiver will be neutral, positive, or hostile toward your message.

Another advantage of profiling your audience is considering the possibility of a secondary audience. For example, let's say you start to write an e-mail message to your supervisor, Sheila, describing a problem you are having. Halfway through the message you realize that Sheila will probably forward this message to her boss, the vice president. Sheila will not want to summarize what you said; instead she will take the easy route and merely forward your e-mail. When you realize that the vice president will probably see this message, you decide to back up and use a more formal tone. You remove your inquiry about Sheila's family, you reduce your complaints, and you tone down your language about why things went wrong. Instead, you provide more background information, and you are more specific in identifying items the vice president might not recognize. Analyzing the task and anticipating the audience help you adapt your message so that you can create an efficient and effective message.

Adapting to the Task and Audience

After analyzing your purpose and anticipating your audience, you must convey your purpose to that audience. Adaptation is the process of creating a message that suits your audience.

One important aspect of adaptation is tone. Tone, conveyed largely by the words chosen for the message, determines how a receiver feels upon reading or hearing it.

> Writers improve the tone of a message by emphasizing reader benefits, cultivating a polite "you" attitude, and using a conversational tone and inclusive language.

Skilled communicators create a positive tone in their messages by using a number of adaptive techniques, some of which are unconscious. These include spotlighting audience benefits, cultivating a polite "you" attitude, sounding conversational, and using inclusive language. Additional adaptive techniques include using positive expressions and preferring plain language with familiar words.

Audience Benefits

Smart communicators know that the chance of success of any message is greatly improved by emphasizing reader benefits. This means making readers see how the message affects and benefits them personally.

It is human nature for individuals to be most concerned with matters that relate directly to themselves. This is a necessary condition of existence. If we weren't interested in attending to our own needs, we could not survive.

Adapting your message to the receiver's needs means temporarily putting yourself in that person's shoes. This skill is known as empathy. Empathic senders think about how a receiver will decode a message. They try to give something to the receiver, solve the receiver's problems, save the receiver money, or just understand the feelings and position of that person. Which of the following messages is more appealing to the audience?

Empathy involves thinking of how the receiver feels and is likely to respond.

The most successful messages focus on the audience.

Sender Focus	Audience Focus
To enable us to update our shareholder records, we ask that the enclosed card be returned.	So that you may promptly receive dividend cheques and information related to your shares, please return the enclosed card.
Our warranty becomes effective only when we receive an owner's registration.	Your warranty begins working for you as soon as you return your owner's registration.
The Human Resources Department requires that the online survey be completed immediately so that we can allocate our training resource funds.	By filling out the online survey, you can be one of the first employees to sign up for the new career development program.

Polite "You" View

Notice how many of the previous audience-focused messages included the word *you*. In concentrating on receiver benefits, skilled communicators naturally develop the "you" view. They emphasize second-person pronouns (*you, your*) instead of first-person pronouns (*I/we, us, our*). Whether your goal is to inform, persuade, or promote goodwill, the most attention-getting words you can use are *you* and *your*. Compare the following examples.

Because receivers are most interested in themselves, emphasize you whenever possible.

"I/We" View	I have scheduled your vacation to begin May 1.
"You" View	You may begin your vacation May 1.
"I/We" View	We have shipped your order by courier, and we are sure it will arrive in time for the sales promotion on January 15.
"You" View	Your order will be delivered by courier in time for your sales promotion January 15.
"I/We" View	As a financial planner, I care about my clients' well-being.
"You" View	Your well-being is the most important consideration for financial planners like me.

To see if you're really concentrating on the reader, try using the "empathy index." In one of your messages, count all the second-person references; then count all the first-person references. Your empathy index is low if the *I*'s and *we*'s outnumber the *you*'s and *your*'s.

The use of *you* is more than merely a numbers game. Second-person pronouns can be overused and misused. Readers appreciate genuine interest; on the other hand, they resent obvious attempts at manipulation. Some sales messages, for example, become untrustworthy when they include *you* dozens of times in a direct mail promotion. Furthermore, the word can sometimes create the wrong impression. Consider this statement: *You cannot return merchandise until you receive written approval.* The word *you* appears twice, but the reader feels singled out for criticism. In the following version the message is less personal and more positive: *Customers may return merchandise with written approval.* In short, avoid using *you* for general statements that suggest blame and could cause ill will.

In recognizing the value of the "you" attitude, however, writers do not have to sterilize their writing and totally avoid any first-person pronouns or words that show their feelings. Skilled communicators are able to convey sincerity, warmth, and enthusiasm by the words they choose. Don't be afraid to use phrases such as *I'm happy* or *We're delighted,* if you truly are. When speaking face to face, communicators show sincerity and warmth with nonverbal cues such as a smile and pleasant voice tone. In letters, memos, and e-mail messages, however, only expressive words and phrases can show these feelings. These phrases suggest hidden messages that say to readers and customers, "You are important, I am listening, and I'm honestly trying to please you."

Emphasize *you* but don't eliminate all *I* and *we* statements.

Conversational but Professional

Most business e-mails, letters, memos, and reports are about topics that would otherwise be part of a conversation. Thus, they are most effective when they convey an informal, conversational tone instead of a formal, pretentious tone. But messages should not become so conversational that they sound overly casual and unprofessional. With the increasing use of e-mail, a major problem has developed. Sloppy, unprofessional expression appears in many e-mail messages. You'll learn more about e-mail in Chapter 4. At this point, though, we urge you to strive for a warm, conversational tone that does not include slang or overly casual wording such as texting/messaging abbreviations like LOL. The following examples should help you distinguish between three levels of diction.

Strive for conversational expression, but also remember to be professional.

Unprofessional (low-level diction)	Conversational (mid-level diction)	Formal (high-level diction)
badmouth	criticize	denigrate
guts	nerve	courage
pecking order	line of command	dominance hierarchy
ticked off	upset	provoked
rat on	inform	betray
rip off	steal	embezzle/appropriate
TTYL	talk to you later	I'll be in touch soon about this

Unprofessional	If we just hang in there, we can grab the contract.
Conversational	If we don't get discouraged, we can win the contract.
Formal	If the principals persevere, they can acquire the contract.

Your goal is a warm, friendly tone that sounds professional. Talk to the reader with words that are comfortable to you. Avoid long and complex sentences. Use familiar pronouns such as *I, we,* and *you* and an occasional contraction, such as *we're* or *I'll.* Stay away from third-person constructions such as *the undersigned, the writer,* and *the affected party.* Also avoid legal terminology and technical words. Your writing will be easier to read and understand if it sounds like the following conversational examples:

Formal	All employees are herewith instructed to return the appropriately designated contracts to the undersigned.
Conversational	Please return your contracts to me.
Formal	Pertaining to your order, we must verify the sizes that your organization requires prior to consignment of your order to our shipper.
Conversational	We'll send your order as soon as we confirm the sizes you need.
Formal	The writer wishes to inform the above-referenced individual that subsequent payments may henceforth be sent to the address cited below.
Conversational	Your payments should now be sent to us in Sudbury.
Formal	To facilitate ratification of this agreement, your negotiators urge that the membership respond in the affirmative.
Conversational	We urge you to approve the agreement by voting yes.

Positive Language

Positive language creates goodwill and gives more options to receivers.

The clarity and tone of a message are considerably improved if you use positive rather than negative language. Positive language generally conveys more information than negative language. Moreover, positive messages are uplifting and pleasant to read. Positive wording tells what *is* and what *can be done* rather than what *isn't* and what *can't be done.* For example, *Your order cannot be shipped by January 10* is not nearly as informative as *Your order will be shipped January 20.* Notice in the following examples how you can revise the negative tone to reflect a more positive impression.

Negative	We are unable to send your shipment until we receive proof of your payment.
Positive	We look forward to sending your shipment as soon as we receive your payment.
Negative	You will never regret opening an account with us.
Positive	Your new account enables you to purchase high-quality clothing at reasonable prices.
Negative	If you fail to pass the exam, you will not qualify.
Positive	You'll qualify if you pass the exam.
Negative	Although I've never had a paid position before, I have completed a work placement in a law office as an administrative assistant while completing my diploma.
Positive	My work placement experience in a lawyer's office and my recent training in legal procedures and computer applications can be assets to your organization.

Courteous Language

Maintaining a courteous tone involves not just guarding against rudeness but also avoiding words that sound demanding or preachy. Expressions such as *you should*, *you must*, and *you have to* cause people to instinctively react with *Oh, yeah?* One remedy is to turn these demands into rhetorical questions that begin with *Will you please....* Giving reasons for a request also softens the tone.

Even when you feel justified in displaying anger, remember that losing your temper or being sarcastic will seldom help you accomplish your goals as a business communicator: to inform, to persuade, and to create goodwill. When you are irritated, frustrated, or infuriated, keep cool and try to defuse the situation. In dealing with customers in telephone conversations, use polite phrases such as *It was a pleasure speaking with you, I would be happy to assist you with that*, and *Thank you for being so patient*.

Less Courteous	**More Courteous and Helpful**
You must complete the report before Friday.	Will you please complete the report by Friday.
You should organize a car pool in this department.	Organizing a car pool will reduce your transportation costs and help preserve the environment.
This is the second time I've written. Can't you get anything right?	Please credit my account for $450. My latest statement shows that the error noted in my letter of April 2 has not been corrected.
Am I the only one who can read the operating manual?	Let's review the operating manual together so that you can get your documents to print correctly next time.

Inclusive Language

A business writer who is alert and empathic will strive to use words that include rather than exclude people. Some words have been called *sexist* because they seem to exclude females. Notice the use of the masculine pronouns *he* and *his* in the following sentences:

If a physician is needed, *he* will be called.

Every renter must read *his* rental agreement carefully.

Sensitive communicators avoid language that excludes people.

These sentences illustrate an age-old grammatical rule called "common gender." When a speaker or writer did not know the gender (sex) of an individual, masculine pronouns (such as *he* or *his*) were used. Masculine pronouns were understood to indicate both men and women. Today, however, sensitive writers and speakers replace common-gender pronouns with alternate inclusive constructions. You can use any of four alternatives.

Sexist/Non-inclusive	Every lawyer has ten minutes for *his* summation.
Alternative 1	All lawyers have ten minutes for their summations. (Use a plural noun and plural pronoun.)
Alternative 2	Lawyers have ten minutes for summations. (Omit the pronoun entirely.)
Alternative 3	Every lawyer has ten minutes for *a* summation. (Use an article instead of a pronoun.)
Alternative 4	Every lawyer has ten minutes for *his* or *her* summation. (Use both a masculine and a feminine pronoun.)

Note that the last alternative, which includes a masculine and a feminine pronoun, is wordy and awkward. Try not to use it frequently.

Other words are considered sexist because they suggest stereotypes. For example, the nouns *fireman* and *mailman* suggest that only men hold these positions. You can avoid offending your listener or reader by using neutral job titles, such as those shown here:

Non-inclusive Job Titles		Inclusive, Neutral Job Titles	
chairman	stewardess	department head	flight attendant
fireman	waiter, waitress	firefighter	server
mailman	workman	letter carrier	worker
policeman		police officer	

Plain English

Business communicators who are conscious of their audience try to use plain language that expresses clear meaning. They do not use showy words and ambiguous expressions in an effort to dazzle or confuse readers. They write to express ideas, not to impress others.

Some business, legal, and government documents are written in an inflated style that obscures meaning. This style of writing has been given various terms, such as *legalese, federalese, bureaucratese, doublespeak,* and *the official style.* It may be used intentionally to mask meaning. It may be an attempt to show off the writer's intelligence and education. It may be the traditional or accepted way of writing in that field. Or it may result from lack of training. What do you think the manager's intention is in the following message?

> Personnel assigned vehicular space in the adjacent areas are hereby advised that access will be suspended temporarily Friday morning.

Employees will probably have to read that sentence several times before they understand that they are being advised not to park in the lot next door on Friday morning.

To overcome this pretentious style, the federal government requires public servants to use plain language to inform the public about government policies, programs, and services. This means a clear, simple style that uses everyday words. Examples of this plain style are shown below in Figure 2.4. But the plain-English

Inflated, unnatural writing that is intended to impress readers often confuses them.

FIGURE 2.4 Plain English Pointers

- Use the active voice with strong verbs (instead of *the stock was acquired by the investor, write the investor bought the stock*).
- Don't be afraid of personal pronouns (e.g., *I*, *we*, and *you*).
- Bring abstractions down to earth (instead of *asset,* write *one share of IBM common stock*).
- Omit superfluous words (instead of *in the event that,* write *if*).
- Use positive expression (instead of *it is not unlike,* write *it is similar*).
- Prefer short sentences.
- Remove jargon and legalese.
- Keep the subject, verb, and object close together.
- Keep sentence structure parallel.

movement goes beyond word choice. It can also mean writing that is easy to follow and organized into segments with appropriate headings.

The important thing to remember is not to be impressed by important-sounding language and legalese, such as *herein, thereafter, hereinafter, whereas,* and similar expressions. Your writing will be better understood if you use plain language.

Familiar Words

Clear messages contain words that are familiar and meaningful to the receiver. How can we know what is meaningful to a given receiver? Although we can't know with certainty, we can avoid long or unfamiliar words that have simpler synonyms. Whenever possible in business communication, substitute short, common, simple words. Don't, however, give up a precise word if it says exactly what you mean.

Less Familiar Words	Simple Alternatives	Less Familiar Words	Simple Alternatives
ascertain	find out	perpetuate	continue
conceptualize	see	perplexing	troubling
encompass	include	reciprocate	return
hypothesize	guess	stipulate	require
monitor	check	terminate	end
operational	working	utilize	use
option	choice	leverage	use to

OFFICE INSIDER

"Simple changes can have profound results. . . . Plain talk isn't only rewriting. It's rethinking your approach and really personalizing your message to the audience and to the reader."

Notice in Figure 2.5 what a difference revision makes to writing. Before revision the e-mail failed to use familiar language, and many negative ideas could have been expressed positively. After thoughtful revision, keeping in mind the points made in this chapter, the message is shorter, more conversational, and emphasizes audience benefits.

FIGURE 2.5 Improving the Tone in an E-Mail Message

Before

_ Transfer Special Tools Window Help

Send

To: All TechTron Team Members
From: Rayford Williams <ray.williams@techtron.com>
Subject: Company Needs to Reduce Employee Driving Trips to Office
Cc:
Attached:

Our company faces harsh governmental penalties if we fail to comply with the Ministry of the Environment's program to reduce the number of automobile trips made by employees.

The aforementioned program stipulates that we offer incentives to entice employees to discontinue driving their vehicles as a means of transportation to and from this place of employment.

First, we are prepared to offer a full day off without penalty. However, the employee must not drive to work and must maintain a 75 percent vanpool participation rate for six months. Second, we offer a vanpool subsidy of $100 a month, and the vanpool driver will not be limited in the personal use he makes of the vehicle on his own time. Third, employees in the vanpool will not be forced to park in outlying lots.

Pertaining to our need to have you leave your cars at home, all employees are herewith instructed to communicate with Saul Salazar, who will be facilitating the above-referenced program.

Emphasizes sender's rather than receiver's viewpoint

Uses unfamiliar words (aforementioned, stipulates, entice)

Presents ideas negatively (penalty, must not drive, will not be limited, will not be forced) and assumes driver will be male

Doesn't use plain English (pertaining to, herewith, facilitating, above-referenced)

After

Message Transfer Special Tools Window Help

Send

To: All TechTron Team Members
From: Rayford Williams <raywilliams@techtron.com>
Subject: Great Perks for Driving Less
Cc:
Attached:

Focuses on receiver's viewpoint and audience benefits (day off, less driving stress, lower gas bill)

Hi, Team,

Want to earn a full day off with pay, reduce the stress of your commute, and pay a lot less for gas? You can enjoy these and other perks if you make fewer driving trips to the office.

As part of the Ministry of the Environment's Trip Reduction Plan, you can enjoy the following benefits by reducing the number of trips you make to work:

Full Day Off. If you maintain a 75 percent participation rate in our ride-share program for a six-month period, you will receive one day off with pay.

Places options in bulleted list with "you" view

Vanpool Subsidy. By joining a vanpool, you will receive assistance in obtaining a van along with a monthly $100 subsidy. Even better, if you become a vanpool driver, you will also have unlimited personal use of the vehicle off company time.

Preferential Parking. By coming to work in vanpools, you can park close to the building in reserved spaces.

Repeats audience benefits using conversational tone and familiar words

Why not help the environment, reduce your gas bill, and enjoy other perks by joining this program? For more information and to sign up, please contact Saul Salazar at saul.salazar @techtron.com before February 1.

Ray

Rayford Williams
Senior Coordinator, Human Resources
ray.williams@techtron.com
(213) 692-9981

Summing Up and Looking Forward

In this chapter you learned that good business writing is audience centred, purposeful, and economical. To achieve these results, business communicators typically follow a systematic writing process. This process includes three phases: prewriting, writing, and revising. In the prewriting phase, communicators analyze the task and the audience. They select an appropriate channel to deliver the message, and they consider ways to adapt their message to the task and the audience. Effective techniques include spotlighting audience benefits, cultivating the "you" view, using conversational language, and expressing ideas positively. Good communicators also use inclusive language, plain expressions, and familiar words.

The next chapter continues to examine the writing process. It presents additional techniques to help you become a better writer. You'll learn how to eliminate repetitious and redundant wording, as well as how to avoid wordy prepositional phrases, long lead-ins, needless adverbs, and misplaced modifiers. You'll also take a closer look at spell checkers and grammar checkers.

Critical Thinking

1. As a business communicator, you are encouraged to profile or "visualize" the audience for your messages. How is this possible if you don't really know the people who will receive a sales letter or who will hear your business presentation?

2. If adapting your tone to your audience and developing reader benefits are so important, why do we see so much writing that fails to reflect these suggestions?

3. Discuss the following statement: "The English language can be dangerous—it is filled with terms that are easily misinterpreted as derogatory and others that are blatantly insulting."

4. Why is writing in a natural, conversational tone difficult for many people?

5. Is it ethical to always write in a positive tone, as this chapter has advised? What if the message you're conveying is a bad one, such as a firing, demotion, or loss of sales?

Chapter Review

1. Name three ways in which business writing differs from other writing.

2. List the three phases of the business writing process and summarize what happens in each phase. Which phase requires the most time?

3. What factors are important in selecting an appropriate channel to deliver a message?

4. How does profiling the audience help a business communicator prepare a message?

5. What is meant by *audience benefit*? Give an original example.

6. List three specific techniques for developing a warm, friendly, and conversational tone in business messages.

7. Why does positive language usually tell more than negative language? Give an original example.

8. What makes language sexist? Offer some original examples.

9. What are the advantages of using plain English when communicating?

Writing Improvement Exercises

Selecting Communication Channels

Using Figure 2.2, suggest the best communication channels for the following messages. Assume that all channels shown are available. Be prepared to explain your choices.

1. As department manager, you wish to inform four members of a training session scheduled for three weeks from now.

2. As assistant to the vice president, you are to investigate the possibility of developing work placement programs with several nearby colleges and universities.

3. You wish to send price quotes for a number of your products in response to a request from a potential customer in Taiwan.

4. You must respond to a notice from the Canada Revenue Agency insisting that you did not pay the correct amount for last quarter's employee remittance.

5. As a manager, you must inform an employee that continued tardiness is jeopardizing her job.

6. Members of your task force must meet to discuss ways to improve communication among 500 employees at 12 branches of your company. Task force members are from Toronto, Winnipeg, Calgary, Regina, and Halifax.

7. You need to know whether Davinder in Printing can produce a special pamphlet for you within two days.

Audience Benefits and the "You" View

Revise the following sentences to emphasize the perspective of the audience and the "you" view.

8. To prevent us from possibly losing large sums of money, our bank now requires verification of any large cheque presented for immediate payment.

9. We take pride in announcing daily flights to Singapore.

10. So that we may comply with new federal privacy legislation, we are asking you to complete the enclosed waiver.

11. For just $1,195 (CDN) per person, we have arranged a seven-day trip to Las Vegas that includes deluxe accommodations, a Cirque du Soleil performance, and selected meals.

12. I give my permission for you to attend the two-day workshop.

13. We're requesting all employees to complete the enclosed questionnaire so that we may develop a master schedule for summer vacations.

14. I think my background and my education match the description of the manager trainee position you advertised.

15. We are offering an in-house training program for employees who want to improve their writing skills.

16. We are pleased to announce an arrangement with Hewlett-Packard that allows us to offer discounted computers in the student bookstore.

17. We have approved your application for credit, and the account may be used immediately.

18. We are pleased to announce that we have selected you to join our trainee program.

19. Our safety policy forbids us from renting power equipment to anyone who cannot demonstrate proficiency in its use.

20. We will reimburse you for all travel expenses.

21. To enable us to continue our policy of selling name brands at discount prices, we cannot give cash refunds on returned merchandise.

Conversational, Professional Tone

Revise the following sentences to make the tone conversational yet professional.

Example: As per your recent request, the undersigned is happy to inform you that we are sending you forthwith the brochures you requested.

Revision: I'm happy to send you the brochures you requested.

22. Kindly inform the undersigned whether or not your representative will be making a visitation in the near future.

23. Pursuant to your letter of the 12th, please be advised that your shipment was sent 9 June 2012.

24. She was pretty ticked off because the manager accused her of ripping off office supplies.

25. Kindly be informed that your vehicle has been determined to require corrective work.

26. He didn't have the guts to badmouth her to her face.

27. The undersigned respectfully reminds affected individuals that employees desirous of changing their benefits package must do so before December 30.

Positive Expression

Revise the following statements to make them more positive.

28. If you fail to pass the examination, you will not qualify.

29. In your e-mail, you claim that you returned a defective headset.

30. We can't process your application because you neglected to provide your social insurance number.

31. Construction cannot begin until the building plans are approved.

32. It is impossible to move forward without community support.

33. Customers are ineligible for the 10 percent discount unless they show their membership cards.

34. Titan Insurance Company will not process any claim not accompanied by documented proof from a physician showing that the injuries required physiotherapy.

Inclusive Language

Revise the following sentences to eliminate terms that are considered sexist or that suggest stereotypes.

35. Any applicant for the position of fireman must submit a medical report signed by his physician.

36. Every employee is entitled to see his personnel file.

37. All conference participants and their wives are invited to the banquet.

38. At most hospitals in the area, a nurse must provide her own uniform.

39. Representing the community are a businessman and a female doctor.

40. A salesman would have to use all his skills to sell those condos.

41. Every doctor is provided with a parking spot for his car.

Plain Language and Familiar Words

Revise the following sentences to use plain expression and familiar words.

42. Profits are declining because our sales staff is not cognizant of our competitor's products.

43. He hypothesized that the vehicle was not operational because of a malfunctioning gasket.

44. Because we cannot monitor all cash payments, we must terminate the contract.

45. The contract stipulates that management must maintain in perpetuity the retirement plan.

Plain, Positive Language

Can you make the following understandable?

46. If your evidence is not received before June 18, 2013, which is one year from the date of our first letter, your claim, if entitlement is established, cannot be processed before the date of the receipt of the evidence.

2.1 Starting a Wiki

At your company of 45 employees, it's always been a lot of work to organize the annual holiday season party in December. Ten years ago a sign up sheet used to be sent around, which would invariably get lost. Then, money would have to be collected, which took a lot of time. Later, when e-mail came to the company, things became a bit easier. One person sent an e-mail to all employees asking them to respond "yes" or "no" about their attendance at the party. The problem was that some employees didn't respond "yes" but then showed up at the party anyway. One of your colleagues at work recently suggested that this year, someone should start a wiki to make organizing the party easier.

Your Task. Form into teams of 3 to 5. Go to **http://www.wikispaces.com** and create one free membership. Give your new wiki a name (e.g., "BoffLtd.Party2012." Choose one team member to be the wiki organizer. Add other team members as wiki members. Then, start using the wiki by sending messages and receiving responses. Show your evolving wiki to your instructor or to the rest of the class. Is a wiki a more efficient way to get an office party organized than traditional e-mail? Why or why not?

2.2 Weighing the Pros and Cons of Instant Messaging

The company you work for is finding that e-mail response time is beginning to lag. Anecdotally, managers are hearing that employees are taking up to 72 hours to respond to routine e-mail requests for information, updates, etc. Because the company is embarking on its annual "ReThink" exercise, you figure it's time to introduce instant messaging as a way of ensuring rapid response. ReThink, by the way, is the company's way of taking stock of the good and bad things that have happened in the last year, and of brainstorming ideas for future improvements.

Your Task. Form teams of 3 to 5. Go to Google Talk's Web site (**http://www.google.ca/talk/**) and download the instant messaging software. Add your team members as contacts. Start chatting about this year's ReThink. Offer suggestions and make criticisms for five to ten minutes. Now, pick a team leader. Have that team leader send a traditional e-mail to all team-mates asking them to offer suggestions and constructive criticism for this year's ReThink. Now that you've talked about ReThink using instant messaging and using traditional e-mail, which communication channel is more effective? Why? If possible, demonstrate the "thread" of conversation in the instant messaging channel and the e-mail channel to your instructor or class.

2.3 Turning Negatives Into Positives

There has been a lot of bad business news in the past couple of years. Between the recession and the disastrous oil spill in the Gulf of Mexico, the world has witnessed large corporations going bankrupt or having to be bailed out by taxpayers, CEOs losing their jobs due to mismanagement of corporate disasters, and national governments negotiating bailouts (e.g., in Ireland, Greece, Italy). From the point of view of one of the bailed out companies or governments or corporations suffering from bad media publicity, how do you move the focus away from the negative news and toward a more positive perspective?

Your Task. In your school's library databases or on the Internet, using a search term such as "bad publicity," see if you can find a source that gives good advice on how companies or governments can turn negatives into positives. Then, imagine that your college or university has just experienced a horrible health or environmental disaster, or some large-scale scandal that has been reported in the media. Create some business communications for various stakeholders (e.g., students, parents, media, government, corporate partners) that turn negatives into positives. Present your communications to your instructor or to the class.

2.4 When the Audience Is Your Superior

Imagine that you are a new employee working for a large corporation. You've been on the job six months and your best friend suddenly announces she's getting married—next weekend, on a whim. You've known her for 15 years, and you really want to be at her wedding.

Unfortunately, the day and time that the wedding is taking place are unconventional: next Friday at 11:00 a.m. As a result, you'll need to ask for the whole day off.

Your task. Write two e-mails to your boss. In the first one, break the three fundamental rules of good business writing: make the e-mail not audience-oriented, unpurposeful, and uneconomical. In the second e-mail, correct the three broken rules. Once you're finished, put the first e-mail on a handout and see how many of your classmates notice where you've broken the rules. Then, show your classmates your second version and see whether or not they agree about how you decided to improve the e-mail.

Grammar/Mechanics Review—2

The following sentences contain a variety of inaccuracies, including grammar, punctuation, style, and spelling. Revise each sentence making the appropriate corrections. Then, learn about each type of error in the Grammar/Mechanics Handbook at the back of this book. More exercises are located in the handbook to help reinforce your ability to write accurately.

1. In the evening, each of the female nurses are escorted to their car.
2. It must have been him who received the highest score, although its hard to understand how he did it.
3. The Manager asked Hilary and I to fill in for him for 4 hours on Saturday morning.
4. Working out at the Gym and jogging twenty kilometers a week is how she stays fit.
5. 3 types of costs must be considered for proper inventory control; warehousing costs, ordering costs, and stocking costs.
6. If I was him I would fill out the questionaire immediately so that I would qualify for the prize.
7. Higher engine revolutions per kilometre mean better acceleration, however, lower revolutions mean better fuel economy.
8. Our teams day-to-day operations include: setting goals, improvement of customer service, manufacturing quality products and hitting sales targets.
9. If I had saw the shippers bill I would have payed it immediately.
10. Salary, hours, and benefits, these are 3 items about which most all job candidates ask.
11. Do you think it was him who left the package on the boss desk.
12. About 1/2 of Pizza to Gos sixty outlets makes deliverys, the others concentrates on walk-in customers.
13. Every thing accept labour is covered in this 5 year warranty.
14. Our Director of Human Resources felt nevertheless that the applicant should be given a interview.
15. When Keisha completes her degree she plans to apply for employment in: Moose Jaw, Regina, or Saskatoon.

Chapter 2: Before You Write

Grammar/Mechanics Challenge—2

The document in Figure 2.6 contains some writing accuracy issues, including grammar, spelling, punctuation, and style. In addition, it doesn't take into consideration the advice on tone covered in this chapter. Read the document and edit it as you go, identifying inaccuracies and needed changes and fixing them. Your instructor will take up the correct answers with you.

FIGURE 2.6 E-Mail Sample

File Edit Mailbox Message Transfer Special Tools Window Help

Send

To: Max Westerfield <max.westerfield@cola.ca>
From: Gilbert W. Ho <gilbert.ho@cola.ca>
Subject: Analysis of Pepsi XL
Cc:
Bcc:
Attached:

Max,

Herewith is a summation of the research project assigned to Richard Adams and I vis-à-vis Pepsi XL. As you know, this is the reduced-sugar cola drink being introduced by our company's No. 1 competitor.

In just under one year, Pepsi-Cola developed this innovative drink. It contains mix of 50 percent sugar (high-fructose corn syrup) and 50 percent artificial sweetener (aspartame). Apparently, Pepsi-Cola plans to spend over $8 million to introduce the drink and to ascertain consumers' reactions to it. It will be tested on the shelfs of grocerys, mass merchants, and conveneince stores in five citys in Southern Ontario.

The company's spokesperson said, "The 'X' stands for excelent taste, and the 'L' for less sugar." Aimed at young adults who don't like the taste of aspartame but who want to control calorys, the new cola is a hybrid sugar and diet drink. Our studys have shown that similar drinks tried in this country in the 1990s were unsuccessful. However, a 50-calorie low-sugar cola introduced in the United States of America two year ago was well received. In Japan a 40-calorie soda was not successful until it was marketed heavily.

Neither Mr. Adams nor myself hypothesize that this country's consumers will be interested in a midcalorie cola at this time. In fact, all of we analysts in the lab were flabbergasted at Bay Street's favorable response to the Pepsi announcement. Pepsi-Cola's stock value augmented sharply.

If the decision were up to Mr. Adams or I, him and I would take a wait-and-see attitude toward the introduction of our own low-sugar drink. We do not want to badmouth the new drink, but we believe it is smarter to consider our own drink after we monitor the success of Pepsi XL. We cannot send our full report until June 1.

Gil

Gilbert W. Ho
Research and Development
Office: (914) 682-9811
Cell: (914) 358-3802

Sharpening Your Skills for Critical Thinking, Problem Solving, and Decision Making

Gone are the days when management expected workers to follow the leader blindly and do only what they were told. Today, you'll be expected to think critically. You'll be solving problems and making decisions. Much of this book is devoted to helping you solve problems and communicate those decisions to management, fellow workers, clients, governments, and the public. Faced with a problem or an issue, most of us do a lot of worrying before making a decision. All that worrying can become directed thinking by channelling it into the following procedure.

1. **Identify and clarify the problem.** Your first task is to recognize that a problem exists. Some problems are big and unmistakable, such as failure of a courier service to get packages to customers on time. Other problems may be continuing annoyances, such as regularly running out of toner for an office copy machine. The first step in reaching a solution is pinpointing the problem area.

2. **Gather information.** Learn more about the problem situation. Look for possible causes and solutions. This step may mean checking files, calling suppliers, or brainstorming with fellow workers. For example, the courier service would investigate the tracking systems of the airlines carrying its packages to determine what is going wrong.

3. **Evaluate the evidence.** Where did the information come from? Does it represent various points of view? What biases could be expected from each source? How accurate is the information gathered? Is it fact or opinion? For example, it is a fact that packages are missing; it is an opinion that they are merely lost and will turn up eventually.

4. **Consider alternatives and implications.** Draw conclusions from the gathered evidence and pose solutions. Then weigh the advantages and disadvantages of each alternative. What are the costs, benefits, and consequences? What are the obstacles, and how can they be handled? Most important, what solution best serves your goals and those of your organization? Here's where your creativity is especially important.

5. **Choose and implement the best alternative.** Select an alternative and put it into action. Then, follow through on your decision by monitoring the results of implementing your plan. The courier company decided to give its unhappy customers free delivery service to make up for the lost packages and downtime. Be sure to continue monitoring and adjusting the solution to ensure its effectiveness over time.

Career Application

Let's return to the fast-food franchise problem discussed earlier in this chapter, in which some franchise owners are unhappy with the multiple lines for service. Customers don't seem to know where to stand to be next in line. Tempers flare when aggressive customers cut in line, and other customers spend so much time protecting their places in line that they fail to study the menu. Then they don't know what to order when they approach the counter. As a franchise owner, you would like to find a solution to this problem. Any changes in procedures, however, must be approved by all the franchise owners in a district. That means you'll have to get a majority to agree. You know that management feels that the multi-line system accommodates higher volumes of customers more quickly than a single-line system. Moreover, the problem of perception is important. What happens when customers open the door to a restaurant and see a long, single line? Do they stick around to learn how fast the line is moving?

Your Task

- Individually or with a team, use the critical thinking steps outlined here. Begin by clarifying the problem.
- Where could you gather information to help you solve this problem? Would it be wise to see what your competitors are doing? How do banks handle customer lines? Airlines? Sports events?
- Evaluate your findings and consider alternatives. What are the pros and cons of each alternative?
- Choose the best alternative. Present your recommendation to your class and give your reasons for choosing it.

Related Web site: http://www.cfa.ca/About_Us/Code_of_EthicS/

CHAPTER 3

Writing and Revising

Write with your target audience in mind. Ask yourself what information your audience needs and present the key messages in a clear and concise way. People don't take time to read lots of jargon and flowery words.[1]

Shelly Datseris,
Communications Manager,
Rogers Communications

LEARNING OBJECTIVES

1. Contrast formal and informal methods of researching data and generating ideas for messages.

2. Explain how to organize information into outlines.

3. Compare direct and indirect patterns for organizing ideas.

4. Identify components of complete and effective sentences.

5. Revise messages to achieve conciseness, clarity, and impact.

6. Revise message to achieve visual persuasiveness.

7. Describe effective techniques for proofreading routine and complex documents.

Writing naturally, as Shelly Datseris advises, may seem easy. But it's not. It takes instruction and practice. You've already learned some techniques for writing naturally (using a conversational tone, positive language, plain expression, and familiar words). This chapter presents additional writing tips that make your communication not only natural but also effective.

Figure 3.1 reviews the entire writing process. In Chapter 2 we focused on the prewriting stage. This chapter addresses the second and third stages, which include researching, organizing, composing, revising, and proofreading.

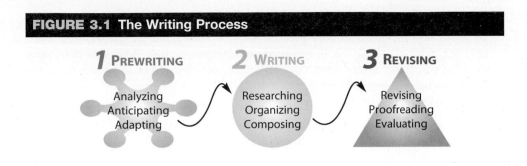

FIGURE 3.1 The Writing Process

1 PREWRITING
Analyzing
Anticipating
Adapting

2 WRITING
Researching
Organizing
Composing

3 REVISING
Revising
Proofreading
Evaluating

Writing: Researching

No experienced businessperson would begin writing a message to a customer or client or manager before collecting the needed information. We call this collection process *research*. Research is necessary before beginning to write because the information you collect helps shape the message. Discovering significant information after a message is completed often means starting over and reorganizing. To avoid frustration and inaccurate messages, collect information that answers this primary question:

- What does the receiver need to know about this topic?

When the message involves action, search for answers to secondary questions:

- What is the receiver to do?
- How is the receiver to do it?
- When must the receiver do it?
- What will happen if the receiver doesn't do it?

Whenever your communication problem requires more information than you have in your head or at your fingertips, you must conduct research. This research may be formal or informal.

Formal Research Methods

Long reports and complex business problems generally require some use of formal research methods. Let's say you are a market specialist for a major soft drink manufacturer, and your boss asks you to evaluate the impact on cola sales of generic ("no name") soft drinks. Or let's assume you must write a term paper for a college class. Both tasks require more data than you have in your head or at your fingertips. To conduct formal research, you could:

- **Search manually.** You'll find helpful background information through manual searching of books, newspapers, magazines, and journals in public and college libraries, as well as your company's files. Other useful sources may include encyclopedias, reference books, handbooks, dictionaries, directories, and almanacs.
- **Search electronically.** Much of the printed material just described is now contained in searchable databases available through the Internet. College and public libraries subscribe to databases that permit you to access most periodical literature. You can also find extraordinary amounts of information, though not always of the best quality, by searching the Web. You'll learn more about using electronic sources in Chapter 9.
- **Go to the source.** For firsthand information, go directly to the source. For the cola sales report, for example, you could find out what consumers really think by conducting interviews or surveys, by putting together questionnaires, or by organizing focus groups. Formal research includes structured sampling and controls that allow investigators to make accurate judgments and valid predictions.

The second stage of the writing process involves research, which means collecting the necessary information to prepare a message.

Formal research may include searching libraries and electronic databases or investigating primary sources.

Good sources of primary information are interviews, surveys, questionnaires, and focus groups.

- **Conduct scientific experiments.** Instead of asking for the target audience's opinion, scientific researchers present choices with controlled variables. Let's say, for example, that the brand-name cola manufacturer wants to determine at what price and under what circumstances consumers would switch from the brand name to a generic brand. The results of such experimentation would provide valuable data for managerial decision making.

Because formal research techniques are particularly necessary for reports, you'll study them more extensively in Chapters 8 and 9.

Informal Research and Idea Generation

Most routine tasks—such as composing e-mails, memos, letters, informational reports, and oral presentations—require data that you can collect informally. Here are some techniques for collecting informal data and for generating ideas:

- **Search company files.** If you are responding to an inquiry, you often can find the answer by investigating your company's files or by consulting colleagues.
- **Talk with your boss.** Get information from the individual making the assignment. What does that person know about the topic? What slant should be taken? What other sources would he or she suggest?
- **Interview the target audience.** Consider talking with individuals at whom the message is aimed. They can provide clarifying information that tells you what they want to know and how you should shape your remarks.
- **Conduct an informal survey.** Gather unscientific but helpful information via questionnaires or telephone surveys. In preparing a memo report predicting the success of a proposed fitness centre, for example, circulate a questionnaire asking for employee reactions.
- **Brainstorm for ideas.** Alone or with others, come up with ideas for the writing task at hand, and record at least a dozen ideas without judging them. Small groups are especially fruitful in brainstorming because people spin ideas off one another.

Writing: Organizing Data

Once you've collected data, you need to find a way to organize it. Organizing includes two processes: grouping and patterning. Well-organized messages group similar items together; ideas follow a sequence that helps the reader understand relationships and accept the writer's views. Unorganized messages proceed without structure or pattern, jumping from one thought to another. Such messages fail to emphasize important points. Puzzled readers can't see how the pieces fit together, and they become frustrated and irritated. Many communication experts regard poor organization as the greatest failing of business writers. A simple technique can help you organize data: the outline.

Outlining

A simple way to organize data is the outline.

In developing simple messages, some writers make a quick ideas list of the topics they wish to cover. They then compose a message at their computers directly from the list.

Most writers, though, need to organize their ideas—especially if the project is complex—into a hierarchy, such as an outline. The beauty of preparing an outline is that it gives you a chance to organize your thoughts before you start to choose specific words and sentences. Figure 3.2 shows a format for an outline.

FIGURE 3.2 Sample Outline

Awards Ceremony Costs

I. Venue
    A. Rentals
        1. Microphone
        2. Screen projector
        3. Tablecloths
    B. Extra staff
        1. Security guard
        2. Set-up, clean-up staff
II. Food
    A. Pre-awards
        1. Nonalcoholic beverages
        2. Appetizers
    B. Post-awards
        1. Alcohol
        2. Dinner
        3. Dessert
III. Awards
    A. Certificates
    B. Cash prizes

The Direct Pattern

After preparing an outline, you will need to decide where in the message you will place the main idea. Placing the main idea at the beginning of the message is called the *direct pattern*. In the direct pattern the main idea comes first, followed by details, explanation, or evidence. Placing the main idea later in the message (after the details, explanation, or evidence) is called the *indirect pattern*. The pattern you select is determined by how you expect the audience to react to the message, as shown in Figure 3.3.

In preparing to write any message, you need to anticipate the audience's reaction to your ideas and frame your message accordingly. When you expect the reader to be pleased, mildly interested, or, at worst, neutral—use the direct pattern. That is, put your main point—the purpose of your message—in the first or second sentence. Compare the direct and indirect patterns in the following memo openings. Notice how long it takes to get to the main idea in the indirect opening.

Business messages typically follow either (1) the direct pattern, with the main idea first, or (2) the indirect pattern, with the main idea following explanation and evidence.

Indirect opening	Bombardier is seeking to improve the process undertaken in producing its annual company awards ceremony. To this end, the Marketing Department, which is in charge of the event, has been refining last year's plan, especially as regards the issue of rental costs and food and beverage costs.
Direct opening	The Marketing Department at Bombardier suggests cutting costs for the annual awards ceremony by adjusting the way we order food and the way we handle rentals.

Tips for Writing Outlines

- Define the main topic in the title.
- Divide the topic into major components, preferably three to five.
- Break the components into subpoints.
- Use details, illustrations, and evidence to support subpoints.
- Don't put a single item under a major component if you have only one subpoint; integrate it with the main item above it or reorganize.
- Strive to make each component exclusive (no overlapping).

FIGURE 3.3 Audience Response Determines Pattern of Organization

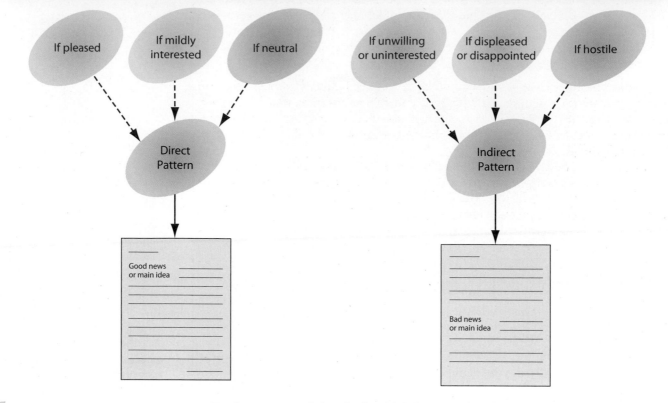

Frontloading saves the reader time, establishes the proper frame of mind, and prevents frustration.

Explanations and details should follow the direct opening. What's important is getting to the main idea quickly. This direct method, also called *frontloading*, has at least three advantages:

- **Saves the reader time.** Many businesspeople can devote only a few moments to each message. Messages that take too long to get to the point may lose their readers along the way.
- **Sets a proper frame of mind.** Learning the purpose up front helps the reader put the subsequent details and explanations in perspective. Without a clear opening, the reader may be thinking, *Why am I being told this?*
- **Prevents frustration.** Readers forced to struggle through excessive text before reaching the main idea become frustrated. They resent the writer. Poorly organized messages create a negative impression of the writer.

The direct pattern works best with audiences that are likely to be receptive.

The direct strategy works best with audiences that are likely to be receptive to or at least not likely to disagree with what you have to say. Typical business messages that follow the direct pattern include routine requests and responses, orders and acknowledgments, non-sensitive memos, e-mails, informational reports, and informational oral presentations. All these tasks have one element in common: none has a sensitive subject that will upset the reader.

The Indirect Pattern

The indirect pattern works best when the audience may be uninterested, unwilling, displeased, or even hostile.

When you expect the audience to be uninterested, unwilling, displeased, or perhaps even hostile, the indirect pattern is more appropriate. In this pattern you don't reveal the main idea until after you have offered explanation and evidence. This approach works well with three kinds of messages: (1) bad news, (2) ideas that require persuasion, and (3) sensitive news, especially when being transmitted to superiors. The indirect pattern has these benefits:

- **Respects the feelings of the audience.** Bad news is always painful, but the pain can be lessened when the receiver is prepared for it.

- **Encourages a fair hearing.** Messages that may upset the reader are more likely to be read when the main idea is delayed. Beginning immediately with a piece of bad news or a persuasive request, for example, may cause the receiver to stop reading or listening.
- **Minimizes a negative reaction.** A reader's overall reaction to a negative message is generally improved if the news is delivered gently.

Typical business messages that could be developed indirectly include letters and memos that decline requests, deny claims, and refuse credit. Persuasive requests, sales letters, sensitive messages, and some reports and oral presentations also benefit from the indirect strategy. You'll learn more about how to use the indirect pattern in Chapters 6 and 7.

In summary, business messages may be organized directly, with the main idea first, or indirectly, with the main idea delayed. Although these two patterns cover many communication problems, they should not be considered universal. Every business transaction is distinct. Some messages are mixed: part good news, part bad; part goodwill, part persuasion. In upcoming chapters you'll practise applying the direct and indirect patterns in typical situations. Then, you'll have the skills and confidence to evaluate communication problems and vary these patterns depending on the goals you wish to achieve.

Effective Sentences

After deciding how to organize your message, you are ready to begin composing it. As you create your first draft, you'll be working at the sentence level of composition. Although you've used sentences all your life, you may be unaware of how they can be shaped and arranged to express your ideas most effectively. First, let's review some basic sentence elements.

Complete sentences have subjects and verbs and make sense.

SUBJECT VERB
This report is clear and concise.

Clauses and phrases, the building blocks of sentences, are related groups of words. Phrases don't have subjects and verbs, while clauses do.

SUBJECT   PHRASE 1   VERB   PHRASE 2
The CEO of that organization sent a letter to our staff.

Clauses can be divided into two groups: independent and dependent. Independent clauses are grammatically complete, while dependent clauses depend for their meaning on independent clauses. In the example below, the clause beginning with *Because* does not make sense by itself, while the clause beginning with *Tracy* does make sense by itself.

VERB 1   SUBJECT VERB 2
Because she writes well, Tracy answers most customer letters.

DEPENDENT CLAUSE   INDEPENDENT CLAUSE

Here's a final example.

VERB 1   SUBJECT VERB 2
When she writes to customers, Naomi uses straightforward language.

DEPENDENT CLAUSE   INDEPENDENT CLAUSE

By learning to distinguish phrases, independent clauses, and dependent clauses, you'll be able to punctuate sentences correctly and avoid three basic sentence faults: the fragment, the run-on sentence, and the comma splice.

Sentence Fragment

Fragments are broken-off parts of sentences and should not be punctuated as sentences.

One error a writer can make is punctuating a fragment as if it were a complete sentence. A fragment is a broken-off part of a sentence that is missing either a subject or a verb.

Fragment	Because most transactions require a permanent record. Good writing skills are critical.
Revision	Because most transactions require a permanent record, good writing skills are critical.
Fragment	The interviewer requested a writing sample. Even though the candidate seemed to communicate well.
Revision	The interviewer requested a writing sample, even though the candidate seemed to communicate well.

Fragments can often be identified by the words that introduce them—words such as *although*, *as*, *because*, *even*, *except*, *for example*, *if*, *instead of*, *since*, *so*, *such as*, *that*, *which*, and *when*. These words introduce dependent clauses. Make sure such clauses always connect to independent clauses.

Run-On Sentence

When two independent clauses are run together without punctuation or a coordinating conjunction, a run-on sentence results.

A sentence with two independent clauses must be joined by a coordinating conjunction (*and*, *or*, *nor*, *but*) or by a semicolon (;). Without a conjunction or a semicolon, the result is a run-on sentence.

Run-on	Some employers still prefer to see a printed résumé a growing number specify that only electronic résumés can be submitted.
Revision 1	Some employers still prefer to see a printed résumé, but a growing number specify that only electronic résumés can be submitted.
Revision 2	Some employers still prefer to see a printed résumé; a growing number specify that only electronic résumés can be submitted.

Comma Splice

When two independent clauses are joined by a comma without a conjunction, a comma splice results.

A comma splice results when a writer joins two independent clauses with a comma. Independent clauses should be joined with a coordinating conjunction (*and*, *or*, *nor*, *but*) or a conjunctive adverb (*however*, *consequently*, *therefore*, and others). Notice that clauses joined by a coordinating conjunction require only a comma. Clauses joined by a conjunctive adverb, however, require a semicolon.

Here are three ways to rectify a comma splice:

Comma splice	Some employees responded by e-mail, others picked up the telephone.
Revision 1	Some employees responded by e-mail, but others picked up the telephone.
Revision 2	Some employees responded by e-mail; however, others picked up the telephone.
Revision 3	Some employees responded by e-mail; others picked up the telephone.

Sentence Length

Because your goal is to communicate clearly, you're better off limiting your sentences to 20 or fewer words. When crafting your sentences, think about the relationship between sentence length and comprehension:

Sentences of 20 or fewer words have the most impact.

Sentence Length	Comprehension Rate
8 words	100%
15 words	90%
19 words	80%
28 words	50%

Instead of grouping clauses with *and*, *but*, and *however*, break some of your sentences into separate segments. Business readers want to grasp ideas immediately. They can do that best when thoughts are separated into short sentences. On the other hand, too many monotonous short sentences will sound unprofessional and may bore or even annoy the reader. Strive for a balance between longer sentences and shorter ones.

Writing: Composing the First Draft

Once you've researched your topic, organized the data, and selected a pattern of organization, you're ready to begin composing. Communicators who haven't completed the preparatory work often suffer from "writer's block" and sit staring at the computer screen. It's easier to get started if you have organized your ideas and established a plan. Composition is also easier if you have a quiet environment in which to concentrate. In a time when many routine messages are tapped out on iPads or BlackBerrys in meetings, on the bus, or at lunch, businesspeople with important messages to compose need to consciously set aside a given time and not allow calls, visitors, or other interruptions. This is a good technique for students as well.

Create a quiet place in which to write.

As you begin composing, keep in mind that you are writing the first draft, not the final copy (see Figure 3.4). Experts suggest that you write quickly, sometimes known as *sprint writing*. According to one university writing centre, "The purpose of the initial draft is to produce raw material, not to dazzle the critics with your finely shaped prose."[2] As you write out each idea, imagine that you are talking to the reader. Don't let yourself get bogged down. If you can't think of the right word, insert a substitute or type "find perfect word later."[3]

Another technique that helps you compose your message is reading it back to yourself, aloud. Sometimes a sentence or group of sentences don't seem complete or persuasive on the screen. However, reading them aloud can cause you to see in which direction you might continue, or if a change in direction is required.

Finally, because these days almost everyone composes electronically, don't forget to save as you go. There's nothing worse than writing for 5 or 15 or 30 minutes only to have your computer lose everything you've written.

FIGURE 3.4 The Writing Process

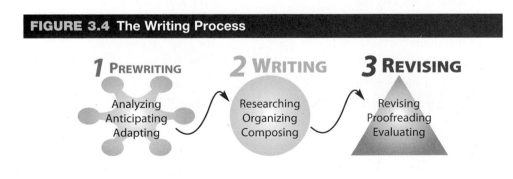

Revising: Understanding the Process of Revision

Once you've composed a complete draft of the business document you are writing, it's time to begin revising the document so it can be sent to its intended audience. Revising means improving the content and sentence structure of your message. It may include adding to, cutting, and changing what you've written. Proofreading involves correcting the grammar, spelling, punctuation, format, and mechanics of your message.

Both revising and proofreading require a little practice to develop your skills. Take a look at Figure 3.5 on page 65. Notice how the revised version of this paragraph is clearer, more concise, and more vigorous because we removed a lot of extra words that were not adding to the message. Major ideas stand out when they are not covered up by unnecessary words.

Many professional writers compose the first draft quickly without worrying about language, precision, or correctness. Then they revise and polish extensively. Other writers prefer to revise as they go—particularly for shorter business documents. Whether you revise as you go or do it when you finish a document, you'll want to focus on concise wording.

> The third phase of the writing process includes revision, proofreading, and evaluating.

> Some communicators write the first draft quickly; others revise and polish as they go.

Concise Wording

In business, time is money. Translated into writing, this saying means that concise messages save reading time and, thus, money. In addition, messages that are written directly and efficiently are easier to read and comprehend. In the revision process, look for shorter ways to say what you mean. Examine every sentence you write. Could the thought be conveyed in fewer words? Notice how the following wordy expressions could be put more concisely.

> Main points are easier to understand in concise messages.

> A wordy phrase can often be reduced to a single word.

Wordy	Concise
at a later date	later
at this point in time	now
afford an opportunity	allow
are of the opinion that	believe, think that
at the present time	now, currently
despite the fact that	though
due to the fact that	because, since
during the time	while
feel free to	please
for the period of	for
fully cognizant of	aware of
in addition to the above	also
in spite of the fact that	even though
in the event that	if
in the amount of	for
in the near future	soon
in view of the fact that	because
inasmuch as	since
more or less	about
until such time as	until

Wordy Prepositional Phrases

Some wordy prepositional phrases may be replaced by single adverbs. For example, *in the normal course of events* becomes *normally* and *as a general rule* becomes *generally*.

Replace wordy prepositional phrases with adverbs whenever possible.

Wordy	DCI approached the merger *in a careful manner*.
Concise	DCI approached the merger carefully.
Wordy	The merger will *in all probability* be effected.
Concise	The merger will probably be effected.
Wordy	We have taken this action *in very few cases*.
Concise	We have seldom taken this action.

Long Lead-Ins

Delete unnecessary introductory words and phrases. The main idea of the sentence often follows the words *that* or *because*.

Avoid long lead-ins that delay the reader from reaching the meaning of the sentence.

Wordy	I am sending you this announcement to let you all know that the office will be closed Monday.
Concise	The office will be closed Monday.
Wordy	You will be interested to learn that you can now be served at our Web site.
Concise	You can now be served at our Web site.
Wordy	I am writing this letter because Dr. Rahib Peshwar suggested that your organization was hiring trainees.
Concise	Dr. Rahib Peshwar suggested that your organization was hiring trainees.

Outdated Expressions

The world of business has changed greatly in the past century. Yet some business writers continue to use antiquated phrases and expressions borrowed from a period when the language of business was exceedingly formal. In the 1800s, letter writers "begged to state" and "trusted to be favoured with" and assured their readers that they "remained their humble servants." Such language was current in the 1800s but it is now out of fashion. Replace outdated expressions such as those shown here with more modern phrasing:

Replace outdated expressions with modern, concise phrasing.

Outdated Expressions	Modern Phrasing
are in receipt of	have received
as per your request	at your request
attached hereto	attached
enclosed please find	enclosed is/are
pursuant to your request	at your request
thanking you in advance	thank you
I trust that	I think, I believe
under separate cover	separately

Chapter 3: Writing and Revising

Needless Adverbs

Eliminating intensifying adverbs such as *very, definitely, quite, completely, extremely, really, actually, somewhat,* and *rather* streamlines your writing. Omitting these intensifiers generally makes you sound more credible and businesslike.

Wordy   We *actually* did not *really* give his plan a *very* fair trial.

Concise   We did not give his plan a fair trial.

Wordy   Professor Anna Pictou offers an *extremely* fine course that students *definitely* appreciate.

Concise   Professor Anna Pictou offers a fine course that students appreciate.

Fillers

Good writers avoid crowding sentences with excess words. Beginning an idea with *there is* usually indicates that writers are having a hard time deciding what the main idea of the sentence should be. Used correctly, *there* indicates a specific place (*I placed the box there*). Used as fillers, *there* and occasionally *it* merely take up space.

Wordy   There are three vice presidents who report directly to the president.

Concise   Three vice presidents report directly to the president.

Wordy   It is the client who should make application for licensing.

Concise   The client should apply for licensing.

Repetitious Words

> **Avoid the monotony of unintentionally repeated words.**

Communicators who want to create vibrant sentences vary their words to avoid unintentional repetition. Notice how monotonous the following announcement sounds:

> Employees will be able to elect an additional six employees to serve with the four previously elected employees who currently comprise the employees' board of directors. To ensure representation, shift employees will be electing one shift employee as their sole representative.

In this example the word *employee* is used six times. In addition, the last sentence begins with the word *representation* and ends with the similar word *representative*. An easier-to-read version follows:

> Employees will be able to elect an additional six representatives to serve with the four previously elected members of the employees' board of directors. To ensure representation, shift workers will elect their own board member.

In the second version, synonyms (*representatives, members, workers*) replaced *employee*. The last sentence was reworked by using a pronoun (*their*) and by substituting *board member* for the repetitious *representative*. Variety of expression can be achieved by searching for appropriate synonyms and by substituting pronouns.

Good writers are also alert to the overuse of the articles *a, an,* and particularly *the*. Often the word *the* can simply be omitted, particularly with plural nouns.

Wordy   The committee members agreed on many rule changes.

Improved   Committee members agreed on many rule changes.

Redundant Words

Repetition of words to achieve emphasis or effective transition is an important writing technique discussed in the previous chapter. The needless repetition, however, of words whose meanings are clearly implied by other words is a writing fault

FIGURE 3.5 Revising for Conciseness

~~This is just a short note to inform you that~~ as you requested, I have ~~made an~~
examined
~~examination of~~ several of our competitors' Web sites. Attached ~~hereto~~ is a summary
comparing
of my findings ~~of my investigation~~. I was ~~really~~ most interested in ~~making a comparison~~
~~of the~~ navigational ~~graphics or~~ cues that ~~were used to~~ guide visitors through the sites.
Since
~~In view of the fact that~~ we will be building our own Web site in ~~the near future~~ *soon*, I was
~~extremely~~ intrigued by the organization, ~~kind of~~ content, and navigation at each ~~and~~
~~every~~ site I visited.

---

called *redundancy*. For example, in the expression *final outcome*, the word *final* is redundant and should be omitted, since *outcome* implies finality. Learn to avoid redundant expressions such as the following:

absolutely essential	*final* outcome
adequate *enough*	*grateful* thanks
advance warning	*mutual* cooperation
basic fundamentals	*necessary* prerequisite
big *in size*	*new* beginning
combined *together*	*past* history
consensus *of opinion*	reason *why*
continue *on*	red *in colour*
each *and every*	refer *back*
exactly identical	repeat *again*
few *in number*	*true* facts

Appropriate Wording

In the world of business, it's important that you choose the most economical or concise words to get your point across (after all, time is money), but it's just as important that these words be appropriate. "Appropriate" in the world of business is easy to explain—it means professional as opposed to friendly, formal or semi-formal as opposed to informal, and precise as opposed to long-winded.

Jargon

Except in certain specialized contexts, you should avoid jargon and unnecessary technical terms. Jargon is special terminology that is peculiar to a particular activity or profession. For example, geologists speak knowingly of *exfoliation*, *calcareous ooze*, and *siliceous particles*. Engineers are familiar with phrases such as *infrared processing flags*, *output latches*, and *movable symbology*. Telecommunication experts use such words and phrases as *protocol*, *mode*, and *asynchronous transmission*. Business professionals are especially prone to using jargon, with words and phrases such as *leverage*, *ramp up*, *in the pipeline*, *cascade*, *pushback*, and *bullish* or *bearish* being just a few of the many you may find in the business section of the newspaper or in your local office.

Ask high-tech shoppers if they want a tablet with a microprocessor containing two or more cores that process multiple data streams into rich multimedia content fast, and you will encounter only blank stares. But ask if they want a tablet with multiple brains that can download songs, play videos, and allow the user to instant message with friends at the same time, and you have made a sale. *In what situations should communicators avoid using complex or technical language?*

Every field has its own special vocabulary. Using that vocabulary within the field is acceptable and even necessary for accurate, efficient communication. Don't use specialized terms, however, if you have reason to believe that your reader or listener may misunderstand them.

Slang

Slang is composed of informal words with arbitrary and extravagantly changed meanings. Slang words quickly go out of fashion because they are no longer appealing when everyone begins to understand them. Consider the following excerpt from an e-mail sent by a ski resort company president to his executive team: "Well guys, the results of our customer survey are in and I'm massively stoked by what I'm hearing. Most of our customers are totally happy with the goods, and I just want to congratulate all my peeps on a job well done!"

The meaning here is considerably obscured by the use of slang. Good communicators, of course, aim at clarity and avoid unintelligible slang.

Clichés

Clichés are expressions that have become exhausted by overuse. These expressions lack not only freshness but also clarity. Most are meaningless to people from other cultures. The following partial list contains representative clichés you should avoid in business writing.

"FYI, Cc: R & D Re: B2B IPO ASAP."

Clichés are dull and sometimes ambiguous.

below the belt	last but not least
better than new	make a bundle
beyond the shadow of a doubt	pass with flying colours
easier said than done	quick as a flash
exception to the rule	shoot from the hip
fill the bill	stand your ground
first and foremost	true to form
hard facts	one in a million
keep your nose to the grindstone	

Instant-Messaging and Texting Speak

Although there has been widespread adoption of communication technology in the workplace (e-mails, instant messages, PDAs, etc.), the technology came in far faster than new rules could be put in place about how it should be used. The boundary between personal use of communication technology (between friends and family) and professional use of communication technology (between coworkers) has been blurred. Not everyone is happy about this blurring, and you can Google "instant-message speak" to get a taste of the debate raging among bloggers, journalists, and others.

What ends up happening is that the shorthand we sometimes use in personal texts, e-mails, and BlackBerry messages—expressions like CUL8R (instead of "see you later")—creeps into our professional workplace messages. You can visit **http://www.webopedia.com/quick_ref/textmessageabbreviations.asp** for hundreds more such abbreviations. It would be unrealistic to insist that such shorthand should never be used, but a rule you definitely should follow as a new business communicator is never to use such shorthand when your message is going to a customer, to another audience outside your company (for example, government), to a manager or other employee higher up than you in the company's hierarchy, or to a fellow employee with whom you've never communicated before. In such cases, continue to use standard, more formal diction.

Precise Verbs

Effective writing creates meaningful images in the mind of the reader. Such writing is marked by concrete and descriptive words. Ineffective writing is often dulled by abstract and generalized words. The most direct way to improve lifeless writing is through using precise verbs. Precise verbs describe action in a way that is understandable for the reader. These verbs deliver the force of the sentence. Select verbs that will help the reader see precisely what is happening.

> **Precise verbs make your writing forceful, clear, and lively.**

General	Our salesperson will *contact* you next week.
Precise	Our salesperson will (*telephone*, *fax*, *e-mail*, *visit*) you next week.
General	The CEO *said* that we should contribute.
Precise	The CEO (*urged*, *pleaded*, *demanded*) that we contribute.
General	We must *consider* this problem.
Precise	We must (*clarify*, *remedy*, *rectify*) this problem.
General	The newspaper was *affected* by the strike.
Precise	The newspaper was (*crippled*, *silenced*, *demoralized*) by the strike.

The power of a verb is diminished when it is needlessly converted to a noun. This happens when verbs such as *acquire*, *establish*, and *develop* are made into nouns (*acquisition*, *establishment*, and *development*). These nouns then receive the central emphasis in the sentence. In the following pairs of sentences, observe how forceful the original verbs are compared with their noun forms.

Weak	*Acquisition* of park lands was made recently by the provincial government. (Noun-centred)
Strong	The provincial government *acquired* park lands recently. (Verb-centred)
Weak	The webmaster and the designer had a *discussion* concerning graphics. (Noun-centred)
Strong	The webmaster and the designer *discussed* graphics. (Verb-centred)
Weak	Both companies must grant *approval* of the merger. (Noun-centred)
Strong	Both companies must *approve* the merger. (Verb-centred)

Concrete Nouns

Concrete nouns help readers visualize the meanings of words.

Nouns name persons, places, and things. Abstract nouns name concepts that are difficult to visualize, such as *automation, function, justice, institution, integrity, form, judgment,* and *environment*. Concrete nouns name objects that are more easily imagined, such as *desk, car,* and *light bulb*. Nouns describing a given object can range from the very abstract to the very concrete—for example, *object, motor vehicle, car, convertible, Mustang*. All of these words or phrases can be used to describe a Mustang convertible. However, a reader would have difficulty envisioning a Mustang convertible when given just the word *object* or even *motor vehicle* or *car*.

In business writing, help your reader "see" what you mean by using concrete language.

General	*a change* in our budget
Concrete	*a 10 percent reduction* in our budget
General	*that company's product*
Concrete	*Motorola's Minitor V pager*
General	*a person* called
Concrete	*Mrs. Tomei, the administrative assistant,* called
General	we *improved* the assembly line
Concrete	we *installed 26 ARC Mate 120iC Series robots* on the assembly line

Vivid Adjectives

Including highly descriptive, dynamic adjectives makes writing more vivid and concrete. Be careful, though, neither to overuse them nor to lose objectivity in selecting them.

General	The report was on time.
Vivid	The *detailed 12-page report* was submitted on time.
General	Clayton needs a better truck.
Vivid	Clayton needs a *rugged, four-wheel-drive Dodge* truck.
General	We enjoyed the movie.
Vivid	We enjoyed the *entertaining* and *absorbing* movie.
Overkill	We enjoyed the *gutsy, exciting, captivating,* and *thoroughly marvellous* movie.

A thesaurus (on your computer or in book form) helps you select precise words and increase your vocabulary.

Designing Documents for Readability

Well-designed documents improve your messages in two important ways. First, they enhance readability and comprehension. Second, they make readers think you are a well-organized and intelligent person. In the revision process, you have a chance to adjust formatting and make other changes so that readers grasp your main points quickly. Significant design techniques to improve readability include appropriate use of white space, margins, typefaces, numbered and bulleted lists, and headings for visual impact.

Employing White Space

Empty space on a page is called *white space*. A page crammed full of text or graphics appears busy, cluttered, and unreadable. To increase white space, use headings, bulleted or numbered lists, short paragraphs, and effective margins. As discussed earlier, short sentences (20 or fewer words) improve readability and comprehension, as do short paragraphs (eight or fewer printed lines). As you revise, think about shortening long sentences. Also consider breaking up long paragraphs into shorter chunks. Be sure, however, that each part of the divided paragraph has a topic sentence.

Numbering and Bulleting Lists for Quick Comprehension

One of the best ways to ensure rapid comprehension of ideas is through the use of numbered or bulleted lists. Lists provide high "skim value." This means that readers can browse quickly and grasp main ideas. By breaking up complex information into smaller chunks, lists improve readability, understanding, and retention. They also force the writer to organize ideas and write efficiently.

In the revision process, look for items that could be converted to lists and follow these techniques to make your lists look professional:

- **Numbered lists:** Use for items that represent a sequence or reflect a numbering system.
- **Bulleted lists:** Use to highlight items that don't necessarily show a chronology.
- **Capitalization:** Capitalize the initial word of each line.
- **Punctuation:** Add end punctuation only if the listed items are complete sentences.
- **Parallelism:** Make all the lines consistent; for example, start each with a verb.

In the following examples, notice that the list on the left presents a sequence of steps with numbers. The bulleted list does not show a sequence of ideas; therefore, bullets are appropriate. Also notice the parallelism in each example. In the numbered list, each item begins with a verb. In the bulleted list, each item follows an adjective/noun sequence. Business readers appreciate lists because they focus attention. Be careful, however, not to use so many that your messages look like grocery lists.

Numbered lists represent sequences; bulleted lists highlight items that may not show a sequence.

Numbered List

Our recruiters follow these steps when hiring applicants:

1. Examine the application.
2. Interview the applicant.
3. Check the applicant's references.

Bulleted List

To attract upscale customers, we feature the following:

- Quality fashions
- Personalized service
- A generous return policy

Adding Headings for Visual Impact

Headings are an effective tool for highlighting information and improving readability. They encourage the writer to group similar material together. Headings help the reader separate major ideas from details. They enable a busy reader to skim familiar or less important information. They also provide a quick preview or review. Headings appear most often in reports, which you will study in greater detail in Chapters 8 and 9. However, main headings, subheadings, and category headings can also improve readability in e-mail messages, memos, and letters. In the following example they are used with bullets to summarize categories.

Our company focuses on the following areas in the employment process:

- **Attracting applicants.** We advertise for qualified applicants, and we also encourage current employees to recommend good people.
- **Interviewing applicants.** Our specialized interviews include simulated customer encounters as well as scrutiny by supervisors.
- **Checking references.** We investigate every applicant thoroughly; we contact former employers and all listed references.

In Figure 3.6 the writer was able to convert a dense, unappealing e-mail message into an easier-to-read version by applying document design. Notice that the all-caps font in the first paragraph makes its meaning difficult to decipher. Justified margins and lack of white space further reduce readability. In the revised version, the writer changed the all-caps font to upper- and lowercase and also used ragged-right margins to enhance visual appeal. One of the best document design techniques in this message is the use of headings and bullets to help the reader see chunks of information in similar groups. All of these improvements are made in the revision process. You can make any message more readable by applying the document design techniques presented here.

FIGURE 3.6 Using Document Design to Improve Readability

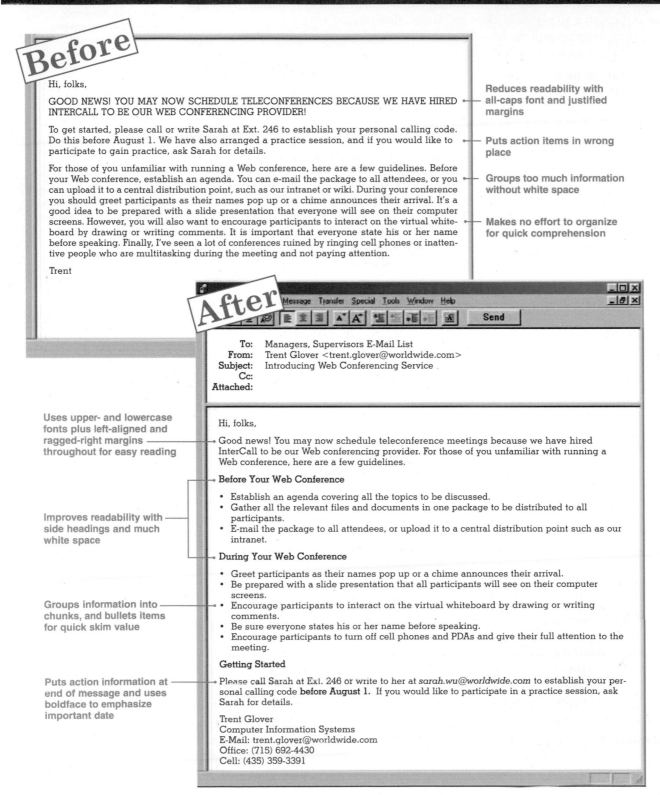

Before

Hi, folks,

GOOD NEWS! YOU MAY NOW SCHEDULE TELECONFERENCES BECAUSE WE HAVE HIRED INTERCALL TO BE OUR WEB CONFERENCING PROVIDER! •→ **Reduces readability with all-caps font and justified margins**

To get started, please call or write Sarah at Ext. 246 to establish your personal calling code. Do this before August 1. We have also arranged a practice session, and if you would like to participate to gain practice, ask Sarah for details. •→ **Puts action items in wrong place**

For those of you unfamiliar with running a Web conference, here are a few guidelines. Before your Web conference, establish an agenda. You can e-mail the package to all attendees, or you can upload it to a central distribution point, such as our intranet or wiki. During your conference you should greet participants as their names pop up or a chime announces their arrival. It's a good idea to be prepared with a slide presentation that everyone will see on their computer screens. However, you will also want to encourage participants to interact on the virtual whiteboard by drawing or writing comments. It is important that everyone state his or her name before speaking. Finally, I've seen a lot of conferences ruined by ringing cell phones or inattentive people who are multitasking during the meeting and not paying attention. •→ **Groups too much information without white space**

•→ **Makes no effort to organize for quick comprehension**

Trent

After

Message Transfer Special Tools Window Help   **Send**

To:	Managers, Supervisors E-Mail List
From:	Trent Glover <trent.glover@worldwide.com>
Subject:	Introducing Web Conferencing Service
Cc:	
Attached:	

Uses upper- and lowercase fonts plus left-aligned and ragged-right margins throughout for easy reading

Hi, folks,

Good news! You may now schedule teleconference meetings because we have hired InterCall to be our Web conferencing provider. For those of you unfamiliar with running a Web conference, here are a few guidelines.

Before Your Web Conference

Improves readability with side headings and much white space

- Establish an agenda covering all the topics to be discussed.
- Gather all the relevant files and documents in one package to be distributed to all participants.
- E-mail the package to all attendees, or upload it to a central distribution point such as our intranet.

During Your Web Conference

- Greet participants as their names pop up or a chime announces their arrival.
- Be prepared with a slide presentation that all participants will see on their computer screens.
- Encourage participants to interact on the virtual whiteboard by drawing or writing comments.

Groups information into chunks, and bullets items for quick skim value

- Be sure everyone states his or her name before speaking.
- Encourage participants to turn off cell phones and PDAs and give their full attention to the meeting.

Getting Started

Puts action information at end of message and uses boldface to emphasize important date

Please call Sarah at Ext. 246 or write to her at *sarah.wu@worldwide.com* to establish your personal calling code **before August 1.** If you would like to participate in a practice session, ask Sarah for details.

Trent Glover
Computer Information Systems
E-Mail: trent.glover@worldwide.com
Office: (715) 692-4430
Cell: (435) 359-3391

Revising: The Proofreading Process

Once you have the message in its final form, it's time to proofread. Don't proofread earlier because you may waste time checking items that are eventually changed or omitted.

What to Watch for in Proofreading

Careful proofreaders check for problems in these areas:

Good proofreaders check spelling, grammar, punctuation, names, numbers, format, and consistency.

- **Spelling.** Now's the time to consult the dictionary. Is *recommend* spelled with one or two *c*'s? Do you mean *affect* or *effect*? Use your computer spell checker, but don't rely on it. See the Communication Workshop section on pages 80–81 to learn more about the benefits and hazards of computer spell checkers.
- **Grammar.** Locate sentence subjects. Do their verbs agree with them? Do pronouns agree with their antecedents? Review the principles in the Grammar/ Mechanics Handbook if necessary. The Communication Workshop discusses grammar checkers more extensively, but we recommend not using them until you've mastered grammar, mechanics, and punctuation on your own.
- **Punctuation.** Make sure that introductory clauses are followed by commas. In compound sentences put commas before coordinating conjunctions (*and, or, but, nor*). Double-check your use of semicolons and colons.
- **Names and numbers.** Compare all names and numbers with their sources, because inaccuracies are not immediately visible. Especially verify the spelling of the names of individuals receiving the message. Most of us immediately dislike someone who misspells our name.
- **Format.** Be sure that letters, printed memos, and reports are balanced on the page. Compare their parts and format with those of standard documents shown in Appendix A. If you indent paragraphs, be certain that all are indented.
- **Consistency.** Make sure all words are spelled and formatted the same way throughout your document. For example, spelling *cheque* the Canadian way three times and then twice the American way (*check*) reduces your credibility as a business writer and confuses readers.

How to Proofread Routine Documents

Routine documents need proofreading.

Most routine messages, including e-mails, require proofreading. Use your keyboard's "down" arrow to reveal one line at a time, focusing your attention at the bottom of the screen. Read carefully for faults such as omitted or repeated words.

For routine messages such as printed letters or memos, a safer proofreading method is reading from a printed copy. You're more likely to find errors and to observe the tone. Use standard proofreading marks, shown in Figure 3.8 on page 73, to indicate changes.

How to Proofread Complex Documents

Long, complex, important documents demand more careful proofreading. Word processing software makers such as Microsoft include standard proofreading features, such as the Track Changes feature and Insert Comment feature (see Figure 3.7), that make it possible to edit long documents onscreen. While it's good practice for new business writers to first get used to editing on paper before trying to edit on screen, the reality is that in most workplaces today documents are edited using the Track Changes function in Word, which is straightforward to use.

Track Changes shows in different colours any changes you make to the wording of your document. The feature also creates a comment bubble on the right side of

FIGURE 3.7 Proofreading Features in Microsoft Word

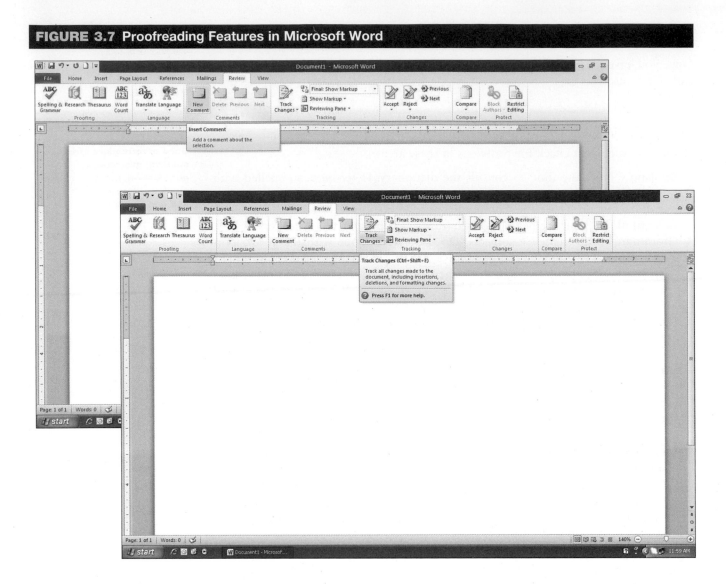

the screen that explains what has been changed. The advantage of Track Changes is that it shows you both the new improved wording and the older wording that has been left behind.

If you are going to proofread on paper (for example during a peer editing session in your business communication course), the process of proofreading is described below.

- Print a copy, preferably double-spaced.
- Allow adequate time to proofread carefully. A common excuse for sloppy proofreading is lack of time.
- Be prepared to find errors. One student confessed, "I can find other people's errors, but I can't seem to locate my own." Psychologically, we don't expect to find errors, and we don't want to find them. You can overcome this obstacle by anticipating errors and congratulating, not criticizing, yourself each time you find one.

FIGURE 3.8 Proofreading Marks

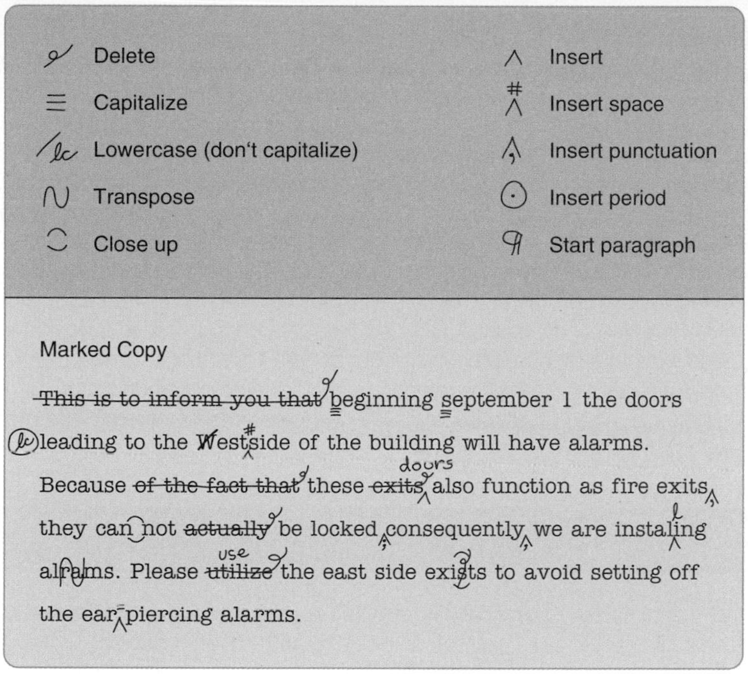

✐	Delete	∧	Insert
≡	Capitalize	#⁄∧	Insert space
/lc	Lowercase (don't capitalize)	∧	Insert punctuation
∩	Transpose	⊙	Insert period
◡	Close up	¶	Start paragraph

Marked Copy

~~This is to inform you that~~ beginning september 1 the doors ⓁⒸ leading to the W̶est side of the building will have alarms. Because ~~of the fact that~~ these ~~exits~~ doors also function as fire exits, they can not ~~actually~~ be locked consequently, we are installing alarms. Please ~~utilize~~ use the east side exits to avoid setting off the ear piercing alarms.

- Read the message at least twice—once for meaning and the second time to identify grammar, mechanics, and style errors. For very long documents (book chapters and long articles or reports), read a third time to verify consistency in formatting.
- For documents that must be perfect, read complex passages of the message aloud. Spell names and difficult words, note capitalization, and read punctuation.
- Use standard proofreading marks, shown in Figure 3.8, to indicate changes. A more complete list of proofreading marks appears in Appendix B.

Your word processing program probably also includes a style or grammar checker. These programs generally analyze aspects of your writing style, including readability level and use of passive voice, trite expressions, split infinitives, and wordy expressions. Most programs use sophisticated technology to identify significant errors. In addition to finding spelling and typographical errors, grammar checkers can find subject–verb disagreement, word misuse, spacing irregularities, punctuation problems, and many other faults. But they won't find everything, as you will see in the workshop at the end of this chapter. While grammar and spell checkers can help you a great deal, you are the final proofreader.

Summing Up and Looking Forward

This chapter explained the second phase of the writing process including researching, organizing, composing, revising, and proofreading. Before beginning a message, every writer collects data, either formally or informally. Information for a message can then be organized into a list or an outline. Depending on the expected reaction of the receiver, the message can be organized directly (for positive reactions) or indirectly (for negative reactions or when persuasion is necessary).

Once a message has been composed, it should be revised before it's sent. To revise for clarity and conciseness, look for wordy phrases that can be shortened and eliminate long lead-ins, outdated expressions, and empty fillers. Also watch for repetitive words and redundancies. Use jargon only when it is clear to receivers, and avoid slang and clichés altogether. The best writing includes precise verbs, concrete nouns, and vivid adjectives. After revising, you're ready for the last step in the writing process: proofreading. Watch for irregularities in spelling, grammar, punctuation, names and numbers, and format. Although routine messages are often proofread on the screen, you should practise proofreading from a printed copy. Complex documents should be proofread several times. Also, complex documents should be revised with readability and visual persuasiveness in mind (e.g., white space and graphic highlighting).

In Chapters 2 and 3 you've studied the writing and revision process. Now it's time for you to put these techniques to work. Chapter 4 introduces you to writing e-mails and memos, the most frequently used forms of communication for most businesspeople. Later chapters present letters and reports.

Critical Thinking

1. "A real writer can sit down at a computer and create a perfect document the first time." Do you agree or disagree? Why?

2. "Carefully written short messages often take longer to write than longer messages." Do you agree or disagree? Why?

3. Because clichés are familiar and have been used for long periods of time, do they help clarify writing?

4. If your boss writes in a flowery, formal tone and relies on outdated expressions, should you follow that style also?

5. Is it unethical to help a friend revise a report when you know that the friend will be turning that report in for a grade?

6. Why is audience analysis so important in choosing the direct or indirect pattern of organization for a business message?

7. In what ways do you imagine that writing on the job differs from the writing you do in your academic studies?

8. How are speakers different from writers in the manner in which they emphasize ideas?

9. Why are short sentences and short paragraphs appropriate for business communication?

10. When might it be unethical to use the indirect method of organizing a message?

Chapter Review

1. How is revising different from proofreading?

2. Why is conciseness especially important in business?

3. What is a long lead-in? Give an original example.

4. What's wrong with using adverbs such as *very*, *really*, and *actually*?

5. What is a redundancy? Give an example.

6. What is jargon? When can it be used? What are examples in your field?

7. What happens when a verb (such as *describe*) is converted to a noun expression (*give a description*)? Provide an original example.

8. Should you proofread when you are writing or after you finish? Why?

9. What six areas should you especially pay attention to when you proofread?

10. How does the proofreading of routine and complex documents differ?

11. What three steps are included in the second phase of the writing process?

12. Distinguish between formal and informal methods of researching data for a business message.

13. What is the difference between a list and an outline?

14. What is frontloading, and what are its advantages?

15. When is the indirect method appropriate, and what are the benefits of using it?

Writing Improvement Exercises

Wordiness

Revise the following sentences to eliminate wordy phrases, outdated expressions, and long lead-ins.

Example: This is to notify you that at a later date we may be able to submit the report.

Revision: We may be able to submit the report later.

1. In the event that the response is at all favourable, we will in all probability start our Web site in the month of January. *We will start the website in January if there is good response*

2. This is to advise you that beginning with the date of April 1 all charges made after that date will be charged to your new credit card number. *All charges after April 1 will be charged to your new #*

3. Pursuant to your request, enclosed please find a copy of your August statement. *Enclosed is a copy of your August statement*

4. In view of the fact that our sales are increasing in a gradual manner, we must secure a loan in the amount of $50,000. *Increasing sales mean we must get a $50,000 loan.*

5. This is to let you know that you should feel free to use your credit card for the purpose of purchasing household items for a period of 60 days. *You can use your credit card for the next 60 days to buy household items*

Needless Adverbs, Fillers, Repetitious Words

Revise the following sentences to eliminate needless adverbs, fillers (such as *there is* and *it is*), and unintentional repetition.

6. It is Web-based technology that is really streamlining administrative processes and reducing business costs for businesses.

7. It is certainly clear that there are many younger managers who are very eager but who are actually unprepared to assume management or leadership roles.

8. There are four employees who definitely spend more time in Internet recreational uses on the Internet than they spend on business-related Internet work.

9. There are definitely five advantages that computers have over a human decision maker.

Redundancies, Jargon, Slang, Clichés

Revise the following sentences to eliminate redundancies, jargon, slang, clichés, and any other wordiness.

Example: Last but not least, Tobias collected together as much support material as possible to avoid getting burned in cash losses or bottom-line profits.

Revision: Finally, Tobias collected as much support material as possible to avoid losing cash or profits.

10. First and foremost, we plan to emphasize an instructional training program.

11. It was the consensus of opinion of members of the committee that the committee should meet at 11 a.m. in the morning. *Committee members decided to meet at 11 a.m.*

12. If you will refer back to the contract, you will definitely find that there are specific specifications to prevent anyone from blowing the budget. *The contract guidelines prevent overspending on the budget*

13. This memorandum serves as an advance warning that all books and magazines borrowed from the library must be taken back to the library by June 1. *All materials must be returned by June 1.*

14. In view of the fact that our last presentation failed, we are at this point in time convinced that we must include only the most absolutely essential selling points this time. *This present must include only essential selling points*

15. In the normal course of events, we would wait until such time as we had adequate enough credit reports. *Normally, we wait until we have adequate credit reports.*

Precise Verbs

Revise these sentences, centring the action in the verbs.

Example: Ms. Tulita gave an appraisal of the Web site.

Revision: Ms. Tulita appraised the Web site.

16. The Webmaster made a description of the project. *The Webmaster described the project.*
17. Can you bring about a change in our company travel policy?
18. Web-based customer service will produce the effect of reduction in overall costs.
19. In writing this proposal, we must make application of new government regulations.
20. The board of directors made a recommendation affirming abandonment of the pilot project.
21. An investigator made a determination of the fire damages.
22. We hope to have production of our new line of products by January.
23. The duty of the comptroller is verification of departmental budgets.
24. Please make a correction in my account to reflect my late payment.

Vivid Words

Revise the following sentences to include vivid and concrete language. Add appropriate words.

Example: They said it was a long way off.

Revision: Management officials announced that the merger would not take place for two years.

25. Our new copier is fast.
26. An employee from that company notified us about the change in date.
27. Please contact them soon.
28. They said that the movie they saw was good.
29. Workers improved when they saw the big picture.
30. The report was weak.

Revising Sentences

Revise the following sentences. Identify whether the mistake is a sentence fragment, run-on sentence, or comma splice.

31. When McDonald's tested pizza, Pizza Hut fought back. With aggressive ads ridiculing McPizza.
32. Companies sometimes sue their rivals they also may respond with counterattacks.
33. Aggressive advertisements can backfire that's why marketing directors consider them carefully.
34. Although Tim Hortons is the country's number one doughnut chain. Robin's is popular in Western Canada.
35. About half of Swiss Chalet's outlets make deliveries, the others concentrate on walk-in customers.

Activities and Cases

3.1 Editing Done Three Ways

Return to Activity 2.4 from the last chapter. If you completed this activity, you should have two different documents: the first e-mail and the second e-mail.

Your Task. Using traditional editing as described in this chapter (proofreading marks made with pen or pencil on the page itself), edit your two e-mails. Alternatively, edit two e-mails by one of your classmates. Next, try editing the same two e-mails onscreen. Use Microsoft Word's Track Changes feature. How long did it take you to edit the e-mails this way? Did you prefer this way to the traditional way? Why or why not? Finally, try editing the same two e-mails on-screen using Word's Insert Comment feature. How long did it take you to edit the e-mails this way compared to the other two ways? What are the pros and cons of using only the "Insert Comment" feature? Explain to your fellow students in a short presentation the editing process you've just completed.

3.2 Editing Other Peoples' Writing

Go to Stephen Moore's online article "Exploring Accounting Lecturer Perceptions of 'Good' and 'Poor' NESB Student Writing, located at **http://www-faculty.edfac.usyd.edu.au/ projects/usp_in_tesol/pdf/volume02/article03.pdf.** This academic article looks at the factors accounting professors consider when assessing the writing of their students with non-English-speaking backgrounds.

Your Task. Read the article or skim it, depending on how much time your instructor allows you to complete this activity. On pages 73–76 of the article, you'll see three samples of poor student writing. Using Track Changes, traditional editing symbols, or the Insert Comment feature, edit one of these samples and present your results to your instructor either in an e-mail memo or in a short presentation. If you have time, edit all three of the poor samples, each time using a different method (i.e., Track Changes, traditional symbols, and Insert Comment). Which way is easiest? Fastest? Most accurate? (For this activity, you'll have to cut and paste the samples into a Word document so they can then be edited on-screen. Figure 3.9 shows you one editor's editing of one of the samples using Track Changes.)

FIGURE 3.9 Writing Sample With Track Changes

In nowadaysNowadays, computers have had a significant impact in the re cordingrecording phase of the accounting process (Hoggett, Edwards and Mendlin 2003, p.9). Thus, the first step of in producing Accounting reports can beis easier than before. However, accountants still have challenges becouse the most important step of running a business is making decisions. Furthermore, the improvement of the requirement from different users shows that communication skills play a key role in the busi–ness.

Meanwhile, communication skills can help us to make decisions more easier easily and more confidentlyce. Also, communication skills can help us be an good accountants or a good managers. Finaly, communication skills can help us understand ideas more clearly.

The following sentences contain errors in grammar, punctuation, capitalization, number style, usage, and spelling. Pay special attention to eliminating wordiness. Below each sentence write a corrected version.

Example: Inasmuch as our sales dropped fifty thousand dollars we are now fully cognizant of our competition.

Revision: Because our sales dropped $50,000, we are now aware of our competition.

1. This is to inform you that for a period of 2 weeks we must place a restriction on parking.

2. We made a plan to keep all our customers names and addresses in Mr. Betz database.

3. There are three laptop problems that have been solved; weight, size, and power consumption.

4. In view of the fact that the envelope was addressed to Manuel and I, him and me should receive the free gift.

5. Pursuant to your e-mail message of the 15th please be advised that your shipment was sent June 9. *Your shipment was sent on June 9.*

6. Acting as President the budget was immediately signed by Rashida. *Rashida, the president, signed the budget*

7. Although I'm sure it was him who sent the e-mail message the C.E.O. doesn't seem to care.

8. I am writing this e-mail to let you know that the meeting is May 15th.

9. The companys principle office is in Bella Coola however, most shipments come from Powell River.

10. If you are looking for a laptop that is small in size try the datapro superslim 505 model.

11. We expect 17 employees to attend the 2 meetings on november 2nd.

12. To improve you're language skills the rules of grammar must be applied.

13. The Vice President and the Human Resources Director made a distribution of complementary tickets to the concert.

14. New corporate taxes will effect all corporations in the near future.

15. Dr. Erek M. Sheps who is one of the principle researchers sighted considerable evidence to support his arguement.

Grammar/Mechanics Challenge—3

Document for Revision

The e-mail in Figure 3.10 has faults in grammar, punctuation, conversational language, outdated expressions, sexist language, concise wording, long lead-ins, and many other problems. Use standard proofreading marks (see Appendix B) to correct the errors. Study the guidelines in the Grammar/Mechanics Handbook to sharpen your skills. When you finish, your instructor may show you the revised version of this e-mail.

FIGURE 3.10 Agent's Packages

Agent's Packages

File Edit Mailbox Message Transfer Special Tools Window Help

Send

To: Roxanne Crosley <r.crosley@titleguaranty.ca> Sept. 12, 2013
From: Kay Legault <Klegault@gmail.com>
Subject: Agent's Packages
Cc:
Bcc:
Attached:

Dear Kay:

Pursuant to our telephone conversation this morning, this is to advise that two (2) agent's packages will be delivered to you next week. Due to the fact that new forms had to be printed; we do not have them immediately available.

Although we cannot offer a 50/50 commission split, we are able to offer new agents a 60/40 commission split. There are two new agreement forms that show this commission ratio. When you get ready to sign up a new agent have her fill in these up to date forms.

When you send me an executed agency agreement please make every effort to tell me what agency package was assigned to the agent. On the last form that you sent you overlooked this information. We need this data to distribute commissions in an expeditious manner.

If you have any questions, don't hesitate to call on me.

Yours very truly

Roxanne

The two agent's packages you requested will be delivered to you next week. When you have signed up a new agent, please be sure to include which agency package has been assigned to which agent. Ensuring that forms are completed properly will speed up the time in which you receive your commissions. We would like to offer you a 60/40 commission split. There are two forms enclosed with this ratio so you can start signing agents up immediately. If you have any question, please call me.

Yours truly,
Roxanne

Communication Workshop

Grammar and Spell Checkers

Nearly all word processing programs now include grammar and spell checkers to help writers with their proofreading tasks.

Grammar Checkers

When first introduced, grammar and spelling checkers were not too helpful. They were limited in scope, awkward to use, and identified many questionable "errors." But today's grammar checkers detect a considerable number of legitimate writing lapses. Microsoft Word finds faults in word use (such as *there*, *their*), capitalization, punctuation, subject–verb agreement, sentence structure, singular and plural endings, repeated words, wordy expressions, gender-specific expressions, and many other problems. Still, as Daniel Kies shows in "Evaluating Grammar Checkers: A Comparative Ten-Year Study," most commonly-used grammar checkers do a poor job identifying the most common errors made by college-level writers, and sometimes flag writing that doesn't have an error in it as incorrect.[4]

How does a grammar checker work? Let's say you typed the sentence *The office and its equipment is for sale*. You would see a wavy green line appear under *is*. When you point your cursor at "Tools" in the tool bar and click on "Spelling and Grammar," a box opens up. It identifies the subject–verb agreement error and suggests the verb *are* as a correction. When you click on "Change," the error is corrected.

Spell Checkers

Spell checkers compare your typed words with those in the computer's memory. Microsoft Word uses a wavy red line to underline misspelled words as you type them. Although some writers dismiss spell checkers as an annoyance, most of us are only too happy to have our typos and misspelled words detected. What's annoying is that spell checkers don't find all the problems. In the following poem, for example, only two problems were detected (*your* and *it's*).

I have a spell checkers
    That came with my PC.
It plainly marks four my review
    Mistakes I cannot sea.
I've run this poem threw it,
    I'm sure your pleased too no.
Its letter perfect in it's weigh
    My checker tolled me sew.
                —Anonymous

The lesson to be learned here is that you can't rely totally on any spell (or grammar) checker. Homonyms—words that sound the same but are spelled differently—may not be highlighted because the spell checker doesn't know what meaning you have in mind. That's why you're wise to print out important messages and proofread them word by word.

Career Application

Your boss, Serena Simkus, is developing an in-service training program on word processing. She wants you to analyze the effectiveness of your computer's grammar and spell checkers. Your brief report will become part of a presentation to new employees.

Your Task

- You decide to try out your software with a set of test sentences. At a computer that has grammar- and spell-checking software, type the following four sentences, including all the errors. Print the sentences.

  1. Is the companys office located on riverside drive in new york city.
  2. The manger adviced her to make a consciensous effort to improve.
  3. There house and it's furniture was allready sold before they moved to saskatoon.
  4. My friend and me was going to apply for the job in june but we were to late.

- For each sentence, underline the errors the software identified. Then circle the errors that the software missed. (A word may contain only one error.) Total your underlines and circles. Make notes on the kinds of errors identified and the kinds missed. *Tip:* You should find 20 errors.
- On the basis of your findings, as well as some Web and library research into the pros and cons of grammar and spelling checkers, how would you rate the usefulness of your computer's grammar and spell checkers? What are the strengths and weaknesses?
- What advice would you give to employees about relying on these programs for proof-reading?
- Stage an in-class debate on the topic "Grammar and spell checkers should not be relied upon by business writers."
- Depending on your own opinion, write a memo to your boss, Serena Simkus, suggesting what kind of policy she should adopt on the use of grammar and spell checkers.

Related Web site: Check out the following article from the *Seattle Post-Intelligencer* on the grammar checker debate: http://www.seattlepi.com/business/article/A-Word-to-the-unwise-program-s-grammar-check-1169572.php. After reading the article, what lessons do you take from it? Does the article change your opinion of the efficacy of this software?

Communicating at Work

Watch Your (Digital) Mouth

Amber MacArthur, "Watch your (digital) mouth," *Globe and Mail*, July 21, 2010, globeandmail.com, http://www.theglobeandmail.com/news/technology/ digital-culture/trending-tech/watch-your-digital-mouth/article1647223. © The Globe and Mail Inc. All Rights Reserved.

According to blogger Cindy Alvarez, there are six kinds of angry emails, ranging from name-calling emails to "frustration-laden tirade emails."

Most of us try to resist sending these types of messages, but sometimes the temptation is overwhelming. It's easy to think that anger management can be just a click away.

But if you want to keep your friends, your job, and your sanity, but are prone to writing angry-sounding messages, take ToneCheck for a spin.

This temper-tracking tool professes to "stop email confusion before it happens." The software, developed by Moncton-based company Lymbix, flags emotional words and phrases, and gives users a chance to make changes before hitting send.

Through a number of positive ratings, such as affection and amusement, to a number of negative ratings, such as fear and anger, the tool analyzes messages for "Tone Tolerance." For example, their online demo identifies this example sentence as one that would prompt review.

"It is time to solidify matters or move on."

ToneCheck describes these words as angry and offers the sender a chance to modify the tone within a preview window.

The email add-on is currently only available for Microsoft Outlook. During the beta release, ToneCheck is free. As for other compatibility beyond Windows, ToneCheck is working on supporting web-based clients.

I interviewed Matt Eldridge, founder and CEO of ToneCheck's parent company, Lymbix.

Amber: How did you come up with the idea for ToneCheck?

Matt: I was a partner and Director of Franchising for a dotcom private sale real estate company, and I found I was good at closing deals face to face and over the phone, but when it came to emails I was losing deals. I found that the tone in my emails was being interpreted as aggressive or harsh and because of that, potential franchise buyers were walking away. I thought there must be a solution, some kind of tone checker that I could download into my email to help with this problem, but after a lot of research discovered there was no such solution. I then started to think about spellcheck and grammar check and really belived that a tone check could be the next step in the natural evolution of those tools.

And voila, ToneCheck was born.

Amber: How big of an issue are negative emails?

Matt: Emails that are seen as negative because tone has been misinterpreted are a very big problem. You have a 50/50 chance of somebody ascertaining the correct tone of your email message and seeing as billions of emails are sent each day, we are solving a very big problem. English as second language is a very lucrative market that I am also excited about, as connotation is lost in translation.

Amber: Where do you plan on developing your product next?

Matt: We will expand beyond Outlook as market demand increases. We chose Outlook strategically because of the client's 500 million users. With that kind of market dominance it made the most sense to tackle that beast first. I have always wanted to build a company with mass market appeal and with our suite of solutions, I believe we will do just that.

Amber: What has been the response so far?

Matt: The response has been overwhelming, with amusement, contentment, excitement and gratitude topping the list. We are solving a problem that almost everyone can identify with and because of that we are starting to gain a lot of traction. We want to help the world communicate more clearly and for people to be truly understood!

Summarize the blog posting you've just read in a paragraph of two to three sentences. Answer the following questions, either on your own or in a small group. Be prepared to present your answers in a short presentation or in an e-mail to your instructor.

QUESTIONS:

1. How does what you've learned in this article change your perception of business communication?

2. How might what you've learned in this article change your own communication style?

3. Come up with pro and con arguments for one of the following debate/discussion topics:
   a) Worrying about the tone of your e-mails at work is a waste of time.
   b) Tools like ToneCheck make us into less responsible writers.

E-Mails, Instant Messages, and Memos

E-mail is a powerful way to distribute information among far-flung team members contemporaneously. For example, I work with team members who are based in four countries, but who are often travelling. With e-mail, we're able to share information immediately, without knowing where each of us is at a given moment. And, I'll have a detailed record of who said what, and when. With e-mail, I'm able to maintain a dynamic and successful working relationship with coworkers I seldom meet.[1]

Peter Schneider,
Vice-President of Business and Legal Affairs, Cineflix Productions Inc.

LEARNING OBJECTIVES

1. Understand how organizations exchange paper-based and electronic messages.

2. Know when to send and how to organize e-mails and memos.

3. Describe appropriate formats of e-mails and memos.

4. Analyze the writing process and explain how it helps you produce effective internal messages.

5. Identify smart e-mail practices, including getting started; content, tone, and correctness; netiquette; reading and replying to e-mail; personal use; and other practices.

6. Explain the pros and cons of instant messaging and how to use it professionally.

7. Write information and procedure e-mails and memos.

8. Write request and reply e-mails and memos.

How Organizations Exchange Messages and Information

People working in organizations exchange information both externally and internally. External messages go to customers, suppliers, other businesses, and government agencies. Internal messages go to fellow employees. These internal messages are increasing in number and importance, and as Peter Schneider shows, in complexity, because organizations are downsizing, flattening chains of command, forming work teams, empowering rank-and-file employees, and working internationally. Given more power in making decisions, employees find that they need more information. In today's workplace you will be expected to collect, evaluate, and exchange information in clearly written messages.

Written messages fall into two main categories: paper-based and electronic. Paper-based messages include business letters and memos. Electronic messages include e-mail, instant messaging, and text messaging. Electronic information may also be exchanged through podcasts, blogs, and wikis. Knowing what channel to use and how to prepare an effective message can save you time, reduce stress, and make you look professional.

Communicating With Paper-Based Messages

Although the business world is quickly switching to electronic communication channels, paper-based documents still have definite functions.

- **Business letters.** Writers prepare business letters on letterhead stationery. This is the best channel when a permanent record is necessary, when confidentiality is important, when sensitivity and formality are essential, and when you need to make a persuasive, well-considered presentation. Chapters 5, 6, and 7 cover various business letters that you may write in today's workplace.
- **Interoffice memos.** Paper-based interoffice memos were once the chief form of internal communication. Today, employees use memos primarily to convey confidential information, emphasize ideas, deliver lengthy documents, or lend importance to a message. Memos are especially appropriate for explaining organizational procedures or policies that become permanent guidelines. Later in this chapter you will study various components in everyday interoffice memos.

Communicating With Electronic Messages

A number of electronic communication channels enable businesspeople to exchange information rapidly and efficiently. All of these new electronic channels display your writing skills.

- **E-mail.** E-mail involves the transmission of messages through computers and networks. Users can send messages to a single recipient or broadcast them to multiple recipients. When messages arrive in a simulated mailbox, recipients may read, print, forward, store, or delete them. E-mail is most appropriate for short messages that deliver routine requests and responses. It is inappropriate for sensitive, confidential, or lengthy documents. Used professionally, e-mail is a powerful business tool. You will learn more about safe and smart e-mail practices shortly.
- **Instant messaging.** More interactive than e-mail, instant messaging (IM) involves the exchange of text messages in real time between two or more people logged into an IM service. IM creates a form of private chat room so that individuals can carry on conversations similar to telephone calls. IM is especially useful for back-and-forth online conversations, such as a customer communicating with a tech support person to solve a problem. Like e-mail, instant messaging creates a permanent text record and must be used carefully.

> Downsized organizations, work teams, increased employee empowerment, and global competition mean more emphasis on internal communication.

- **Text messaging.** Sending really short messages (140 or fewer characters) from mobile phones and other wireless devices is called *text messaging*. This method uses Short Message Service (SMS) and is available on most digital mobile phones and some personal digital assistants with wireless telecommunications. SMS gateways exist to connect mobile phones with instant message services, the Web, desktop computers, and even landline telephones. Busy communicators use text messaging for short person-to-person inquiries and responses that keep them in touch while away from the office.
- **Podcasts.** A podcast is a digital media file that is distributed over the Internet and downloaded on portable media players and personal computers. Podcasts are distinguished by their ability to be syndicated, subscribed to, or downloaded automatically when new content is added. In business, podcasts are useful for improving customer relations, marketing, training, product launches, and "viral" marketing (creating online "buzz" about new products).
- **Blogs.** A blog is a Web site with journal entries usually written by one person with comments added by others. It may combine text, images, and links to other blogs or Web pages. Businesses use blogs to keep customers and employees

informed and to receive feedback. Company news can be posted, updated, and categorized for easy cross-referencing. Blogs may be a useful tool for marketing and promotion as well as for showing a company's personal side.

- **Wikis.** A wiki is a Web site that enables multiple users to collaboratively create and edit pages. A wiki serves as a central location where shared documents can be viewed and revised by a large or dispersed team. Because a wiki can be used to manage and organize meeting notes, team agendas, and company calendars, it is a valuable project management tool.

> **Businesspeople are writing more messages than ever before.**

Organizing E-Mails and Memos

E-mail messages and memos are standard forms of communication within organizations. As such, they will probably become your most common business communication channel. These messages perform critical tasks such as informing employees, requesting data, supplying responses, confirming decisions, and giving directions. They generally follow a similar structure and formatting.

Knowing When to Send an E-Mail or a Memo

Before sending any message, you must choose a communication channel, as discussed in Chapter 2. Although both e-mail and memos deliver internal information, they are not interchangeable.

E-mail is appropriate for short, informal messages that request information and respond to inquiries. It is especially effective for messages to multiple receivers and messages that must be archived (saved). An e-mail is also appropriate as a cover document when sending longer attachments. E-mail, however, is not a substitute for face-to-face conversations, telephone calls, business letters, or memorandums. Face-to-face conversations or telephone calls are better channel choices if your goal is to convey enthusiasm or warmth, explain a complex situation, present a persuasive argument, or smooth over disagreements.

Interoffice memos are appropriate for a number of purposes. If you are delivering confidential data, such as salary or employee review information, a memo is suitable. If you are sending a lengthy report to others within your organization, memo formatting is proper. Memos are equally useful when you need to emphasize your ideas or send an internal message that is important or formal.

Finally, when deciding whether to send an e-mail message or a memo, you must also consider your receiver's preference and your organization's choice. Choose a channel that is comfortable to the receiver and appropriate for the organization.

Components of E-Mails and Memos

Whether electronic or hard copy, direct internal messages generally contain four parts: (a) an informative subject line that summarizes the message, (b) an opening that reveals the main idea immediately, (c) a body that explains and justifies the main idea, and (d) an appropriate closing. Remember that direct messages deliver good news or standard information.

> **A subject line must be concise but meaningful.**

Writing the Subject Line. In e-mails and memos, an informative subject line is mandatory. It summarizes the central idea, thus providing quick identification for reading and for filing. In e-mail messages, a good subject line is critical. It often determines whether and when the message is read, and how easily it can be found when someone is searching for it at a later date. Messages without subject lines may be automatically deleted.

What does it take to get your message read? For one thing, stay away from meaningless or dangerous words. A sure way to have your message deleted or ignored is to use a one-word heading such as *Issue*, *Problem*, *Important*, or *Help*. Including a word such as *Free* is dangerous because it may trigger spam filters. Try to make your subject line "talk" by including a verb. Explain the purpose of the message and how it relates to the reader. Remember that a subject line is usually written in an abbreviated style, often without articles (*a, an, the*). It need not be a complete sentence, and it does not end with a period.

Poor Subject Line	Improved Subject Line
Trade Show	Need You to Showcase Two Items at Our Next Trade Show
Staff Meeting	Rescheduling Staff Meeting for 1 P.M. on May 12
Important!	Please Respond to Job Satisfaction Survey
Parking Permits	Obtain New Employee Parking Permits From HR

Opening With the Main Idea. Most e-mails and memos cover non-sensitive information that can be handled in a straightforward manner. Begin by frontloading; that is, reveal the main idea immediately. Even though the purpose of the e-mail or memo is summarized in the subject line, that purpose should be restated—and amplified—in the first sentence. Busy readers want to know immediately why they are reading a message. As you learned in Chapter 3, most messages should begin directly. Notice how the following indirect opener can be improved by frontloading.

Frontloading means revealing the main idea immediately.

Indirect Opening	For the past six months, the Human Resources Development Department has been considering changes in our employee benefit plan.
Direct Opening	Please review the following proposal regarding employee benefits and let me know by May 20 if you approve these changes.

Explaining in the Body. The body provides more information about the reason for writing. It explains and discusses the subject logically. Effective e-mail messages and memos generally discuss only one topic. Limiting the topic helps the receiver act on the subject and file it appropriately. A writer who, for example, describes a computer printer problem and also requests permission to attend a conference runs a 50 percent failure risk. The reader may respond to the printer problem but delay or forget about the conference request.

Designed for easy comprehension, the body explains one topic.

The body of e-mails and memos should have high "skim value." This means that information should be easy to read and comprehend. As covered in the section on document design in Chapter 3, many techniques improve readability. You can use white space, bulleted lists, enumerated lists, appropriate typefaces and fonts, and headings. In the revision stage, you will see many ways to improve the readability of the body of your message.

Graphic highlighting (bullets, numbered lists, headings) makes information easier to read and review.

Closing With a Purpose. Generally, close an e-mail or a memo with (a) action information, dates, or deadlines; (b) a summary of the message; or (c) a closing thought. Here again the value of thinking through the message before actually writing it becomes apparent. The closing is where readers look for deadlines and action language. An effective memo or e-mail closing might be *Please submit your written report to me by June 15 so that we can have your data before our July planning session.*

In more complex messages, a summary of main points may be an appropriate closing. If no action request is made and a closing summary is unnecessary, you might end with a simple concluding thought (*I'm glad to answer your questions* or *This sounds like a useful project*). You need not close messages to coworkers with goodwill statements such as those found in letters to customers or clients. However, some closing thought is often necessary to prevent a feeling of abruptness. Closings can show gratitude or encourage feedback with remarks such as *I sincerely appreciate your help* or *What are your ideas on this proposal?* Other closings look

Chapter 4: E-Mails, Instant Messages, and Memos

forward to what's next, such as *How would you like to proceed?* Avoid closing with overused expressions such as *Please let me know if I may be of further assistance.* This ending sounds mechanical and insincere.

Putting It All Together. To see the development of a complete internal message, look at Figure 4.1. It shows the first draft and revision of an e-mail that Madeleine Espinoza, senior marketing manager, wrote to her boss, Keith Milton.

FIGURE 4.1 Revising an E-Mail

Before

To:	Keith Milton <keith.milton@apex.com>
From:	Madeleine Espinoza <madeleine.espinoza@apex.com>
Subject:	Problems
Cc:	
Attached:	

— Uses one-word, meaningless subject line

Pursuant to your request, I am responding. Your inquiry of April 29 suggested that you wanted to know how to deal with the database problems.

— Fails to reveal purpose quickly

In my opinion the biggest problem is that it contains a lot of outdated information, including customers who haven't purchased anything in five or more years. Another problem is that the old database is not compatible with the new software that is being used by our mailing service, and this makes it difficult to merge files. After much thought, I think I can solve both problems by starting a new database. This would be the place where we put the names of all new customers. And we would have it keyed using Access software. The problem with outdated information could be solved by finding out if the customers in our old database wish to continue receiving our newsletter and product announcements. Finally we would rekey the names of all active customers in the new database. Does this make sense?

— Buries two problems and three-part solution in difficult-to-read paragraph

— Forgets to conclude with next action and end date

Maddy — **Does not provide full contact information**

After

Provides informative subject line summarizing purpose

To:	Keith Milton <keith.milton@apex.com>
From:	Madeleine Espinoza <madeleine.espinoza@apex.com>
Subject:	How to Improve Our Customer Database
Cc:	
Attached:	

Opens with concise purpose and highlights two problems

Keith,

As you requested, I am submitting my recommendations for improving our customer database. The database has two major problems. First, it contains many names of individuals who have not made purchases in five or more years. Second, the format is not compatible with the new Access software used by our mailing service.

The following three steps, however, should solve both problems:

Organizes body in numbered list for readability

1. **Start a new database.** Effective immediately, enter the names of all new customers in a new database using Access software.

2. **Determine the status of customers in our old database.** Send out a mailing asking whether recipients wish to continue receiving our newsletter and product announcements.

3. **Rekey the names of active customers.** Enter the names of all responding customers in our new database so that we have only one active database.

Closes with key benefit, deadline, and next action

These changes will enable you, as team leader, to send mailings only to active customers. Please let me know by May 10 whether you think these recommendations are workable. If so, I will investigate costs.

Maddy

Provides name and full contact information

Madeleine M. Espinoza
Senior Marketing Manager
E-Mail: madeleine.espinoza@apex.com
Office: (658) 348-8835
Cell: (632) 348-9820

Although it contained solid information, the first draft was so wordy and dense that the main points were lost.

In the revision stage, Madeleine realized that she needed to reorganize her message into an opening, body, and closing. She desperately needed to improve the readability. In studying what she had written, she recognized that she was talking about two main problems. She discovered that she could present a three-part solution. These ideas didn't occur to her until she had written the first draft. Only in the revision stage was she able to see that she was talking about two separate problems as well as a three-part solution. The revision process can help you think through a problem and clarify a solution.

As she revised, Madeleine was more aware of the subject line, opening, body, and closing. She used an informative subject line and opened directly by explaining why she was writing. Her opening outlined the two main problems so that her reader understood the background of the recommendations that followed. In the body of the message, Madeleine identified three corrective actions, and she highlighted them for improved readability. Notice that she listed her three recommendations using numbers with boldface headings. Bullets don't always transmit well in e-mail messages. Madeleine closed her message with a deadline and a reference to the next action to be taken.

Formatting E-Mails and Memos

E-mails and hard-copy memos are similar in content and development, but their formats are slightly different. Because e-mail is still an evolving communication channel, its formatting and usage conventions are somewhat fluid. On the other hand, formatting memos has become much easier because of software templates. Whereas students used to learn how to create memos from scratch (see Appendix A for details), students today are just as often encouraged to choose a template in their word processing program (e.g., Microsoft Word's Professional Memo template) and begin filling in their content. Once in the workforce, people are usually encouraged to use a company memo template. While memo formatting is standard and rarely varies, e-mail users and experts do not always agree, for instance, on what's appropriate for salutations and closings. The following suggestions can guide you in formatting most e-mails, but always check with your organization to observe its practices.

Guide Words. E-mail programs provide a set of guide words to help you create your message. Following the guide word *To*, writers who have already been in touch with someone by e-mail generally insert the recipient's name, which is recognized by the program, which then provides the person's e-mail address. For example, after the *To*, I type in *Mark Philly* and the e-mail program provides his e-mail address, *mphilly@accountpro.com*. In some cases, you may be given someone's e-mail address on a scrap of paper and actually have to type it in after the *To*. Either way, it's a good idea to leave typing the receiver's address or name until after you've typed your message—this will prevent you from pressing *Send* by mistake and sending an embarrassing, angry, or incomplete e-mail. By the way, the order of *Date, To, From, Subject,* and other guide words varies depending on your e-mail program and whether you are sending or receiving the message.

Most e-mail programs automatically add the current date after *Date*. On the *Cc* line (which stands for *carbon copy* or *courtesy copy*), you can type the address of anyone who is to receive a copy of the message. Remember, though, to send copies only to those people directly involved with the message. Most e-mail programs also include a line for *Bcc (blind carbon copy)*. This sends a copy without the addressee's knowledge. Savvy writers today use *Bcc* for the names and addresses of a list of receivers, a technique that avoids revealing the addresses to the entire group. On the subject line, identify the subject of the memo. Be sure to include enough information to be clear and compelling.

> Although e-mail formatting style is not set in stone, all messages contain *To, From, Date,* and *Subject* lines.

Hi, Kevin,   Thank you, Haley,

Greetings, Amy,   Dear Mr. Cotter,

Leslie,   Dear Leslie,

In addition to being friendly, a greeting provides a visual cue marking the beginning of the message. Many messages are transmitted or forwarded with such long headers that finding the beginning of the message can be difficult. A greeting helps, even if is just the receiver's name, as shown in Figures 4.1 and 4.2.

FIGURE 4.2 E-Mail Request

CONSIDERING GERRY WAYKAMP FOR MARKETING DIVISION

File Edit Mailbox Message Transfer Special Tools Window Help

B I U | | **Send**

To: Brent Atkins <batkins@pyramid.com>   August 14, 2012
From: Patricia Wille <wille@accountpro.com>
Subject: CONSIDERING GERRY WAYKAMP FOR MARKETING DIVISION ———— *Subject line is specific*
Cc:
Bcc:
Attached:

Dear Pat: ———— *Includes salutation because message is going to outsider*

Could you please answer a few questions we have related to the position Gerry Waykamp applied for in our Marketing Division here at Pyramid?

1. Our starting salary for the position is in the range of $44,000 to $49,000. Given Gerry's experience with you, is this range reasonable? ———— *Double spaces between paragraphs*

2. Is Gerry responsible for managing accounts with your organization or writing copy?

3. Does Gerry have any experience in public relations campaigns with your organization? ———— *Lists questions to improve readability*

Thanks for sending him to interview for our junior account coordinator job. His interview was very successful; and his résumé suggests that he has the education, background, and experience we need.

The interview committee agreed that Pyramid would benefit from adding him to our team. So that we can prepare an offer for Gerry, please let me know your answers to these questions by Wednesday, August 18. ———— *Includes end date to motivate action*

All the best,

Brent Atkins, Director, Finance ———— *Closes politely*
Pyramid Financial
1890 boul Rene-Levesque O.
Montreal, QC H3Z 2V5
E batkins@pyramid.com
T (514) 555-2367
F (514) 555-2360

Tips for Formatting E-Mails

- After *To*, type the receiver's e-mail address.
- After *From*, type your name—your e-mail program should insert it automatically.
- After *Subject*, provide a specific description of your message.
- Insert the names of anyone receiving carbon or blind copies.
- Include a salutation (such as *Dear Pat, Hi Pat, Greetings*) or weave the receiver's name into the first line.
- Double-space between paragraphs.
- Do not type in all caps or in all lowercase letters.
- Include a complimentary close including your name (and contact information if an automatic signature block has not been enabled in your e-mail program).

Body. When keying the body of an e-mail, use standard caps and lowercase characters—never all uppercase or all lowercase characters. Cover just one topic, and try to keep the total message under one screen in length. Remember to double-space between paragraphs. For longer messages prepare a separate file to be attached and use the e-mail only as a cover document. To assist you in preparing your message, many e-mail programs have basic text-editing features, such as cut, copy, paste, and word-wrap. However, avoid graphics, font changes, boldface, and italics unless you are sure your reader's system can handle them. As more and more programs offer HTML formatting options, writers are able to use all the graphics, colours, and fonts available in their word processing programs.

Closing Lines. Some people sign off their e-mails with a cordial expression such as *Cheers, All the best,* or *Warm regards.* Regardless of the closing, be sure to sign your name. Messages without names become very confusing when forwarded or when they are part of a thread (string) of responses. To avoid further confusion, include a signature block with your contact information. This might include your name, title, organization, address, e-mail address, telephone number, cell phone number, and fax number. Decide what information is most important. Then prepare a signature block with five or fewer lines. Although you might be tempted to omit your e-mail address, it is wise to include it because some systems do not transmit your address automatically. When your message is forwarded, your e-mail address may be lost.

> Closing lines (or a signature block) should name the writer and provide sufficient information for identification.

Formatting Interoffice Memos

In the past interoffice memos were the primary communication channel for delivering information within organizations. Although e-mail is more often used today, memos are still useful for important internal messages that require a permanent record or formality. For example, organizations use memos to deliver changes in procedures, official instructions, reports, and long internal documents.

Memo Templates. Some organizations use memo templates. In addition to the name of the organization, these templates include the basic elements of *Date, To, From,* and *Subject.* Large organizations may include other identifying headings, such as *File Number, Floor, Extension, Location,* and *Distribution.*

> Hard-copy memos are useful for internal messages that require a permanent record or formality.

If you are preparing a memo on plain paper, set 1-inch top and bottom margins and left and right margins of 1.25 inches. Provide a heading that includes the name of the company plus "Memo" or "Memorandum." Begin the guide words a triple space (two blank lines) below the last line of the heading. Key in bold the guide words **Date:**, **To:**, **From:**, and **Subject:** at the left margin. The guide words may appear in all caps or with only the initial letter capitalized. Triple-space (set two blank lines) after the last line of the heading. Do not justify the right margins. As discussed in the document design section of Chapter 3, ragged-right margins in printed messages are easier to read. Single-space the message, and double-space between paragraphs, as shown in Figure 4.3.

Preparing Memos as E-Mail Attachments. E-mail has become increasingly important for exchanging internal messages. However, it is inappropriate for long documents or for items that require formality or permanence. For such messages, writers may prepare the information in standard memo format and send it as an attachment with a cover e-mail.

> To deliver a long or formal document, send a cover e-mail with an attachment.

In preparing e-mail attachments, be sure to include identifying information. Because the cover e-mail message may become separated from the attachment, the attachment must be fully identified. Preparing the e-mail attachment as a memo provides a handy format that identifies the date, sender, receiver, and subject.

FIGURE 4.3 Interoffice Memo That Responds to a Request

↓ 1 inch

HOLLYWOOD NORTH AUDIENCE SERVICES

↓ 2 blank lines

MEMORANDUM

↓ 2 blank lines

Aligns all heading words with those following Subject

Date: November 11, 2012

↓ 1 blank line

To: Stephanie Sato, President

↓ 1 blank line

From: Sundance Richardson, Special Events Manager   *S.R.*

Provides writer's initials after printed name and title

↓ 1 blank line

Subject: Improving Web Site Information

↓ 1 or 2 blank lines

In response to your request for ideas to improve our Web site, I am submitting the following suggestions. Because interest in our audience member, seat-filler, and usher services is growing constantly, we must use our Web site more strategically. Here are three suggestions.

Provides ragged line endings—not justified

First, our Web site should explain our purpose. We specialize in providing customized and responsive audiences for studio productions and award shows. The Web site should distinguish between audience members and seat fillers. Audience members have a seat for the entire taping of a TV show. Seat fillers sit in the empty seats of celebrity presenters or performers so that the front section does not look empty to the home audience.

Leaves side margins of 1.25 inches

Second, I suggest that our Web designer include a listing such as the following so that readers recognize the events and services we provide:

Event	Audience Members Provided Last Year	Seat Fillers and Ushers Provided Last Year
Juno Awards	75	15
Much Music Video Awards	120	n/a
Canadian Country Music Association Awards	85	20
CBC's *Battle of the Blades*	250	25

Lists data in columns with headings and white space for easy reading

Third, our Web site should provide answers to commonly asked questions such as the following:

- Do audience members or seat fillers have to pay to attend the event?
- How often do seat fillers have to move around?
- Will seat fillers be on television?

Our Web site can be more informative and boost our business if we implement some of these ideas. Are you free to talk about these suggestions at 10 a.m. on Tuesday, November 19?

Omits a closing and signature

Tips for Formatting Interoffice Memos

Use MS Word's templates to select a memo format and begin filling in the template. If a template is not available, follow these steps:

- On plain paper, set 1-inch top and bottom margins.
- Set left and right margins of 1.25 inches.
- Include an optional company name and the word *MEMO* or *MEMORANDUM* as a heading. Leave 2 blank lines after this heading.
- Set one tab to align entries evenly after *Subject*.
- Leave 1 or 2 blank lines after the subject line.
- Single-space all but the shortest memos. Double-space between paragraphs.
- For a two-page memo, use a second-page heading with the addressee's name, page number, and date.
- Handwrite your initials after your typed name.
- Place bulleted or numbered lists flush left or indent them 0.5 inches.

Using the Writing Process to Create Effective Internal Messages

Internal e-mails and hard-copy memos usually carry direct messages that are neither sensitive nor persuasive. Although these messages are straightforward, they require careful writing to be clearly and quickly understood. By following the three-phase writing process, you can speed up your efforts and greatly improve the product.

Analyzing, Anticipating, and Adapting

In the prewriting phase, you will spend some time analyzing your task. It is amazing how many of us are ready to put our pens or computers into gear before engaging our minds. Before writing, ask yourself these important questions:

- **Do I really need to write this e-mail or memo?** A phone call or a quick visit to a nearby coworker might solve the problem—and save the time and expense of a written message. On the other hand, some written messages are needed to provide a permanent record.
- **Why am I writing?** Know why you are writing and what you hope to achieve. This will help you recognize what the important points are and where to place them.
- **How will the reader react?** Visualize the reader and the effect your message will have. In writing e-mails and memos, imagine that you are sitting and talking with your reader. Avoid speaking bluntly, failing to explain, or ignoring your reader's needs. Consider ways to shape the message to benefit the reader. Also be careful about what you say because your message may very well be forwarded to someone else—or may be read by your boss.
- **How can I save my reader's time?** Think of ways to make your message easier to comprehend at a glance. Use bullets, lists, headings, and white space to improve readability.

Researching, Organizing, and Composing

Phase 2, writing, involves gathering documentation, organizing, and actually composing the first draft. Although some of your e-mails and memos will be short, you can ensure a more effective message by following these steps:

Gather background information; organize it into an outline; compose your message; and revise for clarity, correctness, and feedback.

- **Conduct research.** Check the files, talk with your boss, and possibly consult the target audience to collect information before you begin to write. Gather any documentation necessary to support your message.
- **Organize your information.** Make a brief outline of the points you want to cover in your message. For short messages jot down notes on the document you are answering or make a scratch list at your computer.
- **Compose your first draft.** At your computer compose the e-mail from your outline. As you compose, avoid amassing huge blocks of text. No one wants to read endless lines of type.

Revising, Proofreading, and Evaluating

Phase 3, revising, involves putting the final touches on your message. Careful and caring writers will ask a number of questions as they do the following:

- **Revise for clarity and conciseness.** Viewed from the receiver's perspective, are the ideas clear? Do they need more explanation? If the message is passed on to others, will they need further explanation? Consider having a colleague critique your message if it is an important one.
- **Revise for readability.** Did you group related information into paragraphs, preferably short ones? Paragraphs separated by white space look inviting. Does each paragraph begin with the main point, and is that point backed up by details? Can

you add paragraph headings to improve readability? Can you form bullet points or lists to make the message easy to skim and comprehend?

- **Proofread for correctness.** Are the sentences complete and punctuated properly? Did you overlook any typos or misspelled words? Remember to use your spell checker and grammar checker to proofread your message before sending it.
- **Plan for feedback.** How will you know whether this message is successful? You can improve feedback by asking questions (such as *Are you comfortable with these suggestions?* or *What do you think?*). Remember to make it easy for the receiver to respond by providing your e-mail address or phone number.

Best Practices for Using E-Mail Smartly, Safely, and Professionally

The stratospheric growth of e-mail continues unabated. In 2000, the Internet handled about 10 billion e-mails a day. According to the website Tech Watch, by 2008 that number had gone up to 210 billion per day.[2] The number is clearly much higher today, given the regular use of BlackBerrys, iPhones, and other personal digital assistants. Statistics Canada reports that 81 percent of Canadian private-sector enterprises use e-mail, while 100 percent of Canadian public-sector workplaces do the same.[3] Companies acknowledge that e-mail has become an indispensable means of internal communication as well as an essential link to customers and suppliers.

At the same time, as a recent high-profile case demonstrates, companies are also finding the widespread use of e-mail problematic. A major Canadian bank recently sued ten of its former employees for what it claimed was illegal use of BlackBerrys it had assigned these employees.[4] The employees used the communication devices to send e-mails to each other discussing the setting up of a new and rival company to the bank. The employees obviously didn't realize that the e-mails sent using the BlackBerrys were not private, and that the bank was fully within its rights to store these e-mails.

Today, the average e-mail may remain in the company's computer system for several years. And, in an increasing number of cases, the only impression a person has of the e-mail writer is from a transmitted message; they never actually meet. That's why it's important to take the time to organize your thoughts, compose carefully, and ensure correct grammar and punctuation.

Savvy e-mail business communicators are also learning its dangers. They know that their messages can travel (intentionally or unintentionally) to unexpected destinations. A quickly drafted note may end up in the boss's mailbox or forwarded to an unintended receiver. Making matters worse, computers—like elephants—never forget. Even erased messages can remain on hard drives. The case involving the bank discussed above is a cautionary tale for any company-employed business writer naive enough to assume e-mail is a simple, private, two-way communication system.

Smart E-Mail Practices

Despite its dangers and limitations, e-mail is increasingly the channel of choice for sending routine business messages. In large part, this increased popularity is a result of the advent of personal digital assistants (PDAs—BlackBerry and iPhone are the best-known kinds) that make it possible for people to carry their e-mail with them wherever they go. However, other channels of communication are still more effective for complex data or sensitive messages.

Getting Started. The following pointers will help you get off to a good start in using e-mail safely and effectively.

- **Get the address right.** E-mail addresses can be long and complex, often including letters, numbers, dashes, and underscores. Omit one character or misread the letter *l* for the number *1*, and your message will be returned. Solution: use your electronic address book frequently and use the reply feature in your e-mail program—most e-mail programs include the correct e-mail address from the original message in the reply message. And double-check every address that you key in manually.

- **Avoid misleading subject lines.** With an abundance of "spam" (junk e-mail) clogging inboxes and the fear of computer viruses that are spread by e-mail attachments, many e-mail users ignore or delete messages with unclear subject lines. Make sure your subject line is specific and helpful. Generic tags such as "HELLO" and "GREAT DEAL" may cause your message to be deleted before it is opened.
- **Apply the top-of-screen test.** When readers open your message and look at the first screen, will they see what is most significant? Your subject line and first paragraph should convey your purpose.

Content, Tone, and Correctness. Although e-mail seems as casual as a telephone call, it's not. A telephone call has its own set of rules, as does a letter, but neither of these sets of rules applies to e-mail. Concentrating on tone, content, and correctness will help to reduce the potential for misinterpretation of e-mail messages. As well, since e-mail also produces a permanent record, think carefully about what you say and how you say it.

> Avoid sending e-mails that are longer than one screen.

- **Be concise.** Don't burden readers with unnecessary information. Many e-mail recipients read dozens or even hundreds of e-mails every day. A concise message is appreciated. Organized and compelling messages will help to hold the reader's interest even if the e-mail contains many ideas.
- **Send only appropriate information.** Because e-mail seems like a telephone call or a person-to-person conversation, writers sometimes send sensitive, confidential, inflammatory, or potentially embarrassing messages. Information you consider appropriate, funny, or appealing may not be interpreted the same way by your audience. By sending an inappropriate message, you are also creating a permanent record that often does not go away even when deleted. Every message sent at work is a corporate communication for which both you and your employer are responsible.
- **Don't use e-mail to avoid contact.** Breaking bad news or resolving an argument through e-mail is not recommended. With e-mail you cannot rely on nonverbal communication, active listening techniques, and other face-to-face communication methods to ensure correct understanding of emotion and meaning. Imagine being fired by e-mail or having your job performance evaluated through e-mail. It's also not a good channel for dealing with conflict with supervisors, subordinates, or others. If there's any possibility of hurt feelings, pick up the telephone or pay the person a visit.

> E-mail should not be used for bad news or angry messages.

- **Never respond when you're angry.** Always allow some time to compose yourself before responding to an upsetting message. You'll often come up with different and better alternatives after thinking about what was said. If possible, iron out differences in person.
- **Care about correctness.** People are still judged by their writing, whether electronic or paper-based. Sloppy e-mail messages (with missing apostrophes, haphazard spelling, and stream-of-consciousness writing) make readers work too hard. Readers quickly lose respect for writers of poor e-mails.
- **Resist humour and personal jokes.** Without the nonverbal cues conveyed by your face and your voice, humour can easily be misunderstood.

> Avoid humorous or sarcastic expressions that may be misunderstood.

Netiquette. Although e-mail is an evolving communication channel, a number of rules of polite online interaction apply.

- **Limit the tendency to copy to your distribution list.** Send copies only to people who really need to see the message. It is unnecessary to document every business decision and action with an electronic paper trail.

- **Limit the tendency to reply to the entire cc list.** Think carefully about whether your reply needs to be seen by everyone or just the person who sent you the message.
- **Don't automatically forward junk e-mail.** Internet jokes and other unnecessary messages such as warnings about new viruses, chain letters, or unusual fund-raising campaigns are tiresome and valueless.
- **Consider using identifying labels.** When appropriate, add one of the following labels to the subject line: "ACTION" (Action required, please respond); "FYI" (For your information, no response needed); "RE" (This is a reply to another message); "URGENT" (Please respond immediately; but note that this label is sometimes poorly used because a phone call or face-to-face meeting is a better option). These labels should be agreed upon among employees.
- **Use capital letters only for emphasis or for titles.** Avoid writing entire messages in all caps, which is equivalent to shouting.
- **Announce attachments.** If you're sending a lengthy attachment, tell your receiver. Consider summarizing or highlighting important aspects of the attachment briefly in the e-mail. Make sure the receiver can open the attachment you send; maximum file sizes are sometimes an issue within companies when sending external messages. Some file formats cannot be opened on all computers.
- **Consider asking for permission before forwarding.** For messages containing private or project specific information, obtain approval before forwarding to others.

"Have a seat. There are 342 email messages ahead of you."

Reading and Replying to E-Mail. The following tips can save you time and frustration when reading and answering e-mails.

- **Scan all messages in your inbox before replying to each individually.** Because subsequent messages often affect the way you respond, read them all first, especially all those from the same sender.
- **Print only when necessary.** Generally, read and answer most messages online without printing. Use folders to archive messages that should be saved. Print only those messages that are complex, controversial, or involve significant decisions and follow-up.
- **Acknowledge receipt.** If you can't reply immediately, say when you can (*Will respond Friday*).

- **Don't automatically return the sender's message.** When replying, cut and paste the relevant parts. Avoid irritating your recipients by returning the entire "thread" or sequence of messages on a topic, unless the thread needs to be included to provide context for your remarks.
- **Revise the subject line if the topic changes.** When replying or continuing an e-mail exchange, revise the subject line as the topic changes.
- **Respond to messages quickly and efficiently.** Set yourself a goal of replying to all messages on the day they are received. After answering e-mails, file them in a project-specific folder if necessary.

Personal Use. Remember that office computers are meant for work-related communication.

- **Don't use company computers for personal matters.** Unless your company specifically allows it, never use your employer's computers for personal messages, personal shopping, or entertainment.
- **Assume that all e-mail is monitored.** Employers can and do monitor e-mail.

Other Smart E-Mail Practices. Depending on your messages and audience, the following tips promote effective electronic communication.

- **Use graphic highlighting to improve readability of longer messages.** When a message is longer, help the reader with headings, bulleted lists, and perhaps an introductory summary that describes what will follow. Although these techniques lengthen a message, they shorten reading time.
- **Consider cultural differences.** When using this global tool, be especially clear and precise in your language. Remember that figurative clichés (*pull up stakes, playing second fiddle*), sports references (*hit a home run, play by the rules*), and slang (*cool, stoked*) can cause confusion abroad.
- **Double-check before hitting the Send button.** Have you included everything? Avoid the necessity of sending a second message, which makes you look careless. Edit for grammar and style and ensure your answer makes sense before sending.

Improving E-Mail and Memo Readability With Listing Techniques

Because readers of e-mails and memos are usually in a hurry, they want important information to stand out. One of the best ways to improve the readability of any message is by listing items. The information in e-mails and memos often lends itself to listing. A list is a group or series of related items, usually three or more. Since lists require fewer words than complete sentences, they can be read and understood quickly and easily. In writing lists, keep these general points in mind.

- **Make listed items parallel.** Listed items must all relate to the same topic, and they must be balanced grammatically. If one item is a single word but the next item requires a paragraph of explanation, the items are not suitable for listing.
- **Use bullets, numbers, or letters appropriately.** Numbers (1, 2, 3) and letters (a, b, c) suggest a hierarchy or sequence of operation; bullets merely separate.
- **Use generally accepted punctuation.** Most writers use a colon following the introduction to most lists. However, they don't use a colon if the listed items follow a verb or a preposition (for example, *the colours are red, yellow, and blue*). Use end punctuation only after complete sentences, and capitalize the first word of items listed vertically.

> You can improve the readability of a message by listing items in parallel.

Parallelism

Instead of This	Try This
She likes *sleeping, eating,* and *to work*.	She likes *sleeping, eating,* and *working*.
We are hiring the following: *sales clerks, managers who will function as supervisors,* and *people to work in offices*.	We are hiring the following: *sales clerks, supervising managers,* and *office personnel*.

Instructions

Instead of This	Try This
Here are the instructions for operating the copy machine. First, you insert your copy card in the slot. Then you load paper in the upper tray. Last, copies are fed through the feed tray.	Follow these steps to use the copy machine: 1. *Insert* your copy card in the slot. 2. *Load* paper in the upper tray. 3. *Feed* copies through the feed tray.

Listed Items With Headings

Instead of This

On May 16 we will be in Regina, and Dr. Susan Dillon is the speaker. On June 20, we will be in Saskatoon, and Dr. Diane Minger is the speaker.

Try This

Date	City	Speaker
May 16	Regina	Dr. Susan Dillon
June 20	Saskatoon	Dr. Diane Minger

Listed Items for Emphasis Within Sentences

Instead of This	Try This
To keep exercising, you should make a written commitment to yourself, set realistic goals for each day's workout, and enlist the support of a friend.	To keep exercising, you should (a) make a written commitment to yourself, (b) set realistic goals for each day's workout, and (c) enlist the support of a friend.

Bulleted Items

Instead of This

Our goal

- is to recruit intensely competitive sales reps
- is to use reps who know our products
- recruit intelligent reps who are quick to learn

Try This

Our goal is to recruit sales reps who are

- Intensely competitive
- Familiar with our products
- Intelligent and quick to learn

Using Instant Messaging Professionally

Businesspeople use instant messaging to exchange ideas in real time in a private chat room.

Instant messaging (IM) enables you to use the Internet to communicate in real time in a private chat room with one or more individuals. It is like live e-mail or a text telephone call. More and more workers are using it as a speedy communication channel to exchange short messages.

How Instant Messaging Works

To send an instant message, you might use Yahoo! Messenger, Google Talk, Jabber, or Microsoft's Windows Live Messenger. These are public IM services. Once the software is installed, you enter your name and password to log on. The software checks to see if any of the users in your contact list are currently logged in. If the server finds any of your contacts, it sends a message back to your computer. If the person you wish to contact is online, you can click that person's name and a window opens into which you can enter text. You enter a message, such as that shown in Figure 4.4, and click **Send**. Because your IM software has the Internet address and port number for the computer of the person you addressed, your message is sent directly to that person's computer. All communication occurs directly between the two computers without the need of a server.

Unlike e-mail, IM provides no elaborate page layout options. The text box is short, and pressing the "Enter" key "sends" the message. Obviously, it is designed for brief, fast text interaction.

Weighing the Pros and Cons of Instant Messaging

Once primarily a consumer tool, instant messaging is increasingly being used by knowledge workers for many reasons. People like instant messaging because of its immediacy. Unlike e-mail, messages do not need to be downloaded from a mail server. In addition, a user knows right away whether a message was delivered. Proponents of instant messaging say that it avoids phone tag and eliminates the downtime associated with personal telephone conversations. Because it replaces expensive long-distance telephone and fax calls, instant messaging saves money. Another benefit of instant messaging includes "presence functionality." Coworkers can locate each other online, thus avoiding wild goose chases hunting down someone who is out of the office. Many people consider instant messaging a productivity booster because it enables them to get answers quickly and helps them multitask.

Despite its popularity among workers, some organizations forbid employees to use instant messaging for a number of reasons. Employers consider instant messaging yet another distraction in addition to the interruptions caused by the

FIGURE 4.4 Instant Message for Brief, Fast Communication

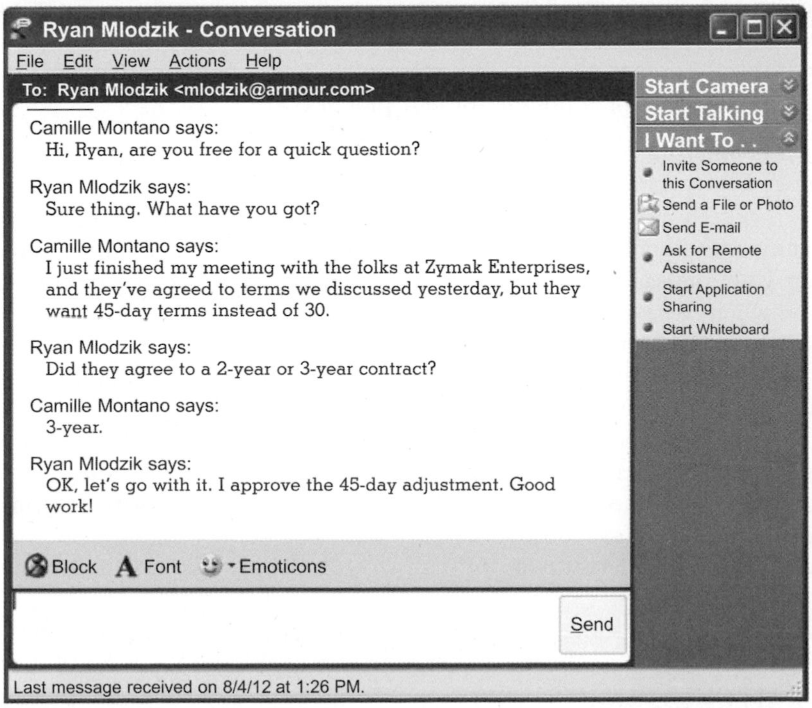

FIGURE 4.5 Pros and Cons of Instant Messaging

Pros	Cons
Speed: Connects people immediately.	**Security:** Imperils privileged information.
Cost savings: Reduces telephone bills.	**Litigation:** Endangers companies with possibility of disclosure in lawsuits.
Presence functionality: Locates people online.	**Control:** Requires companies to establish and enforce usage rules.
Convenience: Provides quick answers to short questions.	**Compliance:** Forces organizations to monitor and track conversations to meet legal requirements.
Productivity booster: Speeds project completion; enables multitasking.	**Productivity thief:** Distracts workers; encourages frivolous time wasting.

telephone, e-mail, and the Web. Organizations also fear that privileged information and company records will be revealed through public instant messaging systems, which hackers can easily penetrate. Organizations worry about "phishing" schemes, viruses, malware, and *spim* (IM spam). Like e-mail, instant messages are subject to discovery (disclosure); that is, they can become evidence in lawsuits. Finally, companies fear instant messaging because it forces them to face the daunting task of tracking and storing messaging conversations to comply with legal requirements. The pros and cons of instant messaging are summarized in Figure 4.5.

For some organizations IM is not an essential business tool and not worth the risks involved. They simply block its use. Other companies, however, see instant messaging as a beneficial communication tool. They are investing in *enterprise-class IM systems*. Such systems enable workers to exchange instant messages within a closed-loop structure. These systems provide an audit trail and greater security. Organizations can selectively retain, archive, and destroy IM conversations to meet compliance laws.

Best Practices for Instant Messaging

Instant messaging can definitely save time and simplify communications with coworkers and customers. Before using it on the job, however, be sure you have permission. Do not use public systems without checking with your supervisor. If your organization does allow instant messaging, you can use it efficiently and professionally by following a number of best practices.

- Learn about your organization's IM policies. Are you allowed to use instant messaging? With whom may you exchange messages?
- Make yourself unavailable when you need to complete a project or meet a deadline.
- Organize your contact lists to separate business contacts from family and friends.
- Keep your messages simple and to the point. Avoid unnecessary chitchat, and know when to say goodbye.
- Don't use IM to send confidential or sensitive information.
- Be aware that instant messages can be saved. As with e-mail, don't say anything that would damage your reputation or that of your organization.
- If personal messaging is allowed, keep it to a minimum. Your organization may prefer that personal chats be done during breaks or the lunch hour.
- Show patience by not blasting multiple messages to coworkers if a response is not immediate.
- Keep your presence status up to date so that people trying to reach you don't waste their time.
- Beware of jargon, slang, and abbreviations, which, although they may reduce keystrokes, may be confusing and appear unprofessional.
- Respect your receivers by employing proper grammar, spelling, and proofreading.

Writing Information and Procedure E-Mails and Memos

Although you may exchange instant messages, most of your writing tasks on the job will probably involve preparing e-mails and the odd interoffice memo. Some of the most frequent messages that you can expect to be writing as a business communicator are (a) information and procedure messages and (b) request and reply messages.

In this book we suggest a number of writing plans for various messages. These plans provide a skeleton; they are the bones of a message. You will provide the flesh. Simply plugging in phrases or someone else's words won't work. Good writers provide details and link their ideas with transitions to create fluent and meaningful messages. However, a writing plan helps you get started and gives you ideas about what to include. At first, you may rely on these plans considerably. As you progress, these plans will become less important. Later in the book, no plans are provided.

Writing Plan for Information and Procedure E-Mails and Memos

- **Subject line:** Summarize the content of the message.
- **Opening:** Expand the subject line by stating the main idea concisely in a full sentence.
- **Body:** Provide background data and explain the main idea. Consider using lists, bullets, or headings to improve readability. In describing a procedure or giving instructions, use command language (*do this, don't do that*).
- **Closing:** Request a specific action, summarize the message, or present a closing thought. If appropriate, include a deadline and a reason.

Information and procedure messages distribute routine information, describe procedures, and deliver instructions. They typically flow downward from management to employees and relate to the daily operation of an organization. In writing these messages, you have one primary function: conveying your idea so clearly that no further explanation (return message, telephone call, or personal visit) is necessary.

Information and procedure messages generally flow downward from management to employees.

You have already seen the development of a routine information message in Figure 4.1 on page 88. It follows the writing plan with an informative subject line, an opening that states the purpose directly, and a body that organizes the information for maximum readability. The closing in an information message depends on what was discussed. If the message involves an action request, it should appear in the closing—not in the opening or in the body. If no action is required, the closing can summarize the message or offer a closing thought.

Procedure messages must be especially clear and readable. Figure 4.6 shows the first draft of an interoffice memo written by Troy Bell. His memo was meant to announce a new procedure for employees to follow in advertising open positions. However, the tone was negative, the explanation of the problem rambled, and the new procedure was unclear. Notice, too, that Troy's first draft told readers what they *shouldn't* do (*Do not submit your advertisements for new employees directly to an Internet job bank or a newspaper*). It is more helpful to tell readers what they *should* do. Finally, Troy's first memo closed with a threat instead of showing readers how this new procedure would help them.

In the revision Troy improves the tone considerably. The subject line contains a *please*, which is always nice to include even if one is giving an order. The subject line also includes a verb and specifies the purpose of the memo. Instead of expressing his

FIGURE 4.6 Procedure Memo

Before

Date: January 5, 2012
To: Ruth DiSilvestro, Manager
From: Troy Bell, Human Resources
Subject: Job Advertisement Misunderstanding ●————— Vague, negative subject line

We had no idea last month when we implemented new hiring procedures that ●————— Fails to pinpoint main idea in opening
major problems would result. Due to the fact that every department is now placing
Internet advertisements for new-hires individually, the difficulties occurred. This
cannot continue. Perhaps we did not make it clear at the time, but all newly hired
employees who are hired for a position should be requested through this office.

Do not submit your advertisements for new employees directly to an Internet job ●————— New procedure is hard to follow
bank or a newspaper. After you write them, they should be brought to Human
Resources, where they will be centralized. You should discuss each ad with one of
our counsellors. Then we will place the ad at an appropriate Internet site or other
publication. If you do not follow these guidelines, chaos will result. You may pick ●————— Uses threats instead of showing benefits to reader
up applicant folders from us the day after the closing date in an ad.

After

MEMORANDUM

Date: January 5, 2012

To: Ruth DiSilvestro, Manager

From: Troy Bell, Human Resources ᵀᴮ

Subject: Please Follow New Job Advertisement Procedure

Employs informative, courteous, upbeat subject line —————

To find the right candidates for your open positions as fast as possible, we are
implementing a new routine. Effective today, all advertisements for departmental
job openings should be routed through the Human Resources Department.

Combines "you" view with main idea in opening —————

A major problem resulted from the change in hiring procedures implemented last
month. Each department is placing job advertisements for new-hires individually,
when all such requests should be centralized in this office. To process applications
more efficiently, please follow this procedure:

Explains why change in procedures is necessary —————

1. Write an advertisement for a position in your department.

2. Bring the ad to Human Resources and discuss it with one of our counsellors.

Lists easy-to-follow steps and starts each step with a verb —————

3. Let Human Resources place the ad at an appropriate Internet job bank or submit it to a newspaper.

4. Pick up applicant folders from Human Resources the day following the closing date provided in the ad.

Closes by reinforcing benefits to reader —————

Following these guidelines will save you work and will also enable Human
Resources to help you fill your openings more quickly. Call Ann Edmonds at
Ext. 2505 if you have questions about this procedure.

---

ideas with negative words and threats, Troy revises his message to explain objectively and concisely what went wrong.

Troy realizes that his original explanation of the new procedure is vague. Messages explaining procedures are most readable when the instructions are broken down into numbered steps listed chronologically. Each step should begin with an action verb in the command mode. Notice in Troy's revision in Figure 4.6 that numbered items begin with *Write, Bring, Let,* and *Pick up*. It is sometimes difficult to force all the steps in a procedure into this kind of command language. Troy struggles, but by trying different wording, he finally finds verbs that work.

Procedures and instructions are often written in numbered steps using command language (*Do this, don't do that*).

Why should you go to so much trouble to make lists and achieve parallelism? Because readers can comprehend what you have written much more quickly, parallel language also makes you look professional and efficient.

In writing information and procedure messages, be careful of tone. Today's managers and team leaders seek employee participation and cooperation. These goals can't be achieved, though, if the writer sounds like a dictator or an autocrat. Avoid making accusations and assigning blame. Rather, explain changes, give reasons, and suggest benefits to the reader. Assume that employees want to contribute to the success of the organization and to their own achievement. Notice in the Figure 4.6 revision that Troy tells readers that they will save time and have their open positions filled more quickly if they follow the new procedures.

Writing Request and Reply E-Mails and Memos

Business organizations require information as their fuel. To make operations run smoothly, managers and employees request information from each other and then respond to those requests. Knowing how to write requests and responses efficiently and effectively can save you time and make you look good.

Writing Plan for Request E-Mails and Memos

- **Subject line:** Summarize the request and note the action desired.
- **Opening:** Begin with the request or a brief statement introducing it.
- **Body:** Provide background, justification, and details. If asking questions, list them in parallel form.
- **Closing:** Request action by a specific date. If possible, provide a reason. Express appreciation, if appropriate.

Writing Direct E-Mail and Memo Requests

If you are requesting routine information or action within an organization, the direct approach works best. Generally, this means asking for information or making the request without first providing elaborate explanations and justifications. Remember that readers are usually thinking, "Why me? Why am I receiving this?" They can understand the explanation better once they know what you are requesting.

If you are seeking answers to questions, you have three options for opening the message: (a) ask the most important question first, followed by an explanation and then the other questions, (b) use a polite command (*Please answer the following questions regarding*), or (c) introduce the questions with a brief statement (*Your answers to the following questions will help us . . .*).

In the body of the memo, explain and justify your request. When you must ask many questions, list them, being careful to phrase them similarly. Be courteous and friendly. In the closing include an end date (with a reason, if possible) to promote a quick response.

The e-mail shown in Figure 4.7 requests information. The subject line uses a verb in noting the action desired (*Need Your Reactions to Our Casual-Dress Policy*). The reader knows immediately what is being requested. The message opens with a polite command followed by a brief explanation. Notice that the questions are highlighted with bullets to provide the high "skim value" that is important in business messages. The reader can quickly see what is being asked. The message concludes with an end date and a reason. Providing an end date helps the reader know how to plan a response so that action is completed by the date given. Expressions such as

> Use the direct approach in routine requests for information or action, opening with the most important question, a polite command, or a brief introductory statement.

FIGURE 4.7 Request E-Mail

To: Taylor Manning <tmanning@lugo.com>
From: William Lugo <wlugo@lugo.com>
Subject: Need Your Reactions to Our Casual-Dress Policy
Cc:
Attached:

Taylor,

Should we revamp our casual-dress policy? I'm asking you and other members of our management team to consider the questions below as we decide whether to change our policy here at Lugo & Associates.

As you know, we adopted a casual business attire program several years ago. Some employees saw it as an employment benefit. To others, it was a disaster because they didn't know how to dress casually and still look professional. Since we originally adopted the policy, times have changed and the trend seems to be moving back toward more formal business attire. Here are some questions to consider:

• What is acceptable to wear on dress-down days?
• Should our policy restrict body art (tattoos) and piercing?
• How should supervisors react when clothing is offensive, tasteless, revealing, or sloppy?
• Is it possible to develop a uniform definition of acceptable casual attire?
• Do the advantages of a dress-down policy outweigh the disadvantages?
• Should we refine our dress-down policy or eliminate it?

Please give careful thought to these questions and be ready to discuss each at our management meeting September 14.

Bill

William P. Lugo
CEO, Lugo & Associates
340 Portage Ave., Winnipeg, MB R3C 2X7
Office (403) 555-2388   Cell (403) 555-6654

Annotations:
- Provides functional subject line noting desired action
- Opens directly by immediately describing the request
- Explains reasoning behind request and gives details
- Lists questions in parallel form and uses bullets to produce high "skim value"
- Closes with end date and reason

---

do it whenever you can or *complete it as soon as possible* make little impression on procrastinators or very busy people. It is always wise to provide a specific date for completion. Dates can be entered on calendars to serve as reminders.

Replying to E-Mail and Memo Requests

A lot of business correspondence reacts or responds to previous messages. When replying to an e-mail or other message, be sure to follow the three-phase writing process. Analyze your purpose and audience, collect whatever information is necessary, and organize your thoughts. Make a brief outline of the points you plan to cover following this writing plan:

> **Overused and long-winded openers bore readers and waste their time.**

Writing Plan for E-Mail and Memo Replies

● **Subject line:** Summarize the main information from your reply.
● **Opening:** Start directly by responding to the request with a summary statement.
● **Body:** Provide additional information and details in a readable format.
● **Closing:** Add a concluding remark, summary, or offer of further assistance.

Writers sometimes fall into bad habits in replying to messages. Here are some trite and long-winded openers that are best avoided:

In response to your message of the 15th . . . (States the obvious.)

Thank you for your memo of the 15th in which you . . . (Suggests the writer can think of nothing more original.)

I have before me your memo of the 15th in which you . . . (Unnecessarily identifies the location of the previous message.)

Pursuant to your request of the 15th . . . (Sounds old-fashioned.)

This is to inform you that . . . (Delays getting to the point.)

Instead of falling into the trap of using one of the preceding shopworn openings, start directly by responding to the writer's request. If you agree to the request, show your cheerful compliance immediately. Consider these good-news openers:

Direct opening statements can also be cheerful and empathic.

Yes, we will be glad to . . . (Sends message of approval by opening with "Yes.")

Here are answers to the questions you asked about . . . (Sounds straightforward, businesslike, and professional.)

You are right in seeking advice about . . . (Opens with words that every reader enjoys seeing and hearing.)

We are happy to assist you in . . . (Shows writer's helpful nature and goodwill.)

As you requested, I am submitting . . . (Gets right to the point.)

After a direct and empathic opener, provide the information requested in a logical and coherent order. If you are answering a number of questions, arrange your answers in the order of the questions. In providing additional data, use familiar words, short sentences, short paragraphs, and active-voice verbs. Figure 4.3 on page 92 illustrates an interoffice memo that replies to a request. Notice that the writer organized her suggestions into separate paragraphs with the introductory words *First*, *Second*, and *Third*. The writer also designed the document with columns, white space, and bullets to further improve readability. The message concludes with what is to happen next.

In responding to requests, your primary goal is to answer the request clearly and completely so that additional messages are unnecessary.

Summing Up and Looking Forward

Organizations exchange messages externally and internally. Paper-based messages include business letters and interoffice memos. Electronic messages include e-mails, instant messages, text messages, podcasts, blogs, and wikis. Internal messages in today's workplace usually take the form of e-mail, interoffice memos, and, to a lesser extent, instant messages. E-mails and memos use a standardized format to request and deliver information.

Because messages are increasingly being exchanged electronically, this chapter presented many techniques for sending and receiving safe and effective e-mails and instant messages. However, businesspeople are still using interoffice memos to convey confidential information, emphasize ideas, deliver lengthy documents, or lend importance to a message. In this chapter you learned to apply the direct strategy in writing internal messages that inform, describe procedures, request, and respond. In the next chapter you will extend the direct strategy to writing letters.

Critical Thinking

1. "E-mail is no longer a cutting-edge tool," says a recent newspaper article. "But it is clear that some people still do not know how to use it effectively."[5] What have you heard are the major complaints about the use of business e-mail?

2. What do you think this statement means? *Instant messaging and texting could be the dial tone of the future.* Do you agree or disagree? Why or why not?

3. Why are lawyers and technology experts warning companies to store, organize, and manage computer data, including e-mail, with greater diligence?

4. Discuss the ramifications of the following statement: *Once a memo or any other document leaves your hands, you have essentially published it.*

5. *Ethical Issue*: Should managers have the right to monitor the e-mail messages of employees? Why or why not? What if employees are warned that e-mail could be monitored? If a company sets up an e-mail policy, should only in-house transmissions be monitored? Only outside transmissions?

Chapter Review

1. Name the major forms of electronic communication and describe each briefly.
2. Are e-mails and memos interchangeable as communication channels? Explain.
3. How are the structure and format of e-mails and memos similar and different?
4. What questions should you ask yourself before writing an e-mail or memo?
5. What pointers would you offer a new business e-mail writer?
6. What e-mail etiquette suggestions show respect for others?
7. What are the most important practices when sending instant messages at work?
8. Describe the writing plan for an information or procedure message.
9. Describe the writing plan for a request message.
10. Describe the writing plan for a reply message.

Writing Improvement Exercises

Message Openers

Compare the following sets of message openers. Circle the letter of the opener that illustrates a direct opening. Be prepared to discuss the weaknesses and strengths of each.

1. An e-mail message inquiring about Web hosting:

   a. We are considering launching our own Web site because we feel it is the only way to keep up with our competition and make our product more visible in a crowded market. We have a lot of questions and need information about Web hosting.

   b. Please answer the following questions about hosting our new Web site, which we hope to launch to increase our product visibility in a crowded market.

2. An e-mail message announcing a professional development program:

   a. Employees interested in improving their writing and communication skills are invited to a training program beginning October 4.

   b. For the past year we have been investigating the possibility of developing a communication skills training program for some of our employees.

3. An e-mail message announcing a study:

   a. We have noticed recently a gradual but steady decline in the number of customer chequing accounts. We are disturbed by this trend, and for this reason I am asking our Customer Relations Department to conduct a study and make recommendations regarding this important problem.

   b. Our Customer Relations Department will conduct a study and make recommendations regarding the gradual but steady decline of customer chequing accounts.

4. A memo announcing a new procedure:

   a. Some customer representatives in the field have suggested that they would like to enter their reports from the field instead of coming back to the office to enter them in their computers. That's why we have made a number of changes. We would like you to use the following procedures.

   b. Customer representatives may now enter their field reports using the following procedures.

Opening Paragraphs

The following opening paragraphs to memos are wordy and indirect. After reading each paragraph, identify the main idea. Then, write an opening sentence that illustrates a more direct opening. Use a separate sheet if necessary.

5. Several staff members came to me and announced their interest in learning more about severance plans and separation policies. As most of you know, these areas of concern are increasingly important for most Human Resources professionals. A seminar entitled "Severance & Separation Benefits" is being conducted February 11. The following employees are attending the seminar: Dave Neufeld, Tayreez Mushani, and Gail Switzer.

   Because

6. Your employee association has secured discounts on auto repair, carpet purchases, travel arrangements, and many other services. These services are available to you if you have a Buying Power Card. All employees are eligible for their own private Buying Power Cards.

   All employees are eligible for great discounts with their Buying Power Cards.

Lists

Write lists as indicated below.

7. Use the following information to compose a single sentence that includes an introductory statement and a list with letters (*a*, *b*, *c*). Do not list the items vertically.

   The home page of a Web site should orient readers. This page should tell them what the site is about. It should also tell about the organization of the site. Finally, it should tell them how to navigate the site.

   Web site home page should include (a) site description (b) site organization (c) site navigation

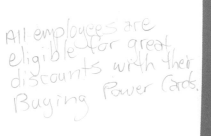

8. Use the following information to compose a bulleted vertical list with an introductory statement.

   To use the conventional inline skate heel brake, you should do these things. First, you should move one leg slightly forward. Then the ball of your foot should be lifted. Finally, the heel should be dragged to complete the braking action.

9. Use the following information to compose a sentence containing a list.

   Your equipment lease will mature in a month. When it does, you must make a decision. Three options are available to you. If you like, you may purchase the equipment at fair market value. Or the existing lease may be extended, again at fair market value. Finally, if neither of these options is appealing, the equipment could be sent back to the leasing company.

Activities and Cases

4.1 Document Critique: Dealing with Excessive E-mail

The following e-mail from Stella Soto requests feedback from her managerial staff; however, her first draft suffers from many writing faults.

Your Task. Analyze the message. List its weaknesses and then outline an appropriate writing plan. If your instructor directs, revise the message.

Date: December 18, 2012
To: Amsoft Manager List
From: Stella Soto <stella.soto@amsoft.com>
Subject: E-Mail Problems
Cc:
Bcc:

Dear Managers,

As Amsoft vice president, I am troubled by a big problem. I am writing this note to ask for your help and advice to address an urgent problem—the problem of excessive e-mail. If you will do me the favour of answering the questions below, I'm sure your ideas will assist us in the development of a plan that should benefit your staff, yourself, and our organization will be improved. Your responses in writing to these questions (preferably by December 22) will help me prepare for our supervisory committee meeting on January 4. Everyone had the expectation that e-mail would be a great big productivity tool. I'm afraid that its use is becoming extremely excessive. For our organization it is actually cutting into work time. Did you know that one study found that the average office worker is spending 2 hours a day on e-mail? In our organization we may be spending even more then this. Its exceedingly difficult to get any work done because of writing and answering an extra ordinary number of e-mails coming in each and every day. Excessive e-mail is sapping the organization's strength and productivity. I would like to have your answers to some questions before the above referenced dates to help us focus on the problem.

Can you give a ballpark figure for how many e-mail messages you receive and answer on a personal basis each day? Think about how many hours the staff members in your department spend on e-mail each day. Approximately how many hours would you estimate? Do you have any ideas about how we can make a reduction in the volume of e-mail messages being sent and received within our own organization? Do you think that e-mail is being used by our employees in an excessive manner?

I'm wondering what you think about an e-mail-free day once a week. How about Fridays? I appreciate your suggestions and advice in developing a solution to the problem of controlling e-mail and making an improvement in productivity.

Stella

1. List at least five weaknesses of this message.

2. Outline a writing plan for this message.

4.2 Document Critique: Facts About Corporate Instant Messaging

The following interoffice memo reports information from a conference, but it is poorly written.

Your Task. Analyze the memo. List its weaknesses and then outline an appropriate writing plan. If your instructor directs, revise the memo.

Date: March 4, 2012
To: Trevor Kurtz, CEO
From: Emily Lopez-Rush
Subject: Instant Messaging

Thanks for asking me to attend the Instant Messaging Conference. It was sponsored by Pixel Link and took place March 2. Do you think you will want me to expand on what I learned at the next management council meeting? I believe that meeting is March 25.

Anyway, here's my report. Jason Howard, the conference leader told us that over 80 million workers are already using instant messaging and that it was definitely here to stay. But do the risks outweigh the advantages? He talked about benefits, providers, costs involved, and risks. The top advantages of IM are speed, documentation, and it saves costs. The major problems are spam, security, control, and disruptive. He said that the principal IM providers for consumers were Windows Live Messenger and Yahoo Messenger. Misuse of IM can result in reductions in productivity. However, positive results can be achieved with appropriate use. Although some employees are using consumer IM services, for maximum security many organizations are investing in enterprise-level IM systems, and they are adopting guidelines for employees. These enterprise-level IM systems range in cost from $30 to $100 per user licence. The cost depends on the amount of functionality.

This is just a summary of what I learned. If you want to hear more, please do not hesitate to call.

1. List at least five weaknesses of this interoffice memo.
2. Outline a writing plan for this memo.

4.3 Document Critique: Planning a Charity Golf Event

The following e-mail from Seth Jackson requests information about planning a charity golf tournament. His first draft must be revised.

Your Task. Analyze the message. List its weaknesses and then outline an appropriate writing plan. If your instructor directs, revise the message. Could this message benefit from category headings?

Date: February 1, 2012
To: Kaitlin Merek <kmerek@monarch.ca>
From: Seth Jackson <seth.jackson@cox.ca>
Subject: Need Help!

The Children's Resource Centre badly needs funds. We have tried other things, but now we want to try a charity golf event. In view of the fact that you have expertise in this area and since you volunteered to offer your assistance, I am writing this e-mail to pick your brain, so to speak, in regard to questions that have to do with five basic fundamentals in the process of preparation. I'm going to need your answers these areas before February 15. Is that possible? Maybe you would rather talk to me. Should I contact you?

In regard to the budget, I have no idea how to estimate costs. For example, what about administrative costs. How about marketing? And there are salaries, cell-phone rentals, copiers, and a lot of other things.

I also need help in choosing a golf course. Should it be a public course? Or a private course? Resort? One big area that I worry about is sponsors. Should I go after one big sponsor? But let's say I get Pepsi to be a sponsor. Then do I have to ban Coke totally from the scene?

Another big headache is scoring. I will bet you can make some suggestions for tabulating the golf results. And posting them. By the way, did you see that Tiger Woods is back in the winner's circle?

I have noticed that other golf tournaments have extra events, such as a pairing party to introduce partners. Many also have an awards dinner to award prizes. Should I be planning extra events?

Seth Jackson
Philanthropy and Gifts Coordinator
Children's Resource Centre

1. List at least five weaknesses of this request e-mail.
2. Outline a writing plan for this message.

4.4 Document Critique: New Process for Reporting Equipment Repairs

The following is a manager's first draft of an e-mail describing a new process for reporting equipment repairs. The message is addressed to one employee, but it will also be sent to others.

Your Task. Analyze the message. List its weaknesses and then outline an appropriate writing plan. If your instructor directs, revise the message.

Date: April 25, 2012
To: Faith Benoit <Faith.Benoit@stcc.ca>
From: Mia Murillo <Mia.Murillo@stcc.ca>
Subject: Repairs
Cc:
Bcc:

We have recently instituted a new procedure for all equipment repairs. Effective immediately, we are no longer using the "Equipment Repair Form" that we formerly used. We want to move everyone to an online database system. These new procedures will help us repair your equipment faster and keep track of it better. You will find the new procedure at http://www.BigWebDesk.ca. That's where you log in. You should indicate the kind of repair you need. It may be for AudioVisual, Mac, PC, or Printer. Then you should begin the process of data entry for your specific problem by selecting **Create New Ticket.** The new ticket should be printed and attached securely to the equipment. Should you have questions or trouble, just call Sylvia at Extension 255. You can also write to her at *Sylvia.Freeman@stcc.ca*. The warehouse truck driver will pick up and deliver your equipment as we have always done in the past.

1. List at least five weaknesses of this e-mail message.

2. Outline a writing plan for this message.

4.5 Memo That Informs: Change in Insurance Premiums

Compose as Memo addressed to all employees

You are the benefits manager for a national furniture retail chain, The Home Centre, headquartered in Richmond, British Columbia. Most of the full-time employees who work for the chain pay into an employee benefits plan. This plan includes dental and vision care, prescription drug coverage, and other benefits. One of the most expensive benefits employees pay for is long-term disability (LTD) insurance. Recently, your insurance provider, Cansafe, has informed you that due to the high number of recent long-term disability claims, premiums for long-term disability insurance will have to rise substantially, on the order of 15 percent. For the average employee, this means an increase of more than $20 per month.

Your Task. Your job requires you to write a well-organized memo informing The Home Centre employees about the impending increase. From past experience, you know that employees who are closer to retirement are big supporters of long-term disability insurance, whereas younger employees tend to be frustrated by the high premiums.

Related Web site: Sun Life's site has a useful description of LTD insurance at http://www.sunlife.ca/Plan/Health/Disability+insurance?vgnLocale=en_CA.

4.6 E-Mail That Informs and Requests: Dress Code Controversy

WEB

TEAM

As the Montreal-based director of Human Resources at Sensational, you have not had a good week. The national media recently reported the fact that Sensational—a leading women's fashion chain—has been taken before the Nova Scotia Human Rights Commission to defend against a claim by a young woman. The young woman recently applied for a job at a Halifax Sensational location and was told in a pre-interview with a manager that "she'd never be hired if she wore her headdress to work." Citing the Commission's Web site claim that "It's against the law to fire an employee because he wears clothing that is required by his religion," the young woman lodged a complaint.[6] Head office in Vancouver has been in damage-control mode ever since.

Your Task. Quickly realizing the effects the negative media reporting will have, you draft an e-mail to all employees. The purpose of the e-mail is to reaffirm that Sensational abides by and supports all Canadian human rights legislation, and at the same time, that employees should not talk to any media that may ask them for comments. You realize that these two messages are somewhat contradictory (one positive, one negative), but you feel time is of the essence.

Related Web site: Nova Scotia Human Rights Commission (http://www.gov.ns.ca/humanrights/)

4.7 Response E-Mail or Memo: Office Romance Off Limits?

Where can you find the hottest singles scene today? Some would say in your workplace. Because people are working long hours and have little time for outside contacts, relationships often develop at work. Estimates suggest that one third to one half of all romances begin at the office. Your boss is concerned about possible problems resulting from workplace relationships. What happens if a relationship between a superior and subordinate results in perceived favouritism? What happens if a relationship ends in a nasty breakup? Your boss would like to simply ban all relationships between employees. However, that's not likely to work. He asks you, his assistant, to learn what guidelines could be established regarding office romances.

Your Task. Using research databases or the Internet, look for articles about workplace romance. From various articles, select four or five suggestions that you could make to your boss in regard to protecting an employer. Why is it necessary for a company to protect itself? Discuss your findings and reactions with your team. Individually or as a group, submit your findings and reactions in a well-organized, easy-to-read e-mail or memo to your boss (your instructor). You may list main points from the articles you research, but use your own words to write the message.

4.8 Request E-Mail or Memo: Old Habits Die Hard *Read for background*

Over five years ago, the province of Manitoba introduced The Non-Smokers Health Protection Act to make "smoking … prohibited in all enclosed public places and indoor workplaces." The legislation was mostly popular, but some companies in the province have been finding that their employees are not necessarily obeying the law at all times.

Your Task. As Lindsay Harapa, director of Human Resources, write an e-mail attaching a memo to all department managers of Imperial Foods, a large food products company in Winnipeg. Remind employees of the provincial law, and tell the managers that you want them to set up departmental committees to mediate any smoking conflicts before complaints surface. Explain why this is a good policy.

Related Web site: Highlights of Manitoba's legislation can be found at http://www.gov.mb.ca/healthyliving/smokingban.html.

4.9 Response E-Mail: Enforcing Smoking Ban

As director of the accounting department for Imperial Foods, you must respond to Ms. Harapa's memo in the preceding activity. You could have called Ms. Harapa, but you prefer to have a permanent record of this message. You are having difficulty enforcing the smoking ban in restrooms. Only one men's room serves your floor, and 9 of your 27 male employees are smokers. You have already received complaints, and you see no way to enforce the ban in the restrooms. You have also noticed that smokers are taking longer breaks than other employees. Smokers complain that they need more time because they must walk to an outside area. Smokers are especially unhappy when the weather is cold, rainy, or snowy. Moreover, smokers huddle near the building entrances, creating a negative impression for customers and visitors. Your committee members can find no solutions; in fact, they have become polarized in their meetings to date. You need help from a higher authority.

Your Task. Write an e-mail to Ms. Harapa appealing for solutions. Perhaps she should visit your department or invite a city bylaw officer to give a talk to the department.

4.10 Response E-Mail: Rescheduling Interviews to Accommodate a Travelling Boss

Your boss, Michael Kaufman, has scheduled three appointments to interview applicants for the position of project manager. All of these appointments are for Thursday, May 5. However, he now must travel to Toronto that week. He asks you to reschedule all the appointments for one week later. He also wants a brief background summary for each candidate.

Although frustrated, you call each person and are lucky to arrange these times. Saul Salazar, who has been a project manager for nine years with Summit Enterprises, agrees to come at 10:30 a.m. Kaitlyn Grindell, who is a systems analyst and a consultant to many companies, will come at 11:30. Mary Montgomery, who has an MA degree and six years of experience as senior project coordinator at High Point Industries, will come at 9:30 a.m. You are wondering whether Mr. Kaufman forgot to include Grace Ho, operations personnel officer, in these interviews. Ms. Ho usually is part of the selection process.

Your Task. Write an e-mail to Mr. Kaufman including all the information he needs.

4.11 Procedure Memo: Standardizing Purchase Requests

The purchasing department handles purchases for a growing family company. Some purchase orders arrive on the proper forms, but others are memos or handwritten notes that are barely legible. The owner wants to establish a standard procedure for submitting purchase requests. The purchase requests must now be downloaded from the company intranet. To provide the fastest service, employees should fill out the purchase request. Employees must include the relevant information: date, quantities, catalogue numbers, complete descriptions, complete vendor mailing address and contact information, delivery requirements, and shipping methods. The purchasing department should receive the original, and the sender should keep a copy. An important step in the new procedure is approval by the budget manager on the request form.

Your Task. As assistant manager in the purchasing department, write an interoffice memo or e-mail to all employees informing them of the new procedure.

4.12 Information Memo

You are the manager of Dream Come True Vacations. Your travel company, in conjunction with the Mexican Tourist Bureau, will be hosting a dinner and presentation evening on Mexico. This presentation evening will be a wonderful opportunity for your agents to become educated on popular Mexican destinations and attractions and Mexican culture. It will be held on April 5 in Lobby A of the Westin Hotel, Ottawa, and is an event not to miss, since so many of Dream Come True's clients have been choosing Mexico as their preferred vacation destination. The cost of the meal will be covered by the Mexican Tourist Bureau. It is important to let your staff know that they should R.S.V.P. to Juan Martez at martez@mexicantouristbureau.com by March 20 so that appropriate arrangements can be made for meal planning and seating. Given the expense of the evening, this is a staff-only event. Several destination representatives and travel counsellors from Mexico will be present that evening and will be available to answer any questions on leisure products offered to Canadian clients. The evening will begin with cocktails at 6:00 p.m., followed by a four-course Mexican-style meal at 7:00 p.m. A presentation will be delivered after dinner. Fabulous door prizes, including an all-inclusive week on the Mayan Riviera, will be given out at the end of the evening.

Your Task. As manager of Dream Come True Vacations, draft an interoffice memo to your staff informing them of the event and the importance of attending. Provide all the relevant information. Stress the fact that this evening will be a worthwhile opportunity to network with partners in the travel industry and to become more familiar with the types of products offered to clients, such as hotels, excursions, and on-site activities.

4.13 E-Mail Overload

Besides the workplace e-mail issues discussed in this chapter, another issue that has generated a lot of attention is the issue of e-mail as a "work-extending technology." Because many people can access their desk at all hours of the day and night, on weekends, and during holidays, they tend to work more than before. Sometimes the level of "work extension" is so high that it creates stress. Imagine you are a new employee at a large financial services company. Your company issued you a BlackBerry PDA in your first week of work and made it known that you were expected to be "available as much as possible." Grateful to be hired so quickly out of college, you didn't think about the consequences of agreeing to be available "as much as possible." However, a year later, you find that a number of consequences have affected your life: lack of sleep, lack of time to unwind after the work week, addiction to e-mail checking and sending, and so on. You'd like to see if you can make some changes. You decide to do some research, using the Internet as well as research databases (available at your workplace) on the topic of "work-extending technology."

Your Task. Write an e-mail to your boss in which you briefly inform him or her about what you've found. Based on what you've found, request some changes to be made in how you interface with your BlackBerry.

4.14 Request IM: Don't Abuse the Casual-Friday Policy

You work in a government ministry as manager of 25 customer service representatives. You've been with the ministry for ten years, and two years ago your fellow managers adopted a policy allowing casual dress (e.g., short skirts, shorts, t-shirts, jeans) on Fridays. Any employee wishing to "dress down" could do so by bringing along a donation for the local food bank. Also two years ago, the ministry installed instant messaging software so that employees could be in touch with each other more quickly and more informally. Over the past few months, you've noticed employees abusing the casual-Friday policy by wearing casual clothing on other days of the week.

Your Task. Send an instant message early on a Monday morning to your 25 customer service reps informing them that the casual-Friday policy needs to be followed. Assume that a trouble-making customer service rep named Ed responds to your message, as does Yanique, a very young recently hired rep. Create an IM conversation, imagining what Ed's and Yanique's responses will be to your message and how you will reply. How will you stay on top of this situation and ensure that your directions are being followed?

Grammar/Mechanics Review—4

The following sentences contain errors in grammar, punctuation, capitalization, number style, usage, and spelling. Below each sentence write a corrected version.

1. As a matter of fact the italian alphabet has only twenty one letters.
2. About one hundred of Tim Hortons seven hundred forty canadian resterants is serving the new toffee donut.
3. Meanwhile, the highly-advertised McDonald's 1.99 hamburger promotion, which was pushed heavy by its Canadian Headquarters, turned out to be a major dissappointment.
4. A powerful reason for Burger Kings new success is, a hefty 2 patty burger thats being promoted as an extra big Big Mac.
5. Experts say the 2 smartest dogs are scottish border collies and golden retrievers; on the other hand the dumbest are afghan hounds.
6. After listening carefully to your advise, we paid several months rent in advance.
7. 2 sizes of batteries—see Page Sixteen in the instruction booklet—may be used in this flashlight.
8. When convenent, will you please send me 3 copys of the companys color logo?

9. The first book ever wrote on a typewriter was "Tom Sawyer."

10. A tacky tee shirt in the Niagara falls souvenir shop reads "my parents went to niagara falls and all I got was this t-shirt.

11. In Maclean's I saw an article titled How to develop the exercise habit."

12. Appearing next is the President and Sales Manager both of whom were personally invited by myself.

13. Production cost and markup is important to the manufacturer and to we vendors.

14. That stack of papers have been laying on your desk for at least three week's.

15. The only canadian Prime Minister to win a Nobel peace prize is Lester B. Pearson in 1957.

Grammar/Mechanics Challenge—4

Document for Revision

The following memo has faults in grammar, punctuation, spelling, capitalization, number form, repetition, wordiness, and other areas. Use standard proofreading marks (see Appendix B) to correct the errors. When you finish, your instructor can show you the revised version of this memo.

Lux Hotels and Spas Inc.

Memo

DATE: March 2, 2012
TO: Department Heads, Managers, and Supervisors
FROM: James Robbins, Director, Human Resources
SUBJECT: Submitting Appraisals of Performance by April 15th

Please be informed that performance appraisals for all you're employees' are due, before April 15th. These appraisal are esspecially important and essential this year. Because of job changes, new technologys and because of office re-organization.

To complete your performance appraisals in the most effective way, you should follow the procedures described in our employee handbook, let me briefly make a review of those procedures;

1. Be sure each and every employee has a performance plan with 3 or 4 main objective.

2. For each objective make an assessment of the employee on a scale of 5 (consistently excedes requirements) to 0 (does not meet requirements at all).

3. You should identify 3 strengths that he brings to the job.

4. Name 3 skills that he can improve. These should pertain to skills such as Time Management rather then to behaviors such as habitual lateness.

5. The employee should be met with to discuss his appraisal.

6. Finish the appraisal and send the completed appraisal to this office.

We look upon appraisals like a tool for helping each worker assess his performance. And enhance his output. If you would like to discuss this farther, please do not hessitate to call me.

Communication Workshop

Whose Computer or BlackBerry or iPhone Is It, Anyway?

Many companies today provide their employees with computers and/or PDAs with Internet access. Should employees be able to use those devices for online shopping, personal messages, personal work, and listening to music or playing games?

But It's Harmless

According to a recent poll, one-third of Canadian workers have Internet access at work and four out of five of these say they log on for personal reasons, such as sending personal e-mails, checking out news or sports headlines, comparison shopping, checking investments, and making online purchases. While the poll did not determine whether this activity occurred during work or in the employee's spare time, the potential for abuse and evidence of abuse have led a growing number of employers in Canada to consider developing policies governing Internet use and also to monitor the online activities of employees.[7] To justify much of this personal activity, workers claim that pursuing personal online activities is performance enhancing, as it keeps them at their desks rather than in the shopping malls or at the water cooler.

Companies Cracking Down

Employers are less happy about increasing use of bandwidth for personal online activities. The growth of electronic monitoring has been significant since 1998 in both Canada and the United States. In fact, the number of companies in the United States reviewing e-mail and computer files stored on hard drives has doubled from the late 1990s.[8]

What's Reasonable?

Some companies try to enforce a "zero tolerance" policy, prohibiting any personal use of company equipment, while others allow some personal activity. In Canada under the Privacy Act and Charter of Rights and Freedoms, employees have a "reasonable expectation" of privacy in the workplace, but that expectation can be met simply by notifying employees that they are being monitored.[9] Currently many employers provide no guidelines on reasonable Internet use. As well, what some employers regard as a firing offence others view as acceptable personal use. As Paul Kent-Snowsell, a Vancouver lawyer specializing in Internet cases, warns, "It has always been cause for dismissal if you're not using company time to do company work."[10] At the same time, Robert Lendvai, marketing director for Ottawa's Kyberpass Corporation, a maker of network security software, indicates that while Canadian corporations use the security features of his company's software, only about one in five activates the monitoring capabilities.[11]

Career Application

As an administrative assistant at Big C Technologies in Vancouver, you have just received an e-mail from your boss asking for your opinion. It seems that many employees have been shopping online; one person actually received four personal packages couriered to him in one morning. Although reluctant to do so, management is considering installing monitoring software that not only tracks Internet use but also allows extensive blocking of Web sites, such as porn, hate, and game sites.

Your Task
- In teams or as a class, research and discuss the problem of workplace abuse of e-mail and the Internet.
- Should full personal use be allowed?
- In terms of equipment, are computers and their links to the Internet similar to office telephones?

- Should employees be allowed to access the Internet for personal use if they use their own private e-mail accounts?
- Should management be allowed to monitor all Internet use?
- Should employees be warned if e-mail is to be monitored?
- What specific reasons can you give to support an Internet crackdown by management?
- What specific reasons can you give to oppose a crackdown?

Decide whether you support or oppose a crackdown. Explain your views in an e-mail or a memo to your boss, Roberta Everson (reverson@bigc.com), or in a traditional in-class debate.

Related Web sites: Visit the WebSpy site (http://www.webspy.com) for a detailed look at Internet surveillance software available for purchase by corporations and organizations. For information on Canada's privacy laws and regulations, visit the Web site of the Office of the Privacy Commissioner of Canada (http://www.privcom.gc.ca).

CHAPTER 5

Letters

Who cares about composing well crafted business letters today? Didn't that mode of communication start to die in the 1980s when the fax machine began to rule our lives? Surely after the advent of sophisticated voice mail systems in the early 1990s, the mailed business letter was destined for obsolescence! If nothing else, the explosion of email users must have put this archaic form of correspondence out of its misery by now! Think again. Believe it or not, there is at least one group of people who are still impressed when they receive a well written letter in the ordinary mail. They are called prospective clients/customers.[1]

Reg Pirie,
*Lead Partner, Pirie Management
Consultants Inc.*

LEARNING OBJECTIVES

1. Explain why business letters are important in delivering positive messages outside an organization.
2. Write letters that request information and action.
3. Write letters that make claims.
4. Write letters that reply to requests.
5. Write letters that reply to claims.
6. Write letters of recommendation.
7. Write goodwill messages.

Letters that fail to get to the point or are badly written are a concern for employees and managers everywhere. For example, a bank's profitability can depend on the quality of information it provides to its customers. Without clear, well-written messages that transmit information concisely, banks and insurance companies risk alienating current customers and losing potential customers. This fact was demonstrated by the work of the Government of Canada's Task Force on the Future of the Canadian Financial Services Sector. In one of its research reports, "Assessing Financial Documents for Readability," the task force concluded that, based on "readability scores, almost all the documents assessed in these studies are Difficult and Complex."[2] Since then, financial services companies have strived to use plain language in both their internal and external messages.

Messages that meander slowly toward their point have little appeal for most of us. Readers want to know why a message was written and how it involves them. And they want that information up front.

Sending Letters Outside Your Organization

Most of the workplace messages you write will probably be positive. That is, they will deal with routine matters that require straightforward answers using the direct method. As communication channels continue to evolve, you will be using both electronic and paper-based channels to send positive, routine messages. Chapter 4 discussed electronic messages and memos dealing primarily with internal communication. This chapter focuses on positive external messages via the channel of business letters.

Understanding the Power of Business Letters

Positive, straightforward letters help organizations conduct everyday business and convey goodwill to outsiders. Such letters go to suppliers, government agencies, other businesses, and, most important, customers. The letters to customers receive a high priority because these messages encourage product feedback, project a favourable image of the organization, and promote future business.

Even with the new media available today, a letter remains one of the most powerful and effective ways to get your message across. Although e-mail is incredibly successful for both internal and external communication, many important messages still call for letters. Below are some reasons that business letters are still very much a part of business.

Business Letters Produce a Permanent Record. Many business transactions require a permanent record. Business letters fulfill this function. For example, when a company enters into an agreement with another company, business letters introduce the agreement and record decisions and points of understanding. Although telephone conversations and e-mails may be exchanged, important details are generally recorded in business letters that are kept in company files. Business letters deliver contracts, explain terms, exchange ideas, negotiate agreements, answer vendor questions, and maintain customer relations. Business letters are important for any business transaction that requires a permanent written record.

Business Letters Can Be Confidential. Carefree use of e-mail was once a sign of sophistication. Today, however, communicators know how dangerous it is to entrust confidential and sensitive information to digital channels. A writer in *The New York Times* recognized the unique value of letters when he said, "Despite the sneering term *snail mail*, plain old letters are the form of long-distance communication least likely to be intercepted, misdirected, forwarded, retrieved, or otherwise inspected by someone you didn't have in mind."[3]

Business Letters Convey Formality and Sensitivity. Business letters presented on company stationery carry a sense of formality and importance not possible with e-mail. They look important. They carry a nonverbal message saying the writer considered the message to be so significant and the receiver so prestigious that the writer cared enough to write a real message. Business letters deliver more information than e-mail because they are written on stationery that usually is printed with company information such as logos, addresses, titles, and contact details.

Business Letters Deliver Persuasive, Well-Considered Messages. When a business communicator must be persuasive and can't do it in person, a business letter is more effective than other communication channels. Letters can persuade people to change their actions, adopt new beliefs, make donations, contribute their time, and try new products. Direct-mail letters remain a powerful tool to promote services and products, boost online and retail traffic, and solicit contributions. Business letters represent deliberate as opposed to rushed communication. They give you a chance to think through what you want to say, organize your thoughts, and write a well-considered argument.

Letters communicate with outsiders and produce a formal record.

Information and Action Requests

Many business messages are written to request information or action. Although the specific subject of each inquiry may differ, the similarity of purpose in routine requests enables writers to use the following writing plan.

> **Writing Plan for an Information or Action Request**
>
> - **Opening:** Ask the most important question first or express a polite command.
> - **Body:** Explain the request logically and courteously. Ask other questions if necessary.
> - **Closing:** Request a specific action with an end date, if appropriate, and show appreciation.

Opening Directly

The most emphatic positions in a letter are the openings and closings. Readers tend to look at them first. The writer should capitalize on this tendency by putting the most significant statement first. The first sentence of an information request is usually a question or a polite command. It should not be an explanation or justification, unless resistance to the request is expected. When the information requested is likely to be forthcoming, immediately tell the reader what you want. This saves the reader's time and may ensure that the message is read. A busy executive who skims the mail, quickly reading subject lines and first sentences only, may grasp your request rapidly and act on it. A request that follows a lengthy explanation, on the other hand, may never be found.

Readers find the openings and closings of letters most valuable.

A letter inquiring about hotel accommodations, shown in Figure 5.1, begins immediately with the most important idea. Can the hotel provide meeting rooms and accommodations for 250 people? Instead of opening with an explanation of who the writer is or how the writer happens to be writing this letter, the letter begins directly.

If several questions must be asked, you have two choices. You can ask the most important question first, as shown in Figure 5.1. An alternative opening begins with a summary statement, such as *Will you please answer the following questions about providing meeting rooms and accommodations for 250 people from May 25 through May 29, 2013*. Notice that the summarizing statement sounds like a question but has no question mark. That's because it's really a command disguised as a question. Rather than bluntly demanding information (*Answer the following questions*), we often soften commands by posing them as questions. Such statements, called rhetorical questions, should not be punctuated as questions because they do not require answers.

Details in the Body

The body of a letter that requests information should provide necessary details and should be easy to read. Remember that the quality of the information obtained from a request letter depends on the clarity of the inquiry. If you analyze your needs, organize your ideas, and frame your request logically, you are likely to receive a meaningful answer that doesn't require a follow-up message. Whenever possible, itemize the information to improve readability. Notice that the questions in Figure 5.1 are bulleted, and they are parallel. They demonstrate an excellent use of graphic highlighting.

The body of a request letter may contain an explanation or a list of questions.

Closing With an Action Request

Use the final paragraph to ask for specific action, to set an end date if appropriate, and to express appreciation. As you learned in working with e-mails and memos, a request for action is most effective when an end date and reason for that date are supplied, as shown in Figure 5.1.

The ending of a request letter should tell the reader what you want done and when.

FIGURE 5.1 Letter That Requests Information

Letterhead

GEOTECH

770 Cherry Avenue
Corner Brook, NL A2L 3W5

Dateline

August 20, 2012

Inside address

Ms. Jane Mangrum, Manager
Vancouver Hilton Hotel
6333 North Scottsdale Road
Vancouver, BC V5H 1W4

Salutation

Dear Ms. Mangrum:

Direct opening

Can the Vancouver Hilton provide meeting rooms and accommodations for about 250 GeoTech sales representatives from May 25 through May 29, 2013?

Your hotel received strong recommendations because of its excellent resort and conference facilities. Our spring sales conference is scheduled for next May, and I am collecting information for our planning committee. Will you please answer these additional questions regarding the Vancouver Hilton.

Body

- Does the hotel have a banquet room that can seat 250?

- Do you have at least four smaller meeting rooms, each to accommodate a maximum of 75?

- What kind of computer facilities are available for presentations?

- Is there a shuttle from the airport to the hotel?

Closing

I would appreciate answers to these questions and any other information you can provide about your resort facilities by September 1. Our planning committee meets in mid-September to finalize details.

Sincerely,

Marlene Frederick

Author's name and identification

Marlene Frederick
Corporate Travel Administrator
mfrederick@geotech.ca

Reference initials

MF:gdr

Tips for Formatting Letters

Most business writers today use a software template such as Microsoft Word's Professional Letter template, and simply pour in their content. If you don't have access to a template, follow the steps below.

- Start the date on line 13 or 1 blank line below the letterhead.
- For block style, like the letter in Figure 5.1, begin all lines at the left margin.
- For modified block style, like the letter in Figure 5.2 (page 123), begin the date and closing lines at the centre.
- Leave side margins of 2.5 to 3 cm (1 to 1.5 inches) depending on the length of the letter.
- Single-space the body and double-space between paragraphs.

It's always appropriate to end a request letter with appreciation for the action taken. However, don't fall into a cliché trap, such as *Thanking you in advance, I remain …* or the familiar *Thank you for your cooperation*. Your appreciation will sound most sincere if you avoid mechanical, tired expressions.

Claims

In business many things can go wrong—promised shipments are late, warranted goods fail, or service is disappointing. When you as a customer must write to identify or correct a wrong, the letter is called a *claim*. Straightforward claims are those to which you expect the receiver to agree readily. But even these claims often require a letter. While your first action may be a telephone call or an e-mail, you may not get the results you seek. Written claims are generally taken more seriously, and they also establish a record of what happened. Below is the writing plan for a straightforward claim that uses a direct approach.

Claim letters register complaints and usually seek correction of a wrong.

> ### Writing Plan for a Simple Claim
>
> - **Opening:** Describe clearly the desired action.
> - **Body:** Explain the nature of the claim, explain how the claim is justified, and provide details regarding the action requested.
> - **Closing:** End pleasantly with a goodwill statement and include an end date if appropriate.

Opening With Action

If you have a legitimate claim, you can expect a positive response from a company. Smart businesses today want to hear from their customers. That's why you should open a claim letter with a clear statement of the problem or with the action you want the receiver to take. You might expect a replacement, a refund, a new order, credit to your account, correction of a billing error, free repairs, free inspection, or cancellation of an order.

The direct strategy is best for simple claims that require no persuasion.

When the remedy is obvious, state it immediately (*Please send us 24 Royal hot-air popcorn poppers to replace the 24 hot-oil poppers sent in error with our order shipped January 4*). When the remedy is less obvious, you might ask for a change in policy or procedure or simply for an explanation (*Because three of our employees with confirmed reservations were refused rooms at your hotel on September 16, would you please clarify your policy regarding reservations and late arrivals*).

Explaining in the Body

In the body of a claim letter, explain the problem and justify your request. Provide the necessary details so that the difficulty can be corrected without further correspondence. Avoid becoming angry or trying to lay blame. Bear in mind that the person reading your letter is seldom responsible for the problem. Instead, state the facts logically, objectively, and unemotionally; let the reader decide on the causes.

Providing details without getting angry improves the effectiveness of a claim letter.

Include copies of all pertinent documents such as invoices, sales receipts, catalogue descriptions, and repair records. (By the way, be sure to send copies and not your originals, which could be lost.) When service is involved, cite names of individuals spoken to and dates of calls. Assume that a company honestly wants to satisfy its customers—because most do. When an alternative remedy exists, describe it (*If you are unable to send 24 Royal hot-air popcorn poppers immediately, please credit our account now and notify us when they become available*).

Closing Pleasantly

Conclude a claim letter with a courteous statement that promotes goodwill and expresses a desire for continued relations. If appropriate, include an end date (*We realize that mistakes in ordering and shipping sometimes occur. Because we've enjoyed your prompt service in the past, we hope that you will be able to send us the hot-air poppers by January 15*).

Written claims submitted promptly are taken more seriously than delayed ones.

Finally, in making claims, act promptly. Delaying claims makes them appear less important. Delayed claims are also more difficult to verify. By taking the time to put your claim in writing, you indicate your seriousness. A written claim also starts a record of the problem, should later action be necessary. Be sure to keep a copy of your letter.

Putting It All Together

Figure 5.2 shows a hostile claim letter that vents the writer's anger but accomplishes little else. Its tone is belligerent, and it assumes that the company intentionally overcharged the customer. Furthermore, it fails to tell the reader how to remedy the problem. The revision tempers the tone, describes the problem objectively, and provides facts and figures. Most importantly, it specifies exactly what the customer wants done.

Notice that the letter in Figure 5.2 is shown with the return address typed above the date. This personal business style may be used when typing on paper without a printed letterhead. Notice, too, that this letter uses modified block style. The return address, date, and closing lines start at the centre.

Replying to Requests

Before responding to requests, gather facts, check figures, and seek approval if necessary.

Often, your messages will respond favourably to requests for information or action. A customer wants information about a product. A supplier asks to arrange a meeting. Another business inquires about one of your procedures. But before responding to any inquiry, be sure to check your facts and figures carefully. Any letter written on company stationery is considered a legally binding contract. If a policy or procedure needs authorization, seek approval from a supervisor or executive before writing the letter. In complying with requests, you'll want to apply the same direct pattern you used in making requests.

> ### Writing Plan for a Reply Letter
> - **Subject line:** Identify previous correspondence.
> - **Opening:** Deliver the most important information first.
> - **Body:** Arrange information logically, explain and clarify it, provide additional information if appropriate, and build goodwill.
> - **Closing:** End pleasantly.

Subject Line Efficiency

Use the subject line to refer to previous correspondence.

An information response letter should contain a subject line, which helps the reader recognize the topic immediately. Knowledgeable business communicators use a subject line to refer to earlier correspondence so that in the first sentence, the most important spot in a letter, they are free to emphasize the main idea. Notice in Figure 5.3 that the subject line identifies the subject completely.

Opening Directly

In the first sentence of an information response, deliver the information the reader wants. Avoid wordy, drawn-out openings (*I have before me your letter of February 6, in which you request information about . . .*). More forceful and more efficient is an opener that answers the inquiry (*Here is the information you wanted about . . .*). When agreeing to a request for action, announce the good news promptly (*I will be happy to speak to your business communication class on the topic of . . .*).

Arranging Information Logically in the Body

A good way to answer questions is to number or bullet each one.

When answering a group of questions or providing considerable data, arrange the information logically and make it readable by using lists, tables, headings, boldface, italics, or other graphic devices. When customers or prospective customers inquire about products or services, your response should do more than merely supply answers. You'll also want to promote your organization and products. Be sure to present the promotional material with attention to the "you" view and to

FIGURE 5.2 Direct Claim Letter

Dear Sweet Sounds:

Sounds angry; jumps to conclusions

You call yourselves Sweet Sounds, but all I'm getting from your service is sour notes! I'm furious that you have your salespeople slip in unwanted service warranties to boost your sales.

Forgets that mistakes happen

When I bought my Panatronic DVD player from Sweet Sounds, Inc., in August, I specifically told the salesperson that I did NOT want a three-year service warranty. But there it is on my credit card statement this month! You people have obviously billed me for a service I did not authorize. I refuse to pay this charge.

Fails to suggest solution

How can you hope to stay in business with such fraudulent practices? I was expecting to return this month and look at flat-screen TVs, but you can be sure I'll find an honest dealer this time.

Sincerely,

Brent K. Royer

1201 North Plum Street
Steinbach, MB R3L 2N7
September 3, 2012

Personal business letter style

Mr. Sam Lee, Customer Service
Sweet Sounds, Inc.
2003 East Street
Toronto, ON M2T 1G5

Dear Mr. Lee:

Please credit my VISA account, No. 0000-0046-2198-9421, to correct an erroneous charge of $299.

States simply and clearly what to do

On August 8 I purchased a Panatronic DVD player from the Sweet Sounds, Inc., outlet in Steinbach. Although the salesperson discussed a three-year extended warranty with me, I decided against purchasing that service for $299. However, when my credit card statement arrived this month, I noticed an extra $299 charge from Sweet Sounds, Inc. I suspect that this charge represents the warranty I declined.

Explains objectively what went wrong

Doesn't blame or accuse

Enclosed is a copy of my sales invoice along with my VISA statement on which I circled the charge. Please authorize a credit immediately and send a copy of the transaction to me at the above address.

Documents facts

I'm enjoying all the features of my DVD player and would like to be shopping at Sweet Sounds for a flat-screen TV shortly.

Uses friendly tone

Suggests continued business once problem is resolved

Sincerely,

Brent K. Royer

Brent K. Royer

Enclosure

FIGURE 5.3 Information Response Letter

TRG MEDIATION SERVICES

930 Taylor Avenue
Regina, Saskatchewan
S4A 2Y4

February 6, 2012

Ms. Irene McKenzie
The Regina Leader-Post
4980 Washington Avenue
Regina, Saskatchewan
S4L 4W6

Dear Ms. McKenzie:

SUBJECT: YOUR FEBRUARY 1 LETTER REQUESTING INFORMATION ON THE ROLE OF
MEDIATION SERVICES COMPANIES IN THE LABOUR-MANAGEMENT
RELATIONSHIP

Here are answers to your questions about mediation services. We are eager to supply you with this information so that you can publish accurate news about the role mediators play in the labour-management relationship.

1. TRG is a mediation services company that provides assistance to businesses and individuals during labour disputes. Agencies such as ours provide professional mediators to help both sides in labour-management disputes reach acceptable settlement terms. Without mediation services, many of these disputes would undoubtedly proceed to job action. Our mediators deal with disputes of all sorts from harassment complaints to wage and contract negotiations.

2. We do not handle mediation services for person-to-person disputes such as divorce or automobile accident insurance.

3. Many collective agreements include mediation as a required step in the negotiation process once contract talks have broken down. We do not, however, make decisions about the outcome of a settlement as an arbitrator would.

4. TRG uses the methods of principled negotiation as articulated by the Harvard School of Business and others. Principled negotiation urges the participants in a dispute to search for ways that each participant can win rather than dwelling on win-lose scenarios. Our mediators are trained to help participants find the "win-win."

You'll find additional information in the enclosed booklet, "Understanding and Using Mediation Services." To speak with me personally, just call (306) 598-2300. We look forward to seeing your article in print.

Sincerely,

Debbie Wills-Garcia

Debbie Wills-Garcia
Vice President

DWG:rio
Enclosure

Margin annotations:

Identifies previous correspondence

Answers each inquiry fully and logically in list form

Builds goodwill by providing extra information and ends cordially without clichés

---

reader benefits (*You can use our standardized tests to free you from time-consuming employment screening*). You'll learn more about special techniques for developing sales and persuasive messages in Chapter 6.

Closing Pleasantly

To avoid abruptness, include a pleasant closing remark that shows your willingness to help the reader. Provide extra information if appropriate. Tailor your remarks to fit this letter and this reader. Since everyone appreciates being recognized as an individual, avoid form-letter closings (e.g., *If we may be of further assistance, . . .*).

Airline troubles continue to mount as weary air travel-lers complain of lost luggage, long delays, cancelled flights, and soaring ticket prices. In one customer-service debacle, major U.S. carriers shut down 3,700 flights in a single month after failing to meet safety inspections mandated by the Federal Aviation Administration. The grounded flights affected hundreds of thousands of passengers, underscoring the airline industry's last-place finish in a Consumer Satisfaction Index survey conducted by the University of Michigan. *What guidelines should airline companies follow when writing adjustment letters to disgruntled customers?*

Replying to Claims

As you learned earlier, when an organization receives a claim, it usually means that something has gone wrong. In responding to a claim, you have three goals:

- To rectify the wrong, if one exists
- To regain the confidence of the customer
- To promote future business and goodwill

Responding to customer claims means rectifying the wrong, regaining customer confidence, and promoting future business.

If you decide to grant the claim, your response letter will represent good news to the reader. Use the direct strategy described in the following writing plan.

> **Writing Plan for Replying to a Claim**
>
> - **Subject line (optional):** Identify the previous correspondence.
> - **Opening:** Grant request or announce the adjustment immediately. Include resale or sales promotion if appropriate.
> - **Body:** Provide details about how you are complying with the request. Try to regain the customer's confidence, and include resale or sales promotion if appropriate.
> - **Closing:** End positively with a forward-looking thought, express confidence in future business relations, and avoid referring to unpleasantness.

Revealing Good News in the Opening

Instead of beginning with a review of what went wrong, present the good news immediately. When Amy Hopkins responded to Sound, Inc.'s claim about a missing shipment, her first draft, shown at the top of Figure 5.4, was angry. No wonder. Sound, Inc., had apparently provided the wrong shipping address, and the goods were returned. But once Amy and her company decided to send a second shipment and comply with the customer's claim, she had to give up the anger and strive to retain the goodwill and the business of this customer. The improved version of her letter announces that a new shipment will arrive shortly.

Readers want to learn the good news immediately.

If you decide to comply with a customer's claim, let the receiver know immedi-ately. Don't begin your letter with a negative statement (*We are very sorry to hear that you are having trouble with your Sno-Flake ice crusher*). This approach reminds the reader of the problem and may rekindle the heated emotions or unhappy feelings

Be enthusiastic, not grudging, when granting a claim.

FIGURE 5.4 Customer Claim Response

Sir:

In response to your recent complaint about a missing shipment, it's very difficult to deliver merchandise when we have been given the wrong address.

Fails to reveal good news immediately; blames customer

Our investigators looked into your problem shipment and determined that it was sent immediately after we received the order. According to the shipper's records, it was delivered to the warehouse address given on your stationery: 3590 University Avenue, Saint John, New Brunswick E2M 1G7. Unfortunately, no one at that address would accept delivery, so the shipment was returned to us. I see from your current stationery that your company has a new address. With the proper address, we probably could have delivered this shipment.

Creates ugly tone with negative words and sarcasm

Sounds grudging and reluctant in granting claim

Although we feel that it is entirely appropriate to charge you shipping and restocking fees, as is our standard practice on returned goods, in this instance we will waive those fees. We hope this second shipment finally catches up with you.

Sincerely,

Amy Hopkins

EW ELECTRONIC WAREHOUSE
930 Abbott Park Place
Saint John, New Brunswick E3L 0T7

February 21, 2012

Mr. Jeremy Garber
Sound, Inc.
2293 Second Avenue
Saint John, NB E3M 2R5

Dear Mr. Garber:

Uses customer's name in salutation

SUBJECT: YOUR FEBRUARY 20 LETTER ABOUT YOUR PURCHASE ORDER

You should receive by February 28 a second shipment of the speakers, headphones, and other electronic equipment that you ordered January 20.

Announces good news immediately

The first shipment of this order was delivered January 28 to 3590 University Avenue, Saint John, NB. When no one at that address would accept the shipment, it was returned to us. Now that I have your letter, I see that the order should have been sent to 2293 Second Avenue, Saint John, New Brunswick E3M 2R5. When an order is undeliverable, we usually try to verify the shipping address by telephoning the customer. Somehow the return of this shipment was not caught by our normally painstaking shipping clerks. You can be sure that I will investigate shipping and return procedures with our clerks immediately to see if we can improve existing methods.

Regains confidence of customer by explaining what happened and by suggesting plans for improvement

As you know, Mr. Garber, our volume business allows us to sell wholesale electronics equipment at the lowest possible prices. However, we do not want to be so large that we lose touch with valued customers like you. Over the years our customers' respect has made us successful, and we hope that the prompt delivery of this shipment will earn yours.

Closes confidently with genuine appeal for customer's respect

Sincerely,

Amy Hopkins

Amy Hopkins
Distribution Manager

c David Cole
Shipping Department

experienced when the claim was written. Instead, focus on the good news. The following openings for various letters illustrate how to begin a message with good news.

> You may take your Sno-Flake ice crusher to Ben's Appliances at 310 First Street, Moose Jaw, where it will be repaired at no cost to you.

> Thanks for your letter about your new Winter-Buster tires. You are certainly justified in expecting them to last more than 12,000 km.

> We agree with you that the warranty on your iPod Nano should be extended for six months.

> The enclosed cheque for $325 demonstrates our desire to satisfy our customers and earn their confidence.

In announcing that you will grant a claim, be sure to do so without a grudging tone—even if you have reservations about whether the claim is legitimate. Once you decide to comply with the customer's request, do so happily. Avoid half-hearted or reluctant responses (*Although the Sno-Flake ice crusher works well when it is used properly, we have decided to allow you to take yours to Ben's Appliances for repair at our expense*).

Explaining Compliance in the Body

In responding to claims, most organizations sincerely want to correct a wrong. They want to do more than just make the customer happy. They want to stand behind their products and services; they want to do what's right.

Most businesses comply with claims because they want to promote customer goodwill.

In the body of the letter, explain how you are complying with the claim. In all but the most routine claims, you should also seek to regain the confidence of the customer. You might reasonably expect that a customer who has experienced difficulty with a product, with delivery, with billing, or with service has lost faith in your organization. Rebuilding that faith is important for future business.

How to rebuild lost confidence depends on the situation and the claim. If procedures need to be revised, explain what changes will be made. If a product has defective parts, explain how the product is being improved. If service is faulty, describe genuine efforts to improve it. Notice in Figure 5.4 that the writer promises to investigate shipping procedures to see if improvements might prevent future mishaps.

Sometimes the problem is not with the product but with the way it's being used. In other instances customers misunderstand warranties or inadvertently cause delivery and billing mix-ups by supplying incorrect information. Remember that rational and sincere explanations will do much to regain the confidence of unhappy customers.

Because negative words suggest blame and fault, avoid them in letters that attempt to build customer goodwill.

In your explanation avoid emphasizing negative words such as *trouble*, *regret*, *misunderstanding*, *fault*, *defective*, *error*, *inconvenience*, and *unfortunately*. Keep your message positive and upbeat.

Deciding Whether to Apologize

Whether to apologize is a debatable issue. Some writing experts argue that apologies remind customers of their complaints and are therefore negative. These writers avoid apologies; instead they concentrate on how they are satisfying the customer. Real letters that respond to customers' claims, however, often include apologies.[4] If you feel that your company is at fault and that an apology is an appropriate goodwill gesture, by all means include it. Be careful, though, not to admit negligence. You'll learn more about responding to negative letters in Chapter 7.

Showing Confidence in the Closing

End your letter by looking ahead positively.

End positively by expressing confidence that the problem has been resolved and that continued business relations will result. You might mention the product in a favourable light, suggest a new product, express your appreciation for the customer's business, or anticipate future business. It's often appropriate to refer to the desire to be of service and to satisfy customers. Notice how the following closings illustrate a positive, confident tone.

Your Sno-Flake ice crusher will help you remain cool and refreshed this summer. For your additional summer enjoyment, consider our Smoky Joe tabletop gas grill, shown in the enclosed summer catalogue. We genuinely value your business and look forward to your future orders.

We hope that this refund cheque convinces you of our sincere desire to satisfy our customers. Our goal is to earn your confidence and continue to justify that confidence with quality products and matchless service.

You were most helpful in telling us about this situation and giving us an opportunity to correct it. We sincerely appreciate your cooperation.

In all your future dealings with us, you will find us striving our hardest to earn your confidence by serving you with efficiency and sincere concern.

Letter of Recommendation

Letters of recommendation may be written to nominate people for awards and for membership in organizations. More frequently, though, they are written to evaluate present or former employees. The central concern in these messages is honesty. Thus, you should avoid exaggerating or distorting a candidate's qualifications to cover up weaknesses or to destroy the person's chances. Ethically and legally, you have a duty to the candidate as well as to other employers to describe that person truthfully and objectively. You don't, however, have to endorse everyone who asks. Since recommendations are generally voluntary, you can—and should—resist writing letters for individuals you can't truthfully support. Ask these people to find other recommenders who know them better.

Some businesspeople today refuse to write recommendations for former employees because they fear lawsuits. Other businesspeople argue that recommendations are useless because they're always positive. Despite the general avoidance of negatives, well-written recommendations do help match candidates with jobs. Hiring companies learn more about a candidate's skills and potential. As a result, they are able to place a candidate properly. Therefore, you should learn to write such letters because you will surely be expected to do so in your future career.

For letters of recommendation, use the direct strategy as described in the following writing plan.

Writing Plan for a Letter of Recommendation

- **Opening:** Identify the applicant, the position, and the reason for writing. State that the message is confidential. Establish your relationship with the applicant. Describe the length of employment or relationship.
- **Body:** Describe job duties. Provide specific examples of the applicant's professional and personal skills and attributes. Compare the applicant with others in his or her field.
- **Closing:** Summarize the significant attributes of the applicant. Offer an overall rating. Draw a conclusion regarding the recommendation.

Identifying the Purpose in the Opening

Begin an employment recommendation by identifying the candidate and the position sought, if it is known. State that your remarks are confidential, and suggest that you are writing at the request of the applicant. Describe your relationship with the candidate, as shown here:

> Ms. Cindy Rosales, whom your organization is considering for the position of media trainer, requested that I submit confidential information on her behalf. Ms. Rosales worked under my supervision for the past two years in our Video Training Centre.

Letters that recommend individuals for awards may open with more supportive statements, such as the following:

> I'm very pleased to nominate Robert Walsh for the Employee-of-the-Month award. For the past 16 months, Mr. Walsh served as staff accountant in my division. During that time he distinguished himself by. . . .

Describing Performance in the Body

The body of an employment recommendation should describe the applicant's job performance and potential. Employers are particularly interested in such traits as communication skills, organizational skills, people skills, the ability to work with a team, the ability to work independently, honesty, dependability, ambition, loyalty, and initiative. In describing these traits, be sure to back them up with evidence. One of the biggest weaknesses in letters of recommendation is that writers tend to make global, non-specific statements (*He was careful and accurate* versus *He completed eight financial statements monthly with about 99 percent accuracy*). Employers prefer definite, task-related descriptions:

> As a training development specialist, Ms. Rosales demonstrated superior organizational and interpersonal skills. She started as a Specialist I, writing scripts for interactive video modules. After six months she was promoted to team leader. In that role she supervised five employees who wrote, produced, evaluated, revised, and installed 14 computer/videodisc training courses over a period of 18 months.

A good recommendation describes general qualities ("organizational and interpersonal skills") backed up by specific evidence that illustrates those qualities.

Be especially careful to support any negative comments with verification (not *He was slower than other customer service reps* but *He answered 25 calls an hour, while most service reps average 40 calls an hour*). In reporting deficiencies, be sure to describe behaviour (*Her last two reports were late and had to be rewritten by her supervisor*) rather than evaluate it (*She is unreliable and her reports are careless*).

Evaluating in the Conclusion

In the final paragraph of a recommendation, you should offer an overall evaluation. Indicate how you would rank this person in relation to others in similar positions. Many managers add a statement indicating whether they would re-hire the applicant, given the chance. If you are strongly supportive, summarize the candidate's best qualities. In the closing you might also offer to answer questions by telephone. Such a statement, though, could suggest that the candidate has weak skills and that you will make damaging statements orally but not in print. Here's how our sample letter might close:

The closing of a recommendation presents an overall ranking and may provide an offer to supply more information by telephone.

> Ms. Rosales is one of the most productive employees I have supervised. I would rank her in the top 10 percent of all the media specialists with whom I have worked. Were she to return to Waterloo, we would be pleased to re-hire her. If you need additional information, call me at (519) 555-3019.

General letters of recommendation, written when the candidate has no specific position in mind, often begin with the salutation *To Prospective Employers*. More specific recommendations, to support applications to known positions, address an individual. When the addressee's name is unknown, consider using the simplified letter format, shown in Figure 5.5, which avoids a salutation.

Figure 5.5 illustrates a complete employment letter of recommendation and provides a summary of writing tips. After naming the applicant and the position sought, the letter describes the applicant's present duties. Instead of merely naming positive qualities (*He is personable, possesses superior people skills, works well with a team, is creative, and shows initiative*), these attributes are demonstrated with specific examples and details.

FIGURE 5.5 Recommendation Letter

Kelowna Health Sciences Centre

2404 Euclid Avenue   Kelowna, BC V1Y 4S3   Phone: 250 768-3434 www.khsc.bc.ca

March 2, 2012

Vice President, Human Resources
Healthcare Enterprises
1200 Riel Blvd. N.
Winnipeg, MB R3C 2X4

RECOMMENDATION OF LANCE W. OLIVER

At the request of Lance W. Oliver, I submit this confidential information in support of his application for the position of assistant director in your Human Resources Department. Mr. Oliver served under my supervision as assistant director of Patient Services at Kelowna Health Sciences Centre for the past three years.

Mr. Oliver was in charge of many customer service programs for our 770-bed hospital. A large part of his job involved monitoring and improving patient satisfaction. Because of his personable nature and superior people skills, he got along well with fellow employees, patients, and physicians. His personnel record includes a number of "Gotcha" citations, given to employees caught in the act of performing exemplary service.

Mr. Oliver works well with a team, as evidenced by his participation on the steering committee to develop our "Service First Every Day" program. His most significant contributions to our hospital, though, came as a result of his own creativity and initiative. He developed and implemented a patient hotline to hear complaints and resolve problems immediately. This enormously successful telephone service helped us improve our patient satisfaction rating from 7.2 last year to 8.4 this year. That's the highest rating in our history, and Mr. Oliver deserves a great deal of the credit.

We're sorry to lose Mr. Oliver, but we recognize his desire to advance his career. I am confident that his resourcefulness, intelligence, and enthusiasm will make him successful in your organization. I recommend him without reservation.

Mary E. O'Rourke

MARY E. O'ROURKE, DIRECTOR, Patient Services

MEO:rtd

Illustrates simplified letter style

Identifies applicant and position

Supports general qualities with specific details

Summarizes main points and offers evaluation

Mentions confidentiality of message

Explains relationship to writer

Describes and interprets accomplishments

Tips for Writing Letters of Recommendation

- Identify the purpose and confidentiality of the message.
- Establish your relationship with the applicant.
- Describe the length of employment and job duties, if relevant.
- Provide specific examples of the applicant's professional and personal skills.
- Compare the applicant with others in his or her field.
- Offer an overall rating of the applicant.
- Summarize the significant attributes of the applicant.
- Draw a conclusion regarding the recommendation.

Goodwill Messages

Messages that express thanks, recognition, and sympathy should be written promptly.

Goodwill messages, which include thanks, recognition, and sympathy, seem to intimidate many communicators. Finding the right words to express feelings is sometimes more difficult than writing ordinary business documents. Writers tend to procrastinate when it comes to goodwill messages, or else they send a ready-made card or pick up the telephone. Remember, though, that the personal sentiments of the sender are always more expressive and more meaningful to readers than are printed cards or oral messages. Taking the time to write gives more importance to our well-wishing. Personal notes also provide a record that can be re-read, and treasured.

In expressing thanks, recognition, or sympathy, you should always do so promptly. These messages are easier to write when the situation is fresh in your mind. They also mean more to the recipient. And don't forget that a prompt thank-you note carries the hidden message that you care and that you consider the event to be important. You will learn to write four kinds of goodwill messages—thanks, congratulations, praise, and sympathy. Instead of writing plans for each of them, we recommend that you concentrate on the five Ss. Goodwill messages should be

Goodwill messages are most effective when they are selfless, specific, sincere, spontaneous, and short.

- **Selfless.** Be sure to focus the message solely on the receiver, not the sender. Don't talk about yourself; avoid such comments as *I remember when I.* . . .
- **Specific.** Personalize the message by mentioning specific incidents or characteristics of the receiver. Telling a colleague *Great speech* is much less effective than *Great story about RIM marketing in Washington.* Take care to verify names and other facts.
- **Sincere.** Let your words show genuine feelings. Rehearse in your mind how you would express the message to the receiver orally. Then transform that conversational language to your written message. Avoid pretentious, formal, or flowery language (*It gives me great pleasure to extend felicitations on the occasion of your firm's 20th anniversary*).
- **Spontaneous.** Keep the message fresh and enthusiastic. Avoid canned phrases (*Congratulations on your promotion, Good luck in the future*). Strive for directness and naturalness, not creative brilliance.
- **Short.** Although goodwill messages can be as long as needed, try to accomplish your purpose in only a few sentences. What is most important is remembering an individual. Such caring does not require documentation or wordiness. Individuals and business organizations often use special note cards or stationery for brief messages.

Thanks

When someone has done you a favour or when an action merits praise, you need to extend thanks or show appreciation. Letters of appreciation may be written to customers for their orders, to hosts and hostesses for their hospitality, to individuals for kindnesses performed, and especially to customers who complain. After all, complainers are actually providing you with "free consulting reports from the field." Complainers who feel that they were listened to often become the greatest promoters of an organization.[5]

Send letters of thanks to customers, hosts, and individuals who have performed kind acts.

Because the receiver will be pleased to hear from you, you can open directly with the purpose of your message. The letter in Figure 5.6 thanks a speaker who addressed a group of marketing professionals. Although such thank-you notes can be quite short, this one is a little longer because the writer wants to lend importance to the receiver's efforts. Notice that every sentence relates to the receiver and offers enthusiastic praise. And, by using the receiver's name along with contractions and positive words, the writer makes the letter sound warm and conversational.

Written notes that show appreciation and express thanks are significant to their receivers. In expressing thanks, you generally write a short note on special note paper or heavy card stock. The following messages provide models for expressing thanks for a gift, for a favour, and for hospitality.

To Express Thanks for a Gift

Thanks, Laura, to you and the other members of the department for honouring me with the elegant Waterford crystal vase at the party celebrating my twentieth anniversary with the company.

Identify the gift, tell why you appreciate it, and explain how you will use it.

The height and shape of the vase are perfect to hold roses and other bouquets from my garden. Each time I fill it, I'll remember your thoughtfulness in choosing this lovely gift for me.

FIGURE 5.6 Thank-You for a Favour

The Canada-Japan Society of British Columbia

302-1107 Homer Street, Vancouver, BC V6B 2Y1   www.canadajapansociety.bc.ca   604 681-0295

March 20, 2012

Mr. Bryant Huffman
Marketing Manager
Ballard Power Systems
4343 North Fraser Way
Burnaby, BC V5J 5J9

Dear Bryant:

You have our sincere gratitude for providing The Canada-Japan Society of B.C. with one of the best presentations our group has ever heard.

> Explains purpose and delivers praise

Your description of the battle Ballard Power waged to begin marketing products in Japan was a genuine eye-opener for many of us. Nine years of preparation establishing connections and securing permissions seems an eternity, but obviously such persistence and patience pay off. We now understand better the need to learn local customs and nurture relationships when dealing in Japan.

> Personalizes the message by using specifics rather than generalities

In addition to your good advice, we particularly enjoyed your sense of humour and jokes—as you must have recognized from the uproarious laughter. What a great routine you do on faulty translations!

> Spotlights the reader's talents

We're grateful, Bryant, for the entertaining and instructive evening you provided for our marketing professionals. Thanks!

> Concludes with compliments and thanks

Cordially,

Judy Hayashi

Judy Hayashi
Program Chair, CJSBC

JRH:grw

To Send Thanks for a Favour

Tell what the favour means using sincere, simple statements.

I sincerely appreciate your filling in for me last week when I was too ill to attend the planning committee meeting for the spring exhibition.

Without your participation much of my preparatory work would have been lost. It's comforting to know that competent and generous individuals like you are part of our team, Mark. Moreover, it's my very good fortune to be able to count you as a friend. I'm grateful to you.

To Extend Thanks for Hospitality

Jeffrey and I want you to know how much we enjoyed the dinner party for our department that you hosted Saturday evening. Your charming home and warm hospitality, along with the lovely dinner and sinfully delicious chocolate dessert, combined to create a truly memorable evening.

Most of all, though, we appreciate your kindness in cultivating togetherness in our department. Thanks, Jennifer, for being such a special person.

Compliment the fine food, charming surroundings, warm hospitality, excellent host and hostess, and good company.

Should you Respond to Goodwill Messages?

By all means, respond to such messages. These messages are attempts to connect personally; they are efforts to reach out, to form professional and/or personal bonds. Failing to respond to notes of congratulations and most other goodwill messages is like failing to say "You're welcome" when someone says "Thank you." Responding to such messages is simply the right thing to do. Avoid minimizing your achievements with comments that suggest you don't really deserve the praise or that the sender is exaggerating your good qualities.

To Answer a Congratulatory Note

Thanks for your kind words regarding my award, and thanks, too, for sending me the newspaper clipping. I truly appreciate your thoughtfulness and warm wishes.

"It's a thank you letter from our office supply vendor. It used up all our fax paper."

To Respond to a Pat on the Back

Your note about my work made me feel good. I'm grateful for your thoughtfulness.

Take the time to respond to any goodwill message you may receive. Usually your response will be an e-mail or a phone call, regardless of what channel the original goodwill message used.

Sympathy

Most of us can bear misfortune and grief more easily when we know that others care. Notes expressing sympathy are probably more difficult to write than any other kind of message. Commercial "In sympathy" cards make the task easier—but they are far less meaningful. Grieving friends want to know what you think—not what Hallmark's card writers think. To help you get started, you can always glance through cards expressing sympathy. They will supply ideas about the kinds of thoughts you might wish to convey in your own words. In writing a sympathy note, (1) refer to the death or misfortune sensitively, using words that show you understand what a crushing blow it is; (2) in the case of a death, praise the deceased in a personal way; (3) offer assistance without going into excessive detail; and (4) end on a reassuring, forward-looking note. Sympathy messages may be typed, although handwriting seems more personal. In either case, use note paper or personal stationery.

Sympathy notes should refer to the misfortune sensitively and offer assistance.

To Express Condolences

We are deeply saddened, Gayle, to learn of the death of your husband. Warren's kind nature and friendly spirit endeared him to all who knew him. He will be missed.

Although words seem empty in expressing our grief, we want you to know that if we can help you or lighten your load in any way, you just have to let us know.

We hope that the treasured memories of your many happy years together, along with the support of your family and many friends, will provide strength and comfort in the months ahead.

In condolence notes, mention the loss tactfully and recognize the good qualities of the deceased. Assure the receiver of your concern. Offer assistance. Conclude on a positive, reassuring note.

Summing Up and Looking Forward

In this chapter you learned to write letters that request information and action and letters that make claims. You also saw how you should respond positively to information requests and customer claims. Finally, you learned how to write recommendation and goodwill messages. Virtually all of these routine letters use the direct strategy. They open immediately with the main idea followed by details and explanations. But not all letters will carry good news. Occasionally, you must deny requests and deliver bad news. In Chapter 7 you will learn to use the indirect strategy in conveying negative news.

Critical Thinking

1. What is wrong with using the indirect pattern for writing routine requests and replies? If the reader understands the message, why make a big fuss over the organization?

2. Since brevity is valued in business writing, is it ever wise to respond with more information than requested? Why or why not?

3. Is it insensitive to include resale or sales promotion information in a letter that responds to a claim letter from a customer?

4. Which is more effective in claim letters—anger or objectivity? Why?

5. Why is it important to regain the confidence of a customer when you respond to a claim letter?

6. Is it appropriate for businesspeople to write goodwill messages expressing thanks, recognition, and sympathy to business acquaintances? Why or why not?

Chapter Review

1. Why do businesspeople still write letters when e-mail is so much faster?
2. What determines whether you write a letter directly or indirectly?
3. What are the two most important positions in a letter?
4. List two ways that you could begin an inquiry letter that asks many questions.
5. What three elements are appropriate in the closing of a request for information?
6. What is a claim letter? Give an original example.
7. What are the three goals when responding to a customer claim letter?
8. Why do some companies comply with nearly all claims?
9. What information should the opening in a letter of recommendation include?
10. The best goodwill messages include what five characteristics?

Writing Improvement Exercises

Letter Openers
Which of the following entries represents an effective direct opening?

___ 1. a. Permit me to introduce myself. I am Alexa Alexander, and I represent TelCom. With the travel season approaching quickly, have you thought about upgrading your telecommunications system to meet the expected increased demand?

___ b. Have you thought about upgrading your telecommunications system to meet the expected increased demand in the upcoming travel season?

___ 2. a. Thank you for your letter of December 2 in which you inquired about the availability of No. 19 bolts of fabric.

___ b. We have an ample supply of No. 19 bolts in stock.

___ 3. a. Yes, the Princess Cruise Club is planning a 15-day Mediterranean cruise beginning October 20.

___ b. This will acknowledge receipt of your letter of December 2 in which you ask about our Mediterranean cruise schedule.

___ 4. a. Your letter of July 9 requesting a refund has been referred to me because Mr. Halvorson is away from the office.

___   b. Your refund cheque for $175 is enclosed.

___ 5. a. We sincerely appreciate your recent order for plywood wallboard panels.

___   b. The plywood wallboard panels that you requested were shipped today by GoFast Express and should reach you by August 12.

Direct Openings

Revise the following openings so that they are more direct. Add information if necessary.

6. Hello! My name is Nalini Tomei, and I am the assistant manager of Body Trends, a fitness equipment centre in Montreal. My manager has asked me to inquire about the upright and semi-recumbent cycling machines that we saw advertised in the June issue of *Your Health* magazine. I have a number of questions.

7. Because I've lost your order form, I have to write this letter. I hope that it's all right to place an order this way. I am interested in ordering a number of things from your summer catalogue, which I still have although the order form is missing.

8. Pursuant to your letter of January 15, I am writing in regard to your inquiry about whether we offer our European-style patio umbrella in colours. This unique umbrella is a very popular item and receives a number of inquiries. Its 3-metre canopy protects you when the sun is directly overhead, but it also swivels and tilts to virtually any angle for continuous sun protection all day long. It comes in two colours: off-white and forest green.

9. I am pleased to receive your inquiry regarding the possibility of my acting as a speaker at the final meeting of your business management club on April 30. The topic of online résumés interests me and is one on which I think I could impart helpful information to your members. Therefore, I am responding in the affirmative to your kind invitation.

10. We have just received your letter of March 12 regarding the unfortunate troubles you are having with your Magnum HD PVR. In your letter you ask if you may send the flawed unit to us for inspection. Although we normally handle all service requests through our local dealers, in your circumstance we are willing to take a look at your unit here at our plant in Edmonton. Therefore, please send it to us so that we may determine what's wrong.

Closing Paragraph

The following concluding paragraph to a claim letter response suffers from faults in strategy, tone, and emphasis. Revise and improve.

11. As a result of your complaint of June 2, we are sending a replacement shipment of laser printers by Excellent Express. Unfortunately, this shipment will not reach you until June 5. We hope that you will not allow this troubling incident and the resulting inconvenience and lost sales you suffered to jeopardize our future business relations. In the past we have been able to provide you with quality products and prompt service.

Activities and Cases

5.1 Information Request: Can I Do a Co-op Placement at Your Firm?

You are a second-semester interior design student at Algonquin College in Ottawa. As part of your four-year applied degree program, you are required to complete a 20-week co-op term. Rather than using the services of the college's co-op office, which normally helps students find co-op positions, you've decided to strike out on your own. Being fluently bilingual, you decide you'd like to move to Montreal for your co-op term. You've narrowed your search down to one well-known design firm, Leroux + Smythe, and you have a lot of questions. For example, has the firm used co-op students before? If so, what typical tasks did the students perform? Another question you'd like answered is whether the firm can pay a salary or at least an honorarium for your 20-week placement. Also, you'd like to know what kinds of clients the firm has for its design services. Finally, you're interested in finding out the amount of French you'll have to write and speak during your placement. You decide to write the company a letter requesting information.

1. What should you include in the opening of this information request?
2. What should the body of your letter contain?
3. How can your phrase your questions most effectively?
4. How should you close this letter?

Your Task. Using your own return address, write a personal business letter requesting information about a co-op placement to Claudette Garneau, Manager Human Resources, Leroux + Smythe, 1450 rue Maclennan, Montreal, QC H3X 2Y4.

Related Web site: Information on Algonquin College's program in interior design is available at http://www2.algonquincollege.com/mediaanddesign/program/bachelor-of-applied-arts-interior-design/. Information on co-op placements is available at http://www.algonquincollege.com/coop.

5.2 Claim Request: Free Samples Are Surprisingly Costly

As marketing manager of Caribou Mountain Ranch, you are very ticked off at Quantum Enterprises. Quantum provides imprinted promotional products for companies. Your resort was looking for something special to offer in promoting its vacation packages. Quantum offered free samples of its promotional merchandise, under its "No Surprise" policy.

You figured, what could you lose? So on January 11 you placed a telephone order for a number of samples. These included three kinds of jumbo tote bags and a square-ended barrel bag with fanny pack, as well as a deluxe canvas attaché case and two colours of garment-dyed sweatshirts. All items were supposed to be free. You did think it odd that you were asked for your company's MasterCard number, but Quantum promised to bill you only if you kept the samples.

When the items arrived, you weren't pleased, and you returned them all on January 21 (you have a postal receipt showing the return). But your February credit card statement showed a charge of $239.58 for the sample items. You called Quantum in February and spoke to Lane, who assured you that a credit would be made on your next statement. However, your March statement showed no credit. You called again and received a similar promise. It's now April and no credit has been made. You decide to write and demand action. Circle the correct choice in the following items.

1. To open this claim letter, you should
   a. Provide a complete chronology of what happened with all the dates and facts.
   b. Tell Quantum how sick and tired you are of this game it is playing.
   c. Explain carefully how much of your valuable time you have spent on trying to resolve this matter.
   d. Describe the action you want taken.

2. In writing this claim letter, you should assume that Quantum
   a. Regularly uses this trick to increase its sales.
   b. Made an honest mistake and will rectify the problem.
   c. Has no intention of crediting your account.
   d. Reacts only when threatened seriously.

3. In the body of this claim letter, you should
   a. Describe briefly what has taken place.
   b. Refer to specific dates and names of people contacted.
   c. Enclose copies of any relevant documents.
   d. All of the above.

4. The closing of this claim letter should
   a. Refer to your lawyer, whom Quantum will hear from if this matter is not settled.
   b. Explain what action you want taken and by when.
   c. Make sure that Quantum knows that you will never use their products again.
   d. Threaten to spread the word among the travel industry that Quantum can't be trusted.

Your Task. After circling your choices, write a claim letter that documents the problem and states the action you want taken. Add any information you feel is necessary. Address your letter to Ms. Kayla Tutshi, Customer Service, Quantum Enterprises, 1505 Victory Drive, Kamloops, BC V2C 4X3.

5.3 Information Request: Helping Raise Puppies to Become Dog Guides

As an assistant in the Corporate Social Responsibility Office of your corporation, you have been given an unusual task. Your manager wants to expand the company's philanthropic and community relations mission and especially employee volunteerism. She heard about the Lions Foundation of Canada Dog Guides, a program in which trainers breed and raise puppies for dog guide training. She thinks this would be an excellent outreach program for the company's employees. They could give back to the community in their role as foster parents to a future dog guide, groomers/bathers of dog guides in training, kennel workers, or special events workers. To pursue the idea, she asks you to request information about the program and ask questions about whether a company could sponsor a program encouraging employees to act as volunteers. She hasn't thought it through very carefully and relies on you to raise logical questions, especially about costs for volunteers.

Your Task. Write an information request to Sandy Turney, Executive Director, Lions Foundation of Canada Dog Guides, P.O. Box 907, Oakville, ON L6J 5E8. Include an end date and a reason.

For more information on the dog guide program go to http://www.dogguides.com/ doghome.htm.

5.4 Information Request: Culture Vultures Seeking Adventure

You just saw a great television program about cheap travel in Europe, and you think you'd like to try it next summer. The program described how some people want to get away from it all; others want to see a little of the world. Some want to learn a different language; some want to soak up a bit of culture. The "get-away" group, the program advised, should book a package trip to a Contiki resort where they relax and soak up the sun. But "culture vultures" and FITs (free independent travellers) should select the countries they want to visit and plan their own trips. You decide to visit France, Spain, and Portugal.

Begin planning your trip by gathering information from the country's tourist office or Web site. Many details need to be worked out. What about visas? How about inoculations? Since your budget will be limited, you need to stay in hostels whenever possible. Where are they? Are they private? Some hostels accept only people who belong to their organization. You really need to get your hands on a list of hostels for every country before departure. You are also interested in any special transport passes for students, such as a Eurail Pass. And while you are at it, find out if they have any special guides for student travellers. All this information can be secured from a tourist office.

Your Task. Using the Internet, you found an address for information: Tourist Office of Spain in Canada, 3402–2 Bloor Street West, Toronto, ON M4W 3E2 (**http://www.spain.info/ca/ TourSpain**). Write a letter requesting information. If you prefer another country, find its tourist office address. Because this is a personal business letter, include your return address above the date.

5.5 Information Request: Meeting in Haines Junction at the Dalton Trail Lodge

Do this

Your company, Software Solutions, has just had an enormously successful two-year sales period. The CEO has asked you, as marketing manager, to arrange a fabulous conference/ retreat as a thank-you gift for all 20 engineers, product managers, and salespeople. She wants the company to host a four-day combination sales conference/vacation/retreat at some spectacular location. She suggests that you start by inquiring at the Dalton Trail Lodge in Haines Junction, Yukon. You check its Web site and get some good information. However, you decide to write a letter so that you can have a permanent, formal record of all the resorts you investigate. You estimate that your company will require about 20 rooms. You'll also need about three conference rooms for one and a half days. You want to know room rates, conference facilities, and outdoor activity possibilities for families. You have two time periods that would be possible: September 18–22 or October 4–8. You know that these are off-peak times, and you wonder if you can get a good room rate. What is the most economical way to get to Haines Junction from Software Solutions' headquarters in Prince George, B.C.? One evening you will want to host a banquet for about 140 people. The CEO wants a report from you by April 1.

Your Task. Write a well-organized information request to Dalton Trail Lodge, c/o Grayling Camp Enterprises, Box 5331, Haines Junction, YT Y0B 1L0.

Related Web site: http://www.daltontrail.com.

5.6 Information Request: Computer Code of Conduct

As an assistant in your college's or university's campus computer centre, you have been asked by your supervisor to help write an updated code of conduct for use of the centre facilities. This code will spell out which behaviour and activities are allowed in your centre and which are not. The first thing you are to do is conduct a search on the Internet to see what other college or university computing centres have written as conduct codes.

Your Task. Search the Internet employing variations of the keywords "computer code of conduct." Print two or three codes that seem appropriate. Write an e-mail to the director of an educational computer centre asking for further information about its code and its effectiveness. Include at least five significant questions. Attach your printouts to your letter.

5.7 Information Request: Backpacking Cuisine

Assume that you are Marc Vannault, manager of a health spa and also an ardent backpacker. You are organizing a group of hikers for a wilderness trip to Yukon. One item that must be provided is freeze-dried food for the three-week trip. You are unhappy with the taste and quality of backpacking food products currently available. You expect to have a group of hikers who are older, affluent, and natural-food enthusiasts. Some are concerned about products containing preservatives, sugar, and additives. Others are on diets restricting cholesterol, fat, and salt.

You heard that Outfitters, Inc., offers a new line of freeze-dried products. You want to know what they offer and whether they have sufficient variety to serve all the needs of your group. You need to know where their products can be purchased and what the cost range is. You'd also like to try a few of their items before placing a large order. You are interested in how they produce the food products and what kinds of ingredients they use. If you have any items left over, you wonder how long they can be kept and still be usable.

Your Task. Write an information request letter to Karie Osborne, Outfitters, Inc., 1169 Willamette Street, Canmore, AB T0L 2P2.

5.8 Direct Claim: Neglected Landscape

As project manager at South Shore Property Management, you are in charge of landscaping maintenance for many clients, including Bluenose Business Park. Recently two tenants called to complain that their lawns had not been cut for two weeks and that weeds were growing in the parking lot. You drove out to see for yourself, and sure enough, Bluenose was looking quite bedraggled. You also noticed that fallen tree branches from a recent windstorm were lying on the ground. Back in the office, you checked the files and saw that Stephen's Landscaping Service had been hired to mow lawns and service the grounds at Bluenose. You checked further and saw that the original contract called for a fee of $350 per month. However, the latest bill paid was $450. You can't understand why the price was increased without your knowledge. After leaving several telephone messages at Stephen's Landscaping and receiving no response, you decide to write a claim letter and attach it to an e-mail.

Your Task. Decide what you want to do in this situation. Send an appropriate letter (with e-mail cover) explaining your claim or complaint to Stephen Johnstone, Stephen's Landscaping Service, 240 Howe Rd., Dartmouth, NS, B3V 1M2. Add any necessary details.

5.9 Claim Letter: Undersized French Doors

As Julie Chen, owner of Smart Interiors, you recently completed a kitchen remodel that required double-glazed, made-to-order oak French doors. You ordered them by telephone on July 2 from Custom Wood, Inc. When they arrived on July 25, your carpenter gave you the bad news: the doors were cut too small. Instead of measuring a total of 3.23 square metres, the doors measured 3.13 square metres. In your carpenter's words, "No way can I stretch those doors to fit these openings!" You waited three weeks for these doors, and your clients wanted them installed immediately. Your carpenter said, "I can rebuild this opening for you, but I'm going to have to charge you for my time." His extra charge came to $455.50.

You feel that the people at Custom Wood should reimburse you for this amount, since it was their error. In fact, you actually saved them money by not returning the doors. You decide to write to Custom Wood and enclose a copy of your carpenter's bill. You wonder whether you should also include a copy of Custom Wood's invoice, even though it does not show the exact door measurements. You are a good customer of Custom Wood, having used their quality doors and windows on many other jobs. You're confident that it will grant this claim.

Your Task. Write a claim letter to Jay Brandt, Marketing Manager, Custom Wood, Inc., 401 Main Street, Vancouver, BC V1L 2E6.

5.10 Direct Claim: Can't Attend Management Seminar

Assiniboine Executive Training Institute offered a seminar titled "Enterprise Project Management Protocol" that sounded terrific. It promised to teach project managers how to estimate scope of work, report status, write work packages, and cope with project conflicts. Because your company often is engaged in large cross-functional projects, it decided to send four key managers to the seminar to be held June 1–2 at the Assiniboine headquarters in Winnipeg. The fee was $2,200 each, and it was paid in advance. About six weeks before the seminar, you learned that three of the managers would be tied up in projects that would not be completed in time for them to attend.

Your Task. On your company letterhead, write a claim letter to Addison Firchuk, Registrar, Assiniboine Executive Training Institute, Suite 901–100 Lombard Avenue, Winnipeg, MB R3B 0X2. Ask that the seminar fees for three employees be returned because they cannot attend. Give yourself a title and supply any details necessary.

5.11 Claim Letter: Deep Desk Disappointment

Assume that you are Monica Keil, President, Keil Consulting Services, 423 Lawrence Avenue, Montreal, QC H5L 2E3. Since your consulting firm is doing very well, you decide to splurge and purchase a fine executive desk for your own office. You order an expensive desk described as "North American white oak embellished with hand-inlaid walnut cross-banding." Although you do not ordinarily purchase large, expensive items by mail, you are impressed by the description of this desk and by the money-back guarantee promised in the catalogue.

When the desk arrives, you know that you have made a mistake—it is not the high-quality product that you had anticipated. The wood finish is rough, the grain looks splotchy, and many of the drawers do not pull out easily. The advertisement has promised "full suspension, silent ball bearing drawer slides." You are disappointed with the desk and decide to send it back, taking advantage of the money-back guarantee.

Your Task. Write a letter to Rodney Harding, Marketing Manager, Big Spruce Wood Products, P.O. Box 488, Sandpoint, BC V5N 7L8. You want your money refunded. You're not sure whether the freight charges can be refunded, but it's worth a try. Supply any details needed.

5.12 Information Response: Avoiding Employee Gifts That Are Re-gifted

A friend of yours, Megan Stowe, is an executive with a large insurance company. One day in late October, you see her at an industry conference in St. John's, Newfoundland. Afterward, you decide to head down to Water Street for a coffee at a nearby café. After the usual small talk, she says, "You know, I'm beginning to hate the holidays. Every year it gets harder to choose presents for our staff. Once we gave fruitcakes, which I thought were tasty and elegant, but it turns out a lot of our people re-gifted them to other people before Christmas." As an executive training coach, you say, "Well, what's your gift goal? Do you want to encourage your employees? Are you just saying thanks? Or do you want your gifts to act as a retention tool to keep good people on your team?" Megan responds, "I never thought of it that way. Our company doesn't really have a strategy for holiday gifts. It's just something we do every year. Do you have any ideas?"

As it turns out, you have a lot of ideas. You've developed a gift list based on the reasons talented people stay in organizations. Megan asks you to get in touch next week explaining some of the gift ideas. She thinks she will be able to retain your services for this advice.

Your Task. Using your library databases and the Internet, research articles and information on corporate gift giving. As a consultant, prepare a letter with a sampling of gift-giving ideas addressed to Megan Stowe, Vice President, Human Resources, London Life Insurance Company, 255 Dufferin Ave., London, ON N6A 4K1.

5.13 Information Response: Scannable Résumés

As part of a team of interns at SportMax head office, you have been asked to revise a form letter to send to job applicants who inquire about your résumé-scanning techniques. The following poorly written response to an inquiry was pulled from the file.

Dear Mr. Chouxfleur:

Your letter of April 11 has been referred to me for a response. We are pleased to learn that you are considering employment here at SportMax, and we look forward to receiving your résumé, should you decide to send same to us.

You ask if we scan incoming résumés. Yes, we certainly do. Actually, we use SmartTrack, an automated résumé-tracking system. SmartTrack is wonderful! You know, we sometimes receive as many as 30 résumés a day, and SmartTrack helps us sort, screen, filter, and separate the résumés. It also processes them, helps us organize them, and keeps a record of all of these résumés. Some of the résumés, however, cannot be scanned, so we have to return those—if we have time.

The reasons that résumés won't scan may surprise you. Some applicants send photocopies or faxed copies, and these can cause misreading, so don't do it. The best plan is to send an original copy. Some people use coloured paper. Big mistake! White paper (8 1/2 × 11-inch) printed on one side is the best bet. Another big problem is unusual type fonts, such as script or fancy gothic or antique fonts. They don't seem to realize that scanners do best with plain, readable fonts such as Helvetica, Arial, or Times New Roman in a 10- to 14-point size.

Other problems occur when applicants use graphics, shading, italics, underlining, horizontal and vertical lines, parentheses, and brackets. Scanners like plain résumés! Oh yes, staples can cause misreading. And folding of a résumé can also cause the scanners to foul up. To be safe, don't staple or fold, and be sure to use wide margins and a quality printer (no ancient dot matrixes!!).

When a hiring manager within SportMax decides to look for an appropriate candidate, he is told to submit keywords to describe the candidate he has in mind for his opening. We tell him (or sometimes her) to zero in on nouns and phrases that best describe what they want. Thus, my advice to you is to try to include those words that highlight your technical and professional areas of expertise.

If you do decide to submit your résumé to us, be sure you don't make any of the mistakes described herein that would cause the scanner to misread it.

Sincerely,

Your Task. As a team, discuss how this letter could be improved. Decide what information is necessary to send to potential job applicants. Search for additional information that might be helpful. Then, submit an improved version to your instructor. Although the form letter should be written so that it can be sent to anyone who inquires, address this one to René Chouxfleur, 629 Cathedral Street, Vancouver, BC V3L 2F3.

5.14 Information Response: Backpacking Cuisine

As Karie Osborne, owner of Outfitters, Inc., producer of freeze-dried backpacking foods, answer the inquiry of Marc Vannault (see Activity 5.7). You are eager to have Mr. Vannault sample your new all-natural line of products containing no preservatives, sugar, or additives. You want him to know that you started this company two years ago after you found yourself making custom meals for discerning backpackers who rejected typical camping fare. Some of your menu items are excellent for individuals on restricted diets. Some dinners are cholesterol-, fat-, and salt-free, but he'll have to look at your list to see for himself.

You will send him your complete list of dinner items and the suggested retail prices. You will also send him a sample "Saturday Night on the Trail," a four-course meal that comes with fruit candies and elegant appetizers. All your food products are made from choice ingredients in sanitary kitchens that you supervise personally. They are flash-frozen in a new vacuum process that you have patented. Although your dried foods are meant to last for years, you don't recommend that they be kept beyond 18 months because they may deteriorate. This could happen if a package were punctured or if the products became overheated.

Your Task. Respond to Marc Vannault, 322 East Drive, Penticton, BC V2A 1T2. By the way, your products are currently available at High-Country Sports Centre, 19605 Rocky Mountain Highway, Calgary, AB T8L 1Z8. Large orders may be placed directly with you, and you offer a five percent discount on direct orders.

5.15 Information Response: Massage Necessary

As a general practitioner, you've noticed that many of your patients have begun to ask for a letter stating that you've recommended they have massage therapy. The reason your patients need the letter is that some insurance plans will not reimburse for massage expenses unless a medical doctor has said—in writing—that the treatment is necessary. Rather than writing a new letter each time a patient makes this request, you decide to develop a template that can be stored on your computer. The only thing that will have to change is the date and the name of the patient.

Your Task. Write a short information response letter that can be sent to any insurance plan/ company. In the letter, figure out a way to say that your patient needs massage for an under- lying condition, not for a workplace or accident-related injury (sometimes insurance com- panies will not pay if the condition requiring treatment is a result of an accident or something that happened at work).

5.16 Order Response: Unfortunately, We're Fully Booked . . .

As the sales manager of the Dalton Trail Lodge in Haines Junction, Yukon, you sometimes wish you had an infinite number of rooms to offer prospective guests. It seems to often happen that people all want to stay at the lodge at the same times. You recently received a letter from Software Solutions in Prince George, B.C. (Activity 5.5). Unfortunately, you have to tell Software Solutions that both dates it requested are already fully booked at the lodge. That's the bad news. The good news as you see it is that the periods immediately after the ones requested by Software Solutions are free (i.e., September 25–29 and October 11–15). You are very eager to get the booking, even though you are aware that the dates of the lodge's availability don't exactly match up with Software Solutions' request.

Your Task. Because you consider time to be of the essence, you decide to reply via e-mail to this letter. In your e-mail, you encourage Software Solutions to get in touch via telephone or by reply e-mail so that a solution to the situation can be reached more quickly.

CRITICAL THINKING

5.17 Claim Response: Undersized French Doors

As Jay Brandt, manager of Custom Wood, Inc., you have a problem. Your firm manufactures quality pre-cut and custom-built doors and frames. You have received a letter dated August 3 from Julie Chen (Activity 5.9). Ms. Chen is an interior designer, and she complains that the oak French doors she recently ordered for a client were made to the wrong dimensions.

Although they were the wrong size, she kept the doors and had them installed because her clients were without outside doors. However, her carpenter charged an extra $455.50 to install them. She claims that you should reimburse her for this amount, since your company was responsible for the error. You check her July 2 order and find that the order was filled correctly. In a telephone order, Ms. Chen requested doors that measured 3.13 square metres and that's what you sent. Now she says that the doors should have been 3.23 square metres.

Your policy forbids refunds or returns on custom orders. Yet, you remember that around July 2 you had two new people working the telephones taking orders. It's possible that they did not hear or record the measurements correctly. You don't know whether to grant this claim or refuse it. But you do know that you must look into the training of telephone order takers and be sure that they verify all custom-order measurements. It might also be a good idea to have your carpenters call a second time to confirm custom measurements.

Ms. Chen is a successful interior designer and has provided Custom Wood with a number of orders. You value her business but aren't sure how to respond. You'd like to remind her that Custom Wood has earned a reputation as a premier manufacturer of wood doors and frames. Your doors feature prime woods, meticulous craftsmanship, and award-winning designs. And the engineering is ingenious.

Your Task. Decide how to treat this claim and whether to respond by letter or e-mail. The addresses are Julie Chen, Smart Interiors, 3282 Richmond Road, Vancouver, BC V5Y 2A8 and jchen@smartinteriors.ca. You might mention that you have a new line of greenhouse win- dows that are available in three sizes. Include a brochure describing these windows.

5.18 Claim Response: Deep Desk Disappointment

As Rodney Harding, Marketing Manager of Big Spruce Wood Products, it is your job to reply to customer claims, and today you must respond to Monica Keil, President of Keil Consulting Services (Activity 5.11). You are disturbed that she is returning the executive desk (Invoice No. 3499), but your policy is to comply with customer wishes. If she doesn't want to keep the desk, you will certainly return the purchase price plus shipping charges. Desks are occasion- ally damaged in shipping, and this may explain the marred finish and the sticking drawers.

You want Ms. Keil to give Big Spruce Wood Products another chance. After all, your office furniture and other wood products are made from the finest hand-selected woods by master artisans. Since she is apparently furnishing her office, send her another catalogue and invite her to look at the traditional conference desk on page 10-E. This is available with a matching credenza, file cabinets, and accessories. She might be interested in your furniture-leasing plan, which can produce substantial savings.

Your Task. Write to Monica Keil, President, Keil Consulting Services, 423 Lawrence Avenue, Montreal, Quebec H5L 2E3 or mkeil@keilconsulting.ca. In granting her claim, promise that you will personally examine any furniture she may order in the future.

5.19 Recommendation Letter: Telling It Like It Is

You are a business communication professor at a community college. Your students do a co-op semester from May to August as part of their program. In March, some of your students start asking for recommendation letters. This spring in particular has been heavy with requests, and one sticks in your mind. Jeff Brown, a second-year student, who has been in two of your classes, asks for a recommendation letter. He is applying for entry-level customer service jobs in the banking industry. You are Jeff's business communication professor, and you've got little to complain about. Jeff has been averaging an A in your two courses, his writing and speaking skills are superior, he thinks critically, solves problems in original ways, and is a good team player. Unfortunately, he's managed to demonstrate all of these strong skills and maintain his high average while continually skipping classes and arriving late for the classes he does show up to. You want to give Jeff a good recommendation, but you realize that in the work world, absenteeism and showing up late aren't treated as lightly as at college.

Your Task. Write a general letter of recommendation for Jeff Brown.

5.20 Thanks for the Favour: I Got a Job!

You are Jeff Brown from Activity 5.19. It took you only three weeks of co-op job hunting and you landed a great job with Scotiabank. You'd like to thank your business communication professor for the recommendation letter s/he wrote for you in early March. You're busy with end of term and final exams, though, so you put writing the thank-you letter off till late April, more than six weeks since the recommendation letter was written.

Your Task. Write a letter thanking your professor.

5.21 Response to Thanks: Congratulations on Your New Job

As the professor from Activity 5.19, you've just received Jeff Brown's handwritten letter of thanks. You're off for your vacation at this point, and only checking in at the office once a week. You don't have Jeff's mailing address, but you do have his e-mail address.

Your Task. Send Jeff an e-mail responding to his letter of thanks.

5.22 Sympathy Message: For a Friend Who Can't Work Anymore

Your best friend at work, Alice Palumbo, was diagnosed with breast cancer some months ago. Her treatments appeared to be effective at first, and she continued to work even though her hair had fallen out and she was feeling weak. It's now six months since her original diagnosis and Alice has begun to miss at first whole days and then whole weeks of work. Your supervisor sends an e-mail memo one day informing everyone on your team that Alice is taking a long-term leave of absence.

Your Task. Write Alice a sympathy message.

5.23 Information Request

You are in the second year of the Hairstylist program at Algonquin College and will be graduating shortly. You and your sister have inherited a small amount of money from an aunt who recently passed away, and you are looking for ways to put your inheritance to good use. Your sister is graduating from the Esthetician program at the same college, and together you would like to purchase a hair salon and aesthetics franchise called Hair Clippers and Best Face Forward. There are already two successful franchises in Ottawa; one is located in the west end, the other in downtown Ottawa. You and your sister would like to obtain information on opening another franchise in the east end, close to where the two of you are living. Some of the information you would like to gather includes the total investment required to start the franchise, whether a portion of the investment can be financed, and whether you can rent your own equipment. You would also like to know whether the east end would be a feasible location, whether training is available, and, since this is your first venture operating a small business, the nature of support provided to franchisees. You would appreciate any other information that Hair Clippers and Best Face Forward can offer, since you are also contemplating other investment options.

Your Task. Write an information request letter or e-mail, using modified block style, to Martha Jones, Business Manager, Hair Clippers and Best Face Forward Franchise, 53 St. Laurent Boulevard, Ottawa, ON K2R 5R3, asking for detailed information on starting your own franchise business. Include at least five significant questions.

Grammar/Mechanics Review—5

The following sentences contain errors in grammar, punctuation, capitalization, number style, usage, and spelling. Below each sentence write a corrected version.

1. Every secretaries desk will be equipped with the most latest computer and printer.

2. We ordered new stationary about 2 months ago but I can find no correspondance or invoice related to our order.

3. Anyone of the Vice Presidents are authorized to sign cheques; however for amounts that are over 10 thousand dollars 2 signatures are required.

4. To be admitted an application must be submitted before April 1st.

5. Although twenty percent of the Companys sales now come from outside North America, the Company expects to increase that number to thirty percent, by 2010.

6. The sierra club recommend investing in "socially responsible" companys such as the mountain equipment coop.

7. Some organizations worry that valueable company information may be stole over the internet.

8. Did you know that an ostriches eye is bigger than it's brain.

9. Jennifer completed a b.com. degree in Accounting, before taking a job with the PriceWaterhouseCoopers in Kingston.

10. Because she had took many computer courses Erin had numerous job opportunitys from which to chose.

11. The number of students taking Second Language courses are increasing everyyear.

12. To ensure valid survey results each of the fortune 500 companies were sent a questionnaire by the researchers.

13. When Doreen Sparx became Vice President of Customer Support the customer contact centre was receiving more than ten thousand calls a month.

14. Amy miller president of quad graphics met privately with her director of marketing.

15. Some of my business electives Courses includes: marketing, small business management, and Mandarin for business.

Document for Revision

The following e-mail has faults in grammar, punctuation, spelling, number form, and wordiness. Use standard proofreading marks (see Appendix B) to correct the errors. When you finish, your instructor can show you the revised version of this e-mail.

TO: <bspring@cmail.ca>

SUBJECT: Your January 11 Letter Requesting Information About New All-Natural Products

Dear Mr. Spring, We have received your letter of January 11 in which you inquire about our all-natural products. Needless to say, we are pleased to be able to answer in the affirmative. Yes, our new line of freeze dried back-packing foods meet the needs of older adults and young people as well. You asked a number of questions, and here are answers to you're questions about our products.

- Our all natural foods contains no perservatives, sugars or additives. The inclosed list of dinner items tell what foods are cholesterol-, fat-, and salt-free.

- Large orders recieve a five percent discount when they're placed direct with Outfitters, Inc. You can also purchase our products at Centre Sportif Estrie, 1960 rue Fabre, Sherbrooke, QC, .J1L 3C7.

- Outfitters, Inc., food products are made in our sanitary kitchens which I personally supervise. The foods are flash froze in a patented vacum process that retain freshness, texture and taste.

- Outfitters, Inc. food products are made from choice ingredients that combines good taste and healful quality.

- Our foods stay fresh and tasty for up to 18 months.

Mr. Spring, I started Outfitters, Inc., two years ago after making custom meals for discerning back-packers who rejected typical camping fare. What a pleasure it is now to share my meals with back-packers like you.

I hope you'll enjoy the sample meal we recently mailed you. "Saturday Night on the Trail" is a four-coarse meal complete with fruit candys and elegant appetizers. Please call me personally at (604) 459-3342 to place an order, or to ask other questions about my backpacking food products.

Sincerely,

Retailer Cleans Up Its Act

For years companies have been aware of the corporate social responsibility (CSR) movement. Corporate social responsibility is defined as "a company's environmental, social and economic performance and the impacts of the company on its internal and external stakeholders."[6] In a recent high-profile case in Saskatoon, a women's clothing retailer, Sensational, was picketed by local community members for what they claimed was "a lack of responsibility" around environmental issues. Apparently, in a bid to distinguish itself from the competing stores in the area, the store wrapped all its customers' purchases in multiple layers of tissue paper, and then put this package inside a huge plastic carrying bag with its name printed on the side. Soon, local sidewalk garbage cans began to overflow with the unnecessary packaging offered by this retailer. Members of a vigilant community group wrote a letter to the retailer asking that it reconsider its packaging practices, but they never heard anything back. Five months later, the protest took place, and the media covered the protest. The retailer was unhappy, to say the least, about the negative media coverage.

Career Application

In class discussion, consider these questions:
- Why are companies increasingly interested in social responsibility?
- Should employees be encouraged to report suspected irresponsible behaviour of their employers?
- What are the advantages and disadvantages of detailed codes of social responsibility for companies?

Your Task

You are the assistant manager of Sensational. Your boss, the manager, asks you to research corporate social responsibility, especially recent cases and policies in Canada, and draft a memo summary for the team by next week. She also implies that if she likes what she sees, she'll send it to head office in Vancouver. Using library databases and the Web, research corporate social responsibility in Canada and write an e-mail attaching a draft memo to your boss, Sherry Cardinal, as instructed.

Related Web site: For a good example of a corporate social responsibility code, visit the Canadian Business for Social Responsibility (CBSR) Web site at http://www.cbsr.ca and look for The GoodCompany Guidelines under Resources.

CHAPTER 6

Persuasive Messages

Information overload and the need to reprioritize are being experienced across all sectors in business today—it's the new normal. Persuading others to buy into your priorities is best done by looking for common interests and aligning collective goals. Acknowledge and provide support to those who are critical to your success and your agenda will become their agenda.[1]

Jose Ribau,
General Manager, Consumer Deposits & Payments, CIBC

LEARNING OBJECTIVES

1. Use the indirect strategy to persuade.

2. Request favours persuasively.

3. Write convincing claim request messages.

4. Present persuasive new ideas within organizations.

5. Analyze techniques used in sales messages.

6. Compose carefully planned online sales messages.

The ability to persuade is a primary factor in personal and business success.

Persuasion is the ability to make people think or do what you would like them to think or do. Developing the ability to persuade is a key factor in the success you achieve in your business messages, in your career, and in your interpersonal relations. As Jose Ribau implies, persuasive individuals are highly valued in today's successful organizations. He suggests that everyone make persuasive communication skills a priority. Persuasive individuals become decision makers, managers, executives, and entrepreneurs because their ideas generally prevail. This chapter will examine techniques for presenting ideas persuasively.

Using the Indirect Pattern in Persuasive Requests

Requests for large favours generally require persuasive strategies.

Persuasion is necessary when resistance is anticipated or when ideas require preparation before they can be presented effectively. For example, asking for a favour implies that you want someone to do something for nothing—or for very little. Common examples are requests for the donation of time, money, energy, a name, resources, talent, skills, or expertise. On occasion, everyone needs to ask a favour. Small favours, such as asking a coworker to lock up the office for you on Friday, can be straightforward and direct.

Little resistance is expected. Larger favours, though, require careful planning and an indirect strategy. A busy executive is asked to serve on a committee to help disadvantaged children. A florist is asked to donate table arrangements for a charity fundraiser. A well-known author is asked to speak before a local library group. In each instance persuasion is necessary to overcome natural resistance.

The letters shown in Figure 6.1 (p. 148) illustrate two versions of a favour request. Genevieve Oestriker works for an organization without funds hoping to entice a well-known authority, Ann Cunningham, to speak before its regional conference. Such a request surely requires indirectness and persuasion, but the ineffective version begins with a direct appeal. Even worse, the reader is given an opportunity to refuse the request before the writer has a chance to present reasons for accepting. Moreover, this letter fails to convince the reader that she has anything to gain by speaking to this group. Finally, the closing suggests no specific action to help her accept, should she be so inclined.

A favour request is doomed to failure if the writer does not consider its effect on the reader. In the more effective version, notice how the writer applies the indirect strategy. The opening gains the reader's attention and makes her want to read more regarding the reaction to her presentation. By showing how Ms. Cunningham's interests are related to the organization's, the writer builds interest before presenting the request. The request is then followed by language that reduces resistance, showing Ms. Cunningham how she will benefit from accepting this invitation. This successful letter concludes with a specific action closing. A writing plan for a persuasive request is shown below.

Writing Plan for a Persuasive Request

- **Gain attention** in the opening.
- **Build interest** in the body.
- **Reduce resistance** in the body.
- **Motivate action** in the closing.

The Components of an Indirect Persuasive Request

The indirect pattern described above contains separate strategies, but in a successful persuasive message all four appear together as a unified whole. And the order of the four strategies is not set in stone. Not every persuasive situation will require you to build interest before you reduce resistance, for example. However, most persuasive messages begin by gaining attention and end by motivating action.

Gain Attention. In the opening of the message, which is usually brief, you gain the reader's attention through a strategy such as describing a problem, making an unexpected statement, mentioning a reader benefit, paying the reader a compliment, or posing a stimulating question. For example, in a persuasive request message sent by a local seniors' investment club to a financial planner, the writer might begin by paying the planner a compliment: *A number of our club's members have used your services in the past and have had nothing but praise for your professionalism.*

Build Interest. The message's body is intended to keep the reader's attention and persuade him or her that the request is reasonable. This section is often the longest part of the message, as it includes strategies such as the use of facts and statistics, expert opinion, listing of direct benefits to the receiver, examples, and specific details, as well as indirect benefits to the receiver. In the investment club example, the writer may begin building interest by stating, *You may be interested to know that while 5 of our 25 members have used your services before, the other 20 members of the club are either without a financial planner or else considering changing planners.*

Reduce Resistance. A crucial part of a persuasive message's body, yet one that is often left out by unsophisticated writers, is the writer putting himself or

FIGURE 6.1 Persuasive Favour Request

Before

Dear Ms. Cunningham:

Would you be willing to speak to the members of the Ottawa chapter of the Canadian Restaurant and Foodservices Association? We hate to ask such a busy person, but we hoped you might be free on June 10 and would be able to come up from Toronto to join us in Ottawa.

Fails to pique interest; provides easy excuse

You would address our members on the topic of avoiding the seven cardinal sins in food service. This is a topic we understand you presented at your local chapter with some success. Although we can offer you only a $300 honorarium, we will also include dinner.

Does not promote direct and indirect benefits

Our group is informal, but I'm sure they would be interested in a 45-minute speech. Please let me know if you can join us at 7 p.m. at the Empire Grill in Ottawa.

Does not anticipate objections; fails to make it easy to respond

After

Canadian Restaurant and Foodservices Association
200–180 Sparks St. Ottawa, ON K9A 2V7 (613) 351-4300 www.crfa.ca

February 23, 2012

Ms. Ann Cunningham, Manager
Four Seasons Hotels and Resorts
1165 Leslie St. Toronto,
ON M3C 2K8

Dear Ms. Cunningham:

News of the excellent presentation you made at your local chapter of the Canadian Restaurant and Foodservices Association has reached us here in Ottawa, and we are very impressed.

Piques reader's interest with praise — *Gains attention*

Running a successful restaurant operation, as we all know, is tough even on a good day. The intense pace is frenzied, from scrubbing the vegetables early in the morning to latching the front door at day's end. In all this haste, it is easy to lapse into food service faults that can land an operation in big trouble. Your presentation focusing on seven cardinal sins in the food service industry certainly captured our attention.

Builds interest

The Ottawa chapter of the Canadian Restaurant and Foodservices Association asked me to invite you to be the featured speaker at our June 10 dinner on the topic of "Avoiding the Seven Cardinal Sins in Food Service." By sharing your expertise, you can help other restaurant operators recognize and prevent potential problems involving discrimination, workplace safety, hiring practices, and so forth. Although we can offer you only a small honorarium of $300 plus your travel expenses, we can promise you a big audience of enthusiastic restaurateurs eager to hear your presentation.

Notes indirect benefit
Notes direct benefit
Builds desire and reduces resistance

Our relaxed group doesn't expect a formal address; the members are most interested in hearing about best practices and solutions to prospective problems. To make your talk easy to organize, I have enclosed a list of questions our members submitted. Most talks are about 45 minutes long.

Offsets reluctance by making the talk informal and easy to organize

Can we count on you to join us for dinner at 7 p.m. June 10 at the Empire Grill in Ottawa? Just call me at (613) 241-1343 before March 15 to make arrangements.

Motivates action — *Makes it easy to accept*

Sincerely,

Genevieve Oestriker

Genevieve Oestriker
Chapter President, CRFA

herself in the receiver's shoes and asking, What kinds of problems might the receiver have with my request? For example, the investment club message writer may guess that the financial planner is a busy person with many engagements. This is his most likely source of resistance. In order to counter this perceived resistance, the writer adds a short section that anticipates and names this resistance and then counters it with a benefit. For example, the letter may read *Even though we understand you have a busy schedule of daily meetings with clients, we believe an hour spent talking to us about trends in retirement planning could lead to a new client base.*

Motivate Action. Finally, no persuasive message is complete without the sender closing by telling the receiver exactly what he or she wants, and when he or she wants it. The trick in this section is to sound confident but not pushy, to motivate the reader to say yes. In essence, a persuasive message should end with a specific request that is confident but not demanding. In the investment club example, the message might end, *The club meets at 1 p.m. on the last Friday of each month, in this case the 31st. Lunch is included. We would be grateful if you responded as soon as possible confirming your acceptance of our invitation. Please call Mr. David Taylor at (613) 686-3704 or reply to this message.*

Convincing Claim and Complaint Messages

Let's say you buy a new car and the transmission repeatedly requires servicing. When you finally get tired of taking it in for repair, you decide to write to the car manufacturer's district office, asking that the company install a new transmission in your car. You know that your request will be resisted. You must convince the manufacturer that replacement, not repair, is needed. Routine claim messages, such as those you wrote in Chapter 5, are straightforward and direct. Persuasive claims, on the other hand, are generally more effective when they are indirect.

Use persuasion when you must change attitudes or produce action.

The organization of an effective persuasive claim or complaint message centres on the closing and the persuasion. First, decide what action you want taken to satisfy the claim. Then, decide how you can prove the worth of your claim. Plan carefully the reasoning you will follow in convincing the reader to take the action you request. If the claim is addressed to a business, the most effective appeals are generally to the organization's pride in its products and its services. Refer to its reputation for integrity and your confidence in it. Show why your claim is valid and why the company will be doing the right thing in granting it. Most organizations are sincere in their efforts to showcase quality products and services that gain consumer respect.

The most successful appeals are to a company's pride in its products and services.

Although claim letters are often complaint letters, try not to be angry. Hostility and emotional threats toward an organization do little to achieve the goal of a claim message. Claims are usually referred to a customer service department. The representative answering the claim probably had nothing to do with the design, production, delivery, or servicing of the product or service. An abusive message may serve only to offend, making it hard for the representative to evaluate the claim rationally.

Claim messages should avoid negative and emotional words and should not attempt to fix blame.

A writing plan for an indirect claim follows the pattern below.

> ### Writing Plan for a Persuasive Claim or Complaint
>
> - **Gain attention** in the opening by paying the receiver a compliment.
> - **Build interest** in the body by explaining and justifying the claim or complaint with convincing reasons and without anger.
> - **Reduce resistance** in the body by subtly suggesting the responsibility of the receiver. Appeal to the receiver's sense of fairness or desire for customer satisfaction.
> - **Motivate action** in the closing by explaining exactly what action you want taken and when.

Observe how the claim letter shown in Figure 6.2 illustrates the preceding suggestions. When Arte International Furnishings in Concord, Ontario, purchased two VoIP systems, it discovered that they would not work without producing an annoying static sound. The company's attempt, via the Internet, to return the VoIP systems has been ignored by the retailer. Despite these difficulties, notice the writer's positive opening, her well-documented claims, and her specific request for action.

Persuading within Organizations

When it comes to persuasion, the power relationships at work determine how we write—whether we choose a direct or indirect approach, for example. We may consider what type and amount of support we include, depending on whether we wish

FIGURE 6.2 Persuasive Claim

ARTE INTERNATIONAL FURNISHINGS
2335 Jane St., Concord, ON L4K 2H8   www.arteinternational.ca

February 16, 2012

Customer Service
ZTech Electronics
387 Brimley Rd., Scarborough, ON
MIE 3V9

Dear ZTech Customer Service:

Your VoIP Expandable Telephone System came highly recommended and seemed to be the answer to increasingly expensive telephone service. Here at Arte International Furnishings we were looking for a way to reduce our local and long-distance telephone charges. The VoIP system was particularly attractive to us because it offered Internet phone service with unlimited calling in North America, including Mexico. Our business in fine furnishings and unique objets d'art requires us to make and receive national and international calls.

Begins with compliment; keeps tone objective, rational, and unemotional

On February 8 we purchased two VoIP systems (SGU #IP7402-2) for our main office here in Concord and for our Designer's Walk showroom. Each system came with two cordless handsets and charging docks. Although we followed all the installation instructions, we discovered that an irritating static sound interfered with every incoming and outgoing telephone call.

Provides identifying data and justifies claim

This static is surprising and disappointing because the product description promised the following: "You will experience excellent signal clarity with Frequency Hopping Digital Spread Spectrum (FHDSS) transmission and a frequency of 5.8GHz. Ninety-five channel auto-search ensures a clear signal."

Explains why claim is valid and suggests responsibility of receiver

On February 10 we filled out a Return Merchandise Authorization form at your Web site. However, we are frustrated that we have had no response. We are confident that a manufacturer with your reputation for reliable products and superior customer service will want to resolve this matter quickly.

Expresses disappointment and appeals to receiver's reputation and customer service

Please authorize the return of these two systems and credit our account for $377.24, which represents the original cost plus taxes and shipping. Attached is a copy of the invoice with our credit card number.

Explains what action to take

Sincerely,

Marilyn Easter

Marilyn Easter
President

Enclosure

Tips for Making Claims

- Begin with a compliment, point of agreement, statement of the problem, or brief review of action you have taken to resolve the problem.
- Provide identifying information.
- Prove that your claim is valid; explain why the receiver is responsible.
- Enclose document copies supporting your claim.
- Appeal to the receiver's fairness, ethical and legal responsibilities, and desire for customer satisfaction.
- Describe your feelings and your disappointment.
- Avoid sounding angry, emotional, or irrational.
- Close by telling exactly what you want done.

to persuade subordinates or superiors. The authority of our audience may also help us decide whether to adopt a formal or informal tone.

Persuading Subordinates. Instructions or directives moving downward from superiors to subordinates usually require little persuasion. Employees expect to be directed in how to perform their jobs. These messages (such as information about procedures, equipment, or customer service) follow the direct pattern, with the purpose immediately stated. However, employees are sometimes asked to perform in a capacity outside their work roles or to accept changes that are not in their best interests (such as pay cuts, job transfers, or reduced benefits). Occasionally, superiors need to address sensitive workplace issues such as smoking-cessation or exercise programs. Similarly, supervisors may want to create buy-in when introducing a healthier cafeteria menu. In these instances, a persuasive memo using the indirect pattern may be most effective.

The goal is not to manipulate employees or to deceive them with trickery. Rather, the goal is to present a strong but honest argument, emphasizing points that are important to the receiver or the organization. In business, honesty is not just the best policy—it is the only policy. People see right through puffery and misrepresentation. For this reason, the indirect pattern is effective only when supported by accurate, honest evidence.

Persuading the Boss. Another form of persuasion within organizations centres on suggestions made by subordinates. Convincing management to adopt a procedure or invest in a product or new equipment generally requires skillful communication. Managers are just as resistant to change as others are. Providing evidence is critical when subordinates submit recommendations to their bosses. "The key to making a request of a superior," advises communication consultant Patricia Buhler, "is to know your needs and have documentation [facts, figures, evidence]." Another important factor is moderation. "Going in and asking for the world off the cuff is most likely going to elicit a negative response," she adds.[2] Equally important is focusing on the receiver's needs. How can you make your suggestion appealing to the receiver?

Obviously, when you set out to persuade someone at work who has more clout than you, do so carefully. Use words like *suggest* and *recommend*, and craft sentences to begin with these words: *It might be a good idea if....* That lets you offer suggestions without threatening the person's authority.

In Figure 6.3 you see a persuasive memo written by Marketing Assistant Monica Cho, who wants her boss to authorize the purchase of a multi-function colour laser copier. She has researched the prices, features, and maintenance costs of the machines. They often serve as copiers, faxes, scanners, and printers and can cost several thousand dollars. Monica has found an outstanding deal offered by a local office supplier. Because Monica knows that her boss, Samuel Neesen, favours "cold, hard facts," she lists current monthly costs for copying at Copy Quick to increase her chances of gaining approval. Finally, she calculates the amortization of the purchase price and monthly costs of running the new colour copier.

Notice that Monica's memo isn't short. A successful persuasive message will typically take more space than a direct message because proving a case requires evidence. In the end, Monica chose to send her memo as an e-mail attachment accompanied by a polite, short e-mail message because she wanted to keep the document format in Microsoft Word intact. She also felt that the message was too long to paste into her e-mail program. Monica's persuasive memo and her e-mail include a subject line that announces the purpose of the message without disclosing the actual request. By delaying the request until she has had a chance to describe the problem and discuss a solution, Monica prevents the reader's premature rejection.

The strength of this persuasive document, though, is in the clear presentation of comparison figures showing how much money the company can save by purchasing a remanufactured copier. Buying a copier that uses low-cost solid ink instead of expensive laser cartridges is another argument in this machine's favour. Although the organization pattern is not obvious, the memo begins with an attention-getter (a frank

Internal persuasive messages present honest arguments detailing specific reader or company benefits.

When selling an idea to management, writers often are successful if they make a strong case for saving or earning money.

FIGURE 6.3 E-Mail Cover Note With Attached Persuasive Memo

To: Samuel Neesen <samuel.neesen@smartmachinetools.ca>
From: Monica Cho <monica.cho@smartmachinetools.ca>
Subject: Saving Time and Money on Copying and Printing ●───── Opens with catchy subject line
Attached: Refurbished Color Copiers.docx (10KB)

Sam,

Attached is a memo that details our potential savings from purchasing a refurbished colour laser copier. After doing some research, I discovered that these sophisticated machines aren't as expensive as one might think.

Please look at my calculations and let me know what you suggest that we do to improve our ●───── Does not reveal recommendation but leaves request for action to the attached memo
in-house production of print matter and reduce both time and cost for external copying.

Monica

Monica Cho ●───── Provides an electronic signature with contact information
Marketing Assistant * Smart Machine Tools, Inc.
2400 King St. N. * Waterloo, ON N3G 5B2
519 466-6001 office / 519-466-7001 fax
monica.cho@smartmachinetools.ca

MEMORANDUM ●───── Use Microsoft Word's memo templates to create a professional-looking memo

Date: April 18, 2012
↓ 1 blank line
To: Samuel Neesen, Vice President
↓ 1 blank line
From: Monica Cho, Marketing ᴍ·ᴄ
↓ 1 blank line
Subject: Saving Time and Money on Copying ●───── Describes topic without revealing request
↓ 1 or 2 blank lines

Summarizes problem ───── We are losing money on our current copy services and wasting the time of employees as well. Because our aging Canon copier is in use constantly and can't handle our growing printing volume, we find it increasingly necessary to send major jobs out to Copy Quick. Moreover, whenever we need colour copies, we can't handle the work ourselves. Just take a look at how much we spend each month for outside copy service:

Uses headings and columns for easy comparison

Copy Costs: Outside Service
10,000 B&W copies/month made at Copy Quick	$700.00
1,000 colour copies/month, $0.25 per copy (avg.)	$250.00
Salary costs for assistants to make 32 trips	$480.00
Total	$1,430.00

Proves credibility of request with facts and figures

To save time and money, I have been considering alternatives. Large-capacity colour laser copiers with multiple features (copy, e-mail, fax, LAN fax, print, scan) are expensive. However, reconditioned copiers with all the features we need are available at attractive prices. From Copy City we can get a fully remanufactured Xerox copier that is guaranteed and provides further savings because solid-colour ink sticks cost a fraction of laser toner cartridges. We could copy and print in colour for roughly the same cost as black and white. After we make an initial payment of $300, our monthly costs would look like this:

Copy Costs: Remanufactured Copier
Paper supplies for 11,000 copies	$160.00
Ink sticks and copy supplies	$100.00
Labour of assistants to make copies	150.00
Monthly financing charge for copier (purchase price of $3,105 – $300 amortized at 10% with 36 payments)	93.74
Total	$503.74

Provides more benefits ───── As you can see, a remanufactured Xerox 8860MFP copier saves us more than $900 per month. For a limited time Copy City is offering a free 15-day trial offer, a free copier stand (a $250 value), free starter supplies, and free delivery and installation. We have office space available, and my staff is eager to add a second machine. ●───── Highlights most important benefit / Counters possible resistance

Makes it easy to grant approval ───── Please call me at Ext. 630 if you have questions. This copier is such a good opportunity that I have prepared a purchase requisition authorizing the agreement with Copy City. With your approval before May 1, we could have our machine by May 10 and start saving time and more than $900 every month. Fast action will also help us take advantage of Copy City's free start-up incentives. ●───── Repeats main benefit with motivation to act quickly description of the problem), builds interest (with easy-to-read facts and figures), provides benefits, and reduces resistance. Notice that the conclusion tells what action is to be taken, makes it easy to respond, and repeats the main benefit to motivate action.

Writing Sales and Marketing Messages

Sales messages use persuasion to promote specific products and services. In our coverage we will be most concerned with sales messages delivered by mail. Many of the concepts you will learn about sales persuasion, however, can be applied to radio and TV advertising, as well as to print, online, and wireless media. Smart companies strive to develop a balanced approach to their overall marketing strategy, including both online e-marketing and direct mail when appropriate.

Traditional direct-mail marketing uses snail mail; electronic marketing uses e-mail, Web documents, and fax.

Toward the end of this chapter, you will learn about preparing online sales messages. However, we will give most emphasis to traditional direct-mail campaigns featuring letters. Sellers feel that "even with all the new media we have available today, a letter remains one of the most powerful ways to make sales, generate leads, boost retail traffic, and solicit donations."[3] Moreover, experts know that most recipients do look at their direct mail; in fact, about 80 percent of such promotional mail pieces are read. Hard-copy sales letters are still recognized as "the most personal, one-to-one form of advertising there is."[4]

Sales letters are generally part of a package that may contain a brochure, price list, illustrations, testimonials, and other persuasive appeals. Professionals who specialize in traditional direct-mail services have made a science of analyzing a market, developing an effective mailing list, studying the product, preparing a sophisticated campaign aimed at a target audience, and motivating the reader to act. You have probably received many direct-mail packages, often called "junk mail."

We are most concerned here with the sales letter: its strategy, organization, and evidence. Because sales letters are usually written by specialists, you may never write one on the job. Why, then, learn how to write a sales letter? In many ways, every letter we create is a form of sales letter. We sell our ideas, our organizations, and ourselves. When you apply for a job, you are both the seller and the product. Learning the techniques of sales writing will help you be more successful in any communication that requires persuasion and promotion. Furthermore, you will recognize sales strategies, thus enabling you to become a more perceptive consumer of ideas, products, and services.

Learning to write sales letters helps you sell yourself and your ideas as well as become a smarter consumer.

Your primary goal in writing a sales message is to get someone to devote a few moments of attention to it.[5] You may be promoting a product, a service, an idea, or yourself. In each case the most effective messages will follow a writing plan. This is the same recipe we studied earlier, but the ingredients are different.

Writing Plan for a Sales Message: AIDA

Professional marketers and salespeople follow the AIDA pattern (attention, interest, desire, and action) when persuading consumers. In addition to telemarketing and personal selling, this pattern works very well for written messages.

- **Opening:** Gain *attention*. Offer something valuable; promise a benefit to the reader; ask a question; or provide a quotation, fact, product feature, testimonial, startling statement, or personalized action setting.
- **Body:** Build *interest*. Describe central selling points and make rational and emotional appeals. Elicit *desire* in the reader and reduce resistance. Use testimonials, money-back guarantees, free samples, performance tests, or other techniques.
- **Closing:** Motivate *action*. Offer a gift, promise an incentive, limit the offer, set a deadline, or guarantee satisfaction.

The AIDA pattern (attention, interest, desire, and action) is used in selling because it is highly effective.

Trying to sell a micro car to Canadians has been a gamble for Daimler AG, manufacturer of the luxurious Mercedes-Benz brand but also maker of the diminutive Smart Fortwo. Prompted by skyrocketing gasoline prices, European and Asian drivers have long embraced small automobiles. But SUV-, truck- and van-loving Canadians? Although the Smart is well engineered and sells briskly in over 30 countries, its promoters have had to work hard to win over Canadians, especially those not living in large urban centres. *What might rural or suburban Canadian car buyers worry about most when they see an automobile such as the Smart? What strategies might reduce their resistance?*

Attention. One of the most critical elements of a sales letter is its opening paragraph, the attention-getter. This opener should be short (one to five lines), honest, relevant, and stimulating. Marketing pros have found that eye-catching typographical arrangements or provocative messages, such as the following, can hook a reader's attention:

- **Offer:** A free trip to Hawaii is just the beginning!
- **Benefit:** Now you can raise your sales income by 50 percent or even more with the proven techniques found in....
- **Open-ended suggestive question:** Do you want your family to be safe?
- **Quotation or proverb:** Necessity is the mother of invention.
- **Compliment:** Life is full of milestones. You have reached one. You deserve....
- **Fact:** A recent *Maclean's* poll says that three quarters of Canadians are not happy with the quality of financial advice they're receiving.
- **Product feature:** Electronic stability control, ABS, and other active and passive safety features explain why the ultra-compact new Smart Fortwo has achieved a four-star crash rating in Quebec.
- **Testimonial:** The most recent J.D. Power survey of "initial quality" shows that BMW ranks at the top of brands with the fewest defects and malfunctions, ahead of Chrysler, Hyundai, Lexus, Porsche, and Toyota.
- **Startling statement:** Let the poor and hungry feed themselves! For just $100 they can.
- **Personalized action setting:** It's 6:30 p.m. and you are working overtime to meet a pressing deadline. Suddenly your copier breaks down. The production of your colour-laser brochures screeches to a halt. How you wish you had purchased the Worry-Free-Anytime service contract from Canon.

Other openings calculated to capture attention might include a solution to a problem, an anecdote, a personalized statement using the receiver's name, or a relevant current event.

Build interest by describing the benefits a product or service offers and by making rational or emotional appeals.

Interest. In this phase of your sales message, you should describe clearly the product or service. Think of this part as a promise that the product or service will deliver to satisfy the audience's needs. In simple language, emphasize the central selling points that you identified during your prewriting analysis. Those selling points can be developed using rational or emotional appeals.

Rational appeals are associated with reason and intellect. They translate selling points into references to making or saving money, increasing efficiency, or making the best use of resources. In general, rational appeals are appropriate when a product is expensive, long lasting, or important to health, security, and financial success. Emotional appeals relate to status, ego, and sensual feelings. Appealing to the emotions is sometimes effective when a product is inexpensive, short-lived, or nonessential. Many clever sales messages, however, combine emotional and rational strategies for a dual appeal. Consider these examples:

Rational Appeal

You can buy the things you need and want, pay household bills, pay off higher-cost loans and credit cards—as soon as you are approved and your Credit-Line account is opened.

Emotional Appeal

Leave the urban bustle behind and escape to sun-soaked Bermuda! To recharge your batteries with an injection of sun and surf, all you need is your bathing suit, a little suntan lotion, and your Credit-Line card.

Dual Appeal

New Credit-Line cardholders are immediately eligible for a $100 travel certificate and additional discounts at fun-filled resorts. Save up to 40 percent while lying on a beach in picturesque, sun-soaked Bermuda, the year-round resort island.

A physical description of your product is not enough, however. Experience salespeople know that no matter how well you know your product, no one is persuaded by cold, hard facts alone. In the end, "People buy because of the product benefits."[6] Your job is to translate those cold facts into warm feelings and reader benefits. Let's say a sales letter promotes a hand cream made with Vitamin A and aloe and cocoa butter extracts. Those facts become *Nature's hand helpers—including soothing aloe and cocoa extracts, and firming Vitamin A—form invisible gloves that protect your sensitive skin against the hardships of work, harsh detergents, and constant environmental assaults.*

Desire. The goal at this stage in the sales message is to elicit desire in the reader and to overcome resistance. To make the audience want the product or service and to anticipate objections, focus strongly on reader benefits. Here the promises of the attention and interest sections are covered in great detail. Marketing pros use a number of techniques to elicit desire in their audience and to overcome resistance.

- **Testimonials:** *Thanks to your online selling workshop, I was able to increase the number of my sales leads from 3 per month to 12 per week!*—Carlton Strong, Summerside, P.E.I.
- **Names of satisfied users (with permission, of course):** Enclosed is a partial list of private pilots who enthusiastically subscribe to our service.
- **Money-back guarantee or warranty:** We offer the longest warranties in the business—all parts and service on-site for two years!
- **Free trial or sample:** We are so confident that you will like our new accounting program that we want you to try it absolutely free.
- **Performance tests, polls, or awards:** Our Audi R8 supercar won World Design Car of the Year and World Performance Car of the Year awards—the first time a single car has received trophies in more than one category.

Rational appeals focus on making or saving money, increasing efficiency, or making good use of resources.

Emotional appeals focus on status, ego, and sensual feelings.

In addition, you need to anticipate objections and questions the receiver may have. When possible, translate these objections into selling points (*If you are worried about training your staff members on the new software, remember that our offer includes $1,000 of on-site, one-on-one instruction*). Be sure, of course, that your claims are accurate and do not stretch the truth.

When price is an obstacle, consider these suggestions:

- Delay mentioning price until after you have created a desire for the product.
- Show the price in small units, such as the price per issue of a magazine.
- Demonstrate how the reader saves money by, for instance, subscribing for two or three years.
- Compare your prices with those of a competitor.
- If applicable, offer advantageous financing terms.

Techniques for motivating action include offering a gift or incentive, limiting an offer, and guaranteeing satisfaction.

Action. All the effort put into a sales message is wasted if the reader fails to act. To make it easy for readers to act, you can provide a reply card, a stamped and pre-addressed envelope, a toll-free telephone number, a convenient Web address, or a promise of a follow-up call. Because readers often need an extra push, consider including additional motivators, such as the following:

- **Offer a gift:** You will receive a free iPod nano with the purchase of any new car.
- **Promise an incentive:** With every new, paid subscription, we will plant a tree in one of Canada's pollution-busting boreal forests.
- **Limit the offer:** Only the first 100 customers receive free cheques.
- **Set a deadline:** You must act before June 1 to get these low prices.
- **Guarantee satisfaction:** We will return your full payment if you are not entirely satisfied—no questions asked.

The final paragraph of the sales letter carries the call to action. This is where you tell readers what you want done and give them reasons for doing it. Most sales letters also include postscripts because they make irresistible reading. Even readers who might skim over or bypass paragraphs are drawn to a P.S. Therefore, use a postscript to reveal your strongest motivator, to add a special inducement for a quick response, or to re-emphasize a central selling point.

Putting It All Together

Sales letters are a preferred marketing medium because they can be personalized, directed to target audiences, and filled with a more complete message than other advertising media. However, direct mail is expensive. That is why the total sales message is crafted so painstakingly.

Figure 6.4 shows a sales letter addressed to a target group of small-business owners. To sell the new magazine *Small Business Canada*, the letter incorporates all four components of an effective persuasive message. Notice that the personalized action-setting opener places the reader in a familiar situation (getting into an elevator) and draws an analogy between failing to reach the top floor and failing to achieve a business goal.

The writer develops a rational central selling point (a magazine that provides valuable information for a growing small business) and repeats this selling point in all the components of the letter. Notice, too, how a testimonial from a small-business executive lends support to the sales message, and how the closing pushes for action. Because the price of the magazine is not a selling feature, it is mentioned only on the reply card. This sales letter saves its strongest motivator—a free booklet—for the high-impact P.S. line.

FIGURE 6.4 Sales Letter

small business Canada

29 Sicamous Way, Aldergrove, BC V4W 3N5

April 15, 2012

Mr. Moe Prakesh
2300 Leslie St.
Thornhill, ON L2X 3E5

Dear Mr. Prakesh:

Puts reader into action setting

You walk into the elevator and push the button for the top floor. The elevator glides upward. You step back and relax.

Gains attention

But the elevator never reaches the top. A glitch in its electronics prevents it from processing the information it needs to take you to your destination.

Suggests analogy

Do you see a similarity between your growing company and this elevator? You are aiming for the top, but a lack of information halts your progress. Now you can put your company into gear and propel it toward success with a new publication—*Small Business Canada*.

Builds interest

Emphasizes central selling point

This first-of-its-kind magazine brings you marketing tips, hard-headed business pointers, opportunities, and inspiration. This is the kind of current information you need today to be where you want to be tomorrow. One executive wrote:

Uses testimonial for credibility

As president of a small manufacturing company, I read several top business publications, but I get my "bread and butter" from *Small Business Canada*. I'm not interested in a lot of "pie in the sky" and theory. I find practical problems and how to solve them in *SBC*.

—Mitchell M. Perry, Ste-Anne-de Bellevue, QC

Elicits desire and counters resistance

Mr. Perry's words are the best recommendation I can offer you to try *SBC*. In less time than you might spend on an average business lunch, you can learn the latest in management, operations, finance, taxes, business law, compensation, and advertising.

Repeats central sales pitch in last sentence

To evaluate *Small Business Canada* without cost or obligation, let me send you a free issue. Just initial and return the enclosed card to start receiving a wealth of practical information that could keep your company travelling upward to its goal.

Motivates action

Cordially,

Cheryl Owings

Cheryl Owings
Vice President, Circulation

Spotlights free offer in P.S. to prompt immediate reply

P. S. Act before May 15 and I will send you our valuable booklet *Managing for Success*, revealing more than 100 secrets for helping small businesses grow.

Writing and Designing Online Sales Messages

To make the best use of limited advertising dollars while reaching a great number of potential customers, many businesses are turning to the Internet and to e-mail marketing campaigns in particular. Much like traditional direct mail, e-mail marketing can attract new customers, keep existing ones, encourage future sales, cross-sell, and cut costs. As consumers become more comfortable and secure with online purchases, they will receive more e-mail sales messages.

Selling by E-Mail

If your organization requires an online sales message, try using the following techniques gleaned from the best-performing e-mails.

Communicate only with those who have given permission! By sending messages only to "opt-in" folks, you greatly increase your "open rate"—those e-mail messages that will be opened. E-mail users detest spam. However, receivers are surprisingly receptive to offers tailored specifically for them. Remember that today's customer is somebody—not anybody.

Today's promotional e-mail often comes with colourful and eye-catching graphics and a minimum of text. To allow for embedded images, sound, and even video, the e-mail is coded in HTML and can be viewed in an e-mail program or an Internet browser. Software programs make it easy to create e-newsletters for e-mail distribution. Figure 6.5 shows one such promotional message in HTML format by

FIGURE 6.5 E-Mail Sales Message to Opt-In Recipients

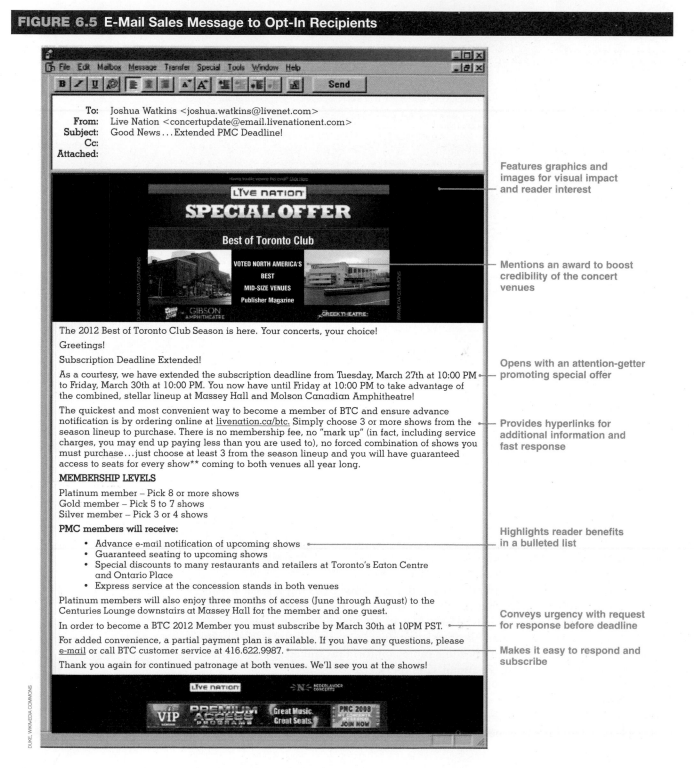

live music search engine Live Nation. It was sent by e-mail to customers who had bought tickets from Live Nation. They had to create an account and sign up to receive e-newsletters and periodic promotions like this one.

The principles you have learned to apply to traditional sales messages also work with electronic promotional tools. However, some fundamental differences are obvious when you study Figure 6.5. Online sales messages are much shorter than direct mail, feature colourful graphics, and occasionally even have sound or video clips. They offer a richer experience to readers who can click hyperlinks at will to access content that interests them. When such messages are sent out as ads or periodic e-newsletters, they may not have salutations or closings. Rather, they may resemble Web pages.

Here are a few guidelines that will help you create effective online sales messages:

- **Craft a catchy subject line.** Offer discounts or premiums: *Spring Sale: Buy now and save 20 percent!* Promise solutions to everyday work-related problems. Highlight hot new industry topics. Invite readers to scan a top-ten list of items such as issues, trends, or people.
- **Keep the main information "above the fold."** E-mail messages should be top heavy. Primary points should appear early in the message so that they capture the reader's attention.
- **Make the message short, conversational, and focused.** Because on-screen text is taxing to read, be brief. Focus on one or two central selling points only.
- **Convey urgency.** Top-performing e-mail messages state an offer deadline or demonstrate why the state of the industry demands action on the reader's part. Good messages also tie the product to relevant current events.
- **Sprinkle testimonials throughout the copy.** Consumers' own words are the best sales copy. These comments can serve as call-outs or be integrated into the copy.
- **Provide a means for opting out.** It is polite and a good business tactic to include a statement that tells receivers how to be removed from the sender's mailing database.

Using Blogs, Wikis, and Other New Media to Convey Company and Product Information

Businesses increasingly look to blogs, wikis, social media, and RSS (Really Simple Syndication) feeds to convey their persuasive and promotional messages to partner firms and customers. These new tools can also be useful internally when communicating with employees.

Blogs. In the right hands, blogs can be powerful marketing tools. Information technology giant Hewlett-Packard invites guest bloggers to contribute to its site as advisors to small businesses, for example. Executives, HP employees, and outside experts discuss a wide range of technology- and company-related topics. Although not overtly pushing a marketing message, ultimately HP wants to generate goodwill; hence, the blogs serve as a public relations tool.[7] Nearly half of the CEOs questioned in one survey said they believe blogs are useful for external public relations, and 59 percent said they find blogs valuable for internal communication.[8] Many companies now use blogs to subtly market their products and develop a brand image.

Wikis. Wikis generally facilitate collaboration inside organizations, but they also do so between companies, thus generating goodwill. A wiki contains digital information available on a Web portal or on a company's protected intranet where visitors can add or edit content. One big advantage of wikis is the ease of information and file sharing. Perhaps the best-known wiki is the online encyclopedia Wikipedia.

In business, wiki users can quickly document and publish a complex process to a group of recipients. Ziba Design of Portland, Oregon, launched what it calls "virtual studios," popular online meeting spots where the agency and its clients share files, exchange design ideas, and post news.[9] Ziba Design is providing a valuable service to its customers and, in turn, is learning about their needs. You will find out more about wikis as collaboration tools in Chapter 10.

RSS (Really Simple Syndication). RSS is yet another tool for keeping customers and business partners up-to-date. Many companies now offer RSS feeds, a format for distributing news or information about recent changes on their Web sites, in wikis, or in blogs. Recipients subscribe to content they want using RSS reader software. Alternatively, they receive news items or articles in their e-mail.[10] The RSS feeds help users keep up with their favourite Web magazines, Web sites, and blogs. As a promotional tool, this medium can create interest in a company and its products.

Podcasting. Podcasting is emerging as an important Internet marketing tool. Business podcasts are content-rich audio or video files featuring company representatives, business experts, or products and services. They can be distributed by RSS or downloaded from company Web sites and played back on a computer or an MP3 player.

Social Media. Social media such as Twitter and Facebook are a very important part of marketing today. As Tamar Weinberg, author of *The New Community Rules: Marketing on the Social Web,* has shown, Twitter, for example, has been used successfully by both large and small companies to increase sales and to perform other functions such as crisis management.[11] Clearly, business communicators today—especially those who work in publicity, advertising, marketing, and sales— have to become experts at the relatively new communication genres such as social media, whose interfaces are radically different than that of the traditional letter: more flexible, colourful, touchable, changeable, and so on.

Summing Up and Looking Forward

The ability to persuade is a powerful and versatile communication tool. In this chapter you learned to apply the indirect strategy in writing claim letters, making favour requests, writing persuasive suggestions within organizations, and writing sales letters. You also learned basic techniques for developing successful online sales messages. The techniques suggested here will be useful in many other contexts beyond the writing of these business documents. You will find that logical organization of arguments is also extremely effective in expressing ideas orally or any time you must overcome resistance to change.

Not all business messages are strictly persuasive. Occasionally, you must deny requests and deliver bad news. In the next chapter you will learn to use the indirect strategy in conveying negative news.

Critical Thinking

1. Why is the ability to persuade a significant trait in both business and personal relations?

2. The organization of a successful persuasive claim centres on the reasons and the closing. Why?

3. Why not just write all favour requests directly? Discuss.

4. In a world of depleted forests and overflowing landfills, why does junk mail still thrive? Is it ethical? Should something be done to curb it?

5. Some individuals will never write a sales letter. Why is it nevertheless important for them to learn the techniques for doing so?

Chapter Review

1. What is the difference between direct and indirect benefits to individuals we may want to persuade?

2. Explain how you would decide whether to use the direct pattern or the indirect pattern.

3. List eight tips for making claims and complaints.

4. What are the most important considerations when trying to persuade people within your organization?

5. List at least ten ways to gain a reader's attention in the opening of a sales letter

6. Name six writing techniques that reduce resistance in a sales message.

7. Name five techniques for motivating action in the closing of a sales message.

8. Describe the main advantages of using business podcasts, blogs, wikis, and social media.

9. What techniques do writers of successful online sales messages use?

Strategies

For each of the following situations, check the appropriate writing strategy.

Direct Strategy	Indirect Strategy	
_____	_____	1. An invitation to a nationally known information technology expert to discuss the latest technology trends with the campus community
_____	_____	2. An announcement that must convince employees to stop smoking, start exercising, and opt for a healthy diet to lower health care expenses and reduce absenteeism
_____	_____	3. A request to another company for verification of employment regarding a job applicant
_____	_____	4. A letter to a cleaning service demanding a refund for sealing a dirty tiled floor and damaging a fresh paint job
_____	_____	5. A request for information about a wireless office network
_____	_____	6. A letter to a grocery store requesting permission to display posters advertising a school fundraising car wash
_____	_____	7. A request for a refund of the cost of a computer program that does not perform the functions it was expected to perform
_____	_____	8. A request for correction of a routine billing error on your company credit card
_____	_____	9. An invitation to your boss or business partner to join you for dinner
_____	_____	10. A memo to employees describing the schedule and menu selections of a new mobile catering service

Activities and Cases

6.1 Persuasive Claim: Exchanging Copiers

Analyze the following poorly written persuasive claim and list at least five major weaknesses. Outline an appropriate writing plan for a persuasive claim. After class discussion, your instructor may ask you to rewrite this message, rectifying its weaknesses. Address your letter to International Copy Services, 1506 Fourth Street S.W., Calgary, AB T7L 2E3. Assume that you are writing on your company's letterhead. Use your word processing software's professional letter template.

Three months ago we purchased four of your Regal Model SP-270F photocopiers, and we've had nothing but trouble ever since.

Our salesperson, Jason Woo, assured us that the SP-270F could easily handle our volume of 3,000 copies a day. This seemed strange since the sales brochure said that the SP-270F was meant for 500 copies a day. But we believed Mr. Woo. Big mistake! Our four SP-270F copiers are down constantly; we can't go on like this. Because they're still under warranty, they eventually get repaired. But we're losing considerable business in downtime.

Your Mr. Woo has been less than helpful, so I telephoned the district manager, Heidi Berger. I suggested that we trade in our SP-270F copiers (which we got for $2500 each) for two S-55 models (at $13,500 each). However, Ms. Berger said she would have to charge 50 percent depreciation on our SP-270F copiers. What a rip-off! I think that 20 percent depreciation is more reasonable since we've had the machines only three months. Ms. Berger said she would get back to me, and I haven't heard from her since.

I'm writing to your headquarters because I have no faith in either Mr. Woo or Ms. Berger, and I need action on these machines. If you understood anything about business, you would see what a sweet deal I'm offering you. I'm willing to stick with your company and purchase a more expensive model—but I can't take such a loss on the SP-270F copiers. The SP-270F copiers are relatively new; you should be able to sell them with no trouble. And think of all the money you'll save by not having your repair technicians making constant trips to service our SP-270F copiers! Please let me hear from you immediately.

1. List at least five faults.
2. Outline a writing plan for a persuasive request.
   Opening:
   Body:
   Closing:

6.2 Favour Request: Inviting a Speaker
Analyze the following poorly written invitation. List its weaknesses and outline a writing strategy. If your instructor directs, revise it.

Dear Dr. Schulz:

Because you're a local Nanaimo author, we thought it might not be too much trouble for you to speak at our Canadian Association of Independent Management banquet May 5. Some of us business students here at Glenbow Valley College admired your book *Beyond Race and Gender*, which appeared last spring and became such a hit across the country. One of our instructors said you were now the country's management guru. What exactly did you mean when you said that Canada is the "Mulligan stew" of the Americas?

Because we have no funds for honoraria, we have to rely on local speakers. Dr. Lester Pierfont and Deputy Mayor Shirley Slye were speakers in the past. Our banquets usually begin at 6:30 with a social hour, followed by dinner at 7:30 and the speaker from 8:30 until 9:00 or 9:15. We can arrange transportation for you and your wife if you need it.

We realize that you must be very busy, but we hope you'll agree. Please let our advisor, Duncan Rankin, have the favour of an early response.

1. List at least five weaknesses.
2. Outline a writing plan for a favour request.
   Opening:
   Body:
   Closing:

6.3 Persuasive Suggestion: Asking for Tuition Reimbursement
Analyze the poorly written e-mail in Figure 6.6. List its weaknesses. If your instructor directs, revise it.

1. List at least five weaknesses in this e-mail.
2. Outline a writing plan for this e-mail.
   Opening:
   Body:
   Closing:

FIGURE 6.6 Tuition Help

Tuition Help

File Edit Mailbox Message Transfer Special Tools Window Help

B / U | | | | | | | | | | | **Send**

To: Jeanette Fillion   June 5, 2012
From: Tony Keough
Subject: Tuition Help
Cc:
Bcc:
Attached:

Mark Hollett and I, along with other Riverfront employees, have been eager to return to college, but we can't afford the costs of tuition and books.

Many of us were forced to go to work before we could complete our university degrees. We know that the continuing education divisions of some universities provide good courses that we could take at night. Mark and I—and we think many other employees as well—would like to enroll in these courses. Would Riverfront be interested in helping us with a tuition-reimbursement program?

We've heard about other local companies (Worldwide Trust, Dominion Securities, Mid Mountain Group, and others) that offer reimbursement for fees and books when employees complete approved courses with a C or higher. Mark and I have collected information, including a newspaper clipping that we're enclosing. Surveys show that tuition-reimbursement programs help improve employee morale and loyalty. They also result in higher productivity because employees develop improved skills.

We'd like a chance to talk over this worthwhile employee program with you at your convenience.

6.4 Sales Letter: Analyzing the Pitch

Read the following sales letter and analyze its effectiveness by answering the questions listed after the letter.

Dear Friend of University of Prince Edward Island,

You are part of a special group of alumni—doctors, lawyers, bankers, managers, professors— who have a wide variety of credit cards available to them. For this reason I am inviting you to choose the superior benefits of the UPEI *Platinum Preferred* Visa credit card.

The UPEI Alumni Association has planned, in association with Atlantic Bank, a superior credit card with excellent benefits, personalized customer care, and best of all, no annual fee.

Each purchase made with your UPEI *Platinum Preferred* Visa card leads directly to a contribution to the UPEI Alumni Association. This extra benefit costs nothing, but allows the Association to continue its vital work on campus and in the community.

Yours sincerely,

Margaret Simpson
Director of Alumni Relations
UPEI Alumni Association

a. What technique captures the reader's attention in the opening? Is it effective?
b. What are the central selling points? *No annual fee, personal cust care, ev benefits*
c. Does the letter use rational, emotional, or a combination of appeals? Explain. *lacking*

d. What technique builds interest in the product? Are benefits obvious?

e. How is price handled? *Mentioned in body but not emphasized for max benefit*

f. Does the letter anticipate reader resistance and offer counterarguments? *None*

g. What action is the reader to take? How is the action made easy? *Nothing*

Your Task. Revise the above letter, adding any improvements you think necessary based on your answers to the above questions.

6.5 Persuasive Claim: Excessive Legal Fees

You are the business manager for McConnell's, a producer of gourmet ice cream. McConnell's has 12 ice-cream shops in the Toronto area and a reputation for excellent ice cream. Your firm was approached by an independent ice-cream vendor who wanted to use McConnell's name and recipes for ice cream to be distributed through grocery stores and drugstores. As business manager you worked with a law firm, Peretine, Valcon, and Associates, to draw up contracts regarding the use of McConnell's name and quality standards for the product.

When you received the bill from Louis Peretine, you couldn't believe it. The bill itemized 38 hours of attorney preparation, at $300 per hour, and 55 hours of paralegal assistance, at $75 per hour. The bill also showed $415 for telephone calls, which might be accurate because Mr. Peretine had to converse with McConnell's owners, who were living in Ireland at the time. However, you doubt that an experienced attorney would require 38 hours to draw up the contracts in question.

Perhaps some error was made in calculating the total hours. Moreover, you have checked with other businesses and found that excellent legal advice can be obtained for $200 per hour. McConnell's would like to continue using the services of Peretine, Valcon, and Associates for future legal business. Such future business is unlikely if an adjustment is not made on this bill.

Your Task. Write a persuasive request to Louis Peretine, Legal Counsel, Peretine, Valcon, and Associates, 2690 Whyte Avenue, Toronto, ON M2N 2E6.

TEAM

6.6 Persuasive E-Mail: Scheduling Meetings More Strategically

The following message, with names changed, was actually sent.

Your Task. Based on what you have learned in this chapter, improve this e-mail. Expect the staff to be somewhat resistant because they have never before had meeting restrictions.

From: Dina Waterman <dwaterman@promosell.ca>
To: All Managers
Cc:
Subject: Scheduling Meetings

Please be reminded that travel in the greater Vancouver area is time consuming. In the future we are asking that you set up meetings that

1. Are of critical importance

2. Consider travel time for the participants

3. Consider phone conferences (or video or e-mail) in lieu of face-to-face meetings

4. Meetings should be at the location where most of the participants work and at the most opportune travel times

5. Travelling together is another way to save time and resources.

We all have our traffic horror stories. A recent one is that a certain manager was asked to attend a one-hour meeting in Ladner. This required one hour of travel in advance of the meeting, one hour for the meeting, and two and a half hours of travel through Vancouver afterward. This meeting was scheduled for 4 p.m. Total time consumed by the manager for the one-hour meeting was four and a half hours.

Thank you for your consideration.

6.7 Persuasive Internal E-Mail Request: Convincing Your Boss to Blog

You have just read Steve Rubel's *Micro Persuasion* blog, in which he cites an interesting study of chief executives and blogging.[12] It turns out that a majority of CEOs believe blogs to be useful for internal (59 percent) and external communication (47 percent). However, only 7 percent of the CEOs interviewed actually blog, although 18 percent expect to host a company blog within two years.

Your boss, Simon Dawkins, is a technophobe who is slow in adopting the latest information technology. You know that it will be a difficult sell, but you believe that corporate blogging is an opportunity not to be missed.

Your Task. Decide what industry your company is part of, then write a persuasive e-mail message to Simon Dawkins attempting to convince him that blogging is a useful public-relations and internal communication tool and that he or someone he officially designates should start a company blog. Anticipate Dawkins' fears. Naturally, a blogger has to be prepared even for unflattering comments. If your instructor directs, visit the blogs of companies such as Google (**http://googleblog.blogspot.com/**), Microsoft (**http://blogs.msdn.com/**), or Rogers (**http://redboard.rogers.com/**). You can search for company blogs in Google. Select the **More** tab on top of the screen and click **Blogs**.

6.8 Persuasive Favour Request: Helping Out a Worthy Charity

You have been a supporter of the World Partnership Walk since you were 17 years old. Now, five years later, you have graduated from college and are working as the office manager for a small Ottawa-based law firm, Fraser, Ahmet, and Grandpre. Last year, you were able to persuade the three partners in the firm to become local corporate sponsors for the Ottawa World Partnership Walk. This year, you'd like to be more ambitious and recruit other local law firms to make a corporate donation. This year's walk happens at a busy time: soon after the annual Terry Fox Run and just before the annual AIDS Walk Ottawa. Still, you believe the World Partnership Walk is worthy of support by area law firms.

Your Task. Write a letter that you will personalize and send to 15 small and medium-sized Ottawa-area law firms requesting that they become corporate sponsors for this year's World Partnership Walk.

Related Web site: For more information on the World Partnership Walk, go to http://www.worldpartnershipwalk.com.

WEB ## 6.9 Persuasive E-Mail: Overusing Overnight Shipments

As office manager of Cambridge Software, write a memo persuading technicians, engineers, programmers, and other employees to reduce the number of overnight or second-day mail shipments. Your Federal Express, Canada Post, and other shipping bills have been higher than expected, and you feel that staff members are overusing these services.

Encourage employees to send messages by e-mail. Sending an e-mail costs almost nothing, whether it's sent locally or halfway around the world. Storing larger documents on secure FTP sites is another easy way to share documents. Attaching smaller documents—whether as Word files or as PDF documents—is replacing faxing and couriering in today's business world. Obviously, there's a huge difference between the "almost nothing" cost of an e-mail and potentially hundreds of dollars for overnight courier service. If employees have to send a package, they should, whenever possible, obtain the courier service account number of the recipient and use it for charging the shipment.

Your Task. Ask employees to decide whether receivers are really going to mind receiving an e-mail document they have to read on screen or print out. You'd like to reduce overnight delivery services voluntarily by 50 percent over the next two months. Unless a sizable reduction occurs, there may be significant consequences (e.g., suspension of courier privileges). Address your e-mail to all employees.

6.10 Persuasive Letter or E-Mail: Persuading Your Member of Parliament

Assume you are upset about an issue of national importance, and you want your MP to know your position. Choose an issue about which you feel strongly: student loans, pension reform, human rights in other countries, environmental protection, the federal debt, employment insurance, taxation of common-law couples, the federal deficit, or some other area regulated by the federal government. Then write to your MP explaining your views.

For best results, consider these tips: (1) Use the proper form of address, such *as The Honourable John Smith*, *Dear Minister Smith* if you are writing to a cabinet minister, and *The*

Honourable Joan Doe, *Dear Ms. Doe* if you are writing to an MP. (See http://www.pch.gc.ca/ pgm/ceem-cced/prtcl/address2-eng.cfm for a full discussion of correct forms of address.) (2) Identify yourself as a member of his or her riding. (3) Immediately state your position (*I urge you to support/oppose ... because*). (4) Present facts and illustrations and how they affect you personally. If legislation were enacted, how would you or your organization be better off or worse off? Avoid generalities. (5) Offer to provide further information. (6) Keep the letter polite, constructive, and brief.

Your Task. Obtain your MP's address. Use a search term such as *"Canadian government"* (enclosing your search term in quotation marks ensures that the words will be searched as a unit). Decide whether you should write an e-mail or a letter. Remember that although e-mail messages are fast they don't carry as much influence as personal letters.

6.11 Sales Letter: Fitness at the Local Brewery

Health research shows that 33 percent of Canadians between age 20 and 64 are overweight.[13] Long-term health risks could be reduced if overweight employees shed their excess weight.

As a sales representative for Fitness Associates, you think your fitness equipment and programs could be instrumental in helping people lose weight. With regular exercise at an on-site fitness centre, employees lose weight and improve overall health. As employee health improves, absenteeism is reduced and overall productivity increases. And employees love working out before or after work. They make the routine part of their work day, and they often have work buddies who share their fitness regimen.

Though many companies resist spending money to save money, fitness centres need not be large or expensive to be effective. Studies show that moderately sized centres coupled with motivational and training programs yield the greatest success. For just $30,000, Fitness Associates will provide exercise equipment including stationary bikes, weight machines, and treadmills. Their fitness experts will design a fitness room, set up the fitness equipment, and design appropriate programs. Best of all, the one-time cost is usually offset by cost savings within one year of centre installation. For additional fees, FA can also provide fitness consultants for employee fitness assessments. FA specialists will also train employees on proper use of equipment, and they will clean and manage the facility—for an extra charge, of course.

Your Task. Write a sales letter to Ms. Kathleen Stewart, Human Resources VP, Good Times Brewing Company, 3939 Brewery Row, Moose Jaw, SK S6H 0V9. Assume you are writing on company letterhead. Ask for an appointment to meet with her. Send her a brochure detailing the products and services that Fitness Associates provides. As an incentive, offer a free fitness assessment for all employees if Good Times Brewing installs a fitness facility by December 1.

6.12 Sales Letter: Persuading an Old Friend to Switch to ACCuracy Plus

You are the owner of Software Solutions, a Prince George, B.C.–based software consultancy. Recently, at a major industry trade show in Chicago, you were introduced to a new accounting software package, ACCuracy Plus. Quickly realizing its merits, you signed a deal with the American manufacturer to become the exclusive sales agent for the software in Canada, west of Ontario. Now that you own the right to sell the software, you have to make some sales. One day, while brainstorming possible clients, you remember your old friend from college, Tim Thom. While reading the newspaper last year you found out that Tim Thom has been promoted to VP Operations for Health & Co., a Victoria-based national retail chain selling vitamins, supplements, and natural foods. Even though you haven't seen or spoken to Tim in over eight years, you used to be good friends, and you believe a persuasive sales letter about your new software will not go unanswered. The question is, should you make a strong pitch for a sale, or should you just pitch for a get-together over lunch?

Your Task. Write a persuasive sales letter to Tim Thom, where you try to interest him in switching from his current accounting software to ACCuracy Plus.

Related Web sites: To build interest in ACCuracy Plus, browse the Internet for the features of its competitors such as AccPac (http://www.accpac.com) and Dynamics GP (http://www.microsoft.com/dynamics/gp/default.mspx). Be careful not to plagiarize when you write your letter.

6.13 New Media Alumni Campaign

Your college or university has traditionally been very conservative in contacting its alumni about donations. For example, there is a paper-based alumni magazine that is mailed out three times a year to all alumni. Also, there is a paper-based letter mailer that goes out once a year to alumni asking them to donate to the scholarship and building funds. Recognizing that social media, blogs, and other new media are revolutionizing the way people get their information, entertain themselves, and plan their lives, the new alumni director at your institution decides that something has to change.

Your Task. As the new alumni coordinator, examine the alumni websites of various post-secondary institutions, but not your own, looking for evidence of new media presence/use. Then, create a persuasive online sales campaign (which may include a traditional Web page, or a social media page, or a combination of the two) whose goal is to persuade recent alumni (who've graduated in the past five years) to stay connected with your institution and to make a regular donation. What can you offer these people in return for their time and money?

WEB

Related Web Site: Visit http://www.alumnifutures.com/2011/03/chiclets.html for a critique of the omnipresent links to social media on alumni Web sites.

CRITICAL THINKING

6.14 Claim Request: Not-So-Automatic Refund

You work for Signet Hotels, a large chain of hotels and resort properties. A recent business trip took you to Argentina, where you had two days off and a chance to do a lot of shopping. The Argentine peso is currently trading at one third the value of the Canadian dollar, so everything you purchased was a third of the cost of buying it in Canada. You bought some souvenirs for your family, some clothing for yourself (including a leather jacket), and an anniversary gift for your partner: an expensive silver bowl. In total, your purchases came to about 1,000 Argentine pesos, or $300 Canadian. At three of the stores in which you shopped, you were offered the opportunity for rebate of your sales tax, through a company called Global Blue Tax Free. In essence, if you fill out some paperwork and save your receipts, once you get to the airport, Global is supposed to give you your tax back. You figure you'll get back about 200 pesos or $70 Canadian. When you get to the airport in Buenos Aires, everything goes smoothly. Global asks if you'd like your refund issued via cheque or directly onto your credit card. You choose the credit card option. Back in Canada, you wait for two months without receiving the refund on your credit card statement.

Your Task. Write a short claim request e-mail to the Manager of Refunds at Global Blue Tax Free.

Related Web site: http://www.global-blue.com

6.15 Indirect Persuasive Request

Tommy Tuna's is the hottest restaurant in town. It's busy every night of the week and reservations are highly recommended. The head chef at Tommy Tuna's is very popular and many articles have been written about her in the local newspaper. The restaurant serves innovative and creative seafood dishes that are beautifully presented. It's also expensive: entrees start at $25 and the average bill for two people is more than $100. To celebrate your parents' twenty-fifth wedding anniversary, you decided to take them to Tommy Tuna's. You discussed it with your brother and decided that you would share the cost of their meal as an anniversary present to them. Knowing how busy this restaurant is, you called several weeks in advance and made a reservation for four people. You knew that this would be a very expensive night, but you were eager to do something special for your parents.

Your group arrived at Tommy Tuna's five minutes early for your 7 p.m. reservation. You were surprised that you were kept waiting more than 20 minutes for a table. Nonetheless, everyone was in a good mood and your parents were thrilled that you had organized this evening for them. Unfortunately, when the hostess finally led you to your table, you were disappointed to find that you were seated in the back near the washroom. Not only that, the hostess had to move two tables together—one round one and one square one—to accommodate your group. The different shapes of the tables made the seating arrangements awkward and left little room for everyone to fit comfortably. You mentioned this to the hostess but she didn't offer to move you to another table and she made no effort to improve the situation. In fact, she was a bit rude and said that there was a lineup of people at the door who would be more than willing to take your table! You wanted to speak to the manager but your mother insisted that the table was fine and encouraged everyone to sit down and enjoy the evening. Not wanting to upset her, you took your place at the table.

Although the table was very crowded and it wasn't in the best location, your family had a terrific dinner. Your parents were very happy and everyone had a great evening. Dinner for the four of you came to $325, and you and your brother split the cost of the bill. However, you can't help but think about the way you were treated at the beginning of the evening. You decide to write a letter to the general manager to let him know of your experience.

Your Task. Decide what action you want taken by the restaurant, then write a persuasive request letter to Captain Tommy, General Manager, Tommy Tuna's, 4523 Trout Trail, Ottawa, ON K2F 3VH.

Grammar/Mechanics Review—6

The following sentences contain errors in grammar, punctuation, capitalization, number style, usage, and spelling. Below each sentence write a corrected version.

1. Not one of the job candidates who we interviewed last week have written a thank-you message.
2. You would of laughed if you could of saw Carlos and I fixing the bosses printer.
3. Either the Marketing Director or the Sales Manager have to approve our departments budget for the next fiscal year.
4. Looking into the mirror of his new toyota prius Glenn slipped on his ray-ban sunglasses, and thought that he looked very cool.
5. Most wifes are listed as beneficiarys on insurance policys of their husbands'.
6. The CEO hisself is willing to support whomever we nominate as our represenative.
7. Our salesperson told Jacqueline and I that a wide range of services are available if we sign up.
8. Somebody on the boys team left their shoes on the bus.
9. $1,600 are more than I can afford to pay for rent although I do like that 3 bedroom apartment.
10. Flying over the rain forests of indonesia the trees formed a menacing, green carpet.
11. 4 candidates submitted applications, however only one had the neccessary skills.
12. Our Manager cautioned Samuel and I not to take the CEOs angry remarks personal.
13. Every employee who completes the course satisfactory, are entitled to have their fees reimbursed.
14. The following benefits are available to cardholders; travel planning, free checking account and low monthly interest.
15. Tornado warnings has been posted for the residence of: windsor barrie and sudbury.

Grammar/Mechanics Challenge—6

Document for Revision

The following persuasive internal memo has faults in grammar, punctuation, spelling, number form, wordiness, and negative words. Use standard proofreading marks (see Appendix B) to correct the errors. When you finish, your instructor can show you the revised version of this memo.

Memo

Beverage Inc.

To: Sara W. Morrisseau, Vice President
From: Jackson Pardell, Market Research
CC:
Date: August 5, 2012
Re: ANALYSIS OF GULPIT XL

Here is a summery of the research of Clemence Willis' and myself. Regarding the reduced sugar sports drink being introduced by our No. 1 compititor, GulpIT.

In just under a years time GulpIT developed this new drink, it combines together a mixture of 50 percent sugar and 50 percent artificial sweetener. Apparently GulpIT plans to spend over $8 million to introduce the drink, and to assess consumers reactions to it. It will be tested on the shelfs of convience stores grocerys and other mass merchants in five citys in the Atlantic provinces.

The companys spokesperson said, "The 'X' stands for excelent taste, and the 'L' stands for less sugar." Aimed at young adult's who don't like the taste of sweetener but who want to control calories. The new sports drink is a hybrid sugar and diet drink. Our studys show that simular drinks tryed in this country in the 1980's were unsucessful. On the other hand a 50 calorie low sugar sports drink introduced in Europe two year ago was well received, similarly in Japan a 40 calorie soda is now marketed sucessfully by a cola manufactuerer.

However our research in regard to trends and our analysis of GulpIT XL fails to indicate that this countrys consumers will be interested in a midcalorie sports drink. Yet the Toronto Stock Exchanges response to GulpITs announcement of it's new drink was not unfavourable.

In view of the foregoing the writer and his colleague are of the opinion that we should take a wait and see attitude. Toward the introduction of our own low sugar sports drink.

Communication Workshop

Eight Steps to Resolving Workplace Conflicts

"No part of life is conflict free. We don't always agree with people around us—our families, friends, neighbours or the people we work with every day."[14] Although all workplaces suffer from conflict from time to time, some people think that workplace conflict is escalating.

Several factors may be tied to increasing problems at work. One factor is our diverse workforce. Sharing ideas that stem from a variety of backgrounds, experiences, and personalities may lead to better problem solving, but it can also lead to conflict. Another factor related to increased conflict is the trend toward participatory management. In the past only bosses had to resolve problems, but now more employees are making decisions and facing conflict. This is particularly true of teams. Working together harmoniously involves a great deal of give and take, and conflict may result if some people feel that they are being taken advantage of. Finally, a significant source of workplace problems is increasing levels of stress. Statistics Canada reports that more than one third of working Canadians (34%) "cited too many demands or too many hours as the most common source of workplace stress." Other sources of workplace stress include "poor interpersonal relations" and "risk of accident and injury."[15]

When problems do arise in the workplace, it's important for everyone to recognize that conflict is a normal occurrence and that it won't disappear if ignored. Conflict must be confronted and resolved. Effective conflict resolution requires good listening skills, flexibility, and a willingness to change. Individuals must be willing to truly listen and seek to understand rather than immediately challenge the adversary. In many workplace conflicts, involving a third party to act as a mediator is necessary.

Although problems vary greatly, the following steps offer a good basic process for resolving conflicts.[16]

1. **Be proactive.** Arrange a time when conflicting parties are willing to have a conversation in a non-threatening environment.

2. **Listen to all sides.** Encourage each individual to describe the situation from his or her perspective.

3. **Diagnose before responding.** To promote empathic communication, follow this rule: No one may respond without first accurately summarizing the other person's previous remarks.

4. **Focus on interests.** Brainstorm together to develop multiple options for meeting the interests of each of the conflicting parties. Try to see each other as allies, rather than opponents, in solving the problem.

5. **Negotiate a solution.** Ensure that both parties are agreeable to the chosen solution.

6. **Communicate the solution formally.** It is important to formalize the agreement on paper or in some other way.

7. **Implement the solution and plan follow-up communication.** Meet again on an agreed-upon date to ensure satisfactory resolution of the conflict. The deadline makes it more likely that both parties will follow through on their part of the deal.

8. **Live the solution.** Act on the solution in the workplace.

Career Application

As leader of your work team, you were recently confronted by an angry team member. Julie, a story editor on your film production team, is upset because, for the third time in as many weeks, she was forced to give up part of her weekend for work. This time it was for a black-tie affair that everyone in the office tried to avoid. Julie is particularly angry with Yannick, who should have represented the team at this awards dinner. But he uttered the magic word: family. "Yannick says he has plans with his family, and it's like he gets to do anything," Julie complains to you. "I don't resent him or his devotion to his family. But I do resent it when my team constantly expects me to give up my personal time because I don't have kids. That's my choice, and I don't think I should be punished for it."[17]

Your Task

Using the principles outlined above, work out a conflict resolution plan for Julie and Yannick. Your instructor may wish to divide your class into three-person teams to role-play Julie, Yannick, and the team leader. Add any details to make a realistic scenario.

- What are the first steps in resolving this conflict?
- What arguments might each side present?
- What alternatives might be offered?
- What do you think is the best solution?
- How could it be implemented with the least friction?

Negative Messages

Despite the fact that we sometimes have to send negative messages at work, it is imperative to turn the situation around and focus on lessons learned and experience gained. Just think, if not for bad news, good news would not be as good![1]

Maria Duncan,
*Director, Business & Administration,
CBC English Television A & E*

LEARNING OBJECTIVES

1. Describe a plan for resolving business problems.
2. List the four components of an indirect bad-news message.
3. Learn various strategies for writing indirect negative messages.
4. Distinguish between the direct and the indirect pattern for business messages.
5. Apply the indirect pattern in refusing requests, refusing claims, and announcing bad news to customers and employees.
6. Identify situations in which the direct pattern is appropriate for breaking bad news.
7. Explain when the indirect strategy may be unethical.

Strategies for Breaking Bad News

Letters, e-mails, and memos that carry negative news can have a significant impact on a company's success. As Maria Duncan suggests, the correct way to go about writing a bad-news message is to think positively. Because bad news disappoints, irritates, and sometimes angers the receiver, such messages must be written in a way that explains the bad news but retains goodwill at the same time.

The direct strategy, which you learned to apply in earlier chapters, presents the main idea first, even when it's bad news. The direct pattern appeals to efficiency-oriented writers who don't want to waste time with efforts to soften the effects of bad news.[2] Many business writers, however, prefer to use the indirect pattern in delivering negative messages. The indirect pattern is especially appealing to relationship-oriented writers. They care about how a message will affect its receiver.

Although the major focus of this chapter will be on developing the indirect pattern, you'll first learn the procedure that many business professionals follow in resolving business problems. It may surprise you. Then you'll study models of

If your message delivers bad news, consider using the indirect strategy.

messages that use the indirect pattern to refuse requests, refuse claims, and announce bad news to customers and employees. Finally, you'll learn to identify instances in which the direct pattern may be preferable in announcing bad news.

Resolving Business Problems

Problems with customers are generally resolved by first calling and then confirming with a follow-up letter.

In all businesses, things occasionally go wrong. Goods are not delivered, a product fails to perform as expected, service is poor, clients are incorrectly invoiced, or customers are misunderstood. All businesses offering products or services must sometimes deal with troublesome situations that cause unhappiness to customers and to employees. Whenever possible, these problems should be dealt with immediately and personally. One study found that a majority of business professionals resolve problems in the following manner:

1. Call the individual involved.
2. Describe the problem and apologize.
3. Explain why the problem occurred, what you are doing to resolve it, and how you will prevent it from happening again.
4. Follow up with a message that documents the phone call and promotes goodwill.[3]

OFFICE INSIDER

"As soon as you realize there is a problem, let your client know by phone or, if possible, in person. It's better to let them hear bad news from you than to discover it on their own because it establishes your candor."

Dealing with problems immediately is very important in resolving conflict and retaining goodwill. Sending letters is generally too slow for problems that demand immediate attention. That said, either a letter or an e-mail, if you can communicate in this faster channel, is important (1) when personal contact is impossible, (2) to establish a record of the incident, (3) to formally confirm follow-up procedures, and (4) to promote good relations.

A bad-news follow-up e-mail is shown in Figure 7.1 (p. 175). Consultant Robert Buch found himself in the embarrassing position of explaining why he had given out the name of his client to a salesperson. The client, Data.com, Inc., had hired his firm, Buch Consulting Services, to help find an appropriate service for outsourcing its payroll functions. Without realizing it, Robert had mentioned to a potential vendor (Payroll Services, Inc.) that his client was considering hiring an outside service to handle its payroll. An overeager salesperson from Payroll Services immediately called on Data.com, thus angering the client. The client had hired the consultant to avoid this very kind of intrusion. Data.com did not want to be hounded by vendors selling their payroll services.

When he learned of the problem, the first thing consultant Robert Buch did was call his client to explain and apologize. But he also followed up with the e-mail shown in Figure 7.1. The e-mail not only confirms the telephone conversation but also adds the right touch of formality and permanence. It sends the nonverbal message that the matter is being taken seriously.

Using the Indirect Pattern in Negative Messages

The indirect pattern softens the impact of bad news.

When sending a bad-news message that will upset or irritate the receiver, many business communicators use the indirect pattern. Revealing bad news indirectly shows sensitivity to your reader. Whereas good news can be announced quickly, bad news generally should be revealed gradually. By preparing the reader, you soften the impact. A blunt announcement of disappointing news might cause the receiver to stop reading and toss the message aside.

The indirect pattern enables you to keep the reader's attention until you have been able to explain the reasons for the bad news. The most important part of a bad-news letter is the explanation, which you'll learn about shortly. The indirect plan consists of four main parts.

FIGURE 7.1 Bad-News Follow-Up Message

Confirming our Earlier Conversation

File   Edit   Mailbox   Message   Transfer   Special   Tools   Window   Help

B *I* U ... | Send

To: Noelle Vanier <noelle.vanier@data.com>   October 23, 2012
From: Robet Buch <robert.buch@buchconsulting.com>
Subject: Confirming our Earlier Conversation
Cc:
Bcc:
Attached:

Dear Noelle:

Opens with agreement and apology →

You have every right to expect complete confidentiality in your transactions with an independent consultant. As I explained in today's telephone call, I am very distressed that you were called by a salesperson from Payroll Services, Inc. This should not have happened, and I apologize to you again for inadvertently mentioning your company's name in a conversation with a potential vendor, Payroll Services, Inc.

Explains what caused problem and how it was resolved →

All clients of Buch Consulting are assured that their dealings with our firm are held in the strictest confidence. Because your company's payroll needs are so individual and because you have so many contract workers, I was forced to explain how your employees differed from those of other companies. The name of your company, however, should never have been mentioned. I can assure you that it will not happen again. I have informed Payroll Services that

Promises to prevent recurrence →

it had no authorization to call you directly and its actions have forced me to reconsider using its services for my future clients.

Closes with forward look →

A number of other payroll services offer excellent programs. I'm sure we can find the perfect partner to enable you to outsource your payroll responsibilities, thus allowing your company to focus its financial and human resources on its core business. I look forward to seeing you in person soon when you may choose from a number of excellent payroll outsourcing firms.

Sincerely,

Robert Buch, Senior Consultant
Buch Consulting Services
3091 Geddes Road, Suite 404
Vancouver, BC V5S 1E4
Voice: 604.499.2341
Web: www.buchconsulting.com

Tips for Resolving Problems and Following Up
- Whenever possible, call or see the individual involved. Don't e-mail instead.
- Describe the problem and apologize.
- Explain why the problem occurred.
- Explain what you are doing to resolve it.
- Explain how it will not happen again.
- Follow up with a letter that documents the personal message.
- Look forward to positive future relations.

Writing Plan for a Negative Message: BREC

- **Buffer** opening
- **Reasons** for bad news
- **Explain** any bad news
- **Close** pleasantly

Buffer the Opening

A buffer is a device that reduces shock or pain. To buffer the pain of bad news, begin your message with a neutral but meaningful statement that makes the reader continue reading. The buffer should be relevant and concise. Although it should avoid revealing the bad news immediately, it should not convey a false impression that good news follows. It should provide a natural transition to the explanation

A buffer opens a bad-news letter with a neutral, concise, relevant, and upbeat statement.

that follows. The individual situation, of course, will help determine what you should put in the buffer. Here are some possibilities for opening bad-news messages.

A good buffer may include the best news, a compliment, appreciation, facts regarding the problem, a statement indicating understanding, or an apology.

- **Best news.** Start with the part of the message that represents the best news. For example, in a memo that announces a new service along with a cutback in mailroom hours, you might write *To ensure that your mail goes out with the last pickup, we're starting a new messenger pickup service at 2:30 p.m. daily beginning June 1.*
- **Compliment.** Praise the receiver's accomplishments, organization, or efforts, but do so with honesty and sincerity. For instance, in a letter declining an invitation to speak, you could write *I admire the United Way for its fundraising projects in our community. I am honoured that you asked me to speak Friday, November 5.*
- **Appreciation.** Convey thanks to the reader for doing business, for sending something, for a service or job well done, for showing confidence in your organization, for expressing feelings, or simply for providing feedback. In a letter terminating an employee's contract, you might say *Thank you for your work on the past two seasons of* Riley's Cove. *Your efforts contributed to a wonderful television program enjoyed across Canada.* Avoid thanking the reader, however, for something you are about to refuse.
- **Agreement.** Make a relevant statement with which both reader and receiver can agree. A letter that rejects a potential student's application for admission to a college may state *In today's economy everyone agrees on the importance of a top-quality postsecondary education. We were glad to receive your recent application....*
- **Facts.** Provide objective information that introduces the bad news. For example, in a memo announcing cutbacks in the hours of the employees' cafeteria, you might say *During the past five years the number of employees eating breakfast in our cafeteria has dropped from 32 percent to 12 percent.*
- **Understanding.** Show that you care about the reader. In announcing a product defect, the writer can still manage to express concern for the customer: *We know you expect superior performance from all the products you purchase from OfficeCity. That's why we're writing personally about the Excell printer cartridges you recently ordered.*
- **Apology.** A study of letters responding to customer complaints revealed that 67 percent carried an apology of some sort.[4] If you do apologize, do it early, briefly, and sincerely. For example, a manufacturer of ice cream might respond to a customer's complaint with *We're genuinely sorry that you were disappointed with the price of the ice cream you recently purchased from one of our vendors. Your opinion is important to us, and we appreciate your giving us the opportunity to look into the problem you describe.*

Present Your Reasons

The most important part of a bad-news message is the section that explains why a negative decision is necessary. Without sound reasons for denying a request or refusing a claim, a message will fail, no matter how cleverly it is organized or written. As part of your planning before writing, you analyzed the problem and decided to refuse a request for specific reasons. Before disclosing the bad news, try to explain those reasons. Providing an explanation reduces feelings of ill will and improves the chances that the reader will accept the bad news.

Bad-news messages should explain reasons before stating the negative news.

- **Be cautious in explaining.** If the reasons are not confidential or legally questionable, you can be specific: *Growers supplied us with a limited number of patio roses, and our demand this year was twice that of last year.* In refusing a speaking engagement, tell why the date is impossible: *On January 17 we have a board of directors meeting that I must attend.*
- **Cite reader benefits.** Readers are more open to bad news if in some way, even indirectly, it may help them. Readers also accept bad news better if they recognize that someone or something else benefits, such as other workers or the environment: *Although we would like to consider your application, we prefer to fill managerial positions from within.* Avoid trying to show reader benefits, though, if they appear insincere: *To improve our service to you, we're increasing our brokerage fees.*

Readers accept bad news more readily if they see that someone benefits.

Société Générale, pictured here among the skyscrapers of Paris, suffered the worst loss in banking history when a junior employee liquidated more than $7 billion in a fraudulent trading scheme. In a letter to the bank's customers, CEO Daniel Bouton opened immediately with the bad news: "It is my duty to inform you that Société Générale has been a victim of a serious internal fraud committed by an imprudent employee in the Corporate and Investment Banking Division." Bouton went on to reveal a disaster-response plan and assured customers that lost funds would be replaced with emergency funding from the international banking community. *Should the bank have buffered this bad news by revealing it more gradually in the letter?*

- **Explain company policy.** Readers don't like blanket policy statements prohibiting something: *Company policy prevents us from making cash refunds* or *Proposals may be accepted from local companies only* or *Company policy requires us to promote from within.* Instead of hiding behind company policy, gently explain why the policy makes sense: *We prefer to promote from within because it rewards the loyalty of our employees. In addition, we've found that people familiar with our organization make the quickest contribution to our team effort.* By offering explanations, you demonstrate that you care about your readers and are treating them as important individuals.
- **Choose positive words.** Because the words you use can affect a reader's response, choose carefully. Remember that the objective of the indirect pattern is to hold the reader's attention until you've had a chance to explain the reasons justifying the bad news. To keep the reader in a receptive mood, avoid expressions that might cause the reader to tune out. Be sensitive to negative words such as *claim, error, failure, fault, impossible, mistaken, misunderstand, never, regret, unwilling, unfortunately,* and *violate.*
- **Show that the matter was treated seriously and fairly.** In explaining reasons, demonstrate to the reader that you take the matter seriously, have investigated carefully, and are making an unbiased decision. Customers are more accepting of disappointing news when they feel that their requests have been heard and that they have been treated fairly. Avoid deflecting responsibility, known as "passing the buck," or blaming others within your organization. Such unprofessional behaviour makes the reader lose faith in you and your company.

Cushion the Bad News

Although you can't prevent the disappointment that bad news brings, you can reduce the pain somewhat by breaking the news sensitively. Be especially considerate when the reader will suffer personally from the bad news. A number of thoughtful techniques can lessen the impact.

- **Position the bad news.** Instead of spotlighting it, enclose the bad news between other sentences, perhaps among your reasons. Try not to let the refusal begin or end a paragraph—the reader's eye will linger on these high-visibility spots. Another technique that reduces shock is putting a painful idea in a subordinate clause: *Although another candidate was hired, we appreciate your interest in our*

> **Techniques for cushioning bad news include positioning it strategically, using the passive voice, emphasizing the positive, implying the refusal, and suggesting alternatives or compromises.**

organization and wish you every success in your job search. Subordinate clauses often begin with words such as *although, as, because, if,* and *since.*

- **Use the passive voice.** Passive-voice verbs enable you to describe an action without connecting the action to a specific person. Whereas the active voice focuses attention on a person (*We don't give cash refunds*), the passive voice highlights the action (*Cash refunds are not given because …*). Use the passive voice for the bad news. In some instances you can combine passive-voice verbs and a subordinate clause: *Although ice-cream vendors cannot be required to lower their prices, we are happy to pass along your comments for their consideration.*

- **Accentuate the positive.** As you learned earlier, messages are far more effective when you describe what you can do instead of what you can't do. Rather than *We will no longer accept requests for product changes after June 1,* try a more positive appeal: *We are accepting requests for product changes until June 1.*

- **Imply the refusal.** It's sometimes possible to avoid a direct statement of refusal. Often, your reasons and explanations leave no doubt that a request has been denied. Explicit refusals may be unnecessary and at times cruel. In this refusal to contribute to a charity, for example, the writer never actually says no: *Because we will soon be moving into new offices, all our funds are earmarked for moving and furnishings. We hope that next year we'll be able to support your worthwhile charity.* This implied refusal is effective even though the bad news is not stated. The danger of an implied refusal, of course, is that it can be so subtle that the reader misses it. Be certain that you make the bad news clear, thus preventing the need for further correspondence.

- **Suggest a compromise or an alternative.** A refusal is not so harsh—for the sender or the receiver—if a suitable compromise, substitute, or alternative is available. In denying permission to a class to visit a research facility, for instance, this writer softens the bad news by proposing an alternative: *Although class tours of the entire research facility are not given due to safety and security reasons, we do offer tours of parts of the facility during our open house in the fall.*

You can further reduce the impact of the bad news by refusing to dwell on it. Present it briefly (or imply it), and move on to your closing.

Close Pleasantly

After explaining the bad news sensitively, close the message with a pleasant statement that promotes goodwill. The closing should be personalized and may include a forward look, an alternative, good wishes, special offers, resale information, or an off-the-subject remark.

Closings to bad-news messages might include a forward look, an alternative, good wishes, special offers, and resale or sales promotional information.

- **Forward look.** Anticipate future relations or business. A letter that refuses a contract proposal might read: *Thank you for your bid. We look forward to working with your talented staff when future projects demand your special expertise.*

- **Alternative.** If an alternative exists, end your letter with follow-through advice. For example, in a letter rejecting a customer's demand for replacement of landscaping plants, you might say *We will be happy to give you a free inspection and consultation. Please call 746-8112 to arrange a date for a visit.*

- **Good wishes.** A letter rejecting a job candidate might read: *We appreciate your interest in our company. Good luck in your search to find the perfect match between your skills and job requirements.*

- **Special offers.** When customers complain—primarily about food products or small consumer items—companies often send coupons, samples, or gifts to restore confidence and to promote future business. In response to a customer's complaint about a frozen dinner, you could write *Thank you for your loyalty and for sharing in our efforts to make Green Valley frozen entrées the best they can be. We appreciate your input so much that we'd like to buy you dinner. We've enclosed a coupon to cover the cost of your next entrée.*

- **Resale or sales promotion.** When the bad news is not devastating or personal, references to resale information or promotion may be appropriate: *The laptops* *you ordered are unusually popular because they have more plug-ins for peripheral devices than any other laptop in their price range. To help you locate additional accessories for these computers, we invite you to visit our Web site at ..., where our online catalogue provides a huge selection of peripheral devices such as stereo speakers, printers, personal digital assistants, and digital pagers.*

Avoid endings that sound superficial, insincere, inappropriate, or self-serving. Don't invite further correspondence (*If you have any questions, do not hesitate ...*), and don't rehash the bad news.

Refusing Requests

Most of us prefer to be let down gently when we're being refused something we want. That's why the indirect pattern works well when you must turn down requests for favours, money, information, action, and so forth. The following writing plan is apvpropriate when you must deny a routine request or claim.

The indirect strategy is appropriate when refusing requests for favours, money, information, or action.

> ### Writing Plan for Refusing Requests or Claims
>
> - **Buffer:** Start with a neutral statement on which both reader and writer can agree, such as a compliment, an appreciative comment, a quick review of the facts, or an apology.
> - **Transition:** Include a key idea or word that acts as a transition to the reasons.
> - **Reasons:** Present valid reasons for the refusal, avoiding words that create a negative tone. Include resale or sales promotion material if appropriate.
> - **Bad news:** Soften the blow by de-emphasizing the bad news, using the passive voice, accentuating the positive, or implying a refusal.
> - **Alternative:** Suggest a compromise, alternative, or substitute if possible.
> - **Closing:** Renew good feelings with a positive statement. Avoid referring to the bad news, and look forward to continued business.

Two versions of a request refusal are shown in Figure 7.2 on the next page. A magazine writer requested salary information for an article, but this information could not be released. The ineffective version begins with needless information that could be implied. The second paragraph creates a harsh tone with such negative words as *sorry*, *must refuse*, *violate*, and *liable*. Since the refusal precedes the explanation, the reader probably will not be in a receptive frame of mind to accept the reasons for refusing. Notice, too, that the bad news is emphasized by its placement in a short sentence at the beginning of a paragraph. It stands out and adds more weight to the rejection already felt by the reader.

Moreover, the refusal explanation is overly graphic, containing references to possible litigation. The tone at this point is threatening and unduly harsh. Then, suddenly, the author throws in a self-serving comment about the high salary and commissions of his salespeople. Instead of offering constructive alternatives, the ineffective version reveals only tiny bits of the desired data. Finally, the closing sounds too insincere and doesn't build goodwill.

In refusing requests, avoid a harsh tone or being too explicit; offer constructive alternatives whenever possible.

In the more effective version of this refusal, the opening reflects the writer's genuine interest in the request. But it does not indicate compliance. The second sentence acts as a transition by introducing the words *salespeople* and *salaries*, repeated in the following paragraph. Reasons for refusing this request are objectively presented in an explanation that precedes the refusal. Notice that the refusal (*Although specific salaries and commission rates cannot be released*) is a subordinate clause in a long sentence in the middle of a paragraph. To further soften the blow, the letter offers an alternative. The cordial closing refers to the alternative, avoids mention of the refusal, and looks to the future.

FIGURE 7.2 Refusing a Request

Before

Salary Information Request

File Edit Mailbox Message Transfer Special Tools Window Help

B *I* U 📷 ≣ ≣ ≣ A˅ A˄ ⋮≣ ⋮≣ ⋮≣ ⋮≣ 🖊 | **Send**

To: <Sylvia.Marcus@bmw.ca>   January 15, 2012
From: <Lloyd.Kenniston@CanonElectronics.ca>
Subject: Salary Information Request
Cc:
Bcc:
Attached:

Dear Ms. Marcus:

States obvious information ——→ I have your e-mail of October 21 in which you request information about the salaries and commissions of our top young salespeople.

Sounds harsh, blunt, and unnecessarily negative ——→ I am sorry to inform you that we cannot reveal data of this kind. I must, therefore, refuse your request. To release this information would violate our private employee contracts. Such disclosure could make us liable for damages, should any employee seek legal recourse. I might say, however, that our salespeople are probably receiving the highest combined salary and commissions of any salespeople in this field.

Switches tone ——→ If it were possible for us to help you with your fascinating research, we would certainly be happy to do so.

Sincerely yours,

After

Salary Information Request

File Edit Mailbox Message Transfer Special Tools Window Help

B *I* U 📷 ≣ ≣ ≣ A˅ A˄ ⋮≣ ⋮≣ ⋮≣ ⋮≣ 🖊 | **Send**

To: <Sylvia.Marcus@bmw.ca>   January 15, 2012
From: <Lloyd.Kenniston@CanonElectronics.ca>
Subject: Salary Information Request
Cc:
Bcc:
Attached:

Dear Ms. Marcus:

The article you are now researching for *Business Management Weekly* sounds fascinating, and we are flattered that you wish to include our organization. We do have many outstanding young salespeople, both male and female, who are commanding top salaries.   ← Buffer shows interest, and transition sets up explanation

Each of our salespeople operates under an individual salary contract. During salary negotiations several ← Explanation gives good reasons for refusing request
years ago, an agreement was reached in which both sales staff and management agreed to keep the terms ←
of these individual contracts confidential. Although specific salaries and commission rates cannot be   ← Subordination and passive voice used
released, we can provide you with a ranked list of our top salespeople for the past five years. Three of the ← Refusal is softened by substitute
current top salespeople are under the age of thirty-five.

Attached is a fact sheet regarding our top salespeople. We wish you every success, and we hope to see ← Closing is pleasant and forward-looking
our organization represented in your article.

Cordially,

Lloyd Kenniston
Executive Vice President
Canon Electronics

Attachment: Sales Fact Sheet

FIGURE 7.3 E-Mail That Refuses a Request

Opens with relevant but neutral buffer

Transition picks up key word *licensed*

De-emphasized refusal diverts attention to reader benefits

Closes with an off-the-subject but friendly remark

To: Staff Computer Users   Fri, 23 Nov 2012 15:29:40
From: Karl Straka
Subject: PERSONAL COPYING OF LICENSED SOFTWARE
Cc:
Bcc:
Attached:

Hi all,

A number of staff have expressed interest in the licensed graphics program PhotoPro. We recently installed this program on the computers in our Document Production Department.

Like many licensed products, this program requires that each purchased copy be used only on a single machine. The agreement forbids not only copies for home use but also copies for additional machines within the office. One can easily understand why a software company must protect its programs from indiscriminate copying. If an organization purchased one program and then made multiple copies for other computers within the company or for employees to take home, the software company could not earn enough profit to make the development of any future software program worthwhile.

When we purchased the PhotoPro program, we agreed to limit its use to a single machine in our department. Although this program must not be copied, we look forward to using it for many of your projects here in the Document Production Department.

When you have a chance, please drop by to see our new graphics and presentation capabilities.

Best,

Karl

It's always easier to write refusals when alternatives can be offered to soften the bad news. But often no alternatives are possible. The refusal shown in Figure 7.3 involves a delicate situation in which a manager has been asked by his superiors to violate a contract. Several of the engineers for whom he works have privately asked him to make copies of a licensed software program for them. They apparently want this program for their personal computers. Making copies is forbidden by the terms of the software licensing agreement, and the manager refuses to do this. Rather than saying no to each engineer who asks him, he sends all affected staff the e-mail shown in Figure 7.3.

The opening tactfully avoids suggesting that any engineer has actually asked to copy the software program. These professionals may prefer not to have their private requests made known. A transition takes the reader to the logical reasons against copying. Notice that the tone is objective, neither preaching nor condemning. The refusal is softened by being linked with a positive statement (*Although this program must not be copied, we look forward to using it for many of your projects here …*). To divert attention from the refusal, the memo ends with a friendly, off-the-subject remark.

Refusing Claims

All businesses offering products or services will receive occasional customer claims for adjustments. Claims may also arise from employees. Most of these claims are valid, and the customer or employee receives a positive response. Even unwarranted claims are sometimes granted because businesses genuinely want to create a good public image and to maintain friendly relations with employees.

Although most customer claims are granted, occasionally some must be refused.

Some claims, however, cannot be approved because the customer or employee is mistaken, misinformed, unreasonable, or possibly even dishonest. Messages responding to these claims deliver bad news. The indirect strategy breaks bad news with the least pain. It also allows the sender to explain why the claim must be refused before the reader realizes the bad news and begins resisting.

In the letter shown in Figure 7.4, the writer denies a customer's claim for the difference between the price the customer paid for speakers and the price she saw advertised locally (which would have resulted in a cash refund of $151). While Premier Sound Sales does match any advertised lower price, the price-matching policy applies only to exact models. This claim must be rejected because the advertisement the customer submitted shows a different, older speaker model.

The letter to Wanda Vandermark opens with a buffer that agrees with a statement in the customer's letter. It repeats the key idea of product confidence as a transition to the second paragraph. Next comes an explanation of the price-matching

FIGURE 7.4 Refusing a Claim

Premier Sound Sales

5920 Jasper Boulevard
Edmonton, Alberta T2C 2A6
Telephone: (780) 499-2341

Fax: (780) 499-5904
Web: www.premiersound.ca
E-mail: premier1@flash.ca

May 24, 2012

Ms. Wanda Vandermark
4205 54th Avenue S.E.
Calgary, Alberta T3L 2W4

Dear Ms. Vandermark:

You're absolutely right! We do take pride in selling the finest products at rock-bottom prices. The X Flex speakers you purchased last month are premier concert hall speakers. They're the only ones we present in our catalogue because they're the best.

Begins by agreeing with receiver

We have such confidence in our products and prices that we offer the price-matching policy you mention in your letter of May 20. That policy guarantees a refund of the price difference if you see one of your purchases offered at a lower price for 30 days after your purchase. To qualify for that refund, customers are asked to send us an advertisement or verifiable proof of the product price and model. As our catalogue states, this price-matching policy applies only to the same models.

Explains price-matching policy

Our X Flex AM-5 II speakers sell for $749. You sent us a local advertisement showing a price of $598 for X Flex speakers. This advertisement, however, described an earlier version, the X Flex AM-4 model. The AM-5 speakers you received have a wider dynamic range and smoother frequency response than the AM-4 model. Naturally, the improved model you purchased costs a little more than the older AM-4 model advertised by your local dealer. Your speakers have a new three-chamber bass module that virtually eliminates harmonic distortion. The AM-5 speakers are also 20 percent more compact than the AM-4 model.

Without actually saying no, shows why claim can't be honoured

You bought the finest compact speakers on the market, Ms. Vandermark. If you haven't installed them yet, you may be interested in ceiling mounts, shown in the enclosed catalogue on page 48. We value your business and invite your continued comparison shopping.

Renews good feelings by building confidence in wisdom of purchase

Sincerely yours,

Melanie Tang

Melanie Tang
Customer Care Specialist

Enclosure

policy. The writer does not assume that the customer is trying to pull a fast one. Nor does the writer suggest that the customer is a dummy who didn't read or understand the price-matching policy.

The safest path is a neutral explanation of the policy along with precise distinctions between the customer's speakers and the older ones. The writer also gets a chance to re-sell the customer's speakers and demonstrate what a quality product they are. By the end of the third paragraph, it's evident to the reader that her claim is unjustified.

Notice how most of the components in an effective claim refusal are woven together in this letter: buffer, transition, explanation, and pleasant closing. The only missing part is an alternative, which was impossible in this situation.

Announcing Bad News to Customers and Employees

In addition to resolving claims, organizations occasionally must announce bad news to customers or to their own employees. Bad news to customers might involve rate increases, reduced service, changed procedures, new locations, or technical problems. Bad news within organizations might involve declining profits, lost contracts, public relations controversies, or changes in policy.

Whether you use a direct or an indirect pattern in delivering that news depends primarily on the anticipated reaction of the receiver. When the bad news affects customers or employees personally—such as a reduction in available overtime hours, a change in a shift premium, or relocation plans—you can generally lessen its impact and promote better relations by explaining reasons before revealing the bad news.

> **The choice of a direct or indirect strategy depends on the expected reaction of the receiver.**

Writing Plan for Announcing Bad News to Customers and Employees

- **Buffer:** Open with a compliment, appreciation, facts, or good news with a neutral statement on which the reader and the writer can agree.
- **Transition:** Include a key idea or word that leads from the opening to the reasons.
- **Reasons:** Explain the logic behind the bad news; use positive words and try to show reader benefits if possible.
- **Bad news:** Position the bad news so that it does not stand out. Consider implying the bad news.
- **Alternative:** Suggest a compromise, alternative, or substitute if possible.
- **Closing:** Look forward positively. Provide information about an alternative, if appropriate.

In many businesses today, employee extended health care plans are increasing in cost. Midland, Inc., had to announce a substantial increase to its employees; Figure 7.5 (p. 184) shows two versions of its bad-news message. The first version opens directly with the bad news. No explanation is given for why employee monthly deductions are rising. Although Midland has been absorbing the increasing costs in the past and has not charged employees, it takes no credit for this. Instead, the tone of the memo is defensive and unsatisfying to receivers.

The improved version of this bad-news memo, shown at the bottom of Figure 7.5, uses the indirect pattern. Notice that it opens with a relevant, upbeat buffer regarding extended health care benefits—but says nothing about increasing monthly costs. For a smooth transition, the second paragraph begins with a key idea from the opening (comprehensive package). The reasons section discusses rising costs with explanations and figures. The bad news (*you will be paying $109 a month*) is clearly presented but embedded within the paragraph.

Throughout, the writer strives to show the fairness of the company's position. The ending, which does not refer to the bad news, emphasizes how much the

> **In announcing bad news to employees, consider starting with a neutral statement or something positive.**

FIGURE 7.5 Memo That Announces Bad News to Employees

Before

MEMO TO: Staff

Beginning January 1 the monthly deduction from your paycheque for extended health benefits will be increased to $109 (up from $42 last year).

Every year extended benefits costs go up. Although we considered dropping other benefits, Midland decided that the best plan was to keep the present comprehensive package. Unfortunately, we can't do that unless we pass along some of the extra cost to you. Last year the company was forced to absorb the total increase in extended health premiums. However, such a plan this year is inadvisable.

We did everything possible to avoid the sharp increase in costs to you this year. A rate schedule describing the increases in payments for your family and dependents is enclosed.

Hits readers with bad news without any preparation

Does not explain why costs are rising

Fails to take credit for absorbing previous increases

Sounds defensive; fails to give reasons

After

DATE:	November 6, 2012
TO:	Fellow Employees
FROM:	Eduardo Martinez, President *EM*
SUBJECT:	MAINTAINING QUALITY BENEFITS PACKAGE

Begins with positive buffer

Extended health benefits programs have always been an important part of our commitment to employees here at Midland, Inc. We're proud that our total benefits package continues to rank among the best in our industry.

Explains why costs are rising

Such a comprehensive package does not come without cost. In the last decade extended health premiums have risen over 50 percent among companies belonging to our group insurance plan. Other insurance plans have been even harder hit. We're told that several factors fuel the cost spiral: greater number of services offered such as therapeutic massage and acupuncture, increased average age of program users, and increased underwriting of drug purchases for program members.

Reveals bad news clearly but embeds it in paragraph

Just two years ago our monthly extended health benefits cost for each employee was $415. It rose to $469 last year. We were able to absorb that jump without increasing your contribution. But this year's hike to $539 forces us to ask you to share the increase. To maintain your current extended health benefits, you will be paying $109 a month. The enclosed rate schedule describes the cost breakdown for families and dependents.

Ends positively by stressing the company's major share of the costs

Midland continues to pay the major portion of the extended health benefit program ($430 each month). We think it's a wise investment.

Enclosure

company is paying and what a wise investment it is. Notice that the entire memo demonstrates a kinder, gentler approach than that shown in the first draft. Of prime importance in breaking bad news to employees is providing clear, convincing reasons that explain the decision.

When to Use the Direct Pattern

Many bad-news messages are best organized indirectly, beginning with a buffer and reasons. The direct pattern, with the bad news first followed by the reasons and a pleasant closing, may be more effective, though, in situations such as the following:

- **When the bad news is not damaging.** If the bad news is insignificant (such as a small increase in cost) and doesn't personally affect the receiver, then the direct strategy certainly makes sense.
- **When the receiver may overlook the bad news.** With the crush of e-mails and other communications today, many readers skim messages, looking only at the opening. If they don't find substantive material, they may discard the message. Rate increases, changes in service, new policy requirements—these critical messages may require boldness to ensure attention.
- **When organization policy suggests directness.** Some companies expect all internal messages and announcements—even bad news—to be straightforward and presented without frills.
- **When the receiver prefers directness.** Busy managers may prefer directness. Such shorter messages enable the reader to get in the proper frame of mind immediately. If you suspect that the reader prefers that the facts be presented immediately, use the direct pattern.
- **When firmness is necessary.** Messages that must demonstrate determination and strength should not use delaying techniques. For example, the last in a series of collection letters that seek payment of overdue accounts may require a direct opener.

Figure 7.6 shows an example of a typical direct bad-news message. Notice how much shorter this message is than the indirect-style messages we've been examining.

The direct pattern is appropriate when the bad news is not damaging, when the receiver might overlook the bad news, when the organization expects directness, when the receiver prefers directness, or when firmness is necessary.

FIGURE 7.6 Direct Bad-News Message

TelCo

December 2012

Dear Valued TelCo Home Phone Customers,

As of January 1, 2013, basic telephone service rates will be rising by 1.5 percent.

This change is taking place as a result of a recent CRTC decision, as well as for competitive reasons within the industry.

We appreciate your continued loyalty.

Toula Vassopoulos

Toula Vassopoulos
Customer Service Manager

Collection Letters

One of the most important processes in business is the collection process. Collection is the steps a company takes to ensure that its unpaid invoices get paid. The first phase in the collection process is usually the sending of a short reminder letter or e-mail that lets the client or customer know that his or her invoice is outstanding. Best practices stipulate that a copy of the outstanding invoice should be attached to this short reminder message, in case the client has misplaced the original.

An understanding of how to write a direct negative message becomes useful in the second step in the collection process. If the client or customer with the outstanding invoice does not reply in a timely manner to the short reminder message, it is time to write a direct bad-news message demanding payment. Figure 7.7 shows a typical example of such a message.

FIGURE 7.7 Collection Letter

FRASER, AHMET, AND GRANDPRE

3017–66 Avenue Northwest, Suite 222
Edmonton, AB T6H 1Y2

August 14, 2012

Tom Przybylski
Unity Ltd.
9 Givins Dr., Unit 5
Edmonton, AB T2A 4X3

Dear Mr. Przybylski:

Re: Invoice No. 443-2010

Outstanding Amount Due: $19,567.87

You are indebted to the firm of Fraser, Ahmet, and Grandpre in the amount of $19,567.87, for services rendered and for which you were invoiced on March 30, 2012. A copy of the outstanding invoice is enclosed for your reference, as is a copy of a reminder letter sent to you on July 2, 2012.

Unless we receive a certified cheque or money order, payable to Fraser, Ahmet, and Grandpre, in the amount of $19,567.87, or unless satisfactory payment arrangements are made within seven (7) business days, we are left no choice but to pursue collection of the amount owing. We are not prepared to continue carrying your accounts receivable and we will take all necessary steps for the recovery of this amount from you.

We do not wish to proceed in this fashion and would appreciate your cooperation instead. We look forward to hearing from you on or before August 21, 2012.

Yours sincerely,

Pat McAfee

Pat McAfee
Office Manager/Collections Clerk

The main objective of a bad-news collection letter is to receive payment, but at the same time to make sure that the goodwill of the client or customer is retained. According to the Web site of Credit Guru Inc. (http://www.creditguru.com), a company that offers advice on the collection process, the main features of a well-written collection letter are a reminder of the dates of the invoice, a reminder of the total amount outstanding, a request for immediate payment or payment by a specified date, a request for the payment to be sent by the quickest means (e.g., courier), and finally, a sense of urgency coupled with an unapologetic and non-threatening tone.[5]

Ethics and the Indirect Pattern

You may worry that the indirect pattern is unethical or manipulative because the writer deliberately delays the main idea. But consider the alternative. Breaking bad news bluntly can cause pain and hard feelings. By delaying bad news, you soften the blow somewhat, as well as ensure that your reasoning will be read while the receiver is still receptive. Your motives are not to deceive the reader or to hide the news. Rather, your goal is to be a compassionate, yet effective, communicator.

The key to ethical communication lies in the motives of the sender. Unethical communicators intend to deceive. For example, Victoria's Secret, the clothing and lingerie chain, once offered free $10 gift certificates. However, when customers tried to use the certificates, they found that they were required to make a minimum purchase of $50 worth of merchandise.[6] For this misleading, deceptive, and unethical offer, the chain paid a $100,000 fine. Although the indirect strategy provides a setting in which to announce bad news, it should not be used to avoid or misrepresent the truth.

> **The indirect strategy is unethical only if the writer intends to deceive the reader.**

Summing Up and Looking Forward

When faced with delivering bad news, you have a choice. You can announce it immediately, or you can delay it by presenting a buffer and reasons first. Many business communicators prefer the indirect strategy because it tends to preserve goodwill. In some instances, however, the direct strategy is more effective in delivering bad news.

In this chapter you learned to write follow-up bad-news messages as well as to apply the indirect strategy in refusing requests, denying claims, and delivering bad news to employees. This same strategy is appropriate when you make persuasive requests or when you try to sell something. Now that you have completed your instruction in writing business e-mails, letters, and memos, you're ready to learn about writing longer business documents such as proposals and reports. Chapter 8 introduces informal reports and Chapter 9 discusses proposals and formal reports.

Critical Thinking

1. A survey of business professionals revealed that most respondents reported that every effort should be made to resolve business problems in person.[7] Why is this logical? Why is this problematic?

2. Does bad news travel faster and farther than good news? Why? What implications would this have for companies responding to unhappy customers?

3. Consider times when you have been aware that others have used the indirect pattern in writing or speaking to you. How did you react?

4. Why is the "reasons" section of a bad-news message so important?

5. Some people feel that all employee news, good or bad, should be announced directly. Do you agree or disagree? Why?

Chapter Review

1. List the four steps that many business professionals follow in resolving business problems.

2. List the four main parts of the indirect pattern for revealing bad news.

3. What is a buffer?

4. List seven possibilities for opening bad-news messages.

5. List at least five words that might affect readers negatively.

6. How can the passive voice be used effectively in bad-news messages? Provide an original example.

7. What is the danger in implying a refusal?

8. List five techniques for closing a bad-news message.

9. What determines whether you announce bad news to customers or employees directly or indirectly?

10. List five instances when bad news should be announced directly.

Activities and Cases

7.1 Follow-up Apology: Naming-Rights-for-Computer-Sales Agreement Goes Sour

As the director of partnerships for Inspire Canada, the largest retailer of computers in the country, you signed an agreement four months ago in July with Macdonald College, a community college in Picton, Ontario. The agreement stipulated that, in exchange for the naming rights to the college's new academic building (now known as the Inspire Canada Information Centre), your company would provide computer hardware, software, and printers at a deep discount to the college for a five-year period. But now you have a difficult situation on your hands.

Over the past two months, the president of the college has been calling you almost weekly to complain about the problematic rollout of the agreement between Inspire Canada and the college. "Your company's name is on our building, and the media have painted you as a great corporate responsibility success story, but you haven't kept your half of the agreement," is a typical message you've received from the president. She has told you that your computer equipment has been shipped late in 90 percent of orders, causing severe problems for students and professors in September. Also, printers have malfunctioned in 85 percent of the labs on campus, causing widespread late submission of assignments. In response, you recently called the president and told her that Inspire is "doing everything it can to improve shipping procedures." You also promised to look into the printer problem.

Discuss the following options in resolving this business problem.

1. Following a telephone call to this unhappy customer, what should you do next?

    a. Leave it. A telephone call is enough. You did what you could to explain the problem, and words will not solve the problem anyway.

    b. Wait to see whether this customer calls again. After all, the next move is up to her. Respond only after repeated complaints.

    c. Send a short e-mail message repeating your apology and explanation.

    d. Immediately send a letter that apologizes, explains, and shows how seriously you have taken the problem and the customer's complaint.

2. You decide to write a follow-up letter. To open this letter, you should begin with

    a. A neutral statement, such as This letter is in response to your telephone complaint.

    b. A defensive statement that protects you from legal liability, such as As I mentioned on the telephone, you are the only customer who has complained about shipping problems.

    c. An apologetic statement that shows you understand and take responsibility for the problem.

    d. An off-the-subject remark, such as We're happy to hear that the college has increased its enrollment this fall.

3. In the body of the follow-up letter, you should

    a. Explain why the problem occurred.

    b. Describe what you are doing to resolve the problem.

    c. Promise that you will do everything possible to prevent the problem from happening again.

    d. All of the above

4. In the closing of this letter, you should

    a. Avoid apologizing because it may increase your legal liability.

    b. Show appreciation for the customer's patience and patronage.

    c. Explain that company policy prohibits you from revealing the exact nature of the shipping and printer problems.

    d. Provide an action deadline.

Your Task. After circling your choices and discussing them in your class, write a follow-up message to Dr. Marianne Porter, President, Macdonald College, 35 Regent St., Picton, ON K0K 3BC or mporter@macdonald.ca. In your message, be proactive about solutions, but consider also that Dr. Porter has implied she may leak the story to the local and national media and/or seek the advice of the college's lawyer.

Chapter 7: Negative Messages

7.2 Request Refusal: Lease Payments Cannot Be Applied to Purchase

Analyze the following letter. List its weaknesses, and then revise it.

Dear Mr. Cervello:

Unfortunately, we cannot permit you to apply the lease payments you've been making for the past ten months toward the purchase of your Sako 600 copier.

Company policy does not allow such conversion. Have you ever wondered why we can offer such low leasing and purchase prices? Converting lease payments to purchases would mean overall higher prices for our customers. Obviously, we couldn't stay in business long if we agreed to proposals such as yours.

You've had the Sako 600 copier for ten months now, Mr. Cervello, and you say that you like its versatility and reliability. Perhaps we could interest you in another Sako model, such as the Sako 400 series. It may be closer to your price range. Do give us a call.

Sincerely,

---

1. List at least five faults in this letter.
2. Outline a plan for writing a refusal to a request.

Your Task. Revise this refusal. Send your message to Mr. Walter Cervello, Vice President of Operations at Copiers Plus, 508 W. Inverary Road, Kingston, ON K2G 1V8 or wcervello@copiersplus.ca. You might mention that many customers are pleased with the Sako copiers, including the Sako 400 series that has nearly as many features as the Sako 600 series. You'd like to demonstrate the Sako 400. Supply any additional information.

7.3 Customer Bad News: Costly SUV Upgrade

Steven Chan, a consultant from Regina, Saskatchewan, was surprised when he picked up his rental car from Budget at the Calgary airport over Easter weekend. He had reserved a full-size car, but the rental agent told him he could upgrade to a Ford Excursion for an additional $25 a day. "She told me it was easy to drive," Mr. Chan reported. "But when I saw it, I realized it was huge—like a tank. You could fit a full-size bed inside."

On his trip Mr. Chan managed to scratch the paint and damage the rear-door step. He didn't worry, though. He thought the damage would be covered because he had charged the rental on his American Express card. He knew that the company offered backup car rental insurance coverage. To his dismay, he discovered that its car rental coverage excluded large SUVs. "I just assumed they'd cover it," he confessed. He wrote to Budget to complain about not being warned that certain credit cards may not cover damage to large SUVs or luxury cars.

Budget agents always encourage renters to sign up for Budget's own "risk product." They don't feel that it is their responsibility to study the policies of customers' insurance carriers and explain what may or may not be covered. Moreover, they try to move customers into their rental cars as quickly as possible and avoid lengthy discussions of insurance coverage. Customers who do not purchase insurance are at risk. Mr. Chan does not make any claim against Budget, but he is upset about being "pitched" to upgrade to the larger SUV, which he didn't really want.[8]

Your Task. As a member of the customer care staff at Budget, respond to Mr. Chan's complaint. Budget obviously is not going to pay for the SUV repairs, but it does want to salvage his goodwill and future business. Offer him a coupon worth two days' free rental of any full-size sedan. Write to Steven Chan, 201–548 Hillsdale Street, Regina, SK S32 0A2.

7.4 Request Refusal: Adieu to Cadillacs in Paris

"As I'm sure you've noticed, Cadillac has been on a bit of a roll lately with the worldwide launch of the all-new Seville and the much-awaited launch of the Escalade," begins the GM invitation letter. This letter has been sent to many of the top automotive journalists in the country, inviting them to join GM's executives on a five-day all-expenses-paid press trip to Paris. Such excursions are not unusual. Automakers routinely sponsor reporters' trips to ensure favourable local coverage from the big auto shows in Paris, Frankfurt, Geneva, and Tokyo.

GM particularly wants reporters at the Paris show. This is the show where it hopes to position Cadillac as a global luxury car manufacturer. The invitation letter, mailed in July, promises a "sneak peak at Cadillac's first major concept vehicle in nearly ten years." But GM has only 20 spots available for the trip, and journalists have to request one of the spots. Suddenly, in late July, GM finds itself in the midst of an expensive strike. "All at once, what had seemed like a good idea is starting to look fiscally irresponsible," says J. Christopher Preuss, Cadillac spokesperson. Although exact figures are not available, some estimates are that the Paris trip could easily cost $12,000 per reporter. That's a large bill for a company facing a prolonged, damaging strike.

Your Task. As part of a group of interns working in the communications division of GM, you and your team have been asked to draft a letter to the journalists who signed up for the trip. Announce that GM must back out. About the best thing they can expect now is an invitation to the gala unveiling and champagne reception GM will sponsor in January at the annual Detroit auto show. At that time GM will brief reporters about Cadillac's "new vision" and unveil the eye-popping Escalade. Mr. Preuss is embarrassed about cancelling the Paris trip, but he feels GM must do what is financially prudent. Prepare a draft of the letter for the signature of J. Christopher Preuss. Address the first letter to Rodney M. Olafson, *The Chronicle-Journal*, 75 S. Cumberland Street, Thunder Bay, ON P7B 1A3.

7.5 Request Refusal: The End of Free Credit Reports

WEB

You are part of the customer service team at Experian, the largest supplier of consumer and business credit information in the world. Experian took over TRW Information Systems & Services back in 1996. Experian currently employs more than 11,000 people in North America, the United Kingdom, Continental Europe, Africa, and Asia Pacific. As a service to consumers, Experian at one time provided complimentary credit reports. However, it now offers them only in certain locations and to certain groups of people.

Experian's Web site explains its new policy in its FAQ (frequently asked question) section. Your supervisor says to you, "I guess not everyone is able to learn about our new policy by going to our Web site, because we still receive a lot of phone requests for free reports. I'm unhappy with a letter we've been using to respond to these requests. I want you to compose a draft of a new form letter that we can send to people who inquire. You should look at our Web site to see who gets free reports and in what locations."

Because you are fairly new to Experian, you ask your boss what prompted the change in policy. She explains, "It was a good idea, but it got out of hand. So-called 'credit repair' companies would refer their clients to us for free credit reports, and then they advised their clients to dispute every item on the report. We had to change our policy. But you can read more about it at our Web site."

Your Task. You resolve to study the Experian Web site closely. Your task is to write a letter refusing the requests of people who want free credit reports. But you must also explain the reasons for the change in policy, as well as its exceptions. Decide whether you should tell consumers how to order a copy and how to pay for it. Although your letter will be used repeatedly for such requests, address your draft to Ms. Cherise Benoit, 250 Rue Bruce, Montreal, QC H2X 1E1. Sign it with your boss's name, Elisabeth Bourke.

7.6 Bad News for Customers: These Funds Are Worth Holding On To

You are a financial planner in Hamilton, Ontario, with over 200 clients. Since you began your practice as a financial planner, you have been a strong believer in BMC's mutual funds, which are heavily invested in the financial services sector. Over the past few years, though, these funds have been underperforming dismally. For example, in 2009, when the S&P/TSX Index was 10.5 percent, BMC funds were averaging 2.2 percent; in 2011 when the index was at 11.9 percent, BMC funds averaged 2.5 percent; and in 2012 when the Index is at 10.9 percent, BMC funds are averaging –0.1 percent. BMC funds have been criticized in major newspapers of late, and for the past few months you have had at least five clients per week calling to sell their funds. You believe BMC funds are still a good value because the financial services sector will rebound soon. Also, with Canadian demographic trends pointing to a large retired population in the next decade, you believe BMC funds are a smart investment.

Your Task. Write a letter to your clients in which you discuss the recent bad news about BMC funds, but at the same time, in which you attempt to put this bad news into a broader context.

Related Web site: For general information on Canadian mutual fund performance, go to http://www.morningstar.ca.

7.7 Claim Refusal: Wilted Landscaping

As Flora Powell, owner of Town & Country Landscaping, you must refuse the following request. Paul and Judy Alexander have asked that you replace the landscaping around the home they recently purchased in Canmore, Alberta. You had landscaped that home nearly a year ago for the former owner, Mrs. Hunter, installing a sod lawn and many shrubs, trees, and flowers. It looked beautiful when you finished, but six months later, Mrs. Hunter sold the property and moved to Calgary. Four months elapsed before the new owners moved in. After four months of neglect and a hot, dry summer, the newly installed landscaping suffered.

You guarantee all your work and normally would replace any plants that do not survive. Under these circumstances, however, you do not feel justified in making any refund because your guarantee necessarily presumes proper maintenance on the part of the property owner. Moreover, your guarantee is made only to the individual who contracted with you—not to subsequent owners. You would like to retain the goodwill of the new owners, since this is an affluent neighbourhood and you hope to attract additional work here. On the other hand, you can't afford to replace the materials invested in this job. You believe that the lawn could probably be rejuvenated with deep watering and fertilizer.

Your Task. Write to Mr. and Mrs. Paul and Judy Alexander, 3318 Clearview Drive, Canmore, AB T2N 3E4 or thealexanders@gmail.com refusing their claim. You would be happy to inspect the property and offer suggestions to the Alexanders. In reality, you wonder whether the Alexanders might not have a claim against the former owner or the escrow agency for failing to maintain the property. Clearly, however, the claim is not against you.

7.8 Refusing a Claim: Evicting a Noisy Neighbour

As Robert Hsu, you must deny the request of Arman Aryai, one of the tenants in your three-storey office building. Mr. Aryai, a Chartered Accountant, demands that you immediately evict a neighbouring tenant who plays loud music throughout the day, interfering with Mr. Aryai's conversations with clients and with his concentration. The noisy tenant, Bryant Haperot, seems to operate an entertainment booking agency and spends long hours in his office.

You know you can't evict Mr. Haperot immediately because of his lease. Moreover, you hesitate to do anything drastic because paying tenants are hard to find. You called your lawyer, and he said that the first thing you should do is talk to the noisy tenant or write him a letter asking him to tone it down. If this doesn't work within 30 days, you could begin the eviction process.

Your Task. Decide on a course of action. Because Mr. Aryai doesn't seem to answer his telephone, you must write to him. You need a permanent record of this decision anyway. Write to Arman Aryai, CA, Suite 203, Pico Building, 1405 Bower Boulevard, Vancouver, BC V6L 1Y3 or aryai@aplusaccountants.ca. Deny his request, but tell him how you plan to resolve the problem.

7.9 Customer Bad News: Olympus Refuses Customer's Request to Repeat World Trip

Olympus Customer Service Manager Charlie Smith can't believe what he reads in a letter from Brian P. Coyle. This 27-year-old Ottawa resident actually wants Olympus to foot the bill for a repeat round-the-world trip because his Stylus Epic camera malfunctioned and he lost 12 rolls of film!

As soon as Smith saw the letter and the returned camera, he knew what was wrong. Of the 2 million Stylus Epic cameras made last year, 20,000 malfunctioned. A supplier squirted too much oil in the shutter mechanism, and the whole lot was recalled. In fact, Olympus spent almost $1 million to remove these cameras from store shelves. Olympus also contacted all customers who could be reached. In addition to the giant recall, the company quickly redesigned the cameras so that they would work even if they had excess oil. But somehow Coyle was not notified of the recall. When Smith checked the warranty files, he learned that this customer had not returned his warranty. Had the customer done so, he would have been notified in August, well before his trip.

Although Smith is sorry about the mishap, he thinks that a request for $20,000 to replace "lost memories" is preposterous. Olympus has never assumed any responsibility beyond replacing a camera. This customer, however, seems to have suffered more than a routine loss of snapshots. Therefore, Smith decides to sweeten the deal by offering to throw in a digital camera valued at $600, more than double the cost of the Stylus Epic. One of the advantages of a digital camera is that it contains an LCD panel that enables the photographer to view stored images immediately. No chance of losing memories with this digital camera!

Your Task. As the assistant to Customer Service Manager Smith, you must write a letter that refuses the demand for $20,000 but retains the customer's goodwill. Tell this customer what you will do, and be sure to explain how Olympus reacted immediately when it discovered the Stylus Epic defect. Write a sensitive refusal to Brian P. Coyle, 594 Swindon Way, Ottawa, ON K1P 5V5.

7.10 Credit Refusal: Cash Only at Goodlife Fitness Clubs

As manager of the Moncton GoodLife Fitness Club, you must refuse the application of Monique Cooper for an Extended Membership. This is strictly a business decision. You liked Monique very much when she applied, and she seems genuinely interested in fitness and a healthful lifestyle. However, your Extended Membership plan qualifies the member for all your testing, exercise, recreation, yoga, and aerobics programs. This multi-service program is expensive for the club to maintain because of the huge staff required. Applicants must have a solid credit rating to join. To your disappointment, you learned that Monique's credit rating is decidedly negative. Her credit report indicates that she is delinquent in payments to four businesses, including Pros Athletic Club, your principal competitor.

You do have other programs, including your Drop In and Work Out plan, which offers the use of available facilities on a cash basis. This plan enables a member to reserve space on the racquetball and handball courts. The member can also sign up for yoga and exercise classes, space permitting. Because Monique is far in debt, you would feel guilty allowing her to plunge in any more deeply.

Your Task. Refuse Monique Cooper's credit application, but encourage her cash business. Suggest that she make an inquiry to the credit-reporting company Experian to learn about her credit report. She is eligible to receive a $10 credit report if she mentions this application. Write to Monique Cooper, 303 Magnetic Blvd., Moncton, NB, E1A 4B8 or mcooper@mymail.ca.

7.11 Employee Bad News: Strikeout for Expanded Office Teams

Assume you are Walter Carvello, vice president of operations at Copiers Plus, 508 W. Inverary Road, Kingston, ON K2G 1V8. Recently several of your employees requested that their spouses or friends be allowed to participate in Copiers Plus's intramural sports teams. Although the teams play only once a week during the season, these employees claim that they can't afford more time away from friends and family. Over 100 employees currently participate in the eight coed volleyball and softball teams, which are open to company employees only. The teams were designed to improve employee friendships and to give employees a regular occasion to have fun together.

If non-employees were to participate, you're afraid that employee interaction would be limited. And while some team members might have fun if spouses or friends were included, you're not so sure all employees would enjoy it. You're not interested in turning intramural sports into "date night." Furthermore, the company would have to create additional teams if many non-employees joined, and you don't want the administrative or equipment costs of more teams. Adding teams would also require changes to team rosters and game schedules, which could be a problem for some employees. You do understand the need for social time with friends and families, but guests are welcome as spectators at all intramural games. Besides, the company already sponsors a family holiday party and an annual company picnic.

Your Task. Write an e-mail or hard-copy memo to the staff denying the request of several employees to include non-employees on Copiers Plus's intramural sports teams.

7.12 Employee Bad News: Refusing Holiday Season Event

In the past your office has always sponsored a holiday season party at a nice restaurant. As your company has undergone considerable downsizing and budget cuts during the past year, you know that no money is available for holiday entertaining.

Your Task. As executive vice president, send an e-mail to Dina Gillian, office manager. Dina asked permission to make restaurant reservations for this year's holiday party. Refuse Dina, but offer some alternatives. How about a potluck dinner?

7.13 Customer Bad News: Image Consultant Plays Bad Guy

As the owner of Polished Pro Image Consultants, you hate the part of your job that requires you every so often to write collection letters. Your work is all about making people look good, so when they don't pay their bills, it's difficult for you to get in touch with them—it's as if nothing you taught them has sunk in. Still, as a small business owner, you cannot afford a collections clerk, and you dread the cost of hiring a third-party collection agency to take care of your outstanding accounts. Recently, you provided extensive consulting services to David M. Fryer, a local businessperson who will be running in the next election to be the local Member of Parliament. You billed Mr. Fryer for 18 hours at $100 per hour for in-person consulting, plus another 10 hours at $50 per hour for telephone consulting. In total, your invoice dated May 14, 2011, amounted to $2,300 plus HST. A reminder e-mail you sent to Mr. Fryer on June 30 went unanswered, and you've decided now that August has arrived, it's time to act. The only thing holding you back is that Mr. Fryer is prominent in your community, and while you definitely want your invoice paid, you're not sure you want to get on his bad side.

Your Task. Write a collection letter to Mr. David M. Fryer, President, Hexago Plastics, 230 Queen St., Saint John, NB E3K 4N6.

7.14 Employee Bad News: The Worst Publicity Ever

Sometimes relaying negative news using new communications technology can turn into a public relations disaster. A case in the United States demonstrates just how bad things can become.

Your Task. Do two sets of secondary research: first, type the phrase "e-mail termination radio shack" into an Internet search engine such as Google. How many articles about the infamous Radio Shack "firing by e-mail" situation can you find? Next, type the same phrase into an online research database in your college or university library. How many articles can you find now? Develop a three-slide PowerPoint presentation in which you offer (a) a short explanation of what happened, (b) a short explanation of the difference in tone between the articles you found via the Internet and those you found via the research database, and (c) a suggestion to Radio Shack and other employers about a better channel and message they can use when delivering negative messages such as the one in this case.

7.15 Announcing Bad News to Customers

You are the owner of Miss Twinkle's Treats, a small bakery in London, Ontario. The delicious cakes, squares, cookies, and breads that Miss Twinkle's is known for are made from scratch daily at your location on the outskirts of the city. Although you operate a small storefront, most of your business comes from supplying local restaurants and coffee shops with your tantalizing treats. You own a small truck that is used to deliver orders to your customers throughout the London area. Although Miss Twinkle's is financially successful, rising costs have severely undercut your profits over the past few months. You know that you are not the only business owner dealing with rising prices—many of your suppliers have raised their prices over the last year. Specifically, the higher price of wheat and sugar has resulted in a drastic increase in your production costs. Previously, you did not charge for deliveries made to your wholesale clients. However, you now feel that you have no choice but to add a delivery charge to each order to cover your increased costs and the rising price of gas.

Your Task. As the owner of Miss Twinkle's Treats, write a letter to your clients in which you announce a $20 charge per delivery. See if you can come up with an offer or special to placate your customers. Use the indirect writing strategy and explain your reasons for introducing the charge.

7.16 Employee Bad News: Refusing the Use of Instant Messaging on the Job

As the vice president of the Green Group, an environmental firm, you've had a request from team leader Emily Tsonga. She wants to know whether her team can use instant messaging on the job. Emily is working on the plans for an environmentally friendly shopping centre, Westbury Mall. Her team project is moving ahead on schedule, and you have had excellent feedback from the shopping centre developers.

Emily's team is probably already using instant messaging through public systems, and this worries you. You are concerned about security, viruses, and wasted time. However, the company has been considering a secured "enterprise-level" instant messaging system. The principal drawbacks are that such a system is expensive, requires administration, and limits use to organizational contacts only. You are not sure your company will ever adopt such a system.

You will have to refuse Emily's request, but you want her to know how much you value her excellent work on developing sustainability and green building techniques for the Westbury Mall project. You know you cannot get by with a quick refusal. You must give her solid reasons for rejecting her request.

Your Task. Send an e-mail to Emily Tsonga at etsonga@greengroup.ca refusing her request. See Chapter 4 for more information on the pros and cons of instant messaging. Also do research on the Internet or in a library database to understand better the risks of instant messaging.

Grammar/Mechanics Review—7

The following sentences contain errors in grammar, punctuation, capitalization, number style, usage, and spelling. Below each sentence write a corrected version.

1. The first province by province report describing Canada's tobacco use and tobacco control laws were recently released.

2. The report which was compiled by statistics canada showed adult smoking rates that varied from 5% of the population in alberta, to twelve percent in quebec.

3. As expected quebecs pattern of deaths related to smoking was nearly twice that of albertas.

4. Hailed by anti-tobacco groups as proof of the need for more stricter National regulations the report was dismissed by the tobacco industry as "old news".

5. Statistics canada said that the comparisons might stimulate changes in some provinces, but that the report was not part of any particular policy drive.

6. "Children are particularly vulnerable to second-hand smoke because they breathe faster than adults inhale more air proportionate to their body mass and their lungs are still growing and developing reported ugnat et al in the Canadian journal of public health.

7. Most likely to attract attention, are data related to smoking among High School students.

8. The 8 provinces with the lowest cigarette taxs has a higher than average number of smokers.

9. The provinces of newfoundland and british columbia have the highest provincial tobacco taxes at $22 a pack rank in the middle on percentage of smokers.

10. The québec-based "ACTI-Menu" health programs non smoking campaign encourages smokers who want to quit to pair up with a non smoking partner. Both partners sign a pledge with the smoker agreeing not to smoke for the period of march 1st to april 12th.

11. Walker Merryman a spokesperson for the tobacco institute said "This report is more rehash than research, it is not terribly useful for understanding why kids smoke".

12. Anti-tobacco supporters are urging government to support a proposal to severely restrict: advertising marketing and distribution of tobacco products.

13. The province of quebec however faces the biggest problem, nearly twenty-four percent of it's students who were daily smokers 15 to 19 years of age, reported smoking within the month in which they were surveyed.

14. In 2004 7% of young people aged 10 to 19 were beginning to smoke.

15. The governments tobacco education and information officer explained that its hard to restrict smoking when the provinces economy is linked so close to gaming which is linked to tobacco.

Chapter 7: Negative Messages

Document for Revision

The e-mail in Figure 7.8 has faults in grammar, punctuation, spelling, number form, and negative words. Use standard proofreading marks (see Appendix B) to correct the errors. When you finish, your instructor can show you the revised version of this message.

FIGURE 7.8 Order Confirmation

Order Confirmation

File   Edit   Mailbox   Message   Transfer   Special   Tools   Window   Help

B / U | | | | A A | | | | | | Send

To: Ragu Raghavan   May 3, 2012
From: Andy Weiss
Subject: Order Confirmation
Cc:
Bcc:
Attached:

Dear Mr. Raghavan:

soon receive

You will be recieving shortly the handimaid service and utility carts you ordered along with 5 *five* recycling stack bins. Unfortunately, the heavy duty can crusher is not available *out of stock* but it will be sent from the factory in St John's Newfoundland and should reach you by May 31st.

You may place any future orders, by using our toll free telephone number (1-800-577-9241), or our toll-free fax number (1-800-577-2657). If you need help with any items ask for one of the following sales represenatives, Ben Crowchild, Susan Fried, or Rick Woo. When the items you order are in our currant catalogue it will be shipped the same day you place you're order. For products to be custom imprinted please provide a typed or printed copy with your order.

Remember we are the only catalogue sales company that guarantees your full satisfaction. If you are not pleased we'll arrange for a prompt refund, credit or replacement. We'll also refund or credit all shipping costs associated with the returned items. We want your business!

Communication Workshop

Intercultural Issues: Presenting Bad News in Other Cultures

To minimize disappointment, Canadians generally prefer to present negative messages indirectly. Other cultures may treat bad news differently, as illustrated in the following:

- In Germany business communicators occasionally use buffers but tend to present bad news directly.
- British writers tend to be straightforward with bad news, seeing no reason to soften its announcement.
- In Latin countries the question is not how to organize negative messages but whether to present them at all. It is considered disrespectful and impolite to report bad news to superiors. Therefore, reluctant employees may fail to report accurately any negative situations to their bosses.
- In Thailand the negativism represented by a refusal is completely alien; the word *no* does not exist. In many cultures negative news is offered with such subtleness or in such a positive light that it may be overlooked or misunderstood by literal-minded Americans.
- In many Asian and some Latin cultures, one must look beyond an individual's actual words to understand what is really being communicated. One must consider the communication style, the culture, and especially the context. Consider the following phrases and their possible meanings:

Phrase	Possible Meaning
I agree.	I agree with 15 percent of what you say.
We might be able to.	Not a chance!
We will consider it.	*We* will consider it, but *the real decision maker* will not.
That is a little too much.	That is outrageous!
Yes.	Yes, I'm listening. *OR*: Yes, you have a good point. *OR*: Yes, I understand, but I don't necessarily agree.

Career Application

Interview fellow students or work colleagues who are from other cultures. Collect information regarding the following questions:

- How is negative news handled in their cultures?
- How would typical business communicators refuse a request for a business favour (such as a contribution to a charity)?
- How would typical business communicators refuse a customer's claim?
- How would an individual be turned down for a job?

Your Task

Report the findings of your interviews in a class discussion or memo report. In addition, collect samples of foreign business letters. You might ask foreign students, your campus admissions office, or local export/import companies whether they would be willing to share business letters from other countries. You can also use the Internet and search terms such as "Business Etiquette" or "Business Letters or Writing" and "Africa" or "Asia" for example. Compare letter styles, formats, tone, and writing strategies. How do these elements differ from those in typical North American business letters?

Reporting Data

Chapter 8
Informal Reports

Chapter 9
Proposals and Formal Reports

COMMUNICATION TECHNOLOGY IN THE NEWS

BlackBerry Etiquette Has Yet to Be Defined

Source: Richard Baum, "Blackberry etiquette has yet to be defined." *Regina Leader Post*, May 15, 2010, page G4. All rights reserved. Republication or redistribution of Thomson Reuters content, including by framing or similar means, is expressly prohibited without the prior written consent of Thomson Reuters. Thomson Reuters and its logo are registered trademarks or trademarks of the Thomson Reuters group of companies around the world. © Thomson Reuters 2010. Thomson Reuters journalist are subject to an Editorial Handbook which requires fair presentation and disclosure of relevant interests.

Do you check your BlackBerry during work meetings? Do you do it furtively under the table, while your colleagues are distracted by a presentation?

Do you leave it in front of you so you can give it the occasional peck whenever it buzzes? Or are you bold enough in the board room to hold it up while you type your replies, a practice that's provoked comedian Jerry Seinfeld to respond, "Can I just pick up a magazine and read it in front of your face while you're talking to me?"

Unless you work in a company that bans BlackBerry use in meetings, you've seen all these behaviours. Most likely, you've been that person. But is it bad etiquette? Don't the pressures of time and overflowing inboxes make this a necessary evil of the 21st century workplace?

Other journalists who have taken time out from deleting e-mail to investigate this burning issue have concluded that polite society abhors the employee whose eyes wander from the PowerPoint presentation to the new e-mail alert.

But as someone who struggles to ignore the siren buzz of the BlackBerry, I demand leave to appeal this collective ruling by the media's finest minds. After all, every new technology that transforms communications encounters resistance from the old guard. Surely the cool kids accept that it is possible to concentrate on a meeting and accept e-mail requests for other meetings at the same time?

It didn't take much Googling to find some research that confirmed my hunch: while 68 per cent of the baby-boom generation born before 1964 think that the use of smartphones during meetings is distracting, just 49 per cent of the under-30s see a problem. As this 2008 LexisNexis survey helpfully points out, that's less than half. If the person running your meeting is a Generation Y'er, there's a better than even chance that she won't mind you checking your e-mail.

Still, most of us have bosses who are too old to skateboard to work. What does Generation X think of BlackBerry peckers? I asked John Freeman, a member of that demographic and the author of *The Tyranny of E-mail*:

"You never have everyone's full attention in a meeting any longer, and I think that's why meetings are becoming so ineffective," he wrote in a non-tyrannical e-mail.

"Whether it's the lot who try to thumb under the table, or those who brazenly do it in the open, the message, from a significant group of those gathered, is—I have other things to do. Which totally defeats the purpose of meeting: you want to create a sense of group purpose. And on top of that it's rude."

But John, I can multitask. It may look like I'm updating my Facebook status under the table, but a co-worker has sent me an urgent question and I can answer that and concentrate on your presentation at the same time. Surely I can get an expert on multitasking to back me up here.

I called Clifford Nass, a professor of communication at Stanford University in California. Nass was part of a group that researched the concentration skills of students who frequently multitasked while consuming media. Did he find that those of us who listen and e-mail at the same time are an elite brigade of hyper-efficient workers? Not exactly.

"The more you multitask, the worse you become at it," he said. According to the Stanford team's research, there's a cost to memory and attention when you switch from one task to another. And that cost increases for people who multitask heavily.

So the science suggests that the appearance of not paying attention when you check your e-mail in a meeting mirrors the reality: however much you think you're paying attention to two things at once, you're not.

And yet the BlackBerry sits there in my pocket, calling to me throughout the meeting: Check me! Check me! What can I do?

"You have to become more cognisant that what you're doing is likely to be offensive to others," said Robert Gordon, who coaches adults with attention deficit hyperactivity disorder (ADHD).

BlackBerry Etiquette Has Yet to Be Defined (*contd.*)

Gordon, who is based in Toronto, says the strategy for executives struggling with ADHD is to separate them from their distractions. So in the case of a BlackBerry, that means shutting it off. I make a final plea. Rob, there are parts of many meetings that aren't relevant to me. What if I check my e-mail then?

"Then the onus falls on the person calling the meeting to be more focused on the agenda," he said.

So there's the answer. It's not my fault I'm rudely checking my BlackBerry. It's your fault for not making the meeting more interesting. And that's just plain bad etiquette.

Summarize the article you've just read in a two- to three-sentence paragraph. Answer the following questions, either on your own or in a small group. Be prepared to present your answers in a short presentation or in an e-mail to your instructor.

QUESTIONS:

1. How does what you've learned in this article change your perception of business communication?

2. How might what you've learned in this article change your own communication style?

3. Come up with pro and con arguments for the following debate/discussion topic: BlackBerrys and other "time-saving" communication devices should be banned from workplace meetings and presentations.

Informal Reports

As a project manager, I find that progress reports are excellent tools to keep clients up to speed. These reports detail the project's progression and provide valuable insight into whether the objectives are being met and if any fine-tuning is required in the assignment of resources and responsibilities.[1]

Heather Jack,
Project Manager, Bell Canada

© CHRIS SCHMIDT/ISTOCKPHOTO.COM

LEARNING OBJECTIVES

1. Describe business report basics, including functions, organization, formats, and delivery methods.

2. Develop informal reports by gathering data effectively and understanding effective style.

3. Identify six kinds of informal reports.

4. Write informal informational reports.

5. Write informal analytical reports.

Understanding Report Basics

Good report writers, as Heather Jack implies, are good at simplifying facts so that anyone can understand them. Collecting information and organizing it clearly and simply into meaningful reports are skills that all successful businesspeople today require. In this age of information, reports play a significant role in helping decision makers solve problems. You can learn to write good reports by examining basic techniques and by analyzing appropriate models.

Because of their abundance and diversity, business reports are difficult to define. They may range from informal e-mail trip reports to formal 200-page financial forecasts. Some reports may be presented orally in front of a group using presentation software, while many reports appear as e-mails, memos, and letters. Still others consist primarily of numerical data, such as tax reports or profit-and-loss statements. Although reports vary in length, content, format, organization, and level of formality, they all have one common purpose: they are systematic attempts to answer business questions and solve business problems in writing or in presentation format. In this chapter we'll concentrate on informal written reports.

> **Informal reports are relatively short (under ten pages) and are usually written in memo or letter format. Sometimes, they are attached to e-mails or presented in the body of the e-mail itself if the context is quite informal.**

Functions of Reports

Most reports can be classified into two functional categories: information reports and analytical reports.

Information Reports

Reports that present data without analysis or recommendations are primarily informational. Although writers collect and organize facts, they are not expected to analyze the facts (i.e., say what the facts mean) for readers. A trip report describing an employee's visit to a conference, for example, simply presents information. Other reports that present information without analysis could involve routine operations (e.g., an incident report in a fast-food restaurant), compliance with regulations (e.g., a status update on a new government regulation rollout in a bank), or company policies and procedures (e.g., a status update on employee reaction to enforcement of a new company policy in a manufacturing company).

Analytical Reports

Reports that provide analysis and conclusions as well as data are analytical. If requested, writers also supply recommendations. Analysis is the process of breaking down a problem into its parts in order to understand it better and solve it (for example, each time you write an outline, as shown in Figure 3.2 on page 57, you are analyzing a problem). Analytical reports attempt to provide the insight necessary to persuade readers to act or change their opinions. For example, a recommendation report that compares several potential locations for an employee fitness club might recommend one site, but not until after it has analyzed and discussed the alternatives. This analysis should persuade readers to accept the writer's choice. Similarly, a feasibility report that analyzes the ability of a private chef school to open a satellite campus in a nearby city will either say yes this can be done or no it can't, but it will also discuss the alternative course of action.

Report Organization

Like e-mails, letters, and memos, reports may be organized directly or indirectly. The reader's expectations and the content of a report determine its pattern of development, as shown in Figure 8.1.

Direct Pattern. When the purpose for writing is presented close to the beginning, the organizational pattern is direct. Information reports, such as the e-mail shown in Figure 8.3, are usually arranged directly. They open with an introduction, followed by the facts and a summary. In Figure 8.3 the writer explains what happened at a work conference. The e-mail begins with an introduction. It then presents the facts, which are listed using bullets for greater readability. The e-mail ends with a summary and a complimentary close.

Analytical reports may also be organized directly, especially when readers are supportive or are familiar with the topic. Many busy executives prefer this pattern because it gives them the results of the report immediately. They don't have to spend time wading through the facts, findings, discussion, and analyses to get to the two items they are most interested in—the conclusions and recommendations. You should be aware, though, that unless readers are familiar with the topic, they may find the direct pattern confusing. Some readers prefer the indirect pattern because it seems logical and mirrors the way we solve problems.

Indirect Pattern. When the conclusions and recommendations, if requested, appear at the end of the report, the organizational pattern is indirect. Such reports usually begin with an introduction or description of the problem, followed by

FIGURE 8.1 Audience Analysis and Report Organization

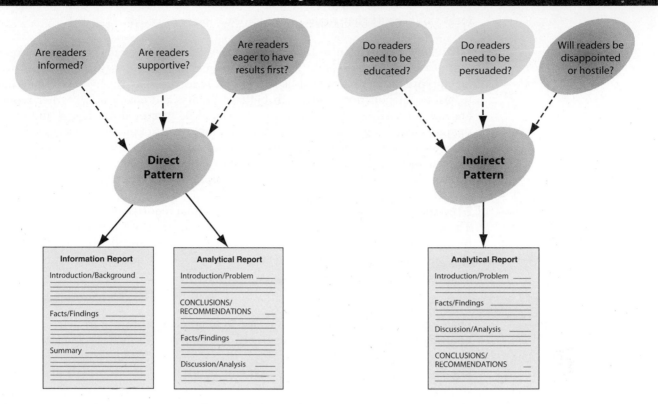

facts and interpretation from the writer. They end with conclusions and recommendations. This pattern is helpful when readers are unfamiliar with the problem. It is also useful when readers must be persuaded or when they may be disappointed in or hostile toward the report's findings. The writer is more likely to retain the reader's interest by first explaining, justifying, and analyzing the facts and then making recommendations. This pattern also seems most rational to readers because it follows the normal thought process: problem, alternatives (facts), solution.

Report Formats

The format of a report is governed by its length, topic, audience, and purpose. After considering these elements, you will probably choose from among the following five formats.

How you format a report depends on its length, topic, audience, and purpose.

Letter Format. Use letter format for short (usually eight or fewer pages) informal reports addressed outside an organization. Prepared using a company's letterhead, a letter report contains a date, inside address, salutation, and complimentary close. Although they may carry information similar to that found in correspondence, letter reports usually are longer and show more careful organization than most letters. They also include headings.

Memo Format. For short informal reports that stay within organizations, memo format is appropriate. Memo reports begin with essential background information, using standard headings: *Date*, *To*, *From*, and *Subject*, as shown in the recommendation report in Figure 8.5 (p. 213). Like letter reports, memo reports differ from regular memos in length, use of headings, and deliberate organization. Note that the writer attaches the report to an e-mail message, which introduces the attachment.

Template Format. Templates (either company-produced or available online from Microsoft Word, for example) are often used for repetitive data, such as monthly sales reports, performance appraisals, merchandise inventories, expense claims, and personnel and financial reports. Standardized headings on these forms save time for the writer. Preprinted forms also make similar information easy to locate and ensure that all necessary information is provided.

Digital Format. In today's less formal workplace, informal reports are often sent as e-mails. For example, the progress report in Figure 8.4 (p. 211) is sent from an employee to her manager. It is perhaps more formal than the average e-mail (i.e., it has an introduction, body with bulleted points, and conclusion). Other reports are not primarily meant to be printed but will be projected or viewed and edited digitally. Increasingly, businesses encourage employees to upload reports to the company intranet or FTP site, especially for team-based writing. Firms provide software that enables workers to update information about their activities, progress on a project, and other information about their on-the-job performance.

Manuscript Format. For longer, more formal reports, use manuscript format. These reports are usually printed on plain paper instead of letterhead stationery or memo forms. They begin with a title followed by systematically displayed headings and subheadings. You will see examples of proposals and formal reports using manuscript format in Chapter 9.

Report Delivery

Written reports can be delivered in person, by mail, or electronically.

Once reports are written, you must decide what channel to use to deliver them to your readers. Written business reports can be delivered in the following ways:

By E-Mail. Reports in any format can be attached to an e-mail message (or sometimes even drafted in the body of the message). When using this channel, you will introduce the report and refer clearly to the attachment in the body of your e-mail message. Figure 8.9 (p. 218) shows an e-mail message that announces the enclosed minutes report and goes to a recipient outside the organization.

Online. You might choose to make your report available online. Many report writers today are making their reports available to their readers on the Web. One common method for doing this involves saving the report in Portable Document Format (PDF) and then uploading it to the company's Web site, FTP site, or intranet. This is an inexpensive method of delivery and allows an unlimited number of readers access to the report. If the report contains sensitive or confidential information, access to the document can be password protected.

In Person. If you are located close to the reader, deliver your report in person. This delivery method works especially well when you would like to comment on the report or clarify its purpose. Delivering a report in person also makes the report seem more important or urgent.

By Mail. Some reports are delivered by mail. You can send your reports by interoffice mail, Canada Post, or a commercial delivery service such as UPS or FedEx.

By Fax. You can fax your report to your reader, but be sure to seek the recipient's permission. Very long reports can overwhelm most fax machines. Be sure to include a cover page that identifies the sender and introduces the report.

Guidelines for Writing Informal Reports

Your natural tendency in preparing a report may be to sit down and begin writing immediately. If you follow this urge, however, you will very likely have to rewrite or even start again. Reports take planning, beginning with defining the project and gathering data. The following guidelines will help you plan your project.

Defining the Project

Begin the process of report writing by defining your project. Do this by stating, in writing, the problem to be solved, the question to be answered, or the task to be completed. Then, move on to writing a statement of purpose. Ask yourself this question: Am I writing this report to inform, to analyze, to solve a problem, or to persuade? The answer should be a clear, accurate statement identifying your purpose—why you are writing the report. In informal reports the statement of purpose may be only one sentence; that sentence usually becomes part of the introduction. Notice how the following introductory statement describes the purpose of the report:

> This report presents information regarding professional development activities coordinated and supervised by the Human Resources Department between the first of the year and the present.

After writing a statement of purpose, analyze who will read your report. If your report is intended for your immediate supervisors and they are supportive of your project, you need not include extensive details, historical development, definition of terms, or persuasion. Other readers, however, may require background information and persuasive strategies.

The expected audience for your report influences your writing style, research method, vocabulary, areas of emphasis, and communication strategy. Remember, too, that your audience may consist of more than one set of readers. Reports are often distributed to secondary readers who may need more details than the primary reader.

Begin a report by being able to state the problem to be solved, question to be answered, or task to be completed. Then, draft a statement of purpose. Be able explain why you are writing the report.

Gathering Data

A professional report is based on solid, accurate, verifiable facts. Typical sources of factual information for informal reports include (1) company records; (2) observation; (3) surveys, questionnaires, and inventories; (4) interviews; and (5) secondary research.

The facts for reports are often obtained from company records, observation, surveys, interviews, and secondary research.

Company Records. Many business-related reports begin with an analysis of company records and files. From these records you can observe past performance and methods used to solve previous problems. You can collect pertinent facts that will help determine a course of action. For example, if a telecommunications company is interested in revamping the design of the bills it sends to customers, the project manager assigned to this task would want to gather examples of previous bill designs to ensure that improvements are made and old designs aren't reused.

Observation. Another logical source of data for many problems lies in personal observation and experience. For example, if you were writing a report on the need for additional computer equipment, you might observe how much the current equipment is being used and for what purpose.

Surveys, Questionnaires, and Inventories. Primary data from groups of people can be collected most efficiently and economically by using surveys, questionnaires, and inventories. For example, if you were part of a committee investigating the success of a campus recycling program, you might begin by using a questionnaire to survey use of the program by students and faculty. You might also do some informal telephoning to see if departments on campus know about the program and are using it.

Interviews. Talking with individuals directly concerned with the problem produces excellent primary information. Interviews also allow for one-on-one communication, thus giving you an opportunity to explain your questions and ideas in eliciting the most accurate information. For example, a food company adding a new low-fat organic bar to its nutrition bar line would solicit interview or focus-group feedback before releasing the new product to the market. Questions posed to people paid to taste the sample bar might include "Did you find the bar tasty? nutritious? healthy?" and "Did you find the packaging attractive? easy to open?"

The Ritz-Carlton, Moscow, has quickly become a hotel hot spot for five-star travellers. Located within walking distance of Red Square and the Kremlin, the 11-storey luxury hotel features marble bathrooms, regal amenities, a dedicated concierge staff, and a panoramic view of one of the world's most historic cities. The guest rooms and suites, along with the hotel's ultra-mod rooftop lounge, offer unparalleled comfort with a touch of contemporary ambiance. Recently, Four Seasons Hotels and Resorts, the Ritz-Carlton chain's main competitor, has announced plans to build a brand new hotel in central Moscow. *What data sources might the Ritz-Carlton management team use to develop an informal recommendation report about how to stay ahead of the competition?*

Secondary Research. You will probably be interested in finding examples from other organizations that shed light on the problem identified in your report. For example, an automobile parts manufacturer eager to drum up new business in the hybrid and electric vehicle market could do in-house research or pay for professional research into hybrid and electric vehicle manufacturing. Hundreds of articles on this topic are available electronically through online library databases and other online resources. From a home, office, or library computer, you can obtain access to vast amounts of information provided by governments, newspapers, magazines, and companies from all over the world. Also, you may decide to use the Internet to conduct secondary research on your topic. Using search engines such as Google or Yahoo will also yield hundreds of results on any topic.

When doing secondary research on the Internet, an extra step must be taken that isn't necessary when using library databases. You need to verify the accuracy of your sources. Because the Internet is a public space where anyone can post information, you must be able to separate credible, useful information from opinion and noncredible sources. You do this by asking yourself a number of questions, which are discussed in more detail in the Communication Workshop at the end of this chapter.

Using an Appropriate Writing Style

Like other business messages, reports can range from informal to formal, depending on their purpose, audience, and setting. Research reports from consultants to their clients tend to be rather formal. Such reports must project an impression of objectivity, authority, and impartiality. But a report to your boss describing a trip to a conference (as in Figure 8.3 on p. 210) would probably have informal elements. You can see the differences between formal and informal styles in Figure 8.2.

In this chapter we are most concerned with an informal writing style. Your informal reports will probably be written for familiar audiences and involve non-controversial topics. You may use first-person pronouns (*I, we, me, my, us, our*) and contractions (*I'm, we'll*). You'll emphasize active-voice verbs and strive for shorter sentences using familiar words.

Whether you choose a formal or informal writing style, remember to apply the writing techniques you have learned in earlier chapters. The same techniques you have been using to compose effective memos, letters, and e-mails apply to developing outstanding reports. Business reports must be clear and concise. They should be written using topic sentences, support sentences, and transitional expressions to

FIGURE 8.2 Report-Writing Styles

	Informal Writing Style	Formal Writing Style
Use for ...	Short, routine reports	Theses
	Reports for familiar audiences	Research studies
	Noncontroversial reports	Controversial or complex reports (especially to outsiders)
	Most reports for company insiders	
Effect is ...	Feeling of warmth, personal involvement, closeness	Impression of objectivity, accuracy, professionalism, fairness
		Distance created between writer and reader
Characteristics are ...	Use of first-person pronouns (*I, we, me, my, us, our*)	Absence of first-person pronouns; use of third-person (*the researcher, the writer*)
	Use of contractions (*can't, don't*)	Absence of contractions (*cannot, do not*)
	Emphasis on active-voice verbs (*I conducted the study*)	Use of passive-voice verbs (*the study was conducted*)
	Shorter sentences; familiar words	Complex sentences; long words
	Occasional use of humour, metaphors	Absence of humour and figures of speech
	Occasional use of colourful speech	Reduced use of colourful adjectives and adverbs
	Acceptance of author's opinions and ideas	Elimination of "editorializing" (author's opinions, perceptions)

build coherence. Avoid wordiness, outdated expressions, slang, jargon, and clichés in your reports. Finally, proofread all business reports carefully to make sure that they contain no errors in spelling, grammar, punctuation, names and numbers, or format.

Being Objective

Reports are convincing only when the facts are believable and the writer is credible. You can build credibility in a number of ways:

- **Present both sides of an issue.** Even if you favour one possibility, discuss both sides and show through logical reasoning why your position is superior. Remain impartial, letting the facts prove your point.
- **Separate fact from opinion.** Suppose a supervisor wrote *Our department works harder and gets less credit than any other department in the company*. This opinion is difficult to prove, and it damages the credibility of the writer. A more convincing statement might be *Our productivity has increased 6 percent over the past year, and I'm proud of the extra effort my employees are making*. After you have made a claim or presented an important statement in a report, ask yourself *Is this a verifiable fact?* If the answer is no, rephrase your statement to make it sound more reasonable.
- **Be sensitive and moderate in your choice of language.** Don't exaggerate. Instead of saying *most people think ...*, it might be more accurate to say *Some people think ....* Better yet, use specific figures such as *Sixty percent of employees agree ....* Also avoid using labels and slanted expressions. Calling someone a *loser*, a *control freak*, or an *elitist* demonstrates bias. If readers suspect that a writer is prejudiced, they may discount the entire argument.
- **Cite sources.** Tell your readers where the information came from. For example, *In a telephone interview with Blake Spence, director of transportation, October 15, he said ...,* or The Wall Street Journal *(August 10, p. 40) reports that ....* By referring to respected sources, you lend authority and credibility to your statements. Your words become more believable and your argument more convincing. In Chapter 9 you will learn how to document your sources properly.

Using Headings Effectively

Headings are helpful to both the report reader and the writer. For the reader they serve as an outline of the text, highlighting major ideas and categories. They also act as guides for locating facts and pointing the way through the text. Moreover, headings provide resting points for the mind and for the eye, breaking up large chunks of text into manageable and inviting segments. For the writer, headings force organization of the data into meaningful blocks.

You may choose functional or talking headings. Functional headings (such as *Introduction*, *Discussion of Findings*, and *Summary*) help the writer outline a report; they are used in the progress report shown in Figure 8.4 (p. 211). But talking headings (such as *Students Perplexed by Shortage of Parking* or *Short-Term Parking Solutions*) provide more information to the reader. Many of the examples in this chapter use functional headings for the purpose of instruction. To provide even greater clarity, you can make headings both functional and descriptive, such as *Recommendations: Shuttle and New Structures*. Whether your headings are talking or functional, keep them brief and clear. Here are general tips on displaying headings effectively:

- **Consistency.** The cardinal rule of headings is that they should be consistent. In other words, don't use informational headings in three of four cases and a talking heading in the fourth case. Or, don't use bolded headings for 80 percent of your report and underlined headings for the other 20 percent.
- **Strive for parallel construction.** Use balanced expressions such as *Visible Costs* and *Invisible Costs* rather than *Visible Costs* and *Costs That Don't Show*.
- **Use only short first- and second-level headings.** Many short business reports contain only one or two levels of headings. For such reports use first-level headings (centred, bolded) and/or second-level headings (flush left, bolded). See Figure 9.4 in the next chapter for examples of how such headings look on the page.
- **Capitalize and underline carefully.** Most writers use all capital letters (without underlines) for main titles, such as the report, chapter, and unit titles. For first- and second-level headings, they capitalize only the first letter of main words. For additional emphasis, they use a bold font.
- **Keep headings short but clear.** Try to make your headings brief (no more than eight words) but understandable. Experiment with headings that concisely tell who, what, when, where, and why.
- **Don't enclose headings in quotation marks.** Quotation marks are appropriate only for marking quoted words or words used in a special sense, such as slang. They are unnecessary in headings.
- **Don't use headings as antecedents for pronouns such as *this, that, these,* and *those*.** For example, when the heading reads *Laser Printers*, don't begin the following sentence with *These are used in tandem with desktop publishing software.*

Six Kinds of Informal Reports

You are about to examine six categories of informal reports frequently written in business. In many instances the boundaries of the categories overlap; distinctions are not always clear cut. Individual situations, goals, and needs may make one report take on some characteristics of a report in another category. Still, these general categories, presented here in a brief overview, are helpful to beginning writers. The reports will be illustrated and discussed in more detail below.

- **Information reports.** Reports that collect and organize information are informative or investigative. They may record routine activities such as daily, weekly, and monthly reports of sales or profits. They may investigate options, performance, or equipment. Although they provide information, they do not analyze that information.
- **Progress reports.** Progress reports monitor unusual or non-routine activities. For example, progress reports would keep management informed about a committee's preparations for a trade show 14 months from now. Such reports

usually answer three questions: (1) Is the project on schedule? (2) Are corrective measures needed? (3) What activities are next?

- **Justification/recommendation reports.** Recommendation and justification reports are similar to information reports in that they present information. However, they offer analysis in addition to data. They attempt to solve problems by evaluating options and offering recommendations. Usually these reports revolve around a significant company decision.
- **Feasibility reports.** When a company or organization must decide whether to proceed with a plan of action based on a previously accepted recommendation, it may require a feasibility report that establishes how possible the plan is. For example, a company has decided to redesign its Web site, but how feasible is it to have the redesign accomplished in six months' time? A feasibility report would examine the practicality of implementing the recommendation or proposal.
- **Summary reports.** A summary condenses the primary ideas, conclusions, and recommendations of a longer report or publication. Employees may be asked to write summaries of technical or research reports. Students may be asked to write summaries of periodical articles or books to sharpen their writing skills.
- **Minutes of meetings.** A record of the proceedings and action points of a meeting is called "the minutes." Although informal business meetings today take place without minutes being recorded, many companies, organizations, clubs, committees, and boards still require minutes to be recorded. The person delegated to take notes at a meeting usually turns them into the minutes, distributes them to the participants after the meeting, asks for revisions, and then files the report. You'll find more information on meetings in Chapter 10.

Information Reports

Writers of information reports provide information without drawing conclusions or making recommendations. Some information reports are highly standardized, such as police reports, hospital admittance reports, monthly sales reports, or statistical reports on government program use. Many of these are fill-in reports using prepared forms or templates for recurring data and situations. Other information reports are more personalized, as illustrated in Figure 8.3 (p. 210). They often include these sections:

Information reports usually contain three parts: introduction, findings, and summary.

Introduction. The introduction to an information report may be called *Introduction* or *Background*. In this section do the following: (1) explain why you are writing, (2) describe what methods and sources were used to gather information and why they are credible, (3) provide any special background information that may be necessary, (4) give the purpose of the report, if known, and (5) offer a preview of your findings. You'll notice in Figure 8.3 that not all five of these criteria are met, nor is a heading included, because it is a short, informal information report. However, if you were writing an information report for a client in manuscript format, you would use the heading *Introduction* and try to fit in all five criteria.

Findings. The findings section of a report may also be called *Observations, Facts, Results,* or *Discussion.* Important points to consider in this section are organization and display. Consider one of these methods of organization: (1) chronological, (2) alphabetical, (3) topical, or (4) most important to least important. You'll notice that in Figure 8.3, the writer uses a chronological method of organization.

To display the findings effectively, number paragraphs, underline or boldface key words, or use other graphic highlighting methods such as bullets. Be sure that words used as headings are parallel in structure. If the findings require elaboration, either include this discussion with each segment of the findings or place it in a separate section entitled *Discussion*.

Summary. A summary section is optional. If it is included, use it to summarize your findings objectively and impartially. The information report shown in Figure 8.3 summarizes the facts laid out in bullet format by looking for commonalities (networking

FIGURE 8.3 Information Report—E-Mail Format

Software Expo 2012 Report

File   Edit   Mailbox   Message   Transfer   Special   Tools   Window   Help

To: Mitch Freeman <mfreeman@softsolutions.ca>   June 30, 2012
From: Nancy Pinto <npinto@softsolutions.ca>
Subject: Software Expo 2012 Report
Cc:
Bcc:
Attached:

Hi Mr. Freeman,

As requested, here's a brief trip report describing the details of my recent time spent at Software Expo 2012 in San Francisco.

I arrived in San Francisco on June 18 and, after lunch, began attending expo activities:

- Microsoft Seminar—info on expected launch of new Windows version (June 18 pm)

- Breakfast Meeting—Jerry Schwartz of AccPac (June 19 am)

- Industry Roundtable on the Future of Accounting Software—useful networking opportunity (June 19 am)

- Lunch Meeting—Lisa O'Toole of Microsoft (June 19 pm)

- Software Fair—useful networking opportunity (June 19 pm)

- Dinner Meeting—Tom Nzobugu and Bill McKay of SAS (June 19 pm)

In essence, Software Expo continues to be a great networking opportunity. It's important for our company to have a presence at this high-profile show, especially because of the competitive nature of our business. I made a number of useful contacts, and I think I've located two hot new software products without current licensing or sales and distribution agreements in Canada.

Regards,

Nancy

---

opportunities) and putting these facts into perspective (all Expo events led to exposure for Nancy's company). In addition, the significance of the facts is explained (Nancy may have found some new products for her company to sell in Canada).

Notice how easy this information report is to read. Short paragraphs, ample use of graphic highlighting, white space, and concise writing all contribute to improved readability.

Progress Reports

Progress reports monitor unusual or non-routine projects. Most progress reports include these four parts:

- The purpose and nature of the project
- A complete summary of the work already completed
- A thorough description of work currently in progress, including personnel, methods, and obstacles, as well as attempts to remedy obstacles
- A forecast of future activities in relation to the scheduled completion date, including recommendations and requests

In Figure 8.4 Maria Robinson explains the construction of a realty company branch office. She begins with a statement summarizing the construction progress in relation to the expected completion date. She then updates the reader with a brief recap of past progress. She emphasizes the present status of construction and concludes by describing the next steps to be taken.

> **Progress reports tell management whether non-routine projects are on schedule.**

FIGURE 8.4 Progress Report—E-Mail Format

CONSTRUCTION PROGRESS OF MISSISSAUGA BRANCH OFFICE   _ □ X

File   Edit   Mailbox   Message   Transfer   Special   Tools   Window   Help   _ ⊞ X

B   I   U   **Send**

To: Dorothy Prevatt <dprevatt@prealty.ca>   April 20, 2012
From: Maria Robinson <mrobinson@prealty.ca>
Subject: CONSTRUCTION PROGRESS OF MISSISSAUGA BRANCH OFFICE
Cc:
Bcc:
Attached:

Dear Ms. Prevatt,

Construction of Prevatt Realty's Mississauga branch office has entered Phase 3. Although we are one week behind the contractor's original schedule, the building should be ready for occupancy August 15.   *Introduces report with a summary*

Past Progress

Phase 1 involved development of the architect's plans; this process was completed February 5. Phase 2 involved submission of the plans for local building permit approval. The plans were then given to four contractors for estimates. The lowest bidder was Holst Brothers Contractors. This firm began construction on March 25.   *Describes completed work concisely*

Present Status

Phase 3 includes initial construction procedures. The following steps have been completed as of April 20:

1. Demolition of existing building 273 Lakeshore Boulevard
2. Excavation of foundation footings for the building and for the surrounding wall
3. Installation of steel reinforcing rods in building pad and wall
4. Pouring of concrete foundation   *Itemizes current activities*

The contractor indicated that he was one week behind schedule for the following reasons:

1. The building inspectors required additional steel reinforcement not shown on the architect's blueprints.
2. The excavation of the footings required more time than the contractor anticipated because the Number 4 footings were all below grade.

Future Schedule

Despite some time lost in Phase 3, we are substantially on target for the completion of this office building by August 1. Phase 4 includes framing, drywalling, and plumbing.   *Projects future activities*

Tips for Writing Progress Reports

- Identify the purpose and the nature of the project immediately.
- Supply background information only if the reader must be educated.
- Describe the work completed.
- Discuss the work in progress, including personnel, activities, methods, and locations.
- Identify problems and possible remedies.
- Consider future activities.
- Close by giving the expected date of completion.

Some business communicators use progress reports to do more than merely report progress. These reports can also be used to offer ideas and suggest possibilities. Let's say you are reporting on the progress of redesigning the company Web site. You might suggest a different way to handle customer responses. Instead of making an official recommendation, which might be rejected, you can lay the foundation for a change within your progress report. Progress reports can also be used to build the image of a dedicated, conscientious employee.

Justification/Recommendation Reports

Both managers and employees must occasionally write reports that justify or recommend something, such as buying equipment, changing a procedure, hiring an employee, consolidating departments, or investing funds. Large organizations sometimes prescribe how these reports should be organized; they use forms of templates with conventional headings. At other times, such reports are not standardized. For example, an employee takes it upon himself to write a report suggesting improvements in telephone customer service because he feels strongly about it. When you are free to select an organizational plan yourself, however, let your audience and topic determine your choice of direct or indirect structure.

For non-sensitive topics and recommendations that will be agreeable to readers, you can organize directly according to the following sequence:

- In the introduction identify the problem or need briefly.
- Announce the recommendation, solution, or action concisely and with action verbs.
- Discuss pros, cons, and costs. Explain more fully the benefits of the recommendation or steps to be taken to solve the problem.
- Conclude with a summary specifying the recommendation and action to be taken.

Justin Brown applied the preceding process in writing the recommendation report shown in Figure 8.5. Justin is operations manager in charge of a fleet of trucks for a large parcel delivery company in Richmond, B.C. When he heard about a new Goodyear smart tire with an electronic chip, Justin thought his company should give the new tire a try. His recommendation report begins with a short introduction to the problem followed by his two recommendations. Then he explains the product and how it would benefit his company. He concludes by highlighting his recommendation and specifying the action to be taken.

Feasibility Reports

Feasibility reports examine the practicality and advisability of following a course of action. They answer this question: Will this plan or proposal work? Feasibility reports are typically internal reports written to advise on matters such as consolidating departments, offering a wellness program to employees, or hiring an outside firm to handle a company's accounting or computing operations. These reports may also be written by consultants called in to investigate a problem. The focus in these reports is on the decision: stopping or proceeding with the proposal. Since your role is not to persuade the reader to accept the decision, you'll want to present the decision immediately. In writing feasibility reports, consider this plan:

- Announce your decision immediately.
- Describe the background and problem necessitating the proposal.
- Discuss the benefits of the proposal.
- Describe any problems that may result.
- Calculate the costs associated with the proposal, if appropriate.
- Show the time frame necessary for implementation of the proposal.

Elizabeth Webb, customer service manager for a large insurance company in London, Ontario, wrote the feasibility report shown in Figure 8.6. Because her company had been losing customer service reps (CSRs) after they were trained, she talked with the vice president about the problem. He didn't want her to take time away from her job to investigate what other companies were doing to retain their CSRs. Instead, he suggested that they hire a consultant to investigate what other companies were doing to keep their CSRs. The vice president then wanted to know whether the consultant's plan was feasible. Although Elizabeth's report is only one page long, it provides all the necessary information: background, benefits, problems, costs, and time frame.

FIGURE 8.5 Justification/Recommendation Report—Memo Format

Applies memo format for short, informal internal report

Interoffice Memo   *Pacific Trucking, Inc.*

DATE: July 19, 2012
TO: Bill Montgomery, Vice President
FROM: Justin Brown, Operations Manager   *JB*
SUBJECT: Pilot Testing Smart Tires

Next to fuel, truck tires are our biggest operating cost. Last year we spent $211,000 replacing and retreading tires for 495 trucks. This year the costs will be greater because prices have jumped at least 12 percent and because we've increased our fleet to 550 trucks. Truck tires are an additional burden since they require labour-intensive paperwork to track their warranties, wear, and retread histories. To reduce our long-term costs and to improve our tire tracking system, I recommend that we do the following:

Introduces problem briefly

Presents recommendations immediately

- Purchase 24 Goodyear smart tires.
- Begin a one-year pilot test on four trucks.

How Smart Tires Work

Smart tires have an embedded computer chip that monitors wear, performance, and durability. The chip also creates an electronic fingerprint for positive identification of a tire. By passing a hand-held sensor next to the tire, we can learn where and when a tire was made (for warranty and other information), how much tread it had originally, and its serial number.

Justifies recommendation by explaining product and pros and cons

How Smart Tires Could Benefit Us

Although smart tires are initially more expensive than other tires, they could help us improve our operations and save us money in four ways:

1. **Retreads.** Goodyear believes that the wear data is so accurate that we should be able to retread every tire three times, instead of our current two times. If that's true, in one year we could save at least $27,000 in new tire costs.
2. **Safety.** Accurate and accessible wear data should reduce the danger of blowouts and flat tires. Last year, drivers reported six blowouts.
3. **Record keeping and maintenance.** Smart tires could reduce our maintenance costs considerably. Currently, we use an electric branding iron to mark serial numbers on new tires. Our biggest headache is manually reading those serial numbers, decoding them, and maintaining records to meet safety regulations. Reading such data electronically could save us thousands of dollars in labour.
4. **Theft protection.** The chip can be used to monitor each tire as it leaves or enters the warehouse or yard, thus discouraging theft.

Enumerates benefits for maximum impact and readability

Explains recommendation in more detail

Summary and Action

Specifically, I recommend that you do the following:
- Authorize the special purchase of 24 Goodyear smart tires at $450 each, plus one electronic sensor at $1,200.
- Approve a one-year pilot test in our Lower Mainland territory that equips four trucks with smart tires and tracks their performance.

Specifies action to be taken

Tips for Memo Reports

- Use memo format for most short (ten or fewer pages) informal reports within an organization.
- Leave side margins of 1 to 1¼ inches.
- Sign your initials on the FROM line.
- Use an informal, conversational style.
- For a receptive audience, put recommendations first.
- For an unreceptive audience, put recommendations last.

Summary Reports

In today's knowledge economy, information is what drives organizations. Information is important because without it, business decisions cannot be made. Because there is a huge amount of information available today on any given topic (e.g., the millions of pages of Internet material), people who make decisions don't always have the time to read and review all the information on a particular problem, issue, or topic. Therefore, decision makers need the essential elements of an issue or problem presented in a short, logical, easy-to-understand format that helps them quickly grasp what's vital.

Any time you take what someone else has written or said and reduce it to a concise, accurate, and faithful version of the original—in your own words—you are summarizing. A well-written summary report does three things: (1) it provides all

A summary condenses the primary ideas, conclusions, and recommendations of a longer publication.

FIGURE 8.6 Feasibility Report

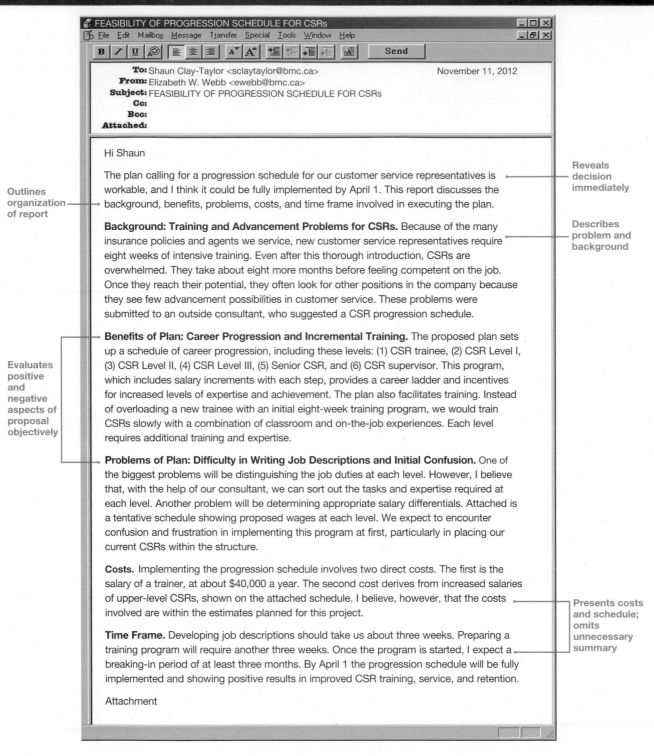

Outlines organization of report

Evaluates positive and negative aspects of proposal objectively

Reveals decision immediately

Describes problem and background

Presents costs and schedule; omits unnecessary summary

FEASIBILITY OF PROGRESSION SCHEDULE FOR CSRs

File   Edit   Mailbox   Message   Transfer   Special   Tools   Window   Help

Send

To: Shaun Clay-Taylor <sclaytaylor@bmc.ca>   November 11, 2012
From: Elizabeth W. Webb <ewebb@bmc.ca>
Subject: FEASIBILITY OF PROGRESSION SCHEDULE FOR CSRs
Cc:
Bcc:
Attached:

Hi Shaun

The plan calling for a progression schedule for our customer service representatives is workable, and I think it could be fully implemented by April 1. This report discusses the background, benefits, problems, costs, and time frame involved in executing the plan.

Background: Training and Advancement Problems for CSRs. Because of the many insurance policies and agents we service, new customer service representatives require eight weeks of intensive training. Even after this thorough introduction, CSRs are overwhelmed. They take about eight more months before feeling competent on the job. Once they reach their potential, they often look for other positions in the company because they see few advancement possibilities in customer service. These problems were submitted to an outside consultant, who suggested a CSR progression schedule.

Benefits of Plan: Career Progression and Incremental Training. The proposed plan sets up a schedule of career progression, including these levels: (1) CSR trainee, (2) CSR Level I, (3) CSR Level II, (4) CSR Level III, (5) Senior CSR, and (6) CSR supervisor. This program, which includes salary increments with each step, provides a career ladder and incentives for increased levels of expertise and achievement. The plan also facilitates training. Instead of overloading a new trainee with an initial eight-week training program, we would train CSRs slowly with a combination of classroom and on-the-job experiences. Each level requires additional training and expertise.

Problems of Plan: Difficulty in Writing Job Descriptions and Initial Confusion. One of the biggest problems will be distinguishing the job duties at each level. However, I believe that, with the help of our consultant, we can sort out the tasks and expertise required at each level. Another problem will be determining appropriate salary differentials. Attached is a tentative schedule showing proposed wages at each level. We expect to encounter confusion and frustration in implementing this program at first, particularly in placing our current CSRs within the structure.

Costs. Implementing the progression schedule involves two direct costs. The first is the salary of a trainer, at about $40,000 a year. The second cost derives from increased salaries of upper-level CSRs, shown on the attached schedule. I believe, however, that the costs involved are within the estimates planned for this project.

Time Frame. Developing job descriptions should take us about three weeks. Preparing a training program will require another three weeks. Once the program is started, I expect a breaking-in period of at least three months. By April 1 the progression schedule will be fully implemented and showing positive results in improved CSR training, service, and retention.

Attachment

the important points from the original without introducing new material; (2) it has a clear structure that often reflects the structure of the original material; and (3) it is independent of the original, meaning the reader of the summary can glean all essential information in the original without having to refer to it.

The ability to summarize well is a valuable skill for a number of reasons. Businesspeople are under pressure today to make decisions based on more information than ever before. Someone who can summarize that information into its key parts is way ahead of someone who cannot. Second, summarizing is a key communication task in many businesses today. For instance, as in the example below, a

VP of Human Resources asks one of his HR consultants to do research on the use of BlackBerrys in the workplace, as the company they work at has been experiencing some problems. Third, the ability to summarize makes you a better writer. As you learn to pick apart the structure of articles, reports, and essays written by professional writers such as journalists, you can introduce their tricks of the trade into your own writing. Finally, as part of writing the more complex reports discussed in Chapter 9, you will have to write executive summaries of your own work. Why not learn how to do this by summarizing other peoples' writing first?

There are four steps to writing an effective summary:

- **Read the material carefully for understanding.** Ideally, you will read the original three times: the first time to understand the topic; the second time with a pen, pencil, or highlighter in hand to underline the main points (usually no more than three in an article-length piece); and the third time to see the overall pattern.
- **Lay out the structure of your summary.** Simply write the main points you've underlined or highlighted in a list. For example, the HR consultant summarizing the Regina *Leader-Post* article in Figure 8.7 (also found at the beginning of this chapter) has identified three main points, one overall pattern, and one solution or conclusion. To lay out the structure of her summary, she would write:

1. There is evidence that younger workers don't view the use of BlackBerrys during meetings as a distraction from what's going on.
2. Experts agree that using BlackBerrys during meetings is distracting.
3. Experts also agree that multitasking becomes inefficient after a certain point.
4. The solution to using BlackBerrys at work is to recognize that this behaviour is potentially offensive to others and to separate oneself from the source of one's distraction.

FIGURE 8.7 Marked-Up Article for Summary

BlackBerry etiquette has yet to be defined

Richard Baum

Reuters

Saturday, May 15, 2010

Do you check your BlackBerry during work meetings? Do you do it furtively under the table, while your colleagues are distracted by a presentation?

Do you leave it in front of you so you can give it the occasional peck whenever it buzzes? Or are you bold enough in the board room to hold it up while you type your replies, a practice that's provoked comedian Jerry Seinfeld to respond, "Can I just pick up a magazine and read it in front of your face while you're talking to me?"

Unless you work in a company that bans BlackBerry use in meetings, you've seen all these behaviours. Most likely, you've been that person. But is it bad etiquette? Don't the pressures of time and overflowing inboxes make this a necessary evil of the 21st century workplace?

Other journalists who have taken time out from deleting e-mail to investigate this burning issue have concluded that polite society abhors the employee whose eyes wander from the PowerPoint presentation to the new e-mail alert.

But as someone who struggles to ignore the siren buzz of the BlackBerry, I demand leave to appeal this collective ruling by the media's finest minds. After all, every new technology that transforms communications encounters resistance from the old guard. Surely the cool kids accept that it is possible to concentrate on a meeting and accept e-mail requests for other meetings at the same time?

It didn't take much Googling to find some research that confirmed my hunch: <u>while 68 per cent of the baby-boom generation born before 1964 think that the use of smartphones meetings is distracting, just 49 per cent of the under-30s-see-a-problem.</u> As this 2008 LexisNexis survey helpfully points out, that's less than half. If the person running your meeting is a Generation Y'er, there's a better than even chance that she won't mind you checking your e-mail.

Main Point # 1

Evidence = Survey

Still, most of us have bosses who are too old to skateboard to work. What does Generation X think of BlackBerry Peckers? I asked John Freeman, a member of that demographic and the author of The Tyranny of Email:

"You never have everyone's full attention in a meeting any longer, and I think that's why meetings are becoming so ineffective" he wrote in a non-tyrannical e-mail.

"Whether it's the lot who try to thumb under the table, or those who brazenly do it in the open, the message, from a significant group of those gathered, is -- I have other things to do. Which totally defeats the purpose of meeting: you want to create a sense of group purpose. And on top of that it's rude."

But John, I can multitask. It may look like I'm updating my Facebook status under the table, but a co-worker has sent me an urgent question and I can answer that and concentrate on your presentation at the same time. Surely I can get an expert on multitasking to back me up here.

I called Clifford Nass, a professor of communication at Stanford University in California. Nass was part of a group that researched the concentration skills of students who frequently multitasked while consuming media. Did he find that those of us who listen and e-mail at the same time are an elite brigade of hyper-efficient workers? Not exactly.

"The more you multitask, the worse you become at it," he said. According to the Stanford team's research, there's a cost to memory and attention when you switch from one task to another. And that cost increases for people who multitask heavily.

So the science suggests that the appearance of not paying attention when you check your e-mail in a meeting mirrors the reality: however much you think you're paying attention to two things at once, you're not.

And yet the BlackBerry sits there in my pocket, calling to me throughout the meeting: Check me! Check me! What can I do?

"You have to become more cognisant that what you're doing is likely to be offensive to others," said Robert Gordon, who coaches adults with attention deficit hyperactivity disorder (ADHD).

Gordon, who is based in Toronto, says the strategy for executives struggling with ADHD is to separate them from their distractions. So in the case of a BlackBerry, that means shutting it off. I make a final plea. Rob, there are parts of many meetings that aren't relevant to me. What if I check my e-mail then?

"Then the onus falls on the person calling the meeting to be more focused on the agenda," he said.

So there's the answer. It's not my fault I'm rudely checking my BlackBerry. It's your fault for not making the meeting more interesting. And that's just plain bad etiquette.

- **Write a first draft.** In this step, you take your list from the step before (which may use the original author's exact language in many parts) and convert it into your own words. Our summary writer might write something like this:

  As requested, I've researched ~~the topic of~~ current opinion on the use of BlackBerrieys in the workplace.

  One useful article I found was by Richard Baum in the Regina *Leader-Post*. In his article ~~called~~ "BlackBerry etiquette has yet to be defined" (May 15, 2010), Baum makes ~~a number of main points and supports his~~ the following points ~~with~~ using two types of evidence.

  - Baum's main point is that there is a difference of opinion in the workplace. Younger workers see BlackBerry use as okay, while older workers don't. He ~~s~~cites a LexisNexis survey from 2008 to back up this point.

  - The second point Baum makes is that the use of BlackBerrys in meetings and presentations is distracting. He supports this point with quotes from experts like authors and professors.

  - The next point ~~made by~~ Baum makes is that multitasking with a BlackBerry (one of the device's selling points) becomes inefficient after a certain point. Again he uses a professor of communication to support this point.

  - Baum's conclusion is that BlackBerrieys do need to be put away at certain points in order not to create distractions that irritates other workers and leads to less efficiency at work.

  I appreciated the opportunity to provide this summary. If there's anything else you need, please let me know.

  Sincerely,

  Bailey Bingley

- **Proofread and revise.** The final step of writing a summary, like any written document, is to proofread for grammar, spelling, punctuation, and style mistakes and to rewrite where necessary. In the example above, the summary writer found

FIGURE 8.8 Descriptive Summary Report

BLACKBERRY RESEARCH YOU REQUESTED `_ □ ✕`

File Edit Mailbox Message Transfer Special Tools Window Help `_ 🗗 ✕`

| B | I | U | 🖉 | | ≣ | ≣ | ≣ | | A˄ | A˅ | | ˙≣ | ˙≣ | ˙≣ | ˙≣ | | 🖻 | | **Send** |

To: John Swiderski <jswiderski@bmc.ca>   January 14, 2012
From: Bailey Bingley <bbingley@bmc.ca>
Subject: BlackBerry research you requested
Cc:
Bcc:
Attached:

Hi John,

As requested, I've researched current opinion on the use of BlackBerrys in the workplace.

One useful article I found was by Richard Baum in the Regina *Leader-Post*. In his article "BlackBerry etiquette has yet to be defined" (May 15, 2010), Baum makes the following points using two types of evidence.

- Baum's main point is that there is a difference of opinion in the workplace. Younger workers see BlackBerry use as okay, while older workers don't. He cites a Lexis-Nexis survey from 2008 to back up this point.

- The second point Baum makes is that the use of BlackBerrys in meetings and presentations is distracting. He supports this point with quotes from experts like authors and professors.

- The next point Baum makes is that multitasking with a BlackBerry (one of the device's selling points) becomes inefficient after a certain point. Again he uses a professor of communication to support this point.

- Baum's conclusion is that BlackBerrys do need to be put away at certain points in order not to create distractions that irritate other workers and lead to less efficiency at work.

I appreciated the opportunity to provide this summary. If there's anything else you need, please let me know.

Sincerely,

Bailey Bingley

---

a number of mistakes in her draft (shown with strikethrough.) A proofread and revised final version of this descriptive summary report appears in Figure 8.8.

Minutes of Meetings

Minutes provide a summary of the proceedings of meetings. Traditional minutes, illustrated in the attachment shown in Figure 8.9, are written for large groups and legislative bodies. If you are the secretary of a meeting, you'll want to write minutes that do the following:

- Provide the name of the group, as well as the date, time, and place of the meeting.
- Identify the names of attendees and absentees, if appropriate.
- Describe the disposition of previous minutes.
- Record old business, new business, announcements, and reports.
- Include the precise wording of motions; record the vote and action taken.
- Conclude with the name and signature of the person recording the minutes.

> **Meeting minutes record summaries of old business, new business, announcements, and reports, as well as the precise wording of motions.**

Notice in Figure 8.9 that secretary Carol Allen tries to summarize discussions rather than capture every comment. However, when a motion is made, she records it verbatim. She also shows in parentheses the names of the individual making the motion and the person who seconded it. By using all capital letters for "MOTION" and "PASSED," she makes these important items stand out for easy reference.

Informal minutes are usually shorter and easier to read than formal minutes. They may be formatted with three categories: summaries of topics discussed, decisions reached, and action items (showing the action item, the person responsible, and the due date).

FIGURE 8.9 Minutes of Meeting—E-Mail Attachment Format

International Association of Administrative Professionals

Western Canada Division
Planning Committee Meeting
Conference Room B, Brunswick Plaza Hotel
November 4, 2012, 10 a.m.

Present: Carol Allen, Kim Jobe, LeeAnn Johnson, Barbara Leonard, Lee Schultz, Doris Williamson, Margaret Zappa

Shows attendees and absentees →

Absent: Ellen Williams

The meeting was called to order by Chair Kim Jobe at 10:05 a.m. Minutes from the July 11 meeting were read and approved.

← Describes disposition of previous minutes

Old Business

Summarizes discussion; does not record every word →

LeeAnn Johnson and Barbara Leonard reviewed the information distributed at the last meeting about hotels being considered for the Banff conference. LeeAnn said that the Fairmont Banff Springs has ample conference rooms and remodelled interiors. Barbara reported that the Mount Royal Hotel also has excellent banquet facilities, adequate meeting facilities, and rooms at $162 per night.
MOTION: To recommend that IAAP hold its International Convention at the Mount Royal Hotel, July 21–24, 2013. (Allen/Leonard). PASSED 6–1.

Reports

Lee Schultz reported on convention exhibits and her desire to involve more companies and products. Discussion followed regarding how this might be accomplished.
MOTION: That IAAP office staff develop a list of possible convention exhibitors. The list should be submitted at the next meeting. (Leonard/Schultz). PASSED 7–0.

← Highlights motions, showing name of person making motion and person seconding it

New Business

Summarizes new business and announcements →

The chair announced three possible themes for the convention, all of which focused on technology and the changing role of administrative assistants. Doris Williamson suggested the following possible title: "Vision Without Boundaries." Carol Allen suggested a communication theme. Several other possibilities were discussed. The chair appointed a subcommittee of Doris and Margaret to bring to the next committee meeting two or three concrete theme ideas.

Margaret Zappa thought that IAAP should be doing more to help members stay ahead in the changing workplace. She suggested workshops to polish skills in spreadsheet, database, presentations, and scheduling software.
MOTION: To recommend to IAAP that it investigate offering fee-based technology workshops at the national and regional conventions. (Zappa/Schultz). PASSED 5–2.

The meeting was adjourned at 11:50 by Kim Jobe.

Respectfully submitted,

← Shows name of person recording minutes

Carol Allen, Secretary

Minutes of November 4, 2012 meeting

File   Edit   Mailbox   Message   Transfer   Special   Tools   Window   Help

B I U   Send

To: <IAAP Boards>   November 16, 2012
From: Carol Allen <callen@iaap.ca>
Subject: Minutes of November 4, 2012 meeting
Cc:
Bcc:
Attached: Minutes Nov 12 2012.doc

Hi all,

Please find attached minutes of our last meeting.

Let me know if you have any questions or comments.

Regards,

Carol

Carol Allen
Secretary, IAAP Western Division
callen@iaap.ca
604 555-2993

Summing Up and Looking Forward

This chapter presented six types of informal business reports: information reports, progress reports, justification/recommendation reports, feasibility reports, summaries, and minutes of meetings. Information reports generally provide data only. But justification/recommendation reports as well as feasibility reports and sometimes summary reports are more analytical in that they also evaluate the information, draw conclusions, and make recommendations. This chapter also discussed a number of possible formats, delivery methods, and style choices for reports. The chapter's model documents illustrating six informal sample reports would be considered relatively informal. Longer, more formal reports are necessary for major investigations and research leading to important decisions. These reports and proposals, along with suggestions for research methods, are presented in Chapter 9.

Critical Thinking

1. What's the difference between a report and a regular e-mail or other message?

2. Of the reports presented in this chapter, which require indirect development and which require direct development?

3. Is it a good idea to provide analysis all the time when asked to write reports, or are there times when it's okay just to present information?

4. Compare and contrast justification/recommendation reports and feasibility reports. How can you easily remember the difference?

5. *Providing a summary is both an exercise in information gathering and an analytical task.* Discuss this statement and provide examples to back it up.

Chapter Review

1. List six kinds of informal reports and describe the goal of each one.

2. Explain the difference between providing information and providing an analysis of information.

3. Why are there two different patterns of organization for informal reports?

4. List the main report formats and give a realistic example of each one.

5. Match each situation below with the appropriate informal report.

   a. Your supervisor asks you to read a long technical report and write a report that condenses the important points.

   b. You want to tell management about an idea you have for improving a procedure that you think will increase productivity.

   c. You just attended a meeting at which you were the only person taking notes. The person who ran the meeting sends you an e-mail asking if you could remind him of the important decisions that were made.

   d. As Engineering Department office manager, you have been asked to describe your highly regarded computer system for another department.

   e. As a police officer, you are writing a report of an arrest.

   f. At a mail-order catalogue company, your boss asks you to investigate ways to reduce the time that customers are kept waiting for service representatives to take their telephone orders. She wants your report to examine the problem and offer solutions.

6. If you were about to write the following reports, where would you gather information? Be prepared to discuss the specifics of each choice.

   a. You are a student representative on a curriculum committee. You are asked to study the course requirements in your major and make recommendations.

   b. As department manager, you must write job descriptions for several new positions you wish to establish in your department.

   c. You are proposing to management that a copier in your department be replaced.

   d. You must document the progress of a 12-month advertising campaign to alter the image of a clothing manufacturer's jeans.

7. What three questions do progress reports typically address?

8. What is the purpose of a meeting minutes report?

9. Information reports generally contain what three parts?

10. What items should you include in an article summary that your employer asks you to write?

11. What is the main difference between a descriptive summary and an evaluative summary?

Writing Improvement Exercises

1. **Practise Summarizing.** Summarize the magazine article below in a 150-word e-mail to your business partner.
2. **Practise Summarizing.** Summarize the newspaper article on page 221 in a 150-word e-mail to your boss.
3. **Practise Summarizing/Role Play.** Choose a newspaper or magazine article related to business and summarize it. Look ahead to Figure 11.3 (p. 312) and turn your article summary into an oral presentation outline. Give your summary as a short presentation to your class, as if they were your work colleagues at a weekly staff meeting.

Patients rewarded

by Greg Fjetland, November 22, 2004

After her 13-year-old daughter Jessica was diagnosed with a rare brain tumour, Marlene Petersen of Kelowna, B.C., felt almost overwhelmed by the demands on her time. New to the province, with four other children at home and as many as six medical appointments for Jessica on just one day, "You can imagine how stressful the situation was," says Petersen. Fortunately, she was able to make use of a new health service launched in October.

NavaHealth, a for-profit, privately owned company, leads B.C. residents through the labyrinthine health-care system by providing support and patient advocacy. With NavaHealth's president Elisabeth Riley helping her to understand Jessica's treatment, Petersen found coping with her daughter's illness far less overwhelming. "There's so much information coming at you, you can't remember it all," says Petersen. "You have questions that you forget to ask. And your emotions get in the way."

NavaHealth is the brainchild of Riley, currently dean of the School of Health Sciences at the British Columbia Institute of Technology. Riley began the planning for NavaHealth after she was laid off in the summer of 2002 from her position as president and CEO of the Children's & Women's Health Centre of B.C. in Vancouver. She realized from her long experience in the health sector that a service gap was widening. "The medical system is increasingly complex," says Riley. "It's not the fault of the system; it's just that medicine is so complex. We had only a doctor and a nurse in the system 50 years ago, and now look at how many health professionals and alternatives there are."

So Riley laid the groundwork for her new enterprise, including hiring IT professionals to create a database for health information and hiring registered nurses as "health navigators." With 10 navigators now working throughout British Columbia, NavaHealth provides services in person, by phone and e-mail. Navigators not only will accompany clients to appointments—the doctors are informed first—but can point out a wide range of appropriate services, including directing the client to community support services such as grief counselling, or private services such as contractors to adapt a home for handicap needs.

Riley is the sole owner of NavaHealth. She charges $100 an hour for the services of a navigator, which she splits with the RN. After an initial free consultation, payment is on a fee-for-service basis. Riley says she funded the launch of NavaHealth entirely out of her pocket. She watches her budget carefully: when a reporter calls her long distance on her cellphone, she calls him back on her land line to reduce the charges.

Helping patients comprehend their medical options is a large market, but where Riley might really strike gold is in targeting her services at what she calls the Sandwich Generation: those adults with both aging parents and children at home to care for. It's a market strongly supported by the demographics of the mid-life baby boomers who live in one part of the country while their parents live elsewhere. "Anyone who has had to balance the demands of caring for an aging parent along with demands from their work and their own family, knows how challenging that can be," Riley says.

While the British Columbia Medical Association doesn't have an official position on patients hiring paid consultants to accompany them to the doctor's office, BCMA president Dr. Jack Burak admits to some concerns. First, it's not a service that all patients can afford equally, and secondly, a patient with a paid advocate may expect a longer appointment with a doctor who has only limited time available. "I don't know how you meld those two concerns," Burak says.

Riley says the market will decide. Since opening her doors, she's received inquiries for her service from across the country and she estimates NavaHealth will break even within six months. Riley intends to expand her service nationwide with head offices in every province within five years. Now that's a healthy ambition.

SOURCE: GRET FJETLAND, "PATIENTS REWARDED," CANADIAN BUSINESS, NOVEMBER 22, 2004. REPRINTED WITH PERMISSION.

TONY WONG

BUSINESS REPORTER, May 25, 2005

David Morton has had just about every kind of request from executives moving to Toronto on short-term assignments and looking for housing. For a Fortune 500 company executive with a substantial monthly budget of $40,000, Morton was able to find a mansion in Rosedale, considered one of Toronto's best neighbourhoods.

The client's main requests were that the backyard be big enough for his children and their dog, and that the home be recently renovated.

While living in Rosedale isn't the typical request, Morton, the owner of MAC Furnished Rentals Inc., can place you in furnished accommodation for a short-term stay in Toronto from $3,000 a month all the way up to the $40,000 range and beyond.

"They could be moving for a new posting, to fill a short-term position, to look after a maternity leave—the reasons vary," said Morton, who has more than 100 units in Ottawa, Toronto and Sudbury.

According to a Royal LePage Relocation Services study released yesterday, the corporate-housing market in Canada was a $230 million business in 2004.

The most expensive city to relocate to was Vancouver, where it cost an average of $2,950 a month for furnished accommodation, or about $98 per night. Toronto was in close second place at $2,935, followed by Fort McMurray at $2,905.

Toronto has the largest supply of units, but Calgary, with less than a quarter of the population, comes in a close second because of the highly mobile oil and gas industry.

Royal LePage places Fort McMurray, with a population of just 56,000, in third place, but calls it the "corporate-housing capital of Canada," with the lowest vacancy rate driven by the boom in oil-sands production.

In Fort McMurray, the average stay is 90 days, compared with 47 in Toronto and 58 in Vancouver.

"The amount of corporate activity out of (Fort McMurray) is staggering," said Robert Peterman, director of assignment solutions for Royal LePage. "You're talking about one of the biggest oil-production areas in the world, and most of it is coming from that area."

Peterman said the corporate-housing market has grown significantly over the past several years, thanks to an improving economy.

Morton said his company, which started five years ago, has grown about 20 per cent annually.

While the Toronto area has experienced a surge of growth over the past several years, some of that was curtailed last year. Some smaller players left the business due to competition from rising vacancy rates caused by heavy condominium development and a downturn caused by the increase in the Canadian dollar, boosting prices for foreign filmmakers and other visitors, said Royal LePage.

While the market is generally made up of small, independent operators, the returns are now attractive enough to garner the attention of bigger chains, said Peterman.

"The corporate-housing market in Canada is extremely fragmented," Royal LePage said in its report. "Local suppliers range from independent investors with a single furnished suite to large full-suite hotels. Amenities, services and quality vary enormously."

In Toronto, several developers are looking at specially built suite lodges specifically for the corporate, long-term-stay market.

"If you look a few years back, most of the big firms had their own furnished apartments they could move their executives to," said Morton.

With corporate downsizing in the 1990s, the furnished apartments were sold, leaving a vacuum in the market that was filled by operators such as Morton.

Peterman said companies generally use furnished apartments over hotels as a "lifestyle choice" rather than a cost-saving issue, although it is generally cheaper to use corporate accommodations rather than place employees in hotel rooms.

"Some people do prefer living out of hotels. But if you are moving somewhere for three months, you generally would probably prefer to live in a bigger unit with a full kitchen and more of a home-like atmosphere," said Peterman.

It's also something of a misconception to think that placing an employee on temporary assignment rather than relocating him or her entirely is always more cost effective, Peterman said: "You've got to pay for accommodations, and then there are the bi-weekly trips back home, so this can add up pretty quickly."

Activities and Cases

TEAM

8.1 Evaluating Headings and Titles

Identify the following report headings and titles as "talking" or "functional/descriptive." Discuss the usefulness and effectiveness of each.

a. Problem

b. Need for Tightening Computer ID System

c. Annual Budget

d. How Direct Mail Can Deliver Profits for Your Business

e. Case History: Rotunda Palace Hotel Focuses on Improving Service to Customers

f. Solving Our Networking Problems with an Extranet

g. Comparing Copier Volume, Ease of Use, and Speed

h. Alternatives

8.2 Information Report: The Less Glamorous Side of Being an Entrepreneur

You and three friends have decided to open a consulting business in Kitchener, Ontario. You're all recent business college grads and, rather than work for a large corporation, you'd like to strike out on your own. The area you'd like to concentrate on is branding for not-for-profit organizations and educational institutions. Your three friends have already staked out the glamorous side of things, including business development, which leaves you with the "nuts and bolts." The company has been registered, but none of its banking issues have been dealt with. Your partners ask you to send them an e-mail about which bank has "the best deal" as well as "any other stuff you can find out."

Your Task. Write an e-mail information report to your three partners investigating opening up a business account at two financial institutions. Do some more research into what it takes to start a small business and include this information in your report.

Related Web site: The government of Ontario maintains an excellent site on starting a small business in that province; see http://www.ontariocanada.com/ontcan/1medt/ smallbiz/en/sb_yrguide_main_en.jsp.

8.3 Information Report: Canadian Tech Company Expands into Asia

You work in business development for Hydrogenics, a Mississauga, Ontario–based producer of clean energy products. Hydrogenics already has an office in Tokyo, but the owners feel they need to expand its Asian operations. Your boss has asked you to investigate the partnership opportunities available for investors in Korea and China. He gives you a tight deadline of one week, and asks for the report to be sent to him via e-mail with any attachments you think are important.

Your Task. Investigate the mechanics of opening an office and/or investing in Korea and China. Report your findings in an e-mail to your boss, Bob Khan.

Related Web sites: Important background information can be found at http://www. hydrogenics.com, http://www.investkorea.org, and http://www.fdi.gov.cn/pub/ FDI_EN/default.htm.

8.4 Information Report: What I Did and Found Out at a Recent Conference

Using the Internet, find an upcoming professional conference in your area of study—for example, a human resources conference, a marketing and sales conference, a financial services conference, a management conference, and so on. Examine the schedule of events. Then, assume you have attended this conference. When you get back to your city, your manager asks you to send him a report on what you experienced and found out.

Your Task. In e-mail format, write the information report requested by your manager.

8.5 Progress Report: Making Headway Toward Your Educational Goal

You made an agreement with your parents (or spouse, relative, or partner) that you would submit a progress report at this time describing the headway you have made toward your educational goal (employment, certificate, diploma, degree).

Your Task. In memo format write a progress report that fulfills your promise to describe your progress toward your educational goals. Address your progress report to your parents, spouse, relative, or partner. In your memo (1) describe your goal; (2) summarize the work you have completed thus far; (3) discuss thoroughly the work currently in progress, including your successes and anticipated obstacles; and (4) forecast your future activities in relation to your scheduled completion date.

8.6 Progress Report: Designing a Template for HR

WEB

You are the assistant to the Director of Human Resources at BASF's head office in Mississauga, Ontario. At a recent meeting of the management board, it was decided that the employee review process required an overhaul. Instead of once-yearly meetings with their immediate superior to "discuss any issues," the company has decided to institute a more accountable process in which all employees (including managers) must write a yearly progress report.

Your Task. Develop a template report for your boss, Sue Swinton, Director of Human Resources, that can be filled out by all BASF Canada employees at all ten locations once a year. Keep in mind that employees are generally unenthusiastic about the employee review process. In other words, your template must be easy to fill out and logical.

Related Web sites: BASF Canada's site is at http://www2.basf.us/basf-canada/index_e.shtm. You may also want to research best practices in performance management and the employee review process.

8.7 Recommendation Report: What Is It About Advertising?

WEB

You are the CEO of a mid-size Oakville, Ontario–based advertising agency named Slam! Your company is in the enviable position of having secured the advertising contract for the 2015 Pan/Parapan American Games in Toronto. The problem is, you can't seem to keep your employees around long enough to ensure continuity within projects. It seems as though the advertising business is a revolving door: new college and university grads are eager to work for you, but six months later, once you've trained them, they leave for more lucrative jobs at other agencies. You're too busy to figure out a solution or policy; in fact you're so busy you haven't got around to hiring a human resources manager. Instead you ask your research manager to write you a report on some possible solutions.

Your Task. As the research manager at Slam!, research and write a short e-mail recommendation report for your boss outlining some possible solutions to the "revolving door" problem. Your boss's thriftiness is well known, so you'll have to be careful about how you phrase any expensive solutions.

Related Web site: An article at the following URL provides some general solutions to employee retention: http://www.bcjobs.ca/re/hr-resources/human-resource-advice/recruitment-and-retention/employee-retention-ideas--ideas-for-retaining-top-performers; however, you should also do other research on the topic of employee retention. Be careful not to plagiarize from your sources when completing this report. Information on the Pan/Parapan American Games can be found at http://www.toronto2015.org/.

8.8 Recommendation Report

CRITICAL THINKING

As a management trainee at a small, family-owned resort, you have been assigned to spend a week at a time in each of the many food service areas. This week you are working as acting assistant manager for Room Service from 4 a.m. to 11 a.m. You have noticed a serious shortage of staff during the hours from 6 a.m. to 8 a.m., when most breakfast orders come in. Often guests have to call two or three times for their orders; some end up cancelling. You have had several visits from angry guests, and even your staff is disgruntled. Because of your schedule, you don't get to speak personally to Dal Lewis, the Manager of Food and Beverage, but you must make sure he knows about the situation.

Your Task. Write a short e-mail recommendation report to Dal Lewis clearly explaining the extent of the problem and outlining some possible solutions.

8.9 Justification/Recommendation Report: Solving a Campus Problem

TEAM

In any organization, room for improvement always exists. Your college or university campus is no different. You are the member of a student task force that has been asked to identify problems and suggest solutions.

In groups of two to five, investigate a problem on your campus, such as inadequate parking, slow registration, poor class schedules, an inefficient bookstore, a weak job-placement program, unrealistic degree requirements, or a lack of internship programs. Within your group develop a solution to the problem. If possible, consult the officials involved to ask for their input in arriving at a feasible solution. Do not attack existing programs; instead, strive for constructive discussion and harmonious improvements.

Your Task. After reviewing persuasive techniques discussed in Chapter 6, write a justification/recommendation report in memo or letter format. Address your report to the college or university president.

8.10 Justification/Recommendation Report: Developing a Company E-Mail and Web-Use Policy

As a manager in a midsize financial services firm, you are aware that members of your department frequently use e-mail and the Internet for private messages, shopping, games, and other personal activities. In addition to the strain on your company's computer network, you worry about declining productivity, security problems, and liability issues. When you walked by one worker's computer and saw what looked like pornography on the screen, you knew you had to do something. Although workplace privacy is a controversial issue for unions and employee-rights groups, employers have legitimate reasons for wanting to know what is happening on their computers. A high percentage of lawsuits involve the use and abuse of e-mail. You think that the executive council should establish some kind of e-mail and Web-use policy. The council is generally receptive to sound suggestions, especially if they are inexpensive. You decide to talk with other managers about the problem and write a justification/recommendation report.

In teams of two to five, discuss the need for an e-mail and Web-use policy. Using the Web, find sample policies used by other firms. Look for examples of companies struggling with lawsuits over e-mail abuse. Find information about employers' rights to monitor employees' e-mail and Web use. Use this research to determine what your company's e-mail and Web-use policy should cover. Each member of the team should present and support his or her ideas regarding what should be included in the policy and how to best present your ideas to the executive council.

Your Task. Write a convincing justification/recommendation report in memo or letter format to the executive council based on the conclusions you draw from your research and discussion. Decide whether you should be direct or indirect.

8.11 Justification/Recommendation Report: Diversity Training— Does It Work?

Employers recognize the importance of diversity awareness and intercultural sensitivity in the workplace because both are directly related to productivity. It is assumed that greater harmony also minimizes the threat of lawsuits. An interest in employee diversity training has spawned numerous corporate trainers and consultants, but after many years of such training, some recent studies seem to suggest that they may be ineffective or deliver mixed results at best. A 2009 article in the trade magazine *Canadian HR Reporter* concluded that diversity training does not necessarily change bias, for example, against lesbian, gay, and transgendered employees.[2]

Search the Internet and your library's databases for information about diversity training. Examine articles favourable to diversity training and those that exhibit a more pessimistic view of such efforts.

Your Task. As a group of two to five members, write a memo report to your boss (address it to your instructor) and define diversity training. Explain which measures companies take to make their managers and workers culturally aware and respectful of differences. If you have personally encountered such training, draw on your experience in addition to your research. Your report should answer the question *Does diversity training work?* If yes, recommend steps your company should take to become more sensitive to minorities. If no, suggest how current practices could be improved to be more effective.

8.12 Justification Report: Evaluating Your Curriculum

You have been serving as a student member of a curriculum advisory committee. The committee is expected to examine the course requirements for a degree, diploma, or certificate in your area.

Your Task. In teams of three to five, decide whether the requirements are realistic and practical. What improvements can your team suggest? Interview other students, faculty members, and employers for their suggestions. Prepare a justification report in e-mail or memo format to send to the president of your college or university proposing your suggestions. You anticipate that the head of your faculty or department may need to be persuaded to make any changes. Consider delaying your recommendations until after you have developed a foundation of explanation and reasons.

8.13 Justification Report: Purchasing New Equipment

In your work or your training position, identify equipment that needs to be purchased or replaced (e.g., computer, printer, modem, DVD player, copier, digital camera, etc.). Gather information about two different models or brands.

Your Task. Write a justification report comparing the two items. Establish a context by describing the need for the equipment. Discuss the present situation, emphasizing the current deficiencies. Describe the advantages of acquiring the new equipment.

8.14 Feasibility Report: CEO Not Convinced by Assistant's Recommendations

The CEO of Slam! (from Activity 8.7) is not convinced. He received his research manager's recommendation report, which was well written and persuasive, but he doesn't yet believe that the recommendations she made (e.g., increasing pay, benefits, and vacation time) are practical or warranted. Still, her recommendation report was persuasive enough that the CEO has decided to spend money on a consultant's services. He wants a feasibility report written on the practicality of his research manager's suggestions.

Your Task. As the performance management consultant hired by Slam!'s CEO, write a short feasibility report, in manuscript format, to your client. Keep in mind that Slam! has roughly 35 employees working on the creative side of advertising, but it also has 15 employees working in account management and finance who are likely to be suspicious if their creative colleagues are "showered with gifts." Are there non-monetary compromise solutions that would make the CEO's attempts to retain employees feasible and effective?

8.15 Summary Report: Condensing an Article About E-Mail Privacy

Your boss is worried because the company has no formal e-mail policy. Should employees be allowed to use e-mail for personal messages? May management monitor the messages of employees? She asks you to research this topic (or another topic on which you and your instructor agree).

Your Task. Using library databases, find a useful newspaper, magazine, or other periodical article (around 1,000 words). In a one-page document, summarize the major points of the article. Also evaluate its strengths and weaknesses. Attach this summary document to an e-mail that you send to your boss, Justine Toller, Division Manager.

8.16 Summary Report: What Are They Saying About Us?

As the Director of Foreign Operations for Beijing-based China Mining Corp., you have to be a savvy communicator. One the one hand, your domestic market is in desperate need of more sources of minerals and metals to feed a rapidly expanding industrial base. On the other hand, the domestic supply of many metals and minerals is just about used up and you are forced to search for sources in other parts of the world. The problem—and this is where your savvy communicating comes in—is convincing the rest of the world that investment by China is okay. In particular, you've heard rumours that some Canadians are not happy about the prospect of their natural resources being controlled by foreign companies. You're just about to travel to Canada for some important meetings with government and mining industry leaders, but before you do, you want solid information on what Canadians are thinking and saying.

Your Task. As Director Huang's Canadian office manager in Calgary, you are asked via e-mail to quickly summarize "a few articles" that provide a picture of current Canadian opinion on foreign control of natural resources. After researching newspaper, magazine, and other periodical articles, reply to Mr. Huang with a short descriptive summary report.

8.17 Minutes: Recording the Proceedings of a Meeting

Ask your instructor to let you know when the next all-faculty or division or departmental meeting is taking place on your campus. Or, ask your student association or student council representative to let you know when the next association or council meeting is taking place. Or, next time you're at work or at your co-op job, ask your boss to let you sit in on a meeting. Volunteer to act as note-taker or secretary for this meeting.

Your Task. Record the proceedings of the meeting you attend in an informal meeting minutes report. Focus on reports presented, motions/action items, votes, and decisions reached.

Chapter 8: Informal Reports

8.18 Role Play: Everyone's Taking Minutes

Next time you have a group or team related to one of your school assignments, videotape or audiotape one of your group or team meetings. Then, turn that meeting into a scripted skit. Perform the skit in front of your class.

Your Task. As an audience member, watch the skit discussed above. Assume you are the note-taker at the meeting. Create a minutes report for the meeting you just watched. Are there any elements of a meeting the group/team missed (e.g., motions, action statements, etc.)?

8.19 Longer Report: Solving a Problem

Choose a business or organization with which you are familiar and identify a problem, such as poor quality, indifferent service, absenteeism at organization meetings, uninspired cafeteria food, outdated office equipment, unresponsive management, lack of communication, under-appreciated employees, wasteful procedures, or a similar problem.

Your Task. Describe the problem in detail. Assume you are to report to management (or to the leadership of an organization) about the nature and scope of the problem. Decide which kind of report to prepare (information, recommendation, justification), and choose the format. How would you gather data to lend authority to your conclusions and recommendations? Determine the exact topic and report length after consultation with your instructor.

Grammar/Mechanics Review—8

The following sentences contain errors in grammar, punctuation, capitalization, number style, usage, and spelling. Pay special attention to eliminating expletives (*there is*, *there are*). Below each sentence write a corrected version.

Example: There were 2 employees who volunteered to head the united way campaign.

Revision: Two employees volunteered to head the United Way campaign.

1. There are three Vice Presidents who report directly to the company President.
2. Although the meeting was first scheduled for May 2nd its been rescheduled for May 10th.
3. As a matter of fact there are figures that suggest that a medium size dog costs exactly six thousand four hundred dollars to raise for eleven years.
4. There were exhibitors at the Trade Show, who came from as far as australia and japan, to promote there products.
5. If there have been many customers who are complaining we must revamp delivery schedules.
6. Would you please remove the charge of 78 dollars from my July statement?
7. "Large companies," says Tate Steinke director of transportation at big rigs freight "are looking for ways to shrink shipping costs.
8. There were 25 Zoomout Cameras awarded as prizes at the end of the year awards' ceremony.
9. Because there are so many ontarians and quebeckers who flock to florida the price of rental units rises in the winter.
10. After travelling north on highway 101 exit at pritchard valley road, and follow the signs to birds hill estates.
11. In canada sixty-eight percent of the land is wilderness, however in africa only twenty-eight percent is wilderness.
12. On december 21st did we pay forty-two dollars a share to acquire 1/4th of the stocks in genetics, inc.
13. By eliminating 1 olive from each salad served in the first class section transway airlines saved forty thousand dollars.
14. There are many foreign language software programs that we stock including: russian, chinese, japanese, and dutch programs.
15. There is no canadian football league team that plays it's home games in a domed stadium that have ever won a grey cup.

Document for Revision

The progress report shown in Figure 8.10 has faults in grammar, punctuation, spelling, number form, wordiness, and word use. Use standard proofreading marks (see Appendix B) to correct the errors. When you finish, your instructor can show you the revised version of this report.

FIGURE 8.10 Progress Report

Progress Report on Sites for "Great Canadian Cook Off" Series

File   Edit   Mailbox   Message   Transfer   Special   Tools   Window   Help

B / U | | | | | A A | | | | | A | **Send**

To: John Peters <jpeters@zedfilms.ca>   January 10, 2012
From: Kalare Jegsee <kjegsee@zedfilms.ca>
Subject: Progress Report on Sites for "Great Canadian Cook Off" Series
Cc:
Bcc:
Attached:

This email will outline the progress of my location search for our "Great Canadian Cook Off" series, which begins to shooting in April. My location search has been undertaken in the downtown Toronto area, because the gratest number of restaurants are found there.

What I've done so Far: As requested by you, I've searched for restaurants that have a professional kitchen, that are not crampped in size, and which are avaliable for rental during our shoting period and renting for less than $1,000 per day. This required a week's worth of telephoning around the city to narrow down the possibilities. After my phoning I had narrowed down the search to five restaurants: Lisa's; On the Avenue; Trattoria Umberto, Avignon; and also the Mackenzie House. At this point I have had meetings with the owners of the first two restaurants named above. Bot Lisa's and On the Avenue fit our criterias, but Lisas is pretty cramped in size.

What I still Need To Do: As you can see from what I've said above, there are three restaurants I've yet to visit. I have meetings scheduled for this Thursday and Friday at all three. I realized while visiting Lisa's and On the Avenue that we should probably be add another criteria which is; what kind of front-of-house facilities do they have. In other words, if the dining area itself is not attractive (we may be using this for extra shots, e.g. one on one interviews), there isn't much points going with this location. So I will keep this extra criteria in mind when I meet with the other 3 restaurants.

I'll send u a final report narrowing my list of five down to 2 by early next week (probably Monday!). Please let me know if you have any questions.

Cheers,

Kalare

Web Evaluation: Hoax? Scholarly Research? Advocacy?

Most of us tend to think that any information turned up via a Web search engine has somehow been evaluated as part of a valid selection process.[3] Not true. The truth is that the Internet is rampant with unreliable sites that reside side by side with reputable sites. Anyone with a computer and an Internet connection can publish anything on the Web.

Unlike library-based research materials, information at many sites has not undergone the editing or scrutiny of scholarly publication procedures. The information we read in journals and most reputable magazines is reviewed, authenticated, and evaluated. That's why we have learned to trust these sources as valid and authoritative. But information on the Web is much less reliable. Some sites are obvious hoaxes. Others exist to distribute propaganda. Still others want to sell you something. To use the Web meaningfully, you must scrutinize what you find. Here are specific questions to ask as you examine a site:

- **Currency.** What is the date of the Web page? When was it last updated? Is some of the information obviously out of date? If the information is time sensitive and the site has not been updated recently, the site is probably not reliable.
- **Authority.** Who publishes or sponsors this Web page? What makes the presenter an authority? Is a contact address available for the presenter? Learn to be skeptical about data and assertions from individuals whose credentials are not verifiable.
- **Content.** Is the purpose of the page to entertain, inform, convince, or sell? Who is the intended audience, judging from content, tone, and style? Can you assess the overall value of the content compared with that of the other resources on this topic? Web presenters with a skewed point of view cannot be counted on for objective data.
- **Accuracy.** Do the facts that are presented seem reliable to you? Do you find errors in spelling, grammar, or usage? Do you see any evidence of bias? Are footnotes provided? If you find numerous errors and if facts are not referenced, you should be alerted that the data may be questionable.

For more information on evaluating Web sites, check out the University of California at Berkeley's excellent Web site at **http://www.lib.berkeley.edu/TeachingLib/Guides/Internet/Evaluate.html**.

Career Application

As interns at a news-gathering service, you have been asked to assess the quality of the following Web sites. Which of these could you recommend as sources of valid information?

- Beef Nutrition (**http://www.beefnutrition.org)**
- Edmunds—Where Smart Car Buyers Start (**http://www.edmunds.com**)
- I Hate Windows (**http://www.ihatewindowsxp.com**)
- EarthSave International (**http://www.earthsave.org**)
- The Vegetarian Resource Group (**http://www.vrg.org/nutshell/nutshell.htm**)
- The White House (**http://www.whitehouse.gov**)
- The White House (**http://www.whitehouse.com**)
- The Anaheim White House (**http://www.anaheimwhitehouse.com**)
- National Anti-Vivisection Society (**http://www.navs.org**)
- Dow Chemical Company (**http://www.dow.com**)
- Dow: A Chemical Company on the Global Playground (**http://www.dowethics.com**)
- Smithsonian Institution (**http://www.si.edu**)
- Drudge Report (**http://www.drudgereport.com**)
- Canadian Cancer Society (**http://www.cancer.ca**)
- CraigsList (**http://www.craigslist.com**)

Your Task

If you are working with a team, divide the preceding list among team members. If you are working individually, select four of the sites. Answer the questions in the preceding checklist as you evaluate each site. Summarize your evaluation of each site in a memo report to your instructor or in team or class discussion. Consider the following questions:

- What evidence can you find to determine whether these sites represent hoaxes, personal opinion, or reliable information?
- Are the sources for factual information clearly listed so that they can be verified?
- Can you tell who publishes or sponsors the page?
- Are the organization's biases clearly stated?
- Is advertising clearly differentiated from informational content?
- Would you use these sites for scholarly research? Why or why not?

CHAPTER 9

Proposals and Formal Reports

A research supplier report needs to clearly and concisely articulate insights and implications from the study, and no report is complete without actionable recommendations. I am particularly impressed if the writer demonstrates a good knowledge and understanding of the confectionery category and our business in particular. The quality of the final report is very important. It reflects on me personally, as I am the person managing the study. The report's quality will strongly influence my decision about whether to hire the same research company for future studies.[1]

Len Willschick,
Manager, Consumer and Market Intelligence, Wrigley Canada

© LISE GAGNE/ISTOCKPHOTO.COM

LEARNING OBJECTIVES

1. Identify and explain the parts of informal and formal proposals.

2. Describe the preparatory steps for writing a formal report.

3. Collect data from secondary sources, including print and electronic sources.

4. Understand how to use the Web and online databases to locate reliable data.

5. Discuss how to generate primary data from surveys, interviews, observation, and experimentation.

6. Understand the need for accurate documentation of data and the consequences of plagiarism.

7. Describe how to organize report data, create an outline, and write effective titles.

8. Illustrate data using tables, charts, and graphs.

9. Sequence 13 parts of a formal report.

> **Proposals are persuasive offers to solve problems, provide services, or sell equipment.**

> **Both large and small companies today often use requests for proposals (RFPs) to solicit competitive bids on projects.**

Proposals are persuasive offers to solve problems, provide services, or sell equipment or other products. Let's say that the City of Fredericton wants to upgrade the computers and software in its human resources department. If it knows exactly what it wants, it prepares a request for proposal (RFP) specifying its requirements. It then publicizes the RFP, and companies interested in bidding on the job submit proposals. RFPs were traditionally publicized in newspapers, but today they're published on special Web sites, such as **http://www.merx.com**, which is the best-known Canadian RFP site.

Both large and small companies, organizations, and agencies are increasingly likely to use RFPs to solicit competitive bids on their projects. This enables them to compare "apples to apples." That is, they can compare the prices different companies would charge for completing the same project. RFPs also work for companies in situations where needs are not clear. An RFP can be issued stating broad expectations and goals within which bidding companies offer innovative solutions and price quotes. In most cases, a proposal also acts as a legal statement of work from which a contract for services is developed.

Many companies earn a sizable portion of their income from sales resulting from proposals. It's important to realize that not all proposals are solicited—that is, published in the newspaper or on Web sites. Unsolicited proposals are also important business documents. For example, if I'm a consultant who specializes in coaching and team-building skills, I can send an unsolicited proposal to a large organization such as a bank, offering my services.

The ability to write effective proposals, whether solicited or unsolicited, is especially important today. In writing proposals, the most important thing to remember is that they are sales presentations. They must be persuasive, not merely mechanical descriptions of what you can do. You may recall from Chapter 6 that effective persuasive sales messages build interest by emphasizing benefits for the reader, reduce resistance by detailing your expertise and accomplishments, and motivate action by making it easy for the reader to understand and respond.

Informal Proposals

Proposals may be informal or formal; the distinction is primarily in length and format. Informal proposals are often presented in letter format. Sometimes called letter proposals, they contain six principal parts: introduction, background, proposal, staffing, budget, and authorization. The informal letter proposal shown in Figure 9.1 (p. 232) illustrates all six parts of a letter proposal. This proposal is addressed to a Calgary dentist who wants to improve patient satisfaction.

Informal proposals may contain an introduction, background information, the plan, staffing requirements, a budget, and an authorization request.

Introduction

Most proposals begin by explaining briefly the reasons for the proposal, highlighting the writer's qualifications, and briefly previewing the price and timeline of the job to be undertaken. To make your introduction more persuasive, use persuasive techniques to gain the reader's attention. One proposal expert suggests these possibilities:

Effective proposal openers capture interest by promising extraordinary results or resources or by identifying key benefits, issues, or outcomes.

- Hint at extraordinary results with details to be revealed shortly.
- Promise low costs or speedy results.
- Mention a remarkable resource (well-known authority, new computer program, well-trained staff) available exclusively to you.
- Identify a serious problem (worry item) and promise a solution, to be explained later.
- Specify a key issue or benefit that you feel is the heart of the proposal.[2]

For example, Dana Swensen, in the introduction of the proposal shown in Figure 9.1, focused on a key benefit. In this proposal to conduct a patient satisfaction survey, Dana thought that the client, Dr. Larocque, would be most interested in specific recommendations for improving service to her patients. But Dana didn't hit on this benefit until after the first draft had been written. Indeed, it's often a good idea to put off writing the introduction to a proposal until after you have completed other parts. For longer proposals the introduction also describes the scope and limitations of the project, as well as outlining the organization of the material to come.

Background

The background section identifies the problem and discusses the goals or purposes of the project. The background is also the place to go over some recent history. In other words, briefly summarize what circumstances led to you writing the proposal. For example, in Figure 9.1, the "history" of the situation is alluded to in the

FIGURE 9.1 Informal Proposal

SWENSEN RESEARCH ASSOCIATES

One Providence Plaza
Calgary, Alberta T1A 4E5
(403) 628-3011
www.sra.ca

May 15, 2012

Dr. Marie Larocque
1789 Clarkston Avenue
Calgary, AB T1L 5G4

Dear Dr. Larocque:

Introduction grabs attention with "hook" that focuses on key benefit

Helping you improve your practice is of the highest priority to us at Swensen Research Associates. We are pleased to submit the following proposal outlining our plan to help you more effectively meet your patients' needs by analyzing their views about your practice. This project can be completed for you by July 2 at a cost of $4,872.00.

Background and Goals

Discusses circumstances leading to proposal and identifies four goals of survey

We understand that you have been incorporating a total quality management system in your practice. Although you have every reason to believe your patients are pleased with the service you provide, you would like to give them an opportunity to discuss what they like and possibly don't like about your service. Based on our conversations, we understand that you would like the patient surveys to allow you to do the following:

- Determine the level of their satisfaction with you and your staff
- Elicit suggestions for improvement
- Learn more about how your patients discovered you
- Compare your "preferred" and "standard" patients

Proposed Plan

To help you achieve your goals, Swensen Research proposes the following plan:

Plan is divided into logical segments for easy reading and interest building

Survey. A short but thorough questionnaire will probe for the data you desire. This questionnaire will measure your patients' reactions to such elements as courtesy, professionalism, accuracy of billing, friendliness, and waiting time. After you approve it, the questionnaire will be sent to a carefully selected sample of 300 patients whom you have separated into groupings of "preferred" and "standard."

Analysis. Survey data will be analyzed by demographic segments, such as patient type, age, and gender. Our experienced team of experts, using state-of-the-art computer programs and advanced statistical measures, will study the (1) degree of patient satisfaction, (2) reasons for satisfaction or dissatisfaction, and (3) relationship between your "preferred" and "standard" patients. Moreover, our team will give you specific suggestions for making patient visits more pleasant.

Report. You will receive a final report with the key findings. The report will include tables summarizing all responses categorized by "preferred" and "standard" clients. Our staff will also draw conclusions based on these findings.

---

sentence *We understand that you have been incorporating a total quality management system in your practice.*

In a proposal, your aim is to convince the reader that you understand the problem completely. Thus, if you are responding to an RFP, this means repeating its language. For example, if the RFP asks for the *design of a maintenance program for high-speed mail-sorting equipment*, you would use the same language in explaining the purpose of your proposal. This section might include segments entitled *Basic Requirements*, *Most Critical Tasks*, and *Most Important Secondary Problems*.

FIGURE 9.1 *(Continued)*

Dr. Marie Larocque   Page 2   May 15, 2012

Schedule. With your approval, the following schedule has been arranged for your patient satisfaction survey:

Questionnaire development and mailing	June 1–16
Deadline for returning questionnaire	June 24
Data tabulation and processing	June 24–26
Completion of final report	July 2

Uses past-tense verbs to show that work has already started on the project

Our Team

Swensen Research Associates is a nationally recognized, experienced research consulting firm specializing in survey investigation. I have assigned your customer satisfaction survey to Dr. Kelly Miller, our director of research. Dr. Miller was trained at Queen's University and has successfully supervised our research program for the past nine years. Before joining SRA, she was a marketing analyst with Procter & Gamble Company.

Assisting Dr. Miller will be a team headed by Jacob Malau, our vice president for operations. Mr. Malau earned a bachelor's degree in computer science and a master's degree in marketing from the University of Calgary. Within our organization he supervises our computer-aided telephone interviewing (CAT) system and manages our 30-person professional interviewing staff.

Staffing section builds credibility and reduces resistance by describing outstanding staff and facilities

Our Cost

	Estimated Hours	Rate	Total
Professional and administrative time			
Questionnaire development	3	$150/hr.	$ 450.00
Data processing and tabulation	16	50/hr.	800.00
Analysis of findings	15	150/hr.	2250.00
Preparation of final report	5	150/hr.	750.00
Mailing costs			390.00
HST			232.00
Total cost			$ 4872.00

Budget section itemizes costs carefully because a proposal is a contract offer

Authorization

Patient satisfaction is vital to the success of your practice. Our professionally designed and administered client survey will help you determine how best to meet the needs of your patients, thereby assuring the success of your practice. Specific results from your survey can be ready for you by July 2. Please sign the enclosed duplicate copy of this letter and return it to us with a retainer of $2,320 so that we may begin developing your survey immediately. The rates in this offer are in effect only until September 1. Thank you for giving us this chance to help you better serve your patients.

Authorization section summarizes benefits, makes response easy, and provides deadline

Sincerely,

Dana H. Swensen

Dana H. Swensen, President

DHS:pm
Enclosure

Plan

In the plan section, you should discuss your methods for solving the problem. In some proposals this is tricky, because you want to disclose enough of your plan to secure the contract without giving away so much information that your services aren't needed. Without specifics, though, your proposal has little chance, so you must decide how much to reveal. Explain what you propose to do and how it will benefit the reader. Remember, too, that a proposal is a sales presentation. Sell your methods, product, and "deliverables"—items that will be left with the client. In

The plan section must give enough information to secure the contract but not so much detail that the services are not needed.

this section some writers specify how the project will be managed, how its progress will be audited, and what milestones along the way will indicate the project is progressing as planned. Most writers also include a schedule of activities or a timetable showing when events take place.

Staffing

The staffing section of a proposal describes the credentials and expertise of the project leaders and the company as a whole. A well-written staffing section describes the capabilities of the whole company. Although the example in Figure 9.1 does not do so, staffing sections often list other high-profile jobs that have been undertaken by the company, as a way of building interest and reducing resistance. For example, before she mentioned Dr. Miller and Mr. Malau, Dana Swensen could have said, *Among our well-known clients are Husky Energy and the Calgary Board of Education.*

The staffing section may also identify the size and qualifications of the support staff, along with other resources such as computer facilities and special programs for analyzing statistics. In longer proposals, résumés of key people may be provided. The staffing section is a good place to endorse and promote your staff.

Budget

Because a proposal is a legal contract, the budget must be researched carefully.

A central item in proposals is the budget, a list of project costs. You need to prepare this section carefully because it represents a contract; you can't raise the price later—even if your costs increase. You can—and should—protect yourself with a deadline for acceptance. In the budget section some writers itemize hours and costs; others present a total sum only. A proposal to install a complex computer system might, for example, contain a detailed line-by-line budget. In the proposal shown in Figure 9.1, Dana Swensen felt that she needed to justify the budget for her firm's patient-satisfaction survey, so she itemized the costs. But the budget included for a proposal to conduct a one-day seminar to improve employee communication skills might be a lump sum only. Your analysis of the project and your audience will help you decide what kind of budget to prepare.

Authorization

Informal proposals need to close with a request for approval or authorization. In addition, the closing should remind the reader of key benefits and motivate action. It might also include a deadline date beyond which the offer is invalid. At some companies, such as Hewlett-Packard, authorization to proceed is not part of the proposal. Instead, it is usually discussed after the customer has received the proposal. In this way the customer and the sales account manager are able to negotiate terms before a formal agreement is drawn. Either way, learning to write an authorization section—which must find a way of saying you want the job without appearing too greedy or needy—is an important persuasive exercise.

Formal Proposals

Formal proposals differ from informal proposals in size and format. Formal proposals respond to big projects and may range from 5 to 200 or more pages. To facilitate comprehension and reference, they are organized into many parts. In addition to the six basic parts just described, formal proposals contain some or all of the following additional parts: copy of the RFP, letter of transmittal, abstract and/or executive summary, title page, table of contents, figures, and appendixes containing such items as detailed budgets and staffing information. In this book we will not discuss formal proposals in detail because it is unlikely that a business communicator in an entry-level position would have to write such a detailed proposal. Formal proposal writing is usually handled either by consultants or by employees with significant experience in this area.

Well-written proposals win contracts and business for companies and individuals. In fact, many companies, especially those that are run on a consulting model, depend entirely on proposals to generate their income. Companies such as Microsoft, Hewlett-Packard, and IBM employ staffs of people that do nothing but prepare proposals to compete for new business. For more information about industry standards and resources, visit the Web site of the Association of Proposal Management Professionals (**http://www.apmp-canada.ca/**).

Preparing to Write Formal Reports

Whenever business research is part of a business problem (as in the example in Figure 9.1 concerning Swensen Research Associates and Dr. Marie Larocque), a formal report (or presentation, or both) is usually the main deliverable to the client. We can define a formal business report, then, as a written solution to a business issue or problem. These formal reports typically have three overall characteristics: a formal tone, a traditional structure, and considerable length. Formal research reports in business serve a very important function. They provide management with vital data, analysis, and recommendations for decision making. In this section we will consider the entire process of writing a formal report: preparing to write; researching, generating, documenting, organizing, and illustrating data; and presenting the final report.

Like proposals and informal reports (which you studied in Chapter 8), formal reports begin with a definition of the project. Probably the most difficult part of this definition is limiting the scope of the report. Every project has limitations. Decide at the outset what constraints influence the range of your project and how you will achieve your purpose. How much time do you have for completing your report? How much space will you be allowed for reporting on your topic? How accessible are the data you need? How thorough should your research be?

If you are writing about low morale among employees who work shifts, for example, how many of your 475 employees should you interview? Should you limit your research to company-related morale factors, or should you consider external factors over which the company has no control? In investigating variable-rate mortgages, should you focus on a particular group, such as first-time homeowners in a specific area, or should you consider all mortgage holders? The first step in writing a report, then, is determining the precise boundaries of the topic.

Once you have defined the project and limited its scope, write a statement of purpose. The statement of purpose should describe the goal, scope, significance, and limitations of the report. Notice how the following statement includes all four criteria:

> The purpose of this report is to explore employment possibilities for entry-level paralegal workers in the city of St. John's. It will consider typical salaries, skills required, opportunities, and working conditions. This research is significant because of the increasing number of job openings in the electronic health records field. This report will not consider health care sector secretarial employment, which represents a different employment focus.

WORKPLACE IN FOCUS

Hailed as the largest science experiment in history, the Large Hadron Collider is a multibillion-dollar atom-smasher out to uncover the origins of the universe. Buried 100 metres below Meyrin, Switzerland, the massive particle accelerator uses barrel-shaped solenoids and supercooled magnets to recreate conditions believed to have existed during the Big Bang. Physicists at CERN built the collider to investigate the existence of extra dimensions and "dark matter"—an invisible mass that may comprise much of the universe. Despite public fears that the atomic project could unleash an Earth-swallowing black hole, scientists backing the collider have issued formal reports affirming its safety. *Why is it important for CERN to provide accurate documentation in its safety reports?*

Researching Secondary Data

> **Primary data come from firsthand experience and observation; secondary data from reading articles, books, Web sites, reports, and statistics.**

One of the most important steps in the process of writing a report is doing research that will help solve the business problem at hand. A report is only as good as its data, so you'll want to spend considerable time collecting data before you begin writing.

Data fall into two broad categories, primary and secondary. Primary data result from firsthand experience and observation. Secondary data come from reading what others have experienced and observed. One of the best-known organizations that researches primary data is Consumers Union (**http://www.consumerreports.org**), a nonprofit organization headquartered in Yonkers, New York. After testing all kinds of consumer goods in its National Testing and Research Center—everything from cars to computers to fitness equipment—Consumers Union publishes its results in its best-selling magazine, *Consumer Reports*. Once published, the primary data generated in the Yonkers lab becomes secondary data. Now anyone—a student, a parent, or a newspaper reporter—can use the data. Secondary data are easier and less expensive to develop than primary data, which might involve interviewing large groups or sending out questionnaires.

Secondary research is where nearly every research project should begin. Often, something has already been written about your topic. Reviewing secondary sources can save time and effort and help you avoid costly primary research to develop data that already exist. Most secondary material is available in online databases conveniently located in your school or company library.

Print Resources

Although we're seeing a steady movement away from print to electronic data, some information is still available only in print.

> **Although researchers are increasingly turning to electronic data, some data are available only in print.**

If you are an infrequent library user, begin your research by talking with a reference librarian about your project. These librarians won't do your research for you, but they will steer you in the right direction. And they are very accommodating. Many libraries also help you understand their computer, cataloguing, and retrieval systems by providing brochures, handouts, and workshops.

Books. Although sometimes outdated depending on how quickly a particular body of knowledge changes, books provide excellent in-depth data and interpretation on many subjects. For example, if you are investigating best practices in Web site design, you will find numerous books with valuable information in your nearest library. Books are located through online catalogues that can be accessed in the library, on any campus computer, or from home with an Internet connection and valid password. Most library catalogues today enable you to learn not only whether a book is in the library's holdings but also whether it is currently available.

Periodicals. Magazines, newspapers, and journals are called periodicals because of their recurrent or periodic publication. Journals are compilations of scholarly articles. Articles in journals and other periodicals will be extremely useful to you because they are concise, limited in scope, and current, and can supplement information in books. For example, if you want to understand the latest trends and research in the business communication field, you would browse through recent volumes of the *Journal of Business Communication*. Periodical research in paper format is especially useful these days when following current issues. For example, if you're studying the fluctuating prices of commodities like food and energy, a reputable newspaper's business section would be a good place to start to get oriented to the topic.

Online Databases

As a writer of business reports today, you will most likely do much of your secondary research using online databases. Many researchers turn to databases first because they are fast, focused, and available online. Databases are exactly what they sound like: large collections of information in electronic format. In this case, the information is almost every article published in every newspaper, magazine, academic journal, and trade journal. A huge amount of information, by any measure. By using these online resources you can look for the secondary data you require without ever leaving your office or home.

The strength of databases lies in the fact that they are current and field specific. For example, if you go to the George Brown College Library Web site (**http://library .georgebrown.ca/**), you will instantly see the "Start Your Research" title and right underneath it a box that says "Articles & Databases." From here, you can choose the area of you research (e.g., Business, Health, Hospitality, Technology) and press "Go." Doing so will take you to a list of databases of information in your particular area of research. If you then click on "Business," a list of forty-five different databases appears. These business databases contain articles from magazines, newspapers, and academic journals, but they also contain statistical information, encyclopedia information, company information, and various other important business information. Your own library will have similar resources. Libraries pay for these databases partly through your tuition fees. If you do not have access to an institution's databases, your local public library will also have databases available for your use.

Learning how to use an online database takes some practice. We suggest you go to your favourite library Web site and experiment with online databases. Choose a topic like *trends in business communication* and see what you come up with. Try to find one current article from a newspaper, a magazine, and a journal. Do you get better results when you use the basic or the advanced search function? Do you get better results by separating the topic into parts, for example, *trends* and *business* and *communication*, or by typing in the whole phrase at once? If you're having trouble, you can always sign up for a free guided seminar at your library, or ask a librarian for help next time you're there.

The Web

The best-known area of the Internet is the World Wide Web. Growing at a dizzying pace, the Web includes an enormous collection of Web sites around the world. With trillions of pages of information available on the Web, chances are good that if you have a question, an answer exists online. Web offerings include online

Books provide historical, in-depth data; periodicals provide limited but current coverage.

Most researchers today begin by looking in online databases, which are collections of almost every article published in any publication.

Review information online through research databases that are accessible by computer and searchable.

The World Wide Web is a collection of hypertext pages that offer information and links to trillions of pages.

databases, magazines, newspapers, library resources, sound and video files, and many other information resources. You can expect to find such items as product and service facts, public relations material, mission statements, staff directories, press releases, current company news, government information, selected article reprints, collaborative scientific project reports, stock research, financial information, and employment information. The Web is indeed a vast network of resources at your fingertips.

The Web is unquestionably one of the greatest sources of information now available to anyone needing simple facts quickly and inexpensively. But finding relevant, credible information can be frustrating and time consuming. The constantly changing contents of the Web and its lack of organization irritate budding researchers. Moreover, content isn't always reliable. Anyone posting a Web site is a publisher without any quality control or guarantee. The problem of gathering information is complicated by the fact that the total number of Web sites recently surpassed 100 million, growing at a rate of about 4 million new addresses each month.[3] Therefore, to succeed in your search for information and answers, you need to understand how to browse the Web and use search engines. You also need to understand how to evaluate the information you find.

Web Browsers and URLs. Searching the Web requires a Web browser, such as Microsoft Internet Explorer, Safari, or Firefox. Browsers are software programs that enable you to view the graphics and text of, as well as access links to, Web pages. To locate the Web page of a specific organization, you need its Web site address, or URL (Uniform Resource Locator). URLs are case and space sensitive, so be sure to type the address exactly as it is printed. For most companies, the URL follows the pattern of **http://www.xyzcompany.com**. Your goal is to locate the top-level Web page (called the *home page* and, in certain cases, *portal*) of an organization's site. On this page you will generally find an overview of the site contents or a link to a site map. If you can't guess a company's URL, you can usually find it quickly using Google (**http://www.google.ca**).

Web access has gone mobile in the last few years, as increasingly sophisticated smartphones and PDAs (personal digital assistants) now offer nearly the same functions as desktop and laptop computers do. Mobile browsers, also called mini browsers, are small versions of their bigger cousins, Internet Explorer or Firefox. Businesspeople can surf Web pages and write e-mail on the go with devices such as the popular BlackBerry and iPhone, which fit into their pockets. Similarly, users can listen to podcasts, digital recordings of radio programs, and other audio and video files on demand. Podcasts are distributed for downloading to a computer or an MP3 audio player such as the iPod and can be enjoyed anywhere you choose.

Search Engines. The Web is packed with amazing information. Instead of visiting libraries or searching reference books when you need to find something, you can now turn to the Web for all kinds of facts. However, you will need a good search engine, such as Google, Yahoo, or MSN. A search engine is a service that indexes, organizes, and often rates and reviews Web pages. Some search engines rely on people to maintain a catalogue of Web sites or pages. Others use software to identify key information. They all begin a search based on the keywords you enter. The most-used search engine at this writing is Google. It has developed a cult-like following with its "uncanny ability to sort through millions of Web pages and put the sites you really want at the top of its results pages."[4]

Web Search Tips and Techniques. To conduct a thorough Web search for the information you need, use these tips and techniques:

● **Use two or three search engines.** Different Internet search engines turn up different results. However, at this writing, Google consistently turns up more reliable "hits" than other search engines.

- **Know your search engine.** When connecting to a search service for the first time, always read the description of its service, including its FAQs (Frequently Asked Questions), Help, and How to Search sections.
- **Understand case sensitivity.** Generally use lowercase for your searches, unless you are searching for a term that is typically written in upper- and lowercase, such as a person's name.
- **Use nouns as search words and as many as eight words in a query.** The right key words—and more of them—can narrow your search considerably.
- **Use quotation marks.** When searching for a phrase, such as *cost-benefit analysis,* most search engines will retrieve documents having all or some of the terms. This AND/OR strategy is the default of most search engines. To locate occurrences of a specific phrase, enclose it in quotation marks.
- **Omit articles and prepositions.** Known as "stop words," articles and prepositions don't add value to a search. Instead of *request for proposal,* use *proposal request.*
- **Proofread your search words.** Make sure you are searching for the right thing by proofreading your search words carefully. For example, searching for *sock market* will come up with substantially different results than searching for *stock market.*
- **Save the best.** To keep better track of your favourite Web sites, save them as bookmarks or favourites.
- **Keep trying.** If a search produces no results, check your spelling. Try synonyms and variations on words. Try to be less specific in your search term. If your search produces too many hits, try to be more specific. Think of words that uniquely identify what you are looking for, and use as many relevant keywords as possible. Use a variety of search engines, and repeat your search a few days later.

Blogs (Weblogs), Wikis, and Social Networks

The Web continues to grow and expand, offering a great variety of virtual communities and collaboration tools. Mentioned most frequently are blogs, wikis, and social networking sites. Far from being mere entertainment for "wired" teens, these resources are affecting the way we do business today.

Blogs, wikis, and informal online networks can be used to generate primary or secondary data.

One of the newest ways to locate secondary information on the Web is through the use of *Weblogs,* more commonly referred to as *blogs.* A Google search yields dozens of definitions. A Cornell University glossary defines the term as a "journal on the web, which may be public or private, individual or collaborative."[5] An individual's opinions or news are posted regularly in reverse chronological order, allowing visitors to comment.

Blogs are used by business researchers, students, politicians, the media, and many others to share and gather information. Marketing firms and their clients are looking closely at blogs because blogs can produce unbiased consumer feedback faster and more cheaply than such staples of consumer research as focus groups and surveys.[6] Employees and executives at companies such as Google, Rogers, IBM, and Hewlett-Packard maintain blogs. They use blogs to communicate internally with employees and externally with clients.[7]

A blog is an online diary or journal that allows visitors to leave public comments. At this time, writers have posted 70 million blogs, up nearly 30 percent in one year.[8] However, only about half of these blogs are active, meaning that posts were published within the last three months. Although blogs may have been overrated in their importance, they do represent an amazing new information stream if used wisely. Be sure to evaluate all blog content using the checklist provided in the Communication Workshop at the end of Chapter 8.

At least as important to business as blogs are new communication tools such as wikis and social networking sites. A wiki is collaborative software, typically a collection of Web pages, that can be edited by a group of users tapping into the same technology that runs the well-known online encyclopedia Wikipedia. Large companies, such as British Telecom (BT), encourage their employees to team up to author software, launch branding campaigns, and map cell phone stations. Most projects are facilitated with the help of wikis, a tool that is especially valuable across vast geographic distances and multiple time zones.[9]

Far from being only entertaining leisure sites, social networks such as Facebook and Twitter are used by businesses to enable teams to form spontaneously and naturally and then to assign targeted projects to them. Idea generators are easy to spot. A BT executive considers these contributors invaluable, adding that "a new class of supercommunicators has emerged."[10] However, these exciting new online tools require sound judgment when researchers wish to use them. For example, if using social networking to promote a product as a marketer, are you ethically compromised by invading the privacy of unsuspecting members of the public?

Generating Primary Data

Primary data come from firsthand experience.

Although you'll begin a business report by searching for secondary data, you'll need primary data to give a complete, up-to-date, and original picture. Business reports that solve specific current problems typically rely on primary, firsthand data. If, for example, management wants to discover the cause of increased employee turnover in its Toronto office, it must investigate conditions in Toronto by collecting recent information. Providing answers to business problems often means generating primary data through surveys, interviews, observation, or experimentation.

Surveys

Surveys yield efficient and economical primary data for reports.

Surveys collect data from groups of people. When companies develop new products, for example, they often survey consumers to learn their needs. The advantages of surveys are that they gather data economically and efficiently. Mailed surveys reach big groups nearby or at great distances. Moreover, surveys are easy to respond to because they're designed with closed-ended, quantifiable questions. It's easy to pick an answer on a professionally designed survey, thus improving the accuracy of the data.

Surveys, of course, have disadvantages. Most of us rank them as an intrusion on our increasingly important private time, so response rates may be no higher than 10 percent. Furthermore, those who do respond may not represent an accurate sample of the overall population, thus invalidating generalizations for the group. Let's say, for example, that an insurance company sends out a survey questionnaire asking about provisions in a new policy. If only older people respond, the survey data cannot be used to generalize what people in other age groups might think. A final problem with surveys has to do with truthfulness. Some respondents exaggerate their incomes or distort other facts, thus causing the results to be unreliable. Nevertheless, surveys are still considered the best way to generate data for business and student reports.

Interviews

Interviews with experts produce useful report data, especially when little has been written about a topic.

Some of the best report information, particularly on topics about which little has been written, comes from individuals. These individuals are usually experts or veterans in their fields. Consider both in-house and outside experts for business reports. Tapping these sources will call for in-person, e-mail, or telephone interviews. To elicit the most useful data, try these techniques:

- **Locate an expert.** Ask managers and other individuals whom they consider to be most knowledgeable about a particular field or industry. Check Web sites of professional organizations and consult articles about the topic or related topics. Most people enjoy being experts or at least recommending them. You could also post an inquiry to an Internet group. Choose your groups carefully, though, to avoid being flooded with unwanted correspondence.
- **Prepare for the interview.** Learn about the individual you're interviewing as well as the background and terminology of the topic. Let's say you're interviewing a corporate communication expert about producing an in-house company blog.

You ought to be familiar with terms such as *font* and software such as WordPress or Movable Type. In addition, be prepared by making a list of questions that pinpoint your areas of interest in the topic. Ask the interviewee if you may record the talk.

- **Make your questions objective and friendly.** Don't get into a debating match with the interviewee. And remember that you're there to listen, not to talk! Use open-ended, rather than yes-or-no, questions to draw experts out.
- **Watch the time.** Tell interviewees in advance how much time you expect to need for the interview. Don't overstay your appointment.
- **End graciously.** Conclude the interview with a general question, such as *Is there anything you'd like to add?* Express your appreciation, and ask permission to phone or e-mail later if you need to verify points.

Observation and Experimentation

Some kinds of primary data can be obtained only through firsthand observation and investigation. How long does a typical caller wait before a customer service representative answers the call? How is a new piece of equipment operated? Are complaints of sexual harassment being taken seriously? Observation produces rich data, but that information is especially prone to charges of subjectivity. One can interpret an observation in many ways. Thus, to make observations more objective, try to quantify them. For example, record customer telephone wait time for 60-minute periods at different times throughout a week. Or compare the number of sexual harassment complaints made with the number of investigations undertaken and resulting actions.

Experimentation produces data suggesting causes and effects. Informal experimentation might be as simple as a pretest and post-test in a college course. Did students expand their knowledge as a result of the course? More formal experimentation is undertaken by scientists and professional researchers who control variables to test their effects. Assume, for example, that Mordens' of Winnipeg Candy Manufacturing wants to test the hypothesis (which is a tentative assumption) that chocolate lifts people out of depression. An experiment testing the hypothesis would separate depressed individuals into two groups: those who ate chocolate (the experimental group) and those who did not (the control group). What effect did chocolate have? Such experiments are not done haphazardly, however. Valid experiments require sophisticated research designs, careful attention to matching the experimental and control groups, and ethical considerations.

> Some of the best report data come from firsthand observation and investigation.

Documenting Data and Plagiarism

One of the most common complaints of college and university professors is that their students don't understand the importance of documentation. Documentation is the act of showing where your information came from, whether in a business report or in an academic essay. Young people who have grown up with the Internet sometimes find it hard to understand that *all* information, whether it comes from a book, a magazine, a newspaper, a pamphlet or brochure, a Web site, or a blog, is the property of someone else. If you use it and don't say that you've used it, you're stealing.

Put yourself in the shoes of a journalist. She makes her living by writing for a magazine. If you take a phrase or a sentence or a paragraph from what she's written and place it in your report without acknowledging that fact, you're infringing on the journalist's rights—you're stealing from her. Not documenting sources is dishonest, ethically problematic, and illegal. The crime is called plagiarism, and all colleges and universities have strict policies against it, including penalties such as a zero grade on the plagiarized assignment. If your instructor has not already discussed your institution's policy, you should ask him or her to do so.

Plagiarism is the act of not documenting your sources, of taking another person's ideas or published words and not acknowledging that fact. Any time you quote directly, paraphrase, or summarize information from a source, you must document it. Documentation in a business report serves three purposes:

- **Strengthens your argument.** Including good data from reputable sources will convince readers of your credibility and the logic of your reasoning.
- **Protects you.** Acknowledging your sources keeps you honest. It's unethical and illegal to use others' ideas without proper documentation.
- **Instructs the reader.** Citing references enables readers to pursue a topic further and make use of the information themselves.

Documentation is achieved through citations. A citation is the method used to show from where the idea or phrase or sentence was borrowed. The original reason behind citations (before plagiarism became a big problem) was to allow anyone reading your work to find your sources should he or she wish to do additional research. If someone says to you, "But you didn't cite it!" he or she means you didn't include a proper citation.

For example, in a report that reads *In a recent Vancouver Province article, Blake Spence, Director of Transportation, argues that the TTC must be modernized and expanded to cope with the influx of tourists expected during the 2015 Pan American Games (A17)*, the citation is the combination of the lead-in, *Blake Spence … argues*, and the page reference, *(A17)*. The basic elements of an in-text citation are the author's name and the page number. There will be times when you don't have these two pieces of information. For more information on such cases, as well as the two main citation methods—footnote/endnote (or Chicago style) and parenthetic (or APA and MLA style)—please read Appendix C. Also study Figure 9.16 (pages 252–261) to see how sources are documented there. Besides in-text citations, you will cite each source you've used (primary and secondary) at the end of your report on a page called the "Works Cited" or "References" page. There is a specific format for how this is done, also found in Appendix C.

Citing Electronic Sources. Now that research has become an extension of our fingertips (we log on and search the Internet as if it's part of us, unlike earlier generations of students, who experienced a separation between themselves and research sources—they had to physically get to a library, wander around, find books and magazines on shelves, flip through pages to find material, copy that material into a notebook, then go back home and copy it on a typewriter or computer—it's no surprise that plagiarism is on the rise. As a recent article in the *Ottawa Citizen* points out, 53 percent of undergraduate students in Canada admit to "copying a few sentences from a written source or the Internet" without citing.[11]

Precisely because it's so easy to do, Internet plagiarism is a difficult problem to root out. Some students today even believe that they're not doing anything wrong by copying information from the Internet. Unfortunately, the reality is that this act constitutes academic dishonesty, and all academic institutions penalize dishonesty with a range of penalties, from a zero on the assignment to revoking admission from a course or a program to displaying evidence of academic dishonesty on academic transcripts. It's your responsibility as a business communicator, both at school and at work, not to plagiarize from the Internet.

Standards for researchers using electronic sources are still evolving. When citing electronic media, you should hold the same goals as for print sources. That is, you want to give credit to the author and to allow others to locate the same or updated information easily. However, since electronic sources are less stable than books or magazines, citation experts recommend more information be provided when citing electronic sources than when citing print sources. Since electronic sources can be changed easily, multiple publication dates may need to be included as well as the date on which the source was used. Most citation experts suggest similar information be cited for an electronic source, including the author's name (when available), document title, Web page or online database title, access date, and Web address. See Appendix C for more detailed information and examples of citing electronic sources.

Organizing and Outlining Data

Once you have collected the data for a report and recorded that information on notes or printouts, you are ready to organize it into a coherent plan of presentation. First, you should decide on an organizational strategy, and then, following your plan, you will want to outline the report. Poorly organized reports lead to frustration; therefore, it is important to organize your report carefully so that readers will understand, remember, or be persuaded.

Organizational Strategies

The readability and effectiveness of a report are greatly enhanced by skillful organization of the information presented. As you begin the process of organization, ask yourself two important questions: (a) Where should I place the conclusions/recommendations? and (b) How should I organize the findings?

Where to Place the Conclusions and Recommendations. As you recall from earlier instruction, the direct strategy requires that we present main ideas first. In formal reports that would mean beginning with your conclusions and recommendations. For example, if you were studying five possible locations for a proposed shopping centre, you would begin with the recommendation of the best site. Use this strategy when the reader is supportive and knowledgeable. However, if the reader isn't supportive or needs to be informed, the indirect strategy may be better. This strategy involves presenting facts and discussion first, followed by conclusions and recommendations. Since formal reports often seek to educate the reader, this order of presentation is often most effective. Following this sequence, a study of possible locations for a shopping centre would begin with data regarding all proposed sites followed by an analysis of the information and conclusions drawn from that analysis.

> In the direct strategy, conclusions and recommendations come first; in the indirect strategy, they are last.

How to Organize the Findings. After collecting your facts, you need a coherent plan for presenting them. Below we describe three organizational patterns: chronological, geographical, and topical. You will find these and other patterns summarized in Figure 9.2. The pattern you choose depends on the material collected and the purpose of your report.

> Organize report findings chronologically, geographically, topically, or by one of the other methods shown in Figure 9.2.

- **Chronological order.** Information sequenced along a time frame is arranged chronologically. This plan is effective for presenting historical data or for describing a procedure. Agendas, minutes of meetings, progress reports, and procedures are usually organized by time. A description of the development of a multinational company, for example, would be chronological. A report explaining how to obtain federal funding for a project might be organized chronologically. Often topics are arranged in a past-to-present or present-to-past sequence.
- **Geographical or spatial arrangement.** Information arranged geographically or spatially is organized by physical location. For instance, a report analyzing a company's national sales might be divided into sections representing geographical areas such as the East Coast, Quebec, Southern Ontario, Northern Ontario, Prairies, and the West Coast.
- **Topical or criteria arrangement.** Some subjects lend themselves to arrangement by topic or criteria. A report analyzing changes that need to be made to improve a company's Web site is an example. The report could be organized by "Possible Models and Competitor Models" or by the criteria used to judge effective Web sites, such as "Usability," "Navigation," "Content," and "Other Design Issues."

Outlines and Headings

Most writers agree that the clearest way to show the organization of a report topic is by recording its divisions in an outline. Although the outline isn't part of the final report, it is a valuable tool for the writer. It reveals at a glance

> Outlines show the organization and divisions of a report.

FIGURE 9.2 Organizational Patterns for Report Findings

Pattern	Development	Use
Chronology	Arrange information in a time sequence to show history or development of topic.	Useful in showing time relationships, such as five-year profit figures or a series of events leading to a problem
Geography/Space	Organize information by regions or areas.	Appropriate for topics that are easily divided into locations, such as East Coast and West Coast, etc.
Topic/Function	Arrange by topics or functions.	Works well for topics with established categories, such as a report about categories of company expenses
Compare/Contrast	Present problem and show alternative solutions. Use consistent criteria. Show how the solutions are similar and different.	Best used for "before and after" scenarios or for problems with clear alternatives
Journalism Pattern	Arrange information in paragraphs devoted to *who*, *what*, *when*, *where*, *why*, and *how*. May conclude with recommendations.	Useful with audiences that need to be educated or persuaded
Value/Size	Start with the most valuable, biggest, or most important item. Discuss other items in descending order.	Useful for classifying information in, for example, a realtor's report on home values
Importance	Arrange from most to least important or build from least to most important.	Appropriate when persuading the audience to take a specific action or change a belief
Simple/Complex	Begin with simple concept; proceed to more complex idea.	Useful for technical or abstract topics
Best Case/Worst Case	Describe the best and worst possible outcomes.	Useful when dramatic effect is needed to achieve results; helpful when audience is uninterested or uninformed
Convention	Organize the report using a prescribed plan that all readers understand.	Useful for many operational and recurring reports such as weekly sales reports

FIGURE 9.3 Outline Format

FORMS OF BUSINESS OWNERSHIP

I. Sole proprietorship (*first main topic*)
    A. Advantages of sole proprietorship (*first subdivision of Topic I*)
        1. Minimal capital requirements (*first subdivision of Topic A*)
        2. Control by owner (*second subdivision of Topic A*)
    B. Disadvantages of sole proprietorship (*second subdivision of Topic I*)
        1. Unlimited liability (*first subdivision of Topic B*)
        2. Limited management talent (*second subdivision of Topic B*)
II. Partnership (*second main topic*)
    A. Advantages of partnership (*first subdivision of Topic II*)
        1. Access to capital (*first subdivision of Topic A*)
        2. Management talent (*second subdivision of Topic A*)
        3. Ease of formation (*third subdivision of Topic A*)
    B. Disadvantages of partnership (*second subdivision of Topic II*)
        1. Unlimited liability (*first subdivision of Topic B*)
        2. Personality conflicts (*second subdivision of Topic B*)

the overall organization of the report. As you learned in Chapter 3, outlining involves dividing a topic into major sections and supporting those with details. Figure 9.3 shows a short outline for a report about forms of business ownership. Rarely is a real outline so perfectly balanced; some sections are usually longer than others.

The main points used to outline a report often become the main headings of the written report, amplified with facts, statistics, quotations, and other data. In Chapter 8 you studied tips for writing functional and talking headings. Formatting those headings depends on what level they represent. Major headings, as you can see in Figure 9.4, are centred and typed in bold font. Second-level headings start at the left margin, and third-level headings are bolded, situated at the beginning of a paragraph, and followed by a period.

FIGURE 9.4 Levels of Headings in Reports

2-inch top margin

REPORT, CHAPTER, AND PART TITLES

2 blank lines

The title of a report, chapter heading, or major part (such as CONTENTS or NOTES) should be centred in all caps. If the title requires more than one line, arrange it in an inverted triangle with the longest lines at the top. Begin the text a triple space (two blank lines) below the title, as shown here.

2 blank lines

First-Level Subheading

1 blank line

Headings indicating the first level of division are centred and bolded. Capitalize the first letter of each main word. Whether a report is single-spaced or double-spaced, most typists triple-space (leaving two blank lines) before and double-space (leaving one blank line) after a first-level subheading.

1 blank line

Every level of heading should be followed by some text. For example, we could not jump from "First-Level Subheading," shown above, to "Second Level Subheading," shown below, without some discussion between.

Good writers strive to develop coherency and fluency by ending most sections with a lead-in that introduces the next section. The lead-in consists of a sentence or two announcing the next topic.

2 blank lines

Second-Level Subheading

Headings that divide topics introduced by first-level subheadings are bolded and begin at the left margin. Use a triple space above and a double space after a second-level subheading. If a report has only one level of heading, use either first- or second-level subheading style.

Always be sure to divide topics into two or more subheadings. If you have only one subheading, eliminate it and absorb the discussion under the previous major heading. Try to make all headings within a level grammatically equal. For example, all second-level headings might use verb forms (*Preparing, Organizing,* and *Composing*) or noun forms (*Preparation, Organization,* and *Composition*).

1 blank line

Third-level subheading. Because it is part of the paragraph that follows, a third-level subheading is also called a "paragraph subheading." Capitalize only the first word and proper nouns in the subheading. Bold the subheading and end it with a period. Begin typing the paragraph text immediately following the period, as shown here. Double-space before a paragraph subheading.

Places major headings in the centre

Capitalizes initial letters of main words

Does not indent paragraphs because report is single-spaced

Starts at left margin

Makes heading part of paragraph

Chapter 9: Proposals and Formal Reports

Illustrating Data

Effective graphics clarify numerical data and simplify complex ideas.

Tables, charts, graphs, illustrations, and other visual aids play an important role in clarifying, summarizing, and emphasizing information. Numerical data become meaningful, complex ideas are simplified, and visual interest is provided by the appropriate use of graphics. Here are general tips for making the most effective use of visual aids:

- Clearly identify the contents of the visual aid with meaningful titles and numbering (e.g., *Figure 1 Internet Use at Canadian Companies*).
- Refer the reader to the visual aid by discussing it in the text and mentioning its location and figure number (e.g., *as Figure 1 below shows...*).
- Locate the visual aid close to its reference in the text.
- Strive for vertical placement of visual aids. Readers are disoriented by horizontal pages in reports.
- Give credit to the source if appropriate (e.g., *Source: Statistics Canada*).

Tables

Tables permit systematic presentation of large amounts of data, while charts enhance visual comparisons.

Probably the most frequently used visual aid in reports is the table. A table presents quantitative information in a systematic order of columns and rows. Here are tips for designing good tables, one of which is illustrated in Figure 9.5:

- Provide clear heads for the rows and columns.
- Identify the units in which figures are given (percentages, dollars, units per worker-hour, and so forth) in the table title, in the column or row head, with the first item in a column, or in a note at the bottom.
- Arrange items in a logical order (alphabetical, chronological, geographical, highest to lowest) depending on what you need to emphasize.
- Use *N/A* (not available) for missing data.
- Make long tables easier to read by shading alternate lines or by leaving a blank line after groups of five.

Bar Charts

Bar charts enable readers to compare related items, see changes over time, and understand how parts relate to a whole.

Although they lack the precision of tables, bar charts enable you to make emphatic visual comparisons. Bar charts can be used to compare related items, illustrate changes in data over time, and show segments as part of a whole. Figures 9.6 through 9.9 show vertical, horizontal, grouped, and segmented bar charts that highlight income for an entertainment company called MPM. Note how the varied bar charts present information in different ways.

FIGURE 9.5 Table Summarizing Precise Data

Figure 1
DYNAMO PRODUCTS
Number of Computers Sold, 2012

Region	1st Qtr.	2nd Qtr.	3rd Qtr.	4th Qtr.	Yearly Totals
Atlantic	13 302	15 003	15 550	16 210	60 065
Central	12 678	11 836	10 689	14 136	49 339
Prairie	10 345	11 934	10 899	12 763	45 941
Pacific	9 345	8 921	9 565	10 256	38 087
Total	45 670	47 694	46 703	53 365	193 432

FIGURE 9.6 Vertical Bar Chart

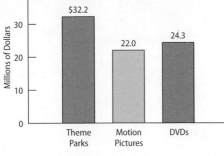

Figure 1

2012 MPM INCOME BY DIVISION

Source: *Industry Profiles* (New York: DataPro, 2012), p. 225.

FIGURE 9.7 Horizontal Bar Chart

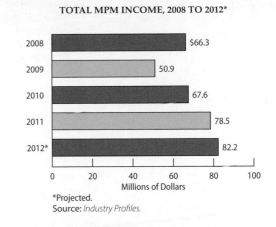

Figure 2

TOTAL MPM INCOME, 2008 TO 2012*

*Projected.
Source: *Industry Profiles.*

FIGURE 9.8 Grouped Bar Chart

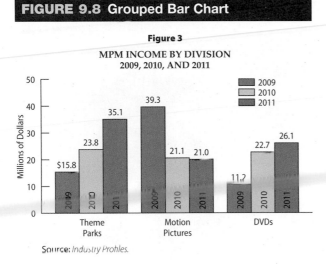

Figure 3

MPM INCOME BY DIVISION
2009, 2010, AND 2011

Source: *Industry Profiles.*

FIGURE 9.9 Segmented 100% Bar Chart

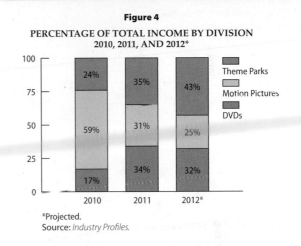

Figure 4

PERCENTAGE OF TOTAL INCOME BY DIVISION
2010, 2011, AND 2012*

*Projected.
Source: *Industry Profiles.*

Many suggestions for tables also hold true for bar charts. Here are a few additional tips:

- Keep the length of each bar and segment proportional.
- Include a total figure in the middle of a bar or at its end if the figure helps the reader and does not clutter the chart.
- Start dollar or percentage amounts at zero.

Line Charts

The major advantage of line charts is that they show changes over time, thus indicating trends. Figures 9.10 through 9.12 show line charts that reflect revenue trends for the major divisions of MPM. Notice that line charts do not provide precise data. Instead, they give an overview or impression of the data. Experienced report writers use tables to list exact data; they use line charts or bar charts to spotlight important points or trends.

Simple line charts (Figure 9.10) show just one variable. Multiple line charts combine several variables (Figure 9.11). Segmented line charts (Figure 9.12), also called surface charts, illustrate how the components of a whole change over time.

Here are tips for preparing line charts:

- Begin with a grid divided into squares.
- Arrange the time component (usually years) horizontally across the bottom; arrange values for the other variable vertically.

Line charts illustrate trends and changes in data over time.

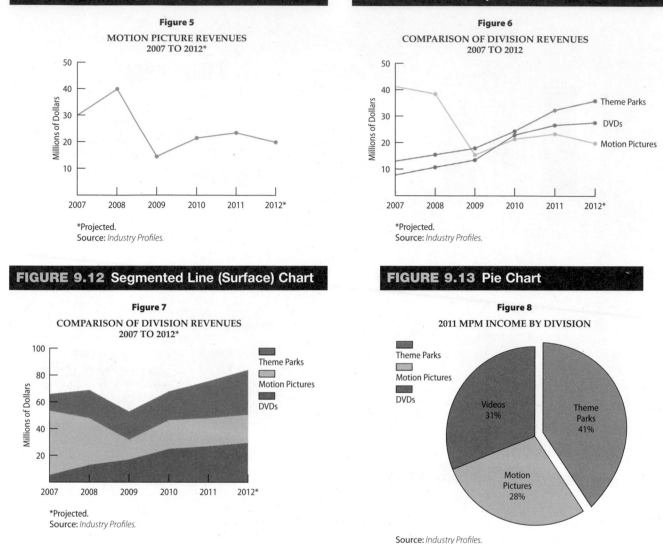

FIGURE 9.10 Simple Line Chart

Figure 5

MOTION PICTURE REVENUES
2007 TO 2012*

*Projected.
Source: *Industry Profiles.*

FIGURE 9.11 Multiple Line Chart

Figure 6

COMPARISON OF DIVISION REVENUES
2007 TO 2012

Theme Parks
DVDs
Motion Pictures

*Projected.
Source: *Industry Profiles.*

FIGURE 9.12 Segmented Line (Surface) Chart

Figure 7

COMPARISON OF DIVISION REVENUES
2007 TO 2012*

Theme Parks
Motion Pictures
DVDs

*Projected.
Source: *Industry Profiles.*

FIGURE 9.13 Pie Chart

Figure 8

2011 MPM INCOME BY DIVISION

Theme Parks
Motion Pictures
DVDs

Videos
31%

Theme
Parks
41%

Motion
Pictures
28%

Source: *Industry Profiles.*

- Draw small dots at the intersections to indicate each value at a given year.
- Connect the dots and add colour if desired.
- To prepare a segmented (surface) chart, plot the first value (e.g., *DVD income*) across the bottom; add the next item (e.g., *motion picture income*) to the first figures for every increment; for the third item (e.g., *theme park income*) add its value to the total of the first two items. The top line indicates the total of the three values.

Pie Charts

Pie charts are most useful in showing the proportion of parts to a whole.

Pie, or circle, charts help readers visualize a whole and the proportion of its components, or wedges. Pie charts, though less flexible than bar or line charts, are useful in showing percentages, as Figure 9.13 illustrates. For the most effective pie charts, follow these suggestions:

- Begin at the 12 o'clock position, drawing the largest wedge first. (Computer software programs don't always observe this advice, but if you're drawing your own charts, you can.)
- Include, if possible, the actual percentage or absolute value for each wedge.
- Use four to eight segments for best results; if necessary, group small portions into one wedge called "Other."
- Distinguish wedges with colour, shading, or cross-hatching.
- Keep all labels horizontal.

FIGURE 9.14 Flow Chart

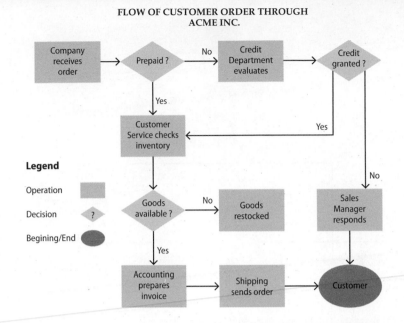

FLOW OF CUSTOMER ORDER THROUGH
ACME INC.

Flow charts are useful for clarifying procedures.

Flow Charts

Procedures are simplified and clarified by diagramming them in a flow chart, as shown in Figure 9.14. Whether you need to describe the procedure for handling a customer's purchase order or outline steps in solving a problem, flow charts help the reader visualize the process. Traditional flow charts use the following symbols:

Flow charts use standard symbols to illustrate a process or procedure.

- Ovals to designate the beginning and end of a process
- Diamonds to denote decision points
- Rectangles to represent major activities or steps

Organization Charts

Many large organizations are so complex that they need charts to show the chain of command, from the boss down to managers and employees. The chart in Figure 9.15 defines the hierarchy of authority from the board of directors to individual managers.

Using Your Computer to Produce Charts

Designing effective bar charts, pie charts, figures, and other graphics is easy with today's software. Spreadsheet programs such as Excel as well as presentation graphics programs such as Microsoft PowerPoint allow even non-technical people to design quality graphics. These graphics can be printed directly on paper for written reports or used for transparency masters and slides for oral presentations. The benefits of preparing visual aids on a computer are near-professional quality, shorter preparation time, and substantial cost savings. To prepare computer graphics, follow these steps:

- Assemble your data, usually in table form (such as that in Figure 9.5, p. 246).
- Choose a chart type, such as a pie chart, grouped bar chart, vertical bar chart, horizontal bar chart, organization chart, or some other graphic.
- To make a pie chart, key in the data or select the data from an existing file.
- Add a title for the chart as well as any necessary labels.
- To make a bar or line chart, indicate the horizontal and vertical axes (reference lines or beginning points).
- Verify the legend, which your program may generate automatically.
- Print the final chart on paper or import into another program.

FIGURE 9.15 Organization Chart

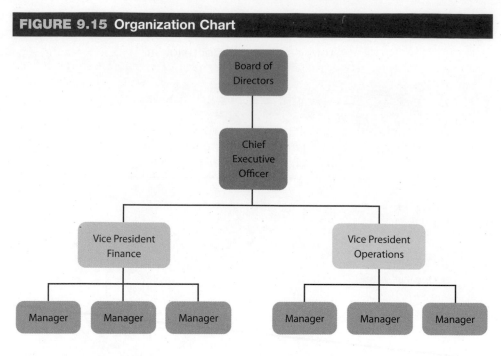

Photographs, Maps, and Illustrations

Some business reports include photographs, maps, illustrations, and other graphics to serve specific purposes. Photos, for example, add authenticity and provide a visual record. An environmental engineer may use photos to document hazardous waste sites. Maps enable report writers to depict activities or concentrations geographically, such as dots indicating sales reps in states across the country. Illustrations and diagrams are useful in indicating how an object looks or operates. A drawing showing the parts of a printer with labels describing their functions, for example, is more instructive than a photograph or verbal description. With today's computer technology, photographs, maps, illustrations, and other graphics can be scanned and inserted directly into business reports.

Presenting the Final Report

Long reports are generally organized into three major divisions: (1) prefatory parts, (2) body, and (3) supplementary parts. Following is a description of the order and content of each part. Refer to the model formal report in Figure 9.16 (starting on p. 252) for illustrations of most of these parts.

Prefatory Parts

- **Title fly.** A single page with the title begins a formal report. In less formal reports, the title fly is omitted. Our model report does not include this optional part. Compose the title of your report carefully so that it shows immediately what the report covers and what it does not cover.
- **Title page.** In addition to the title, the title page shows the author, the individual or organization who authorized the report, the recipient of the report, and the date.
- **Letter or memo or e-mail of authorization.** If a letter or memo authorized the report, it may be included in the prefatory material. This optional part is omitted from the model in Figure 9.16.
- **Letter or memo of transmittal.** This is the first impression the reader receives of the report; it should be given serious consideration. Use the direct strategy and include some or all of the suggestions here: (a) "hand over" the report to the person who authorized it; (b) briefly describe the project; (c) highlight the report's findings, conclusions, and recommendations, if the reader is expected to

A letter or memo of transmittal presents formally hands over the report to its recipient. It presents a brief summary of the report, expresses appreciation for the job, and offers to do more work if necessary.

be supportive; and (d) close with appreciation for the assignment, instructions for the reader's follow-up actions, acknowledgment of help from others, or an offer to answer any questions or provide more assistance.

- **Table of contents.** Identify the name and location of every part of the report except the title fly, title page, and table of contents itself. Use spaced periods (dot leaders) to join each part with its page number. Include a list of figures at the bottom of the title page.
- **Executive summary or abstract.** A summary condensing the entire report is a timesaving device summarizing the purpose, findings, and recommendations for busy readers who may not have time to read the entire report.

Body of Report

Introduction. After the prefatory parts, begin the body of the report with an introduction that includes all of the following items that apply in your particular situation:

1. Background information on how the report originated and why it was authorized
2. Description of the problem that prompted the report and the specific research questions to be answered
3. Purpose of the report
4. Scope (boundaries) and limitations or restrictions of the research
5. Sources and methods of collecting data
6. Summary of findings, if the report is written directly
7. Preview of the major sections of the report to follow, thus providing coherence and transition for the reader

A letter or memo of transmittal presents an overview of the report, suggests how to read it, describes limitations, acknowledges assistance, and expresses appreciation.

Findings. This is the main section of the report and contains numerous headings and subheadings. It is unnecessary to use the title *Findings*; many business report writers prefer to begin immediately with the major headings into which the body of the report is divided. Present your findings objectively, avoiding the use of first-person pronouns (*I, we*). Include tables, charts, and graphs to illustrate findings. Analytic and scientific reports may include another section entitled *Implications of Findings*, in which the findings are analyzed and related to the problem. Less formal reports contain the author's analysis of the research findings within the findings section itself. In other words, most business research reports present data and follow the presentation by analyzing what the data means.

Conclusions and recommendations. If the report has been largely informational, it ends with a summary of the data presented. However, the report will usually also analyze its research findings; in that case it should end with conclusions drawn from the analyses. An analytic report frequently poses research questions. The conclusion to such a report reviews the major findings and answers the research questions. If a report seeks to determine a course of action, it may end with conclusions and recommendations. Recommendations regarding a course of action may be placed in a separate section or incorporated with the conclusions. Recommendations should be numbered in order of descending importance (i.e., the most important recommendation first) and should begin with a present-tense verb (e.g., *Purchase, Inform, Reduce*, etc.).

Supplementary Parts of a Report

- **Footnotes or endnotes.** See Appendix C for details on how to document sources. In the footnote method, the source notes appear at the foot of each page. In the endnote method, they are displayed immediately after the text on a page called "Notes." The trend today is away from the footnote or endnote method and toward the parenthetic method, which works all citations directly into the text of the report.

Endnotes, a bibliography, and appendixes may appear after the body of the report.

- **Works Cited.** Most formal reports include a Works Cited page that lists all sources consulted in the report research. See Appendix C for more information.
- **Appendix.** The appendix (or appendixes if there's more than one) contains any supplementary information needed to clarify the report. Charts and graphs illustrating significant data are generally part of the report proper. However, extra information that might be included in an appendix could consist of such items as a sample questionnaire, a questionnaire cover letter, correspondence relating to the report, maps, other reports, and optional tables.

FIGURE 9.16 Model Formal Report

The title page is usually arranged in four evenly balanced areas. If the report is to be bound on the left, move the left margin and centre point 0.5 cm to the right. Notice that no page number appears on the title page, although it is counted as "page i." In designing the title page, be careful to avoid anything unprofessional, such as too many type fonts, italics, oversized print, and inappropriate graphics. Keep the title page simple and professional.

**ECONOMIC IMPACT OF ROXBURY INDUSTRIAL PARK
ON THE CITY OF WINNIPEG** — Includes report title in all caps with longer line above shorter line

Prepared for
The Standing Committee on Property and Development
Winnipeg City Council
Winnipeg, Manitoba — Highlights name of report recipient

Prepared by
Brigitte Morceaux
Senior Research Consultant
Petit, Morceaux Industrial Consultants — Identifies report writer

January 10, 2012

— Omits page number

FIGURE 9.16 *(Continued)* **Letter of Transmittal**

A letter or memo of transmittal announces the report topic and explains who authorized it. It describes the project briefly and previews the conclusions, if the reader is supportive. Such messages generally close by expressing appreciation for the assignment, suggesting follow-up actions, acknowledging the help of others, or offering to answer questions. The margins for the transmittal should be the same as for the report, about 3 cm on all sides.

PETIT, MORCEAUX INDUSTRIAL CONSULTANTS

588 Main Street   www.petitmorceaux.com
Winnipeg, Manitoba R2L 1E6   (204) 549-1101

January 12, 2012

Councillor Richard Moody
Chairperson
Standing Committee on Property and Development
City of Winnipeg
Winnipeg, MB R2L 1E9

Dear Councillor Moody:

[Announces report and identifies authorization] The attached report, requested by the Standing Policy Committee on Property and Development in a letter dated May 20, describes the economic impact of Roxbury Industrial Park on the City of Winnipeg. We believe you will find the results of this study useful in evaluating future development of industrial parks within the city limits.

[Gives broad overview of report purposes] This study was designed to examine economic impact in three areas:

(1) Current and projected tax and other revenues accruing to the city from Roxbury Industrial Park

(2) Current and projected employment generated by the park

(3) Indirect effects on local employment, income, and economic growth

[Describes primary and secondary research] Primary research consisted of interviews with 15 Roxbury Industrial Park tenants and managers, in addition to a 2011 survey of over 5000 RIP employees. Secondary research sources included the Annual Budget of the City of Winnipeg, other government publications, periodicals, books, and online resources. Results of this research, discussed more fully in this report, indicate that Roxbury Industrial Park exerts a significant beneficial influence on the Winnipeg metropolitan economy.

[Offers to discuss report; expresses appreciation] I would be pleased to discuss this report and its conclusions with you at your request. My firm and I thank you for your confidence in selecting our company to prepare this comprehensive report.

Sincerely,

Brigitte Morceaux

Brigitte Morceaux
Senior Research Consultant

BM:mef

Attachment

FIGURE 9.16 *(Continued)* **Table of Content and List of Figures**

Because the table of contents and the list of figures for this report are small, they are combined on one page. Notice that the titles of major report parts are in all caps, while other headings are a combination of upper- and lowercase letters. The style duplicates those within the report. Word processing programs enable you to generate a contents page automatically, including leaders and accurate page numbering—no matter how many times you revise.

TABLE OF CONTENTS

LIST OF FIGURES

Uses leaders to guide eye from heading to page number

Indents secondary headings to show levels of outline

Includes tables and figures in one list for simplified numbering

iii

FIGURE 9.16 *(Continued)* **Executive Summary**

An executive summary or abstract highlights report findings, conclusions, and recommendations. Its length depends on the report it summarizes. A 100-page report might require a 10-page summary. Shorter reports may contain single-page summaries, as shown here. Unlike letters of transmittal (which may contain personal pronouns and references to the writer), summaries are formal and impersonal. They use the same margins as the body of the report.

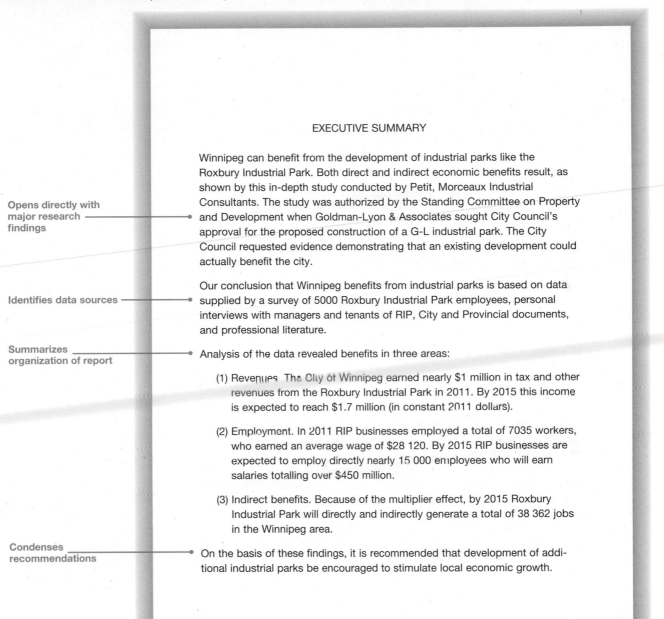

EXECUTIVE SUMMARY

Winnipeg can benefit from the development of industrial parks like the Roxbury Industrial Park. Both direct and indirect economic benefits result, as shown by this in-depth study conducted by Petit, Morceaux Industrial Consultants. The study was authorized by the Standing Committee on Property and Development when Goldman-Lyon & Associates sought City Council's approval for the proposed construction of a G-L industrial park. The City Council requested evidence demonstrating that an existing development could actually benefit the city.

Opens directly with major research findings

Our conclusion that Winnipeg benefits from industrial parks is based on data supplied by a survey of 5000 Roxbury Industrial Park employees, personal interviews with managers and tenants of RIP, City and Provincial documents, and professional literature.

Identifies data sources

Analysis of the data revealed benefits in three areas:

Summarizes organization of report

(1) Revenues. The City of Winnipeg earned nearly $1 million in tax and other revenues from the Roxbury Industrial Park in 2011. By 2015 this income is expected to reach $1.7 million (in constant 2011 dollars).

(2) Employment. In 2011 RIP businesses employed a total of 7035 workers, who earned an average wage of $28 120. By 2015 RIP businesses are expected to employ directly nearly 15 000 employees who will earn salaries totalling over $450 million.

(3) Indirect benefits. Because of the multiplier effect, by 2015 Roxbury Industrial Park will directly and indirectly generate a total of 38 362 jobs in the Winnipeg area.

Condenses recommendations

On the basis of these findings, it is recommended that development of additional industrial parks be encouraged to stimulate local economic growth.

iv

FIGURE 9.16 *(Continued)* Introduction

The introduction of a formal report contains the title printed 5 cm from the top edge. Titles for major parts of a report (such as Problem, Background, Findings, *and* Conclusions*) are centred in all caps. First-level headings (such as* Employment *on page 3 of the report) are printed with bold upper- and lowercase letters. Second-level headings (such as* Distribution *on page 3) begin at the left side. See Figure 9.4 (page 245) for an illustration of heading formats.*

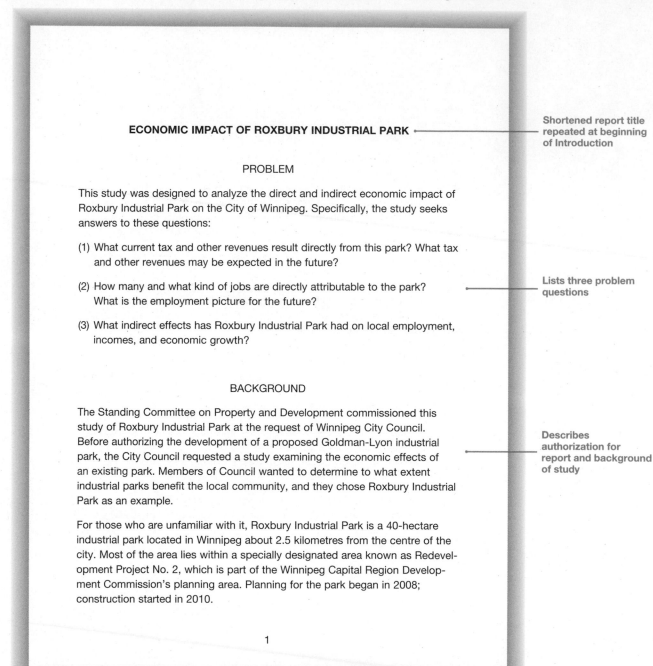

ECONOMIC IMPACT OF ROXBURY INDUSTRIAL PARK ——— Shortened report title repeated at beginning of Introduction

PROBLEM

This study was designed to analyze the direct and indirect economic impact of Roxbury Industrial Park on the City of Winnipeg. Specifically, the study seeks answers to these questions:

(1) What current tax and other revenues result directly from this park? What tax and other revenues may be expected in the future?

(2) How many and what kind of jobs are directly attributable to the park? What is the employment picture for the future? ——— Lists three problem questions

(3) What indirect effects has Roxbury Industrial Park had on local employment, incomes, and economic growth?

BACKGROUND

The Standing Committee on Property and Development commissioned this study of Roxbury Industrial Park at the request of Winnipeg City Council. Before authorizing the development of a proposed Goldman-Lyon industrial park, the City Council requested a study examining the economic effects of an existing park. Members of Council wanted to determine to what extent industrial parks benefit the local community, and they chose Roxbury Industrial Park as an example. ——— Describes authorization for report and background of study

For those who are unfamiliar with it, Roxbury Industrial Park is a 40-hectare industrial park located in Winnipeg about 2.5 kilometres from the centre of the city. Most of the area lies within a specially designated area known as Redevelopment Project No. 2, which is part of the Winnipeg Capital Region Development Commission's planning area. Planning for the park began in 2008; construction started in 2010.

1

FIGURE 9.16 *(Continued)* **Introduction and Discussion**

Notice that this formal report is single-spaced. Many businesses prefer this space-saving format. However, some organizations prefer double-spacing, especially for preliminary drafts. If you single-space, do not indent paragraphs. If you double-space, do indent the paragraphs. Page numbers may be centred near the bottom of the page or placed near the upper right corner at the margin. Strive to leave comfortable top, bottom, and side margins. References follow the MLA citation style. Notice that citations appear as references in the "Works Cited" section with a corresponding parenthetical reference to the author in the text of the report at the appropriate location.

The park now contains 14 building complexes with over 25 000 square metres of completed building space. The majority of the buildings are used for office, research and development, marketing and distribution, or manufacturing uses. Approximately 5 hectares of the original area are yet to be developed.

Provides specifics for data sources

MLA-style parenthetical citation

Data for this report came from a 2011 survey of over 5000 Roxbury Industrial Park employees, interviews with 15 RIP tenants and managers, the Annual Budget of the City of Winnipeg, current books, articles, journals, and online resources. Projections for future revenues resulted from analysis of past trends and *Estimates of Revenues for Debt Service Coverage, Redevelopment Project Area 2* (Miller 78–79).

DISCUSSION OF FINDINGS

Previews organization of report

Uses topical arrangement

The results of this research indicate that major direct and indirect benefits have accrued to the City of Winnipeg and surrounding municipal areas as a result of the development of Roxbury Industrial Park. The research findings presented here fall into three categories: (a) revenues, (b) employment, and (c) indirect effects.

Revenues

Places figure close to textual reference

Roxbury Industrial Park contributes a variety of tax and other revenues to the City of Winnipeg. Figure 1 summarizes revenues.

Figure 1

REVENUES RECEIVED BY THE CITY OF WINNIPEG
FROM ROXBURY INDUSTRIAL PARK

Current Revenues and Projections to 2015

	2011	2015
Property taxes	$604 140	$1 035 390
Revenues from licences	126 265	216 396
Business taxes	75 518	129 424
Provincial service receipts	53 768	92 134
Licences and permits	48 331	82 831
Other revenues	64 039	111 987
Total	$972 061	$1 668 162

Source: City of Winnipeg Chief Financial Officer. *2011 Annual Financial Report*. City of Winnipeg, Jan. 2012. Web. 6 Jan. 2012.

2

FIGURE 9.16 *(Continued)* **Discussion**

Only the most important research findings are interpreted and discussed for readers. The depth of discussion depends on the intended length of the report, the goal of the writer, and the expectations of the reader. Because the writer wants this report to be formal in tone, she avoids I *and* we *in all discussions.*

Sales and Use Revenues

As shown in Figure 1, the city's largest source of revenues from RIP is the property tax. Revenues from this source totalled $604 140 in 2011, according to the City of Winnipeg Standing Committee on Finance (City of Winnipeg 103). Property taxes accounted for more than half of the park's total contribution to the City of $972 061.

Continues interpreting figures in table

Other Revenues

Other major sources of City revenues from RIP in 2011 include revenues from licences such as motor vehicle in lieu fees, trailer coach licences ($126 265), business taxes ($75 518), and provincial service receipts ($53 768).

Projections

Total City revenues from RIP will nearly double by 2015, producing an income of $1.7 million. This projection is based on an annual growth rate of 1.4 percent in constant 2011 dollars.

Employment

One of the most important factors to consider in the overall effect of an industrial park is employment. In Roxbury Industrial Park the distribution, number, and wages of people employed will change considerably in the next five years.

Sets stage for next topics to be discussed

Distribution

A total of 7035 employees currently work in various industry groups at Roxbury Industrial Park, as shown below in Figure 2. The largest number of workers (58 percent) is employed in manufacturing and assembly operations. In the next largest category, the computer and electronics industry employs 24 percent of the workers. Some overlap probably exists because electronics assembly could be included in either group. Employees also work in publishing (9 percent), warehousing and storage (5 percent), and other industries (4 percent).

Although the distribution of employees at Roxbury Industrial Park shows a wide range of employment categories, it must be noted that other industrial parks would likely generate an entirely different range of job categories.

3

FIGURE 9.16 *(Continued)* **Discussion**

If you use figures or tables, be sure to introduce them in the text (for example, as shown below in Figure 3). Although it's not always possible, try to place them close to the spot where they are first mentioned. To save space, you can print the title of a figure at its side. Because this report contains few tables and figures, the writer named them all "Figures" and numbered them consecutively.

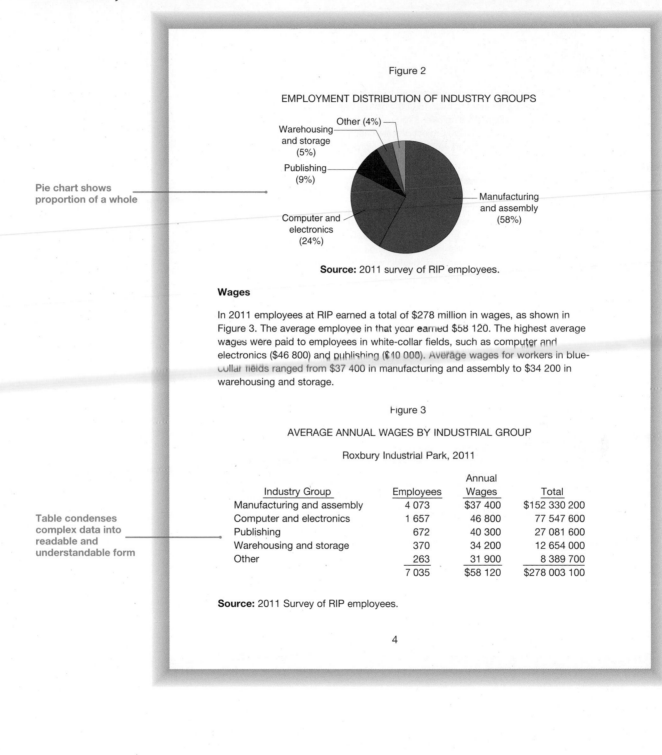

Pie chart shows proportion of a whole

Figure 2

EMPLOYMENT DISTRIBUTION OF INDUSTRY GROUPS

Other (4%)
Warehousing and storage (5%)
Publishing (9%)
Computer and electronics (24%)
Manufacturing and assembly (58%)

Source: 2011 survey of RIP employees.

Wages

In 2011 employees at RIP earned a total of $278 million in wages, as shown in Figure 3. The average employee in that year earned $58 120. The highest average wages were paid to employees in white-collar fields, such as computer and electronics ($46 800) and publishing ($40 000). Average wages for workers in blue-collar fields ranged from $37 400 in manufacturing and assembly to $34 200 in warehousing and storage.

Figure 3

AVERAGE ANNUAL WAGES BY INDUSTRIAL GROUP

Roxbury Industrial Park, 2011

Table condenses complex data into readable and understandable form

Industry Group	Employees	Annual Wages	Total
Manufacturing and assembly	4 073	$37 400	$152 330 200
Computer and electronics	1 657	46 800	77 547 600
Publishing	672	40 300	27 081 600
Warehousing and storage	370	34 200	12 654 000
Other	263	31 900	8 389 700
	7 035	$58 120	$278 003 100

Source: 2011 Survey of RIP employees.

4

FIGURE 9.16 *(Continued)* Discussion, Conclusions, and Recommendations

After discussing and interpreting the research findings, the writer articulates what she considers the most important conclusions and recommendations. Longer, more complex reports may have separate sections for conclusions and resulting recommendations. In this report they are combined. Notice that it is unnecessary to start a new page for the conclusions.

Projections

By 2015 Roxbury Industrial Park is expected to more than double its number of employees, bringing the total to over 15 000 workers. The total payroll in 2012 will also more than double, producing over $450 million (using constant 2011 dollars) in salaries to RIP employees. These projections are based on an 8 percent growth rate, along with anticipated increased employment as the park reaches its capacity (Miller 78–79).

Clarifies information and explains what it means in relation to original research questions

Future development in the park will influence employment and payrolls. As Ivan Novak, RIP project manager, stated in an interview, much of the remaining five hectares is planned for medium-rise office buildings, garden offices, and other structures for commercial, professional, and personal services (September 2011). Average wages for employees are expected to increase because of an anticipated shift to higher-paying white-collar jobs. Industrial parks often follow a similar pattern of evolution (Badri 38–45). Like many industrial parks, RIP evolved from a warehousing centre into a manufacturing complex.

CONCLUSIONS AND RECOMMENDATIONS

Summarizes conclusions and recommendations

Analysis of tax revenues, employment data, personal interviews, and professional literature leads to the following conclusions and recommendations about the economic impact of Roxbury Industrial Park on the City of Winnipeg:

1. Property tax and other revenues produced nearly $1 million in income to the City of Winnipeg in 2011. By 2015 revenues are expected to produce $1.7 million in city income.

2. RIP currently employs 7035 employees, the majority of whom are working in manufacturing and assembly. The average employee in 2011 earned $38 120.

3. By 2015 RIP is expected to employ more than 15 000 workers producing a total payroll of over $450 million.

4. Employment trends indicate that by 2015 more RIP employees will be engaged in higher-paying white-collar positions.

On the basis of these findings, we recommend that the City Council of Winnipeg authorize the development of additional industrial parks to stimulate local economic growth.

5

FIGURE 9.16 *(Continued)* Works Cited

WORKS CITED

Arranges references in
alphabetical order

Badri, Mahmood A. "Infrastructure, Trends, and Economic Effects of Industrial
    Parks." *www.industryweek.com.* Penton Media, Inc., 1 Apr. 2000: 38–45. Web.
    15 Dec. 2011.

City of Winnipeg Chief Financial Officer. *2011 Annual Financial Report.* City of Winnipeg,
    Jan. 2012. Web. 6 Jan. 2012.

Follows Modern
Language Association
documentation style

Miller, Arthur M. *Estimates of Revenues for Debt Service Coverage, Redevelop-
    ment Project Area No. 2.* Winnipeg, MB: Rincon Press, 2011. Print.

Novak, Ivan M. E-mail interview. 30 Sept. 2011.

Summing Up and Looking Forward

Proposals are offers to solve problems, provide services, or sell equipment or goods. Both small and large businesses today write proposals to generate income. Informal proposals may be as short as 2 pages; formal proposals may be 200 pages or more. Regardless of the size, proposals contain standard parts that must be developed persuasively.

Formal reports present well-organized information systematically. The information may be collected from primary or secondary sources. All ideas borrowed from others must be documented. Good reports contain appropriate headings and illustrations.

Written reports are vital to decision makers. But oral reports can be equally important. In Chapters 10 and 11 you will learn how to organize and give oral presentations, as well as how to conduct meetings and communicate effectively on the phone.

Critical Thinking

1. Why is the writing of proposals an important function in many businesses?

2. Is information obtained on the Web as reliable as information obtained from journals, newspapers, and magazines? Explain.

3. Should all reports be written so that they follow the sequence of investigation—that is, description of the initial problem, analysis of issues, data collection, data analysis, and conclusions? Why or why not?

4. Distinguish between primary and secondary data. Which data are more likely to be useful in a business report?

5. Who is hurt by plagiarism? Discuss.

6. How do charts and graphical elements help a reader in a report?

Chapter Review

1. What are the six principal parts and functions of an informal proposal?

2. How are formal proposals different from informal proposals?

3. What is the first step in writing a formal report?

4. Do formal business reports generally rely more heavily on primary or secondary data?

5. List three sources of secondary information, and be prepared to discuss how valuable each might be in writing a formal report about updating your company's accounting procedures.

6. Define these terms: *browser, URL, search engine*.

7. List four levels of headings, and explain how they are different.

8. Pie charts are most helpful in showing what?

9. Line graphs are most effective in showing what?

10. List three reasons for documenting data in a business report.

11. List the parts of a formal report. Be prepared to discuss each.

Writing Improvement Exercises

1. **Detecting and Eliminating Plagiarism.** A student doing business research comes across the *Canadian Business* article reprinted in Chapter 8 (p. 220). She uses the article's second paragraph in a report. Below is an extract from her report. Identify where and why she has plagiarized and revise her report so that no plagiarism exists.

   ### New Health Care Solutions

   One of the most exciting business opportunities in the field of health care is the provision of private consulting services. For example, NavaHealth, a for-profit, privately owned company, leads B.C. residents through the labyrinthine health care system by providing support and patient advocacy. The owner of this company has had to invest heavily, but she plans to make a profit in less than a year.

2. **Detecting and Eliminating Plagiarism.** A student doing business research comes across the *Toronto Star* article reprinted in Chapter 8 (p. 221). He uses the article's fifth paragraph in an essay. Below is an extract from his essay. Identify where and why he has plagiarized and revise his essay so that no plagiarism exists.

   As mentioned earlier, one of the fringe benefits of a hot economy is the spin-off effects it creates. One of the spin-off effects of the hot Canadian economy, especially in places like Alberta, is the corporate housing market. A study released recently by Royal LePage Relocation Services states that this market was worth $230 million in Canada in 2004. Another spin-off of the hot economy is corporate travel, corporate retreats, and corporate entertaining, which I will discuss below.

Activities and Cases

9.1 Doing Research

TEAM

Like many business communication skills, research is one that only gets better when it is practised. In this activity you'll act as a consultant to your college or university, which needs some internal research done about the effectiveness of its policies, services, and procedures.

Your Task. Choose one of the research topics below and go through the following six-step procedure:

1. Create a five-question survey and a five-question follow-up interview.

2. After you've shown your survey and interview to your instructor, go out "into the field" and gather data. Try to get at least 15 completed surveys and two completed interviews.

3. Now that you have raw data, analyze the survey data by turning it into two or three of the types of illustration discussed in this chapter (e.g., bar chart, table, line chart).

4. Analyze your interview data by looking for similarities and differences between what the people you interviewed had to say.

5. Once you've completed your primary research and analysis, turn to secondary research. Find two newspaper or magazine articles, one academic article, one book, and one good Web site with information on your topic. How does this information compare with or help to illustrate the information you gathered in your primary research?

6. Finally, present all of the above in a two-page memo or e-mail to your instructor.

   Possible research topics:

CRITICAL THINKING

- Is the cost of tuition at your institution too high?
- How well is your college/university doing in terms of customer service?
- Does your college/university career centre do a good job?
- Assess the usefulness of your college/university library.
- Examine the success of your institution's physical plant: washrooms, hallways, stairwells, elevators, etc.
- Choose a topic of your own in consultation with your instructor.

9.2 Outlining

You work for a recruiting firm that helps businesses find candidates for jobs. Over the years, many clients have asked for suggestions on the best way to interview job candidates. Your supervisor asks you to write a short report on how to become a great interviewer. Here are some ideas you gathered from your own experience and that of other recruiters:

- One of the most important qualities of a successful interview is efficient use of the interview time. Most businesspeople hate the hiring process because it interrupts their daily routine and throws off their schedules. But if you block out an afternoon or a whole day, you don't feel so frustrated. In addition, shutting out all interruptions and setting aside 45 minutes for each interview can also be helpful.
- Interviewing is an inexact art because judging the talents and abilities of people is very subjective. To select the best candidate, you must begin with a list of all the job duties. Then you select the three duties with the highest priorities. Naturally, you would then ask questions to discover what candidate can perform those duties best.
- Every interview should have objectives. What do you want to achieve? One of the most important goals is uncovering the experience that qualifies the candidate to do the job. Another important element is the correlation you see between the candidate and your company's values. A major final objective is selling the candidate on the opportunity with your company.

Your Task. Select the most important information and organize it into an outline such as that shown in Figure 9.3 on page 244. You should have three main topics with three subdivisions under each. Assume that you would gather more information later. Add a title.

9.3 Selecting Visual Aids

In teams, identify the best visual aid (table, bar chart, line chart, pie chart, flow chart, organization chart) to illustrate the following data:

a. Instructions for workers telling them how to distinguish between worker accidents that must be reported to appropriate provincial agencies and those that need not be reported

b. Figures showing what proportion of every provincial tax dollar is spent on education, social services, health care, debt, and other expenses

c. Data showing the academic, administrative, and operation divisions of a college, from the president to department chairs and deans

d. Figures showing the operating profit of a company for the past five years

e. Figures comparing the sales of PVRs, flat-screen TVs, and personal computers for the past five years

f. Percentages showing the causes of forest fires (lightning, 73 percent; arson, 5 percent; campfires, 9 percent; and so on) in the Canadian Rockies

g. Figures comparing the cost of basic TV cable service in five areas of Canada for the past ten years (the boss wants to see exact figures)

9.4 Evaluating Visual Aids

From *Maclean's*, *Canadian Business*, *Businessweek*, *The Economist*, or some other publication, locate one example each of a table, a pie chart, a line chart, a bar chart, and an organization chart. Bring copies of these visual aids to class. How effectively could the data have been expressed in words, without the graphics? Is the appropriate graphic form used? How is the graphic introduced in the text? Your instructor may ask you to submit a short e-mail recommendation report discussing how to improve visual aids.

9.5 Visual Aids in Annual Reports: How Do We Compare with the Best?

You are the assistant to the director of investor relations at Canfinco, a large Canadian company. One of your important shareholders recently wrote a letter to the board of directors complaining about the quality of your annual reports, in particular the quality of the visual aids. Your boss, the director, is now worried about his job. He asks you to do some quick research on how to improve your company's annual report. You figure the best way to do this is to pick a few of Canada's top companies and comb through their annual reports, analyzing their use of visual aids. You choose Telus, Canadian Tire, and Loblaws for your research.

Your Task. Using the Web, find three recent annual reports published by Telus, Canadian Tire, and Loblaws. Read these reports and make notes as you go on the effectiveness of the visual aids and of graphics and layout in general. Critique the readability, clarity, and success in visualizing data of these reports. Are the aids introduced in the text? What similarities do you see among the three reports? E-mail your recommendation report to your boss.

Related Web site: Check out the Canadian Institute of Chartered Accountants (CICA) Web site describing the annual Corporate Reporting Awards it hands out for the best corporate annual reports in Canada. Of particular interest are the judging criteria and the examples of past winners: http://www.cica.ca/news/corporate-reporting-awards/item36127.aspx.

9.6 Annotated Bibliography

Select a business topic or issue that interests you. Controversial or current topics will often work best for this type of exercise, because there will be a lot of information available. For example, the question of whether foreign companies should be allowed to buy Canadian natural resources companies is a current controversial question. In some parts of Canada, the question of whether mandatory retirement should be abolished is also a current topic. Imagine that you have been asked to write an essay, report, or article on the topic you've chosen. What will your next step be?

Your Task. Professional researchers begin the process of writing by compiling an annotated bibliography. This is a list of sources on the topic followed by an annotation, or brief summary. Using your library's online databases—*not* the Web—find five sources (two newspaper articles, two periodical articles, one other) that contain relevant information on your topic. Read each source and summarize it in 75 to 100 words. Compile an annotated bibliography in MLA style, with a citation of your source followed by a brief summary. Format the annotated bibliography as part of a memo you are sending to your instructor (e.g., "As you requested, below is my annotated bibliography on the topic of …").

9.7 Informal Proposal: Don't Give Up Your Day Job

As a struggling student, single parent, or budding entrepreneur, you decide to start your own part-time business (Web site design, word processing, or something similar). Select a company or professional in your city that might need your services. Assess your expertise and equipment. Check out the competition. What are competitors offering, and what do they charge?

Your Task. Prepare a letter proposal offering your services to a specific individual.

9.8 Informal Proposal: Student Views Consulting Inc.

Imagine you are in your last semester of college or university. As part of your business program, there is a course you can take called "Consulting Business Simulation." This course allows students to simulate running a consulting business for a semester. You enroll in the course, and on the first day of class the instructor says, "There's only one requirement in this course and it's worth 100 percent of your grade. You will design, conduct, and write a research proposal and project of your choice for this institution. You won't get paid for it, but you'll have gained a lot of experience that will look good on your résumé." You choose to work with two other students and you call yourselves Student Views Consulting Inc. You decide to tackle the problem of poor customer service at your institution.

Your Task. Write a proposal to the Director of Student Services at your college or university. Propose that your consulting firm carry out a detailed study on current student satisfaction at your institution, which you understand has been problematic lately. For example, there have been questions about how effectively telephone, e-mail, and in-person queries are being handled in various college departments and offices. Also, how the service level at your institution compares to that of competing institutions in the same area has been questioned. Describe the background of this problem and draft a schedule of the work to be done. Cost out this research realistically. When it comes to describing the prior work of Student Views Consulting Inc., make up a realistic list of prior work. Format this proposal as a letter to the Director of Student Services.

9.9 Unsolicited Proposal: Working From Home

You have been working as an administrative/virtual assistant for your company since its inception in 2001. Every day you commute from your home, almost two hours round trip. Most of your work is done at a computer terminal with little or no human contact. You would prefer to eliminate the commute time, which could be better spent working on your programming. You believe your job would be perfect for telecommuting. With a small investment in the proper equipment, you could do all of your work at home, perhaps reporting to the office once a week for meetings and other activities.

Your Task. Research the costs and logistics of telecommuting, and present your proposal to your supervisor, Sidney Greene. Because this is an unsolicited proposal, you will need to be even more persuasive. Convince your supervisor that the company will benefit from this telecommuting arrangement.

9.10 Formal Report: Intercultural Communication

U.S. businesses are expanding into foreign markets with manufacturing plants, sales offices, and branch offices abroad. Unfortunately, most Americans have little knowledge of or experience with people from other cultures. To prepare for participation in the global marketplace, you are to collect information for a report focused on an Asian, Latin American, African, or European country where English isn't regularly spoken. Before selecting the country, though, consider consulting your campus international student program for volunteers who are willing to be interviewed. Your instructor may make advance arrangements seeking international student volunteers.

Your Task. In teams of two to four, collect information about your target country from the library, the Web, and other sources. If possible, invite an international student representing your target country to be interviewed by your group. As you conduct primary and secondary research, investigate the topics listed in Figure 9.17.[12] Confirm what you learn in your secondary research by talking with your interviewee. When you complete your research, write a report for the CEO of your company (make up a name and company). Assume that your company plans to expand its operations abroad. Your report should advise the company's executives of social customs, family life, attitudes, appropriate business attire, religions, economic institutions, and values in the target country. Remember that your company's interests are business oriented; don't dwell on tourist information. Write your report individually or in teams.

9.11 Formal Report: Is Vinyl Back?

Although you and fellow students were probably born long after the introduction of the CD in the early 1980s and regularly download MP3 tracks from iTunes to an iPod, something strange is afoot. Lately, sales of turntables and vinyl long-playing records (LPs) have been picking up. "Classic" bands such as the Beatles and Pink Floyd are not the only ones on vinyl. Contemporary artists such as R.E.M., the White Stripes, the Foo Fighters, and Metallica have released their music on vinyl to enthusiastic audiences. Listeners even claim that music sounds better on vinyl than it does on a CD.[13] Perhaps most surprising, many vinyl fans are not nostalgic baby boomers but their teenage or twenty-something children.

Major music retailers have caught on to the trend. Although Amazon.ca has been selling vinyl records since its founding in 1994, it has recently begun to offer a vinyl-only section on its site. Now, your employer, Best Buy Company, is eager to test vinyl sales at some of its stores. Your manager, José Martinez, was asked by headquarters to explore the feasibility of offering a vinyl selection in his store, and he left this research job to you.

Your Task. This assignment calls for establishing primary data using a survey. Devise a questionnaire and poll young music consumers in your area to find out whether they enjoy and, more important, purchase vinyl records. Examine attitudes toward LPs in the populations and age groups most likely to find them intriguing. After collecting your data, determine whether your Best Buy store could establish a profitable vinyl business. Support your recommendation with conclusions you draw from your survey but also from secondary research detailing the new trend. To illustrate your findings, use pie charts for percentages (e.g., how many LPs are sold in comparison to CDs and other media), line graphs to indicate trends over time (e.g., sales figures in various consumer segments), and other graphics. Prepare a formal report for José Martinez, who will share your report with upper management.

FIGURE 9.17 Intercultural Interview Topics and Questions

Social Customs

1. How do people react to strangers? Are they friendly? Hostile? Reserved?
2. How do people greet each other?
3. What are the appropriate manners when you enter a room? Bow? Nod? Shake hands with everyone?
4. How are names used for introductions? Is it appropriate to inquire about one's occupation or family?
5. What are the attitudes toward touching?
6. How does one express appreciation for an invitation to another's home? Bring a gift? Send flowers? Write a thank-you note? Are any gifts taboo?
7. Are there any customs related to how or where one sits?
8. Are any facial expressions or gestures considered rude?
9. How close do people stand when talking?
10. What is the attitude toward punctuality in social situations? In business situations?
11. What are acceptable eye contact patterns?
12. What gestures indicate agreement? Disagreement?

Family Life

1. What is the basic unit of social organization? Basic family? Extended family?
2. Do women work outside of the home? In what occupations?

Housing, Clothing, and Food

1. Are there differences in the kind of housing used by different social groups? Differences in location? Differences in furnishings?
2. What occasions require special clothing?
3. Are some types of clothing considered taboo?
4. What is appropriate business attire for men? For women?
5. How many times a day do people eat?
6. What types of places, food, and drink are appropriate for business entertainment? Where is the seat of honour at a table?

Class Structure

1. Into what classes is society organized?
2. Do racial, religious, or economic factors determine social status?
3. Are there any minority groups? What is their social standing?

Political Patterns

1. Are there any immediate threats to the political survival of the country?
2. How is political power manifested?
3. What channels are used for expression of popular opinion?
4. What information media are important?
5. Is it appropriate to talk politics in social situations?

Religion and Folk Beliefs

1. To which religious groups do people belong? Is one predominant?
2. Do religious beliefs influence daily activities?
3. Which places have sacred value? Which objects? Which events?
4. How do religious holidays affect business activities?

Economic Institutions

1. What are the country's principal products?
2. Are workers organized in unions?
3. How are businesses owned? By family units? By large public corporations? By the government?
4. What is the standard work schedule?
5. Is it appropriate to do business by telephone?
6. How has technology affected business procedures?
7. Is participatory management used?
8. Are there any customs related to exchanging business cards?
9. How is status shown in an organization? Private office? Secretary? Furniture?
10. Are businesspeople expected to socialize before conducting business?

Value Systems

1. Is competitiveness or cooperation more prized?
2. Is thrift or enjoyment of the moment more valued?
3. Is politeness more important than factual honesty?
4. What are the attitudes toward education?
5. Do women own or manage businesses? If so, how are they treated?
6. What are your people's perceptions of Canadians? Do Canadians offend you? What has been hardest for you to adjust to in Canada? How could Canadians make this adjustment easier for you?

9.12 Formal Report: Quick-Service Restaurant Checkup

The national franchising headquarters for a quick-service chain has received complaints about the service, quality, and cleanliness of one of its restaurants in your area. You have been sent to inspect and to report on what you see.

Your Task. Select a quick-service restaurant in your area. Visit on two or more occasions. Make notes about how many customers were served, how quickly they received their food, and how courteously they were treated. Observe the number of employees and supervisors working. Note the cleanliness of observable parts of the restaurant. Inspect the washroom as well as the exterior and surrounding grounds. Sample the food. Your boss is a stickler for details; he has no use for general statements like *The washroom was not clean*. Be specific. Draw conclusions. Are the complaints justified? If improvements are necessary, make recommendations. Address your report to Lawrence C. Shymko, President.

9.13 Formal Report: Consumer Product Investigation

Study a consumer product that you might consider buying. Are you (or your family) interested in purchasing a DVD player, computer, digital camera, iPod, microwave, car, van, camcorder, or some other product? Your investigation should include primary data collected from interviews with users, owners, salespeople, service technicians, and so forth. You'll also find rich resources on the Web and in sales brochures and pamphlets. Conduct secondary research by studying (and citing) magazine articles in such publications as *Consumer Reports*. Be sure to narrow your topic by setting boundaries to your search. For example, are you interested in an economy van with good mileage that will be driven 80 kilometres daily? Are you in the market for an economical auto-focus camera?

Your Task. In your report include an introduction that discusses why you selected this product and for whom it is intended (for example, a DVD player for a middle-class family who would use it primarily for watching rented DVDs). Perhaps provide some background data about the product gleaned from your reading. In the Discussion section you might discuss such topics as price, warranty, specific features, and service reputation. Draw conclusions from your data and make a recommendation. Address the report to your instructor. Your instructor may ask your class to work in pairs on this project.

WEB

CRITICAL THINKING

9.14 Formal Report: Communication Skills on the Job

Collect information regarding communication skills used by individuals in a particular career field (accounting, management, marketing, office administration, paralegal, and so forth). Interview three or more individuals in a specific occupation in that field. Determine how much and what kind of writing they do. Do they make oral presentations? Do they use PowerPoint? If so, what do they think of its effectiveness? How much time do they spend in telephone communication? How often do they use e-mail? For what? Do they have a PDA? Do they find themselves communicating more or less than in past years? Are they happy or unhappy about the amount of communicating they have to do? What recommendations do they have for training for this position?

Your Task. Write a report that discusses the findings from your interviews. What conclusions can you draw regarding communication skills in this field? What recommendations would you make for individuals entering this field? Your instructor may ask you to research the perception of businesspeople over the past ten years regarding the communication skills of employees. To gather such data, conduct library or online database research.

CRITICAL THINKING

9.15 Informal Proposal: Setting Up a Web Site

As a consultant, you have been asked to investigate the cost of setting up a Web site for Arni Arason, who owns a small wine distribution business in Stratford, Ontario, named Fruit of the Gods Inc. He hopes to begin with a simple, basic Web site, but he wants it to be user friendly, and he wants customers to be able to buy wine from the site with a credit card.

Your Task. Use search engines on the Internet to locate information. Try "Web site development" as a search term. Visit several sites that offer to build Web sites. Focus on those that seem most professional. Look to see when the site was last updated. Read the promotional material and decide whether it is well written. Remember, anyone can post a Web site. Investigate the general characteristics of a Web site, how to create and promote a site, and how to maintain a Web server. Mr. Arason wants a low-cost but high-quality site. Develop cost figures. Draw conclusions and make recommendations in a letter proposal to Mr. Arason.

Related Web site: Drinks Ontario (http://www.drinksontario.com/about-aims.shtml), which Arni Arason hopes to join soon, has some brief background information about the wine distribution business.

WEB

TEAM

9.16 Formal Report: Selecting a Location for a Satellite Campus

The college or university you attend has recently been experiencing unprecedented growth. Student enrollment has been up for five years in a row, research and donation money has been on the increase, and the number of international students applying for admission is also up. The board of directors has asked the director of development to look into the idea of planning a small satellite campus in an outlying area of the city. The question is, where to locate the satellite?

Your Task. Using your own college or university as the example for this report, research and write a formal report offering a recommendation about where to locate a satellite campus. What components (e.g., locations) will you choose to structure your report? What criteria would be important to the board of directors? Price of land? Proximity to public transportation? Proximity to other institutions? Proximity to a large population base? Where will you find data on these criteria?

9.17 Formal Report: All About Wikis

As discussed earlier in this chapter, wikis are becoming increasingly important to businesses that rely on teamwork across time zones and national borders. Some educators also use wikis for collaboration in their college-level classes. You are part of a group of interns from your college working at a large financial institution, Home Bank. Your intern team has collaborated on your finance-related research using a wiki. Your informal wiki has also been helpful when you worked together on a team project for college credit. Your internship supervisor is impressed and would like you to collect more hard data so he can pilot wikis for wider application in collaborative settings at the bank. Your preliminary research suggests that quite a few companies are using wikis, such as Best Buy's Geek Squad, Xerox, and IBM. In fact, IBM conducted a massive online brainstorming session that took two 72-hour sessions and involved 100,000 employees, customers, and business partners in over 160 countries.[14] Your boss is interested in reading about such cases to decide whether to pilot a wiki, and if so, what kind would work for Home Bank. Your team of three to five will investigate.

Your Task. Keep in mind that your boss, Irving E. Pound, will share your report with other managers who may be computer-literate users but are no tech heads. Start with the brief definition of wikis earlier in this chapter. Expand the definition by searching the Web and electronic database articles. First explain what wikis are and how they work, which resources (cost, software, hardware) are needed, how much training is required, and so forth. Examine the use of wikis in business today. How are large and small companies benefiting from collaboration facilitated by wikis? If your instructor directs, the report (or a section thereof) could discuss wikis in education and how instructors harness this new tool. After collecting a sufficient amount of information and data, outline and then write a formal report with a recommendation at the end suggesting whether and how Home Bank would benefit from investing in wiki software.

Grammar/Mechanics Review—9

The following sentences contain errors in grammar, punctuation, capitalization, number style, usage, and spelling. Below each sentence write a corrected version.

1. Each of our applicants are rated on the following factors; skills, experience, education, and people skills.

2. Although Bianca and him agreed to pay two months rent in advance the landlord refused to rent to them.

3. The nations airlines threatened to stop service on Monday at 5 p.m.

4. Our 3 top sales reps, Lucinda, Rafael, and Alasie—received cash bonus's of one thousand dollars each.

5. Did we send 2 copies of the proposal to SuperCom, Inc?

6. If you were me would you step into the managers shoes at this time.

7. Anji wondered whether all two hundred of our brochures would be delivered within the 2 week mailing period?

8. A complete glossary of terms, see page 200 are available to help readers' understand difficult terms.

9. In Globe and Mail you will find an article titled The Blossoming of Internet Chat, however we could not locate it online.

10. Mr Ferranto, Ms Toney, and Miss Cabot has each recieved a new computer.

11. (Direct quotation) The teacher said, A clear conscious is usually the sign of a bad memory.

12. Would you please send me this years rankings of all your stock funds?

13. A host of ethical issues surround business including economic justice, corporate morality and whistleblowing.

14. Greenshield Investments developed it's own code of ethics however its difficult to inforce such a code.

15. For those whom are interested the online version of Canadian News and World Reports university rankings are now available.

Grammar/Mechanics Challenge—9

Document for Revision

The following report executive summary has faults in grammar, punctuation, spelling, number form, wordiness, and word use. Use standard proofreading marks (see Appendix B) to correct the errors. When you finish, your instructor can show you the revised version of this summary.

EXECUTIVE SUMMARY

Problem

The Canadian salmon industry must expand it's markets abroad particularly in regard to Japan. Although consumption of salmon is decreasing in Canada they are increasing in Japan. The problem that is for the canadian salmon industry is developing apropriate marketing strategies to boost its current sale in Japanese markets.

Summary of Findings

This report analyzes the Japanese market which currently consumes six hundred thousand tons of salmon per year, and is growing rapidly. Much of this salmon is supplied by imports which at this point in time total about 35% of sales. Our findings indicate that not only will this expand, but the share of imports will continue to grow. The trend is alarming to Japanese salmon industry leaders, because this important market, close to a $billion a year, is increasingly subject to the influence of foreign imports. Declining catches by Japans own Salmon fleet as well as a sharp upward turn in food preference by affluent Japanese consumers, has contributed to this trend.

Recommendations

Based on our analisys we reccommend the following 5 marketing strategys for the Canadian Salmon industry.

1. Farm greater supplys of atlantic farmed salmon to export.

2. We should market our own value added products.

3. Sell fresh salmon direct to the Tokyo Central Wholesale market.

4. Sell to other Japanese markets also.

5. Direct sales should be made to Japanese Supermarket chains.

Chapter 9: Proposals and Formal Reports

Laying the Groundwork for Team Writing Projects

Chances are very good that you can look forward to some kind of team writing in your future career. You may collaborate voluntarily (seeking advice and differing perspectives) or involuntarily (through necessity or by assignment). Working with other people can be frustrating, particularly when some team members don't carry their weight or when conflict breaks out. Team projects, though, can be harmonious, productive, and rewarding when members establish ground rules at the outset and adhere to guidelines such as those presented here.

Collaboration tools, such as wikis, allow team members to contribute to and edit a text online. Many businesses today turn to wikis to facilitate teamwork. Your instructor may have access to wiki software or to the wiki function in Blackboard.

Preparing to Work Together

Before you discuss the project, talk about how your group will function.

- Limit the size of your team, if possible, to two to five members. Larger groups have more difficulties. An odd number is usually preferable to avoid ties in voting.
- Name a team leader (to plan and conduct meetings), a recorder (to keep a record of group decisions), and an evaluator (to determine whether the group is on target and meeting its goals).
- Decide whether your team will be governed by consensus (everyone must agree) or by majority rule.
- Compare schedules of team members, and set up the best meeting times. Plan to meet often. Avoid other responsibilities during meetings. Team meetings can take place face-to-face or virtually.
- Discuss the value of conflict. By bringing conflict into the open and encouraging confrontation, your team can prevent personal resentment and group dysfunction. Conflict can actually create better final documents by promoting new ideas and avoiding groupthink.
- Discuss how you will deal with members who are not doing their share of the work.

Planning the Document

Once you have established ground rules, you are ready to discuss the project and resulting document. Be sure to keep a record of the decisions your team makes.

- Establish the document's specific purpose and identify the main issues involved.
- Decide on the final form of the document. What parts will it have?
- Discuss the audience(s) for the document and what appeal would help it achieve its purpose.
- Develop a work plan. Assign jobs. Set deadlines.
- Decide how the final document will be written: individuals working separately on assigned portions, one person writing the first draft, the entire group writing the complete document together, or some other method.
- Discuss ways to ensure the accuracy and currency of the information collected.

Collecting Information

The following suggestions help teams gather accurate information:

- Brainstorm for ideas as a group.
- Decide who will be responsible for gathering what information.
- Establish deadlines for collecting information.

Organizing, Writing, and Revising

As the project progresses, your team may wish to modify some of its earlier decisions.

- Review the proposed organization of your final document, and adjust it if necessary.
- Write the first draft. If separate team members are writing segments, they should use the same word processing program to facilitate combining files.
- Meet to discuss and revise the draft(s).
- If individuals are working on separate parts, appoint one person (probably the best writer) to coordinate all the parts, striving for consistent style and format.

Editing and Evaluating

Before the document is submitted, complete these steps:

- Give one person responsibility for finding and correcting grammatical and mechanical errors.
- Meet as a group to evaluate the final document. Does it fulfill its purpose and meet the needs of the audience?

Option: Using a Wiki to Collaborate

Hosting companies such as PBwiki (**http://pbwiki.com/education.wiki**) offer easy-to-use, free wiki accounts to educators to run in their classes without the need of involving the IT department. Blackboard supports a wiki option as long as a college or university selects it with its subscription. A wiki within Blackboard is a page, or multiple pages, that students enrolled in the class can edit and change. They may add other content such as images and hyperlinks. A log allows instructors to track changes and the students' contributions. Ask your instructor about these options.

Career Application

Select a report topic from this chapter or Chapter 8. Assume that you must prepare the report as a team project. If you are working on a long report, your instructor may ask you to prepare individual progress reports as you develop your topic.

Your Task

- Form teams of two to five members.
- Prepare to work together by using the suggestions provided here.
- Plan your report by establishing its purpose, analyzing the audience, identifying the main issues, developing a work plan, and assigning tasks.
- Collect information, organize the data, and write the first draft.
- Decide how the document will be revised, edited, and evaluated.

Tip: For revising and editing, consider using the Microsoft Word tools introduced in Chapter 3 to track changes and make comments.

Your instructor may assign grades not only on the final report but also on your team effectiveness and your individual contribution, as determined by fellow team members and, potentially, by tracking your activities if you are using a wiki.

Developing Speaking Skills

Chapter 10

Communicating in Person: Professionalism, Etiquette, Teamwork, and Meetings

Chapter 11

Business Presentations

COMMUNICATION TECHNOLOGY IN THE NEWS

Finding the Right Words in Awkward Situations

Source: Danielle Harder, "Finding the right words in awkward situations," *Canadian HR Reporter*, January 31, 2011, pp. 22–23. Used with permission.

As a leadership and communications expert, Merge Gupta-Sunderji thought she had heard it all. But when her Calgary-based firm asked clients about the most difficult conversations they've had with employees, she was admittedly surprised.

Take, for example, the female manager who had to talk to a male employee about continually grabbing himself in his private area during meetings. The manager started by showing him Michael Jackson videos and footage of baseball players and asking, "What do you have in common with these guys?"

He didn't know so, eventually, the manager had to be more direct. It turns out he was a former baseball player and completely unaware of either his offensive habit or its impact on co-workers.

While conversations about sensitive issues—such as social habits, body odour, poor performance, gossip or workplace attire—are dreadful, they must happen, says Gupta-Sunderji.

"You have to make the first move," she said. "It's really uncomfortable but it won't go away. You're the manager and this is what you're paid to do."

Advance preparation

It helps to do some homework in advance. Before approaching an employee, be clear about the reason for having the conversation in the first place, says Mitch Fairrais, president of On the Mark, a Toronto consulting firm that offers workshops on navigating difficult talks.

"You need clarity," he says. "Get a clear sense from HR or your organization about what the hope is from you, and reflect back your intentions so everyone is clear."

Many conversations become stuck, says Fairrais, because managers forget the bigger picture: What impact is this poor performance or behaviour having on the company?

Ginger Brunner, president of Dynamic HR in Shawnigan Lake, B.C., once had to discuss personal attire, or lack thereof, with an employee. The woman was fit and wanted to show it off.

"I just had to keep bringing it back to our policies," says Brunner.

Having a productive talk starts by meeting one-on-one, says Fairrais.

"The only time a conversation like this can be good is if you're clear about the other party's view or frame of reference," he says. "You can't do that in a group."

Body language and seating also needs to be just right. It's best to sit—never stand—only a few feet apart with nothing between the two of you, says Fairrais. It's also important to lean in and be present—no checking email, taking a "quick" call or allowing others to butt into the conversation.

"You have to eliminate distractions," he says. "Otherwise, you will not be 'there.'"

It's also helpful to have a game plan, says Gupta-Sunderji. Employers should take a five-step approach, she says. This not only gives managers confidence, it also gives them a road map if the discussion goes off track. It can be helpful if you have the steps written down and mentally check them off as you go along.

First on the list, of course, is to have the conversation. Start by acknowledging any discomfort. A line such as, "I have something to discuss with you that I've really struggled with but it's something I'd want to know about if it were me," works well, says Gupta-Sunderji.

Then, you need to be direct.

"Be respectful, be empathetic, but get to the point," she says. "'There's a strong body odour coming from you' or 'I know you have a sick child but your work is falling behind.'"

The third step is to anticipate and be prepared for emotion, whether it's anger, defensiveness or tears.

"It's natural for people to be upset in these situations. Don't take it personally," says Gupta-Sunderji.

This leads to step four: Express your desire to resolve the issue rather than see it escalate.

"Try saying, 'I see how this has upset you. My goal is to see how we can turn this around so you come in on time so you don't face disciplinary action,'" she says.

How the conversation is framed sets the tone, says Fairrais, who tells clients to shift the talk from being a monologue to a dialogue.

"You could say, 'I have a challenge. It involves my perception of the practices you use in meetings. Here's what those perceptions are. What are your perceptions?'" he says. "It gets their guard down. When you make it about them alone, their guard goes up."

If there are tears or anger, it can help to take a break and resume the conversation later. It's a good idea to think through all potential reactions in advance of the meeting and to practise a response to them, says Fairrais. At the same time, consider what it would be like in the other person's situation.

"You have to be as sincere as possible," he says. "Bring as much clarity and transparency as you can. You don't want them to think you're trying to soft sell something."

Brunner brings a box of tissues and shows she cares.

"Don't forget you're dealing with a person," she says. "Sometimes we get caught up in all of the proper steps and we forget that there's a human on the other side of the table."

At the same time, to be effective, you have to stick to the facts and not get caught up in the emotion. These types of meetings should never go longer than 20 minutes, says Fairrais.

Wrapping it up

It's important to leave the meeting with a plan. That means laying out the problem, the desired change or outcome and the potential consequences as early as possible in the meeting, he says. This leaves time to work on a solution together.

"You really want to focus on the future, not what went wrong," he says. "Find a way to enlist their views. Unless they feel you truly understood them, and they are part of the solution, they will be back again."

As difficult as these discussions can be, if they're not dealt with, the consequences can be far worse, says Brunner.

"The rest of the employees see these things happening," she says. "If they're not being addressed, that sends a really loud message."

Summarize the article you've just read in a two- or three-sentence paragraph. Answer the following questions, either on your own or in a small group. Be prepared to present your answers in a short presentation or in an e-mail to your instructor.

QUESTIONS:

1. How does what you've learned in this article change your perception of business communication?

2. How might what you've learned in this article change your own communication style?

3. Come up with pro and con arguments for the following debate/discussion topic: It's better to not have difficult conversations at work and instead just get on with your job.

CHAPTER 10

Communicating in Person: Professionalism, Etiquette, Teamwork, and Meetings

Before meeting with clients, I gather as much information as possible. The more information, the better prepared I can be to meet their needs. Preparation is key for any meeting. It's important to meet face-to-face with my clients to get to know them on a personal level. In our meetings, we work together to establish client goals, plan for future needs, and monitor client progress.[1]

Orna Spira,
Investment Advisor, CIBC Wood Gundy

LEARNING OBJECTIVES

1. Show that you understand the importance of professional behaviour, business etiquette, and ethics and know what employers want.

2. Demonstrate how to improve face-to-face workplace communication, including using your voice as a communication tool.

3. Explain how to promote positive workplace relations through conversation.

4. Review techniques for offering constructive criticism on the job, responding professionally to workplace criticism, and resolving workplace conflicts.

5. Identify ways to polish professional phone skills.

6. List techniques for making the best use of voice mail.

7. Follow procedures for planning and participating in productive business and professional meetings.

Recognizing the Importance of Professionalism, Business Etiquette, and Ethical Behaviour

Whether we call it *professionalism, business etiquette, ethical conduct, social intelligence,* or *soft skills,* we are referring to a whole range of desirable workplace behaviours.

You have probably been told that being *professional* is important. When you search for definitions, however, you will find a wide range of meanings. Related terms and synonyms, such as *business etiquette* or *protocol, soft skills, social intelligence, polish,* and *civility,* may add to the confusion. However, they all have one thing in common: they describe desirable workplace behaviour. Businesses have an interest in a workforce that gets along and delivers positive results that enhance profits and boost a company's image. As a budding business professional, you have a stake in acquiring skills that will make you a strong job applicant and a valuable, successful employee.

In this section you will learn which professional characteristics most business-people value in workplace relationships and will expect of you. Next you will be asked to consider the link between professional and ethical behaviour on the job. Finally, by knowing what recruiters want, you will have the power to shape yourself into the kind of professional they are looking to hire.

Defining Professional Behaviour

Smooth relations in the workplace and when interacting with business partners or the public are crucial for the bottom line. Therefore, many businesses have established protocol procedures or policies to encourage civility. They are responding to increasing incidents of "desk rage" in the workplace. Here are a few synonyms that attempt to define professional behaviour that will foster positive workplace relations:

Civility. Management consultant Patricia M. Buhler defines rising incivility at work "as behaviour that is considered disrespectful and inconsiderate of others."[2] For an example of a policy encouraging civility, view Wikipedia's guidelines to its editors (**http://en.wikipedia.org/wiki/Wikipedia:CIV**), which offer principles to prevent rudeness and hateful responses on the Internet. The largest wiki ever created, the free encyclopedia must ensure that its more than 75,000 active collaborators get along and respect each other. Interestingly, Wikipedia admits that it is easier to define civility by its opposite: "[I]ncivility . . . consists of personally targeted, belligerent behaviour and persistent rudeness that result in an atmosphere of conflict and stress."[3]

Polish. You may hear businesspeople refer to someone as being *polished* or displaying *polish* when dealing with others. In her book with the telling title *Buff and Polish: A Practical Guide to Enhance Your Professional Image and Communication Style*, Kathryn J. Volin focuses on nonverbal techniques and etiquette guidelines that are linked to career success. For example, she addresses making first impressions, shaking hands, improving one's voice quality, listening, and presentation skills.

Business and Dining Etiquette. Proper business attire, dining etiquette, and other aspects of your professional presentation can make or break your interview, as you will see in Chapter 13. Even a seemingly harmless act such as sharing a business meal can have a huge impact on your career. In the words of one executive, "Eating is not an executive skill . . . but it is especially hard to imagine why anyone negotiating a rise to the top would consider it possible to skip mastering the very simple requirements. . . . [W]hat else did they skip learning?"[4] This means that you will be judged on more than your college-bred expertise. You will need to hone your etiquette skills as a well-rounded future business professional.

Social Intelligence. Occasionally you may encounter the expression *social intelligence*. In the words of one of its modern proponents, it is "The ability to get along well with others and to get them to cooperate with you."[5] Social intelligence points to a deep understanding of culture and life that helps us negotiate interpersonal and social situations. This type of intelligence can be much harder to acquire than simple etiquette. Social intelligence requires us to interact well, be perceptive, show sensitivity toward others, and grasp a situation quickly and accurately.

Soft Skills. Perhaps the most common term for important interpersonal habits is *soft skills*, as opposed to *hard skills*, a term for the technical knowledge in your field. Soft skills are a whole cluster of personal qualities, habits, attitudes (for example, optimism and friendliness), communication skills, and social graces. Employers want managers and employees who are comfortable with diverse coworkers, who can listen actively to customers and colleagues, who can make eye contact, who display good workplace manners, and who possess a host of other interpersonal skills. *Dress for Success* guru John T. Molloy says that 99 out of 100 executives view social skills as prerequisites to success, whether over cocktails, during dinner,

From meetings and interviews to company parties and golf outings, nearly all workplace-related activities involve etiquette. Take Your Dog to Work Day, the ever-popular morale booster that keeps workers chained to their pets instead of the desk, has a unique set of guidelines to help maximize fun. Some etiquette gurus say pets must be well behaved, housebroken, and free of fleas to participate in the four-legged festivity. *Why is it important to follow proper business etiquette?*

or in the boardroom.[6] These skills are immensely important not only to being hired but also to being promoted.

All attempts to explain proper behaviour at work aim at identifying traits that make someone a good employee and a compatible coworker. You will want to achieve a positive image on the job and to maintain a solid reputation. For the sake of simplicity, in the discussion that follows, the terms *professionalism*, *business etiquette*, and *soft skills* will be used largely synonymously.

Understanding the Relationship Between Ethics and Professional Behaviour

Business etiquette is closely related to everyday ethical behaviour.

The wide definition of professionalism also encompasses another crucial quality in a businessperson: *ethics* or *integrity*. Perhaps you subscribe to a negative view of business after learning about companies such as the U.S.'s Enron or Canada's LiveEnt. The collapse of these businesses, along with fraud charges against their executives, has reinforced the cynical perception of business as unethical and greedy. However, for every company that captures the limelight for misconduct, hundreds or even thousands of others operate honestly and serve their customers and the public well. The overwhelming majority of businesses wish to recruit ethical and polished graduates.

The difference between ethics and etiquette is minimal in the workplace. Ethics suggest that no sharp distinction between ethics and etiquette exists. How we approach the seemingly trivial events of work life reflects our character and attitudes when we handle larger issues. Our conduct should be consistently ethical and professional. Harvard University Professor Douglas Chismar believes that "[w]e each have a moral obligation to treat each other with respect and sensitivity every day."[7] He calls on all of us to make a difference in the quality of life, morale, and even productivity at work. When employed appropriately in business, he says, professionalism brings greater good to society and makes for a better workplace.

Figure 10.1 summarizes the many components of professional workplace behaviour[8] and identifies six main dimensions that will ease your entry into the world of work. Follow these guidelines to ensure your success on the job and increase the likelihood of promotion.

FIGURE 10.1 The Six Dimensions of Professional Behaviour

Professional Dimension	What Professionalism Means on the Job
Courtesy and respect	• Be punctual. • Speak and write clearly and in language others can understand. • Apologize for errors or misunderstandings. • Notify the other person promptly when running late. • Accept constructive criticism. • Provide fair and gentle feedback. • Practise active listening.
Appearance and appeal	• Present yourself pleasantly with good hygiene and grooming. • Choose attractive, yet not distracting, business attire. • Understand that appropriate dress and behaviour are the first indication of professionalism and create lasting impressions. • Display proper business and dining etiquette.
Tolerance and tact	• Demonstrate self-control. • Stay away from public arguments and disagreements, including in written documents and e-mail. • Eliminate biases and prejudices in all business dealings. • Keep personal opinions of people private. • Avoid snap judgments, especially when collaborating with others.
Honesty and ethics	• Avoid even the smallest lies at all cost. • Steer clear of conflicts of interest. • Pay for services and products promptly. • Keep confidential information confidential. • Pass up opportunities to badmouth competitors—emphasize your company's benefits, not your competitors' flaws. • Take positive, appropriate actions; avoid resorting to vengeful behaviour when you feel wronged.
Reliability and responsibility	• Be dependable. • Follow through on commitments. • Keep promises and deadlines. • Perform work consistently and deliver effective results. • Make realistic promises about the quantity and quality of work output in a projected time frame.
Diligence and collegiality	• Deliver only work you can be proud of. • Strive for excellence at all times. • Give to customers more than they expect. • Be prepared before meetings and when presenting reports. • Do what needs to be done; do not leave work for others to do. • Show a willingness to share expertise. • Volunteer services to a worthy community or charity group. • Join networking groups and help their members.

Anticipating What Employers Want

Professional polish is increasingly valuable in our knowledge-based economy and will set you apart in competition with others. Hiring managers expect you to have technical expertise in your field. A good résumé and interview may get you in the door. However, soft skills and professional polish will ensure your long-term

> In the workplace we are judged to a great extent on our soft skills and professionalism.

success. Advancement and promotions will depend on your grasp of workplace etiquette and the ability to communicate with your boss, coworkers, and customers. You will also earn recognition on the job if you prove yourself as an effective and contributing team member—and as a well-rounded professional overall.

Even in technical fields such as accounting and finance, employers are looking for professionalism and soft skills. Based on a survey of international accounting executives, *CA Magazine* concluded that "the future is bright for the next generation of accounting and finance professionals provided they are armed with such soft skills as the ability to communicate, deal with change, and work in a team setting."[9] A survey of chief financial officers revealed that a majority believed that communication skills carry a greater importance today than in the past.[10] Increasingly, finance professionals must be able to interact with the entire organization and explain terms without using financial jargon.

Employment advertisements frequently mention team, communication, and people skills.

Employers want team players who can work together productively. If you look at current online or newspaper want ads, chances are you will find requirements such as the following examples:

- Proven team skills to help deliver on-time, on-budget results
- Strong verbal and written communication skills as well as excellent presentation skills
- Excellent interpersonal, organizational, and teamwork skills
- Interpersonal and team skills plus well-developed communication skills
- Good people skills and superior teamwork abilities

In addition, most hiring managers are looking for new hires who show enthusiasm, are eager to learn, volunteer to tackle even difficult tasks, and exhibit a positive attitude. You will not be hired to warm a seat.

This chapter focuses on developing interpersonal skills, telephone and voice mail etiquette, teamwork proficiency, and meeting management skills. These are some of the soft skills that employers seek in today's increasingly interconnected and competitive environments. You will learn many tips and techniques for becoming a professional communicator, valuable team player, and polished meeting participant.

Improving Face-to-Face Workplace Communication

One-dimensional communication technologies cannot replace the richness or effectiveness of face-to-face communication.

Because technology provides many alternate communication channels, you may think that face-to-face communication is no longer essential or even important in business and professional transactions. You've already learned that e-mail is now the preferred communication channel because it is faster, cheaper, and easier than telephone, mail, or fax. Yet, despite their popularity and acceptance, new communication technologies can't replace the richness or effectiveness of face-to-face communication.[11] Imagine that you want to tell your boss how you solved a problem. Would you settle for a one-dimensional e-mail when you could step into her office and explain in person?

Face-to-face conversation has many advantages. It allows you to be persuasive and expressive because you can use your voice and body language to make a point. You are less likely to be misunderstood because you can read feedback instantly and make needed adjustments. In conflict resolution, you can reach a solution more efficiently and cooperate to create greater levels of mutual benefit when communicating face to face.[12] Moreover, people want to see each other to satisfy a deep human need for social interaction. For numerous reasons, communicating in person remains the most effective of all communication channels. In this chapter you'll explore helpful business and professional interpersonal speaking techniques, starting with viewing your voice as a communication tool.

Using Your Voice as a Communication Tool

It's been said that language provides the words, but your voice is the music that makes words meaningful.[13] You may believe that a beautiful or powerful voice is unattainable. After all, this is the voice you were born with, and it can't be changed. Actually, the voice is a flexible instrument. For example, two of Canada's leading theatre companies, the Stratford and Shaw festivals in Ontario, both have speech coaches on staff to teach actors various accents and voice techniques. Celebrities, business executives, and everyday people consult voice and speech therapists to help them shake bad habits or help them speak so that they can be understood and not sound less intelligent than they are. Rather than consult a high-paid specialist, you can pick up useful tips for using your voice most effectively by learning how to control such elements as pronunciation, tone, pitch, volume, rate, and emphasis.

Pronunciation. Pronunciation involves saying words correctly and clearly with the accepted sounds and accented syllables. You'll be at a distinct advantage in your job if, through training and practice, you learn to pronounce words correctly. Some of the most common errors, shown in Figure 10.2, include adding or omitting vowels, omitting consonants, reversing sounds, and slurring sounds. In casual conversation with your friends, correct pronunciation is not a big deal. But on the job you want to sound intelligent, educated, and competent. If you mispronounce words or slur phrases together, you risk being misunderstood as well as giving a poor impression of yourself. How can you improve your pronunciation skills? The best way is to listen carefully to educated people, read aloud from well-written newspapers like *The Globe and Mail* and the *National Post*, look up words in the dictionary, and avoid errors such as those in Figure 10.2.

Tone. The tone of your voice sends a nonverbal message to listeners. It identifies your personality and your mood. Some voices sound enthusiastic and friendly, conveying the impression of an upbeat person who is happy to be with the listener. But voices can also sound controlling, patronizing, slow-witted, angry, or childish. This doesn't mean that the speaker necessarily has that attribute. It may mean that the speaker is merely carrying on a family tradition or pattern learned in childhood. To check your voice tone, record your voice and listen to it critically. Is it projecting a positive quality about you?

> Like an actor, you can change your voice to make it a more powerful communication tool.

> Proper pronunciation means saying words correctly and clearly with the accepted sounds and accented syllables.

FIGURE 10.2 Pronunciation Errors to Avoid

Adding vowel sounds	*athlete* (NOT *ath-a-lete*) *disastrous* (NOT *disas-ter-ous*)
Omitting vowel sounds	*federal* (NOT *fed-ral*) *ridiculous* (NOT *ri-dic-lous*) *generally* (NOT *gen-rally*)
Substituting vowel sounds	*get* (NOT *git*) *separate* (NOT *sep-e-rate*)
Adding consonant sounds	*butter* (NOT *budder*) *statistics* (NOT *sta-stis-tics*) *especially* (NOT *ex-specially*)
Omitting consonant sounds	*library* (NOT *libery*) *perhaps* (NOT *praps*)
Confusing or distorting sounds	*ask* (NOT *aks*) *hundred* (NOT *hunderd*) *accessory* (NOT *assessory*)
Slurring sounds	*didn't you* (NOT *dint ya*) *going to* (NOT *gonna*)

Pitch. Effective speakers use a relaxed, controlled, well-pitched voice to attract listeners to their message. Pitch refers to sound vibration frequency; that is, it indicates the highness or lowness of a sound. In Canada, most speakers and listeners tend to prefer a variety of pitch patterns. Voices are most attractive when they rise and fall in conversational tones. Flat, monotone voices are considered boring and ineffectual. In business, communicators strive for a moderately low voice, which is thought to be pleasing and professional.

Speaking in a moderately low-pitched voice at about 125 words a minute makes you sound pleasing and professional.

Volume and Rate. Volume indicates the degree of loudness or the intensity of sound. Just as you adjust the volume on your iPod or television, you should adjust the volume of your speaking to the occasion and your listeners. When speaking face to face, you generally know whether you are speaking too loudly or softly by looking at your listeners. Are they straining to hear you? To judge what volume to use, listen carefully to the other person's voice. Use it as a guide for adjusting your voice. Rate refers to the pace of your speech. If you speak too slowly, listeners are bored and their attention wanders. If you speak too quickly, listeners can't understand you. Most people normally talk at about 125 words a minute. If you're the kind of speaker who speeds up when talking in front of a group of people, monitor the nonverbal signs of your listeners and adjust your rate as needed.

Emphasis. By emphasizing or stressing certain words, you can change the meaning you are expressing. For example, read these sentences aloud, emphasizing the italicized words:

Matt said the hard drive failed again. (Matt knows what happened.)

Matt *said* the hard drive failed again. (But he may be wrong.)

Matt said the hard drive failed *again*? (Did he really say that?)

As you can see, emphasis affects the meaning of the words and the thought expressed. To make your message interesting and natural, use emphasis appropriately. You can raise your volume to sound authoritative and raise your pitch to sound disbelieving. Lowering your volume and pitch makes you sound professional or reasonable.

Some speakers today are prone to "uptalk." This is a habit of using a rising inflection at the end of a sentence, resulting in a singsong pattern that makes statements sound like questions. Once used exclusively by teenagers, uptalk is increasingly found in the workplace, with negative results. When statements sound like questions, speakers seem weak and tentative. Their messages lack conviction and authority. On the job, managers afflicted by uptalk may have difficulty convincing staff members to follow directions because their voice inflection implies that other valid options are available. If you want to sound confident and competent, avoid uptalk.

"Uptalk," in which sentences sound like questions, makes speakers seem weak and tentative.

Promoting Positive Workplace Relations Through Conversation

In the workplace, conversations may involve giving and taking instructions, providing feedback, exchanging ideas on products and services, participating in performance appraisals, or engaging in small talk about such things as families and sports. Face-to-face conversation helps people work together harmoniously and feel that they are part of the larger organization. There are several guidelines that promote positive workplace conversations, starting with using correct names and titles.

Use Correct Names and Titles. Although the world seems increasingly informal, it's still wise to use titles and last names when addressing professional adults (*Mrs. Smith*, *Mr. Rivera*). In some organizations senior staff members will speak to junior employees on a first-name basis, but the reverse may not be encouraged. Probably the safest plan is to ask your superiors how they want to be addressed. Customers and others outside the organization should always be addressed by title and last name.

When you meet strangers, do you have trouble remembering their names? You can improve your memory considerably if you associate the person with an object, place, colour, animal, job, adjective, or some other memory hook. For example, *computer pro Kevin, Miami Kim, silver-haired Mr. Lee, bulldog Chris, bookkeeper Lynn, traveller Ms. Janis.* The person's name will also be more deeply embedded in your memory if you use it immediately after being introduced, in subsequent conversation, and when you part.

Choose Appropriate Topics. In some workplace activities, such as social gatherings or interviews, you will be expected to engage in small talk. Be sure to stay away from controversial topics with someone you don't know very well. Avoid politics, religion, or current events items that can start heated arguments until you know the person better. To initiate appropriate conversations, read newspapers and listen to radio and TV shows discussing current events. Make a mental note of items that you can use in conversation, taking care to remember where you saw or heard the news items so that you can report accurately and authoritatively. Try not to be defensive or annoyed if others present information that upsets you.

> You will be most effective in workplace conversations if you use correct names and titles, choose appropriate topics, avoid negative and judgmental remarks, and give sincere and specific praise.

Avoid Negative Remarks. Workplace conversations are not the place to complain about your colleagues, your friends, the organization, or your job. No one enjoys listening to whiners. And your criticism of others may come back to haunt you. A snipe at your boss or a complaint about a fellow worker may reach him or her, sometimes embellished or distorted with meanings you did not intend. Be careful about publicizing negative judgments. Remember, some people love to repeat statements that will stir up trouble or set off internal workplace wars. It's best not to give them the ammunition.

"I had to spend the money I budgeted for your raise on a therapist after listening to your endless complaining."

Listen to Learn. In conversations with colleagues, subordinates, and customers, train yourself to expect to learn something from what you are hearing. Being attentive is not only instructive but also courteous. Beyond displaying good manners, you'll probably find that your conversation partner has information that you don't have. Being receptive and listening with an open mind means not interrupting or prejudging. Let's say you very much want to be able to work at home for part of your workweek. You try to explain your ideas to your boss, but he cuts you off shortly after you start. He says, "It's out of the question; we need you here every day." Suppose instead he says, "I have strong reservations about your telecommuting, but maybe you'll change my mind"; and he settles in to listen to your presentation. Even if your boss decides against your request, you will feel that your ideas were heard and respected.

Give Sincere and Specific Praise. A wise person once said, "Man does not live by bread alone. He needs to be buttered up once in a while." Probably nothing promotes positive workplace relationships better than sincere and specific praise. Whether the compliments and appreciation are travelling upward to management, downward to workers, or horizontally to colleagues, everyone responds well to recognition. Organizations run more smoothly and morale is higher when people feel appreciated. In your workplace conversations, look for ways to recognize good work and good people. And try to be specific. Instead of "You did a good job in leading that meeting," try something more specific, such as "Your leadership skills certainly kept that meeting focused and productive."

Offering Constructive Criticism on the Job

No one likes to receive criticism, and most of us don't like to give it either. But in the workplace cooperative endeavours demand feedback and evaluation. How are we doing on a project? What went well? What failed? How can we improve our efforts? Today's workplace often involves team projects. As a team member, you will be called on to judge the work of others. In addition to working on teams, you can also expect to become a supervisor or manager one day. As such, you will need to evaluate subordinates. Good employees seek good feedback from their supervisors. They want and need timely, detailed observations about their work to reinforce what they do well and help them overcome weak spots. But making that feedback palatable and constructive is not always easy. Depending on your situation, you may find some or all of the following suggestions, in addition to the ones listed in the article that opens this unit (p. 274), helpful when you must deliver constructive criticism:

Offering constructive criticism is easier if you plan what you will say, focus on improvement, offer to help, be specific, discuss the behaviour and not the person, speak privately face to face, and avoid anger.

- **Mentally outline your conversation.** Think carefully about what you want to accomplish and what you will say. Find the right words at the right time and in the right setting.
- **Generally, use face-to-face communication.** Most constructive criticism is better delivered in person rather than in e-mails or memos. Personal feedback offers an opportunity for the listener to ask questions and give explanations. Occasionally, however, complex situations may require a different strategy. You might prefer to write out your opinions and deliver them by telephone or in writing. A written document enables you to organize your thoughts, include all the details, and be sure of keeping your cool. Remember, though, that written documents create permanent records—for better or worse.
- **Focus on improvement.** Instead of attacking, use language that offers alternative behaviour. Use phrases such as "Next time, it would great if you could. . . ."
- **Offer to help.** Criticism is accepted more readily if you volunteer to help in eliminating or solving the problem.
- **Be specific.** Instead of a vague assertion such as "Your work is often late," be more specific: "The specs on the Riverside job were due Thursday at 5 p.m., and you didn't hand them in until Friday." Explain how the person's performance jeopardized the entire project.
- **Avoid broad generalizations.** Don't use words such as *should*, *never*, *always*, and other encompassing expressions. They may cause the listener to shut down and become defensive.
- **Discuss the behaviour, not the person.** Instead of "You seem to think you can come to work any time you want," focus on the behaviour: "Coming to work late means that we have to fill in with someone else until you arrive."
- **Use the word *we* rather than *you*.** "We need to meet project deadlines," is better than saying "You need to meet project deadlines." Emphasize organizational expectations rather than personal ones. Avoid sounding accusatory.
- **Encourage two-way communication.** Even if well-planned, criticism is still hard to deliver. It may surprise or hurt the feelings of the employee. Consider ending your message with, "It can be hard to hear this type of feedback. If you'd like to share your thoughts, I'm listening."
- **Avoid anger, sarcasm, and a raised voice.** Criticism is rarely constructive when tempers flare. Plan in advance what you will say and deliver it in low, controlled, and sincere tones.
- **Keep it private.** Offer praise in public; offer criticism in private. "Setting an example" through public criticism is never a wise management policy.

Responding Professionally to Workplace Criticism

As much as we hate giving criticism, we dislike receiving it even more. Yet the workplace requires that you not only provide it but also be able to accept it. When being criticized, you probably will feel that you are being attacked. You can't just sit back and relax. Your heart beats faster, your temperature increases, your face

When being criticized, you should listen, paraphrase, and clarify what is said. If you agree that the criticism is valid, apologize or explain what you will do differently.

reddens, and you respond with the classic "fight or flight" syndrome. You feel that you want to instantly retaliate or escape from the attacker. But focusing on your feelings distracts you from hearing the content of what is being said, and it prevents you from responding professionally. Some or all of the following suggestions will guide you in reacting positively to criticism so that you can benefit from it:

- **Listen without interrupting.** Even though you might want to protest, make yourself hear the speaker out.
- **Determine the speaker's intent.** Unskilled communicators may throw "verbal bricks" with unintended negative-sounding expressions. If you think the intent is positive, focus on what is being said rather than reacting to poorly chosen words.
- **Acknowledge what you are hearing.** Respond with a pause, a nod, or a neutral statement such as "I understand you have a concern." This buys you time. Do not disagree, counterattack, or blame, which may escalate the situation and harden the speaker's position.
- **Paraphrase what was said.** In your own words, restate objectively what you are hearing; for example, "So what you're saying is. . . ."
- **Ask for more information if necessary.** Clarify what is being said. Stay focused on the main idea rather than interjecting side issues.
- **Agree—if the comments are accurate.** If an apology is in order, give it. Explain what you plan to do differently. If the criticism is on target, the sooner you agree, the more likely you will engender respect from the other person.
- **Disagree respectfully and constructively—if you feel the comments are unfair.** After hearing the criticism, you might say, "May I tell you my perspective?" Or you could try to solve the problem by saying, "How can we improve this situation in a way you believe we can both accept?" If the other person continues to criticize, say "I want to find a way to resolve your concern. When do you want to talk about it next?"
- **Look for a middle position.** Search for a middle position or a compromise. Be genial even if you don't like the person or the situation.

> If you feel you are being criticized unfairly, disagree respectfully and constructively; look for a middle position.

Resolving Workplace Conflicts

Conflict is a normal part of every workplace, but it is not always negative. When managed properly, conflict can improve decision making, clarify values, increase group cohesiveness, stimulate creativity, decrease tensions, and reduce dissatisfaction. Unresolved conflict, however, can destroy productivity and seriously reduce morale. You will be better prepared to resolve workplace conflict if you know the five most common response patterns as well as a six-step procedure for dealing with conflict.

Common Conflict Response Patterns. Imagine a time when you were very upset with a workplace colleague, boss, or a teammate. How did you respond? Experts who have studied conflict say that most of us deal with it in one of the following predictable patterns:

> Although avoidance does not solve conflicts, it may be the best response for some situations, such as when the issue is trivial.

- **Avoidance/withdrawal.** Instead of trying to resolve the conflict, one person or the other simply withdraws. Avoidance of conflict generally results in a "lose-lose" situation because the problem festers and no attempt is made to understand the issues causing the conflict. On the other hand, avoidance may be the best response when the issue is trivial, when potential losses from an open conflict outweigh potential gains, or when insufficient time is available to work through the issue adequately.
- **Accommodation/smoothing.** When one person gives in quickly, the conflict is smoothed over and surface harmony results. This may be the best method when the issue is minor, when damage to the relationship would harm both parties, and when tempers are too hot for productive discussion.

- **Compromise.** In this pattern both people give up something of lesser importance to gain something more important. Compromise may be the best approach when both parties stand to gain, when a predetermined "ideal" solution is not required, and when time is short.
- **Competition/forcing.** This approach results in a contest in which one person comes out on top, leaving the other with a sense of failure. This method ends the conflict, but it may result in hurt feelings and potential future problems from the loser. This strategy is appropriate when a decision or action must be immediate and when the parties recognize the power relationship between themselves.
- **Collaboration/problem solving.** In this pattern both parties lay their cards on the table and attempt to reach consensus. This approach works when the involved people have common goals but they disagree over how to reach them. Conflict may arise from misunderstanding or a communication breakdown. Collaboration works best when all parties are trained in problem-solving techniques.[14]

Six-Step Procedure for Dealing with Conflict. Probably the best pattern for resolving conflicts involves collaboration and problem-solving procedures. But this method requires a certain amount of training. Fortunately, experts in the field of negotiation have developed a six-step pattern that you can try the next time you need to resolve a conflict:

1. **Listen.** To be sure you understand the problem, listen carefully. If the other person doesn't seem to be listening to you, you need to set the example and be the first to listen.
2. **Understand the other point of view.** Once you listen, it's much easier to understand the other's position. Show your understanding by asking questions and paraphrasing. This will also verify what you think the other person means.
3. **Show a concern for the relationship.** By focusing on the problem, not the person, you can build, maintain, and even improve relationships. Show an understanding of the other person's situation and needs. Show an overall willingness to come to an agreement.
4. **Look for common ground.** Identify your interests and help the other side to identify its interests. Learn what you have in common, and look for a solution to which both sides can agree.
5. **Invent new problem-solving options.** Spend time identifying the interests of both sides. Then brainstorm to invent new ways to solve the problem. Be open to new options.
6. **Reach an agreement based on what's fair.** Seek to determine a standard of fairness that is acceptable to both sides. Then weigh the possible solutions, and choose the best option.[15]

Telephone and Voice Mail Etiquette

The telephone is the most universal—and, some would say, the most important—piece of equipment in offices today.[16] For many businesspeople, it is a primary contact with the outside world. Some observers predicted that e-mail and faxes would "kill off phone calls."[17] In fact, the amazing expansion of wireless communication has given the telephone a new and vigorous lease on life. Telephones are definitely here to stay. But many of us do not use them efficiently or effectively. In this section we'll focus on traditional telephone techniques as well as voice mail efficiency.

Making Productive Telephone Calls

Before making a telephone call, decide whether the intended call is necessary. Could you find the information yourself? If you wait a while, would the problem resolve itself? Perhaps your message could be delivered more efficiently by some other means. One company found that telephone interruptions consumed about 18 percent of staff members' workdays. Another study found that two-thirds of all calls were less important than the work they interrupted.[18] Alternatives to telephone calls include e-mail, memos, or calls to voice mail systems. If a telephone call must be made, use the following suggestions to make it fully productive.

You can make productive telephone calls by planning an agenda, identifying the purpose, being courteous and cheerful, and avoiding rambling.

- **Plan a mini-agenda.** Have you ever been embarrassed when you had to make a second telephone call because you forgot an important item the first time? Before placing a call, jot down notes regarding all the topics you need to discuss. Following an agenda guarantees not only a complete call but also a quick one. You'll be less likely to wander from the business at hand while rummaging through your mind trying to remember everything.
- **Use a three-point introduction.** When placing a call, immediately (1) name the person you are calling, (2) identify yourself and your affiliation, and (3) give a brief explanation of your reason for calling. For example: "May I speak to Larry Levin? This is Hillary Dahl of Acme Ltd., and I'm seeking information about a software program called Power Presentations." This kind of introduction enables the receiving individual to respond immediately without asking further questions.
- **Be brisk if you are rushed.** For business calls when your time is limited, avoid questions such as "How are you?" Instead, say, "Lisa, I knew you'd be the only one who could answer these two questions for me." Another efficient strategy is to set a "contract" with the caller: "Hi, Lisa, I have only ten minutes, but I really wanted to get back to you."
- **Be cheerful and accurate.** Let your voice show the same kind of animation that you radiate when you greet people in person. In your mind try to envision the individual answering the telephone. A smile can certainly affect the tone of your voice, so smile at that person. Moreover, be accurate about what you say. "Hang on a second; I'll be right back" is rarely true. Better to say, "It may take me two or three minutes to get that information. Would you prefer to hold or have me call you back?"
- **Bring it to a close.** The responsibility for ending a call lies with the caller. This is sometimes difficult to do if the other person rambles on. You may need to use suggestive closing language, such as "I've certainly enjoyed talking with you," "I've learned what I needed to know, and now I can proceed with my work," "Thanks for your help," or "I must go now, but may I call you again in the future if I need . . .?"
- **Avoid telephone tag.** If you call someone who's not in, ask when it would be best for you to call again. State that you will call at a specific time—and do it. If you ask a person to call you, give a time when you can be reached—and then be sure you are in at that time.
- **Leave complete voice mail messages.** Remember that there's no rush when you leave a voice mail message. Always enunciate clearly. And be sure to provide a complete message, including your name, telephone number, and the time and date of your call. Explain your purpose so that the receiver can be ready with the required information when returning your call.

Receiving Productive Telephone Calls

With a little forethought, you can make your telephone a productive, efficient work tool. Developing good telephone manners also reflects well on you and on your organization.

- **Identify yourself immediately.** In answering your telephone or someone else's, provide your name, title or affiliation, and, possibly, a greeting. For example, "Larry Levin, Proteus Software. How may I help you?" Force yourself to speak clearly and slowly. Remember that the caller may be unfamiliar with what you are saying and fail to recognize slurred syllables.

- **Be responsive and helpful.** If you are in a support role, be sympathetic to callers' needs. Instead of "I don't know," try "That's a good question; let me investigate." Instead of "We can't do that," try "That's a tough one; let's see what we can do." Avoid "No" at the beginning of a sentence. It sounds especially abrasive and displeasing because it suggests total rejection.
- **Be cautious when answering calls for others.** Be courteous and helpful, but don't give out confidential information. Better to say, "She's away from her desk" or "He's out of the office" than to report a colleague's exact whereabouts.
- **Take messages carefully.** Few things are as frustrating as receiving a potentially important phone message that is illegible. Repeat the spelling of names and verify telephone numbers. Write messages legibly and record their time and date. Promise to give the messages to intended recipients, but don't guarantee return calls.
- **Explain what you're doing when transferring calls.** Give a reason for transferring, and identify the extension to which you are directing the call in case the caller is disconnected.

Using Cell Phones for Business

Cell phones and smartphones (e.g., BlackBerrys) enable you to conduct business from virtually anywhere at any time. More than a plaything or a mere convenience, the wireless phone has become an essential part of communication in many of today's workplaces. As with many new technologies, a set of rules or protocol on cell phone usage is still evolving. How are these phones best used? When is it acceptable to take calls? Where should calls be made? Most of us have experienced thoughtless and rude cell phone behaviour. To avoid offending, smart business communicators practise cell phone etiquette, as outlined in Figure 10.3. In projecting a professional image, they are careful about location, time, and volume in relation to their cell phone calls.

"Do you mind? I happen to be on the phone!"

Location. Use good judgment in placing or accepting cell phone calls. Some places are dangerous or inappropriate for cell phone use. Turn off your cell phone in your vehicle and when entering a conference room, interview, theatre, place of worship, or any other place where it could be distracting or disruptive to others. Taking a call in a crowded room or bar makes it difficult to hear and reflects poorly on you as a professional. A bad connection also makes a bad impression. Static or dropped signals create frustration and miscommunication. Don't sacrifice professionalism for the sake of a garbled phone call. It's smarter to turn off your phone in an area where the signal is weak and when you are likely to have interference. Use voice mail and return the call when conditions are better.

Time. Often what you are doing is more important than whatever may come over the airwaves to you on your phone. For example, when you are having an important discussion with a business partner, customer, or superior, it is rude to allow yourself to be interrupted by an incoming call. It's also poor manners to practice multi-tasking while on the phone. What's more, it's dangerous. Although you might be able to read and print out e-mails, deal with a customer at the counter, and talk on your wireless phone simultaneously, it's impolite and risky. Lack of attention results in errors and a lack of respect. If a phone call is important enough to accept, then it's important enough to stop what you are doing and attend to the conversation.

> Avoid taking cell phone calls when you are talking with someone else, and avoid "cell yell."

Volume. Many people raise their voices when using their cell phones. "Cell yell" results, much to the annoyance of anyone nearby. Raising your voice is unnecessary since most phones have excellent microphones that can pick up even a whisper. If the connection is bad, louder volume will not improve the sound quality. As in face-to-face conversations, a low, modulated voice sounds professional and projects the proper image.

Making the Best Use of Voice Mail

Voice mail links a telephone system to a computer that digitizes and stores incoming messages. Some systems also provide functions such as automated attendant menus, allowing callers to reach any associated extension by pushing specific buttons on a touch-tone telephone. For example, a ski resort in British Columbia uses voice mail to answer routine questions that once were routed through an operator: *Welcome to Panorama. For information on accommodations, press 1; for snow conditions, press 2; for ski equipment rental, press 3*, and so forth.

> Voice mail eliminates telephone tag, inaccurate message taking, and time-zone barriers; it also allows communicators to focus on essentials.

FIGURE 10.3 Practising Courteous and Responsible Cell Phone Use

Business communicators find cell phones to be enormously convenient and real time-savers. But rude users have generated a backlash against inconsiderate callers. Here are specific suggestions for using cell phones safely and responsibly:

- **Be courteous to those around you.** Don't force those near you to hear your business. Apologize and make amends gracefully for occasional cell phone blunders.

- **Observe wireless-free quiet areas.** Don't allow your cell phone to ring in theatres, restaurants, museums, classrooms, important meetings, and similar places. Use the cell phone's silent/vibrating ring option. A majority of travellers prefer that cell phone conversations *not* be held on most forms of public transportation.

- **Speak in low, conversational tones.** Microphones on cell phones are quite sensitive, thus making it unnecessary to talk loudly. Avoid "cell yell."

- **Take only urgent calls.** Make full use of your cell phone's caller ID feature to screen incoming calls. Let voice mail take those calls that are not pressing.

- **Drive now, talk later.** Pull over if you must make a call. Talking while driving increases the chance of accidents fourfold. In most Canadian provinces, including British Columbia, Newfoundland and Labrador, Nova Scotia, Ontario, Quebec, and Saskatchewan, there are specific laws against driving and using handheld devices. Other provinces and territories are enacting similar laws.[19]

Within some companies, voice mail accounts for 90 percent of all telephone messages.[20] Its popularity results from serving many functions, the most important of which is message storage. Because as many as half of all business calls require no discussion or feedback, the messaging capabilities of voice mail can mean huge savings for businesses. Incoming information is delivered without interrupting potential receivers and without all the niceties that most two-way conversations require. Stripped of superfluous chitchat, voice mail messages allow communicators to focus on essentials. Voice mail also eliminates telephone tag, inaccurate message taking, and time-zone barriers. Critics complain, nevertheless, that automated systems seem cold and impersonal and are sometimes confusing and irritating. In any event, here are some ways that you can make voice mail work more effectively for you.

- **Announce your voice mail.** If you rely principally on a voice mail message system, identify it on your business stationery and cards. Then, when people call, they will be ready to leave a message.
- **Prepare a warm, informative, up-to-date greeting.** Make your mechanical greeting sound warm and inviting, both in tone and content. Identify yourself and your organization so that callers know they have reached the right number. Thank the caller and briefly explain that you are unavailable. Invite the caller to leave a message or, if appropriate, call back. Here's a typical voice mail greeting: "Hi! This is Larry Levin of Proteus Software, and I appreciate your call. You've reached my voice mailbox because I'm either working with customers or talking on another line at the moment. Please leave your name, number, and reason for calling so that I can be prepared when I return your call." Give callers an idea of when you will be available, such as "I'll be back at 2:30" or "I'll be out of my office until Wednesday, May 20." If you screen your calls as a time-management technique, try this message: "I'm not near my phone right now, but I should be able to return calls after 3:30."
- **Test your message.** Call your number and assess your message. Does it sound inviting? Sincere? Understandable? Are you pleased with your tone? If not, says one consultant, have someone else, perhaps a professional, record a message for you.

Becoming a Team Player in Professional Groups and Teams

As we discussed in Chapter 1, the workplace and economy are changing. One significant recent change is the emphasis on teamwork. You might find yourself a part of a work team, project team, customer support team, supplier team, design team, planning team, functional team, cross-functional team, or some other group. All of these teams are being formed to accomplish specific goals, and your career success will depend on your ability to function well in a team-driven professional environment.

Teams can be effective in solving problems and in developing new products. German auto manufacturer BMW likes to "throw together" designers, engineers, and marketing experts to work intensively on a team project. Ten team members, for example, working in an old bank building in London, collaborated on the redesign of the Rolls-Royce Phantom. The result was a best-selling super-luxury automobile that remained true to the Rolls heritage. The new model had twenty-first-century lines with BMW's technological muscle under the hood.[21] Perhaps you can now imagine why forming teams is important.

The Importance of Conventional and Virtual Teams in the Workplace

Businesses are constantly looking for ways to do jobs better at less cost. They are forming teams for the following reasons:

- **Better decisions.** Decisions are generally more accurate and effective because group and team members contribute different expertise and perspectives.

> Organizations are forming teams for better decisions, faster response, increased productivity, greater buy-in, less resistance to change, improved morale, and reduced risks.

- **Faster response.** When action is necessary to respond to competition or to solve a problem, small groups and teams can act rapidly.
- **Increased productivity.** Because they are often closer to the action and to the customer, team members can see opportunities for improving efficiency.
- **Greater buy-in.** Decisions arrived at jointly are usually better received because members are committed to the solution and are more willing to support it.
- **Less resistance to change.** People who have input into decisions are less hostile, less aggressive, and less resistant to change.
- **Improved employee morale.** Personal satisfaction and job morale increase when teams are successful.
- **Reduced risks.** Responsibility for a decision is diffused, thus carrying less risk for any individual.

To connect with distant team members across borders and time zones, many organizations are creating *virtual teams*. These are groups of people who work interdependently with a shared purpose across space, time, and organization boundaries using technology.[22]

> **Virtual teams are groups of people who work interdependently with a shared purpose across space, time, and organization boundaries using technology.**

Virtual teams may be local or global. Many workers today complete their tasks from remote locations, thus creating local virtual teams. Hyundai Motors exemplifies virtual teaming at the global level. For its vehicles, Hyundai completes engineering in Korea, research in Tokyo and Germany, styling in California, engine calibration and testing in Michigan, and heat testing in the California desert.[23] Members of its virtual teams coordinate their work and complete their tasks across time and geographic zones. Work is increasingly viewed as what you do rather than a place you go.

In some organizations, remote coworkers may be permanent employees of the same company or may be specialists called together for temporary projects. Regardless of the assignment, virtual teams can benefit from shared views and skills.

Positive and Negative Team Behaviour

Team members who are committed to achieving the group's purpose contribute by displaying positive behaviour. How can you be a professional team member? The most effective groups have members who are willing to establish rules and abide by those rules. Effective team members are able to analyze tasks and define problems so that they can work toward solutions. They offer information and try out their ideas on the group to stimulate discussion. They show interest in others' ideas by listening actively. Helpful team members also seek to involve silent members. They help to resolve differences, and they encourage a warm, supportive climate by praising and agreeing with others. When they sense that agreement is near, they review significant points and move the group toward its goal by synthesizing points of understanding.

> **Professional team members follow team rules, analyze tasks, define problems, share information, listen actively to others, and try to involve quiet members.**

Not all groups, however, have members who contribute positively. Negative behaviour is shown by those who constantly put down the ideas and suggestions of others. They insult, criticize, and aggress against others. They waste the group's time with unnecessary recounting of personal achievements or irrelevant topics. The team joker distracts the group with excessive joke telling, inappropriate comments, and disruptive antics. Also disturbing are team members who withdraw and refuse to be drawn out. They have nothing to say, either for or against ideas being considered. To be a productive and welcome member of a group, be prepared to perform the positive tasks described in Figure 10.4. Avoid the negative behaviours.

> **Negative team behaviour includes insulting, criticizing, aggressing against others, wasting time, and refusing to participate.**

Characteristics of Successful Professional Teams

The use of teams has been called the solution to many ills in the current workplace.[24] Someone even observed that as an acronym TEAM means "Together, Everyone Achieves More."[25] Yet, many teams do not work well together. In fact, some teams can actually increase frustration, lower productivity, and create employee

FIGURE 10.4 Positive and Negative Team Behaviours

Positive Team Behaviours	Negative Team Behaviours
Setting rules and abiding by them	Blocking the ideas and suggestions of others
Analyzing tasks and defining problems	Insulting and criticizing others
Contributing information and ideas	Wasting the group's time
Showing interest by listening actively	Making inappropriate jokes and comments
Encouraging members to participate	Failing to stay on task
Synthesizing points of agreement	Withdrawing, failing to participate

"Isn't this what teamwork is all about?
You doing all my work for me?"

Small, diverse teams often produce more creative solutions with broader applications than homogeneous teams do.

dissatisfaction. Experts who have studied team workings and decisions have discovered that effective teams share some or all of the following characteristics.

Small Size, Diverse Makeup. Teams may range from 2 to 25 members, although 4 or 5 is optimum for many projects. Larger groups have trouble interacting constructively, much less agreeing on actions.[26] For the most creative decisions, teams generally have male and female members who differ in age, ethnicity, social background, training, and experience. Members should bring complementary skills to a team. The key business advantage of diversity is the ability to view a project and its context from multiple perspectives. Many of us tend to think that everyone in the world is like us because we know only our own experience.[27] Teams with members from a variety of ethnicities and cultures can look at projects beyond the limited view of one culture. Many organizations are finding that diverse teams can produce innovative solutions with broader applications than homogeneous teams can.

Agreement on Purpose. An effective team begins with a purpose. Working from a general purpose to specific goals typically requires a huge investment of time and effort. Meaningful discussions, however, motivate team members to "buy in" to the project.

Agreement on Procedures. The best teams develop procedures to guide them. They set up intermediate goals with deadlines. They assign roles and tasks, requiring all members to contribute equivalent amounts of real work. They decide how they will reach decisions using one of the strategies discussed earlier. Procedures are continually evaluated to ensure movement toward the attainment of the team's goals.

Ability to Confront Conflict. Poorly functioning teams avoid conflict, preferring sulking, gossiping, or backstabbing. A better plan is to acknowledge conflict and address the root of the problem openly. Although it may feel emotionally risky, direct confrontation saves time and enhances team commitment in the long run. To be constructive, however, confrontation must be task oriented, not person oriented. An open airing of differences, in which all team members have a chance to speak their minds, should centre on the strengths and weaknesses of the different positions and ideas—not on personalities. After hearing all sides, team members must negotiate a fair settlement, no matter how long it takes. Good decisions are based on consensus: most members must agree.

Use of Good Communication Techniques. The best teams exchange information and contribute ideas freely in an informal environment. Team members speak clearly and concisely, avoiding generalities. They encourage feedback. Listeners become actively involved, read body language, and ask clarifying questions before responding. Tactful, constructive disagreement is encouraged. Although a team's task is taken seriously, successful teams are able to inject humour into their interactions.

Ability to Collaborate Rather Than Compete. Effective team members are genuinely interested in achieving team goals instead of receiving individual recognition. They contribute ideas and feedback unselfishly. They monitor team progress, including what is going right, what is going wrong, and what to do about it. They celebrate individual and team accomplishments.

Shared Leadership. Effective teams often have no formal leader. Instead, leadership rotates to those with the appropriate expertise as the team evolves and moves from one phase to another. Many teams operate under a democratic approach. This approach can achieve buy-in to team decisions, boost morale, and create fewer hurt feelings and less resentment. But in times of crisis, a strong team member may need to step up as leader.

Acceptance of Ethical Responsibilities. Teams as a whole have ethical responsibilities to their members, to their larger organizations, and to society. Members have a number of specific responsibilities to each other, as shown in Figure 10.5. As a whole, teams have a responsibility to represent the organization's view and respect its privileged information. They should not discuss with outsiders

---

FIGURE 10.5 Ethical Responsibilities of Group Members and Leaders

When people form a group or a team to achieve a purpose, they agree to give up some of their individual sovereignty for the good of the group. They become interdependent and assume responsibilities to one another and to the group. Here are important ethical responsibilities for members to follow:

- **Determine to do your best.** When you commit to the group process, you are obligated to offer your skills freely. Don't hold back, perhaps fearing that you will be repeatedly targeted because you have skills to offer. If the group project is worth doing, it is worth your best effort.
- **Decide to behave with the group's good in mind.** You may find it necessary to set aside your personal goals in favor of the group's goals. Decide to keep an open mind and to listen to evidence and arguments objectively. Strive to evaluate information carefully, even though it may contradict your own views or thwart your personal agendas.
- **Make a commitment to fair play.** Group problem solving is a cooperative, not a competitive, event. Decide that you cannot grind your private ax at the expense of the group project.
- **Expect to give and receive a fair hearing.** When you speak, others should give you a fair hearing. You have a right to expect them to listen carefully, provide you with candid feedback, strive to understand what you say, and treat your ideas seriously. Listeners do not have to agree with you, of course. However, all speakers have a right to a fair hearing.

- **Be willing to take on a participant/analyst role.** As a group member, it is your responsibility to pay attention, evaluate what is happening, analyze what you learn, and help make decisions.
- **As a leader, be ready to model appropriate team behaviour.** It is a leader's responsibility to coach team members in skills and teamwork, to acknowledge achievement and effort, to share knowledge, and to periodically remind members of the team's missions and goals.

© DMITRIY SHIRONOSOV/SHUTTERSTOCK

---

any sensitive issues without permission. In addition, teams have a broader obligation to avoid advocating actions that would endanger members of society at large.

The skills that make you a valuable and ethical team player will serve you well when you run or participate in professional meetings.

Planning and Participating in Productive Business and Professional Meetings

Because you can expect to attend many workplace meetings, learn to make them efficient, satisfying, and productive.

As businesses become more team oriented and management becomes more participatory, people are attending more meetings than ever. One survey of managers found that they were devoting as many as two days a week to various gatherings.[28] Yet meetings are almost universally disliked. Typical comments include "We have too many of them," "They don't accomplish anything," and "What a waste of time!" In spite of employee reluctance and despite terrific advances in communication and team technology, face-to-face meetings are not going to disappear. In discussing the future of meetings, Akio Morita, former chairman of Sony Corporation, said that he expects "face-to-face meetings will still be the number one form of communication in the twenty-first century."[29] So, get used to them. Meetings are here to stay. Our task, then, as business communicators, is to learn how to make them efficient, satisfying, and productive.

Meetings consist of three or more individuals who gather to pool information, solicit feedback, clarify policy, seek consensus, and solve problems. But meetings have another important purpose for you. They represent opportunities. Because they are a prime tool for developing staff, they are career-critical. According to one Canadian company's Web site, "It is . . . true that careers (rightly or wrongly) have been made or broken through performance at meetings."[30] At meetings judgments are formed and careers are made. Therefore, instead of treating them as thieves of your valuable time, try to see them as golden opportunities to demonstrate your leadership, communication, and problem-solving skills. So that you can make the most of these opportunities, here are techniques for planning and conducting successful meetings.

Deciding Whether a Meeting Is Necessary

Call meetings only when necessary, and invite only key people.

No meeting should be called unless the topic is important, can't wait, and requires an exchange of ideas. If the flow of information is strictly one way and no immediate feedback will result, then don't schedule a meeting. For example, if people are merely being advised or informed, send an e-mail, memo, or letter. Leave a telephone or voice mail message, but don't call a costly meeting. Remember, the real expense of a meeting is the lost productivity of all the people attending. To decide whether the purpose of the meeting is valid, it's a good idea to consult the key people who will be attending. Ask them what outcomes are desired and how to achieve those goals. This consultation also sets a collaborative tone and encourages full participation.

Selecting Participants

Problem-solving meetings should involve five or fewer people.

The number of meeting participants is determined by the purpose of the meeting. If the meeting purpose is motivational, such as an employee awards ceremony for Bombardier, then the number of participants is unlimited. But to make decisions, according to studies at 3M Corporation, the best number is five or fewer participants.[31] Ideally, those attending should be people who will make the decision and people with information necessary to make the decision. Also attending should be people who will be responsible for implementing the decision and representatives of groups who will benefit from the decision.

Distributing an Agenda

Before a meeting, pass out a meeting agenda showing topics to be discussed and other information.

At least one day in advance of a meeting, e-mail an agenda of topics to be discussed. Also include any reports or materials that participants should read in advance. For continuing groups, you might also include a copy of the minutes of the previous

FIGURE 10.6 Typical Meeting Agenda

AGENDA
Adventure Travel Canada
Staff Meeting
September 4, 2012
10 to 11 a.m.
Conference Room

I. Call to order; roll call
II. Approval of agenda
III. Approval of minutes from previous meeting

	Person	Proposed Time
IV. Committee reports		
A. Web site update	Kevin	5 minutes
B. Tour packages	Lisa	10 minutes
V. Old business		
A. Equipment maintenance	John	5 minutes
B. Client escrow accounts	Alicia	5 minutes
C. Internal newsletter	Adrienne	5 minutes
VI. New business		
A. New accounts	Sarah	5 minutes
B. Pricing policy for trips	Marcus	15 minutes
VII. Announcements		
VIII. Chair's summary, adjournment		

meeting. To keep meetings productive, limit the number of agenda items. Remember, the narrower the focus, the greater the chances for success. A good agenda, as illustrated in Figure 10.6, covers the following information:

- Date and place of meeting
- Start time and end time
- Brief description of each topic, in order of priority, including the names of individuals who are responsible for performing some action
- Proposed allotment of time for each topic
- Any pre-meeting preparation expected of participants

Getting the Meeting Started

To avoid wasting time and irritating attendees, always start meetings on time—even if some participants are missing. Waiting for latecomers causes resentment and sets a bad precedent. For the same reasons, don't give a quick recap to anyone who arrives late. At the appointed time, open the meeting with a three- to five-minute introduction that includes the following:

Start meetings on time and open with a brief introduction.

- Goal and length of the meeting
- Background of topics or problems
- Possible solutions and constraints
- Tentative agenda
- Ground rules to be followed

A typical set of ground rules might include arriving on time, communicating openly, being supportive, listening carefully, participating fully, confronting conflict frankly, and following the agenda. More formal groups follow parliamentary procedures based on Robert's Rules. For example, in a meeting run using Robert's Rules, there is a way to stop a person from talking too long. It's called "calling the question," which means ending the current discussion and voting on the previous question (or motion) right away. Before you can call the question, however, you have to be recognized by the chair of the meeting, move the "previous question," have your motion seconded, and receive a two-thirds majority vote in favour of calling the question. Most business meetings do not follow Robert's Rules, except perhaps at the highest levels (board meetings), because of the specialized knowledge required to run a meeting in this way.

In most typical business meetings, after establishing basic ground rules, the leader should ask whether participants agree thus far. Ideally, the next step is to assign one attendee to take minutes and one to act as a recorder. The recorder stands at a flipchart or whiteboard and lists the main ideas being discussed and agreements reached.

Moving the Meeting Along

Keep the meeting moving by avoiding issues that sidetrack the group.

After the preliminaries, the leader should say as little as possible. Like a talk show host, an effective leader makes "sure that each panel member gets some air time while no one member steals the show."[32] Remember that the purpose of a meeting is to exchange views, not to hear one person, even the leader, do all the talking. If the group has one member who monopolizes, the leader might say, "Thanks for that perspective, Kurt, but please hold your next point while we hear how Ann would respond to that." This technique also encourages quieter participants to speak up.

To avoid allowing digressions to sidetrack the group, try generating a "parking lot" list. This is a list of important but divergent issues that should be discussed at a later time. Another way to handle digressions is to say, "Folks, we are getting off track here. Forgive me for pressing on, but I need to bring us back to the central issue of...."[33] It's important to adhere to the agenda and the time schedule. Equally important, when the group seems to have reached a consensus, is to summarize the group's position and check to see whether everyone agrees.

Dealing with Conflict

When a conflict develops between two members, allow each to make a complete case before the group.

Conflict is natural and even desirable in workplaces, but it can cause awkwardness and uneasiness. In meetings, conflict typically develops when people feel unheard or misunderstood. If two people are in conflict, the best approach is to encourage each to make a complete case while group members give their full attention. Let each one question the other. Then, the leader should summarize what was said, and the group should offer comments. The group may modify a recommendation or suggest alternatives before reaching consensus on a direction to follow.

Handling Dysfunctional Group Members

To control dysfunctional behaviour, team leaders should establish rules and seat problem people strategically.

When individuals are performing in a dysfunctional role (such as blocking discussion, attacking other speakers, joking excessively, or withdrawing), they should be handled with care and tact. The following specific techniques can help a meeting leader control some group members and draw others out:

- **Lay down the rules in an opening statement.** Give a specific overall summary of topics, time allotment, and expected behaviour. Warn that speakers who digress will be interrupted.
- **Seat potentially dysfunctional members strategically.** Experts suggest seating a difficult group member immediately next to the leader. It's easier to bypass a person in this position. Make sure the person with dysfunctional behaviour is not seated in a power point, such as at the end of table or across from the leader.
- **Avoid direct eye contact.** Direct eye contact is a nonverbal signal that encourages talking. Thus, when asking a question of the group, look only at those whom you wish to answer.
- **Assign dysfunctional members specific tasks.** Ask a potentially disruptive person, for example, to be the group recorder.
- **Ask members to speak in a specific order.** Ordering comments creates an artificial, rigid climate and should be done only when absolutely necessary. But such a system ensures that everyone gets a chance to participate.

- **Interrupt monopolizers.** If a difficult member dominates a discussion, wait for a pause and then break in. Summarize briefly the previous comments or ask someone else for an opinion.
- **Encourage non-talkers.** Give only positive feedback to the comments of reticent members. Ask them direct questions about which you know they have information or opinions.
- **Give praise and encouragement** to those who seem to need it, including the distracters, the blockers, and the withdrawn.[34]

Ending with a Plan

End the meeting at the agreed time or earlier if possible. The leader should summarize what has been decided, who is going to do what, and by what time. It may be necessary to ask people to volunteer to take responsibility for completing action items agreed to in the meeting. No one should leave the meeting without a full understanding of what was accomplished. One effective technique that encourages full participation is "once around the table." Everyone is asked to summarize briefly his or her interpretation of what was decided and what happens next. Of course, this closure technique works best with smaller groups. The leader should conclude by asking the group to set a time for the next meeting. He or she should also assure the group that a report will follow, and thank participants for attending.

> **End the meeting with a summary of accomplishments and a review of action items; follow up by reminding participants of their assigned tasks.**

"That's all very nice, Jefferson, but do you have any other new business?"

Following Up Actively

If minutes were taken, they should be distributed within a couple of days after the meeting. An example of a formal minutes report is found in Figure 8.9 on page 218. Figure 10.7 shows an informal minutes report, which is the kind you'll see more often in the business world today. It is up to the leader to see that what was decided at the meeting is accomplished. The leader may need to call or e-mail people to remind them of their assignments and also to volunteer to help them if necessary.

FIGURE 10.7 Minutes of Meeting, Informal—E-Mail Attachment Format

Grand Beach Homeowners' Association

Board of Directors Meeting
April 12, 2012

MINUTES

Directors Present:	J. Weinstein, A. McGraw, J. Carlson, C. Stefanko, A. Pettus
Directors Absent:	B. Hookym

Summary of Topics Discussed

- Report from Architectural Review Committee. Copy attached.
- Landscaping of centre divider on P.T.H. 59. Three options considered: hiring private landscape designer, seeking volunteers from community, assigning association custodian to complete work.
- Collection of outstanding assessments. Discussion of delinquent accounts and possible actions.
- Use of beach club by film companies. Pros: considerable income. Cons: damage to furnishings, loss of facility to homeowners.
- Nomination of directors to replace those with two-year appointments.

Decisions Reached

- Hire private landscaper to renovate and plant centre divider on P.T.H. 59.
- Attach liens to homes of members with delinquent assessments.
- Submit to general membership vote the question of renting the beach club to film companies.

Action Items

Item	Responsibility	Due Date
1. Landscaping bid	J. Carlson	May 1
2. Lawyer for liens	B. Hookym	April 20
3. Creation of nominating committee	A. Pettus	May 1

Summarizes discussion

Capsulizes decisions rather than showing motions and voting

Highlights items for action

Summing Up and Looking Forward

In this chapter you studied how to use professionalism to your advantage in the workplace. Essentially, professionalism is a type of ethical behaviour, in which you consider the effects of your behaviour on other people before engaging in that behaviour. Also, the chapter discussed using your voice as a communication tool by focusing on pronunciation, tone, pitch, volume, rate, and emphasis. In workplace conversations, you should use correct names and titles, choose appropriate topics, avoid negative remarks, listen to learn, and be willing to offer sincere and specific praise. You studied how to give and take constructive criticism on the job. You also learned about five common response patterns as well as a six-step plan for resolving interpersonal workplace conflicts. The chapter also presented techniques for polishing your professional telephone and voice mail skills, including making and receiving productive telephone calls. You then read about the importance of teamwork and best practices for achieving results when working with other people. Finally, you learned how to plan and participate in productive business and professional meetings.

This chapter focused on developing speaking skills in face-to-face workplace communication. The next chapter covers an additional element of oral communication: giving presentations. Learning to speak before groups is important to your career success because you will probably be expected to do so occasionally. You'll learn helpful techniques and practise applying them so that you can control stage fright and make polished presentations.

Critical Thinking

1. How can we square the empathy needed for ethical professionalism with the individualistic, sometimes greedy, nature of private enterprise (e.g., profit, advancement, etc.)?

2. Is face-to-face communication always preferable to one-dimensional channels of communication such as e-mail and fax? Why or why not?

3. In what ways can conflict be a positive force in the workplace?

4. Commentators often predict that new communications media will destroy old ones. Do you think e-mail, PDAs, and instant messaging will kill off phone calls? Why or why not?

5. Why do so many people hate voice mail when it is an efficient system for recording messages?

6. What's the right course of action when you're the only person on a team doing any actual work?

7. How can business meetings help you advance your career?

Chapter Review

1. Define *soft skills* and list the qualities the term describes.
2. Describe some important aspects of professional behaviour.
3. Name five elements that you control in using your voice as a communication tool.
4. What topics should be avoided in workplace conversations?
5. List six techniques that you consider most important when delivering constructive criticism.
6. If you are criticized at work, what are eight ways in which you can respond professionally?
7. What are five common responses to workplace conflicts? Which response do you think is most constructive?
8. What is a three-point introduction for a telephone call?
9. Name five ways in which callers can practise courteous and responsible cell phone use.
10. When should a business meeting be held?
11. What is an agenda and what should it include?
12. List eight tactics that a meeting leader can use in dealing with dysfunctional participants.

10.1 Constructive Criticism

You work for a large company that is organized into work teams. Your work team, in the company's marketing department, meets weekly for a quick half-hour meeting to review the week's activities and projects. The meetings are run by the team leader, Mandy Miller. The team leader is a position of extra responsibility with a higher salary than that of other marketing staffers. For the past three months, Mandy has been regularly missing or showing up late for meetings. No one has said anything but you. You had a conversation with Mandy in the cafeteria three weeks ago in which you relayed your concerns to her in as positive a way as possible. Mandy has again started to miss meetings. You feel it's appropriate to send an e-mail to the director of the marketing department, letting him know what's been happening, that you've talked to Mandy, and that things haven't improved.

Your Task. Draft an e-mail to your director about the situation with Mandy.

10.2 Meeting Agenda

It's now two months after you've sent your e-mail to the director of marketing. In the meantime, Mandy Miller has been relieved of her extra responsibility as team leader. To your great surprise, your boss has asked you to be the new team leader. You are preparing for your first meeting and you decide to do something Mandy rarely did, which is to e-mail a meeting agenda to your colleagues. Besides discussing the changeover from Mandy to yourself at the meeting, activities to be discussed include the final proofreading of an important catalogue that is going to the printer on Friday and a conference call with your colleagues in the Toronto office on the rollout of 2015 Pan American Games merchandise. You are well liked by your colleagues, and you want to manage this meeting so that it doesn't look like you're "taking over" the department.

Your Task. Draft the agenda for the above meeting.

10.3 Meeting Minutes

Because the weekly marketing team meetings happen so frequently, you're not sure whether it's important to send out formal meeting minutes. Instead, you decide to send out a weekly "Meeting Recap" e-mail after each meeting. At this morning's meeting—your first as team leader—things went well. Mandy made a point of congratulating you on your new position (without sarcasm). You appointed Tom Mavrogianis to be in charge of the catalogue proofread (deadline Thursday afternoon) and Mandy Miller to be in charge of running Friday's conference with the Toronto office. Mandy mentioned she needed the specs on the 2015 Pan American Games caps and T-shirts before the meeting, and you promised to get them to her. Also, an unexpected item of business came up at the meeting when Tom reminded you that it was time to start planning the annual department retreat. Besides Tom, Mandy, and you, Bill Brockton was at the meeting, while Nahla Karim was absent.

Your Task. Draft the minutes report from this meeting.

Activities and Cases

10.1 Voice Rate

As discussed in this chapter, for business presentation purposes, you should be talking at roughly 125 words per minute. This is a different rate than the one you use when you're reading off a computer screen or talking to friends. A good way to practise achieving this ideal rate is to read aloud, as if you were telling a story.

Your Task. Choose one of the newspaper articles from this textbook (pp. 2, 31, 83, 199, 221, 274, and 341). Choose a partner or small group to work with. Stand up in front of your partner or group and read the article aloud as if you were presenting it to a group of people in a workplace setting. Have your partner or one member of your team time you for one minute. This person should say "Stop!" once the minute is over. Remember the last word you said, then go back and count how many words you managed to read in one minute. Is it higher or lower than 125? If it's lower, ask your partner or the people in your group if they thought you were reading too slowly. If it's higher than 125, you're probably reading too quickly; try reading one more time and consciously slow down the rate at which you're speaking. Once you're finished, it's the turn of your partner or someone else in the group to try. When everyone has had a try, let your instructor know. He or she may choose to have the students who come closest to 125 words per minute demonstrate their reading skills for the entire class.

10.2 Voice Quality

Recording your voice gives you a chance to learn how your voice sounds to others and provides an opportunity for you to improve its effectiveness. Don't be surprised if you fail to recognize your own voice.

Your Task. Record yourself reading a newspaper or magazine article.

a. If you think your voice sounds a bit high, practise speaking slightly lower.

b. If your voice is low or expressionless, practise speaking slightly louder and with more inflection.

c. Ask a colleague, teacher, or friend to provide feedback on your pronunciation, pitch, volume, rate, and professional tone.

10.3 Role Play: Delivering and Responding to Criticism

Develop your skills in handling criticism by joining with a partner to role-play critical messages you might deliver and receive on the job.

Your Task. Designate one person "A" and the other "B." Person A should make a list of the kinds of critical messages she or he is likely to receive on the job (e.g., *We need you to be on time regularly*) and identify who might deliver them (e.g., the shift manager). In Scenario 1, Person B should take the role of the critic and deliver the criticism in an unskilled manner. Person A should then respond using techniques described in this chapter. In Scenario 2, Person B again is the critic but delivers the criticism using techniques described in this chapter. Person A responds again. Then A and B reverse roles and repeat Scenarios 1 and 2.

10.4 Role Play: Discussing Workplace Criticism

CRITICAL THINKING

In the workplace, criticism is often delivered thoughtlessly.

Your Task. In teams of two or three, describe a time when you were criticized by an untrained superior or colleague. What made the criticism painful? What goal do you think the critic had in mind? How did you feel? How did you respond? Considering techniques discussed in this chapter, how could the critic have improved his or her delivery? How does the delivery technique affect the way a receiver responds to criticism? Script the situation you've just discussed and present it to the rest of the class in a before-and-after scenario.

10.5 Responding to Workplace Conflicts

TEAM

Experts say that we generally respond to conflict in one of the following patterns: avoidance/withdrawal, accommodation/smoothing, compromise, competition/forcing, or collaboration/problem solving.

Your Task. For each of the following conflict situations, name the appropriate response pattern(s) and be prepared to explain your choice.

a. A company policy manual is posted and updated at an internal Web page. Employees must sign that they have read and understand the manual. A conflict arises when one manager insists that employees should sign electronically. Another manager thinks that a paper form should be signed by employees so that better records may be kept. What conflict response pattern is most appropriate?

b. Jeff and Mark work together but frequently disagree. Today they disagree on what computer disks to purchase for an order that must be submitted immediately. Jeff insists on buying Brand X computer disks. Mark knows that Brand X is made by a company that markets an identical disk at a slightly lower price. However, Mark doesn't have stock numbers for the cheaper disks at his fingertips. How should Mark respond?

c. A manager and his assistant plan to attend a conference together at a resort location. Six weeks before the conference, the company announces a cutback and limits conference support to only one person. The assistant, who has developed a presentation specifically for the conference, feels that he should be the one to attend. Travel arrangements must be made immediately. What conflict response pattern will most likely result?

d. Two vice presidents disagree on a company instant messaging policy. One wants to ban personal messaging totally. The other thinks that an outright ban is impossible to implement. He is more concerned with limiting Internet misuse, including visits to online game, pornography, and shopping sites. The vice presidents agree that they need a policy, but they disagree on what to allow and what to prohibit. What conflict response pattern is appropriate?

e. Customer service rep Jackie comes to work one morning and finds Alexa sitting at Workstation 2. Although the customer service reps have no special workstation assigned to them, Jackie has the most seniority and has always assumed that Workstation 2 was hers. Other workstations were available, but the supervisor told Alexa to use Workstation 2 that morning because she didn't know that Jackie would be coming in. When Jackie arrives and sees "her" workstation occupied, she becomes angry and demands that Alexa vacate the station. What conflict response pattern might be most appropriate for Alexa and the supervisor?

10.6 Rules for Wireless Phone Use in Sales

As one of the managers of Wrigley Canada, a gum and confectionery company, you are alarmed at a newspaper article you just read. A stockbroker for BMO Nesbitt Burns was making cold calls on his personal phone while driving. His car hit and killed a motorcyclist. The brokerage firm was sued and accused of contributing to an accident by encouraging employees to use cellular telephones while driving. To avoid the risk of paying huge damages awarded by an emotional jury, the brokerage firm offered the victim's family a $500,000 settlement.

Your Task. Individually or in teams write an e-mail to Wrigley sales reps outlining company suggestions (or should they be rules?) for safe wireless phone use in cars. Check library databases for articles that discuss cell phone use in cars. Look for additional safety ideas. In your message to sales reps, try to suggest receiver benefits. How is safe cell phone use beneficial to the sales rep?

TEAM

10.7 Role Play: Improving Telephone Skills

Acting out the roles of telephone caller and receiver is an effective technique for improving skills. To give you such practice, your instructor will divide the class into pairs.

Your Task. Read each scenario and rehearse your role silently. Then improvise the role with your partner. After improvising a couple of times, script one of the situations and present it to the rest of the class.

Partner 1

a. You are the HR manager of Datatronics, Inc. Call Elizabeth Franklin, office manager at Computers Plus. Inquire about a job applicant, Chelsea Chavez, who listed Ms. Franklin as a reference.

b. Call Ms. Franklin again the following day to inquire about the same job applicant, Chelsea Chavez. Ms. Franklin answers today, but she talks on and on, describing the applicant in great detail. Tactfully close the conversation.

c. You are now the receptionist for Tom Wing, of Wing Imports. Answer a call for Mr. Wing, who is working in another office, at ext. 134, where he will accept calls.

d. You are now Tom Wing, owner of Wing Imports. Call your lawyer, Michael Murphy, about a legal problem. Leave a brief, incomplete message.

e. Call Mr. Murphy again. Leave a message that will prevent telephone tag.

Partner 2

a. You are the receptionist for Computers Plus. The caller asks for Elizabeth Franklin, who is home sick today. You don't know when she will be able to return. Answer the call appropriately.

b. You are now Ms. Franklin, office manager. Describe Chelsea Chavez, an imaginary employee. Think of someone with whom you've worked. Include many details, such as her ability to work with others, her appearance, her skills at computing, her schooling, her ambition, and so forth.

c. You are now an administrative assistant for lawyer Michael Murphy. Call Tom Wing to verify a meeting date Mr. Murphy has with Mr. Wing. Use your own name in identifying yourself.

d. You are now the receptionist for lawyer Michael Murphy. Mr. Murphy is skiing in Mont-Tremblant and will return in two days, but he doesn't want his clients to know where he is. Take a message.

e. Take a message again.

10.8 Role Play: Investigating Oral Communication in Your Field

Despite the popularity of communications technologies such as PDAs, e-mail, and instant messaging that require people to write, oral communication still plays an important role in the lives of most people working in business.

Your Task. Working in teams of three or four, interview three individuals in your professional field. How is oral communication important in this profession? What are some typical oral communication tasks in a given day, week, or month? As a percentage, how much time is spent communicating orally versus in writing? Besides person-to-person discussions, telephone conversations, and meetings, can this individual name other types of oral communication used at work? Does the need for oral skills change as one advances? What suggestions can this individual make to newcomers to the field for developing proficient oral communication skills? Once you've completed your interviews, script a ten-minute panel discussion between an interviewer and two or three experts on oral communication. Perform the skit in front of the class and discuss it afterward.

10.9 Analyzing a Meeting

You've learned a number of techniques in this chapter for planning and participating in meetings. Here's your chance to put your knowledge to work.

Your Task. Attend a structured meeting of a college, social, business, or other organization. Compare the manner in which the meeting is conducted with the suggestions presented in this chapter. Why did the meeting succeed or fail? Prepare a brief recommendation report for your instructor or be ready to discuss your findings in class.

10.10 Planning a Meeting

In many ways, a typical college or university class or lecture is like a meeting. A number of participants come together to share information and sometimes to solve problems. With the permission of your instructor, plan the next meeting of your class as a business meeting.

Your Task. Ask your instructor for his or her lesson plan for the next class. Based on the lesson plan, in a small team write an agenda for next week's meeting. Distribute this agenda to the rest of your classmates via e-mail at least one day before the meeting. So that your instructor is not the only person talking during the meeting, divide his or her lesson plan into chunks that can be "delivered" by other meeting participants. Assuming that not everyone in the class can have an active role at the meeting, but that everyone does need some sort of responsibility, what will be the responsibility of these "passive" participants? Will you need any visual aids for your meeting? If so, who will be in charge of them?

10.11 Running a Meeting

The best way to learn to run a meeting is to actually do it.

Your Task. Using the agenda your team wrote in Activity 10.13, run part of your next class as a meeting. Many decisions will have to be made. Who will chair the meeting? (It does not necessarily have to be your instructor—in fact it may be better if it's not.) What will the chair say to get the meeting started? What reports will be given at the meeting? How will you generate discussion at this meeting, considering that it's a mock meeting and the participants are your classmates, many of whom may be non-talkers? What will you do if the meeting gets off track? You may want to "plant" one of your team members as a disruptive meeting participant. Does the chair know how to deal with this disruptive person? Consider changing the normal seating arrangement of your class to more closely approximate that of a meeting. Who will take notes at this meeting? How will the meeting end and who will be in charge of following up?

10.12 Spoofing Meetings

One of the most popular ways to demonstrate to students who may not have participated in formal workplace meetings the problems that can often occur is to watch poorly run meetings on video.

Your Task. Search YouTube (**http://www.youtube.com**) for videos about poor meetings. You may also search Google using keywords like "spoof" "meetings" "bad business meetings." Screen five to ten of the videos you find. Make a list of the most commonly shown "bad" meeting behaviours. Why do you think the makers of the videos included these behaviours? Are there other more subtle bad behaviours that might be hard to represent on the screen but that can have a serious impact in meetings? Share your results in a presentation to your class or your instructor.

The following sentences contain errors in grammar, punctuation, capitalization, number style, usage, and spelling. Below each sentence write a corrected version.

1. The five top food service franchisors in the country are the following, mcdonald's, subway sandwiches & salads, burger king, 7-eleven, and tim hartons.

2. Fairlee Wells Corporation which is based in thunder bay ontario and it's german partner has developed a commercial-size cooker to make french fries that taste greasy but are not.

3. Although the time and temperature is set by the user the cooker adjusts itself automatically.

4. The President and Chief Executive of Fairlee Wells said, "this machine is programmed to learn.

5. We rented the 8205 sq. metre building in winnipegs exchange district to many small space tenants.

6. As a manager the most important task is planning.

7. Proper tools and modern equipment makes business's run smooth.

8. Looking back through history, no Prime Minister raises deeper philosophical issues than sir John A. Macdonald.

9. Last Fall, the Kejimkujik National Park based bicycle manufacturer TiCycle installed a network to link 5 PC's in it's factory and retail store.

10. Drove by a series of decisive actions Rogers Wireless membership grew by nearly two and a half million.

11. At the Delta residence inn in Edmonton alberta a 1 bedroom suite costs about one hundred and thirty dollars a night.

12. One of the most popular amenities offerred by top tier extended stay hotels are the free Buffet breakfast.

13. Just between you and I do you prefer a backpacking trip to the rockies or river rafting down the snake river.

14. We had less than fifteen items but others in the grocery store line were over the limit.

15. The President, Ceo, and 3 Managers will tour our facilitys in nova scotia and newfoundland.

Document for Revision

The following report showing meeting minutes has faults in grammar, punctuation, spelling, number form, wordiness, and word use. Use standard proofreading marks (see Appendix B) to correct the errors. When you finish, your instructor can show you the revised version of these minutes.

Canadian Federation of Small Business
Policy Board Committee
February 4, 2012

Present: Debra Chinnapongse, Tweet Jackson, Irene Kishita, Barry Knaggs, Kevin Poepoe, and Ralph Mason

Absent: Alex Watanabe

The meeting was call to order by Chair Kevin Poepo at 9:02 a.m. in the morning. Minutes from the January 6th meeting was read and approve.

Old Business

Debra Chinnapongse discussed the cost of the annual awards luncheon. That honours outstanding members. The ticket price ticket does not cover all the expenses incured. Major expenses include: awards and complementary lunches for the judges, VIP guests and volunteers. CFSB can not continue to make up the difference between income from tickets and costs for the luncheon. Ms. Chinnapongse reported that it had come to her attention that other associations relied on members contributions for their awards' programs.

MOTION: To send a Letter to board members asking for there contributions to support the annual awards luncheon. (Chinapongse/Kishita). PASSED 6-0.

Reports

Barry Knaggs reported that the media relations committee sponsored a get acquainted meeting in November. More than eighty people from various agencys attended.

The Outreach Committee reports that they have been asked to assist the Partnership for Small Business, an Ottawa-based organization in establishing a speakers bureau of Canadian small business owners. It would be available to speak at schools and colleges about small business and employment.

New Business

The chair announced a Planning Meeting to be held in March regarding revising the agri-business plan. In other New Business Ralph Mason reported that the staff had purchased fifty tickets for members, and our committees to attend the Zig Ziglar seminar in the month of March.

Next Meeting

The next meeting of the Policy Boare Committee will be held in early Aprl at the Lord Elgin hotel, Ottawa. At that time the meeting will conclude with a tour of the seaway Networks inc. offices in Kanata.

The meeting adjourned at 10:25 am by Keven Poepoe.

Respectfully submitted,

_____

Communication Workshop

How to Deal With Difficult People at Work

Difficult people in the workplace challenge your patience and your communication skills. In your work life and in your personal life, you may often encounter people who are negative, manipulative, uncooperative, or just plain difficult. Although everyone is irritable or indecisive at times, some people are so difficult that they require us to react with special coping skills. In his well-known book *Coping With Difficult People*, psychologist and management consultant Robert M. Bramson provides helpful advice in dealing with a number of personality types.

Bullies try to overwhelm with intimidation, arrogance, righteous indignation, and outright anger. To cope, try the following:

- Give them time to run down; maintain eye contact.
- Don't worry about being polite; state your opinions forcefully.
- Don't argue or be sarcastic; be ready to be friendly.

Snipers hide behind cover. They attack by teasing and making not-too-subtle digs. To cope, try the following:

- "Smoke" them out; refuse to be attacked indirectly. Ask questions such as "What did you mean by your remark?" and "It sounds as if you're ridiculing me. Are you?"
- Ask the group to confirm or deny the sniper's criticism. "Does anyone else see it that way?" Get other points of view.
- Acknowledge the underlying problem and try to find a feasible solution.

Exploders blow up in frustrated rage; they have an adult tantrum. To cope, try the following:

- Give them time to cool off and regain control on their own.
- If they don't stop, break into the tirade by saying, "Stop!"
- Show that you take them seriously.
- Find a way to take a breather and get some privacy with them.

Complainers find fault with everything. Some complaints are made directly; others are made indirectly to third parties. To cope, try the following:

- Listen attentively, even if you feel guilty or impatient.
- Acknowledge what they are saying and paraphrase to see whether you understand.
- Don't agree or apologize, even if you feel you should.
- Avoid the accusation-defence-reaccusation pattern.
- Try to solve the problem by (a) asking specific informational questions, (b) assigning fact-finding tasks, or (c) asking for the complaint in writing.
- If all else fails, ask the complainer, "How do you want this discussion to end?"

Indecisive stallers are unable to make decisions. Their stalling makes them difficult to work with. To cope, try the following:

- Encourage stallers to tell you about conflicts or reservations that prevent the decision. Listen for clues.
- Help stallers solve their problems by (a) acknowledging past problems non-defensively, (b) examining the facts, and (c) proposing alternative solutions in priority order.
- Give support after a decision has been made.

Career Application

In most workplaces you can expect to meet one or more truly difficult people. To provide practice in dealing with such people, develop a coping plan.

Your Task

In an e-mail memo to yourself, write responses to the following:

1. Describe in detail the behaviour of a person whom you find to be difficult.

2. Analyze and describe your understanding of that behaviour.

3. Review your past interactions with this person. Did you get along better with this person before?

4. Decide what coping behaviour would be appropriate.

5. Acknowledge what you might need to change in yourself to best carry out the most promising coping behaviour.

6. Prepare an action plan explaining what you will do and by what date.

11

Business Presentations

Giving presentations is a skill that can be learned. While it's not rocket science, it also isn't the same as an informal conversation with friends. Identify your audience and the key messages you want them to remember. Put yourself in their chairs. Tell real-life stories to make the presentation come alive and illustrate your points. Make eye contact with the audience, not with your notes or slides. Prepare and rehearse. Prepare and rehearse again. Be yourself and remember that everyone is nervous about standing up and speaking in public.[1]

Lee Jacobson,
Brand Producer and Communications Consultant, Lee Jacobson Consultants

LEARNING OBJECTIVES

1. Discuss two important first steps in preparing effective oral presentations.

2. Explain the major elements in organizing the content of a presentation, including the introduction, body, and conclusion.

3. Identify techniques for gaining audience rapport, including using effective imagery, providing verbal signposts, and sending appropriate nonverbal messages.

4. Discuss types of visual aids, including multimedia slides, handouts, overhead transparencies, and speaker's notes.

5. Explain how to design an impressive multimedia presentation, including adapting text and colour schemes; organizing, composing, and editing your slide show; rehearsing your talk; and keeping audiences engaged.

6. Specify delivery techniques for use before, during, and after a presentation.

Organizations today are interested in hiring people with good presentation skills. Why? The business world is changing. As you have seen, technical skills aren't enough to guarantee success. You also need to be able to communicate ideas effectively in presentations to customers, vendors, members of your team, and management. Your presentations will probably be made to inform, influence, or motivate action.

Speaking skills are useful at every career stage. A recent study found that the number one predictor of success and upward mobility is how much you enjoy public speaking and how effective you are at it.[2] You might, for example, have to make a sales pitch before customers or speak to a professional gathering. You might need to describe your company's expansion plans to your banker, or you might need to persuade management to support your proposed marketing strategy. Speaking skills rank very high on recruiters' wish lists. As reported in an employer study, 70 percent of executives considered oral communication skills very important for high-school graduates entering the job market; 82 percent for two-year college graduates, and a whopping 95 percent for four-year college graduates.[3]

This chapter prepares you to use speaking skills in making effective and professional oral presentations. You will learn what to do before, during, and after your presentation; and how to design effective visual aids and multimedia presentations.

Getting Ready for an Oral Presentation

In getting ready for an oral presentation, you may feel a great deal of anxiety. For many people fear of speaking before a group is almost as great as the fear of pain. We get butterflies in our stomachs just thinking about it. When you feel those butterflies, though, speech coach Dianne Booher advises getting them in formation and visualizing the swarm as a powerful push propelling you to a peak performance.[4] For any presentation, you can reduce your fears and lay the foundation for a professional performance by focusing on five areas: preparation, organization, audience rapport, visual aids, and delivery.

Know Your Purpose

The most important part of your preparation is deciding your purpose. Do you want to sell a group insurance policy to a prospective client? Do you want to persuade management to increase the marketing budget? Do you want to inform customer service reps of three important ways to prevent miscommunication? Whether your goal is to persuade or to inform, you must have a clear idea of where you are going. At the end of your presentation, what do you want your listeners to remember or do?

Eric Evans, a loan officer at TD Canada Trust, faced such questions as he planned a talk for a class in small business management. (You can see the outline for his talk in Figure 11.3, p. 312.) Eric's former business professor had asked him to return to campus and give the class advice about borrowing money from banks in order to start new businesses. Because Eric knew so much about this topic, he found it difficult to extract a specific purpose statement for his presentation. After much thought he narrowed his purpose to this: *To inform potential entrepreneurs about three important factors that loan officers consider before granting start-up loans to launch small businesses.* His entire presentation focused on ensuring that the class members understood and remembered three principal ideas.

Understand Your Audience

A second key element in preparation is analyzing your audience, anticipating its reactions, and making appropriate adaptations. Understanding four basic audience types, summarized in Figure 11.1, helps you decide how to organize your presentation. A friendly audience, for example, will respond to humour and personal experiences. A neutral audience requires an even, controlled delivery style. The talk would probably be filled with facts, statistics, and expert opinions. An uninterested audience that is forced to attend requires a brief presentation. Such an audience might respond best to humour, cartoons, colourful visuals, and startling statistics. A hostile audience demands a calm, controlled delivery style with objective data and expert opinions.

Other elements, such as age, education, experience, and size of audience will affect your style and message content. Analyze the following questions to help you determine your organizational pattern, delivery style, and supporting material.

- How will this topic appeal to this audience?
- How can I relate this information to their needs?
- How can I earn respect so that they accept my message?
- What would be most effective in making my point? Facts? Statistics? Personal experiences? Expert opinion? Humour? Cartoons? Graphic illustrations? Demonstrations? Case histories? Analogies?
- What measures must I take to ensure that this audience remembers my main points?

Preparing for an oral presentation means identifying your purpose and knowing the audience.

Audience analysis issues include size, age, gender, experience, attitude, and expectations.

FIGURE 11.1 Succeeding With Four Audience Types

Audience Members	Organizational Pattern	Delivery Style	Supporting Material
Friendly			
They like you and your topic.	Use any pattern. Try something new. Involve the audience.	Be warm, pleasant, and open. Use lots of eye contact and smiles.	Include humour, personal examples, and experiences.
Neutral			
They are calm, rational; their minds are made up, but they think they are objective.	Present both sides of the issue. Use pro/con or problem/solution patterns. Save time for audience questions.	Be controlled. Do nothing showy. Use confident, small gestures.	Use facts, statistics, expert opinion, and comparison and contrast. Avoid humour, personal stories, and flashy visuals.
Uninterested			
They have short attention spans; they may be there against their will.	Be brief—no more than three points. Avoid topical and pro/con patterns that seem lengthy to the audience.	Be dynamic and entertaining. Move around. Use large gestures.	Use humour, cartoons, colourful visuals, powerful quotations, and startling statistics.
	Avoid darkening the room, standing motionless, passing out handouts, using boring visuals, or expecting the audience to participate.		
Hostile			
They want to take charge or to ridicule the speaker; they may be defensive, emotional.	Organize using a noncontroversial pattern, such as a topical, chronological, or geographical strategy.	Be calm and controlled. Speak evenly and slowly.	Include objective data and expert opinion. Avoid anecdotes and humour.
	Avoid a question-and-answer period, if possible; otherwise, use a moderator or accept only written questions.		

Organizing Content for a Powerful Impact

Good organization and intentional repetition help your audience understand and retain what you say.

Once you have determined your purpose and analyzed the audience, you're ready to collect information and organize it logically. Good organization and conscious repetition are the two most powerful keys to audience comprehension and retention. In fact, many speech experts recommend the following admittedly repetitious, but effective, plan:

Step 1: Tell them what you're going to say.
Step 2: Say it.
Step 3: Tell them what you've just said.

In other words, repeat your main points in the introduction, body, and conclusion of your presentation. Although it sounds boring, this strategy works surprisingly well. Let's examine how to construct the three parts of an effective presentation.

Capture Attention in the Introduction

Attention-grabbing openers include questions, startling facts, jokes, anecdotes, and quotations.

How many times have you heard a speaker begin with *It's a pleasure to be here.* Or *I'm honoured to be asked to speak.* Boring openings such as these get speakers off to a dull start. Avoid such banalities by striving to accomplish three goals in the introduction to your presentation:

- Capture listeners' attention and get them involved.
- Identify yourself and establish your credibility.
- Preview your main points.

If you're able to appeal to listeners and involve them in your presentation right from the start, you're more likely to hold their attention until the finish.

FIGURE 11.2 Nine Winning Techniques for Gaining and Keeping Audience Attention

Experienced speakers know how to capture the attention of an audience and how to maintain that attention during a presentation. You can give your presentations a boost by trying these nine proven techniques.

- **A promise.** Begin with a promise that keeps the audience expectant. For example, *By the end of this presentation I will have shown you how you can increase your sales by 50 percent!*

- **Drama.** Open by telling an emotionally moving story or by describing a serious problem that involves the audience. Throughout your talk include other dramatic elements, such as a long pause after a key statement. Change your vocal tone or pitch. Professionals use high-intensity emotions such as anger, joy, sadness, and excitement.

- **Eye contact.** As you begin, command attention by surveying the entire audience to take in all listeners. Take two to five seconds to make eye contact with as many people as possible.

- **Movement.** Leave the lectern area whenever possible. Walk around the conference table or down the aisles of your audience. Try to move toward your audience, especially at the beginning and end of your talk.

- **Questions.** Keep listeners active and involved with rhetorical questions. Ask for a show of hands to get each listener thinking. The response will also give you a quick gauge of audience attention.

- **Demonstrations.** Include a member of the audience in a demonstration. For example, *I'm going to show you exactly how to implement our four-step customer courtesy process, but I need a volunteer from the audience to help me.*

- **Samples/gimmicks.** If you're promoting a product, consider using items to toss out to the audience or to award as prizes to volunteer participants. You can also pass around product samples or promotional literature. Be careful, though, to maintain control.

- **Visuals.** Give your audience something to look at besides yourself. Use a variety of visual aids in a single session. Also consider writing the concerns expressed by your audience on a flipchart or on the board as you go along.

- **Self-interest.** Review your entire presentation to ensure that it meets the critical *What's-in-it-for-me* audience test. Remember that people are most interested in things that benefit them.

Consider some of the same techniques that you used to open sales letters: a question, a startling fact, a joke, a story, or a quotation. Some speakers achieve involvement by opening with a question or command that requires audience members to raise their hands or stand up. You'll find additional techniques for gaining and keeping audience attention in Figure 11.2.

To establish your credibility, you need to describe your position, knowledge, or experience—whatever qualifies you to speak. Try also to connect with your audience. Listeners are particularly drawn to and identify with speakers who reveal something of themselves. A consultant addressing office workers might reminisce about how he started as a temporary worker; a CEO might tell a funny story in which the joke is on herself.

After capturing attention and establishing yourself, you'll want to preview the main points of your topic, perhaps with a visual aid. You may wish to put off actually writing your introduction until after you have organized the rest of the presentation and crystallized your principal ideas.

Take a look at Eric Evans's introduction, shown in Figure 11.3 (p. 312), to see how he integrated all the elements necessary for a good opening.

"Please don't make me use another water balloon to keep your attention."

Organize the Body

The biggest problem with most oral presentations is a failure to focus on a few principal ideas. Thus, the body of your short presentation (20 or fewer minutes) should include a limited number of main points, say, two to four. Develop each main point with adequate, but not excessive, explanation and details. Too many details can

The best oral presentations focus on a few key ideas.

FIGURE 11.3 Oral Presentation Outline

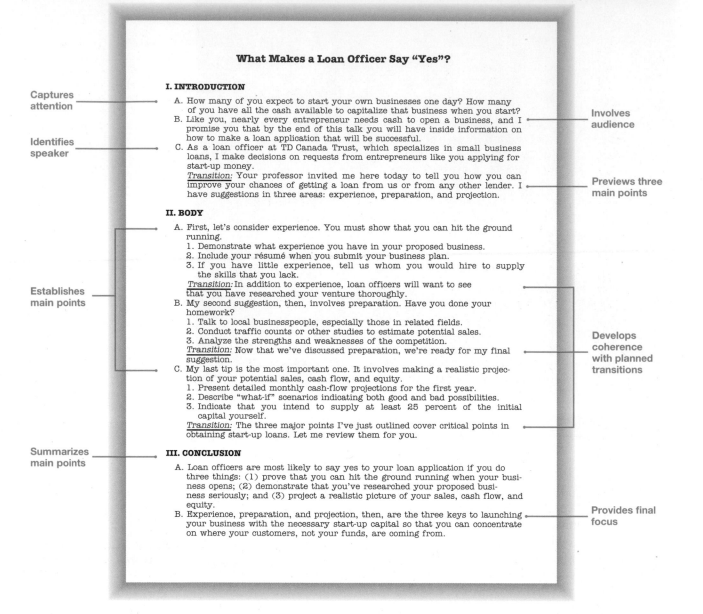

What Makes a Loan Officer Say "Yes"?

Captures attention

Identifies speaker

Establishes main points

Summarizes main points

Involves audience

Previews three main points

Develops coherence with planned transitions

Provides final focus

I. INTRODUCTION

A. How many of you expect to start your own businesses one day? How many of you have all the cash available to capitalize that business when you start?
B. Like you, nearly every entrepreneur needs cash to open a business, and I promise you that by the end of this talk you will have inside information on how to make a loan application that will be successful.
C. As a loan officer at TD Canada Trust, which specializes in small business loans, I make decisions on requests from entrepreneurs like you applying for start-up money.
Transition: Your professor invited me here today to tell you how you can improve your chances of getting a loan from us or from any other lender. I have suggestions in three areas: experience, preparation, and projection.

II. BODY

A. First, let's consider experience. You must show that you can hit the ground running.
  1. Demonstrate what experience you have in your proposed business.
  2. Include your résumé when you submit your business plan.
  3. If you have little experience, tell us whom you would hire to supply the skills that you lack.
  Transition: In addition to experience, loan officers will want to see that you have researched your venture thoroughly.
B. My second suggestion, then, involves preparation. Have you done your homework?
  1. Talk to local businesspeople, especially those in related fields.
  2. Conduct traffic counts or other studies to estimate potential sales.
  3. Analyze the strengths and weaknesses of the competition.
  Transition: Now that we've discussed preparation, we're ready for my final suggestion.
C. My last tip is the most important one. It involves making a realistic projection of your potential sales, cash flow, and equity.
  1. Present detailed monthly cash-flow projections for the first year.
  2. Describe "what-if" scenarios indicating both good and bad possibilities.
  3. Indicate that you intend to supply at least 25 percent of the initial capital yourself.
  Transition: The three major points I've just outlined cover critical points in obtaining start-up loans. Let me review them for you.

III. CONCLUSION

A. Loan officers are most likely to say yes to your loan application if you do three things: (1) prove that you can hit the ground running when your business opens; (2) demonstrate that you've researched your proposed business seriously; and (3) project a realistic picture of your sales, cash flow, and equity.
B. Experience, preparation, and projection, then, are the three keys to launching your business with the necessary start-up capital so that you can concentrate on where your customers, not your funds, are coming from.

obscure the main message, so keep your presentation simple and logical. Remember, listeners have no pages to leaf back through should they become confused.

When Eric Evans began planning his presentation, he realized immediately that he could talk for hours on his topic. He also knew that listeners are not good at separating major and minor points. Thus, instead of submerging his listeners in a sea of information, he sorted out a few principal ideas. In the mortgage business, loan officers generally ask the following three questions of each applicant for a small business loan: (1) Are you ready to "hit the ground running" in starting your business? (2) Have you done your homework? and (3) Have you made realistic projections of potential sales, cash flow, and equity investment? These questions would become his main points, but Eric wanted to streamline them further so that his audience would be sure to remember them. He capsulized the questions in three words: *experience, preparation,* and *projection.* As you can see in Figure 11.3, Eric prepared a sentence outline showing these three main ideas. Each is supported by examples and explanations.

How to organize and sequence main ideas may not be immediately obvious when you begin working on a presentation. In Chapter 9 you studied a number of patterns for organizing written reports. Those patterns, and a few new ones, are equally appropriate for oral presentations:

- **Chronology.** Example: A presentation describing the history of a problem, organized from the first sign of trouble to the present.
- **Geography/space.** Example: A presentation about the changing diversity of the workforce, organized by regions in the country (East Coast, West Coast, and so forth).
- **Topic/function/conventional grouping.** Example: A report discussing mishandled airline baggage, organized by names of airlines.
- **Comparison/contrast (pro/con).** Example: A report comparing organic farming methods with those of modern industrial farming.
- **Journalism pattern.** Example: A report describing how identity thieves can ruin your good name. Organized by *who*, *what*, *when*, *where*, *why*, and *how*.
- **Value/size.** Example: A report describing fluctuations in housing costs, organized by prices of homes.
- **Importance.** Example: A report describing five reasons that a company should move its headquarters to a specific city, organized from the most important reason to the least important.
- **Problem/solution.** Example: A company faces a problem such as declining sales. A solution such as reducing the staff is offered.
- **Simple/complex.** Example: A report explaining genetic modification of plants, organized from simple seed production to complex gene introduction.
- **Best case/worst case.** Example: A report analyzing whether two companies should merge, organized by the best-case result (improved market share, profitability, good employee morale) opposed to the worst-case result (devalued stock, lost market share, poor employee morale).

In the presentation shown in Figure 11.3, Eric arranged the main points by importance, placing the most important point last, where it had maximum effect. When organizing any presentation, prepare a little more material than you think you will actually need. Savvy speakers always have something useful in reserve (such as an extra handout, transparency, or idea)—just in case they finish early.

Organize your report by time, geography, function, importance, or some other method that is logical to the receiver.

Summarize in the Conclusion

Nervous speakers often rush to wrap up their presentations because they can't wait to flee the stage. But listeners will remember the conclusion more than any part of a speech. That's why you should spend some time to make it most effective. Strive to achieve two goals:

Effective conclusions summarize main points and allow the speaker to exit gracefully.

- Summarize the main themes of the presentation, for example "Today, we've attempted to show you/explain for you ..."
- Include a statement that allows you to leave the podium gracefully, such as "Thanks, ladies and gentlemen, for your time and attention. If you have any other questions ..."

Some speakers end limply with comments such as "I guess that's about all I have to say." This leaves bewildered audience members wondering whether they should continue listening. Skilled speakers alert the audience that they are finishing. They use phrases such as *In conclusion*, *As I end this presentation*, or *It's time for me to stop*. Then they proceed immediately to the conclusion. Audiences become justly irritated with a speaker who announces the conclusion but then digresses with one more story or talks on for ten more minutes.

A straightforward summary should review major points and focus on what you want the listeners to do, think, or remember. You might say, *In bringing my presentation to a close, I will restate my major purpose ...*; or *In summary, my major purpose has been to ...*; or *In support of my purpose, I have presented three major points. They are (a) …, (b) …, and (c) ….* Notice how Eric Evans, in the conclusion shown in Figure 11.3, summarized his three main points and provided a final focus to listeners.

If you are promoting a recommendation, you might end as follows: *In conclusion, I recommend that we retain Matrixx Marketing to conduct a telemarketing campaign beginning September 1 at a cost of X dollars. To complete this recommendation, I suggest that we (a) finance this campaign from our operations budget, (b) develop a persuasive message describing our new product, and (c) name Lisa Beck to oversee the project.*

In your conclusion you might want to use an anecdote, an inspiring quotation, or a statement that ties in the attention-capturing opener and offers a new insight. Whatever you choose, be sure to include a closing thought that indicates you are finished. For example, *This concludes my presentation. After investigating many marketing firms, we are convinced that Matrixx is the best for our purposes. Your authorization of my recommendations will mark the beginning of a very successful campaign for our new product. Thank you.*

Building Audience Rapport Like a Pro

Good speakers are adept at building audience rapport. They form a bond with the audience; they entertain as well as inform. How do they do it? Based on observations of successful and unsuccessful speakers, we learn that the good ones use a number of verbal and nonverbal techniques to connect with the audience. Some of their helpful techniques include providing effective imagery, supplying verbal signposts, and using body language strategically.

Effective Imagery

You'll lose your audience quickly if your talk is filled with abstractions, generalities, and dry facts. To enliven your presentation and enhance comprehension, try using some of these techniques:

> Use analogies, metaphors, similes, personal anecdotes, personalized statistics, and worst- and best-case scenarios instead of dry facts.

- **Analogies.** A comparison of similar traits between dissimilar things can be effective in explaining and drawing connections. For example, *Product development is similar to the process of conceiving, carrying, and delivering a baby.* Or, *Downsizing and restructuring are similar to an overweight person undergoing a regimen of dieting, habit changing, and exercise.*
- **Metaphors.** A comparison between otherwise dissimilar things without using the words *like* or *as* results in a metaphor. For example, *Our competitor's CEO is a snake when it comes to negotiating* or *My desk is a garbage dump.*
- **Similes.** A comparison that includes the words like or as is a simile. For example, *Building a business team is like building a sports team—you want people not only with the right abilities, but also with the willingness to work together.* Or, *She's as happy as someone who just won the lottery.*
- **Personal anecdotes.** Nothing connects you faster or better with your audience than a good personal story. In a talk about e-mail techniques, you could reveal your own blunders that became painful learning experiences. In a talk to potential investors, the founder of a new ethnic magazine might tell a story about growing up without enough positive ethnic role models.
- **Personalized statistics.** Although often misused, statistics stay with people—particularly when they relate directly to the audience. A speaker discussing job searching might say, *Look around the room. Only three out of five graduates will find a job immediately after graduation.* If possible, simplify and personalize facts. For example, *The sales of Creemore Springs Brewery totalled 5 million cases last year. That's a full case of Creemore for every man, woman, and child in the Greater Toronto area.*

- **Worst- and best-case scenarios.** Hearing the worst that could happen can be effective in driving home a point. For example, *If we do nothing about our computer backup system now, it's just a matter of time before the entire system crashes and we lose all of our customer contact information. Can you imagine starting from scratch in building all of your customer files again? However, if we fix the system now, we can expand our customer files and actually increase sales at the same time.*
- **Examples.** If all else fails, remember that an audience likes to hear specifics. If you're giving a presentation on office etiquette, for example, instead of just saying, *Rudeness in the workplace is a growing problem,* it's always better to say something like *Rudeness in the workplace is a growing problem. For example, we've heard from some of our clients that our customer service representatives could improve their tone of voice.*

Verbal Signposts

Speakers must remember that listeners, unlike readers of a report, cannot control the rate of presentation or flip back through pages to review main points. As a result, listeners get lost easily. Knowledgeable speakers help the audience recognize the organization and main points in an oral message with verbal signposts. They keep listeners on track by including helpful previews, summaries, and transitions, such as these:

- **Previewing**
  The next segment of my talk presents three reasons for ...
  Let's now consider the causes of ...
- **Switching directions**
  Thus far we've talked solely about ...; now let's move to ...
  I've argued that ... and ..., but an alternate view holds that ...
- **Summarizing**
  Let me review with you the major problems I've just discussed.
  You see, then, that the most significant factors are ...

You can further improve any oral presentation by including appropriate transitional expressions such as *first, second, next, then, therefore, moreover, on the other hand, on the contrary,* and *in conclusion.* These expressions lend emphasis and tell listeners where you are headed. Notice in Eric Evans's outline, in Figure 11.3, that the specific transitional elements are designed to help listeners recognize each new principal point.

Nonverbal Messages

Although what you say is most important, the nonverbal messages you send can also have a potent effect on how well your message is received. How you look, how you move, and how you speak can make or break your presentation. The following suggestions focus on nonverbal tips to ensure that your verbal message is well received.

- **Look terrific.** Like it or not, you will be judged by your appearance. For everything but small, in-house presentations, be sure you dress professionally. The rule of thumb is that you should dress at least as well as the best-dressed person in the company.
- **Animate your body.** Be enthusiastic and let your body show it. Emphasize ideas to enhance points about size, number, and direction. Use a variety of gestures, but try not to consciously plan them in advance.
- **Punctuate your words.** You can keep your audience interested by varying your tone, volume, pitch, and pace. Use pauses before and after important points. Allow the audience to take in your ideas.
- **Get out from behind the podium.** Avoid being planted behind the podium. Movement makes you look natural and comfortable. You might pick a few

places in the room to walk to. Even if you must stay close to your visual aids, make a point of leaving them occasionally so that the audience can see your whole body.

- **Vary your facial expression.** Begin with a smile, but change your expressions to correspond with the thoughts you are voicing. You can shake your head to show disagreement, roll your eyes to show disdain, look heavenward for guidance, or wrinkle your brow to show concern or dismay. To see how speakers convey meaning without words, mute the sound on your TV and watch the facial expressions of any well-known talk show host.

Planning Visual Aids

Before you give a business presentation, consider this wise Chinese proverb: "Tell me, I forget. Show me, I remember. Involve me, I understand." Your goals as a speaker are to make listeners understand, remember, and act on your ideas. To get them interested and involved, include effective visual aids. Some experts say that we acquire 85 percent of all our knowledge visually. Therefore, an oral presentation that incorporates visual aids is far more likely to be understood and retained than one lacking visual enhancement.

Good visual aids have many purposes. They emphasize and clarify main points, thus improving comprehension and retention. They increase audience interest, and they make the presenter appear more professional, better prepared, and more persuasive. Furthermore, research shows that the use of visual aids actually shortens meetings.[5] Visual aids are particularly helpful for inexperienced speakers because the audience concentrates on the aid rather than on the speaker. Good visuals also serve to jog the memory of a speaker, thus improving self-confidence, poise, and delivery.

Types of Visual Aids

Fortunately for today's speakers, many forms of visual media are available to enhance a presentation. Figure 11.4 (p. 317) describes a number of visual aids and compares their degree of formality and other considerations. Four of the most popular visuals are multimedia slides, overhead projectors, handouts, and blackboard/whiteboard.

Multimedia Slides. With today's excellent software programs—such as Microsoft PowerPoint, Prezi, Apple Keynote, Lotus Freelance Graphics, Corel Presentations, and Adobe Presenter—you can create dynamic, colourful presentations with your PC or Mac. The output from these programs is shown on a computer monitor, a TV monitor, an LCD (liquid crystal display) panel, or a screen. With a little expertise and advanced equipment, you can create a multimedia presentation that includes stereo sound, videos, and hyperlinks, as described in the discussion of multimedia presentations below. Multimedia slides can also be uploaded to a Web site or broadcast live over the Internet.

Overhead Projectors. Student and professional speakers alike rely on the overhead projector and document camera for many reasons. Most meeting areas are equipped with projectors and screens. Moreover, acetate transparencies for the overhead are cheap, easily prepared on a computer or copier, and simple to use. Similarly, projecting a page from a book or a newspaper article with a document camera is effective. And, because rooms need not be darkened, a speaker using transparencies or a document camera can maintain eye contact with the audience. A word of caution, though: stand to the side of the projector so that you don't obstruct the audience's view.

FIGURE 11.4 Presentation Enhancers

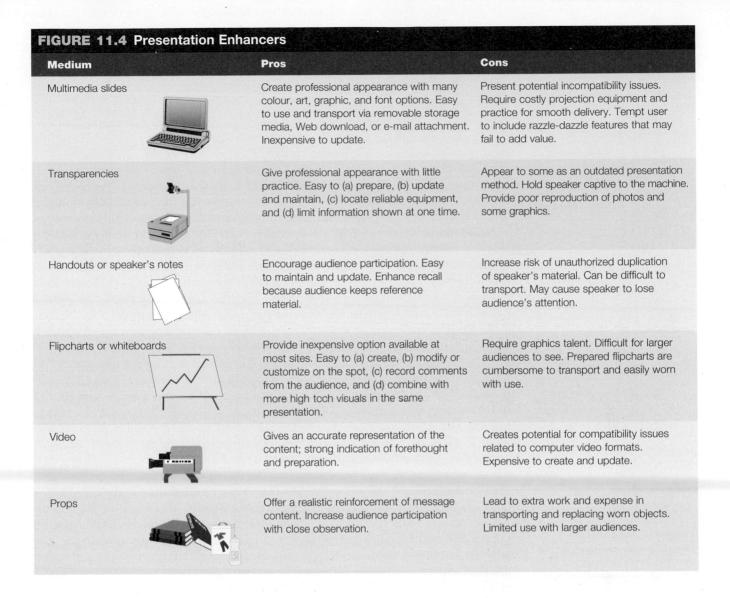

Medium	Pros	Cons
Multimedia slides	Create professional appearance with many colour, art, graphic, and font options. Easy to use and transport via removable storage media, Web download, or e-mail attachment. Inexpensive to update.	Present potential incompatibility issues. Require costly projection equipment and practice for smooth delivery. Tempt user to include razzle-dazzle features that may fail to add value.
Transparencies	Give professional appearance with little practice. Easy to (a) prepare, (b) update and maintain, (c) locate reliable equipment, and (d) limit information shown at one time.	Appear to some as an outdated presentation method. Hold speaker captive to the machine. Provide poor reproduction of photos and some graphics.
Handouts or speaker's notes	Encourage audience participation. Easy to maintain and update. Enhance recall because audience keeps reference material.	Increase risk of unauthorized duplication of speaker's material. Can be difficult to transport. May cause speaker to lose audience's attention.
Flipcharts or whiteboards	Provide inexpensive option available at most sites. Easy to (a) create, (b) modify or customize on the spot, (c) record comments from the audience, and (d) combine with more high tech visuals in the same presentation.	Require graphics talent. Difficult for larger audiences to see. Prepared flipcharts are cumbersome to transport and easily worn with use.
Video	Gives an accurate representation of the content; strong indication of forethought and preparation.	Creates potential for compatibility issues related to computer video formats. Expensive to create and update.
Props	Offer a realistic reinforcement of message content. Increase audience participation with close observation.	Lead to extra work and expense in transporting and replacing worn objects. Limited use with larger audiences.

Handouts. You can enhance and complement your presentations by distributing pictures, outlines, brochures, articles, charts, summaries, or other supplements. Speakers who use computer presentation programs often prepare a set of their slides along with notes to hand out to viewers, with mixed results. Often, the audience doesn't pay attention to the speaker but noisily flips through the printed-out pages of the computer presentation. Timing the distribution of any handout, though, is tricky. If given out during a presentation, your handouts tend to distract the audience, causing you to lose control. Thus, it's probably best to discuss most handouts during the presentation but delay distributing them until after you finish.

Blackboard/Whiteboard. Even though it may seem old-fashioned, effective use of a blackboard and chalk, or a whiteboard and magic markers, is one of the best ways to teach an audience something so that it sticks in people's minds. If you think about it, the reason for this effectiveness is clear. Instead of just using your voice and assuming people will listen, understand, and take notes, if you write down major headings, important concepts, new vocabulary words, and so on, the audience gets a double dose of information: orally through your voice and visually by your writing things on the board. Another reason why using these boards is effective? It makes you look dynamic. You are *doing* something besides just talking.

Designing an Impressive Multimedia Presentation

Imagine those who sit through the more than 30 million PowerPoint presentations that Microsoft estimates are made each day.[6] No doubt, many of them would say this "disease" has reached epidemic proportions. PowerPoint, say its detractors, dictates the way information is structured and presented. They say that the program is turning the nation's businesspeople into a "mindless gaggle of bullet-pointed morons."[7] If you looked up *death by PowerPoint* in your favourite search engine, you would score about 120,000 hits. Writing in *Canadian Business* magazine, Andrew Wahl paints an all too familiar picture: "We've all been there, sitting in some dark, airless space, straining to keep our eyes open during a presentation that drones on and on. A screen glows with a seemingly endless series of slides and charts, bullet points and words streaking and spinning round. But it's all in vain. Befuddled by the barrage of information, you fail to glean anything of use. The presentation ends, the lights come up, and you stumble away in a haze, thirsty for comprehension."[8] Wahl goes on to describe a number of problems with relying too heavily on PowerPoint, but without a doubt the greatest two are the curse of too many words on slides, which leads to audience exhaustion and divided attention, and the curse of the presenter who merely reads his or her slides, often turned away from the audience.

However, text-laden, amateurish slides that distract and bore audiences are the fault of their creator and not the software program itself. The ease with which most of us use PowerPoint has led to a false sense of security. We seem to have forgotten that to be effective, presenters using PowerPoint must first be effective presenters, period. Effective presenters do not overwhelm an audience by assuming it will be happy to read multiple slides with multiple lines or paragraphs of text, nor do they rely so heavily on a screen image that no one is paying attention to or listening to them. In other words, smart business presenters have to keep the attention of their audience by deploying the skills discussed above and in Chapter 10. They cannot assume that simply because they have a well-designed PowerPoint presentation, their actual *presentation* will go well.

> **Computer-aided presentations are economical, flexible, professional, and easy to prepare.**

Of course, learning how to use templates, working with colour, building bullet points, and add multimedia effects are valuable skills. In the sections that follow, you will learn to create an impressive multimedia presentation using the most widely used presentation software program, PowerPoint. With any software program, of course, gaining expertise requires your investment of time and effort. You could take a course or you could teach yourself through an online tutorial such as that at **http://office.microsoft.com/en-us/training/default.aspx**. Another way to master PowerPoint is to read a book such as Faithe Wempen's *PowerPoint 2007 Bible*. If operated by a proficient slide preparer and a skillful presenter, PowerPoint can add a distinct visual impact to any presentation.

Preparing a Visually Appealing PowerPoint Presentation

> **Critics say that PowerPoint is too regimented and produces "bullet-pointed morons."**

Some presenters prefer to create their slides first and then develop the narrative around their slides. Others prepare their content first and then create the visual component. The risk associated with the first approach is that you may be tempted to spend too much time making your slides look good and not enough time preparing your content. Remember that great-looking slides never compensate for thin content. In the following discussion, you will learn how to adjust the content and design of your slides to the situation or purpose and your audience. You will also receive detailed how-to instructions for composing a PowerPoint slide show.

Analyze the Situation and Purpose. Making the best content and design choices for your slides depends greatly on your analysis of the presentation situation and the purpose of your slide show. Will your slides be used during a live presentation? Will they be part of a self-running presentation such as in a store kiosk? Will they be saved on a server so that those with Internet access can watch the presentation at their convenience? Will they be sent as a PowerPoint slide show or

Although videoconferencing, Web seminars, and other virtual-meeting platforms can make business presentations more stimulating and cost-effective, failure to manage these tools may lead to embarrassing career blunders. In one instance, a business executive delivering a virtual presentation became flummoxed when the words "I love you teddy bear" appeared unexpectedly on the computer screen. The instant message, which a love interest had transmitted during the meeting, was visible to all attendees, earning the executive the nickname Teddy Bear. *What precautions should communicators take to ensure the smooth delivery of multimedia presentations?*

a PDF document—also sometimes called a *deck*—to a client instead of a hard-copy report? Are you converting PowerPoint slide shows for viewing on video iPods or BlackBerry devices?

If you are e-mailing the presentation or posting it online as a self-contained file, the slides will typically feature more text than if they were delivered orally. If, on the other hand, you are creating slides for a live presentation, your analysis will include answering questions such as these: *Should I prepare speaker's notes pages for my own use during the presentation? Should I distribute hard copies of my slides to my audience?*

Anticipate Your Audience. Think about how you can design your presentation to get the most positive response from your audience. Audiences respond,

"My presentation lacks power and it has no point. I assumed the software would take care of that!"

for example, to the colours you use. Slide backgrounds for business presentations should be in bold colours such as blue, green, and purple. Because the messages that colours convey can vary from culture to culture, colours must be chosen carefully. In the Western world, blue is the colour of credibility, tranquility, conservatism, and trust. Therefore, it is the background colour of choice for many business presentations. Green relates to interaction, growth, money, and stability. It can work well as a background or an accent colour. Purple can be used as a background or accent colour. It conveys spirituality, royalty, dreams, and humour.[9] As for slide text, adjust the colour so it provides high contrast and is readable. White or yellow, for example, usually works well on dark backgrounds.

Just as you anticipate audience members' reactions to colour, you can usually anticipate their reactions to special effects. Using animation and sound effects—flying objects, swirling text, clashing cymbals, and the like—only because they are available is not a good idea. Special effects distract your audience, drawing attention away from your main points. Add animation features only if doing so helps convey your message or adds interest to the content. When your audience members leave, they should be commenting on the ideas you conveyed—not the cool swivels and sound effects.

Adapt Text and Colour Selections.

Adapt the amount of text on your slide to how your audience will use the slides. As a general guideline, most graphic designers encourage the 6-x-6 rule: "Six bullets per screen, max; six words per bullet, max."[10] You may find, however, that breaking this rule is sometimes necessary, particularly when your users will be viewing the presentation on their own with no speaker assistance.

Adjust the colours based on where the presentation will be given. Use light text on a dark background for presentations in darkened rooms. Use dark text on a light background for presentations in lighted rooms. Avoid using a dark font on a dark background, such as red text on a dark blue background. In the same way, avoid using a light font on a light background, such as white text on a pale blue background. Dark on dark or light on light results in low contrast, making the slides difficult to read.

Organize Your Slides.

When you prepare your slides, translate the major headings in your presentation outline into titles for slides. Then build bullet points using short phrases. In Chapter 4 you learned to improve readability by using graphic highlighting techniques, including bullets, numbers, and headings. In preparing a PowerPoint presentation, you will use those same techniques.

The slides you create to accompany your spoken ideas can be organized with visual elements that will help your audience understand and remember what you want to communicate. Let's say, for example, that you have three points in your presentation. You can create a blueprint slide that captures the three points in a visually appealing way, and then you can use that slide several times throughout your presentation. Near the beginning, the blueprint slide provides an overview of your points. Later, it will provide transitions as you move from point to point. For transitions, you can direct your audience's attention by highlighting the next point you will be talking about. Finally, the blueprint slide can be used near the end to provide a review of your key points.

Compose Your Slide Show.

All presentation programs require you to (a) select or create a template that will serve as the background for your presentation and (b) make each individual slide by selecting a layout that best conveys your message. You can use one of the templates provided with your presentation software program (Figure 11.5), download one from many Web sites, or create one from scratch.

Novice and even advanced users choose existing templates because they are designed by professionals who know how to combine harmonious colours, borders, bullet styles, and fonts for pleasing visual effects. If you prefer, you can alter existing templates so they better suit your needs. Adding a corporate logo, adjusting the colour scheme to better match the colours used on your organization's Web site, and selecting a different font are just some of the ways you can customize existing templates.

Be careful, though, of what one expert labels "visual clichés."[11] Overused templates and even clip art that come with PowerPoint can weary viewers who have seen them repeatedly in presentations. Instead of using a standard template, search for *PowerPoint template* in your favourite search engine. You will see hundreds of template options available as free downloads. Unless your employer requires that presentations all have the same look, your audience will most likely appreciate fresh templates that complement the purpose of your presentation and provide visual variety.

Figure 11.6 illustrates one of the many layout and design options for creating your slides. You can alter layouts by re-positioning, re-sizing, or changing the fonts for the placeholders in which your title, bulleted list, organization chart, video clip, photograph, or other elements appear. As Figure 11.6 shows, you can experiment with graphic elements that will enhance your presentation by making your slides visually more appealing and memorable. Try to avoid long, boring bulleted lists.

Follow the 6-x-6 rule and select background and text colours based on the lightness of the room.

Overused templates and clip art produce "visual clichés" that bore audiences.

FIGURE 11.5 Selecting a Slide Layout in Microsoft PowerPoint

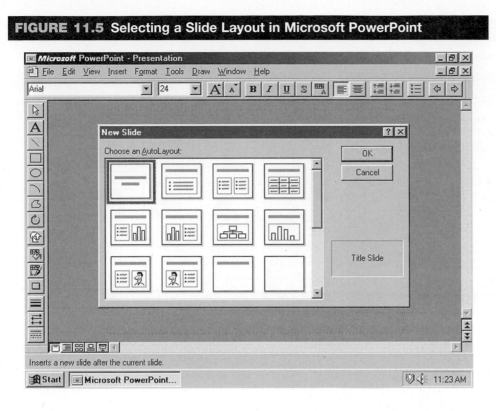

If you look more closely at Figure 11.6, you will notice that the bulleted items on the first slide are not parallel. The slide looks as if the author had been brainstorming or freewriting a first draft. The second and sixth bullet points express the same thought, that shopping online is convenient and easy for customers. Some bullet points are too long. As opposed to that, the bullets on the improved slide are very short, well within the 6-x-6 rule, although they are complete sentences. The photograph in the revised slide adds interest and illustrates the point. You may use stock photos that you can download from the Web for personal or school use without penalty, or consider taking your own pictures if you own a digital camera.

FIGURE 11.6 Revising and Enhancing Slides for Greater Impact

The slide on the left contains bullet points that are not parallel and that overlap meaning. The second and sixth bullet points say the same thing. Moreover, some bullet points are too long. After revision, the slide on the right has a more convincing title illustrating the "you" view. The bullet points are shorter, and each begins with a verb for parallelism. The photo adds interest. Note that the revised slide features a more lively and readable colour scheme, starting with the title.

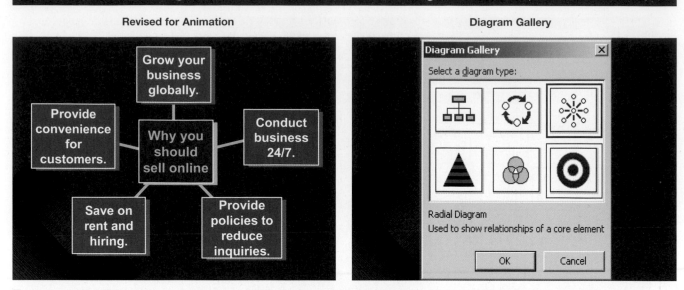

FIGURE 11.7 Converting a Bulleted Slide Into an Animated Diagram

The same content that appears in the Figure 11.6 slides takes on a totally different look when arranged as spokes radiating from a central idea. When presenting this slide, you can animate each item and control its appearance, further enlivening your presentation. PowerPoint provides a Diagram Gallery with six choices for arranging information.

Figure 11.7 shows how to add variety and pizzazz to your slides. Notice that the same information that appeared as bullet points in Figure 11.6 now appears as exciting spokes radiating from the central idea: *Why you should sell online.* This spoke diagram is just one of six common diagram possibilities available in PowerPoint's Diagram Gallery. You can also animate each item in the diagram. Occasionally, try to convert pure text and bullet points to diagrams, charts, and other images to add punch to your slide show. You will keep your audiences interested and help them retain the information you are presenting.

Numeric information is more easily grasped in charts or graphs than in a listing of numbers. Moreover, in most programs, you can animate your graphs and charts. Say, for instance, you have four columns in your bar chart. You can control the entry of each column by determining in what order and how each column appears on the screen. The goal is to use animation strategically to introduce elements of the presentation as they unfold in your spoken remarks. Figure 11.8 shows how a chart can be used to illustrate a concept discussed in the presentation about selling online.

> **Use animation to introduce elements of a presentation as they unfold in your spoken remarks.**

During this composition stage many users fall into the trap of excessive formatting and programming. They fritter away precious time fine-tuning their slides and don't spend enough time on what they are going to say and how they will say it. To avoid this trap, set a limit for how much time you will spend making your slides visually appealing. Your time limit will be based on how many "bells and whistles" (a) your audience expects and (b) your content requires to make it understandable. Remember that not every point or every thought requires a visual. In fact, it is smart to switch off the slides occasionally and direct the focus to yourself. Darkening the screen while you discuss a point, tell a story, give an example, or involve the audience will add variety to your presentation.

Create a slide only if the slide accomplishes at least one of the following purposes:

- Generates interest in what you are saying and helps the audience follow your ideas
- Highlights points you want your audience to remember
- Introduces or reviews your key points
- Provides a transition from one major point to the next
- Illustrates and simplifies complex ideas

In a later section of this chapter, you will find very specific steps to follow as you create your presentation.

FIGURE 11.8 Using a Bar Chart (Column Chart) to Illustrate a Concept

Growth in Online Sales

Online Sales of Three Best-Selling Product Groups 2009-2012

This slide was created using PowerPoint's *Insert, Chart* function. The information presented here is more exciting and easier to comprehend than if it had been presented in a bulleted list.

Revise, Proofread, and Evaluate Your Slide Show. Use PowerPoint's Slide Sorter View to rearrange, insert, and delete slides during the revision process. This is the time when you will focus on making your presentation as clear and concise as possible. If you are listing items, be sure that all items use parallel grammatical form. Figure 11.9 shows how to revise a slide to improve it for conciseness, parallelism, and other features. Study the design tips described in the first slide and determine which suggestions were not followed. Then compare it with the revised slide.

Notice that both slides in Figure 11.9 feature a blue background. This calming colour is the colour of choice for many business presentations (though white is just

FIGURE 11.9 Designing More Effective Slides

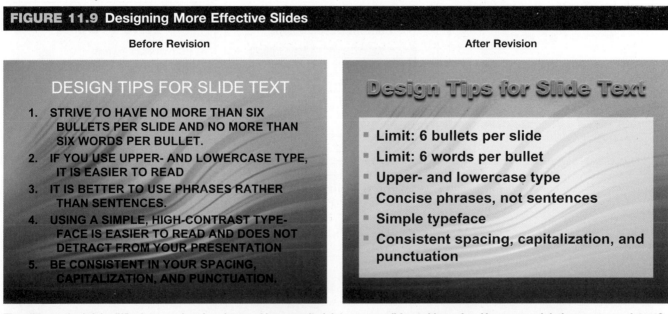

The slide on the left is difficult to read and understand because it violates many slide-making rules. How many violations can you detect? The slide on the right illustrates an improved version of the same information. Which slide do you think viewers would rather read?

as popular an option for its elegance and ease of reading.) However, the background swirls on the first slide are distracting. In addition, the uppercase white font is hard to read and contributes to making the image look busy. Inserting a transparent overlay and choosing a dark font to mute the distracting waves create a cleaner-looking slide.

As you are revising, check carefully to find spelling, grammar, punctuation, and other errors. Use the PowerPoint spell checker, but don't rely on it without careful proofing, preferably from a printed copy of the slide show. Nothing is as embarrassing as projecting errors on a huge screen in front of your audience. Also check for consistency in how you capitalize and punctuate points throughout the presentation.

Finally, critically evaluate your slide show. Consider whether you have done all you can to use the tools PowerPoint provides to communicate your message in a visually appealing way. In addition, test your slides on the equipment and in the room you will be using during your presentation. Do the colours you selected work in this new setting? Are the font styles and sizes readable from the back of the room? Figure 11.10 shows examples of slides that incorporate what you have learned in this discussion.

The dark purple background and the green and blue hues in the slide show shown in Figure 11.10 are standard choices for many business presentations. With an unobtrusive dark background, white fonts are a good option for maximum contrast and, hence, readability. The creator of the presentation varied the slide design to break the monotony of bulleted or numbered lists. Images and animated diagrams add interest and zing to the slides.

FIGURE 11.10 PowerPoint Slides that Demonstrate Best Practices in Multimedia Presentations

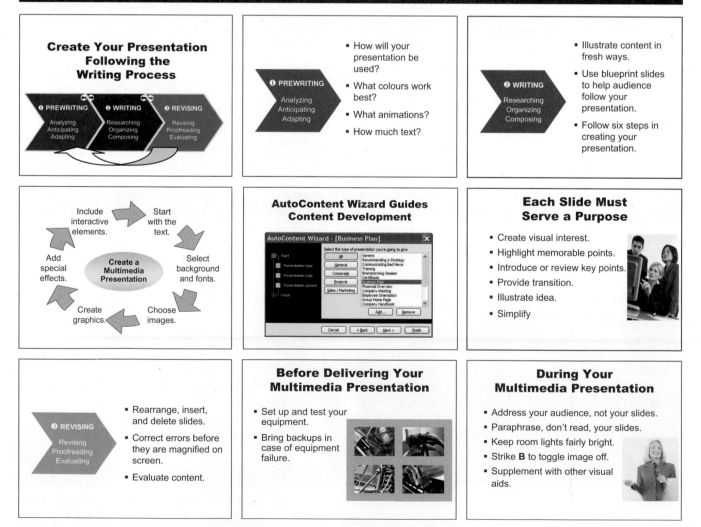

Using PowerPoint Effectively With Your Audience

Many promising presentations have been sabotaged by technology glitches or by the presenter's unfamiliarity with the equipment. Fabulous slides are of value only if you can manage the technology expertly. Apple CEO Steve Jobs is famous for his ability to wow his audiences during his keynote addresses. A journalist described his approach as follows: "Jobs unveils Apple's latest products as if he were a particularly hip and plugged-in friend showing off inventions in your living room. Truth is, the sense of informality comes only after gruelling hours of practice."[12] At one of his recent Macworld rehearsals, for example, he spent more than four hours on stage practising and reviewing every technical and performance aspect of his product launch.

A fabulous slide show can be ruined if you are unfamiliar with the equipment.

Practising and Preparing

Allow plenty of time before your presentation to set up and test your equipment.[13] Confirm that the places you plan to stand are not in the line of the projected image. Audience members don't appreciate having part of the slide displayed on your body. Make sure that all video or Web links are working and that you know how to operate all features the first time you try. No matter how much time you put into pre-show setup and testing, you still have no guarantee that all will go smoothly. Therefore, you should always bring backups of your presentation. Overhead transparencies or handouts of your presentation provide good substitutes. Transferring your presentation to a CD or a USB flash drive that could run from any available notebook might prove useful as well.

Keeping Your Audience Engaged

In addition to using the technology to enhance and enrich your message, here are additional tips for performing like a professional and keeping the audience engaged:

- Know your material, so you are free to look at your audience and to gaze at the screen, not your notes. Maintain genuine eye contact to connect with individuals in the room.
- As you show new elements on a slide, allow the audience time to absorb the information. Then paraphrase and elaborate on what the listeners have seen. Don't insult your audience's intelligence by reading verbatim from a slide.
- Leave the lights as bright as you can. Make sure the audience can see your face and eyes.
- Use a radio remote control (not infrared) so you can move freely rather than remain tethered to your computer. Radio remotes will allow you to be up to 15 metres away from your laptop.
- Maintain a connection with the audience by using a laser pointer to highlight slide items to discuss. Be aware, however, that a dancing laser point in a shaky hand may make you appear nervous. Steady your hand.
- Don't leave a slide on the screen when you are no longer discussing it. In Slide Show, View Show mode, strike *B* on the keyboard to turn off the screen image by blackening it (or press *W* to turn the screen white). Hit the key again to turn the screen back on.

To keep your audience interested, maintain eye contact, don't read from your slides, use a radio remote and a laser pointer, and turn off an image when it has been discussed.

Some presenters allow their PowerPoint slides to steal their thunder. One expert urges speakers to "use their PowerPresence in preference to their PowerPoint."[14] Although multimedia presentations supply terrific sizzle, they cannot replace the steak. In developing a presentation, don't expect your slides to carry the show. You can avoid being upstaged by not relying totally on your slides. Help the audience visualize your points by using other techniques. For example, drawing a diagram on a whiteboard or flipchart can be more engaging than showing slide after slide of static drawings. Demonstrating or displaying real objects or props is a welcome relief from slides. Remember that slides should be used only to help your audience understand the message and to add interest. You are still the main attraction!

Giving Powerful Multimedia Presentations in Eight Steps

We have now discussed many suggestions for making effective PowerPoint presentations, but you may still be wondering how to put it all together. Here is a step-by-step process for creating a powerful multimedia presentation:

1. **Start with the text.** The text is the foundation of your presentation. Express your ideas using words that are clear, concise, and understandable. Once the entire content of your presentation is in place, you are ready to begin adding colour and all the other elements that will make your slides visually appealing.

2. **Select background and fonts.** Select a template that will provide consistent font styles, font sizes, and a background for your slides. You can create your own template or use one included with PowerPoint. You can also download free templates or pay for templates from many online sites. You can't go wrong selecting a basic template design with an easy-to-read font, such as Times New Roman or Arial. As a general rule, use no more than two font styles in your presentation. The point size should be between 24 and 36. Title fonts should be larger than text font. The more you use PowerPoint and find out what works and doesn't work, the more you can experiment with bolder, more innovative background and font options that effectively convey your message.

3. **Choose images that help communicate your message.** Images, such as clip art, photographs, and maps, should complement the text. Never use an image that is not immediately relevant. Microsoft Office Online is accessed in PowerPoint and contains thousands of clip art images and photographs, most of which are in the public domain and require no copyright permissions. Before using images from other sources, determine whether permission from the copyright holder is required. Bear in mind that some people consider clip art amateurish, so photographs are usually preferable. In addition, clip art is available to any user, so it tends to become stale fast.

4. **Create graphics.** PowerPoint includes a variety of tools to help you simplify complex information or to transform a boring bulleted list into a visually appealing graphic. You can use PowerPoint's Draw and AutoShapes tools to create a time line or a flow chart. The Diagram Gallery will help you create an organization chart or a cycle, radial, pyramid, Venn, or target diagram, as well as over a dozen other chart types including line, pie, and bar charts. All of these tools require practice before you can create effective graphics. Remember that graphics should be easy to understand without overloading your audience with unnecessary details or too much text. In fact, consider putting such details in handouts rather than cluttering your slides with them.

5. **Add special effects.** To keep your audience focused on what you are discussing, use PowerPoint's Custom Animation feature to control when objects or text appear on the screen. Animate points in a bulleted list to appear one at a time, for example, or the boxes in a radial diagram to appear as each is discussed. Keep in mind that the first thing your audience sees on every slide should describe the slide's content. With motion paths and other animation options, you can move objects to various positions on the slide; or to minimize clutter, you can dim or remove them once they have served their purpose.

   In addition, as you move from slide to slide in a presentation, you can select transition effects, such as *wipe down*. The animation and transition options range from subtle to flashy—choose them with care so that the visual delivery of your presentation doesn't distract from the content of your message. An option at this step is to purchase a PowerPoint add-in product, such as Presenter, that can add professional-looking special effects to your presentation with very little effort.[15]

6. **Create hyperlinks to approximate the Web browsing experience.** Make your presentation more interactive and intriguing by connecting your PowerPoint presentation, via hyperlinks, to other sources that provide content that will

---

For a powerful presentation, first write the text, and then work on templates, font styles, and colours.

Learn to simplify complex information in visually appealing graphics.

---

enhance your presentation. You can hyperlink to (a) other slides within the presentation or in other PowerPoint files; (b) other programs that will open a second window that displays items such as spreadsheets, documents, or videos; and (c) if you have an Internet connection, Web sites.

Once you have finished discussing the hyperlinked source or watching the video that opened in a second window, close that window and your hyperlinked PowerPoint slide is in view. In this way, you can break up the monotony of typical linear PowerPoint presentations. Instead, your hyperlinked show approximates the viewing experience of a Web user who enters a site through a main page or portal and then navigates at will to reach second- and third-level pages.

7. **Engage your audience by asking for interaction.** When audience response and feedback are needed, interactive tools are useful. Audience response systems may be familiar to you from game shows, but they are also used for surveys and opinion polls, group decision making, voting, quizzes and tests, and many other applications. To interact with your audience, present polling questions. Audience members submit their individual or team responses using handheld devices read by a PowerPoint add-in program. The audience immediately sees a bar chart that displays the response results. If you would like to know more about audience response systems, visit one of the many Web sites devoted to them, for example, **http://www.audienceresponse.com or http://www.turningtechnologies.com**.

8. **Move your presentation to the Internet.** You have a range of alternatives, from simple to complex, for moving your multimedia presentation to the Internet or your company's intranet. The simplest option is posting your slides online for others to access. Even if you are giving a face-to-face presentation, attendees appreciate these "electronic handouts" because they don't have to lug them home. The most complex option for moving your multimedia presentation to the Internet involves a Web conference or broadcast.

Web presentations with slides, narration, and speaker control have emerged as a way for anyone who has access to the Internet to attend your presentation without leaving the office. For example, you could initiate a meeting via a conference call, narrate using a telephone, and have participants see your slides from the browsers on their computers. If you prefer, you could skip the narration and provide a pre-recorded presentation. Web-based presentations have many applications, including providing access to updated training or sales data whenever needed.[16]

Some businesses convert their PowerPoint presentations to PDF documents or send PowerPoint shows (file extension *.PPS), which open directly in Slide Show View, ready to run. Both types of documents are highly suitable for e-mailing. They start immediately, can't be easily changed, and typically result in smaller, less memory-hogging files.

Internet options for slide presentations range from posting slides online to conducting a live Web conference with slides, narration, and speaker control.

Polishing Your Delivery and Following Up

Once you've organized your presentation and prepared visuals, you're ready to practise delivering it. Here are suggestions for selecting a delivery method, along with specific techniques to use before, during, and after your presentation.

Delivery Method

Inexperienced speakers often feel that they must memorize an entire presentation to be effective. Unless you're a professional performer, however, you will sound wooden and unnatural. Moreover, forgetting your place can be embarrassing. Therefore, memorizing an entire oral presentation is not recommended. However, memorizing significant parts—the introduction, the conclusion, and perhaps a meaningful quotation—can be dramatic and impressive.

Chapter 11: Business Presentations

"In this seminar we'll discuss a simple technique for overcoming your fear of speaking in public."

If memorizing won't work, is reading your presentation the best plan? Definitely not. Reading to an audience is boring and ineffective. Because reading suggests that you don't know your topic well, the audience loses confidence in your expertise. Reading also prevents you from maintaining eye contact. You can't see audience reactions; consequently, you can't benefit from feedback.

Neither the memorizing nor the reading method creates convincing presentations. The best plan, by far, is a "notes" method. Plan your presentation carefully and talk from note cards or an outline containing key sentences and major ideas. By preparing and then practising with your notes, you can talk to your audience in a conversational manner. Your notes should be neither entire paragraphs nor single words. Instead, they should contain a complete sentence or two to introduce each major idea. Below the topic sentence(s), outline subpoints and illustrations. Note cards will keep you on track and prompt your memory, but only if you have rehearsed the presentation thoroughly.

Delivery Techniques

> The best method for delivering your presentation is speaking from carefully prepared note cards.

Nearly everyone experiences some degree of stage fright when speaking before a group. "If you hear someone say he or she isn't nervous before a speech, you're talking either to a liar or a very boring speaker," says corporate speech consultant Dianna Booher.[17] In other words, you can capitalize on the adrenaline that is coursing through your body by converting it to excitement and enthusiasm for your performance. But you can't just walk in and "wing it." People who don't prepare suffer the most anxiety and give the worst performances. You can learn to make effective oral presentations by focusing on four areas: preparation, organization, visual aids, and delivery.

> Stage fright is both natural and controllable.

Being afraid is quite natural and results from actual physiological changes occurring in your body. Faced with a frightening situation, your body responds with the fight-or-flight response, discussed more fully in Figure 11.11. You can learn to control and reduce stage fright, as well as to incorporate techniques for effective speaking, by using the following strategies and techniques before, during, and after your presentation.

Before Your Presentation

> Thorough preparation, extensive rehearsal, and stress-reduction techniques can lessen stage fright.

- **Prepare thoroughly.** One of the most effective strategies for reducing stage fright is knowing your subject thoroughly. Research your topic diligently and prepare a careful sentence outline. Those who try to "wing it" usually suffer the worst butterflies—and make the worst presentations.
- **Rehearse repeatedly.** When you rehearse, practise your entire presentation, not just the first half. Place your outline sentences on separate cards. You may also wish to include transitional sentences to help you move to the next topic. Use these cards as you practise, and include your visual aids in your rehearsal. Rehearse alone or before friends and family. Also try rehearsing on audio- or videotape so that you can evaluate your effectiveness.
- **Time yourself.** Most audiences tend to get restless during longer talks. Thus, try to complete your presentation in no more than 20 minutes. Set a timer during your rehearsal to measure your speaking time.
- **Request a lectern.** Every beginning speaker needs the security of a high desk or lectern from which to deliver a presentation. It serves as a note holder and a convenient place to rest wandering hands and arms.
- **Check the room.** Before you talk, make sure that a lectern has been provided. If you are using sound equipment or a projector, be certain they are operational. Check electrical outlets and the position of the viewing screen. Ensure that the seating arrangement is appropriate to your needs.

FIGURE 11.11 Conquer Stage Fright With These Techniques

Ever get nervous before giving a speech? Everyone does! And it is not all in your head, either. When you face something threatening or challenging, your body reacts in what psychologists call the *fight-or-flight response*. This physical reflex provides your body with increased energy to deal with threatening situations. It also creates those sensations—dry mouth, sweaty hands, increased heartbeat, and stomach butterflies—that we associate with stage fright. The fight-or-flight response arouses your body for action—in this case, making a presentation.

Because everyone feels some form of apprehension before speaking, it is impossible to eliminate the physiological symptoms altogether. However, you can reduce their effects with the following techniques:

- **Breathe deeply.** Use deep breathing to ease your fight-or-flight symptoms. Inhale to a count of ten, hold this breath to a count of ten, and exhale to a count of ten. Concentrate on your counting and your breathing; both activities reduce your stress.

- **Convert your fear.** Don't view your sweaty palms and dry mouth as evidence of fear. Interpret them as symptoms of exuberance, excitement, and enthusiasm to share your ideas.

- **Know your topic and come prepared.** Feel confident about your topic. Select a topic that you know well and that is relevant to your audience. Test your equipment and arrive with time to spare.

- **Use positive self-talk.** Remind yourself that you know your topic and are prepared. Tell yourself that the audience is on your side—because it is! Moreover, most speakers appear to be more confident than they feel. Make this apparent confidence work for you.

- **Take a sip of water.** Drink some water to alleviate your dry mouth and constricted voice box, especially if you are talking for more than 15 minutes.

- **Shift the spotlight to your visuals.** At least some of the time the audience will be focusing on your slides, transparencies, handouts, or whatever you have prepared—and not totally on you.

- **Ignore any stumbles.** Don't apologize or confess your nervousness. If you keep going, the audience will forget any mistakes quickly.

- **Don't admit you are nervous.** Never tell your audience that you are nervous. They will probably never notice!

- **Feel proud when you finish.** You will be surprised at how good you feel when you finish. Take pride in what you have accomplished, and your audience will reward you with applause and congratulations. Your body, of course, will call off the fight-or-flight response and return to normal!

- **Greet members of the audience.** Try to make contact with a few members of the audience when you enter the room, while you are waiting to be introduced, or when you walk to the podium. Your body language should convey friendliness, confidence, and enjoyment.

- **Practise stress reduction.** If you feel tension and fear while you are waiting your turn to speak, use stress-reduction techniques, such as deep breathing. Additional techniques to help you conquer stage fright are presented in Figure 11.11.

During Your Presentation

- **Begin with a pause.** When you first approach the audience, take a moment to adjust your notes and make yourself comfortable. Establish your control of the situation.

- **Present your first sentence from memory.** By memorizing your opening, you can immediately establish rapport with the audience through eye contact. You'll also sound confident and knowledgeable.

- **Maintain eye contact.** If the size of the audience overwhelms you, pick out two individuals on the right and two on the left. Talk directly to these people.

- **Control your voice and vocabulary.** This means speaking in moderated tones but loudly enough to be heard. Eliminate verbal static, such as *ah, er, you know*, and *um*. Silence is preferable to meaningless fillers when you are thinking of your next idea.

- **Put the brakes on.** Many novice speakers talk too rapidly, displaying their nervousness and making it difficult for audience members to understand their ideas. Slow down and listen to what you are saying.

- **Move naturally.** You can use the lectern to hold your notes so that you are free to move about casually and naturally. Avoid fidgeting with your notes, your clothing, or items in your pockets. Learn to use your body to express a point.

Eye contact, a moderate tone of voice, and natural movements enhance a presentation.

- **Use visual aids effectively.** Discuss and interpret each visual aid for the audience. Move aside as you describe it so that it can be seen fully. Use a pointer if necessary.
- **Avoid digressions.** Stick to your outline and notes. Don't suddenly include clever little anecdotes or digressions that occur to you on the spot. If it's not part of your rehearsed material, leave it out so that you can finish on time. Remember, too, that your audience may not be as enthralled with your topic as you are.
- **Summarize your main points.** Conclude your presentation by reiterating your main points or by emphasizing what you want the audience to think or do. Once you have announced your conclusion, proceed to it directly.

After Your Presentation

The time to answer questions, distribute handouts, and reiterate main points is after a presentation.

- **Distribute handouts.** If you prepared handouts with data the audience will need, pass them out when you finish.
- **Encourage questions.** If the situation permits a question-and-answer period, announce it at the beginning of your presentation. Then, when you finish, ask for questions. Set a time limit for questions and answers.
- **Repeat questions.** Although the speaker may hear the question, audience members often do not. Begin each answer with a repetition of the question. This also gives you thinking time. Then, direct your answer to the entire audience.
- **Reinforce your main points.** You can use your answers to restate your primary ideas ("I'm glad you brought that up because it gives me a chance to elaborate on..."). In answering questions, avoid becoming defensive or debating the questioner.
- **Keep control.** Don't allow one individual to take over. Keep the entire audience involved.
- **Avoid *Yes, but* answers.** The word *but* immediately cancels any preceding message. Try replacing it with *and*. For example, *Yes, X has been tried. And Y works even better because ...*
- **End with a summary and appreciation.** To signal the end of the session before you take the last question, say something like *We have time for just one more question*. As you answer the last question, try to work it into a summary of your main points. Then, express appreciation to the audience for the opportunity to talk with them.

Summing Up and Looking Forward

This chapter presented techniques for giving effective oral presentations. Good presentations begin with analysis of your purpose and your audience. Organizing the content involves preparing an effective introduction, body, and closing. The introduction should capture the listener's attention, identify the speaker, establish credibility, and preview the main points. The body should discuss two to four main points, with appropriate explanations, details, and verbal signposts to guide listeners. The conclusion should review the main points, provide a final focus, and allow the speaker to leave the podium gracefully. You can improve audience rapport by using effective imagery including examples, analogies, metaphors, similes, personal anecdotes, statistics, and worst/best-case scenarios. In illustrating a presentation, use simple, easily understood visual aids to emphasize and clarify main points. If you employ PowerPoint or other presentation software, you can enhance the presentation by using templates, layout designs, and bullet points, and by not letting your slides overwhelm you and your audience.

In delivering your presentation, outline the main points on note cards and rehearse repeatedly. During the presentation consider beginning with a pause and presenting your first sentence from memory. Make eye contact, control your voice, speak and move naturally, and avoid digressions. After your talk distribute handouts and answer questions. End gracefully and express appreciation.

The final two chapters of this book focus on your ultimate goal—getting a job or advancing in your career. You'll learn how to write a persuasive résumé and how to succeed in an employment interview.

Critical Thinking

1. Why is it necessary to repeat key points in a business presentation?

2. Discuss the advantages and disadvantages of various visual aid options (e.g., projectors, handouts, whiteboards, etc.) Is using the same visual aid as everyone else around you necessarily the best choice in a presentation?

3. If PowerPoint is so effective, why are people speaking out against using it in presentations?

4. How can speakers prevent electronic presentation software from stealing their thunder?

5. What techniques are most effective for reducing stage fright?

Chapter Review

1. The planning of a business presentation should begin with serious thinking about what two factors?

2. Name three goals to be achieved in the introduction of a business presentation.

3. What should the conclusion to a business presentation include?

4. Name three ways for a speaker to use verbal signposts in a presentation. Illustrate each.

5. List seven techniques for creating effective imagery in a presentation. Be prepared to discuss each.

6. List ten ways that a business presentation may be organized.

7. Name specific advantages and disadvantages of presentation software.

8. Why is a PowerPoint slide with less text preferable to one with more text?

9. What delivery method is most effective for speakers?

1. **PowerPoint Practice.** Using the summary you wrote in Chapter 8 for Writing Improvement Exercise 1 (p. 220), develop two electronic presentations to go along with this summary. In the first presentation, make the mistake of having too many words on your slides. In the second presentation, correct this mistake. Give both presentations to your class, and see if students can identify the problematic presentation and tell you why it's problematic.

2. **PowerPoint Practice.** Using the summary you wrote in Chapter 8 for Writing Improvement Exercise 2 (p. 220), develop two electronic presentations to go along with this summary. In the first presentation, make the mistake of having too busy or tacky a design for your slides. In the second presentation, correct this mistake. Give both presentations to your class, and see if students can identify the problematic presentation and tell you why it's problematic.

3. **PowerPoint Practice.** Using the summary you wrote in Chapter 8 for Writing Improvement Exercise 3 (p. 220), develop an electronic presentation to go along with this summary. Present your presentation twice, once making the mistake of reading from the screen or slides and a second time correcting this mistake. See if students can identify the problematic presentation and tell you why it's problematic.

Activities and Cases

CRITICAL THINKING

11.1 It's All About the Audience

As Lee Jacobson reminds us at the beginning of this chapter, it's vital to think about your audience before developing a presentation. Depending on the type of audience, certain elements of your presentation will be emphasized, while others will be downplayed or eliminated altogether.

Your Task. Choose one of the presentation topics below and one of the audience sets below. Spend 15 minutes brainstorming what each presentation will look like; then, in front of a partner, a group, or the entire class, deliver a short improvised presentation in two different ways. Once you're done, see if your partner/group/class can figure out what you've done differently and why you chose to do so.

Topics	Audience sets
Surviving your first year of college/ university	a) Your institution's board of governors b) Your institution's orientation day
The pros and cons of a particular piece of technology	a) A prospective customer b) Your parents
Your recent work experience	a) Your best friend b) A prospective employer
Choose a topic of your own with your instructor's permission	a) A formal audience b) An informal audience

TEAM

11.2 The Pros and Cons of PowerPoint

One of the reasons your boss in a financial services firm purchased new laptops last year was to improve the professionalism of the firm. In other words, he wanted each financial advisor to have a laptop in front of him or her during all client meetings. In his opinion, having a laptop open and on when a client walks into a meeting room is much more effective than simply having a pile of paper sitting on the table. To this end, he made sure the laptops were loaded with the most recent version of Microsoft Office, including PowerPoint. Now that you are to give a presentation to the rest of the staff on the pros and cons of PDAs, you figure you'd better use PowerPoint.

Your Task. Devise two different presentations that discuss the issue of PDAs versus laptops. One of the presentations will use PowerPoint, as described in this chapter. The other presentation will not; instead, it will use other visual aids or no aids at all. Deliver both presentations in front of the same group. Ask the group to rate both of the presentations using the same agreed-upon criteria. Do not intentionally make one presentation less effective than the other. Afterward, discuss the scores each presentation achieved.

11.3 Preparing, Rehearsing, and Critiquing an Oral Presentation

Just as this book's chapters on business writing stress the importance of a revision stage, so too oral communication must be revised if it is to be effective. In other words, until you are a seasoned veteran, you should get into the habit of rehearsing your oral presentations. Likewise, you should get into the habit of offering constructive criticism to your peers and colleagues when they solicit it, and of accepting the same criticism when it is offered to you.

Your Task. In groups of four or five, select an issue with business ramifications that interests you. For example, people have strongly held views on the issue of whether or not Canada should allow privatized health care. Investigate your chosen issue in a couple of newspaper or magazine articles found through library online databases, and prepare an oral presentation based on your research. Rehearse the complete oral presentation in front your group. Your audience members will politely raise their hand and interrupt your presentation each time they believe there needs to be improvement (e.g., your voice trails off, you mispronounce a word, you fidget nervously, your body language is sending the wrong signal, you've lost your train of thought, etc.). Accept their constructive criticism and keep rehearsing. Appoint someone to be note taker each time a presentation is being rehearsed, so that at the end each of you has a list of "notes"—much like a theatre director would give to actors during rehearsal—that you can use to improve future presentations. Are there any common elements among the group members' notes?

11.4 Will Maxing Out My Credit Cards Improve My Credit Rating?

The program chair for the campus business club has asked you to present a talk to the group about consumer credit. He saw a newspaper article saying that only 10 percent of Americans know their credit scores. Many consumers, including students, have dangerous misconceptions about their scores. Not knowing your score could result in denial of credit as well as difficulty obtaining needed services and even a job.

Your Task. Using electronic databases and the Web, learn more about credit scores and typical misconceptions. For example, is a higher or lower credit score better? Can you improve your credit score by marrying well? If you earn more money, will your score get better? If you have a bad score, is it impossible to improve it? Can you improve your score by maxing out all your credit cards? (One survey reported that 28 percent of consumers believed this to be the case!) Prepare an oral presentation appropriate for a student audience. Conclude with appropriate recommendations.

11.5 Critiquing a Speech

Your Task. Go to the CBC Digital Archives at **http://archives.cbc.ca,** and in the search box type the word "speech." Look through the four pages of speeches from Canadian history and choose one that interests you. Then, read up on speech critiques and how the pros review speeches; read Andrew Dlugan's blog at **http://sixminutes.dlugan.com/speech-evaluation-1-how-to-study-critique-speech** or Google "speech critiques." Write a memo report to your instructor critiquing the speech you've chosen in terms of the following:

a. Effectiveness of the introduction, body, and conclusion

b. Evidence of effective overall organization

c. Use of verbal signposts to create coherence

d. Emphasis of two to four main points

e. Effectiveness of supporting facts (use of examples, statistics, quotations, and so forth)

f. Focus on audience benefits

g. Enthusiasm for the topic

11.6 Investigating Oral Presentations in Your Field

One of the best sources of career information is someone in your field.

Your Task. Interview one or two individuals in your professional field. How are oral presentations important in this profession? Does the frequency of oral presentations change as one advances? What suggestions can these people make to newcomers to the field for developing proficient oral presentation skills? What are the most common reasons for giving oral presentations in this profession? Discuss your findings with your class.

11.7 Outlining an Oral Presentation

For many people the hardest part of preparing an oral presentation is developing the outline.

Your Task. Select an oral presentation topic from the list in Activity 11.10 (p. 335) or suggest an original topic. Prepare an outline for your presentation using the following format.

Title
Purpose

        I. INTRODUCTION

Gain attention of audience	A.
Involve audience	B.
Establish credibility	C.
Preview main points	D.

Transition

        II. BODY

Main point	A.
Illustrate, clarify, contrast	1.
	2.
	3.

Transition

Main point	B.
Illustrate, clarify, contrast	1.
	2.
	3.

Transition

Main point	C.
Illustrate, clarify, contrast	1.
	2.
	3.

Transition

        III. CONCLUSION

Summarize main points	A.
Provide final focus	B.
Encourage questions	C.

11.8 Discovering New Presentation Tips

Your Task. Using your library's online databases, perform a subject search for *business presentations*. Read at least three articles that provide suggestions for giving business presentations. If possible, print the most relevant findings. Select at least eight good tips or techniques that you did *not* learn from this chapter. Your instructor may ask you to bring them to class for discussion or to submit a short e-mail or memo report outlining your tips.

11.9 Researching Job-Application Information

Your Task. Using your library's online databases, perform a subject search for one of the following topics. Find as many articles as you can. Then organize and present a five- to ten-minute informative talk to your class.

a. Do recruiters prefer one- or two-page résumés?

b. How do applicant tracking systems work?

c. How are inflated résumés detected, and what are the consequences?

d. What's new in writing cover letters in job applications?

e. What is online résumé fraud?

f. What are some new rules for résumés?

11.10 Choosing a Topic for an Oral Presentation

Your Task. Select a topic from the list below. Prepare a five- to ten-minute oral presentation. Consider yourself an expert who has been called in to explain some aspect of the topic before a group of interested people. Since your time is limited, prepare a concise yet forceful presentation with effective visual aids.

a. What is the career outlook in a field of your choice?

b. How has the Internet changed job searching?

c. What are the advantages and disadvantages of instant messaging as a method of workplace communication?

d. How do employees use online services?

e. What is telecommuting, and for what kind of workers is it an appropriate work alternative?

f. How much choice should parents have in selecting schools for their young children (parochial, private, and public)?

g. What travel location would you recommend for college students at March Break (or another holiday period, or in summer)?

h. What is the economic outlook for a given product (such as domestic cars, laptop computers, digital cameras, fitness equipment, or a product of your choice)?

i. How can your organization or institution improve its image?

j. Why should people invest in a company or scheme of your choice?

k. What brand and model of computer and printer represent the best buy for college students today?

l. What franchise would offer the best investment opportunity for an entrepreneur in your area?

m. How should a job candidate dress for an interview?

n. What should a guide to proper cell phone use include?

o. Are internships worth the effort?

p. How is an administrative assistant different from a secretary?

q. Where should your organization hold its next convention?

r. What is your opinion of the statement "Advertising steals our time, defaces the landscape, and degrades the dignity of public institutions"?[18]

s. How can businesspeople reduce the amount of e-mail spam they receive?

t. What is the outlook for real estate (commercial or residential) investment in your area?

u. What are the pros and cons of videoconferencing for [name an organization]?

v. Are today's communication technologies (e-mail, instant messaging, text messaging, PDAs, etc.) making us more productive or just more stressed out?

w. What kinds of gifts are appropriate for businesses to give clients and customers during the holiday season?

x. How are businesses and conservationists working together to protect the world's dwindling tropical forests?

y. Should employees be able to use computers in a work environment for anything other than work-related business?

11.11 Self-Contained Multimedia Activity: Creating a PowerPoint Presentation (No additional research required)

You are a consultant who has been hired to improve the effectiveness of corporate trainers. These trainers frequently make presentations to employees on topics such as conflict management, teamwork, time management, problem solving, performance appraisals, and employment interviewing. Your goal is to teach these trainers how to make better presentations.

Your Task. Create six visually appealing slides. Base the slides on the following content, which will be spoken during the presentation titled "Effective Employee Training." The comments shown here are only a portion of a longer presentation.

Trainers have two options when they make presentations. The first option is to use one-way communication, where the trainer basically dumps the information on the employees and leaves. The second option is to use a two-way audience-involvement approach. The two-way approach can accomplish many purposes, such as helping the trainer connect with the employees, helping the trainer reinforce key points, increasing the employees' retention rates, and changing the pace and adding variety. The two-way approach also encourages employees to get to know each other better. Because today's employees demand more than just a "talking head," trainers must engage their audiences by involving them in a two-way dialogue.

When you include interactivity in your training sessions, choose approaches that suit your delivery style. Also, think about which options your employees would be likely to respond to most positively. Let's consider some interactivity approaches now. Realize, though, that these ideas are presented to help you get your creative juices flowing. After I present the list, we will think about situations in which these options might be effective. We will also brainstorm to come up with creative ideas we can add to this list.

- Ask employees to guess at statistics before revealing them.
- Ask an employee to share examples or experiences.
- Ask a volunteer to help you demonstrate something.
- Ask the audience to complete a questionnaire or worksheet.
- Ask the audience to brainstorm or list something as fast as possible.
- Ask a variety of question types to achieve different purposes.
- Invite the audience to work through a process or examine an object.
- Survey the audience.
- Pause to let the audience members read something to themselves.
- Divide the audience into small groups to discuss an issue.

11.12 Improving the Design and Content of PowerPoint Slides

Your Task. Identify ways to improve the design and content of the three slides presented in Figure 11.12. Classify your comments under the following categories: (a) colour choices, (b) font choice including style and point size, (c) 6-x-6 rule, (d) listings in parallel grammatical form, (e) consistent capitalization and punctuation, and (f) graphics and images. Identify what needs to be improved and exactly how you would improve it. For example, if you identify category (d) as an area needing improvement, your answer would include a revision of the listing. When you finish, your instructor may show you a revised set of slides.

FIGURE 11.12 PowerPoint Slides Needing Revision

Webcasting Basics

- Inexpensive way to hold conferences and meetings.
- Presenter broadcasts via one of many Webcast platforms available today.
- Participants access meeting from anywhere via Internet connection and free software.
- Capabilities include live Q&A sessions and live polls of audience members.
- Those who missed the event can access stored presentations when convenient.

Voice Quality During Webcast

- The Three Ps are critical
  - Pacing
  - Pausing
  - Passion

Webcasting Pointers

- To engage audience early on, tell personal stories.
- Standing while webcasting adds energy to your voice.
- Remember, smiles are audible.
- Change slides frequently.
- Prepare a brief summary conclusion to follow Q&A session.

Grammar/Mechanics Review—11

The following sentences contain errors in grammar, punctuation, capitalization, number style, usage, and spelling. Below each sentence write a corrected version.

1. On the basis of the Presidents recommendation the Senior Vice President and the Manager were promoted, however there new salarys don't become effective until January 1st.

2. The 2 biggest sellers of blue jeans are finding there market invaded by hotter more fashion conscious manufacturers.

3. Will you please call me before 5 pm CST?

4. Cybertec, Inc. does send items c.o.d. doesn't it?

5. In the not too distant future my friend and me hope to open a clothing outlet in the Bahamas.

6. To start a business at least fifty thousand dollars is needed by us.

7. I bought the book titled On-line Job searches, and read the chapter called Keyword Strategies.

8. If your not on the internet your missing a world of opportunity, and knowledge.

9. If possible send the contract by fax before 6 o'clock p.m.

10. When we analyzed customers complaints we realized that technical support and delivery was responsible for most of the problems.
11. 35 2006 graduates indicated that they would attend the reunion.
12. All things considered the show will be cancelled because it's ratings have sank so low.
13. West Jet airlines offer special menu items: low salt crackers, vegan corn chips, and peanut free trail mix served to cross country passengers flying from Vancouver to ottawa.
14. Men can read smaller print then women; but women can hear better then men.
15. If I was you I would take my father-in-laws advise.

Grammar/Mechanics Challenge—11

Document for Revision

The following executive summary of a report has faults in grammar, punctuation, spelling, number form, wordiness, and word use. Use standard proofreading marks (see Appendix B) to correct the errors. When you finish, your instructor can show you the revised version of this abstract.

EXECUTIVE SUMMARY

Purpose of Report

The purposes of this report is (1) To determine the Sun coast university campus communitys awareness of the campus recycling program and (2) To recommend ways to increase participation. Sun Coasts recycling program was intended to respond to the increasing problem of waste disposal, to fulfil it's social responsibility as an educational institution, and to meet the demands of legislation that made it a requirement for individuals and organizations to recycle.

A Survey was conducted in an effort to learn about the campus communities recycling habits and to make an assessment of the participation in the recycling program that is current. 220 individuals responded to the Survey but twenty-seven Surveys could not be used. Since Sun coast universitys recycling program include only aluminum, glass, paper and plastic at this point in time these were the only materials considered in this Study.

Recycling at Sun coast

Most Survey respondants recognized the importance of recycling, they stated that they do recycle aluminum, glass, paper and plastic on a regular basis either at home or at work. However most respondants displayed a low-level of awareness, and use of the on campus program. Many of the respondants was unfamilar with the location of the bins around campus; and therefore had not participated in the Recycling Program. Other responses indicated that the bins were not located in convenent locations.

Reccommendations for increasing recycling participation

Recommendations for increasing participation in the Program include the following;
1. relocating the recycling bins for greater visability
2. development of incentive programs to gain the participation of on campus groups
3. training student volunteers to give on campus presentations that give an explanation of the need for recycling, and the benefits of using the Recycling Program
4. we should increase Advertising in regard to the Program

Communication Workshop

The Worst Deadly Sin in a Presentation

Audiences appreciate speakers with polished delivery techniques, but they are usually relatively forgiving when mistakes occur. One thing they don't suffer gladly, though, is unethical behaviour. Executives in a comprehensive research survey agreed that the "worst deadly sin" a speaker can commit in a presentation is to demonstrate a lack of integrity.

What kinds of unethical behaviour do audiences reject? They distrust speakers who misrepresent, exaggerate, and lie. They also dislike cover-ups and evasiveness. The following situations clearly signal trouble for speakers because of the unethical actions involved:

- A sales rep, instead of promoting his company's products, suggests that his competitor's business is mismanaged, is losing customers, or offers seriously flawed products.
- A manager distorts a new employee insurance plan, underemphasizing its deficiencies and overemphasizing its strengths.
- A sales rep fabricates an answer to a tough question instead of admitting ignorance.
- A financial planner tries to prove her point by highlighting an irrelevant statistic.

Career Application

In 2002, the largest brokerage firm in the United States, Merrill Lynch, suffered a major blow to its credibility and paid a $100 million settlement. Why? Its analysts privately called particular Internet stocks "crap" or "dogs," while publicly recommending them in presentations to customers.

Your Task

In small groups or with the entire class, discuss what might motivate a speaker to commit "the worst deadly sin." When have you heard presentations in which you doubted the integrity of the speaker? What unethical presentation techniques have you seen on television? What happens when a speaker loses credibility? Research "unethical sales tactics" through a search engine or in library databases and report back to your instructor or the class about one case of a recent unethical business presentation.

UNIT 6

Communicating for Employment

Chapter 12
The Job Search, Résumés, and Cover Letters

Chapter 13
Interviews and Follow-Up

COMMUNICATION TECHNOLOGY IN THE NEWS

Freshen Up That Online Resume With Original "Keywords"

Source: Jenny Lee, "Freshen up that online resume with original 'keywords,'" *Vancouver Sun*, Jan. 3, 2011, pg. C1.

If you are looking for work, using an online resume can be a good idea, but use it wisely. Online profiles and resumes show a clear pattern of overused employment buzzwords, and while at first these words might sound professional, they do little to set you apart, life coach Phyllis Reardon says.

Canadian and U.S. job hunters highlight their "extensive experience," while most of Europe hopes to be seen as "innovative," South Americans want to be seen as "dynamic," as do folks in Spain and India, while the Brits stand alone in their desire to appear "motivated," according to a LinkedIn study of the most overused words and phrases in member profiles.

Are the words extensive experience, innovative, dynamic, motivated, team player, results-oriented, fast-paced, proven track record, multitasker and entrepreneurial liberally sprinkled through your resume? These are Canada's top 10 employment buzzwords according to LinkedIn's records.

"Most Canadians are using the same 10 words in their profiles, and their profile on LinkedIn is playing the role of the modern resume," Reardon said. "While those words are okay in themselves, they can appear a little bit tired. If I was coaching a client, I would say use words which are more descriptive of your working behaviour."

An online resume can reach millions of people, but using it successfully requires savvy.

LinkedIn alone has 85 million members. "Hundreds, if not thousands, of other professionals have those words in their profile, so if you're including them in the hope they will make you stand out, it isn't going to work, said Krista Canfield, LinkedIn's senior PR manager for the Americas.

It's important to use keywords in your summary and descriptions of positions you've held, Canfield said.

An employer looking for an accountant is more likely searching for certain types of accountants rather than a "dynamic" accountant, Canfield said. And someone seeking a corporate tax accountant won't find you if your profile doesn't include the words "corporate" and "tax," she said.

Make sure you're connected to at least 50 people, Canfield said.

"That's the magic number where people start having more of those network effects, first-, second-and third-degree connections," she said. "The starting point could be co-workers, clients, professors if you're a new professional, college classmates, family members—primarily people you know and trust who are vested in your career."

Canfield tells the story of older, established airlines advertising their "low-cost airfare" online when faced with competition from younger airlines such as Virgin, Southwest and JetBlue.

"But no one was searching for that," she said. "They were searching for 'cheap tickets.'"

Put two lenses on your profile, Canfield said. Look at the industry terms you may be proficient at, and then flip to the terms your clients are using.

If you were in sales, you might want to talk about the size of your deals and how frequently you hit your quota, she said.

While some believe employers will search words like "dynamic" in a resume or profile, Reardon said job hunters are better off using words that best describe their behaviour.

Think about how unique you are, Reardon said. "There's no one else like you in the world. Think about what makes you.

"Write a list of the words that describe you and sometimes some of those tired words just may spill out on the page. Let them stay there. Then find synonyms that are more lively that better suit you."

In place of "dynamic," are you adaptable, persuasive, flexible, proactive, enthusiastic? Instead of listing words, describe your behaviours at work, Reardon said. Write up some of your work tasks. Alternatives to "innovative" include entrepreneurial, imaginative, enterprising, open-minded or insightful.

One good exercise is to search your job by title and take a look at your competition.

Freshen Up That Online Resume With Original "Keywords" (*contd.*)

More and more people are using social media to find work. "Research has shown time and time again people procure work more easily through contacts than an employment office. Work has changed and people seeking work must change," Reardon said.

"Networking is the key to success in work. It's a key to success in life and LinkedIn offers the ultimate in networking," said Reardon, noting that she is not paid by LinkedIn.

"Any employer can go right into your name and they have all that information that [at] one time would probably [have been] sitting in somebody's file cabinet."

Reardon sets aside time in the morning and afternoon to blog and post in life-coaching groups. She used to go to conferences to make contacts, but now that is less important to her. "At LinkedIn and the groups I'm in, it's like going into a big conference centre, and every single morning I have access to some of the best minds in the world."

Small-business professionals are among LinkedIn's most active users, Canfield said.

"More than 65 per cent of Fortune 100 companies use LinkedIn's hiring solutions to find talent," she said.

Summarize the article you've just read in a two- or three-sentence paragraph. Answer the following questions, either on your own or in a small group. Be prepared to present your answers in a short presentation or in an e-mail to your instructor.

QUESTIONS:

1. How does what you've learned in this article change your perception of business communication?

2. How might what you've learned in this article change your own communication style or strategy?

3. Come up with pro and con arguments for the following debate/discussion topic: All you need to do to get a job today is have a profile posted on LinkedIn.

The Job Search, Résumés, and Cover Letters

A survey of Canadian human resources professionals suggests the day might come when, rather than dusting off a resume when looking for work, we would be better advised to clean up our Facebook profile. Staffing agency OfficeTeam released results of a survey ... that showed 43 per cent of the HR managers they polled thought it was somewhat or very likely that profiles on websites such as Facebook and LinkedIn will someday replace resumes for getting jobs.[1]

Anonymous,
Victoria Times Colonist, Feb. 18, 2011

LEARNING OBJECTIVES

1. Prepare for employment by identifying your interests, evaluating your assets, recognizing the changing nature of jobs, and choosing a career path.

2. Use traditional and electronic job search techniques.

3. Compare and contrast chronological, functional, and combination résumés.

4. Organize and format the parts of a résumé to produce a persuasive product.

5. Identify techniques that prepare a résumé for computer scanning, faxing, and e-mailing.

6. Write a persuasive cover letter to accompany your résumé.

Whether you are applying for your first permanent position, competing for promotion, or changing careers, you'll be more successful if you understand employment strategies and how to promote yourself with a winning résumé. This chapter provides up-to-date advice on preparing for employment, searching the job market, writing a persuasive résumé, and developing an effective cover letter.

Preparing for Employment

You may think that the first step in finding a job is writing a résumé, but the job search process actually begins long before you are ready to prepare your résumé. Regardless of the kind of employment you seek, you must invest time and effort getting ready. You can't hope to find the position of your dreams without (1) knowing yourself, (2) knowing the job market, and (3) knowing the employment process.

> **Finding a satisfying career means learning about oneself, the job market, and the employment process.**

FIGURE 12.1 The Employment Search

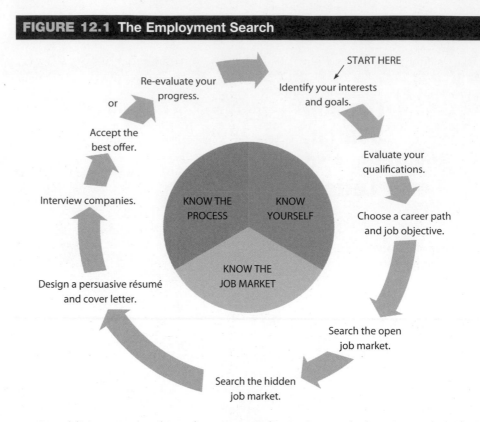

In addition to searching for career information and choosing a specific job objective, you should be studying the job market and becoming aware of the substantial changes in the nature of work. You'll also want to understand how to use the latest online resources in your job search, as the quote at the beginning of this chapter makes clear. When you have finished all this preparation, you're ready to design a persuasive résumé and job application letter and an online profile. These documents should be appropriate for small businesses as well as for larger organizations that may be using résumé-scanning programs. Following these steps, summarized in Figure 12.1 and described in this chapter, gives you a master plan for landing a job you really want.

Identify Your Interests

Analyzing your likes and dislikes helps you make wise employment decisions.

The employment process begins with looking inside yourself to analyze what you like and dislike so that you can make good employment choices. Career counsellors charge large sums for helping individuals learn about themselves. You can do the same kind of self-examination—without spending any money. For guidance in choosing a field that eventually proves to be satisfying, answer the following questions. If you have already chosen a field, think carefully about how your answers relate to that choice.

Answering specific questions can help you choose a career.

- Do I enjoy working with people, data, or things?
- How important is it to be my own boss?
- How important are salary, benefits, and job stability?
- How important are working conditions, colleagues, and job stimulation?
- Would I rather work for a large or small company?
- Must I work in a specific city, geographical area, or climate?
- Am I looking for security, travel opportunities, money, power, or prestige?
- How would I describe the perfect job, boss, and coworkers?

Evaluate Your Qualifications

Assessing your skills and experience prepares you to write a persuasive résumé.

In addition to your interests, assess your qualifications. Employers today want to know what assets you have to offer them. Your responses to the following questions will target your thinking as well as prepare a foundation for your résumé.

Remember that employers seek more than empty assurances; they will want proof of your qualifications.

- What computer skills can I offer? (What specific software programs can I name?)
- What other skills have I acquired in school, on the job, or through activities? How can I demonstrate these skills?
- Do I work well with people? What proof can I offer? (Consider extracurricular activities, clubs, and jobs.)
- Am I a leader, self-starter, or manager? What evidence can I offer?
- Do I speak, write, or understand another language?
- Do I learn quickly? Am I creative? How can I demonstrate these characteristics?
- Do I communicate well in speech and in writing? How can I verify these talents?

Recognize the Changing Nature of Jobs

As you learned in Chapter 1, the nature of the workplace is changing. One of the most significant changes involves the concept of the "job." Following the downsizing in many organizations in the recessions of the early 1990s and the late 2000s, and the movement toward flattened organizations in general, fewer people are employed in permanent positions. Many employees are feeling less job security, although they are doing more work.

In his book *The Canadian Workplace in Transition*, Gordon Betcherman describes a number of ways in which work is being transformed. In Canada, "non-standard" work, including temporary and short-term work, contract work, and self-employed work, is increasing, as is the amount of time people work in a week and the amount of work done outside traditional working hours.[2] At the same time, Canadian corporations are increasing their commitment to flexible work arrangements and employee empowerment.[3]

People are increasingly working for themselves or smaller companies, or they are becoming consultants or specialists who work on tasks or projects under arrangements too fluid to be called "jobs." And because new technologies can spring up overnight, making today's skills obsolete, employers are less willing to hire people into jobs with narrow descriptions.

What do these changes mean for you? For one thing, you should no longer think in terms of a lifelong career with a single company. In fact, you can't even expect reasonably permanent employment for work well done. This social contract between employer and employee is no longer a given. And predictable career paths within companies have largely disappeared. In the new workplace you can expect to work for multiple employers on flexible job assignments associated with teams and projects.

Because of this changing nature of work, you can never become complacent about your position or job skills. Be prepared for constant retraining and updating of your skills. People who learn quickly and adapt to change are valued individuals who will always be in demand especially in a climate of surging change.

Choose a Career Path

Today's job market is vastly different from that of a decade or two ago. As a result of job trends and personal choices, the average Canadian can expect to change careers at least three times and change jobs at least seven times in a lifetime. Some of you probably have not yet settled on your first career choice; others are embarking on a second or perhaps third career. Although you may be changing jobs in the future, you still need to train for a specific career area now. In choosing an area, you'll make the best decisions when you can match your interests and qualifications with the requirements and rewards in specific careers. But where can you find career information? Here are some suggestions:

- **Visit your school career or counselling centre.** Most have literature, inventories, software programs, and Internet connections that allow you to investigate such fields as accounting, finance, office technology, information systems, hotel management, and so forth.

Downsizing and flatter organizations have resulted in people feeling less secure in their jobs.

"Jobs" are becoming more flexible and less permanent.

People can expect to have eight to ten jobs in three or more different careers in a lifetime.

Career information can be obtained at school career centres and libraries, from the Internet, in classified ads, and from professional organizations.

FIGURE 12.2 Results From Online Job Search

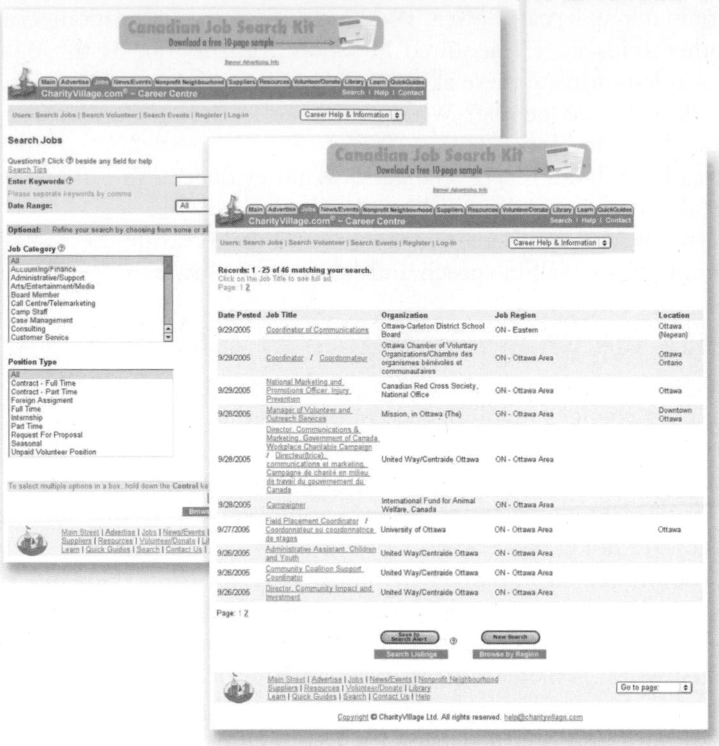

- **Search the Internet.** Many job search sites on the Web (e.g., Workopolis, Monster, and Charity Village) offer career planning information and resources. For example, Workopolis.com helps you link to various career search resources in its "Resource Centre" link. A sample online job site is shown in Figure 12.2.

- **Use your library.** Consult the latest edition of the *Index of Occupational Titles*, the U.S. government's *Occupational Outlook Handbook* (**http://www.bls.gov/oco**), and the Canadian government's National Occupational Classification (**http://www5.hrsdc.gc.ca/NOC-CNP/app/ index.aspx?lc=e**) for information about career duties, qualifications, salaries, and employment trends.

- **Take a summer job, internship, or part-time position in your field.** Nothing is better than trying out a career by actually working in it or in a similar area. Many companies offer internships and temporary jobs to begin training students and to develop relationships with them. These relationships sometimes blossom into permanent positions.

- **Volunteer with a nonprofit organization.** Many colleges and universities encourage service learning opportunities. In volunteering their services, students gain valuable experience, and nonprofits appreciate the expertise and fresh ideas that students bring.

- **Interview someone in your chosen field.** People are usually flattered when asked to describe their careers. Inquire about needed skills, required courses, financial and other rewards, benefits, working conditions, future trends, and entry requirements.

- **Monitor classified ads.** Early in your postsecondary education career, begin monitoring want ads and Web sites of companies in your career area. Check job availability, qualifications sought, duties, and salary range. Don't wait until you're about to graduate to see how the job market looks.

- **Join professional organizations in your field.** Frequently, these organizations offer student membership status and reduced rates. You'll get inside information on issues, career news, and possible jobs.

> Summer and part-time jobs and internships are good opportunities to learn about different careers.

Searching for a Job Electronically

Another significant change in the workplace involves the way we find jobs. Prior to the late 1990s, a job seeker browsed the local newspaper's classified ads, found a likely sounding job listing, prepared a résumé on paper, and sent it out by mail. All that has long since changed. Today, searching for a job electronically has become a common, but not always fruitful, approach. With all the publicity given to Internet job boards (for example, in the quote at the beginning of this chapter) you might think that electronic job searching has totally replaced traditional methods. Not so! Although Web sites such as Workopolis and Monster list millions of jobs (see Figure 12.3 below), actually landing a job is much harder than just clicking a mouse. In addition, these job boards are facing recent competition from social networking sites such as LinkedIn and Facebook.[4]

Employment Web sites list many jobs, but finding a job electronically requires more work than simply clicking a mouse.

FIGURE 12.3 Using the Web to Search for a Job

Both recruiters and job seekers complain about online job boards. Corporate recruiters say that the big job boards bring a flood of candidates, many of whom are not suited for the listed jobs. Workplace experts estimate that the average large corporation can be inundated with up to 2,000 résumés a day.[5] Job candidates grumble that listings are frequently out-of-date and fail to produce leads. Some career advisors call these sites *black holes*,[6] into which résumés vanish without a trace. Applicants worry about the privacy of information posted at big boards. Most important, an independent study has shown that the percentage of hires resulting from job boards is astonishingly low, at somewhere between one and four percent of hires.[7] Workplace expert Liz Ryan advises job seekers not to count on finding a job by devoting all their energy to searching online job boards.[8]

Using the Big Job Boards. Despite these gloomy prospects, you should definitely learn to use job boards if you haven't already to gather job search information, such as résumé, interviewing, and salary tips. Job boards also serve as a jumping-off point in most searches. They can inform you about the kinds of jobs that are available and the skill sets required. With over 40,000 job boards and employment Web sites deluging the Internet, it is hard to know where to start. We have listed a few of the best-known online job sites here:

- **CanadianCareers (http://www.canadiancareers.com)** is a clearing-house site that lists hundreds of online job boards and sites in Canada. For example, if you're in a postsecondary Hospitality program, you can scroll through this site until you get to the "H" section of the listings. Here you'll find a link to the site Hcareers (**http://www.hcareers.ca**), which is exclusively targeted to jobs in the hospitality, tourism, and leisure industry. From this site you can also link to job boards in the public service, federally and provincially.
- **Monster (http://www.monster.ca)** offers access to information on more than 1.1 million jobs worldwide with 275,000 client companies posting jobs. You may search for jobs by keyword, company name, geographic location, and job category. Many consider it to be the Web's premier job site. Of specific interests to students is Monster College (**http://college.monster.com**) with specific help for student job seekers.
- **Workopolis (http://www.workopolis.com)** is, like Monster, a large and well-known job board with many jobs in all major industries. A useful feature on this site is the ability to sign up for a free biweekly newsletter that provides job search tips.
- **Charity Village (http://www.charityvillage.com)** advertises jobs solely in the nonprofit sector. Often overlooked by students and graduates, this site offers a wealth of opportunities in traditional business areas such as accounting, finance, customer service, and marketing, all in the nonprofit sector.

Beyond the Big Job Boards. Besides the big online job boards listed above, savvy candidates know how to use their computers to search for jobs at Web sites such as the following:

Job prospects may be more promising at the Web sites of corporations, professional associations, employers' organizations, niche fields, and, most recently, professional networking sites.

- **Corporate Web sites.** Probably the best way to find a job online is at a company's own Web site. One poll found that 70 percent of job seekers felt they were more likely to obtain an interview if they posted their résumés on corporate sites. In addition to finding a more direct route to decision makers, job seekers thought that they could keep their job searches more private at corporate Web sites than at big job board sites.[9]
- **Association Web sites.** Online job listings have proved to be the single most popular feature of many professional organizations such as the Canadian Professional Sales Association. If you go to the association's Web site at **http://www.cpsa.com** you'll see a large banner ad leading you to the CPSA's job board. Clicking on this link takes you to a rich job board with sales positions

across the country. Even if you have no interest in a sales career, why not try a search for your geographical area and see what jobs exist? You may be surprised. Sometimes job boards at association Web sites are only open to paid-up members, and you'll have to decide whether it's a good idea to join your target association, perhaps as a student member.

- **Professional networking sites.** Perhaps you use MySpace or Facebook to chat with friends. However, users are increasingly tapping into social networking sites to prospect for jobs. Facebook and other sites have started professional offshoots. LinkedIn boasts more than 13 million active users, but smaller sites, such as by-invitation-only Doostang, may have an edge in specialized fields.[10] Finally, international networking sites—Chinese Wealink and German Xing—can help candidates who seek a global reach.

Thousands of job boards listing millions of jobs now flood the Internet. The harsh reality, however, is that landing a job still depends largely on personal contacts. Stanford University sociologist Mark Granovetter found that 70 percent of jobs are discovered through networking.[11] One employment expert believes that overreliance on technology may have made job seekers lazy: "At the end of the day, the job hunt is largely about people and it is about networking—looking at who you know and where they work."[12] Job-search consultant Debra Feldman concurs: "More important than what you know is who knows what you know. Make sure you are on the radar of people who have access to the kind of job leads you want."[13]

Using Traditional Job Search Techniques

Finding the perfect job requires an early start and a determined effort. Whether you use traditional or online job search techniques, you should be prepared to launch an aggressive campaign. And you can't start too early. Students are told early on that a degree or diploma alone doesn't guarantee a good job. They are cautioned that final grades make a difference to employers. And they are advised of the importance of experience and networking. Here are some traditional steps that job candidates take:

> A traditional job search campaign might include checking classified ads and announcements in professional publications, contacting companies, and developing a network of contacts.

- **Study classified ads in local and national newspapers.** Be aware, though, that classified ads are only one small source of jobs. Nearly two-thirds of all jobs, representing the "hidden" job market, are unadvertised.
- **Check announcements in publications of professional organizations.** If you do not have a student membership, ask your professors to share current copies of professional journals, newsletters, and so on. Your college or university library is another good source.
- **Contact companies in which you're interested, even if you know of no current opening.** Write an unsolicited letter and include your résumé. Follow up with a telephone call. Check the company's Web site for employment possibilities and procedures.
- **Sign up for school interviews with visiting company representatives.** Campus recruiters may open your eyes to exciting jobs and locations.
- **Attend career fairs.** Job fairs are invaluable in your quest to learn about specific companies and your future career options. Recruiters say that the more you know about the company and its representatives, the more comfortable you will be in an interview.[14]
- **Ask for advice from your instructors.** They often have contacts and ideas for expanding your job search.
- **Develop your own network of contacts.** Networking still accounts for most of the jobs found by candidates. Therefore, plan to spend a considerable portion of your job search time developing a personal network. The Workshop at the end of this chapter gives you step-by-step instructions for traditional networking as well as some ideas for online networking.

Create a Persuasive Résumé

After reviewing traditional and online employment market and job lead resources, you'll focus on writing a persuasive résumé. Such a résumé does more than merely list your qualifications. It packages your assets into a convincing advertisement that sells you for a specific job. The goal of a persuasive résumé is winning an interview. Even if you are not in the job market at this moment, preparing a résumé now has advantages. Having a current résumé makes you look well organized and professional should an unexpected employment opportunity arise. Moreover, preparing a résumé early can help you recognize weak areas and give you time to bolster your credentials.

Choose a Résumé Style

Your qualifications and career goal will help you choose between two basic résumé styles: chronological and functional.

Chronological résumés focus on past employment; functional résumés focus on skills.

Chronological. Most popular with recruiters is the chronological résumé, shown in Figures 12.7 through 12.10 (pp. 356–359). It lists work history job by job, starting with the most recent position. Recruiters are familiar with the chronological résumé, and as many as 84 percent of employers prefer to see a candidate's résumé in this format.[15] The chronological style works well for candidates who have experience in their field of employment and for those who show steady career growth. But for many students and others who lack extensive experience, the functional résumé format may be preferable.

Functional. The functional résumé, shown in Figure 12.11 (p. 360), focuses attention on a candidate's skills rather than on past employment. Like a chronological résumé, the functional résumé begins with the candidate's name, address, telephone number, job objective, and education. Instead of listing jobs, though, the functional résumé groups skills and accomplishments in special categories, such as *Supervisory and Management Skills* or *Retailing and Marketing Experience*. This résumé style highlights accomplishments and can de-emphasize a negative employment history. People who have changed jobs frequently or who have gaps in their employment records may prefer the functional résumé. Recent graduates with little employment experience often find the functional résumé useful. Older job seekers who want to de-emphasize a long job history and job hunters who are afraid of appearing overqualified may also prefer the functional format. Be aware, though, that online job boards may insist on chronological format. In addition, some recruiters are suspicious of functional résumés, thinking the candidate is hiding something.

Functional résumés are also called skill résumés. Although the functional résumé of Kevin Touhy shown in Figure 12.11 concentrates on skills, it does include a short employment section because recruiters expect it. Notice that Kevin breaks his skills into three categories. An alternative—and easier—method is to make one large list, perhaps with a title such as *Areas of Accomplishment*, *Summary of Qualifications*, or *Areas of Expertise and Ability*.

Decide on Length

Recruiters may say they prefer one-page résumés, but many choose to interview those with longer résumés.

Experts simply do not agree on how long a résumé should be. Conventional wisdom has always held that recruiters prefer one-page résumés. A controlled study of 570 recruiters, however, revealed that they *claimed* they preferred one-page résumés. The recruiters actually *chose* to interview the applicants with two-page résumés.[16] Recruiters who are serious about candidates often prefer a full picture with the kind of details that can be provided in a two-page résumé. On the other hand, recruiters are said to be extremely busy and prefer concise résumés.

Perhaps the best advice is to make your résumé as long as needed to sell your skills to recruiters and hiring managers. Individuals with more experience will naturally have longer résumés. Those with fewer than ten years of experience, those making a major career change, and those who have had only one or two employers will likely have a one-page résumé. Those with ten years or more of related experience may have a two-page résumé. Finally, some senior-level managers and executives with a lengthy history of major accomplishments might have a résumé that is three pages or longer.[17] A recent survey by a global staffing firm found that 61 percent of hiring managers now prefer to receive two-page résumés from experienced candidates for management jobs; 31 percent stated that they would accept three pages. Even applicants for low-level staff jobs may opt for two pages, 44 percent of recruiters said.[18]

Arrange the Parts

Although résumés have standard parts, their arrangement and content should be strategically planned. A customized résumé emphasizes skills and achievements aimed at a particular job or company. It shows a candidate's most important qualifications first, and it de-emphasizes any weaknesses. In arranging your information and qualifications, try to create as few headings as possible; more than six generally looks cluttered. No two résumés are ever exactly alike, but most writers consider including all or some of these items: main heading, career objective, summary of qualifications, education, experience, capabilities and skills, awards and activities, personal information, and references.

The parts of résumés should be arranged with the most important qualifications first.

Main Heading. Your résumé, whether it is chronological or functional, should begin with your name; add your middle initial for a professional look. Following your name, list your contact information, including your complete address, area code and phone number, and e-mail address. If possible, include a telephone number where messages may be left for you. The outgoing message at this number should be in your voice, it should mention your full name, and it should be concise and professional. If you are expecting an important recruiting call on your cell phone, pick up only when you are in a quiet environment and can concentrate. Keep the main heading as uncluttered and simple as possible. Format your name so that it stands out on the page. Don't include the word *résumé*; it is like putting the word *letter* above correspondence.

For your e-mail address, be sure it sounds professional instead of something like *1foxylady@yahoo.com* or *hotdaddy@hotmail.com*. Also be sure that you are using a personal e-mail address. Putting your work e-mail address on your résumé announces to prospective employers that you are using your current employer's resources to look for another job.

Career Objective. Opinion is divided about the effect of including a career objective on a résumé. Recruiters think such statements indicate that a candidate has made a commitment to a career and is sure about what he or she wants to do. Career objectives, of course, make the recruiter's life easier by quickly classifying the résumé. But such declarations can also disqualify a candidate if the stated objective doesn't match a company's job description.[19] A well-written objective customized for the job opening can add value to a chronological or functional résumé.

Career objectives are most appropriate for specific, targeted positions, but they may limit a broader job search.

A person applying for an auditor position might include the following objective: *Seeking an auditor position in an internal corporate accounting department where my accounting skills, computer experience, knowledge of GAAP, and attention to detail will help the company run efficiently and ensure that its records are kept accurately.*

Your objective should also focus on the employer's needs. Therefore, it should be written from the employer's perspective, not your own. Focus on how you can contribute to the organization, not on what the organization can do for you. A typical self-serving objective is *To obtain a meaningful and rewarding position that enables me to learn more about the graphic design field and allows for advancement.* Instead, show how you will add value to the organization with an objective such as *Position with advertising firm designing Web sites, publications, logos, and promotional displays for clients, where creativity, software knowledge, and proven communication skills can be used to build client base and expand operations.*

Also be careful that your career objective doesn't downplay your talents. For example, some consultants warn against using the words *entry-level* in your objective, as these words emphasize lack of experience or show poor self-confidence. Finally, your objective should be concise. Try to limit your objective to no more than two or three lines. Avoid using complete sentences and the pronoun *I*.

If you choose to omit the career objective, be sure to discuss your objectives and goals in your cover letter. Savvy job seekers are also incorporating their objectives into a summary of qualifications, which is discussed next.

Summary of Qualifications.

A Summary of Qualifications section lists your most impressive accomplishments and qualifications in one concise bulleted list.

"The biggest change in résumés over the last decade has been a switch from an objective to a summary at the top," says career expert Wendy Enelow.[20] Recruiters are busy, and smart job seekers add a summary of qualifications to their résumés to save the time of recruiters and hiring managers. Once a job is advertised, a hiring manager may get hundreds or even thousands of résumés in response. A summary at the top of your résumé makes it easier to read and ensures that your most impressive qualifications are not overlooked by a recruiter, who may be skimming résumés quickly. A well-written summary motivates the recruiter to read further.

A summary of qualifications will include three to eight bulleted statements that prove you are the ideal candidate for the position. When formulating these statements, consider your experience in the field, your education, your unique skills, awards you have won, certifications, and any other accomplishments that you want to highlight. Include numbers wherever possible. Target the most important qualifications an employer will be looking for in the person hired for this position. Examples of summaries of qualifications appear in Figures 12.7, 12.8, 12.10, and 12.12.

Education.

The education section shows degrees and grades but does not list all courses a job applicant has taken.

The next component in a chronological résumé is your education—if it is more noteworthy than your work experience. In this section you should include the name and location of schools, dates of attendance, major fields of study, and degrees received. By the way, once you have attended college, you don't need to list high-school information on your résumé.

Your grades and/or class ranking may be important to prospective employers. Sixty-six percent of employers screen candidates by GPA, a recent survey found, and 58 percent of survey respondents stated that they would be less likely to hire candidates with GPAs below 3.0. One way to enhance your GPA is to calculate it in your major courses only (for example, *3.6/4.0 in major*). It is not unethical to showcase your GPA in your major—as long as you clearly indicate what you are doing. Although some hiring managers may think that applicants are hiding something if they omit a poor record of grades, consultant Terese Corey Blanck suggests leaving out a poor GPA. Instead, she advises that students try to excel in internships, show extracurricular leadership, and target smaller, lesser-known companies to offset low grades.[21]

Under *Education* you might be tempted to list all the courses you took, but such a list makes for very dull reading. Refer to courses only if you can relate them to the position sought. When relevant, include certificates earned, seminars attended, workshops completed, and honours earned. If your education is incomplete, include such statements as *B.S. degree expected 5/12* or *80 units completed in 120-unit program*. Title this section *Education, Academic Preparation,* or *Professional Training*. If you are preparing a functional résumé, you will probably put the education section below your skills summaries, as Kevin Touhy has done in Figure 12.11.

Work Experience or Employment History.

The work experience section of a résumé should list specifics and quantify achievements.

If your work experience is significant and relevant to the position sought, this information should appear before your education information. List your most recent employment first and work backward, including only those jobs that you think will help you win the targeted position. A job application form may demand a full employment history, but your résumé may be selective. Be aware, though, that time gaps in your employment history will probably be questioned in the interview. For each position show the following:

- Employer's name, city/town, and province
- Dates of employment (month and year)
- Most important job title
- Significant duties, activities, accomplishments, and promotions

Describe your employment achievements concisely but concretely to make what résumé consultants call "a strong value proposition."[22] Avoid generalities such as *Worked with customers*. Be more specific, with statements such as *Served 40 or more retail customers a day*; *Successfully resolved problems about custom stationery orders*; or *Acted as intermediary among customers, printers, and suppliers*. If possible, quantify your accomplishments, such as *Conducted study of equipment needs of 100 small businesses in Hamilton, ON*; *Personally generated orders for sales of $90,000 annually*; or *Keyed all the production models for a 250-page employee procedures manual*. One professional recruiter said, "I spend a half hour every day screening 50 résumés or more, and if I don't spot some [quantifiable] results in the first 10 seconds, the résumé is history."[23]

Your employment achievements and job duties will be easier to read if you place them in a bulleted list. When writing these bullet points, don't try to list every single thing you have done on the job; instead, customize your information so that it relates to the target job. Make sure your list of job duties shows what you have to contribute and how you are qualified for the position you are applying for. Do not make your bullet points complete sentences, and avoid using personal pronouns (*I, me, my*) in them. If you have performed a lot of the same duties for multiple employers, you don't have to repeat them.

In addition to technical skills, employers seek individuals with communication, management, and interpersonal capabilities. This means you will want to select work experiences and achievements that illustrate your initiative, dependability, responsibility, resourcefulness, flexibility, and leadership. Employers also want people who can work together in teams. Therefore, include statements like *Collaborated with interdepartmental task force in developing ten-page handbook for temporary workers* and *Headed student government team that conducted most successful voter registration in campus history*.

Statements describing your work experience can be made forceful and persuasive by using action verbs, such as those listed in Figure 12.4 and illustrated in Figure 12.5. Starting each of your bullet points with an action verb will help ensure that your bulleted lists are parallel.

FIGURE 12.4 Strengthen Your Résumé With Action Verbs

accelerated	enabled	introduced	reviewed
achieved	encouraged	managed	revitalized
analyzed	engineered	organized	screened
collaborated	established	originated	served
conceptualized	expanded	overhauled	spearheaded
constructed	expedited	pioneered	spurred
converted	facilitated	reduced	strengthened
designed	improved	resolved	targeted
directed	increased	restructured	transformed

Emphasize the skills and aptitudes that prove you are qualified for a specific position.

Capabilities and Skills.

Recruiters want to know specifically what you can do for their companies. Therefore, list your special skills, such as *Proficient in preparing federal, state, and local payroll tax returns as well as franchise and personal property tax returns*. Include your ability to use the Internet, software programs, office equipment, and communication technology tools. If you can speak a foreign language or use sign language, include it on your résumé. Describe proficiencies you have acquired through training and experience, such as *Certified in computer graphics and Web design through an intensive 350-hour classroom program*. Use expressions such as *competent in, skilled in, proficient with, experienced in,* and *ability to*; for example, *Competent in writing, editing, and proofreading reports, tables, letters, memos, manuscripts, and business forms.*

You will also want to highlight exceptional aptitudes, such as working well under stress, learning computer programs quickly, and interacting with customers. If possible, provide details and evidence that back up your assertions; for example, *Mastered PhotoShop in 25 hours with little instruction*. Search for examples of your writing, speaking, management, organizational, and interpersonal skills—particularly those talents that are relevant to your targeted job. For recent graduates, this section can be used to give recruiters evidence of your potential. Instead of *Capabilities*, the section might be called *Skills and Abilities*.

Those job hunters preparing a functional résumé will place more focus on skills than on any other section. A well-written functional résumé groups skills into categories such as *Accounting/Finance Skills, Management/Leadership Skills, Communication/Teamwork Skills,* and *Computer/Technology Skills*. Each skills category includes a bulleted list of achievements and experience that demonstrate the skill, including specific numbers whenever possible. These skills categories should be placed at the beginning of the résumé, where they will be highlighted, followed by education and work experience. The action verbs shown in Figures 12.4 and 12.5 can also be used when constructing a functional résumé.

Awards, honours, and activities are appropriate for the résumé.

Awards, Honours, and Activities.

If you have three or more awards or honours, highlight them by listing them under a separate heading. If not, put them with Activities or in the Education or Work Experience section if appropriate. Include awards, scholarships (financial and other), fellowships, dean's list, and so on. Instead of saying *Recipient of King Scholarship*, give more details: *Recipient of King Scholarship given by Macdonald College to outstanding graduates who combine academic excellence and extracurricular activities*.

It is also appropriate to include school, community, volunteer, and professional activities. Employers are interested in evidence that you are a well-rounded person. This section provides an opportunity to demonstrate leadership and interpersonal skills. Strive to use action statements. For example, instead of saying *Treasurer of business club*, explain more fully: *Collected dues, kept financial records, and paid bills while serving as treasurer of 35-member business management club.*

Personal Data. Today's résumés omit personal data, such as birth date, marital status, height, weight, national origin, health, and religious affiliation. Such information doesn't relate to genuine occupational qualifications, and recruiters are legally barred from asking for such information. Some job seekers do, however, include hobbies or interests (such as skiing or photography) that might grab the recruiter's attention or serve as conversation starters. For example, let's say you learn that your hiring manager enjoys distance running. In that case you may want to mention that you have run a marathon if you share that interest. Many executives play tennis or golf, two sports highly suitable for networking. Naturally, you shouldn't mention time-consuming interests or dangerous pastimes (such as rock climbing, scuba diving, caving, bungee jumping, or motorcycle racing). You could also indicate your willingness to travel or to relocate, since many companies will be interested.

> **Omit personal data not related to job qualifications.**

References. Listing references directly on a résumé takes up valuable space. Moreover, references are not normally instrumental in securing an interview—few companies check them before the interview. Instead, recruiters prefer that you bring to the interview a list of individuals willing to discuss your qualifications. Therefore, you should prepare a separate list, such as that in Figure 12.6, when you begin your job search. Ask three to five instructors, your current employer or previous employers, colleagues or subordinates, and other professional contacts whether they would be willing to answer inquiries regarding your qualifications for employment. Be sure, however, to provide them with an opportunity to refuse. No reference at all is better than a negative one. Better yet, to avoid rejection and embarrassment, ask only those contacts who will give you a glowing endorsement.

> **References are unnecessary for the résumé, but they should be available for the interview.**

FIGURE 12.6 Sample Reference List

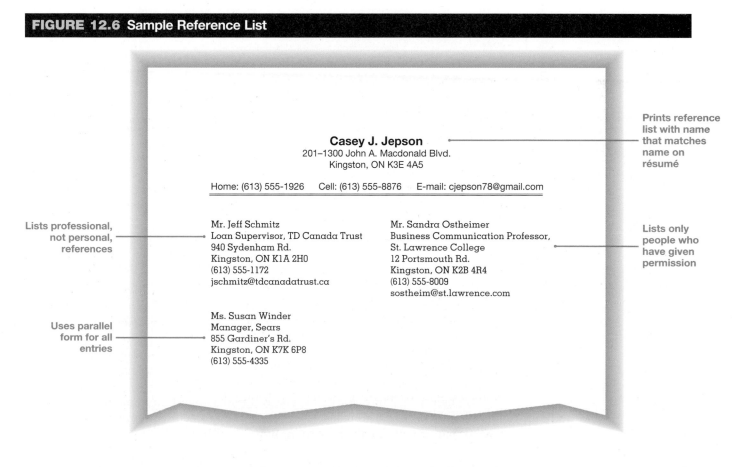

To highlight her skills and capabilities, Casey placed them in the summary of qualifications at the top of her résumé. She used the tables feature of her word processing program to create neat, invisible columns and to fit more information on one page, the length favoured by most recruiters.

Omits objective to keep all options open

Focuses on skills and aptitudes that employers seek

Uses present-tense verbs for current jobs

Arranges employment by job title for easy recognition

Combines activities and awards to show extracurricular involvement

Casey J. Jepson
201–1300 John A. Macdonald Blvd.
Kingston, ON K3E 4A5

Home: (613) 555-1926   Cell: (613) 555-8876   E-mail: cjepson78@gmail.com

SUMMARY OF QUALIFICATIONS
- Over three years' experience in administrative positions, working with business documents and interacting with customers
- Ability to keyboard (65 wpm) and use ten-key calculator (150 kpm)
- Proficient with Microsoft Word, Excel, Access, PowerPoint, FrontPage, and Publisher (passed MOS certification exam)
- Competent in Web research, written and oral communication, records management, desktop publishing, computer software troubleshooting, and proofreading and editing business documents
- Trained in QuickBooks, Flash, Photoshop, and Dreamweaver

EXPERIENCE

Administrative Assistant, Work Study
St. Lawrence College, Kingston, ON
September 2008–present
- Create letters, memos, reports, and forms in Microsoft Word
- Develop customized reports and labels using Microsoft Access
- Maintain departmental Microsoft Excel budget

Loan Support Specialist
TD Canada Trust, Kingston, ON
May 2006–September 2008
- Prepared loan documents for consumer, residential, mortgage, agricultural, and commercial loans
- Ensured compliance with federal, provincial, and bank regulations
- Originated correspondence (oral and written) with customers and insurance agencies
- Ordered and interpreted appraisals, titles, and credit reports
- Created and maintained paper and electronic files for customers

Customer Sales Representative
Sears, Kingston, ON winter seasons 2006–2008
- Answered phones and assisted customers with orders
- Resolved customers' merchandise questions and problems
- Entered catalogue orders into computer system

EDUCATION
St. Lawrence College, Kingston, ON
Major: Administrative Assistant with Help Desk certificate
AA degree expected May 2013. A average

ACTIVITIES AND AWARDS
- Placed first in provincial BPA Administrative Assistant competition
- Served as SLC Student Association Representative for Administrative Assistant program
- Nominated for SLC Ambassador Award (recognizes outstanding students for excellence in and out of classroom)

Do not include personal or character references, such as friends, family, or neighbours, because recruiters rarely consult them. Companies are more interested in the opinions of objective individuals who know how you perform professionally and academically. One final note: most recruiters see little reason for including the statement *References furnished upon request*. It is unnecessary and takes up precious space.

In Figures 12.7 through 12.11, you will find a collection of models for chronological and functional résumés. Use these models to help you organize the content and format of your own persuasive résumé.

Courtney Castro used a chronological résumé to highlight her work experience, most of which was related directly to the position she seeks. Although she is a recent graduate, she has accumulated experience in two part-time jobs and one full-time job. She included a summary of qualifications to highlight her skills, experience, and interpersonal traits aimed at a specific position. Notice that Courtney designed her résumé in two columns with five major categories listed in the left column. In the right column she included bulleted items for each of the five categories. Conciseness and parallelism are important in writing an effective résumé. In the Experience category, she started each item with an active verb, which improved readability and parallel form.

Courtney M. Castro

900 Commercial Dr., Apt 3, Vancouver, BC V6H 2H3

(604) 555-2328
cmcastro77@gmail.com

OBJECTIVE

Seeking position with financial services organization installing accounting software and providing user support, where computer experience and proven communication and interpersonal skills can be used to improve operations.

Includes detailed objective in response to advertisement

Provides a summary of qualifications to list most impressive qualifications

SUMMARY OF QUALIFICATIONS

- Over five years' experience in accounting field
- Extensive experience designing, installing, and providing technical support for accounting software, including ACCPAC, SAP, Great Plains, Peachtree, and Oracle
- Proficient in Word, Access, PowerPoint, Excel, and QuickBooks
- Skilled in technical writing, including proposals, user manuals, and documentation
- Experienced in office administration and management
- Fluent in spoken and written Spanish

Arranges jobs in reverse chronological order

EXPERIENCE

Accounting software consultant. West Coast Software, Burnaby, BC
June 2009 to present
- Design and install accounting systems for businesses such as Century 21 Butler Realty, Capital Financial Services, Pacific Lumber, and others
- Provide ongoing technical support and consultation for regular clients
- Help write proposals such as successful $400,000 government contract

Uses present-tense verbs for current job and past-tense verbs for previous jobs

Uses bulleted lists to make résumé easier to read

Office manager (part-time). Coastal Productions, Vancouver, BC
June 2009 to May 2009
- Conceived and implemented improved order processing and filing system
- Designed and integrated module code pieces to export and convert data from an in-house SQL database to QuickBooks format for automated cheque printing and invoice billing
- Trained three employees to operate QuickBooks software

Specifies relevant activities for targeted position

Shows job titles in bold for readability

Bookkeeper (part-time). Home Roofing, Vancouver, BC
August 2006 to May 2009
- Kept books for roofing and repair company with $240,000 gross income
- Performed all bookkeeping tasks including quarterly internal audit and payroll

EDUCATION

Simon Fraser University, Burnaby, BC
Bachelor Business Administration, June 2013
B⁺ average

Oracle University — currently enrolled in database training seminars leading to Oracle certification

Provides white space around headings to create open look

HONOURS AND ACTIVITIES

- Dean's list, three semesters
- Captain of Simon Fraser's Students in Free Enterprise (SIFE) team

Eric used MS Word to design a traditional chronological print-based résumé that he plans to give to recruiters at the campus job fair or during an interview. Although Eric has work experience not related to his future employment, his résumé looks impressive because he has transferable skills. His internship is related to his future career, and his language skills and study abroad experience will help him score points in competition with applicants. Eric's volunteer experience is also attractive because it shows him as a well-rounded, compassionate individual. Because his experience in his future field is limited, he omitted a summary of qualifications.

Eric Chien
800 ave. Kingston, Montreal, QC H2L 8V9
Home: (514) 555-4811
E-mail: echien79@mcgill.ca

Places education and relevant courses first for emphasis

OBJECTIVE	Seeking a position in public relations or marketing that will possibly involve the use of languages and foreign travel
EDUCATION	*Bachelor of Commerce*, May 2013 Major: Marketing, McGill University, Desautels Faculty of Management Montreal, QC **Study Abroad:** Paris, France Fall 2010
RELATED COURSEWORK	Principles of Marketing Introduction to Macro Economics Business Communication French Conversation Advanced Introduction to Public Relations Organizational Behaviour
PROFESSIONAL EXPERIENCE	**Restaurant Toque, Montreal,** QC Spring 2009–present *Head Waiter (nights and weekends)* • Deliver friendly and professional bilingual customer service • Train and supervise 16 food servers • Handle large amounts of cash and credit card transactions ($20,000 daily); perform accounting duties at the end of shift **Collins Barrow, Montreal,** QC, Fall 2008 *General Office Assistant (part-time)* • Expedited mail, answered phones; provided secretarial support • Filed documents and entered data into computer
INTERNSHIP EXPERIENCE	**Hotel Le Germain, Montreal,** QC Spring 2008 • Conducted research for potential campaigns • Interacted with guests and business partners • Wrote restaurant reviews and other press kit items
HONOURS AND AWARDS	**Breast Cancer Action Montreal,** October 2007–October 2009 • Volunteered at foundation for breast cancer research • Organized local 5K Run for the Cure • Was named "Volunteer of the Month" in Spring 2008
LANGUAGES	Mandarin (understand and speak); French (speak, read, and write)
PROFESSIONAL MEMBERSHIPS	Association des professionnels de la communication et du marketing (Member) The Canadian Public Relations Society, Inc. (Member)
ACTIVITIES	Enjoy watching films, reading, running, and travel

Quantifies responsibilities in numbers and dollar amount

Shows leadership qualities and well-rounded personality

Because Rachel has many years of experience and seeks executive-level employment, she highlighted her experience by placing it before her education. Her summary of qualifications highlighted her most impressive experience and skills. This chronological two-page résumé shows the steady progression of her career to executive positions, a movement that impresses and reassures recruiters.

RACHEL M. CHOWDHRY
85 New Bedford Rd.   rchowdhry@eastlink.ca
Halifax, NS B2T 4T2   (902)555-9887

OBJECTIVE   Senior Financial Management Position

SUMMARY OF
QUALIFICATIONS
- Over 12 years' comprehensive experience in the accounting industry, including over 8 years as a controller
- Chartered Accountant (CA)
- Demonstrated ability to handle all accounting functions for large, midsize, and small firms
- Ability to isolate problems, reduce expenses, and improve the bottom line, resulting in substantial cost savings
- Proven talent for interacting professionally with individuals at all levels, as demonstrated by performance review comments
- Experienced in P&L, audits, taxation, internal control, inventory management, A/P, A/R, and cash management

Lists most impressive credentials first

PROFESSIONAL
HISTORY AND
ACHIEVEMENT

11/08 to present CONTROLLER
United Plastics, Inc., Dartmouth, NS (extruder of polyethylene film for plastic aprons and gloves)
- Direct all facets of accounting and cash management for 160-employee, $3 billion business
- Supervise inventory and production data processing operations and tax compliance
- Talked owner into reducing sales prices, resulting in doubling first quarter 2009 sales
- Created cost accounting by product and pricing based on gross margin
- Increased line of credit with 12 major suppliers

Use action verbs but includes many good nouns for possible computer scanning

Explains nature of employer's business because it is not immediately recognizable

1/06 to 10/08 CONTROLLER
Burgess Inc., Moncton, NB (major manufacturer of flashlight and lantern batteries)
- Managed all accounting, cash, payroll, credit, and collection operations for 175-employee business
- Implemented a new system for cost accounting, inventory control, and accounts payable, resulting in a $100,000 annual savings in computer operations
- Reduced staff from ten persons to five with no loss in productivity
- Successfully reduced inventory levels from $1.1 million to $600,000
- Helped develop new cash management system that significantly increased cash flow

Emphasizes steady employment history by listing dates FIRST

Describes and quantifies specific achievements

8/04 to 11/05 TREASURER/CONTROLLER
Kingston Developers, Halifax, NS (manufacturer of modular housing)
- Supervised accounts receivable/payable, cash management, payroll, insurance
- Directed monthly and year-end closings, banking relations, and product costing
- Refinanced company with long-term loan, ensuring continued operational stability
- Successfully lowered company's insurance premiums by 7 percent

Rachel M. Chowdhry   Page 2

4/00 to 6/04 SUPERVISOR OF GENERAL ACCOUNTING
Levin National Batteries, Dartmouth, NS (local manufacturer of flashlight batteries)
- Completed monthly and year-end closing of ledgers for $2 million business
- Audited freight bills, acted as interdepartmental liaison, prepared financial reports

ADDITIONAL
INFORMATION
Education: Bachelor of Commerce, Dalhousie University, major: Accounting, 1999
Certification: Chartered Accountant (CA), 2000
Personal: Will travel and/or relocate

De-emphasizes education because work history is more important for mature candidates

Recent graduate Kevin Touhy chose this functional format to de-emphasize his meagre work experience and emphasize his potential in sales and marketing. This version of his résumé is more generic than one targeted for a specific position. Nevertheless, it emphasizes his strong points with specific achievements and includes an employment section to satisfy recruiters. The functional format presents ability-focused topics. It illustrates what the job seeker can do for the employer instead of narrating a history of previous jobs. Although recruiters prefer chronological résumés, the functional format is a good choice for new graduates, career changers, and those with employment gaps.

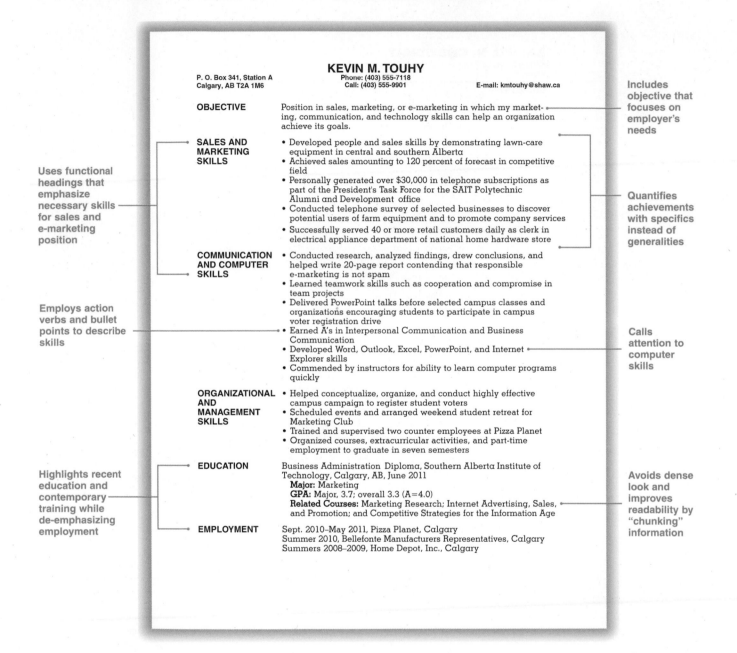

KEVIN M. TOUHY

P. O. Box 341, Station A
Calgary, AB T2A 1M6

Phone: (403) 555-7118
Call: (403) 555-9901

E-mail: kmtouhy@shaw.ca

Includes objective that focuses on employer's needs

OBJECTIVE
Position in sales, marketing, or e-marketing in which my marketing, communication, and technology skills can help an organization achieve its goals.

Uses functional headings that emphasize necessary skills for sales and e-marketing position

SALES AND MARKETING SKILLS
- Developed people and sales skills by demonstrating lawn-care equipment in central and southern Alberta
- Achieved sales amounting to 120 percent of forecast in competitive field
- Personally generated over $30,000 in telephone subscriptions as part of the President's Task Force for the SAIT Polytechnic Alumni and Development office
- Conducted telephone survey of selected businesses to discover potential users of farm equipment and to promote company services
- Successfully served 40 or more retail customers daily as clerk in electrical appliance department of national home hardware store

Quantifies achievements with specifics instead of generalities

COMMUNICATION AND COMPUTER SKILLS
- Conducted research, analyzed findings, drew conclusions, and helped write 20-page report contending that responsible e-marketing is not spam
- Learned teamwork skills such as cooperation and compromise in team projects
- Delivered PowerPoint talks before selected campus classes and organizations encouraging students to participate in campus voter registration drive
- Earned A's in Interpersonal Communication and Business Communication
- Developed Word, Outlook, Excel, PowerPoint, and Internet Explorer skills
- Commended by instructors for ability to learn computer programs quickly

Employs action verbs and bullet points to describe skills

Calls attention to computer skills

ORGANIZATIONAL AND MANAGEMENT SKILLS
- Helped conceptualize, organize, and conduct highly effective campus campaign to register student voters
- Scheduled events and arranged weekend student retreat for Marketing Club
- Trained and supervised two counter employees at Pizza Planet
- Organized courses, extracurricular activities, and part-time employment to graduate in seven semesters

EDUCATION
Business Administration Diploma, Southern Alberta Institute of Technology, Calgary, AB, June 2011
Major: Marketing
GPA: Major, 3.7; overall 3.3 (A=4.0)
Related Courses: Marketing Research; Internet Advertising, Sales, and Promotion; and Competitive Strategies for the Information Age

Highlights recent education and contemporary training while de-emphasizing employment

Avoids dense look and improves readability by "chunking" information

EMPLOYMENT
Sept. 2010–May 2011, Pizza Planet, Calgary
Summer 2010, Bellefonte Manufacturers Representatives, Calgary
Summers 2008–2009, Home Depot, Inc., Calgary

Optimizing Your Résumé for Today's Technologies

Thus far we have aimed our résumé advice at human readers. However, the first reader of your résumé may well be a computer. Hiring organizations today use a variety of methods to process incoming résumés. Some organizations still welcome traditional print-based résumés that may include attractive formatting. Larger organizations, however, must deal with thousands of incoming résumés. Increasingly, they are placing those résumés directly into searchable databases. So that you can optimize your chances, you may need three versions of your résumé: (1) a traditional print-based résumé, (2) a scannable résumé, and (3) a plain-text résumé for e-mailing or online posting. This does not mean that you have to write different résumés. You are merely preparing different versions of your traditional résumé. With all versions, you should also be aware of the significant role of résumé keywords. Finally, you may decide to create an e-portfolio to showcase your qualifications.

Because résumés are increasingly becoming part of searchable databases, you may need three versions.

Designing a Print-Based Résumé

Print-based résumés (also called *presentation résumés*) are attractively formatted to maximize readability. You can create a professional-looking résumé by using your word processing program to highlight your qualifications. The examples in this chapter provide ideas for simple layouts that are easily duplicated. You can also examine résumé templates for design and format ideas. Their inflexibility, however, leads to frustration as you try to force your skills and experience into a predetermined template sequence. What's more, recruiters who read hundreds of résumés can usually spot a template-based résumé. Instead, create your own original résumé that fits your unique qualifications.

Your print-based résumé should use an outline format with headings and bullet points to present information in an orderly, uncluttered, easy-to-read format. An attractive print-based résumé is necessary (a) when you are competing for a job that does not require electronic submission, (b) to present in addition to an electronic submission, and (c) to bring with you to job interviews. Even if a résumé is submitted electronically, nearly every job candidate will want to have an attractive traditional résumé handy for human readers.

Preparing a Scannable Résumé

A scannable résumé is one that is meant to be printed on plain white paper and read by a computer. To screen incoming résumés, many midsize and large companies use automated applicant-tracking software. These systems scan an incoming résumé with optical character recognition (OCR), looking for keywords. The most sophisticated programs enable recruiters and hiring managers to search for keywords, rank résumés based on the number of "hits," and generate reports. Information from your résumé is stored, usually from six months to a year.

Increasing use of scanners requires job candidates to prepare computer-friendly résumés.

Before sending your résumé, find out whether the recipient uses scanning software. If you can't tell from the job announcement, call the company to ask whether it scans résumés electronically. If you don't get a clear answer and you have even the slightest suspicion that your résumé might be read electronically, you will be smart to prepare a plain, scannable version as shown in Figure 12.12.

Applicant-tracking software scans incoming résumés searching for keywords.

Tips for Maximizing Scannability. A scannable résumé must sacrifice many of the graphic enhancements you might have used to make your traditional print résumé attractive. To maximize scannability, follow these steps:

- **Use 10- to 14-point type.** Because touching letters or unusual fonts are likely to be misread, using a large, well-known font such as 12-point Times New Roman or Arial is safest. This may mean that your résumé will require two pages. After printing, inspect your résumé to see whether any letters touch—especially in your name.

Scannable résumés use plain formatting, large fonts, quality printing, and white space.

FIGURE 12.12 Scannable Résumé

Letitia P. Lopez prepared this "plain Jane" résumé free of graphics and fancy formatting so that it would scan well if read by a computer. With the résumé, she included many job titles, skills, traits, and other descriptive keywords that scanners are programmed to recognize. To improve accurate scanning, she avoided bullets, italics, underlining, and columns. If she had more information to include, she could have gone to a second page because a résumé to be scanned need not be restricted to one page.

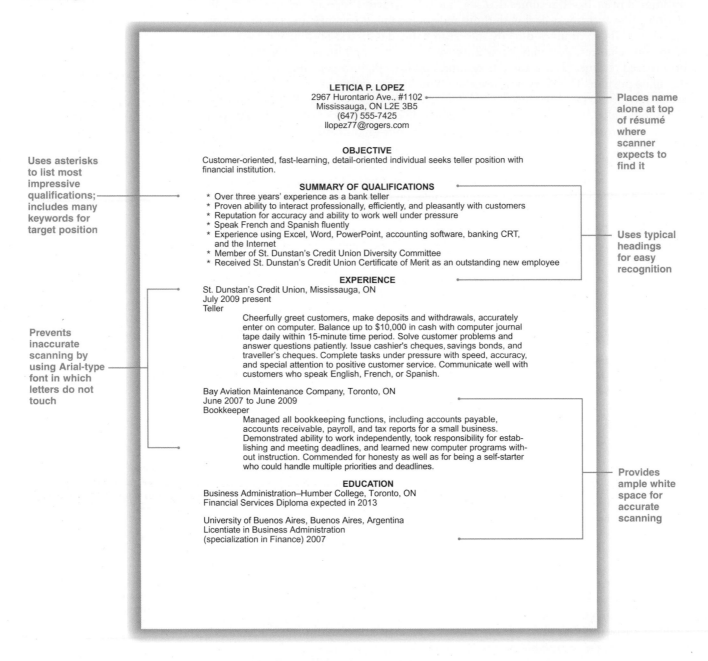

LETICIA P. LOPEZ
2967 Hurontario Ave., #1102
Mississauga, ON L2E 3B5
(647) 555-7425
llopez77@rogers.com

OBJECTIVE

Customer-oriented, fast-learning, detail-oriented individual seeks teller position with financial institution.

SUMMARY OF QUALIFICATIONS

* Over three years' experience as a bank teller
* Proven ability to interact professionally, efficiently, and pleasantly with customers
* Reputation for accuracy and ability to work well under pressure
* Speak French and Spanish fluently
* Experience using Excel, Word, PowerPoint, accounting software, banking CRT, and the Internet
* Member of St. Dunstan's Credit Union Diversity Committee
* Received St. Dunstan's Credit Union Certificate of Merit as an outstanding new employee

EXPERIENCE

St. Dunstan's Credit Union, Mississauga, ON
July 2009 present
Teller

Cheerfully greet customers, make deposits and withdrawals, accurately enter on computer. Balance up to $10,000 in cash with computer journal tape daily within 15-minute time period. Solve customer problems and answer questions patiently. Issue cashier's cheques, savings bonds, and traveller's cheques. Complete tasks under pressure with speed, accuracy, and special attention to positive customer service. Communicate well with customers who speak English, French, or Spanish.

Bay Aviation Maintenance Company, Toronto, ON
June 2007 to June 2009
Bookkeeper

Managed all bookkeeping functions, including accounts payable, accounts receivable, payroll, and tax reports for a small business. Demonstrated ability to work independently, took responsibility for establishing and meeting deadlines, and learned new computer programs without instruction. Commended for honesty as well as for being a self-starter who could handle multiple priorities and deadlines.

EDUCATION

Business Administration–Humber College, Toronto, ON
Financial Services Diploma expected in 2013

University of Buenos Aires, Buenos Aires, Argentina
Licentiate in Business Administration
(specialization in Finance) 2007

Places name alone at top of résumé where scanner expects to find it

Uses asterisks to list most impressive qualifications; includes many keywords for target position

Uses typical headings for easy recognition

Prevents inaccurate scanning by using Arial-type font in which letters do not touch

Provides ample white space for accurate scanning

- **Avoid unusual typefaces, underlining, and italics.** Moreover, don't use borders, shading, or other graphics to highlight text. These features don't scan well. Most applicant-tracking programs, however, can accurately read bold print, solid bullets, and asterisks.
- **Be sure that your name is the first line on the page.** Don't use fancy layouts that may confuse a scanner. Reports generated by applicant-tracking software usually assume that the first line of a résumé contains the applicant's name.
- **List each phone number on its own line.** Your landline and cell phone numbers should appear on separate lines to improve recognition.

- **Provide white space.** To ensure separation of words and categories, leave plenty of white space. For example, instead of using parentheses to enclose a telephone area code, insert blank spaces, such as 416 555-2415. Leave blank lines around headings.
- **Avoid double columns.** When listing job duties, skills, computer programs, and so forth, don't tabulate items into two- or three-column lists. Scanners read across and may convert tables into nonsensical output.
- **Use smooth white paper, black ink, and quality printing.** Avoid coloured or textured paper, and use a high-quality laser or ink-jet printer.
- **Don't fold or staple your résumé.** Send it in a large envelope so that you can avoid folds. Words that appear on folds may not be scanned correctly.

Tips for Maximizing "Hits." In addition to paying attention to the physical appearance of your résumé, you must also be concerned with keywords that produce "hits" or recognition by the scanner. To maximize hits, do the following:

Scanners produce "hits" when they recognize targeted keywords such as nouns describing skills, traits, tasks, and job titles.

- **Focus on specific keywords.** Study carefully any advertisements and job descriptions for the position you want. Select keywords that describe skills, traits, tasks, and job titles. Because interpersonal traits are often requested by employers, consult Figure 12.13. It shows the most frequently requested interpersonal traits, as reported by Resumix, a pioneer in résumé-scanning software.
- **Incorporate words from the advertisement or job description.** Describe your experience, education, and qualifications in terms associated with the job advertisement or job description for this position.
- **Use typical headings.** Include expected categories such as *Objective*, *Summary of Qualifications*, *Education*, *Work Experience*, *Skills*, and *Accomplishments*. Scanning software looks for such headings.
- **Be careful of abbreviations.** Minimize unfamiliar abbreviations, but maximize easily recognized abbreviations—especially those within your field, such as CAD, JPG, or JIT. When in doubt, though, spell out! Computers are less confused by whole words.
- **Describe interpersonal traits and attitudes.** Hiring managers look for keywords and phrases such as *time management skills*, *dependability*, *high energy*, *leadership*, *sense of responsibility*, and *team player*.
- **Use more than one page if necessary.** Computers can easily handle more than one page so include as much as necessary to describe your qualifications and maximize hits.

FIGURE 12.13 Interpersonal Keywords Most Requested by Employers Using Résumé-Scanning Software*

Ability to delegate	Creative	Leadership	Self-accountable
Ability to implement	Customer oriented	Multitasking	Self-managing
Ability to plan	Detail minded	Open communication	Setting priorities
Ability to train	Ethical	Open minded	Supportive
Accurate	Flexible	Oral communication	Takes initiative
Adaptable	Follow instructions	Organizational skills	Team building
Aggressive work	Follow through	Persuasive	Team player
Analytical ability	Follow up	Problem solving	Tenacious
Assertive	High energy	Public speaking	Willing to travel
Communication skills	Industrious	Results oriented	
Competitive	Innovative	Safety conscious	

*Reported by Resumix, a leading producer of résumé-scanning software.

Preparing a Plain-Text Résumé for E-Mailing

A plain-text résumé (also called an ASCII résumé) is an electronic version suitable for e-mailing or pasting into online résumé bank submission forms. Employers prefer plain-text résumés because they avoid possible e-mail viruses and word processing incompatibilities. Usually embedded within an e-mail message, a plain-text résumé (an example is shown in Figure 12.14) is immediately searchable. You should prepare a plain-text résumé if you want the fastest and most reliable way to contact potential employers. Follow these suggestions to create a plain-text résumé:

- **Observe all the tips for a scannable résumé.** A plain-text résumé requires the same attention to content, formatting, and keywords as that recommended for a scannable résumé.
- **Reformat with shorter lines.** Many e-mail programs wrap lines longer than 60 characters. To avoid having your résumé look as if a chain saw attacked it, use a short line length (such as 4 inches).

FIGURE 12.14 Plain-Text Résumé

To be sure her plain-text résumé would transmit well when within an e-mail message, Leticia prepared a special version with all lines starting at the left margin. She used a 4-inch line length to avoid awkward line breaks. To set off her major headings, she used the tilde character on her keyboard. She saved the document as a text file (.txt or .rtf) so that it could be read by different computers. At the end, she included a statement saying that an attractive, fully formatted hard copy of her résumé was available on request.

Starts all lines at left margin

```
LETICIA P. LOPEZ
2967 Hurontario Ave., #1102
Mississauga, ON L2E 3B5
Phone: (647) 555-7425
E-mail: llopez77@rogers.com

~~~~~~~~
OBJECTIVE
~~~~~~~~

Customer-oriented, fast-learning, detail-oriented individual
seeks teller position with financial institution.

~~~~~~~~
SUMMARY OF QUALIFICATIONS
~~~~~~~~

   * Over three years' experience as a bank teller
   * Proven ability to interact professionally, efficiently, and
     pleasantly with customers
   * Reputation for accuracy and ability to work well under
     pressure
   * Speak French and Spanish fluently
   * Experience using Excel, Word, PowerPoint, accounting
     software, banking CRT, and the Internet
   * Member of St. Dunstan's Credit Union Diversity Committee
   * Received St. Dunstan's Credit Union Certificate of Merit as an
     outstanding new employee

~~~~~~~~
EXPERIENCE
~~~~~~~~

St. Dunstan's Credit Union, Mississauga, ON
July 2009 present
Teller
   * Cheerfully greet customers, make deposits and withdrawals
   * Balance up to $10,000 in cash with computer journal tape
     daily within 15-minute time period
   * Solve customer problems and answer questions patiently
   * Issue cashier's cheques, savings bonds, and traveller's cheques
   * Complete tasks under pressure with speed, accuracy, and
     attention to positive customer service
   * Communicate well with customers speaking English, French, or Spanish
```

Sets off headings with the tilde (~) but could have omitted this attempt to improve readability

Uses asterisks instead of bullets, which may not scan well

Shortens lines to avoid awkward line wrap

Creates large empty space that is unavoidable in this format

- **Think about using keyboard characters to enhance format.** In addition to using capital letters and asterisks, you might use spaced equals signs (= = =) and tildes (~ ~ ~) to create lines that separate résumé categories.
- **Move all text to the left.** Do not centre items; start all text at the left margin. Remove tabs.
- **Save your résumé in plain text (.txt) or rich text format (.rtf).** Saving your résumé in one of these formats will ensure that it can be read when pasted in an e-mail message.
- **Test your résumé before sending it to an employer.** After preparing and saving your résumé, copy and paste a copy of it into an e-mail message, send it to yourself, and check to see whether any non-ASCII characters appear. They may show up as question marks, square blocks, or other odd characters. Make any necessary changes.

When sending a plain-text résumé to an employer, be sure that your subject line clearly describes the purpose of your message. In addition, use the professional e-mail techniques you learned in Chapter 4.

Showcasing Your Qualifications in an E-Portfolio

As the workplace becomes increasingly digital, you have yet another way to display your qualifications to prospective employers—the e-portfolio. Resourceful job candidates in certain fields—writers, models, artists, and graphic artists—have been creating print portfolios to illustrate their qualifications and achievements for some time. Now business and professional job candidates in the technology industry in particular are using electronic portfolios to show off their talents.

An e-portfolio is a collection of digital files that can be navigated with the help of menus, much like a personal Web site. It provides viewers with a snapshot of a candidate's performance, talents, and accomplishments. A digital portfolio may include a copy of your résumé, reference letters, special achievements, awards, certificates, work samples, a complete list of your courses, thank-you letters, and anything else that touts your accomplishments. An advanced portfolio might include links to electronic copies of your artwork, film projects, blueprints, and photographs of classwork that might otherwise be difficult to share with potential employers.

Digital portfolios are generally accessed on Web sites, where they are available around the clock to employers. Some colleges and universities not only make Web site space available for student e-portfolios but also provide instruction and resources for scanning photos, digitizing images, and preparing graphics. E-portfolios may also be burned onto CDs and DVDs that you can mail to prospective employers.

E-portfolios have many advantages. On Web sites they can be viewed at employers' convenience. Let's say you are talking on the phone with an employer in another city who wants to see a copy of your résumé. You can simply refer the employer to the Web address where your résumé is posted. E-portfolios can also be seen by many individuals in an organization without circulating a paper copy. But the real reason for preparing an e-portfolio is that it shows off your talents and qualifications more thoroughly than a print résumé does.

Tech-savvy applicants even use videos to profile their skills. A professional-grade video résumé may open doors and secure an interview when other techniques have failed.[24] However, some recruiters are skeptical about digital or video portfolios because they fear that such applications will take more time to view than paper-based résumés do. Non-traditional applications may end up at the bottom of the pile or be ignored. Worse yet, lack of judgment can lead to embarrassment. Aleksey Vayner's video résumé somehow ended up on YouTube in late 2006, causing him to be widely ridiculed. The Yale University student and budding investment banker created a six-minute video titled "Impossible Is Nothing," showing him lifting weights, ballroom dancing, and playing tennis, all the while engaging in shameless puffery.[25]

Experts agree that the new medium will need to mature before smart use guidelines can be established. You can learn more about video résumés by searching the Web.

An e-portfolio offers links to examples of a job candidate's performance, talents, and accomplishments in digital form.

Job candidates generally offer e-portfolios at Web sites, but they may also burn them onto a CD or a DVD.

Applying the Final Touches to Your Résumé

Because your résumé is probably the most important message you will ever write, you will revise it many times. With so much information in concentrated form and with so much riding on its outcome, your résumé demands careful polishing, proofreading, and critiquing.

As you revise, be certain to verify all the facts, particularly those involving your previous employment and education. Don't be caught in a mistake, or worse, a distortion of previous jobs and dates of employment. These items likely will be checked, and the consequences of puffing up a résumé with deception or flat-out lies are simply not worth the risk.

Deception on a résumé, even if discovered much later, can result in firing.

Be Honest and Ethical

A résumé is expected to showcase a candidate's strengths and minimize weaknesses. For this reason, recruiters expect a certain degree of self-promotion. Some résumé writers, however, step over the line that separates honest self-marketing from deceptive half-truths and blatant lies. Distorting facts on a résumé is unethical; lying is illegal. Either practice can destroy a career.

Given the competitive job market, it might be tempting to puff up your résumé. What's more, you wouldn't be alone in telling fibs or outright whoppers. One study found that 44 percent of applicants lied about their work histories, 23 percent fabricated licences or credentials, and 41 percent falsified their educational backgrounds.[26] Another recent study revealed an even higher number of résumé cheats; over 50 percent of applicants lie.[27]

Although recruiters can't check everything, most will verify previous employment and education before hiring candidates. Over half will require official transcripts. InfoCheck, a Canadian résumé verification service, indicates that they do about 800 background checks a month for their corporate customers.

After hiring, the checking process may continue. If hiring officials find a discrepancy in grades or prior experience and the error is an honest mistake, they meet with the new-hire to hear an explanation. If the discrepancy wasn't a mistake, they will likely fire the person immediately. No job seeker wants to be in the unhappy position of explaining résumé errors or defending misrepresentation. Avoiding the following common problems can keep you off the hot seat:

- **Inflated education, grades, or honours.** Some job candidates claim degrees from colleges or universities when in fact they merely attended classes. Others increase their grade point averages or claim fictitious honours. Any such dishonest reporting is grounds for dismissal when discovered.
- **Enhanced job titles.** Wishing to elevate their status, some applicants misrepresent their titles. For example, one technician called himself a programmer when he had actually programmed only one project for his boss. A mail clerk who assumed added responsibilities conferred upon herself the title of supervisor. Even when the description seems accurate, it is unethical to list any title not officially granted.
- **Puffed-up accomplishments.** Some job seekers inflate their employment experience or achievements. One clerk, eager to make her photocopying duties sound more important, said that she assisted the *vice president in communicating and distributing employee directives*. A university graduate who spent the better part of six months watching rented movies on his DVD player described the activity as *Independent Film Study*. That statement may have helped win an interview, but it lost him the job. In addition to avoiding puffery, guard against taking sole credit for achievements that required the efforts of many people. When recruiters suspect dubious claims on résumés, they nail applicants with specific—and often embarrassing—questions during their interviews.
- **Altered employment dates.** Some candidates extend the dates of employment to hide unimpressive jobs or to cover up periods of unemployment and illness. Let's say that several years ago Cindy was unemployed for 14 months between working for Company A and being hired by Company B. To make her employment history

Despite the temptation to fudge the facts a little when applying for a job, it doesn't pay to pad one's résumé. Celebrity chef Robert Irvine, who rose to fame by preparing meals on the Food Network's *Dinner: Impossible* program, lost his spot when executives discovered the TV chef had cooked up far more than sumptuous soufflés and dynamite desserts. Numerous qualifications listed on Irvine's résumé—such as the claim to have cooked for U.S. presidents and Britain's royal family—proved greatly exaggerated or untrue. *What common pitfalls should job seekers avoid when preparing résumés?*

look better, she adds seven months to her tenure with Company A and seven months to Company B. Now her employment history has no gaps, but her résumé is dishonest and represents a potential booby trap for her.

- **Hidden keywords.** One of the latest sneaky tricks involves inserting invisible keywords in electronic résumés. To fool scanning programs into ranking their résumés higher, some job hunters use white type on a white background or they use Web coding to pack their résumés with target keywords. However, newer recruiter search tools detect such mischief, and those résumés are tossed.[28]

If your honest qualifications aren't good enough to get you the job you want, start working now to improve them.

Polishing Your Résumé

While you continue revising, look for other ways to improve your résumé. For example, consider consolidating headings. By condensing your information into as few headings as possible, you will produce a clean, professional-looking document. Study other résumés for valuable formatting ideas. Ask yourself what graphic highlighting techniques you can use to improve readability: capitalization, underlining, indenting, and bulleting. Experiment with headings and styles to achieve a pleasing, easy-to-read message. Moreover, look for ways to eliminate wordiness. For example, instead of *Supervised two employees who worked at the counter*, try *Supervised two counter employees*. Review Chapter 3 for more tips on writing concisely.

In addition to making your résumé concise, make sure that you haven't included any of the following information, which doesn't belong on a résumé:

- Any basis for discrimination (age, marital status, gender, national origin, religion, race, number of children, disability)
- A photograph
- Reasons for leaving previous jobs
- The word *résumé*
- Social insurance number
- Salary history or requirements
- High-school information
- References
- Full addresses of schools or employers (include city and province only)

> Study résumé models for ideas on improving your format.

> **OFFICE INSIDER**
>
> *It sounds basic, but make sure that your résumé is free of typos and other errors. When applying by e-mail, there is more of a tendency to rush and make careless mistakes. For many employers, this shows a lack of attention to detail and is an easy way to eliminate someone from consideration.*

Above all, make sure your print-based résumé look professional. Avoid anything humorous or "cute," such as a help-wanted poster with your name or picture inside. Eliminate the personal pronoun *I* to ensure an objective style. Use high-quality paper in a professional colour, such as white, off-white, or light gray. Print your résumé using a first-rate laser or ink-jet printer. Be prepared with a résumé for people to read as well as one for a computer to read.

Proofreading Your Résumé

After revising, you must proofread, proofread, and proofread again for spelling, mechanics, content, and format. Then have a knowledgeable friend or relative proofread it yet again. This is one document that must be perfect. Because the job market is so competitive, one typo, misspelled word, or grammatical error could eliminate you from consideration.

By now you may be thinking that you'd like to hire someone to write your résumé. Don't! First, you know yourself better than anyone else could know you. Second, you will end up with a generic or a one-time résumé. A generic résumé in today's highly competitive job market will lose out to a customized résumé nine times out of ten. Equally useless is a one-time résumé aimed at a single job. What if you don't get that job? Because you will need to revise your résumé many times as you seek a variety of jobs, be prepared to write (and rewrite) it yourself.

Submitting Your Résumé

If you are responding to a job advertisement, be sure to read the job listing carefully to make sure you know how the employer wants you to submit your résumé. Not following the prospective employer's instructions can eliminate you from consideration before your résumé is even reviewed. Employers will probably ask you to submit your résumé in one of the following ways:

- **Word document.** Recruiters may still ask candidates to send their résumés and cover letters by snail mail. They may also allow applicants to attach their résumés as MS Word documents to e-mail messages, despite the fear of viruses.
- **Plain-text, ASCII document.** As discussed earlier, some employers expect applicants to submit résumés and cover letters as plain-text documents. This format is widely used for posting to an online job board or for e-mail delivery. Plain-text résumés may be embedded within or attached to e-mail messages.
- **PDF document.** For the sake of safety, many hiring managers prefer PDF (portable document format) files. A PDF résumé will look exactly like the original and cannot be easily altered. Newer computers come with Adobe Acrobat Reader pre-installed for easy reading. Converting your MS Word and other documents to a PDF file requires Adobe Acrobat or similar software.
- **Company database.** Some organizations prefer that you complete an online form with your résumé information. This enables them to plug your data into their formats for rapid searching. You might be able to cut and paste your information into the form.
- **Fax.** Although still a popular way of sending résumés, faxing presents problems in blurring and lost information. If you must fax your résumé, use at least a 12-point font to improve readability. Thinner fonts—such as Times, Palatino, New Century Schoolbook, Arial, and Bookman—are clearer than thicker ones. Avoid underlines, which may look broken or choppy when faxed. Follow up with your polished, printed résumé.

Whether you are mailing your résumé the traditional way, submitting it by e-mail, or transmitting it by fax, don't send it on its own. Regardless of the submission format, in most cases a résumé should be accompanied by a cover letter, which will be discussed in the next section.

The Persuasive Cover Letter

To accompany your résumé, you'll need a persuasive cover letter. The cover letter has three purposes: (1) introducing the résumé, (2) highlighting ways your strengths will benefit the reader, and (3) obtaining an interview. In many ways your cover letter is a sales letter; it sells your talents and tries to beat the competition. It will, accordingly, include many of the techniques you learned for sales letters in Chapter 6.

Human resource professionals disagree on how long to make cover letters. Many prefer short letters with no more than four paragraphs; instead of concentrating on the letter, these readers focus on the résumé. Others desire longer letters that supply more information, thus giving them a better opportunity to evaluate a candidate's qualifications and gauge his or her personality. They argue that hiring and training new employees is expensive and time consuming; extra data can guide them in making the best choice the first time. Use your judgment; if you feel, for example, that you need space to explain in more detail what you can do for a prospective employer, do so.

Regardless of its length, a cover letter should have three primary parts: (1) an opening that gets attention, (2) a body that builds interest and reduces resistance, and (3) a closing that motivates action.

Gaining Attention in the Opening

The first step in gaining the interest of your reader is addressing that individual by name. Rather than sending your letter to the "Human Resources Department," try to obtain the name of the appropriate individual. Make it a rule to call the organization for the correct spelling and the complete address. This personal touch distinguishes your letter and demonstrates your serious interest.

How you open your cover letter depends largely on whether your résumé is for a position that is solicited or unsolicited. If an employment position has been announced and applicants are being solicited, you can use a direct approach. If you do not know whether a position is open and you are prospecting for a job, use an indirect approach. Whether direct or indirect, the opening should attract the attention of the reader. Strive for openings that are more imaginative than *Please consider this letter an application for the position of . . .* or *I would like to apply for. . . .*

Openings for Solicited Jobs. Here are some of the best techniques to open a letter of application for a job that has been announced:

- **Refer to the name of an employee in the company.** Remember that employers always hope to hire known quantities rather than complete strangers:

  > Mitchell Sims, a member of your Customer Service Department, told me that DataTech is seeking an experienced customer service representative. The attached summary of my qualifications demonstrates my preparation for this position.

  > At the suggestion of Ms. Claudette Guertin of your Human Resources Department, I submit my qualifications for the position of personnel assistant.

- **Refer to the source of your information precisely.** If you are answering an advertisement, include the exact position advertised and the name and date of the publication. For large organizations it's also wise to mention the section of the newspaper where the ad appeared:

  > Your advertisement in the Careers section of the June 1 *Vancouver Sun* for a junior accountant (competition 10-003) greatly appeals to me. With my accounting training and computer experience, I believe I could serve the City of Richmond well.

  > The September 10 issue of the *National Post* reports that you are seeking a mature, organized, and reliable administrative assistant (competition 10-A54) with excellent communication skills.

Susan Butler, placement director at Carleton University, told me that Open Text Corporation has an opening for a technical writer with knowledge of Web design and graphics.

- **Refer to the job title and describe how your qualifications fit the requirements.** Human resources directors are looking for a match between an applicant's credentials and the job needs:

  Will an honours graduate with a degree in recreation studies and two years of part-time experience organizing social activities for a retirement community qualify for your position of activity director?

  Because of my specialized training in computerized accounting at Simon Fraser University, I feel confident that I have the qualifications you described in your advertisement for an accountant trainee.

Openings for unsolicited jobs show interest in and knowledge of the company, as well as spotlighting reader benefits.

Openings for Unsolicited Jobs. If you are unsure whether a position actually exists, you may wish to use a more persuasive opening. Since your goal is to convince this person to read on, try one of the following techniques:

- **Demonstrate interest in and knowledge of the reader's business.** Show the human resources director that you have done your research and that this organization is more than a mere name to you:

  Since the Canadian Automobile Association is organizing a new information management team for its recently established group insurance division, could you use the services of a well-trained information systems graduate who seeks to become a professional underwriter?

- **Show how your special talents and background will benefit the company.** Human resources directors need to be convinced that you can do something for them:

  Could your rapidly expanding publications division use the services of an editorial assistant who offers exceptional language skills, an honours degree from Brandon University, and two years' experience in producing a school literary publication?

In applying for an advertised job, Kendra Hawkins wrote the solicited cover letter shown in Figure 12.15 (p. 371). Notice that her opening identifies the position and the newspaper completely so that the reader knows exactly what advertisement Kendra refers to. Using features on her word processing program, Kendra designed her own letterhead that uses her name and looks like professionally printed letterhead paper.

More challenging are unsolicited letters of application, such as Donald Vinton's, shown in Figure 12.16 (p. 372). Because he hopes to discover or create a job, his opening must grab the reader's attention immediately. To do that, he capitalizes on company information appearing in the newspaper. Donald purposely kept his application letter short and to the point because he anticipated that a busy executive would be unwilling to read a long, detailed letter. Donald's unsolicited letter "prospects" for a job. Some job candidates feel that such letters may be even more productive than efforts to secure advertised jobs, since "prospecting" candidates face less competition. Notice that Donald's letter uses a standard return address format, placing his street, city, province, and postal code above the date.

Building Interest in the Body

The body of a cover letter should build interest, reduce resistance, and discuss relevant personal traits.

Once you have captured the attention of the reader, you can use the body of the letter to build interest and reduce resistance. Keep in mind that your résumé emphasizes what you have done; your cover letter stresses what you can do for the employer.

Spotlighting reader benefits means matching one's personal strengths to an employer's needs.

Your first goal is to relate your remarks to a specific position. If you are responding to an advertisement, you'll want to explain how your preparation and experience fill the stated requirements. If you are prospecting for a job, you may not know the exact

FIGURE 12.15 Solicited Cover Letter

Uses personally designed letterhead

Kendra A. Hawkins

1880 Bellamy Rd. Toronto, ON M1B 3B4
(416) 555-1289, khawkins@gmail.com

May 23, 2012

Ms. Courtney L. Donahue
Director, Human Resources
Del Rio Enterprises
4839 Brock Rd.
Pickering, ON L2B 3M5

Addresses proper person by name and title

Dear Ms. Donahue:

Identifies job and exact page where ad appeared

Your advertisement for an assistant product manager, appearing May 22 in Section C of the *Toronto Star*, immediately caught my attention because my education and training closely parallel your needs.

According to your advertisement, the job includes "assisting in the coordination of a wide range of marketing programs as well as analyzing sales results and tracking marketing budgets." A recent internship at Ventana Corporation introduced me to similar tasks. Assisting the marketing manager enabled me to analyze the promotion, budget, and overall sales success of two products Ventana was evaluating. My ten-page report examined the nature of the current market, the products' life cycles, and their sales/profit return. In addition to this research, I helped formulate a product merchandising plan and answered consumers' questions at a local trade show.

Relates her experiences to job requirements

Discusses education and experience as they relate to the position

Intensive course work in marketing and management, as well as proficiency in computer spreadsheets and databases, has given me the kind of marketing and computer training that Del Rio probably demands in a product manager. Moreover, my recent retail sales experience and participation in campus organizations have helped me develop the kind of customer service and interpersonal skills necessary for an effective product manager.

Asks for interview and repeats main qualifications

After you have examined the enclosed résumé for details of my qualifications, I would be happy to answer questions. Please call me at (905) 555-1289 to arrange an interview so that we may discuss how my marketing experience, computer training, and interpersonal skills could contribute to Del Rio Enterprises.

Refers reader to enclosed résumé

Sincerely,

Kendra A. Hawkins

Kendra A. Hawkins

Enclosure

requirements. Your employment research and knowledge of your field, however, should give you a reasonably good idea of what is expected for this position.

It's also important to emphasize reader benefits. In other words, you should describe your strong points in relation to the needs of the employer. In one employment survey many human resources professionals expressed the same view: "I want you to tell me what you can do for my organization. This is much more important to me than telling me what courses you took in college or what 'duties' you performed on your previous jobs."[29] Instead of *I have completed courses in business communication, report writing, and technical writing*, try this:

> Courses in business communication, report writing, and technical writing have helped me develop the research and writing skills required of your technical writers.

FIGURE 12.16 Unsolicited Cover Letter

Uses personal business style with return address above date	225 92 St. NW Edmonton, AB T4M 8A9 May 29, 2012

Mr. Richard M. Jannis
Vice President, Operations · — **Addresses proper person by name and title**
Sports World, Inc.
4907 Yellowhead Trail
Edmonton, AB T6G OAP

Dear Mr. Jannis:

Shows resourcefulness and knowledge of company — Today's *Edmonton Journal* reports that your organization plans to expand its operations to include national distribution of sporting goods, and it occurs to me that you will be needing highly motivated, self-starting sales representatives and marketing managers. Here are three significant qualifications I have to offer:

Uses bulleted list to make letter easier to read —

- Four years of formal training in business administration, including specialized courses in sales management, retailing, marketing promotion, and consumer behaviour

- Practical experience in demonstrating and selling consumer products, as well as successful experience in telemarketing — **Keeps letter brief to retain reader's attention**

- Excellent communication skills and a strong interest in most areas of sports (which helped me secure a volunteer position in the marketing department of the Edmonton Oilers organization)

Refers to enclosed résumé — May we talk about how I can put these qualifications, and others summarized in the enclosed résumé, to work for Sports World as it develops its national sales force? I'll call during the week of June 5 to discuss your company's expansion plans and the opportunity for an interview. — **Takes initiative for follow-up**

Sincerely yours,

Donald W. Vinton

Donald W. Vinton

Enclosure

Choose your strongest qualifications and show how they fit the targeted job. And remember, students with little experience are better off spotlighting their education and its practical applications, as these candidates did:

> Because you seek an architect's apprentice with proven ability, I submit a drawing of mine that won second place in the Algonquin College drafting contest last year.

> Successfully transcribing over 100 letters and memos in my college transcription class gave me experience in converting the spoken word into the written word, an exacting communication skill demanded of your legal assistants.

In the body of your letter, you'll also want to discuss relevant personal traits. Employers are looking for candidates who, among other things, are team players, take responsibility, show initiative, and learn easily. Finally, in this section or the next, you should refer the reader to your résumé. Do so directly or as part of another statement, as shown here:

> Please refer to the attached résumé for additional information regarding my education, experience, and references.

> As you will notice from my résumé, I will graduate in June with a bachelor's degree in business administration.

Action in the Closing

After presenting your case, you should conclude with a spur to action. This is where you ask for an interview. If you live in a distant city, you may request an employment application or an opportunity to be interviewed by the organization's nearest representative. However, never ask for the job. To do so would be presumptuous and naive. In requesting an interview, suggest reader benefits or review your strongest points. Sound sincere and appreciative. Remember to make it easy for the reader to agree by supplying your telephone number and the best times to call you. And keep in mind that some human resources directors prefer that you take the initiative to call them. Here are possible endings:

The closing of a cover letter should include a request for an interview.

> I hope this brief description of my qualifications and the additional information on my résumé indicate to you my genuine desire to put my skills in accounting to work for you. Please call me at (416) 488-2291 before 10 a.m. or after 3 p.m. to arrange an interview.

> To add to your staff an industrious, well-trained word processing specialist with proven communication skills, call me at (604) 492-1433 to arrange an interview. I can meet with you at any time convenient to your schedule.

> Next week, after you have examined the attached résumé, I will call you to discuss the possibility of arranging an interview.

Avoiding "I" Dominance

As you revise your application letter, notice how many sentences begin with *I*. Although it's impossible to talk about yourself without using *I*, you can reduce the number of sentences beginning with this pronoun by using two techniques. First, place *I* in the middle of sentences instead of dominating the opening. Instead of *I was the top salesperson in my department*, try *While working in X department, I did Y and Z*, or *among 15 coworkers, I received top ratings from my managers*. Incorporating *I* into the middle of sentences considerably reduces its domination.

Another technique for avoiding "I" dominance involves making activities and outcomes, and not yourself, the subjects of sentences. For example, rather than *I took classes in business communication and computer applications*, say *Classes in business communication and computer applications prepared me to....* Instead of *I enjoyed helping customers*, say *Helping customers taught me to be patient under stress*.

Sending Your Cover Letter by E-Mail or by Fax

More than 90 percent of résumés at Fortune 500 companies arrive by e-mail or are submitted through the corporate Web site.[30] Many applicants using technology make the mistake of not including cover letters with their résumés submitted by e-mail or by fax. A résumé that arrives without a cover letter makes the receiver wonder what it is and why it was sent. Recruiters want you to introduce yourself, and they also are eager to see some evidence that you can write. Some candidates either skip the cover letter or think they can get by with one-line cover letters such as this: *Please see attached résumé, and thanks for your consideration.*

If you are serious about landing the job, take the time to prepare a professional cover letter. If you are sending your résumé by e-mail, you may use the

Serious job candidates send a professional cover letter even if the résumé is submitted online, by e-mail, or by fax.

FIGURE 12.17 E-Mail Cover Letter

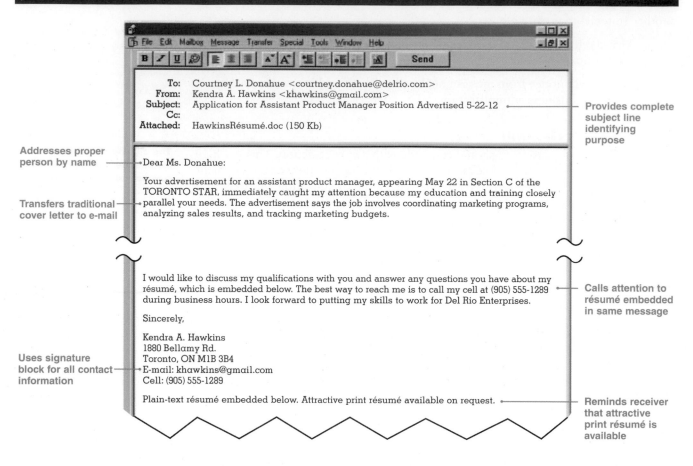

same cover letter you would send by snail mail but shorten it a bit. As illustrated in Figure 12.17, an inside address is unnecessary for an e-mail recipient. Also move your return address from the top of the letter to just below your name. Include your e-mail address and phone number. Remove tabs, bullets, underlining, and italics that might be problematic in e-mail messages. If you are submitting your résumé by fax, you can use the same cover letter you would send by Canada Post; just indicate the delivery method by writing BY FAX above the recipient's address.

Final Tips

Like the résumé, your cover letter must look professional and suggest quality. This means using a traditional letter style, such as block or modified block. Also, be sure to print it on the same bond paper as your résumé. More and more writers today are designing their own letterhead paper, or they adapt one of the templates available with their word processing programs. Be sure to use restraint, though, so that your letterhead looks truly professional, such as that shown in Figure 12.15. Finally, proofread your application letter several times; then, have a friend read it for content and mechanics.

> A cover letter should look professional and suggest quality.

Summing Up and Looking Forward

In today's competitive job market, an employment search begins with identifying your interests, evaluating your qualifications, and choosing a career path. Finding the perfect job will mean a concentrated effort devoted to checking online job boards and networking sites as well as traditional classified advertisements and networking. In applying for jobs, you'll want to submit a persuasive résumé that sells your skills and experience. Whether you choose a chronological or functional résumé style, you should tailor your assets to fit the position sought. If you think your résumé might be scanned, emphasize keywords and keep the format simple. A persuasive cover letter should introduce your résumé and describe how your skills and experiences match those required.

Now, if your résumé and cover letter have been successful, you'll proceed to the employment interview. For some people this is one of life's most stressful experiences, while for others it's an exhilarating experience. The last chapter in this book provides helpful suggestions for successful interviewing and follow-up communication.

Critical Thinking

1. How has the concept of the job changed, and how will it affect your employment search?

2. To what degree is social networking a replacement for the traditional job search?

3. How is a résumé different from a job application form?

4. Some job candidates think that applying for unsolicited jobs can be more fruitful than applying for advertised openings. Discuss the advantages and disadvantages of letters that "prospect" for jobs.

5. *Ethical Issue:* At work, fellow employee Karl lets it slip that he did not complete the degree he claims on his résumé. You have never liked Karl, but he does satisfactory work. You are both competing for the same promotion. You are considering writing an anonymous note to the boss telling him to verify Karl's degree. Use Google or your library database to research Canadian guidelines for whistle-blowing at work. Based on your research, do you think your plan is a good one?

6. A cover letter is a persuasive letter, but do you really want to reduce a potential employer's resistance? Why might this be dangerous?

Chapter Review

1. List at least five questions that you should ask yourself to identify your employment interests.

2. List some Web sites that are useful when looking for work.

3. How are most jobs likely to be found? Through the classified ads? Employment agencies? Networking? Explain.

4. What is the goal of your résumé?

5. What are the advantages and disadvantages of the two résumé types?

6. When does it make sense to include a career objective on your résumé?

7. In a chronological résumé, what information should you include for the jobs you list?

8. In addition to technical skills, what traits and characteristics do employers seek?

9. List some suggestions for making a résumé easily scannable by a computer.

10. What are keywords and why are they important in résumé scanning? Give examples.

11. When sending a cover letter within an e-mail, what changes have to be made to the format of the letter?

12. What are the three purposes of a cover letter?

13. How can you make it easy for a recruiter to reach you?

14. What is an e-portfolio, and why might it be useful?

1. **Cover Letter Opening.** James Nickson has just graduated from college with a three-year diploma in accounting. With the help of his college's career centre, James has begun applying for full-time employment. Below is the opening of one of James's cover letters. Analyze the letter, identify any problems, and rewrite this section of the letter following the guidelines in this chapter.

To whom it may concern,

It was a stroke of luck to find the job advertisement in the local newspaper last week for your company. I've always wanted to work for a company like yours, and this job opening may now give me the opportunity! My name is Jim Nickson and I just graduated in Accounting at a local college.

2. **Cover Letter Body.** Below is the body of James Nickson's cover letter. Analyze the letter, identify any problems, and rewrite this section of the letter following the guidelines in this chapter.

As you can see from my enclosed résumé, I am a strong student, and I am also a good team player. I think these skills would be useful to me in your company. For example, I took a course in Auditing in which I received the highest GPA in the program. Finally, I have worked as a bookkeeper for the past two summers.

3. **Cover Letter Closing.** The closing of James Nickson's cover letter is found below. Analyze the letter, identify any problems, and rewrite this section of the letter following the guidelines in this chapter.

In closing, permit me to be blunt and say that there's nothing I'd like more than the opportunity to work for your company. I know I would be an asset to your organization. I look forward to hearing from you at your earliest convenience.

Best,

Jim Nickson

Activities and Cases

12.1 Interests and Qualifications Inventory

It's often surprising what kind of information you can find out about your fellow classmates in a classroom setting. Imagine you are conducting a study for your college's co-op office or student association about future aspirations of students. The co-op office or student association wants to know the future career interests of the college's students as well as their current qualifications.

Your Task. Choose three people in your class (preferably classmates you don't know very well) and interview them. Ask them the questions listed on page 344 under "Identify Your Interests" and then the questions on page 344 under "Evaluate Your Qualifications." Develop a profile of each of your interviewees, and e-mail this profile to your instructor. Your instructor may choose to share the "inventory" with you in a later class. How might you use this inventory for future networking purposes?

12.2 Evaluating Your Qualifications

Prepare four worksheets that inventory your own qualifications in the areas of employment, education, capabilities and skills, and honours and activities. Use active verbs when appropriate.

a. *Employment.* Begin with your most recent job or internship. For each position list the following information: employer; job title; dates of employment; and three to five duties, activities, or accomplishments. Emphasize activities related to your job goal. Strive to quantify your achievements.

b. *Education.* List degrees, certificates, diplomas, and training accomplishments. Include courses, seminars, or skills that are relevant to your job goal. Calculate your grade point average in your major.

c. *Capabilities and skills.* List all capabilities and skills that recommend you for the job you seek. Use words such as *skilled*, *competent*, *trained*, *experienced*, and *ability to*. Also list five or more qualities or interpersonal skills necessary for a successful individual in your chosen field. Write action statements demonstrating that you possess some of these qualities. Empty assurances aren't good enough; try to show evidence (*Developed teamwork skills by working with a committee of eight to produce a ...*).

d. *Awards, honours, and activities.* Explain any awards so that the reader will understand them. List school, community, and professional activities that suggest you are a well-rounded individual or possess traits relevant to your target job.

12.3 Choosing a Career Path   WEB

Visit your school library, local library, or employment centre. Select an appropriate resource such as Human Resources and Skills Development Canada's National Occupational Classification (**http://www5.hrsdc.gc.ca/noc-CNP/app/index.aspx?lc=e**) to find a description for a position for which you could apply in two to five years. Photocopy or print the pages from the resource you chose that describe employment in the area in which you are interested. If your instructor directs, attach these copies to the cover letter you will write in Activity 12.10. Were you able to find the job that interests you? If not, where else can you find information on this job?

12.4 Searching the Job Market   WEB

Clip a job advertisement from the classified section of a newspaper or print one from a career site on the Web. Select an ad describing the kind of employment you are seeking now or plan to seek when you graduate. Save this advertisement to attach to the résumé you will write in Activity 12.9.

12.5 Résumé Research   WEB

By reading this chapter, you've learned about a number of different types of résumé. But what's reality like on the ground? Do employers care what the résumé looks like as long as it's well written? Or do they care a lot and have particular things they're looking for?

Your Task. Using the material from this chapter, develop a five- to ten-question survey about résumés. For example, do employers care what type of résumé applicants submit? What do employers look for in a résumé? What in a résumé turns them off a prospective candidate? Then identify three to five employers (people you know or who live in your area) and ask them to respond to your survey (this might be easier to do in person than over the phone or by e-mail). Present the results of your primary research in a short memo or e-mail or a presentation. Do your results corroborate or challenge what you learned in this chapter?

12.6 Posting a Résumé on the Web   WEB

Learn about the procedure for posting résumés at job boards on the Web.

Your Task. Prepare a list of at least three online employment sites where you could post your résumé. Describe the procedure involved and the advantages for each site.

12.7 Draft Document: Résumé

Analyze the following résumé. Discuss its strengths and weaknesses. Your instructor may ask you to revise sections of this résumé before showing you an improved version.

Winona Skudra
5349 Main Street
Saskatoon, SK S2N 0B4
Phone: (306) 834-4583 skudraw@lycos.ca.

Seeking to be hired at Meadow Products as an intern in Accounting

SKILLS: Accounting, Internet, MS Office 2007, Excel, PowerPoint, Freelance Graphics

EDUCATION

Now working on B.Comm. in Business Administration. Major, Management and Accounting; GPA is 3.5. Expect to graduate in June, 2014.

EXPERIENCE:

Assistant Accountant, 2007 to present. March and McLennan, Inc., Bookkeeping/Tax Service, Saskatoon. I keep accounting records for several small businesses accurately. I prepare 150 to 200 individual income tax returns each year. For Hill and Hill Trucking I maintain accurate and up-to-date A/R records. And I prepare payroll records for 16 employees at three firms.

Peterson Controls Inc., Saskatoon. Data Processing Internship, 2009 to present. I design and maintain spreadsheets and also process weekly and monthly information for production uptime and downtime. I prepare graphs to illustrate uptime and downtime data.

Saskatoon Curling Club. Accounts Payable Internship, 2008 to 2009. Took care of accounts payable including filing system for the club. Responsible for processing monthly adjusting entries for general ledger. Worked closely with treasurer to give the Board budget/disbursement figures regularly.

Saskatoon High School, Saskatoon. I marketed the VITA program to students and organized volunteers and supplies. Official title: Coordinator of Volunteer Income Tax Assistance Project.

COMMUNITY SERVICE: March of Dimes Drive, Central High School; All Souls Lutheran Church, coordinator for Children's Choir

---

12.8 Draft Document: Cover Letter

Analyze each section of the following cover letter written by an accounting major about to graduate.

Dear Human Resources Director:

Please consider this letter as an application for the position of staff accountant that I saw advertised in the Saskatoon *Star Phoenix*. Although I have had no paid work experience in this field, accounting has been my major in college and I'm sure I could be an asset to your company.

For four years I have studied accounting, and I am fully trained for full-charge bookkeeping as well as electronic accounting. I have completed 36 credits of college accounting and courses in business law, economics, statistics, finance, management, and marketing. In addition to my course work, during the tax season I have been a student volunteer for VITA. This is a project to help individuals in the community prepare their income tax returns, and I learned a lot from this experience. I have also received some experience in office work and working with figures when I was employed as an office assistant for Copy Quick, Inc.

I am a competent and responsible person who gets along pretty well with others. I have been a member of some college and social organizations and have even held elective office.

I feel that I have a strong foundation in accounting as a result of my course work and my experience. Along with my personal qualities and my desire to succeed, I hope that you will agree that I qualify for the position of staff accountant with your company.

Sincerely,

12.9 Résumé

Using the data you developed in Activity 12.2, write your résumé. Aim it at a full-time job, part-time position, or internship. Attach a job listing for a specific position (from Activity 12.4). Revise your résumé until it is perfect.

12.10 Cover Letter

Write an application letter introducing your résumé from Activity 12.9. Revise your application letter until it is perfect.

WEB

12.11 Unsolicited Cover Letter

As you read in this chapter, job applications are not always solicited. As part of your college education, you have no doubt come into contact with periodicals related to your field. For example, you may have read articles in *Canadian Business*, *Report on Business*, *HR Reporter*, *Marketing*, or any number of other magazines. In these magazines, you've come across the names of various businesspeople, either because they were featured in an article or because they were quoted as experts.

Your Task. Using your college library or local public library, read through an issue of a business-related periodical or your local newspaper's business section. Look for a businessperson who is mentioned, quoted, or featured in that periodical. Write that person an unsolicited cover letter asking for an entry-level position or internship either for the summer or upon graduation. Make sure to revise this letter sufficiently, and hand it in to your instructor for comments before actually mailing it.

12.12 Being Wary of Career Advisory Firms With Big Promises and Big Prices

Not long ago employment agencies charged applicants 5 percent of their annual salaries to find jobs. Most agencies have quit this unethical practice, but unscrupulous firms still prey on vulnerable job seekers. Some career advisory firms claim to be legitimate, but they make exaggerated promises and charge inflated fees—an up-front payment of $4,000 is typical, with a typical hourly honorarium of $90 to $125.

Your Task. Using databases and the Web, find examples of current employment scams or danger areas for job seekers. In a presentation to the class or in team discussions, describe three examples of disreputable practices candidates should recognize. Make recommendations to job seekers for avoiding employment scams and disappointment with career advisory services.

12.14 E-Portfolios: Job Hunting in the Twenty-First Century

In high-tech fields digital portfolios have been steadily gaining in popularity and now seem to be going mainstream as universities are providing space for student job seekers to profile their qualifications in e-portfolios online. Although it is unlikely that digital portfolios will become widely used very soon, you would do well to learn about them by viewing many samples—good and bad.

Your Task. Conduct a Google search using the search term *student e-portfolios or student digital portfolios*. You will see long lists of hits, some of which will be actual digital document samples on the Web or instructions for creating an e-portfolio. Your instructor may assign individual students or teams to visit specific digital portfolio sites and ask them to summarize their findings in a memo or in a brief oral presentation. If this is your task, you could focus on the composition of the site, page layout, links provided, colours used, types of documents included, and so forth. A fine site to start from that offers many useful links is maintained by the Center for Excellence in Teaching (CET) at the University of Southern California. Visit **http://www.usc .edu** and type *student e-portfolios* to search the USC Web pages. Click the link to the CET site.

Alternatively, single groups or the whole class could study sites that provide how-to instructions and combine the advice of the best among them to create practical tips for making a digital portfolio. This option would lend itself to team writing, for example, with the help of a wiki.

Grammar/Mechanics Review—12

The following sentences contain errors in grammar, punctuation, capitalization, number style, usage, and spelling. Below each sentence write a corrected version.

1. Please send the softwear to myself or whomever submited the order.

2. All committe members except Tracy and he knew the assignment, and were prepared with there reports when they were do.

3. Was any of the managers absent on the Monday following the 4 day weekend.

4. The Governments crash-worthiness standards all call for the use of two and a half metre 79 kilo dummys.

5. The makers of Saturn however decided to use dummys ranging from nineteen kilo children to 59 kilo females to burly 112 kilo males.

6. The president made an off the record comment but members of the board soon heard it repeated.

7. We retained only a 4 year old printer, however it will be inspected year-by-year.

8. Before five p.m. we must return all 3 computers to our 7th Avenue office.

9. Canada post announced on July 1st that it would increase rates by 4.5%.

10. The three Cs of credit is the following, character, capacity, and capitol.

11. Porter Kohl said that his Father gave him the following advice on making speeches—"Be sincere, be breif; and be seated.

12. Some trucks acceded the 2000 kilogram weight limit, others were under it.

13. Each of the quickly-printed computer books have been priced to sell at ten dollars and ninety-five cents.

14. If you will send the shipment to Elizabeth or I; it's contents will be inspected throughly.

15. The itinerary for Luke and he included 3 countrys holland france and germany.

Chapter 12: The Job Search, Résumés, and Cover Letters

Document for Revision

The following résumé (shortened for this exercise) has faults in grammar, punctuation, spelling, number form, verb form, wordiness, and word use. Use standard proofreading marks (see Appendix B) to correct the errors. When you finish, your instructor can show you the revised version of this résumé.

MEGAN A. Kozlov

245 Topsail Street

St. John's, Newfoundland A1B 3Z4

makozlov@hotmail.com

EDUCATION

Memorial University, St. John's, Newfoundland. Bachelor of Arts Degree expected in June 2012. Major English.

EXPERIENCE:

- Administrative Assistant. Host Systems, St. John's. 2009 too pressent. Responsible for entering data on Macintosh computer. I had to insure accuracy and completness of data that was to be entered. Another duty was maintaining a clean and well-organized office. I also served as Office Courier.

- Lechter's Housewares. Outlook Newfoundland. 2nd Asst. Mgr I managed store in absence of mgr. and asst. mgr. I open and close registers. Ballanced daily reciepts. Ordered some mds. I also had to supervise 2 employes, earning rabid promotion.

- Clerk typist. Sunshine Travel Outlook. 2006–2007. (part time) Entered travel information on IBM PC. Did personalized followup letters to customer inquirys. Was responsible for phones. I also handled all errands as courier.

STRENGTHS

Microsoft Office Applications, transcription, poofreading.

Can type 50 words/per/minute.

I am a fast learner, and very accurate.

Msoffice 07 including Excell, InterNet

Communication Workshop

Network Your Way to a Job in the Hidden Market

Not all jobs are advertised in classified ads or listed in job databases. The "hidden" job market, according to some estimates, accounts for as much as two thirds of all positions available. Companies don't always announce openings publicly because it's time consuming to interview all the applicants, many of whom are not qualified. But the real reason that companies resist announcing a job is that they dislike hiring "strangers." One recruiter says that when she needs to hire, she first looks around among her friends and acquaintances. If she can't find anyone suitable, she then turns to advertising.[31] It's clear that many employers are more comfortable hiring a person they know.

The key to finding a good job, then, is converting yourself from a "stranger" into a known quantity. One way to become a known quantity is by networking. You can use either traditional methods or online resources.

Traditional Networking

- *Step 1: Develop a list.* Make a list of anyone who would be willing to talk with you about finding a job. List your friends, relatives, former employers, former coworkers, classmates from grade school and high school, college friends, members of your religious group, people in social and athletic clubs, present and former teachers, neighbours, and friends of your parents.
- *Step 2: Make contacts.* Call the people on your list or, even better, try to meet with them in person. To set up a meeting, say, "Hi, Aunt Martha! I'm looking for a job and I wonder if you could help me out. When could I come over to talk about it?" During your visit be friendly, well organized, polite, and interested in what your contact has to say. Provide a copy of your résumé, and try to keep the conversation centred on your job search area. Your goal is to get two or more referrals. In pinpointing your request, ask two questions. "Do you know of anyone who might have an opening for a person with my skills?" If not, "Do you know of anyone else who might know of someone who would?"
- *Step 3: Follow up on your referrals.* Call the people whose names are on your referral list. You might say something like, "Hello. I'm Carlos Ramos, a friend of Connie Cole. She suggested that I call and ask you for help. I'm looking for a position as a marketing trainee, and she thought you might be willing to see me and give me a few ideas." Don't ask for a job. During your referral interview ask how the individual got started in this line of work, what he or she likes best (or least) about the work, what career paths exist in the field, and what problems must be overcome by a newcomer. Most important, ask how a person with your background and skills might get started in the field. Send an informal thank-you note to anyone who helps you in your job search, and stay in touch with the most promising contacts. Ask whether you may call every three weeks or so during your job search.

Online Networking

As with traditional networking, the goal is to make connections with people who are advanced in their fields. Ask for their advice about finding a job. Most people like talking about themselves, and asking them about their experiences is an excellent way to begin an online correspondence that might lead to "electronic mentoring" or a letter of recommendation from an expert in the field. Making online connections with industry professionals is a great way to keep tabs on the latest business trends and potential job leads. Here are possible online networking sources:

- **Join a career networking group.** Build your own professional network by joining one or more of the following: **http://www.linkedin.com, http://twitter.com, http://ryze. com**. Some of these sites are fee based, while others are free. Typically, joining a network requires creating a password, filling in your profile, and adding your business contacts. At some sites, you can specify search criteria to locate and then contact individuals directly. At other sites both parties' e-mail addresses are hidden. The site then acts as an intermediary, connecting people only after they agree to share their contact information. Once you

Chapter 12: The Job Search, Résumés, and Cover Letters

have connected with an individual, the content of your discussions and the follow-up will be similar to that of traditional networking. The medium, however, will centre on electronic communication through e-mail and chat room discussions.

- **Participate in a discussion groups and mailing lists.** Two especially good discussion group resources for beginners are Yahoo! Groups (**http://groups.yahoo.com**) and Google Groups (**http://groups.google.com/**). You may choose from groups in a variety of fields including business and computer technology. For example, if you click the *Business/ Finance* listing, you will see links leading to more specialized groups. Click *Employment and Work*, and you will find career groups including construction, customer service, office administration, court reporting, and interior design.
- **Locate relevant blogs.** Blogs are the latest trend for networking and sharing information. A quick Web search will result in hundreds of career-related blogs and blogs in your field of study. Many companies, such as Microsoft, also maintain employment-related blogs. A good list of career blogs can be found at **http://www.quintcareers.com/career-related_blogs.html.** You can also search a worldwide blog directory at **http://www. blogcatalog.com/.** Once you locate a relevant blog, you can read recent postings, search archives, and make replies.

Career Application

Everyone who goes out in the job market needs to develop his or her own network. Assume you are ready to change jobs or look for a permanent position. Begin developing your personal network.

Your Task.

- Conduct at least one referral interview and report on it to your class.
- Join one professional networking site, discussion group, or mailing list. Ask your instructor to recommend an appropriate mailing list for your field. Takes notes on group discussions, and describe your reactions and findings to your class.
- Find a blog related to your career or your major. After monitoring the blog for several days, describe your experience to your class.

13

Interviews and Follow-Up

Nothing delights interviewers more than candidates who have done their homework. They want to know that a candidate has done a little research on the company or industry ... and understands the challenges it is facing. As a bonus, the most heartwarming candidates have actually given a little thought to the job they are applying for.[1]

Michael Stern,
*President, Michael Stern Associates Inc.,
an executive search firm headquartered
in Toronto*

© STOCKLITE/SHUTTERSTOCK

LEARNING OBJECTIVES

1. Distinguish among screening, one-on-one, panel, group, sequential, and stress interviews.

2. Describe what to do before the interview to make an impressive initial contact.

3. Explain how to prepare for employment interviews, including researching the target company.

4. Recognize how to control nonverbal messages and how to fight interview fears.

5. Be prepared to answer common interview questions and know how to close an interview positively.

6. Outline activities that take place after an interview, including thanking the interviewer and contacting references.

7. Write follow-up and other employment messages.

Job interviews, for most of us, are intimidating; no one enjoys being judged and, possibly, rejected. Should you expect to be nervous about an upcoming job interview? Of course. Everyone is uneasy about being scrutinized and questioned. But think of how much more nervous you would be if you had no idea what to expect in the interview and were unprepared.

This chapter presents different kinds of interviews and shows you how to prepare for them. You'll learn how to gather information about an employer, as well as how to reduce nervousness, control body language, and fight fear during an interview. You'll pick up tips for responding to recruiters' favourite questions and learn how to cope with illegal questions and salary matters. Moreover, you'll receive pointers on significant questions you can ask during an interview. Finally, you'll learn what you should do as a successful follow-up to an interview.

Yes, you can expect to be nervous. But you can also expect to succeed in an interview when you know what's coming and when you prepare thoroughly. Remember, it's often the degree of preparation that determines who gets the job.

Succeeding in Various Kinds of Employment Interviews

Job applicants generally face two kinds of interviews: screening interviews and hiring/placement interviews. You must succeed in the first to proceed to the second.

Screening Interviews

Screening interviews screen candidates to eliminate those who fail to meet minimum requirements. Initial screening is often done by telephone or by computer.

    A telephone screening interview may be as short as five minutes. But don't treat it casually. It's not just another telephone call. If you don't perform well during the telephone interview, it may be your last interview with that organization. While the following suggestions are meant for screening interviews, keep them in mind if you must participate in a hiring interview over the telephone. Here's how you can be prepared for a telephone interview:

Screening interviews are intended to eliminate those who fail to meet minimum requirements.

- Keep a list near the telephone of positions for which you have applied.
- Have your résumé, references, a calendar, and a notepad handy.
- If caught off guard, ask if you can call back in a few minutes. Organize your materials and yourself.
- Sell your qualifications and, above all, sound enthusiastic.

    Several Canadian career coaches suggest it is important to politely and directly offer the facts the interviewer seeks, and refrain from volunteering additional information such as salary expectations. Save this kind of information for the probing questions that will occur in first and second interviews. The screening interview is used to "weed out" candidates so they will never reach the next step.

Hiring/Placement Interviews

The most promising candidates selected from screening interviews will be invited to hiring/placement interviews. Although these interviews are the real thing, in many ways they are like a game. Trained interviewers try to uncover any negative information that will eliminate a candidate. The candidate tries to minimize faults and emphasize strengths to avoid being eliminated. Like most games, the more practice you get, the better you perform, because you know what to expect. Hiring/placement interviews are conducted in depth and may take many forms.

In hiring/placement interviews, recruiters try to uncover negative information while candidates try to minimize faults and emphasize strengths.

One-on-One interviews. This is the most common interview type. You can expect to sit down with a company representative or two and talk about the job and your qualifications. If the representative is the hiring manager, questions will be specific and job related. If the representative is from the human resources department, the questions will probably be more general.

Panel Interviews. Panel interviews are typically conducted by people who will be your supervisors and colleagues. Usually seated around a table, interviewers may take turns asking questions. Panel interviews are advantageous because they save time and show you how the staff works together. For these interviews, you can prepare basic biographical information about each panel member. In answering questions, keep eye contact with the questioner as well as with the other team members. Try to take notes during the interview so that you can remember each person's questions and what was important to that individual.[2]

Group Interviews. Group interviews occur when a company interviews several candidates for the same position at the same time. Some employers use this technique to measure leadership skills and communication styles. During a group interview, stay focused on the interviewer, and treat the other candidates with respect.[3]

Sequential Interviews. Sequential interviews allow a candidate to meet individually with two or more interviewers over the course of several hours or days. For example, job candidates seeking tenure-track academic positions undergo sequential interviewing. You must listen carefully and respond positively to all interviewers. Sell your qualifications to each one; don't assume that any interviewer knows what was said in a previous interview. Keep your responses fresh, even when repeating yourself many times over.[4]

Stress interviews. This interview type is meant to test your reactions. If asked rapid-fire questions from many directions, take the time to slow things down. For example, *I would be happy to answer your question, Ms. X, but allow me to finish responding to Mr. Z.* If greeted with silence, another stress technique, you might say *Would you like me to begin the interview? Let me tell you about myself.* Or ask a question such as *Can you give me more information about the position?* The best way to handle stress questions is to remain calm and give carefully considered answers. However, you might also reconsider whether you would want to work for this kind of organization.

Before the Interview

Once you have sent out at least one résumé or filled out at least one job application, you must consider yourself an active job seeker. Being active in the job market means that you must be prepared to be contacted by potential employers. As discussed earlier, employers use screening interviews to narrow the list of candidates. If you do well in the screening interview, you will be invited to an in-person meeting. Here are tips for sounding professional and acting appropriately from the beginning and for preparing for a job interview once it has been scheduled.

Using Professional Phone Techniques

Even with the popularity of e-mail, most employers contact job applicants by phone to set up interviews. Employers can get a better sense of how applicants communicate by hearing their voices over the phone. Therefore, once you are actively looking for a job, anytime the phone rings, it could be a potential employer. Don't make the mistake of letting an unprofessional voice mail message or a lazy roommate ruin your chances. Here's how you can avoid such problems:

- Invest in a good answering machine or voice mail service. Make sure that your outgoing message is concise and professional, with no distracting background sounds. It should be in your own voice and include your full name for clarity. You will find more tips for creating professional outgoing messages in Chapter 10.
- Tell those who might answer your phone at home about your job search. Explain to them the importance of acting professionally and taking complete messages. Family members or roommates can affect the first impression an employer has of you.
- If you have children, prevent them from answering the phone during your job search. Children of all ages are not known for taking good messages!
- If you have put your cell phone number on your résumé, don't answer your cell phone unless you are in a good location to carry on a conversation with an employer. It is hard to pay close attention when you are driving down the highway or eating in a noisy restaurant!

- Use voice mail to screen calls. By screening incoming calls, you can be totally in control when you return a prospective employer's call. Organize your materials and ready yourself psychologically for the conversation.

Making the First Conversation Impressive

Whether you answer the phone directly or return an employer's call, make sure you are prepared for the conversation. Remember that this is the first time the employer has heard your voice. How you conduct yourself on the phone will create a lasting impression. Here are tips to make that first impression a positive one:

- Keep a list near the telephone of positions for which you have applied.
- Treat any call from an employer just like an interview. Use a professional tone and businesslike language. Be polite and enthusiastic, and sell your qualifications.
- If caught off guard by the call, ask whether you can call back in a few minutes. Organize your materials and yourself.
- Have a copy of your résumé available so that you can answer any questions that come up. Also have your list of references, a calendar, and a notepad handy.
- Be prepared for a screening interview. As discussed earlier, this might occur during the first phone call.
- Take good notes during the phone conversation. Obtain accurate directions, and verify the spelling of your interviewer's name. If you will be interviewed by more than one person, get all of their names.
- Before you hang up, reconfirm the date and time of your interview. You could say something like *I look forward to meeting with you next Wednesday at 2 p.m.*

Researching the Target Company

One of the most important steps in being successful at the interview game is gathering information about a prospective employer. In learning about a company, you may uncover information that convinces you that this is not the company for you. It's always better to learn about negatives early in the process. More likely, though, the information you collect will help you tailor your application and interview responses to the organization's needs. Recruiters are impressed by candidates who have done their homework.

For Canadian companies that are publicly held, you can generally learn a great deal from annual reports and financial disclosure reports available at **http://www.sedar.com**. Company information is also available for a cost from Dun and Bradstreet Canada (**http://www.dnb.ca**) and by logging in as a guest at Canadian Business Resource (**http://www.cbr.ca**). One of the best things a job seeker can do is to get into the habit of reading the newspaper regularly. The best place to go for current information on Canadian companies is the business section of the two national newspapers, the *National Post* and *The Globe and Mail*, including these newspapers' websites. Of course, you can also Google a company, which will give you access to its corporate Web site with information such as annual reports and sometimes lists of staff. Your local city or town newspaper will occasionally profile local businesses. Finally, large and small companies alike also maintain their own Web sites, bursting with helpful information. Another way to learn about an organization is to call the receptionist or the interviewer directly. Ask what you can read to prepare for the interview. Here are some specifics to research:

- Find out all you can about company leaders. Their goals, ambitions, and values are often adopted by the entire organization—including your interviewer.
- Investigate the business philosophy of the leaders, such as their priorities, strategies, and managerial approaches. Are you a good match with your target employer? If so, be sure to let the employer know that there is a correlation between its needs and your qualifications.
- Learn about the company's accomplishments and setbacks. This information should help you determine where you might make your best contribution.

- Study the company's finances. Are they so shaky that a takeover is imminent? If so, look elsewhere. Try to get your hands on an annual report. Many larger companies now post them on their Web sites.
- Examine the company's products and customers. What excites you about this company?
- Check out the competition. What are its products, strengths, and weaknesses?
- Analyze the company's advertising, including sales and marketing brochures. One candidate, a marketing major, spent a great deal of time poring over brochures from an aerospace contractor. During his initial interview, he shocked and impressed the recruiter with his knowledge of the company's guidance systems. The candidate had, in fact, relieved the interviewer of his least favourite task—explaining the company's complicated technology.

Learning About Smaller Companies

For smaller companies and those that are not publicly owned, you'll probably have to dig a little deeper. You might start with the local library. Ask the reference librarian to help you locate information. Newspapers might contain stories or press releases with news of an organization. Visit the Better Business Bureau or Chamber of Commerce to discover whether the company has had any difficulties with other companies or consumers. Also, find out what kinds of contributions the company has made to the local community.

Talking with company employees is always a good idea, if you can manage it. They are probably the best source of inside information. Try to be introduced to someone who is currently employed there—but not working in the immediate area where you wish to be hired. Be sure to seek out someone who is discreet.

You know how flattered you feel when an employer knows about you and your background. That feeling works both ways. Employers are pleased when job candidates take an interest in them. Be ready to put in plenty of effort in investigating a target employer, because this effort really pays off at interview time.

Preparing and Practising

After you have learned about the target organization, study the job description or job listing. It not only helps you write a focused résumé but also enables you to match your education, experience, and interests with the employer's position. Learning about the duties and responsibilities of the position will help you practise your best response strategies.

The most successful job candidates never go into interviews cold. They prepare success stories and practise answers to typical questions. They also plan their responses to any problem areas on their résumés. As part of their preparation before the interview, they decide what to wear, and they gather the items they plan to take with them.

Prepare Success Stories. To feel confident and be able to sell your qualifications, prepare and practise success stories. These stories are specific examples of your educational and work-related experience that demonstrate your qualifications and achievements. Look over the job description and your résumé to determine what skills, training, personal characteristics, and experience you want to emphasize during the interview. Then prepare a success story for each one. Incorporate numbers, such as dollars saved or percentage of sales increased, whenever possible. Your success stories should be detailed but brief. Think of them as 30-second sound bites.

Practise telling your success stories until they fluently roll off your tongue and sound natural. Then in the interview be certain to find places to insert them. Tell stories about (a) dealing with a crisis, (b) handling a tough interpersonal situation, (c) successfully juggling many priorities, (d) changing course to deal with changed circumstances, (e) learning from a mistake, (f) working on a team, and (g) going above and beyond expectations.[5]

The best source of inside information is company employees.

Practise success stories that emphasize your most strategic skills, areas of knowledge, strongest personality traits, and key accomplishments.

Practise Answers to Possible Questions. Imagine the kinds of questions you may be asked and work out sample answers. Although you can't anticipate precise questions, you can expect to be asked about your education, skills, experience, and availability. Recite answers to typical interview questions in a mirror, with a friend, while driving in your car, or in spare moments. Keep practising until you have the best responses down pat. Consider recording a practice session to see and hear how you answer questions. Do you look and sound enthusiastic?

Clean Up Any Digital Dirt. Many companies that recruit on campuses are now using Google and Yahoo to screen applicants. The president of a small consulting company in Chicago was about to hire a summer intern when he discovered the student's Facebook page. The candidate described his interests as "smokin' blunts [cigars hollowed out and stuffed with marijuana], shooting people, and obsessive sex."[6] The executive quickly lost interest in this candidate. Even if the student was merely posturing, it showed poor judgment.

Make sure everything posted about you online is professional and positive.

Teasing photographs and provocative comments about drinking, drug use, and sexual exploits make students look immature and unprofessional. Employers have the same access to the Internet as job seekers do, and they are taking a close look: "If what pops up is a ranting blog about the evils of [big business] or a picture of you topless in Cancun with a beer in your hand, you're in trouble," Cynthia Shapiro, an employment expert, says. "Your résumé will land in the trash, and you won't even know what happened."[7] Check out your online presence to see if anything needs to be cleaned up.

Expect to Explain Problem Areas on Your Résumé. Interviewers are certain to question you about problem areas on your résumé. If you have little or no experience, you might emphasize your recent training and up-to-date skills. If you have gaps in your résumé, be prepared to answer questions about them positively and truthfully. If you were fired from a job, accept some responsibility for what happened and explain what you gained from the experience. Don't criticize a previous employer, and don't hide the real reasons. If you received low grades for one term, explain why and point to your improved grades in subsequent terms.

Decide How to Dress. What you wear to a job interview still matters. Even if some employees in the organization dress casually, you should look qualified, competent, and successful. One young applicant complained to his girlfriend about having to wear a suit for an interview when everyone at the company dressed casually. She replied, "You don't get to wear the uniform, though, until you make the team!" Avoid loud colours; strive for a coordinated, natural appearance. Favourite "power" colours for interviews are gray and dark blue. Cover tattoos and conceal body piercings; these can be a turnoff for many interviewers. Don't overdo jewellery, and make sure that what you do wear is clean, pressed, odour-free, and lint-free. Shoes should be polished and scuff-free. Forget about flip-flops.

To summarize, ensure that what you wear projects professionalism and shows your respect for the interview situation.

Gather Items to Bring. Decide what you should bring with you to the interview, and get everything ready the night before. You should plan to bring copies of your résumé, your reference lists, a notebook and pen, money for parking and tolls, and samples of your work, if appropriate. Place everything in a businesslike briefcase to add that final professional touch to your look.

Travelling to and Arriving at Your Interview

The big day has arrived! Ideally you are fully prepared for your interview. Now you need to make sure that everything goes smoothly. That means arriving on time and handling that fear you are likely to feel.

Allow ample time to arrive unflustered, and be congenial to everyone who greets you.

On the morning of your interview, give yourself plenty of time to groom and dress. Then give yourself ample time to get to the employer's office. If something unexpected happens that will to cause you to be late, such as an accident or bridge closure, call the interviewer right away to explain what is happening. Most interviewers will be understanding, and your call will show that you are responsible. On the way to the interview, don't smoke, don't eat anything messy or smelly, and don't load up on perfume or cologne. Arrive at the interview five or ten minutes early. If possible, check your appearance before going in.

When you enter the office, be courteous and congenial to everyone. Remember that you are being judged not only by the interviewer but by the receptionist and anyone else who sees you before and after the interview. They will notice how you sit, what you read, and how you look. Introduce yourself to the receptionist, and wait to be invited to sit. You may be asked to fill out a job application while you are waiting. You will find tips for doing this effectively later in this chapter.

Greet the interviewer confidently, and don't be afraid to initiate a handshake. Doing so exhibits professionalism and confidence. Extend your hand, look the interviewer directly in the eye, smile pleasantly, and say, *I'm pleased to meet you, Mr. Thomas. I am Constance Ferraro.* In this culture a firm, not crushing, handshake sends a nonverbal message of poise and assurance. Once introductions have taken place, wait for the interviewer to offer you a chair. Make small talk with upbeat comments, such as *This is a beautiful headquarters* or *I'm very impressed with the facilities you have here.* Don't immediately begin rummaging in your briefcase for your résumé. Being at ease and unrushed suggest that you are self-confident.

Fighting Fear

Fight fear by practising, preparing thoroughly, breathing deeply, and knowing that you are in charge for part of the interview.

Expect to be nervous before and during the interview. It is natural! Other than public speaking, employment interviews are the most dreaded events in people's lives. One of the best ways to overcome fear is to know what happens in a typical interview. You can further reduce your fears by following these suggestions.

- **Practise interviewing.** Try to get as much interviewing practice as you can—especially with real companies. The more times you experience the interview situation, the less nervous you will be. If offered, campus mock interviews also provide excellent practice, and the interviewers will offer tips for improvement.
- **Prepare thoroughly.** Research the company. Know how you will answer the most frequently asked questions. Be ready with success stories. Rehearse your closing statement. One of the best ways to reduce butterflies is to know that you have done all you can to be ready for the interview.
- **Breathe deeply.** Take deep breaths, particularly if you feel anxious while waiting for the interviewer. Deep breathing makes you concentrate on something other than the interview and also provides much-needed oxygen.
- **Know that you are not alone.** Everyone feels some level of anxiety during a job interview. Interviewers expect some nervousness, and a skilled interviewer will try to put you at ease.
- **Remember that it is a two-way street.** The interviewer isn't the only one who is gleaning information. You have come to learn about the job and the company. In fact, during some parts of the interview, you will be in charge. This should give you courage.

During the Interview

During the interview you will be answering questions and asking your own questions. Your demeanour, body language, and other nonverbal cues will also be on display. The interviewer will be trying to learn more about you, and you should learn more about the job and the organization. Although you may be asked some

An old adage of interviewing says, "You never get a second chance to make a first impression." Until recently, image consultants differed on how much time individuals have to put their best face forward. But a study conducted by two psychologists has concluded that it takes only one-tenth of a second to form judgments about the key character traits of others. In practical terms, this means employers will make inferences about one's likableness, competence, trustworthiness, and aggressiveness in the blink of an eye. *What should job candidates do to make a good first impression during an interview?*

unique questions, many interviewers ask standard, time-proven questions, which means that you can prepare your answers ahead of time.

Sending Positive Nonverbal Messages and Acting Professionally

You have already sent nonverbal messages to your interviewer by arriving on time, being courteous, dressing professionally, and greeting the receptionist confidently. You will continue to send nonverbal messages throughout the interview. Remember that what comes out of your mouth and what is written on your résumé are not the only messages an interviewer receives from you. Nonverbal messages also create powerful impressions. Here are suggestions that will help you send the right non-verbal messages during interviews:

> Send positive nonverbal messages by arriving on time, being courteous, dressing professionally, greeting the interviewer confidently, controlling your body movements, making eye contact, listening attentively, and smiling.

- **Control your body movements.** Keep your hands, arms, and elbows to yourself. Don't lean on a desk. Keep your feet on the floor. Don't cross your arms in front of you. Keep your hands out of your pockets.
- **Exhibit good posture.** Sit erect, leaning forward slightly. Don't slouch in your chair; at the same time, don't look too stiff and uncomfortable. Good posture demonstrates confidence and interest.
- **Practise appropriate eye contact.** A direct eye gaze, at least in North America, suggests interest and trustworthiness. If you are being interviewed by a panel, remember to maintain eye contact with all interviewers.
- **Use gestures effectively.** Nod to show agreement and interest. Gestures should be used as needed, but don't overdo it.
- **Smile enough to convey a positive attitude.** Have a friend give you honest feedback on whether you generally smile too much or not enough.
- **Listen attentively.** Show the interviewer you are interested and attentive by listening carefully to the questions being asked. This will also help you answer questions appropriately.
- **Turn off your cell phone.** Avoid the embarrassment of a ringing cell phone during an interview. Turn it off or leave it at home.
- **Don't chew gum.** Chewing gum during an interview is distracting and unprofessional.
- **Sound enthusiastic and interested—but sincere.** The tone of your voice has an enormous effect on the words you say. Avoid sounding bored, frustrated, or sarcastic during an interview. Employers want employees who are enthusiastic and interested.

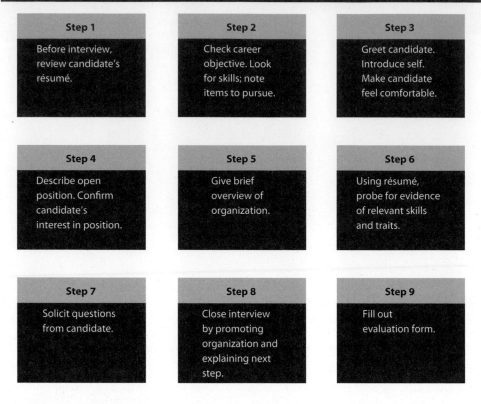

FIGURE 13.1 Steps in an Employment Interview From a Recruiter's Perspective

Step 1	Step 2	Step 3
Before interview, review candidate's résumé.	Check career objective. Look for skills; note items to pursue.	Greet candidate. Introduce self. Make candidate feel comfortable.

Step 4	Step 5	Step 6
Describe open position. Confirm candidate's interest in position.	Give brief overview of organization.	Using résumé, probe for evidence of relevant skills and traits.

Step 7	Step 8	Step 9
Solicit questions from candidate.	Close interview by promoting organization and explaining next step.	Fill out evaluation form.

- **Avoid "empty" words.** Filling your answers with verbal pauses such as *um*, *uh*, *like*, and *basically* communicates that you are not prepared. Also avoid annoying distractions such as clearing your throat repeatedly or sighing deeply.

Above all, remember that employers want to hire people who have confidence in their own abilities. To put yourself into an employer's shoes, so to speak, think of the interview from his or her point of view, as explained below in Figure 13.1. Then, let your body language, posture, dress, and vocal tone prove that you are self-assured.

Answering Typical Questions Confidently

How you answer questions can be as important as the answers themselves.

The way you answer questions can be almost as important as what you say. Use the interviewer's name and title from time to time when you answer: *Ms. Lyon, I would be pleased to tell you about....* People like to hear their own names. But be sure you are pronouncing the name correctly.

Occasionally it may be necessary to re-focus and clarify vague questions. Some interviewers are inexperienced and ill at ease in the role. You may even have to ask your own question to understand what was asked: *By ... do you mean ...?*

Consider closing some of your responses with *Does that answer your question?* or *Would you like me to elaborate on any particular experience?*

Stay focused on the skills and traits that employers seek; don't reveal weaknesses.

Always aim your answers at the key characteristics interviewers seek: expertise and competence, motivation, interpersonal skills, decision-making skills, enthusiasm for the job, and a pleasing personality. And remember to stay focused on your strengths. Don't reveal weaknesses, even if you think they make you look human. You won't be hired for your weaknesses, only for your strengths.

Use proper English and enunciate clearly. Remember, you will definitely be judged by how well you communicate. Avoid slurred words such as *gonna* and *y'know*, as well as slangy expressions such as *yeah*, *like*, and *whatever*. Also

FIGURE 13.2 Interview Actions to Avoid

1. Don't ask for the job. It's naive, undignified, and unprofessional. Wait to see how the interview develops.

2. Don't be negative about your previous employer, supervisors, or colleagues. The tendency is for interviewers to wonder if you would speak about their companies similarly.

3. Don't be a threat to the interviewer. Avoid suggesting directly or indirectly that your goal is to become head honcho, a path that might include the interviewer's job.

4. Don't be late or too early for your appointment. Arrive five minutes before you are scheduled.

5. Don't discuss controversial subjects, and don't use profanity.

6. Don't emphasize salary or benefits. If the interview goes well and these subjects have not been addressed, you may mention them toward the end of the interview.

7. Don't be negative about yourself or others. Never dwell on your liabilities.

8. Don't interrupt. Not only is it impolite but it also prevents you from hearing a complete question or remark.

9. Don't accept an offer until you have completed all your interviews.

eliminate verbal static (*ah*, *and*, *uhm*). As you practise for the interview, a good idea is to record answers to expected interview questions. Is your speech filled with verbal static?

You can't expect to be perfect in an employment interview. No one is. But you can increase your chances of success by avoiding certain topics and behaviours such as those described in Figure 13.2.

Employment interviews are all about questions. And most of the questions are not new. You can actually anticipate 90 to 95 percent of all questions that will be asked before you ever walk into an interview room.[8]

The following questions represent all-time favourites asked of recent graduates and other job seekers. You'll find get-acquainted questions, experience and accomplishment questions, future-oriented questions, squirm questions, and money questions. To get you thinking about how to respond, we've provided an answer or discussion for the first question in each group. As you read the remaining questions in each group, think about how you could respond most effectively.

Questions to Get Acquainted. After opening introductions, recruiters generally try to start the interviewing questioning period with personal questions that put the candidate at ease. They are also striving to gain a picture of the candidate to see if he or she will fit into the organization's culture.

1. Tell me about yourself.

   Experts agree that you must keep this answer short (one to two minutes, tops) but on target. Try practising this formula: "My name is _____. I have completed a _____ degree with a major in _____. Recently I worked for _____ as a _____. Before that I worked for _____ as a _____. My strengths are _____ (interpersonal) and _____ (technical)." Try rehearsing your response in 30-second segments devoted to your education, your work experience, and your qualities/skills. Some candidates end with "Now that I've told you about myself, can you tell me a little more about the position?"

2. What was your area of specialization in college/university, and why did you choose it?

3. If you had it to do over again, would you choose the same major? Why?

4. Tell me about your college/university (or your major) and why you chose it.

5. Do you prefer to work by yourself or with others? Why?

Prepare for get-acquainted questions by practising a short formula response.

6. What are your key strengths?
7. What are some things you do in your spare time? Hobbies? Sports?
8. How did you happen to apply for this job?
9. What particular qualifications do you have for this job?
10. Do you consider yourself a team player? Describe your style as a team player.

Questions to Gauge Your Interest. Interviewers want to understand your motivation for applying for a position. Although they will realize that you are probably interviewing for other positions, they still want to know why you are interested in this particular position with this organization. These types of questions help them determine your level of interest.

1. Why do you want to work for (*name of company*)?

Recruiters want to know how interested you are in this organization and in this specific position.

Questions like this illustrate why you must research an organization thoroughly before the interview. The answer to this question must prove that you understand the company and its culture. This is the perfect place to bring up the company research you did before the interview. Show what you know about the company, and discuss why you would like to become a part of this organization. Describe your desire to work for this organization not only from your perspective but also from its point of view. What do you have to offer?

2. Why are you interested in this position?
3. What do you know about our company?
4. Why do you want to work in the _____ industry?
5. What interests you about our products (services)?

Questions About Your Experience and Accomplishments. After questions about your background and education, the interview generally becomes more specific, with questions about your experience and accomplishments.

1. Why should we hire you when we have applicants with more experience or better credentials?

Employers will hire a candidate with less experience and fewer accomplishments if he or she can demonstrate the skills required.

In answering this question, remember that employers often hire people who present themselves well instead of others with better credentials. Emphasize your personal strengths that could be an advantage with this employer. Are you a hard worker? How can you demonstrate it? Have you had recent training? Some people have had more years of experience but actually have less knowledge because they have done the same thing over and over. Stress your experience using the latest methods and equipment. Be sure to mention your computer training and use of the Internet and Web. Emphasize that you are open to new ideas and learn quickly.

2. Tell me about your part-time jobs, internships, or other experience.
3. What were your major accomplishments in each of your past jobs?
4. Why did you change jobs?
5. What was a typical workday like?
6. What job functions did you enjoy most? Least? Why?
7. Who was the toughest boss you ever worked for and why?
8. What were your major achievements in college/university?
9. Tell me about a difficult situation in a previous work situation and how you dealt with it.

Questions About the Future. Questions that look into the future tend to stump some candidates, especially those who have not prepared adequately. Some of these questions give you a chance to discuss your personal future goals, while others require you to think on your feet and explain how you would respond in hypothetical situations.

1. Where do you expect to be five years from now?

Whatever you do, don't respond that you'd like the interviewer's job. Instead, show an interest in the current job and in making a contribution to the organization. Talk about the levels of responsibility you'd like to achieve. One employment counsellor suggests showing ambition but not committing to a specific job title. Suggest that you will have learned enough to have progressed to a position where you will continue to grow.

2. If you get this position, what would you do to be sure you fit in?
3. If your supervisor gave you an assignment and then left town for two weeks, what would you do?
4. This is a large (or small) organization. Do you think you'd like that environment?
5. If you were aware that a coworker was falsifying data, what would you do?
6. If your supervisor was dissatisfied with your work and you thought it was acceptable, how would you resolve the conflict?
7. Do you plan to continue your education?

Challenging Questions. The following questions may make you uncomfortable, but the important thing to remember is to answer truthfully without dwelling on your weaknesses. As quickly as possible, convert any negative response into a discussion of your strengths.

1. What are your key weaknesses?

It's amazing how many candidates knock themselves out of the competition by answering this question poorly. Actually, you have many choices. You can present a strength as a weakness (*Some people complain that I'm a workaholic or too attentive to details*). You can mention a corrected weakness (*I found that I really needed to learn about the Internet, so I took a course*). You can cite an unrelated skill (*I really need to brush up on my French*). You can cite a learning objective (*One of my long-term goals is to learn more about international management. Does your company have any plans to expand overseas?*). Another possibility is to reaffirm your qualifications (*I have no weaknesses that affect my ability to do this job*).

2. If you could change one thing about your personality, what would it be and why?
3. What would your former boss say about you?
4. What do you want the most from your job? Money? Security? Power?
5. How did you prepare for this interview?
6. Do you feel you achieved the best grade point average of which you were capable in your education?
7. Relate an incident in which you faced an ethical dilemma. How did you react? How did you feel?
8. If your supervisor told you to do something a certain way, and you knew that way was dead wrong, what would you do?

Situational Questions. Questions related to situations help employers test your thought processes and logical thinking. When using situational questions, interviewers will describe a hypothetical situation and ask how you would handle it. Situational questions differ based on the type of position for which you are interviewing.[9] Knowledge of the position and the company culture will help you respond favourably to these questions. Even if the situation sounds negative, keep your response positive. Here are just a few examples:

1. You receive a call from an irate customer who complains about the service she received last night at your restaurant. She is demanding her money back. How would you handle the situation?
2. If you were aware that a coworker was falsifying data, what would you do?

When asked about the future, show ambition and interest in succeeding with this company.

Strive to convert discussion of your weaknesses to topics that show your strengths.

Employers find that situational and behavioural interview questions give them useful information about job candidates.

3. Your supervisor has just told you that she is dissatisfied with your work, but you think it is acceptable. How would you resolve the conflict?

4. Your supervisor has told you to do something a certain way, and you think that way is wrong and that you know a far better way to complete the task. What would you do?

5. Assume that you are hired for this position. You soon learn that one of the staff is extremely resentful because she applied for your position and was turned down. As a result, she is being unhelpful and obstructive. How would you handle the situation?

6. A work colleague has told you in confidence that she suspects another colleague of stealing. What would your actions be?

7. You have noticed that communication between upper management and first-level employees is eroding. How would you solve this problem?

Behavioural Questions. Instead of traditional interview questions, you may be asked to tell stories. The interviewer may say, *Describe a time when ...* or *Tell me about a situation in which....* To respond effectively, learn to use the story-telling or STAR technique. Ask yourself, what the **S**ituation or **T**ask was, what **A**ction you took, and what the **R**esults were.[10] Practise using this method to recall specific examples of your skills and accomplishments. To be fully prepared, develop a coherent and articulate STAR narrative for every bullet point on your résumé. When answering behavioural questions, describe only educational and work-related situations or tasks, and try to keep them as current as possible. Here are a few examples of behavioural questions:

1. Tell me about a time when you solved a difficult problem.

   Tell a concise story explaining the situation or task, what you did, and the result. For example, *When I was at Ace Products, we continually had a problem of excessive back orders. After analyzing the situation, I discovered that orders went through many unnecessary steps. I suggested that we eliminate much of the paper-work. As a result, we reduced back orders by 30 percent.* Go on to emphasize what you learned and how you can apply that learning to this job. Practise your success stories in advance so that you will be ready.

2. Describe a situation in which you were able to use persuasion to successfully convince someone to see things your way.

   The recruiter is interested in your leadership and teamwork skills. You might respond, *I have learned to appreciate the fact that the way you present an idea is just as important as the idea itself. When trying to influence people, I put myself in their shoes and find some way to frame my idea from their perspective. I remember when I....*

3. Describe a time when you had to analyze information and make a recommendation.

4. Describe a time that you worked successfully as part of a team.

5. Tell me about a time you dealt with confidential information.

6. Give me an example of a time when you were under stress to meet a deadline.

7. Tell me about a time when you had to go above and beyond the call of duty in order to get a job done.

8. Tell me about a time you were able to successfully deal with another person even when that person may not have personally liked you (or vice versa).

9. Give me an example of an occasion when you showed initiative and took the lead.

10. Tell me about a recent situation in which you had to deal with an upset customer or coworker.

"Apart from being a CEO and a job bagging bagels, what other work experience do you have?"

Fielding Illegal Questions

Because human rights legislation protects job applicants from discrimination, interviewers may not ask questions such as those in the following list. Nevertheless, you may face an inexperienced or unscrupulous interviewer who does ask some of these questions. How should you react? If you find the question harmless and if you want the job, go ahead and answer. If you think that answering would damage your chance to be hired, try to deflect the question tactfully with a response such as, *Could you tell me how my marital status relates to the responsibilities of this position?* Or you could use the opportunity to further emphasize your strengths. An older worker responding to a question about age might mention experience, fitness, knowledge, maturity, stability, or extensive business contacts. You might also wish to reconsider working for an organization that sanctions such procedures.

You may respond to an illegal question by asking tactfully how it relates to the responsibilities of the position.

Here are some questions that you may or may not want to answer:

1. Are you married, divorced, separated, single, or living common-law?
2. Is your spouse subject to transfer in his/her job? Tell me about your spouse's job.
3. What is your corrected vision? (But it is legal to ask about quality of vision if visual acuity is directly related to safety or some other factor of the job.)
4. Do you have any disabilities? Do you drink or take drugs? Have you ever received psychiatric care or been hospitalized for emotional problems? Have you ever received workers' compensation? (But it is legal to ask if you have any condition that could affect your ability to do the job or if you have any condition that should be considered during selection.)
5. Have you ever been arrested? Have you ever been convicted of a crime? Do you have a criminal record? (But if bonding is a requirement of the job, it is legal to ask if you are eligible.)
6. How old are you? What is your date of birth? Can I see your birth certificate? (But it is legal to ask *Are you eligible to work under Canadian laws pertaining to age restrictions?*)
7. In what other countries do you have a current address? (But it is legal to ask *What is your current address, and how long have you lived there?*)
8. What is your maiden name? (But it is legal to ask *What is your full name?*)
9. What is your religion? How often do you attend religious services? Would you work on a specific religious holiday? Can you provide a reference from a clergyperson or religious leader?
10. Do you have children? What are your child care arrangements? (But it is legal to ask *Can you work the required hours?* and *Are you available for overtime?*)
11. Where were you born? Were you born in Canada? Can you provide proof of citizenship? (But it is legal to ask *Are you legally entitled to work in Canada?*)
12. Were you involved in military service in another country? (But it is legal to ask about Canadian military service.)
13. What is your first language? Where did you receive your language training? (But it is legal to ask if you understand, read, write, and/or speak the language[s] required for the job.)
14. How much do you weigh? How tall are you?
15. What is your sexual orientation?
16. Are you under medical care? Who is your family doctor? Are you receiving therapy or counselling? (But it is legal to make offers of employment conditional on successful completion of a medical exam that is relevant to that job.)

Asking Your Own Questions

At some point in the interview, you will be asked if you have any questions. Your questions should not only help you gain information but also impress the interviewer with your thoughtfulness and interest in the position. Remember that the interview is an opportunity for you to see how you would fit with the company as well. You must be happy with the prospect of working for this organization. You want a position that matches your skills and personality. Use this opportunity

Your questions should impress the interviewer but also draw out valuable information about the job.

to find out whether this job is right for you. Be aware that you don't have to wait for the interviewer to ask you for questions. You can ask your own questions throughout the interview to learn more about the company and position. Here are some questions you might ask:

1. What will my duties be (if not already discussed)?
2. Tell me what it's like working here in terms of the people, management practices, work loads, expected performance, and rewards.
3. Why is this position open? Did the person who held it previously leave?
4. What training programs are available from this organization? What specific training will be given for this position?
5. What are the possibilities for promotion from this position?
6. Who would be my immediate supervisor?
7. What is the organizational structure, and where does this position fit in?
8. Is travel required in this position?
9. How is job performance evaluated?
10. Assuming my work is excellent, where do you see me in five years?
11. How long do employees generally stay with this organization?
12. What are the major challenges for a person in this position?
13. What can I do to make myself more employable to you?
14. What is the salary for this position?
15. When will I hear from you regarding further action on my application?

Ending Positively

After you have asked your questions, the interviewer will signal the end of the interview, usually by standing up or by expressing appreciation that you came. If not addressed earlier, you should at this time find out what action will follow. Demonstrate your interest in the position by asking when it will be filled or what the next step will be. Too many candidates leave the interview without knowing their status or when they will hear from the recruiter. Don't be afraid to say that you want the job!

Before you leave, summarize your strongest qualifications, show your enthusiasm for obtaining this position, and thank the interviewer for a constructive interview and for considering you for the position. Ask the interviewer for a business card, which will provide the information you need to write a thank-you letter, which is discussed later. Shake the interviewer's hand with confidence, and acknowledge anyone else you see on the way out. Be sure to thank the receptionist. Leaving the interview gracefully and enthusiastically will leave a lasting impression on those responsible for making the final hiring decision.

> End the interview by thanking the interviewer, reviewing your strengths for this position, and asking what action will follow.

After the Interview

After leaving the interview, immediately make notes of what was said in case you are called back for a second interview. Write down key points that were discussed, the names of people you spoke with, and other details of the interview. Ask yourself what went really well and what could have been improved. Note your strengths and weaknesses during the interview so that you can work to improve in future interviews. Next, write down your follow-up plans. To whom should you send thank-you letters? Will you contact the employer by phone? If so, when? Then be sure to follow up on those plans, beginning with writing a thank-you letter and contacting your references.

Thanking Your Interviewer

After a job interview you should always send a thank-you message, also called a follow-up message. This courtesy sets you apart from other applicants, some of whom will not bother. Your message also reminds the interviewer of your visit as well as suggesting your good manners and genuine enthusiasm for the job.

> A follow-up thank-you letter shows your good manners and your enthusiasm for the job.

Follow-up messages are most effective if sent immediately after the interview. Experts believe that a thoughtful follow-up note carries as much weight as the cover letter does. Almost nine out of ten senior executives admit that in their evaluation of a job candidate they are swayed by a written thank you.[11] In your thank-you message refer to the date of the interview, the exact job title for which you were interviewed, and specific topics discussed. "An effective thank-you message should hit every one of the employer's hot buttons," author and career consultant Wendy Enelow says.[12] Don't get carried away after a successful interview and send an ill-conceived thank-you e-mail that reads like a text message or sounds too chummy. Smart interviewees don't ruin their chances by communicating with recruiters in hasty, poorly thought-out textspeak from their mobile devices.

In addition to being respectful when following up after an interview, avoid worn-out phrases, such as *Thank you for taking the time to interview me*. Be careful, too, about overusing *I*, especially to begin sentences. Most important, show that you really want the job and that you are qualified for it. Notice how the message in Figure 13.3 conveys enthusiasm and confidence.

If you have been interviewed by more than one person, send a separate letter to each interviewer. It is also a good idea to send a thank-you letter to the receptionist and to the person who set up the interview. Your thank-you letter will probably make more of an impact if prepared in proper business format and sent by regular

FIGURE 13.3 Interview Follow-Up E-Mail

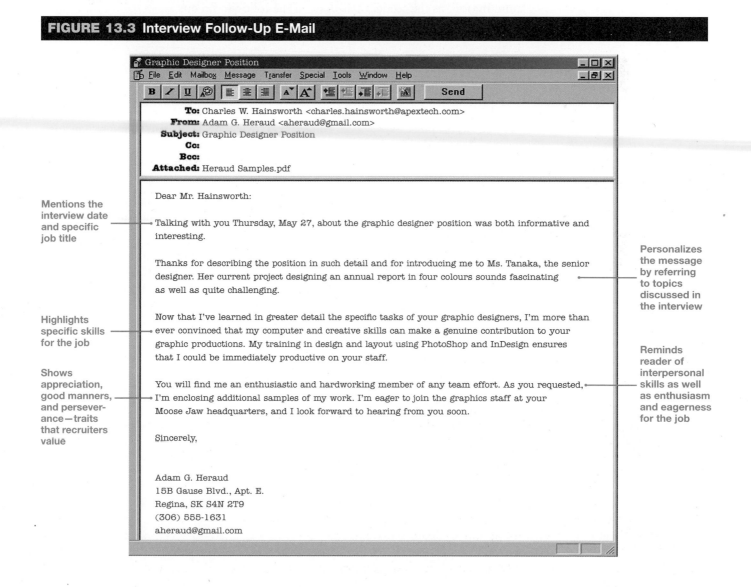

Mentions the interview date and specific job title

Highlights specific skills for the job

Shows appreciation, good manners, and persever-ance—traits that recruiters value

Personalizes the message by referring to topics discussed in the interview

Reminds reader of interpersonal skills as well as enthusiasm and eagerness for the job

To: Charles W. Hainsworth <charles.hainsworth@apextech.com>
From: Adam G. Heraud <aheraud@gmail.com>
Subject: Graphic Designer Position
Cc:
Bcc:
Attached: Heraud Samples.pdf

Dear Mr. Hainsworth:

Talking with you Thursday, May 27, about the graphic designer position was both informative and interesting.

Thanks for describing the position in such detail and for introducing me to Ms. Tanaka, the senior designer. Her current project designing an annual report in four colours sounds fascinating as well as quite challenging.

Now that I've learned in greater detail the specific tasks of your graphic designers, I'm more than ever convinced that my computer and creative skills can make a genuine contribution to your graphic productions. My training in design and layout using PhotoShop and InDesign ensures that I could be immediately productive on your staff.

You will find me an enthusiastic and hardworking member of any team effort. As you requested, I'm enclosing additional samples of my work. I'm eager to join the graphics staff at your Moose Jaw headquarters, and I look forward to hearing from you soon.

Sincerely,

Adam G. Heraud
15B Gause Blvd., Apt. E.
Regina, SK S4N 2T9
(306) 555-1631
aheraud@gmail.com

mail. However, if you know the decision will be made quickly, send your follow-up message by e-mail. One job candidate now makes a follow-up e-mail a practice. She summarizes what was discussed during the face-to-face interview and adds information that she had not thought to mention during the interview.[13]

Contacting Your References

Once you have thanked your interviewer, it is time to alert your references that they may be contacted by the employer. You might also have to request a letter of recommendation to be sent to the employer by a certain date. As discussed in Chapter 12, you should have already asked permission to use these individuals as references, and you should have supplied them with a copy of your résumé, highlighted with sales points.

To provide the best possible recommendation, your references need information. What position have you applied for with what company? What should they stress to the prospective employer? Let's say you are applying for a specific job that requires a letter of recommendation. Professor Orenstein has already agreed to be a reference for you. To get the best letter of recommendation from Professor Orenstein, help her out. Write a letter telling her about the position, its requirements, and the recommendation deadline. Include a copy of your résumé. You might remind her of a positive experience with you that she could use in the recommendation. Remember that recommenders need evidence to support generalizations. Give them appropriate ammunition, as the student has done in the following request:

Dear Professor Orenstein:

Recently I interviewed for the position of administrative assistant in the Human Resources Department of Host International. Because you kindly agreed to help me, I am now asking you to write a letter of recommendation to Host.

The position calls for good organizational, interpersonal, and writing skills, as well as computer experience. To help you review my skills and training, I enclose my résumé. As you may recall, I earned an A in your business communication class last fall; and you commended my research report for its clarity and organization.

Please e-mail your letter to Mr. James Jenkins at Host International (jjenkins@hinternational.com) before July 1 and kindly cc or bcc me. I'm grateful for your support, and I promise to let you know the results of my job search.

Following Up

If you don't hear from the interviewer within five days, or at the specified time, call him or her. Practise saying something like *I'm wondering what else I can do to convince you that I'm the right person for this job* or *I'm calling to find out the status of your search for the _____ position.* You could also e-mail the interviewer to find out how the decision process is going. When following up, it is important to sound professional and courteous. Sounding desperate, angry, or frustrated that you haven't been contacted can ruin your chances. The following follow-up e-mail would impress the interviewer:

Dear Ms. Jamison:

I enjoyed my interview with you last Thursday for the receptionist position. You should know that I'm very interested in this opportunity with Coastal Enterprises. Because you mentioned that you might have an answer this week, I'm eager to know how your decision process is coming along. I look forward to hearing from you.

Sincerely,

In a reference request letter, tell immediately why you are writing. Identify the target position and company.

Specify the job requirements so that the recommender knows what to stress.

A follow-up message inquires courteously and does not sound angry or desperate.

Depending on the response you get to your first follow-up request, you may have to follow up additional times. Keep in mind, though, that some employers won't tell you about their hiring decision unless you are the one hired.[14] Don't harass the interviewer, and don't force a decision. If you don't hear back from an employer within several weeks after following up, it is best to assume that you didn't get the job and to continue with your job search.

Other Employment Documents

Although the résumé and cover letter are your major tasks, other important documents and messages are often required during the employment process. You may need to complete an employment application form and write follow-up letters. You might also have to write a letter of resignation when leaving a job. Because each of these tasks reveals something about you and your communication skills, you will want to put your best foot forward. These documents often subtly influence company officials to offer a job.

Application Form

Some organizations require job candidates to fill out job application forms instead of, or in addition to, submitting résumés. This practice permits them to gather and store standardized data about each applicant. Whether the application is on paper or online, follow the directions carefully and provide accurate information. The following suggestions can help you be prepared:

- Carry a card summarizing vital statistics not included on your résumé. If you are asked to fill out an application form in an employer's office, you will need a handy reference to the following data: graduation dates, beginning and ending dates of all employment; salary history; full names, titles, and present work addresses of former supervisors; full addresses and phone numbers of current and previous employers; and full names, occupational titles, occupational addresses, and telephone numbers of persons who have agreed to serve as references.
- Look over all the questions before starting.
- Fill out the form neatly, using blue or black ink. Many career counsellors recommend printing your responses; cursive handwriting can be difficult to read.
- Answer all questions honestly. Write *Not applicable* or *N/A* if appropriate.
- Use accurate spelling, grammar, and punctuation.
- If asked for the position desired, give a specific job title or type of position. Don't say, *Anything* or *Open*. These answers will make you look unfocused; moreover, they make it difficult for employers to know what you are qualified for or interested in.
- Be prepared for a salary question. Unless you know what comparable employees are earning in the company, the best strategy is to suggest a salary range or to write *Negotiable* or *Open*. See the Communication Workshop at the end of this chapter for tips on dealing with money matters while interviewing.
- Be prepared to explain the reasons for leaving previous positions. Use positive or neutral phrases such as *Relocation*, *Seasonal*, *To accept a position with more responsibility*, *Temporary position*, *To continue education*, or *Career change*. Avoid words or phrases such as *Fired*, *Quit*, *Didn't get along with supervisor*, or *Pregnant*.
- Look over the application before submitting to make sure it is complete and that you have followed all instructions. Sign and date the application.

When applying for jobs, keep with you a card summarizing your important data.

Application or Résumé Follow-Up Letter

If your résumé or application generates no response within a reasonable time, you may decide to send a short follow-up letter such as the following. Doing so (a) jogs the memory of the personnel officer, (b) demonstrates your serious interest, and (c) allows you to emphasize your qualifications or to add new information.

Open by reminding the reader of your interest.

Dear Ms. Lavecchia:

Please know I am still interested in becoming an administrative support specialist with Quad, Inc.

Review your strengths or add new qualifications.

Since I submitted an application [*or* résumé] in May, I have completed my degree and have been employed as a summer replacement for office workers in several downtown offices. This experience has honed my word processing and communication skills. It has also introduced me to a wide range of office procedures.

Please keep my application in your active file and let me know when I may put my formal training, technical skills, and practical experience to work for you.

Rejection Follow-Up Letter

If you didn't get the job and you think it was perfect for you, don't give up. Employment specialists encourage applicants to respond to a rejection. The candidate who was offered the position may decline, or other positions may open up. In a rejection follow-up letter, it is okay to admit you are disappointed. Be sure to add, however, that you are still interested and will contact the company again in a month in case a job opens up. Then follow through for a couple of months—but don't overdo it. You should be professional and persistent, but not a pest. Here's an example of an effective rejection follow-up letter:

Dear Mr. O'Neal:

Subordinate your disappointment to your appreciation at being notified promptly and courteously.

Although I'm disappointed that someone else was selected for your accounting position, I appreciate your promptness and courtesy in notifying me.

Because I firmly believe that I have the technical and interpersonal skills needed to work in your fast-paced environment, I hope you will keep my résumé in your active file. My desire to become a productive member of your Transamerica staff remains strong.

Refer to specifics of your interview.

I enjoyed our interview, and I especially appreciate the time you and Ms. Goldstein spent describing your company's expansion into international markets. To enhance my qualifications, I have enrolled in a course in International Accounting at Conestoga College.

Take the initiative; tell when you will call for an update.

Should you have an opening for which I am qualified, you may reach me at (519) 555-3901. In the meantime, I will call you in a month to discuss employment possibilities.

Sincerely,

Job Acceptance and Rejection Letters

When all your hard work pays off, you will be offered the position you want. Although you will likely accept the position over the phone, it is a good idea to follow up with an acceptance letter to confirm the details and to formalize the acceptance. Your acceptance letter might look like this:

Dear Ms. Madhumali:

Confirm your acceptance of the position with enthusiasm.

It was a pleasure talking with you earlier today. As I mentioned, I am delighted to accept the position of web designer with Innovative Creations, Inc., in your

Richmond office. I look forward to becoming part of the IC team and to starting work on a variety of exciting and innovative projects.

As we agreed, my starting salary will be $46,000, with a full benefits package including health and life insurance, retirement plan, stock options, and three weeks of vacation per year.

Review salary and benefits details.

I look forward to starting my position with Innovative Creations on September 15, 2012. Before that date I will send you the completed tax and insurance forms you need. Thanks again for everything, Ms. Madhumali.

Include the specific starting date.

Sincerely,

If you must turn down a job offer, show your professionalism by writing a sincere letter. This letter should thank the employer for the job offer and explain briefly that you are turning it down. Taking the time to extend this courtesy could help you in the future if this employer has a position you really want. Here's an example of a job rejection letter:

Dear Mr. Opperman:

Thank you very much for offering me the position of sales representative with Bendall Pharmaceuticals. It was a difficult decision to make, but I have accepted a position with another company.

Thank the employer for the job offer and decline the offer without giving specifics. Express gratitude and best wishes for the future.

I appreciate your taking the time to interview me, and I wish Bendall much success in the future.

Resignation Letter

After you have been in a position for a period of time, you may find it necessary to leave. Perhaps you have been offered a better position, or maybe you have decided to return to school full-time. Whatever the reason, you should leave your position gracefully and tactfully. Although you will likely discuss your resignation in person with your supervisor, it is a good idea to document your resignation by writing a formal letter. Some resignation letters are brief, while others contain great detail. Remember that many resignation letters are placed in personnel files; therefore, it should be formatted and written using the professional business letter writing techniques you learned earlier. Here is an example of a basic letter of resignation:

Dear Ms. Patrick:

This letter serves as formal notice of my resignation from Allied Corporation, effective Friday, August 15. I have enjoyed serving as your office assistant for the past two years, and I am grateful for everything I have learned during my employment with Allied.

Confirm exact date of resignation. Remind employer of your contributions.

Please let me know what I can do over the next two weeks to help you prepare for my departure. I would be happy to help with finding and training my replacement.

Offer assistance to prepare for your resignation. Offer thanks and end with a forward-looking statement.

Thanks again for providing such a positive employment experience. I will long remember my time here.

Sincerely,

Although this employee gave a standard two-week notice, you may find that a longer notice is necessary. The higher and more responsible your position, the longer the notice you should give your employer. You should, however, always give some notice as a courtesy.

Writing job acceptance, job rejection, and resignation letters requires effort. That effort, however, is worth it because you are building bridges that later may carry you to even better jobs in the future.

Summing Up and Looking Forward

Whether you face a screening interview or a hiring/placement interview, you must be well prepared. You can increase your chances of success and reduce your stress considerably by knowing how interviews are typically conducted and by investigating the target company thoroughly. Practise answering typical questions, including legal and illegal ones. Consider making an audio or video recording of a mock interview so that you can check your body language and improve your answering techniques.

At the end of the interview, thank the interviewer, review your main strengths for the position, and ask what the next step is. Follow up with a thank-you message and a follow-up call or message, if appropriate. Prepare other employment-related documents as needed, including application forms, application and résumé follow-up letters, rejection follow-up letters, job acceptance and rejection letters, and resignation letters.

You have now completed 13 chapters of rigorous instruction aimed at developing your skills so that you can be a successful business communicator. Remember that this book represents a starting point. For instance, this book has not offered specific suggestions about how to communicate using a PDA device such as a BlackBerry. Your employer may, however, expect you to be able to adapt what you learned about writing e-mails in Chapter 4 to writing with a PDA. Your skills as a business communicator will continue to grow on the job as you apply the principles you have learned and expand your expertise.

Critical Thinking

1. How can recruiters and job seekers connect on the Web, and what are the advantages and potential disadvantages of doing so?

2. Is it normal to be nervous about an employment interview, and what can be done to overcome this fear?

3. What can you do to improve the first impression you make at an interview?

4. In employment interviews, do you think that behavioural questions (such as *Tell me about a business problem you have had and how you solved it*) are more effective than traditional questions (such as *Tell me what you are good at and why*)?

5. Why is it important to ask one's own questions of the interviewer?

6. Why should a job candidate send a thank-you e-mail after an interview?

Chapter Review

1. Name the main purposes of interviews—for job candidates as well as for employers.

2. If you have sent out your résumé to many companies, what information should you keep handy and why?

3. Briefly describe the types of hiring/placement interviews you may encounter.

4. How can you address problem areas on your résumé such as lack of experience, getting fired, or earning low grades?

5. Name at least six interviewing behaviours you can exhibit that send positive nonverbal messages.

6. What is your greatest fear of what you might do or what might happen to you during an employment interview? How can you overcome your fears?

7. Should you be candid with an interviewer when asked about your weaknesses?

8. How can you clarify vague questions from recruiters?

9. How should you respond to questions you believe to be illegal?

10. List the steps you should take immediately following your job interview.

11. Explain the various kinds of follow-up letters.

1. **Scripting Answers to Typical Interview Questions.** You've probably already been through a number of job interviews in your life, but they may not have been formal like the interviews you will go through when you start applying for post-college jobs. Script a one- to two-minute answer to the following interview question, and memorize it. Do not use the template on page 393. Then practise speaking the answer in a natural voice so that you don't appear to have memorized it.

   Question: Tell me about yourself and your previous work experience.

2. **Scripting Answers to Typical Interview Questions.** Script a one- to two-minute answer to the following typical interview question, and memorize it. Then practise speaking the answer in a natural voice so that you don't appear to have memorized it.

   Question: Tell me about a time in a previous job when you faced a difficulty or a criticism or a problem and how you dealt with it.

   Follow-Up Question: What would you do differently if this problem happened again?

3. **Scripting Answers to Typical Interview Questions.** Script a one- to two-minute answer to the following typical interview question, and memorize it. Then practise speaking the answer in a natural voice so that you don't appear to have memorized it.

   Question: Tell me about a former boss or coworker whom you admire a lot and why you admire him or her.

Now that you've memorized these three answers, practise interviewing a partner. As you ask each other questions, surprise each other by slightly modifying the questions so they're not exactly as printed above. This modification will force you to improvise on the spot, a valuable interviewing skill.

Activities and Cases

13.1 Researching an Organization

WEB

Select an organization where you would like to be employed. Assume you've been selected for an interview. Using resources described in this chapter, locate information about the organization's leaders and their business philosophy. Find out about the organization's accomplishments, setbacks, finances, products, customers, competition, and advertising. Prepare a summary report documenting your findings.

13.2 Learning What Jobs Are Really About Through Blogs

WEB

Blogs are becoming an important tool in the employment search process. By accessing blogs, job seekers can learn more about a company's culture and day-to-day activities.

Your Task. Using the Web, locate a blog that is maintained by an employee of a company where you would like to work. Monitor the blog for at least a week. Prepare a short report that summarizes what you learned about the company through reading the blog postings. Include a statement of whether this information would be valuable during your job search.

13.3 Building Interview Skills

Successful interviews require diligent preparation and repeated practice. To be best prepared, you need to know what skills are required for your targeted position. In addition to computer and communication skills, employers generally want to know whether a candidate works well with a team, accepts responsibility, solves problems, is efficient, meets deadlines, shows leadership, saves time and money, and is a hard worker.

Your Task. Consider a position for which you are eligible now or one for which you will be eligible when you complete your education. Identify the skills and traits necessary for this position. If you prepared a résumé in Chapter 12, be sure that it addresses these targeted areas. Now prepare interview worksheets listing at least ten technical and other skills or traits you think a recruiter will want to discuss in an interview for your targeted position.

13.4 Preparing Success Stories

You can best showcase your talents if you are ready with your own success stories that show how you have developed the skills or traits required for your targeted position.

Your Task. Using the worksheets you prepared in Activity 13.3, prepare success stories that highlight the required skills or traits. Select three to five stories to develop into answers to potential interview questions. For example, here's a typical question: "How does your background relate to the position we have open?" A possible response: "As you know, I have just completed an intensive training program in _____. In addition, I have over three years of part-time work experience in a variety of business settings. In one position I was selected to manage a small business in the absence of the owner. I developed responsibility and customer-service skills in filling orders efficiently, resolving shipping problems, and monitoring key accounts. I also inventoried and organized products worth over $200,000. When the owner returned from a vacation trip to Florida, I was commended for increasing sales and was given a bonus in recognition of her gratitude." People relate to and remember stories. Try to shape your answers into memorable stories.

WEB

13.5 Exploring Appropriate Interview Attire

As you prepare for your interview by learning about the company and the industry, don't forget a key component of interview success: creating a favourable first impression by wearing appropriate business attire. Job seekers often have nebulous ideas about proper interview wear. Some wardrobe mishaps include choosing a conservative "power" suit but accessorizing it with beat-up casual shoes or a shabby bag. Grooming glitches include dandruff on dark suit fabric, dirty fingernails, or mothball odour. Women sometimes wrongly assume that any black clothing items are acceptable, even if they are too tight, revealing, sheer, or made of low-end fabrics. Most image consultants agree that workplace attire falls into three main categories: business formal, business casual, and casual. Only business formal is considered proper interview apparel.

Your Task. To prepare for your big day, search your library databases and the Web for descriptions and images of *business formal*. You may research *business casual* and *casual* styles, but for an interview, always dress on the side of caution—conservatively. Compare prices and look for suit sales to buy one or two attractive interview outfits. Share your findings (notes, images, and price ranges for suits, shoes, and accessories) with the class and your instructor.

13.6 Polishing Answers to Interview Questions

Practice makes perfect in interviewing. The more often you rehearse responses to typical interview questions, the closer you are to getting the job.

Your Task. Select three questions from each of the five question categories discussed in this chapter (pp. 393–96). Write your answers to each set of questions. Try to incorporate skills and traits required for the targeted position. Polish these answers and your delivery technique by practising in front of a mirror or with a video or audio recorder.

13.7 Knowing What to Ask

When it is your turn to ask questions during the interview process, be ready.

Your Task. Decide on three to five questions that you would like to ask during an interview. Write these questions out and practise asking them so that you sound confident and sincere.

TEAM

13.8 Role Play: Practising Answering Interview Questions

One of the best ways to understand interview dynamics and to develop confidence is to role-play the parts of interviewer and candidate.

Your Task. Choose a partner from your class. Make a list of five interview questions from those presented in this chapter. In team sessions you and your partner will role-play an actual interview. One acts as interviewer, the other as the candidate. Prior to the Interview, the candidate tells the interviewer what job he/she is applying for, at which company. For the interview, the interviewer and candidate should dress appropriately and sit in chairs facing each other. The interviewer greets the candidate and makes him/her comfortable. The candidate gives the interviewer a copy of his/her résumé. The interviewer asks three (or more, depending on your instructor's time schedule) questions from the candidate's list. The interviewer may also ask follow-up questions if appropriate. When finished, the interviewer ends the meeting graciously. After one interview, reverse roles and repeat.

13.9 Learning to Answer Situational Interview Questions

Situational interview questions can vary widely from position to position. You should know enough about a position to understand some of the typical situations you would encounter on a regular basis.

Your Task. Use your favourite search tool to locate typical job descriptions of a position in which you are interested. Based on these descriptions, develop a list of six to eight typical situations someone in this position would face; then write situational interview questions for each of these scenarios. In pairs of two students, role-play interviewer and interviewee alternating with your listed questions.

13.10 Developing Skill With Behavioural Interview Questions

Behavioural interview questions are increasingly popular, and you will need a little practice before you can answer them easily.

Your Task. Use your favourite search tool to locate lists of behavioural questions on the Web. Select five skills areas such as communication, teamwork, and decision making. For each skills area find three behavioural questions that you think would be effective in an interview. In pairs of two students, role-play interviewer and interviewee alternating with your listed questions. You goal is to answer effectively in one or two minutes. Remember to use the STAR method when answering.

13.11 Answering Puffball and Killer Questions in a Virtual Interview

Two Web sites offer excellent interview advice. At Monster Career Advice (**http://career-advice.monster.com/interview-tips/home.aspx**) you can improve your interviewing skills in virtual interviews. You will find questions, answers, and explanations for interviews in job fields ranging from administrative support to human resources to technology. At WetFeet (**http://www.wetfeet.com**) you can learn how to answer résumé-based questions and how to handle pre-interview jitters, and see dozens of articles filled with helpful tips.

Your Task. Visit one or both of the targeted Web sites. (If the URLs have been changed, use your favourite search tool to locate *Monster Interviews* and *WetFeet Interviews*.)

13.12 Video-Recording an Interview

Seeing how you look during an interview can help you improve your body language and presentation style. Your instructor may act as interviewer, or an outside businessperson may be asked to conduct mock interviews in your classroom.

Your Task. Engage a student or campus specialist to video-record each interview. Review your performance and critique it, looking for ways to improve. Your instructor may ask class members to offer comments and suggestions on individual interviews.

13.13 Handling Difficult Interview Questions

Although some questions are not appropriate in job interviews, many interviewers will ask them anyway—whether intentionally or unknowingly. Being prepared is important.

Your Task. How would you respond in the following scenario? Let's assume you are being interviewed at one of the top companies on your list of potential employers. The interviewing committee consists of a human resources manager and the supervising manager of the department where you would work. At various times during the interview the supervising manager has asked questions that made you feel uncomfortable. For example, he asked whether you were married. You know this question is illegal, but you saw no harm in answering it. But then he asked how old you were. Since you started college early and graduated in two years, you are worried that you may not be considered mature enough for this position. But you have most of the other qualifications required and you are convinced you could succeed on the job. How should you answer this question?

13.14 Saying Thanks for the Interview
You've just completed an exciting employment interview, and you want the interviewer to remember you.

Your Task. Write a follow-up thank-you e-mail to Ronald T. Ranson, Human Resources Manager, Electronic Data Sources, ranson@eds.ca (or a company of your choice).

13.15 Refusing to Take No for an Answer
After an excellent interview with Electronic Data Sources (or a company of your choice), you're depressed to learn that it hired someone else. But you really want to work for the company.

Your Task. Write a follow-up e-mail to Ronald T. Ranson, Human Resources Manager, Electronic Data Sources, ranson@eds.ca (or a company of your choice). Indicate that you are disappointed but still interested.

13.16 Answering Difficult Questions in a Virtual Interview
The Monster Web site offers an entertaining online practice interview with questions ranging from easy to challenging. Even an experienced interviewee is unlikely to get all of these questions right the first time.

Your Task. Visit Monster's Interview section at the URL below. Craft responses to the five bolded questions (without reading Monster's suggestions). After you've crafted your responses, read Monster's suggestions. What do you think of these suggestions?

Related Web site: http://career-advice.monster.ca/job-interview/interview-questions/common-interview-questions-canada/article.aspx.

13.17 Following Up After Submitting Your Résumé
A month has passed since you sent your résumé and cover letter in response to a job advertisement. You are still interested in the position and would like to find out whether you still have a chance.

Your Task. Write a follow-up letter that won't offend the reader or damage your chances of employment.

13.18 Requesting a Reference
Your favourite professor has agreed to be one of your references. You have just arrived home from a job interview that went well, and you must ask your professor to write a letter of recommendation.

Your Task. Write to the professor requesting that a letter of recommendation be sent to the company where you were interviewed. Explain that the interviewer asked that the letter be sent directly to him. Provide data about the job description and about yourself so that the professor can target its content.

13.19 Saying Yes to a Job Offer
Your dream has come true: you have just been offered an excellent position. Although you accepted the position on the phone, you want to send a formal acceptance letter.

Your Task. Write a job acceptance letter to an employer of your choice. Include the specific job title, your starting date, and details about your compensation package. Make up any necessary details.

13.20 Searching for Advice

You can find wonderful, free, and sometimes entertaining information about job search strategies, career tips, and interview advice on the Web.

Your Task. Use a search engine or visit a site such as Workopolis to locate links to job search and résumé sites. From any Web site featuring interview information, make a list of at least five good interview pointers—ones that were not covered in this chapter. Send an e-mail message to your instructor describing your findings.

Related Web site: http://www.workopolis.com.

13.21 Humour and Job Interviews

Job interviews can be stressful occasions, so it's no surprise that comedians have for a long time used job interviews in their routines. The popular Web site YouTube (**www.youtube.com**) has a number of postings under the category "Job Interview Funny."

Your Task. Do some research on YouTube by watching a few funny interview clips. Decide whether there's anything new and useful to be learned from these clips, or whether it has all been covered, and more usefully, by this chapter. If you think there's something new to be learned from the clips you've seen, develop a three- to five-minute presentation in which you use part of a YouTube clip to illustrate your point. Remember, humour has to be used carefully in a classroom or workplace situation. You're using the humour to make a point, not just to get laughs from your audience.

Grammar/Mechanics Review—13

The following sentences contain errors in grammar, punctuation, capitalization, number style, usage, and spelling. Below each sentence write a corrected version.

1. City officials begged the two companys board of directors not to dessert they're locations, and not to abandon local employees.

2. One store listed its Seiko Watch at eighty dollars; while its competitor listed the same watch at seventy-five dollars.

3. Here are a group of participating manufactures who you may wish to contact regarding there Web cites.

4. If we are to remain friends this personal information must be kept strictly between you and I.

5. As soon as the merger is complete we will inform the entire staff, until then its business as usual.

6. Smart organizations can boost profit's allmost one hundred percent by retaining just five percent more of there customers.

7. Many companies sell better at home then abroad; because they lack over-seas experience.

8. The quality of the e-mails, letters, memos and reports in this organization need to be improved.

9. The additional premium you were charged which amounted to fifty-five collars and 40 cents was issued because of you're recent accident.

10. The entire team of thirty-five managers were willing to procede with the proposal for asian expansion.

11. Several copys of the sales' report was sent to the CEO and I immediatley after we requested it.

12. Stored on open shelfs in room 17 is a group of office supplys and at least 7 boxes of stationary.

13. Darren Highsmith who was recently appointed Sales Manager submitted 6 different suggestions for increasing sales.

14. China the worlds fastest growing country will be snapping up personal computers at a thirty percent rate by 2013.

15. Congratulations, your finished!

Document for Revision

The following interview thank-you e-mail (Figure 13.4) has faults in grammar, punctuation, spelling, wordiness, and word use. Use standard proofreading marks (see Appendix B) to correct the errors. When you finish, your instructor can show you the revised version of this e-mail.

FIGURE 13.4 Follow-Up E-Mail

Interview — File Edit Mailbox Message Transfer Special Tools Window Help

B / U ≡ ≡ ≡ A A | Send

To: <AMasters@Biolage.ca> June 4, 2012
From:
Subject: Interview
Cc:
Bcc:
Attached:

Dear Mr. Masters:

I appriciate the opportunity for the interview yesterday for the newly-listed Position of Sales Trainee. It was really a pleasure meeting yourself and learning more about Biolage Enterprises, you have a fine staff and a sophisticated approach to marketing.

You're organization appears to be growing in a directional manner that parralels my interests' and career goals. The interview with yourself and your staff yesterday confirmed my initale positive impressions of Biolage Enterprises and I want to reiterate my strong interest in working with and for you. My prior Retail sales experience as a sales associate with Sears; plus my recent training in Microsoft Word and Excel would enable me to make progress steadily through your programs of training and become a productive member of your sales team in no time at all.

Again, thank-you for your kind and gracius consideration. In the event that you need any additional information from me, all you have to do is give me a call me at (405) 391-7792.

Sincerly yours,

Let's Talk Money: Negotiating a Salary

When to talk about salary causes concern for many job applicants. Some advisors recommend bringing the issue up immediately; others suggest avoiding the topic entirely. What happens if the company asks for salary expectations in the job advertisement? The best plan is to be prepared to discuss salary when required but not to force the issue. The important thing to remember is that almost all salaries are negotiable.

Suggestion No. 1: Avoid discussing salary for as long as possible in the interview process.

The longer you delay salary discussion, the more time you will have to convince the employer that you are worth what you are asking for. Ideally, you should try to avoid discussing salary until you know for sure that the interviewing company is making a job offer. The best time for you to negotiate your salary is between the time you are offered the position and the time you accept it. Wait for the employer to bring salary up first. If salary comes up and you are not sure whether the job is being offered to you, it is time for you to be blunt. Here are some things you could say:

Are you making me a job offer?

What salary range do you pay for positions with similar requirements?

I'm very interested in the position, and my salary would be negotiable.

Tell me what you have in mind for the salary range.

Suggestion No. 2: Know the salary range for similar jobs in similar organizations but be aware of an amount that would motivate you.

Remember that if you provide an amount that is too high you will price yourself out of the market. If the amount is too low you might be sorry. Everyone wants to make money, but salary by itself should not be a reason to take or reject a job. The important thing here is to think in terms of a wide range. Let's say you are hoping to start at between $40,000 and $50,000. To an interviewer, you might say, *I was looking for a salary in the low to high forties.* This technique is called bracketing. In addition, stating your salary range in an annual dollar amount sounds more professional than asking for an hourly wage. Be sure to consider such things as geographic location, employer size, industry standards, the strength of the economy, and other factors to make sure that the range you come up with is realistic.

Suggestion No. 3: When negotiating, focus on what you are worth, not on what you need.

Throughout the interview and negotiation process, focus continually on your strengths. Make sure that the employer knows everything of value that you will bring to the organization. You have to prove that you are worth what you are asking for. Employers pay salaries based on what you will accomplish on the job and contribute to the organization. When discussing your salary, focus on how the company will benefit from these contributions. Don't bring personal issues into the negotiation process. No employer will be willing to pay you more because you have bills to pay, mouths to feed, or debt to get out of.

Suggestion No. 4: Never say no to a job before it is offered.

Why would anyone refuse a job offer before it's made? It happens all the time. Let's say you were hoping for a salary of $45,000. The interviewer tells you that the salary scheduled for this job is $39,000. You respond, *Oh, that's out of the question!* Before being offered the job, you have, in effect, refused it. Instead, wait for the job offer; then start negotiating your salary.

Suggestion No. 5: Ask for a higher salary first, and consider benefits.

Within reason, always try to ask for a higher salary first. This will leave room for this amount to decrease during negotiations until it is closer to your original expectations. Remember to consider the entire compensation package when negotiating. You may be willing to accept a lower salary if benefits such as insurance, flexible hours, time off, and retirement are attractive.

Suggestion No. 6: Be ready to bargain if offered a low starting salary.

Many salaries are negotiable. Companies are often willing to pay more for someone who interviews well and fits their culture. If the company seems right to you and you are pleased with the sound of the open position but you have been offered a low salary, say, *That is somewhat lower than I had hoped but this position does sound exciting. If I were to consider this, what sorts of things could I do to quickly become more valuable to this organization?* Also discuss such things as bonuses based on performance or a shorter review period. You could say something like, *Thanks for the offer. The position is very much what I wanted in many ways, and I am delighted at your interest. If I start at this salary, may I be reviewed within six months with the goal of raising the salary to _____?*

Another possibility is to ask for more time to think about the low offer. Tell the interviewer that this is an important decision, and you need some time to consider the offer. The next day you can call and say, *I am flattered by your offer but I cannot accept, because the salary is lower than I would like. Perhaps you could reconsider your offer or keep me in mind for future openings.*

Suggestion No. 7: Be honest.

Be honest throughout the entire negotiation process. Don't inflate the salaries of your previous positions to try to get more money. Don't tell an employer that you have received other job offers unless it is true. These lies can be grounds for being fired later on.

Suggestion No. 8: Get the final offer in writing.

Once you have agreed on a salary and compensation package, get the offer in writing. You should also follow up with a position acceptance letter, as discussed earlier in this chapter.

Career Application

You've just passed the screening interview and have been asked to come in for a personal interview with the human resources representative and the hiring manager of a company where you are very eager to work. Although you are delighted with the company, you have promised yourself that you will not accept any position that pays less than $45,000 to start.

Your Task

- In teams of two, role-play the position of interviewer and interviewee.
- *Interviewer:* Set the interview scene. Discuss preliminaries, and then offer a salary of $39,000.
- *Interviewee:* Respond to preliminary questions and then counter with a salary request for $42,500.
- Reverse roles so that the interviewee becomes the interviewer. Repeat the scenario.

Business communicators produce numerous documents that have standardized formats. Becoming familiar with these formats is important because business documents actually carry two kinds of messages. Verbal messages are conveyed by the words chosen to express the writer's ideas. Nonverbal messages are conveyed largely by the appearance of a document and its adherence to recognized formats. To ensure that your documents carry favourable nonverbal messages about you and your organization, you'll want to give special attention to the appearance and formatting of your e-mails, letters, envelopes, memos, and fax cover sheets.

E-Mails

Because e-mail is still an evolving communication medium, formatting and usage are fluid. The following suggestions, illustrated in Figure A.1 (p. 414) and also in Figure 4.2 on page 90, may guide you in setting up the parts of an e-mail message. Always check, however, with your organization so that you can observe its practices.

To Line. Include the receiver's e-mail address after *To*. If the receiver's address is recorded in your address book, you just have to click on it. Be sure to enter all addresses carefully, since one mistyped letter prevents delivery.

From Line. Most e-mail programs automatically include your name and e-mail address after *From*.

Cc and Bcc. Insert the e-mail address of anyone who is to receive a copy of the message. *Cc* stands for carbon copy or courtesy copy. Don't be tempted, though, to send needless copies just because it's so easy. *Bcc* stands for *blind carbon copy*. Some writers use *bcc* to send a copy of the message without the addressee's knowledge. Writers also use the *bcc* line for mailing lists. When a message is being sent to a number of people and their e-mail addresses should not be revealed, the *bcc* line works well to conceal the names and addresses of all receivers.

Subject. Identify the subject of the e-mail message with a brief but descriptive summary of the topic. Be sure to include enough information to be clear and compelling. Capitalize the initial letters of principal words, or capitalize the entire line if space permits.

Salutation. Include a brief greeting, if you like. Some writers use a salutation such as *Dear Selina* followed by a comma or a colon. Others are more informal with *Hi, Selina!*, or *Good morning* or *Greetings*. Some writers simulate a salutation by including the name of the receiver in an abbreviated first line, as shown in Figure A.1. Others writers treat an e-mail like a memo and skip the salutation entirely.

Message. Cover just one topic in your message, and try to keep your total message under one screen in length. Single-space and be sure to use both upper- and lowercase letters. Double-space between paragraphs, and use graphic highlighting (bullets, numbering) whenever you are listing three or more items.

Includes descriptive subject line

Incorporates recipient's name in abbreviated first line

Uses single spacing within paragraphs and double spacing between

Closes with name and title to ensure identification

ADDING NEW DEPENDENTS TO YOUR HEALTH COVERAGE

File Edit Mailbox Message Transfer Special Tools Window Help

B / U | | | | A A | | | | | | **Send**

To: <sondra.rios@mail.onyx.com>   November 29, 2012
From: Michael E. Wynn <mewynn@mail.onyx.com>
Subject: ADDING NEW DEPENDENTS TO YOUR HEALTH COVERAGE
Cc:
Bcc:
Attached:

Hi, Sondra

Yes, you may add new dependents to your health plan coverage. Since you are a regular, active employee, you are eligible to add unmarried dependent children (biological, adopted, step, and foster) under age 19 or under age 26, if they are full-time students. You may also be eligible to enroll your domestic partner as your dependent, as part of a pilot program.

For any new dependent, you must submit a completed Verification of Dependent Eligibility Form. You must also submit a photocopy of a document that verifies their eligibility. An acceptable verification document for a spouse is a photocopy of your marriage certificate. For children, submit a photocopy of a birth certificate, adoption certificate, or guardianship certificate. Please call the Health Insurance Unit at Ext. 2558 for more information or to ask for an application form.

Cheers,

Michael E. Wynn
Health Benefits Coordinator

Closing. Conclude an external message with a short expression such as *Cheers* or *Best wishes*, followed by your name. If the recipient is unlikely to know you, it's not a bad idea to include your title and organization. Many e-mail users include a signature file with identifying information embellished with keyboard art. Use restraint, however, because signature files take up precious space. Writers of e-mail messages sent within organizations may omit a closing and even skip their names at the ends of messages because receivers recognize them from identification in the opening lines.

Letters

Business communicators write business letters primarily to correspond with people outside the organization. Letters may go to customers, vendors, other businesses, and the government, as discussed in Chapters 5, 6, and 7. The following information will help you format your letters following conventional guidelines.

Spacing and Punctuation

In the past typists left two spaces after end punctuation (periods, question marks, and so forth). This practice was necessary, it was thought, because typewriters did not have proportional spacing and sentences were easier to read if two spaces separated them. Professional typesetters, however, never followed this practice because they used proportional spacing, and readability was not a problem. Influenced by the look of typeset publications, many writers now leave only one space after end punctuation. As a practical matter, however, it is not wrong to use two spaces.

Letter Placement

The easiest way to place letters on the page is to use the defaults of your word processing program. In Microsoft Word 2007, default side margins are set at 1 inch (2.5 cm). Many companies today find these margins acceptable. If you want to adjust your margins to better balance shorter letters, use the following chart:

Words in Body of Letter	Margin Settings	Blank Lines After Date
Under 200	1.5 inches (4 cm)	4 to 10
Over 200	1 inch (2.5 cm)	2 to 3

Experts say that a ragged-right margin is easier to read than a justified (even) margin. You might want to turn off the justification feature of your word processing program if it automatically justifies the right margin.

Letter Parts

Professional-looking business letters are arranged in a conventional sequence with standard parts. Following is a discussion of how to use these letter parts properly. Figure A.2 illustrates the parts in a block-style letter. (See Chapter 5 for additional discussion of letters and their parts.)

Letterhead. Most business organizations use 8½-by-11-inch paper printed with a letterhead displaying their official name, street address, Web site address, e-mail address, and telephone and fax numbers. The letterhead may also include a logo and an advertising tag line such as *Ebank: A new way to bank.*

Dateline. On letterhead paper you should place the date two blank lines below the last line of the letterhead or 5 cm from the top edge of the paper (line 13). On plain paper place the date immediately below your return address. Since the date goes on line 13, start the return address an appropriate number of lines above it. The most common dateline format is as follows: *June 9, 2012.* Don't use *th* (or *rd*) when the date is written this way. For European or military correspondence, use the following dateline format: *9 June 2012.* Notice that no commas are used.

Addressee and Delivery Notations. Delivery notations such as *FAX TRANSMISSION, FEDERAL EXPRESS, MESSENGER DELIVERY, CONFIDENTIAL,* or *CERTIFIED MAIL* are typed in all capital letters two blank lines above the inside address.

Inside Address. Type the inside address—that is, the address of the organization or person receiving the letter—single-spaced, starting at the left margin. The number of lines between the dateline and the inside address depends on the size of the letter body, the type size (point or pitch size), and the length of the typing lines. Generally, two to ten lines is appropriate.

Be careful to duplicate the exact wording and spelling of the recipient's name and address on your documents. Usually, you can copy this information from the letterhead of the correspondence you are answering. If, for example, you are responding to *Jackson & Perkins Company*, don't address your letter to *Jackson and Perkins Corp.*

Always be sure to include a courtesy title such as *Mr., Ms., Mrs., Dr.,* or *Professor* before a person's name in the inside address—for both the letter and the envelope. Although many women in business today favour *Ms.,* you'll want to use whatever title the addressee prefers.

Remember that the inside address is not included for readers (who already know who and where they are). It's there to help writers accurately file a copy of the message.

Letterhead ——————

peerless **graphics**

8 9 3   D i l l i n g h a m   B o u l e v a r d   S t o n y   P l a i n ,   A B

Phone (403) 667-8880   Fax (403) 667-8830   www.peergraph.com

↓ line 13, or 2 blank lines below letterhead

Dateline ——————— September 13, 2012

↓ 2 to 10 blank lines

Inside address ——————
Mr. T. M. Wilson, President
Visual Concept Enterprises
1256 Lumsden Avenue
Nordegg, AB   T0M 3T0

↓ 1 blank line

Salutation ——————— Dear Mr. Wilson

↓ 1 blank line

Subject line ——————— SUBJECT: BLOCK LETTER STYLE

↓ 1 blank line

This letter illustrates block letter style, about which you asked. All typed lines begin at the left margin. The date is usually placed 5 cm from the top edge of the paper or two lines below the last line of the letterhead, whichever position is lower.

This letter also shows open punctuation. No colon follows the salutation, and no comma follows the complimentary close. Although this punctuation style is efficient, we find that most of our customers prefer to include punctuation after the salutation and the complimentary close.

Body ———————

If a subject line is included, it appears two lines below the salutation. The word SUBJECT is optional. Most readers will recognize a statement in this position as the subject without an identifying label. The complimentary close appears two lines below the end of the last paragraph.

↓ 1 blank line

Sincerely

Mark H. Wong   ↓ 3 to 4 blank lines

Complimentary close
and signature block ———

Modified block style,
mixed punctuation ——— Mark H. Wong
Graphics Designer

↓ 1 blank line

MHW:pil

In block-style letters, as shown above, all lines begin at the left margin. In modified block-style letters, as shown at the left, the date is centred or aligned with the complimentary close and signature block, which start at the centre. The date may also be backspaced from the right margin. Paragraphs may be blocked or indented. Mixed punctuation includes a colon after the salutation and a comma after the complimentary close. Open punctuation, shown above, omits the colon following the salutation and omits the comma following the complimentary closing.

In general, avoid abbreviations (such as *Ave.* or *Co.*) unless they appear in the printed letterhead of the document being answered.

Attention Line. An attention line allows you to send your message officially to an organization but to direct it to a specific individual, officer, or department. However, if you know an individual's complete name, it's always better to use it as the first line of the inside address and avoid an attention line. Here are two common formats for attention lines:

MultiMedia Enterprises
931 Calkins Avenue
Toronto, ON M3W 1E6

Attention Marketing Director

MultiMedia Enterprises
Attention: Marketing Director
931 Calkins Road
Toronto, ON M3W 1E6

Attention lines may be typed in all caps or with upper- and lowercase letters. The colon following *Attention* is optional. Notice that an attention line may be placed two lines below the address block or printed as the second line of the inside address. You'll want to use the latter format if you're composing on a word processor because the address block may be copied to the envelope and the attention line will not interfere with the last-line placement of the postal code. (Mail can be sorted more easily if the postal code appears in the last line of a typed address.)

Whenever possible, use a person's name as the first line of an address instead of putting that name in an attention line. Some writers use an attention line because they fear that letters addressed to individuals at companies may be considered private. They worry that if the addressee is no longer with the company, the letter may be forwarded or not opened. Actually, unless a letter is marked "Personal" or "Confidential," it will very likely be opened as business mail.

Salutation. Place the letter greeting, or salutation, two lines below the last line of the inside address or the attention line (if used). If the letter is addressed to an individual, use that person's courtesy title and last name (*Dear Mr. Lanham*). Even if you are on a first-name basis (*Dear Leslie*), be sure to add a colon (not a comma or a semicolon) after the salutation, unless you are using open punctuation. Do not use an individual's full name in the salutation (not *Dear Mr. Leslie Lanham*) unless you are unsure of gender (*Dear Leslie Lanham*).

For letters with attention lines or those addressed to organizations, the selection of an appropriate salutation has become more difficult. Formerly, *Gentlemen* was used generically for all organizations. With increasing numbers of women in business management today, however, *Gentlemen* is outdated. Because no universally acceptable salutation has emerged as yet, you'll probably be safest with *Ladies and Gentlemen* or *Gentlemen and Ladies*.

One way to avoid the salutation dilemma is to address a document to a specific person. Another alternative is to use the simplified letter style, which conveniently omits the salutation (and the complimentary close).

Subject and Reference Lines. Although experts suggest placing the subject line one blank line below the salutation, many businesses actually place it above the salutation. Use whatever style your organization prefers. Reference lines often show policy or file numbers; they generally appear two lines above the salutation.

Body. Most business letters and memorandums are single-spaced, with double line spacing between paragraphs. Very short messages may be double-spaced with indented paragraphs.

Complimentary Close. Typed two lines below the last line of the letter, the complimentary close may be formal (*Very truly yours*) or informal (*Sincerely* or *Respectfully*). The simplified letter style omits a complimentary close.

Signature Block. In most letter styles, the writer's typed name and optional identification appear three to four blank lines below the complimentary close. The combination of name, title, and organization information should be arranged to achieve a balanced look. The name and title may appear on the same line or on separate lines, depending on the length of each. Use commas to separate categories within the same line, but not to conclude a line.

Sincerely,

Jeremy M. Wood

Jeremy M. Wood, Manager
Technical Sales and Services

Respectfully,

Casandra Baker-Murillo

Casandra Baker-Murillo
Executive Vice President

Courtesy titles (*Mr., Ms., Mrs.,* or *Miss*) should be used before names that are not readily distinguishable as male or female. They should also be used before names containing only initials and international names. The title is usually placed in parentheses, but it may appear without them.

Yours truly,

K. C. Tripton

(Ms.) K. C. Tripton
Project Manager

Sincerely,

Leslie Hill

(Mr.) Leslie Hill
Public Policy Department

Some organizations include their names in the signature block. In such cases the organization name appears in all caps two lines below the complimentary close, as shown here:

Sincerely,
LITTON COMPUTER SERVICES

Shelina A. Simpson

Ms. Shelina A. Simpson
Executive Assistant

Reference Initials. If used, the initials of the typist and writer are typed two lines below the writer's name and title. Generally, the writer's initials are capitalized and the typist's are lowercased, but this format varies.

Enclosure Notation. When an enclosure or attachment accompanies a document, a notation to that effect appears two lines below the reference initials. This notation reminds the typist to insert the enclosure in the envelope, and it reminds the recipient to look for the enclosure or attachment. The notation may be spelled out (*Enclosure, Attachment*), or it may be abbreviated (*Enc., Att.*). It may indicate the number of enclosures or attachments, and it may also identify a specific enclosure (*Enclosure: Form 1099*).

Copy Notation. If you make copies of correspondence for other individuals, you may use *cc* to indicate carbon copy, *pc* to indicate photocopy, or merely *c* for any kind of copy. A colon following the initial(s) is optional.

Second-Page Heading. When a letter extends beyond one page, use plain paper of the same quality and colour as the first page. Identify the second and succeeding pages with a heading consisting of the name of the addressee, the page number, and the date. Use either of the following two formats:

Ms. Rachel Ruiz   2   May 3, 2012

Ms. Rachel Ruiz
Page 2
May 3, 2012

Both headings appear on line 7, followed by two blank lines to separate them from the continuing text. Avoid using a second page if you have only one line or the complimentary close and signature block to fill that page.

Plain-Paper Return Address. If you prepare a personal or business letter on plain paper, place your address immediately above the date. Do not include your name; you will type (and sign) your name at the end of your letter. If your return address contains two lines, begin typing it on line 11 so that the date appears on line 13. Avoid abbreviations other than the two-letter province/territory abbreviation.

580 East Leffels Street
Dartmouth, NS B6R 2F3
December 14, 2012

Ms. Ellen Siemens
Retail Credit Department
Union National Bank
1220 Dunsfield Boulevard
Halifax, NS B4L 2E2

Dear Ms. Siemens:

For letters prepared in the block style, type the return address at the left margin. For modified block-style letters, start the return address at the centre to align with the complimentary close.

Letter and Punctuation Styles

Business letters are generally prepared in one of three formats. The most popular is the block style, but the simplified style has much to recommend it.

Block Style. In the block style, shown in Figure A.2, all lines begin at the left margin. This style is a favourite because it is easy to format.

Modified Block Style. The modified block style differs from block style in that the date and closing lines appear in the centre, as shown at the bottom of Figure A.2. The date may be (1) centred, (2) begun at the centre of the page (to align with the closing lines), or (3) backspaced from the right margin. The signature block—including the complimentary close, writer's name and title, or organization identification—begins at the centre. The first line of each paragraph may begin at the left margin or may be indented five or ten spaces. All other lines begin at the left margin.

Most businesses today use mixed punctuation, shown with the modified block-style letter at the bottom left of Figure A.2. This style requires a colon after the salutation and a comma after the complimentary close. Even when the salutation is a first name, the colon is appropriate.

Envelopes

An envelope should be of the same quality and colour of stationery as the letter it carries. Because the envelope introduces your message and makes the first impression, you need to be especially careful in addressing it. Moreover, how you fold the letter is important.

Return Address. The return address is usually printed in the upper left corner of an envelope, as shown in Figure A.3. In large companies some form of identification (the writer's initials, name, or location) may be typed or handwritten above the company name and return address. This identification helps return the letter to the sender in case of non-delivery.

On an envelope without a printed return address, single-space the return address in the upper left corner. Beginning on line 3 on the fourth space (approximately 12 mm or ½ inch) from the left edge, type the writer's name, title, company, and mailing address.

Mailing Address. On legal-sized No. 10 envelopes (10.5 cm by 24 cm), begin the address on line 13 about 11.5 cm from the left edge, as shown in Figure A.3. For small envelopes (7.5 cm by 15 cm), begin typing on line 12 about 6.2 cm from the left edge.

Canada Post recommends that addresses be typed in all caps without any punctuation. This Postal Service style, shown in the small envelope in Figure A.3, was originally developed to facilitate scanning by optical character readers. Today's OCRs, however, are so sophisticated that they scan upper- and lowercase letters easily. Many companies today prefer to use the same format for the envelope as for the inside address. If the same format is used, writers can take advantage of word

---

FIGURE A.3 Envelope Formats

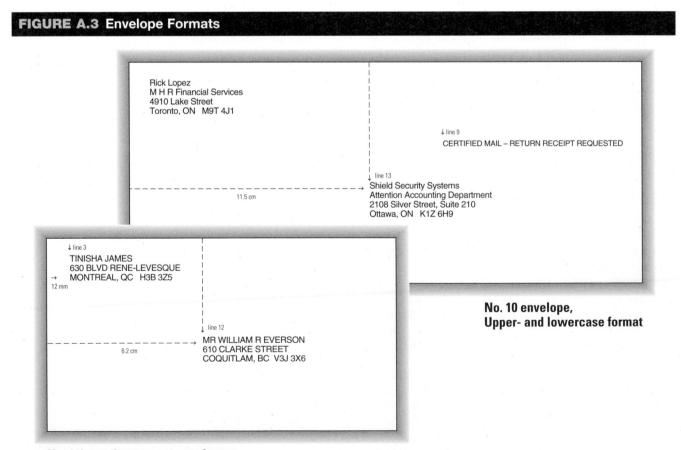

Rick Lopez
M H R Financial Services
4910 Lake Street
Toronto, ON   M9T 4J1

↓ line 9
CERTIFIED MAIL – RETURN RECEIPT REQUESTED

↓ line 13
Shield Security Systems
Attention Accounting Department
2108 Silver Street, Suite 210
Ottawa, ON   K1Z 6H9

11.5 cm

**No. 10 envelope,
Upper- and lowercase format**

↓ line 3
TINISHA JAMES
630 BLVD RENE-LEVESQUE
→ MONTREAL, QC   H3B 3Z5
12 mm

↓ line 12
MR WILLIAM R EVERSON
610 CLARKE STREET
COQUITLAM, BC   V3J 3X6

6.2 cm

No. 6¾ envelope, uppercase format

FIGURE A.4 Abbreviations of Provinces, Territories, and States

Province or Territory	Two-Letter Abbreviation	Province or Territory	Two-Letter Abbreviation
Alberta	AB	Nova Scotia	NS
British Columbia	BC	Nunavut	NU
Manitoba	MB	Ontario	ON
New Brunswick	NB	Prince Edward Island	PE
Newfoundland and		Quebec	QC
Labrador	NL	Saskatchewan	SK
Northwest Territories	NT	Yukon Territory	YT

State or Territory	Two-Letter Abbreviation	State or Territory	Two-Letter Abbreviation
Alabama	AL	Missouri	MO
Alaska	AK	Montana	MT
American Samoa	AS	Nebraska	NE
Arizona	AZ	Nevada	NV
Arkansas	AR	New Hampshire	NH
California	CA	New Jersey	NJ
Colorado	CO	New Mexico	NM
Connecticut	CT	New York	NY
Delaware	DE	North Carolina	NC
District of Columbia	DC	North Dakota	ND
Florida	FL	North Mariana Islands	MP
Georgia	GA	Ohio	OH
Guam	GU	Oklahoma	OK
Hawaii	HI	Oregon	OR
Idaho	ID	Palau	PW
Illinois	IL	Pennsylvania	PA
Indiana	IN	Puerto Rico	PR
Iowa	IA	Rhode Island	RI
Kansas	KS	South Carolina	SC
Kentucky	KY	South Dakota	SD
Louisiana	LA	Tennessee	TN
Maine	ME	Texas	TX
Marshall Islands	MH	Utah	UT
Maryland	MD	Vermont	VT
Massachusetts	MA	Virgin Islands	VI
Michigan	MI	Virginia	VA
Micronesia	FM	Washington	WA
Minnesota	MN	West Virginia	WV
Minor Outlying Islands	UM	Wisconsin	WI
Mississippi	MS	Wyoming	WY

processing programs to "copy" the inside address to the envelope, thus saving keystrokes and reducing errors. Having the same format on both the inside address and the envelope also looks more professional and consistent. For these reasons you may choose to use the familiar upper- and lowercase combination format. But you will want to check with your organization to learn its preference.

In addressing your envelopes for delivery in North America, use the two-letter province, territory, and state abbreviations shown in Figure A.4. Notice that these abbreviations are in capital letters without periods.

Folding. The way a letter is folded and inserted into an envelope sends additional nonverbal messages about a writer's professionalism and carefulness. Most businesspeople follow the procedures shown here, which produce the least number of creases to distract readers.

For large No. 10 envelopes, begin with the letter face up. Fold slightly less than one third of the sheet toward the top, as shown in the diagram. Then fold down the top third to within 6 to 7 mm of the bottom fold. Insert the letter into the envelope with the last fold toward the bottom of the envelope.

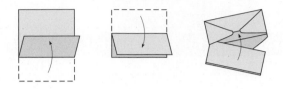

For small No. 8 envelopes, begin by folding the bottom up to within 6 to 7 mm of the top edge. Then fold the right third over to the left. Fold the left third to within 6 to 7 mm of the last fold. Insert the last fold into the envelope first.

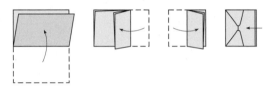

Memos

Memos are important business documents, but they have been largely replaced by mass e-mails. For example, in the past if a company wanted to announce an important policy change to its employees, it would send out a hard-copy memo to each employee's mailbox (or desk or work station). Today, it's increasingly rare to receive hard-copy memos. Nevertheless, you may still find it necessary to create a memo on occasion.

The easiest route is to choose a memo template in Microsoft Word, but if you'd like to design your own memo, follow these instructions:

- Open a Word document and begin typing three centimetres from top of page.
- Right and left margins may be set at 1.5 inches (4 cm).
- Include an optional company name and the word MEMO or MEMORANDUM as a heading. Leave two blank spaces after this heading.
- Create four subheadings on the left side of the page, each separated by one blank line: DATE, TO, FROM, and SUBJECT. The information that comes after each of these subheadings should be stated as clearly and succinctly as possible.
- After the SUBJECT subheading, leave one or two blank lines and begin typing the content of your memo. Single-space between lines and double-space between paragraphs.
- Do not include a closing salutation or signature. This is one of the major differences between, on the one hand, e-mails and letters, and on the other, faxes and memos. Because you've included the FROM subheading at the top, you don't need to repeat your name again at the end of a memo or fax.

Fax Cover Sheet

Documents transmitted by fax are usually introduced by a cover sheet, such as that shown in Figure A.5. As with memos, the format varies considerably, but most important items are incorporated into Microsoft Word's fax templates. Important items in a fax cover sheet are (1) the name and fax number of the receiver, (2) the name and fax number of the sender, (3) the number of pages being sent, and (4) the name, telephone number, and e-mail address of the person to notify in case of unsatisfactory transmission.

When the document being transmitted requires little explanation, you may prefer to attach an adhesive note (such as a Post-it fax transmittal form) to your document instead of a full cover sheet. These notes carry essentially the same information as shown in our printed fax cover sheet. They are perfectly acceptable in most business organizations and can save considerable paper and transmission costs.

FIGURE A.5 Fax Cover Sheet

FAX TRANSMISSION

DATE: _____

TO: _____   **FAX NUMBER:** _____

_____

_____

FROM: _____   **FAX NUMBER:** _____

_____

_____

NUMBER OF PAGES TRANSMITTED INCLUDING THIS COVER SHEET: ___

MESSAGE:

If any part of this fax transmission is missing or not clearly received, please contact:

NAME: _____

PHONE: _____

E-MAIL: _____

In marking your hard-copy assignments, your instructor may use the following symbols or abbreviations to indicate writing areas for improvement. The abbreviations refer to grammar, mechanical, and style issues discussed in Appendix D or in the Grammar/Mechanics Handbook at the end of this book. The symbols are traditional proofreading marks used by professional editors (when working on hard copy instead of using Microsoft Word's Track Changes feature). Knowing this information is valuable, because part of your career may involve reviewing documents for others.

Correction Abbreviations

ART	An article has been used incorrectly or is missing. See G/M Handbook p. 463.
AWK	Your sentence is awkwardly written (see also PREC below). See Appendix D pp. 439–440.
PA	A pronoun does not agree with its antecedent (the noun it replaces). See G/M Handbook pp. 454–455.
PREC	Your sentence is imprecise. See Appendix D pp. 439–440.
PUNCT	A punctuation mark has been used incorrectly or is missing. See G/M Handbook pp. 470–493.
RO	Your sentence has two or more independent clauses without a conjunction or semi-colon, or it uses a comma to join the clauses. See pp. 60; 473–475; 480–481.
SF	Your sentence is actually a fragment of a sentence; either a subject or a verb is missing. See p. 60.
SV	The subject and verb in your sentence do not agree. See pp. 457–458.
WORDY	Your sentence includes repetition or redundancy. See pp. 62–65.
VPR	A pronoun in your sentence is vague. See p. 441.
VT	One of your verbs is in the wrong tense, or you have shifted its tense unnecessarily. See pp. 459–460.

Proofreading Marks

PROOFREADING MARK	DRAFT COPY	FINAL COPY
⹀ Align horizontally	TO: Rick Munoz	TO: Rick Munoz
‖ Align vertically	‖166.32 132.45	166.32 132.45
≛ Capitalize	Coca-cola runs on ms–dos	Coca-Cola runs on MS-DOS
◡ Close up space	meeting at 3 p. m.	meeting at 3 p.m.
⊐⊏ Centre	] Recommendations [	Recommendations
ℛ Delete	in my final judgement	in my judgment
⩗ Insert apostrophe	our companys product	our company's product
⋏ Insert comma	you will of course	you will, of course,
⋏ Insert semicolon	value therefore, we feel	value; therefore, we feel
⹀ Insert hyphen	tax free income	tax-free income
⊙ Insert period	Ms Holly Hines	Ms. Holly Hines
⩔ Insert quotation mark	shareholders receive a bonus	shareholders receive a "bonus"
# Insert space	wordprocessing program	word processing program
/ Lowercase (remove capitals)	the Vice-President	the vice-president
⊏ Move to left	HUMAN RESOURCES	Human Resources
⊐ Move to right	⊏ I. Labour costs	I. Labour costs
◯ Spell out	A. Findings of study ⊐ aimed at 2 depts	A. Findings of study aimed at two departments
¶ Start new paragraph	¶Keep the screen height at eye level.	Keep the screen height at eye level.
⋯ Stet (don't delete)	officials talked openly	officials talked openly
∿ Transpose	accounts recievable	accounts receivable
ᨒ Use boldface	Conclusions	**Conclusions**
— Use italics	The Perfect Résumé	*The Perfect Résumé*
⌐ Start new line	Globex, 23 Acorn Lane	Globex 23 Acorn Lane
⊋ Run lines together	Invoice No., 122059	Invoice No. 122059

Careful writers work hard to document properly any data appearing in reports or messages for many reasons. Citing sources strengthens a writer's argument, as you learned in Chapter 9. Acknowledging sources also shields writers from charges of plagiarism. Moreover, good references help readers pursue further research. Fortunately, word processing programs have taken much of the pain out of documenting data, particularly for footnotes and endnotes.

Source Notes and Content Notes

Before we discuss specific documentation formats, you should know the difference between source notes and content notes. Source notes (also called in-text citations) identify quotations, paraphrased passages, and author references. They lead readers to the sources of cited information, and they must follow a consistent format. Content notes, on the other hand, allow writers to add comments, explain information not directly related to the text, or refer readers to other sections of a report.

Two Documentation Methods for Source Notes

For years researchers have struggled to develop the perfect documentation system—one that is efficient for the writer and crystal-clear to the reader. Most of these systems can be grouped into two methods: the footnote/endnote method and the parenthetic method.

Footnote/Endnote Method

Writers using footnotes or endnotes insert a small superscript (raised) figure into the text close to the place where a reference is mentioned. This number leads the reader to a footnote at the bottom of the page or to an endnote at the end of the report. Footnotes or endnotes contain a complete description of the source document. In this book we have used the endnote method. We chose this style because it least disrupts the text. Most of the individual citation formats in this book follow the traditional style suggested in *The Chicago Manual of Style*, 16th ed. (Chicago: The University of Chicago Press, 2010). Here are some of the most frequently used endnotes, styled in accordance with the *Chicago Manual*. They are numbered here with full-sized numbers; your word processor, however, may show endnotes with superscript figures. Either form is acceptable.

Book, One Author

1. Sara White, *Profiting in the Knowledge Age: A Canadian Guide to the Future* (Toronto: McKnight Publishing, 2001), 25.

Book, Many Authors

2. Manny Colver, Dan Smith, and Jeremy Devport, *Careers in the 21st Century* (Scarborough, ON: ITP Nelson, 2000), 356–58.

Academic Journal Article

3. John Drovich, "Peace in the Middle East," *Canadian Journal of International Studies* 19, no. 5 (2001): 23–45.

Monthly Magazine Article

4. Bill Safer, "Future Leadership," *Canadian Management*, April 2002, 45.

Newspaper Article

5. Trisha Khan, "Beyond 2000: Working in the Next Century," *Winnipeg Free Press*, August 22, 2001, B3.

Government Publication

6. Human Resources Development Canada, *How to Find a Job* (Ottawa: Supply and Services Canada, 2000), 30.

Online Services

7. Loblaw Companies Ltd., *2010 Annual Report*, http://www.loblaw.ca/English/Investor-Centre/financial-reporting/annual-reports/default.aspx, p. 14 (accessed July 28, 2011).

Interview

8. Geoffrey H. Wilson (senior vice president, Investor Relations and Public Affairs, Loblaw Companies Ltd.), personal interview, May 25, 2005.

In referring to a previously mentioned footnote, cite the page number along with the author's last name or a shortened form of the title if no author is given. The Latin forms *ibid.*, *op. cit.*, and *et al.* are rarely seen in business reports today. A portion of a business report using the endnote method for source citation is found in Figure C.1.

Parenthetic Method

Many writers of scholarly works prefer to use a parenthetic style to cite references. In this method a reference to the author appears in parentheses close to the place where it is mentioned in the text. Some parenthetic styles show the author's last name and date of publication (for example, *Cook 2000*), while others show the author's last name and page cited (for example, *Cook 24*). One of the most well-known parenthetic systems is the Modern Language Association (MLA) format. The long report shown in Figure 9.16 (pp. 252–261) illustrates this format. To provide guidance in preparing your academic and business papers, we'll focus on the MLA format.

Which Method for Business?

Students frequently ask, "But what documentation system is most used in business?" Actually no one method dominates. Many businesses have developed their own hybrid systems. These companies generally supply guidelines illustrating their in-house style to employees. Before starting any research project on the job, you'll want to inquire about your organization's preferred documentation style. You can also look in your company's files for examples of previous reports.

These changes are introducing challenges to companies operating both in Canada and abroad. Obviously, all of these employees need specific business and technology skills, but they also need to be aware of, and be sensitive to, the cultures in which they are living and working.[1] The Bank of Montreal has targeted several of these areas in which to enhance services. Chinese-Canadian business has increased 400 percent in the last five years.[2]

Women are increasing their role as both customer and worker. By the year 2003 women are expected to compose 47 percent of the labour force in Canada, as compared with 27 percent in 1961.[3] However, women hold only about 6 percent of the top management positions in organizations in the industrialized world.[4]

Companies that focus on diversity are improving their bottom line. Recently, Federal Express was named in the *Financial Post* as one the 100 best companies to work for in Canada. Canadian Pacific Forest Products received recognition for ensuring that selection committees had diverse membership, for their development of antiharassment policies, and for other diversity initiatives.[5]

Notes

1. Brenda Lynn, "Diversity in the Workplace: Why We Should Care," *CMA Management Accounting Magazine* 70, no. 5 (June 2000): 9–12.

2. Richard Sommer, "Firms Gain Competitive Strength from Diversity (Says Report by Conference Board of Canada)," *Financial Post,* 9 May 2001, 31.

3. British Columbia, Ministry of Education, Skills and Training, *The Impact of Demographic Change* (Victoria: Ministry of Education, Skills, and Training, 2002), 35.

4. R. J. Burke and C. A. McKeen, "Do Women at the Top Make a Difference? Gender Proportions and the Experiences of Managerial and Professional Women," *Human Relations* 49, no. 8 (2002): 1093–1104.

5. British Columbia, 36.

MLA Style—Modern Language Association

The MLA citation style uses parenthetic author references in the text. These in-text citations guide the reader to a bibliography called "Works Cited." Following are selected characteristics of the MLA style. For more information, consult The Modern Language Association of America, *MLA Handbook for Writers of Research Papers*, 7th ed. (New York: The Modern Language Association of America, 2009).

In-Text Citations

Within the text the author's last name and relevant page reference appear in parentheses, such as "(Chartrand 310)." In-text citations should be placed close to the reference they cite. Notice that no separating comma appears. If the author's name is mentioned in the text, cite only the page number in parentheses. If you don't know the author's name (e.g., when quoting from a Web site or blog), use the title of the

Web site section or blog entry you took the information from in your in-text citation. Your goal is to avoid interrupting the flow of your writing. Thus, you should strive to place the parenthetical reference where a pause would naturally occur, but as near as possible to the material documented. Note the following examples:

Author's Name in Text

Peters also notes that stress could be a contributing factor in the health problems reported thus far (135).

Author's Name Unknown

One Web site goes so far as to claim that new communication technologies such as BlackBerrys and multi-purpose cell phones will soon make in-person conversations "a thing of the past" ("Talking Not Cool").

Author's Name in Reference

The study was first published in 1958 (Peters 127–35).

Authors' Names in Text

Others, like Bergstrom and Voorhees (243–51), support a competing theory.

Authors' Names in Reference

Others support a competing theory (e.g., Bergstrom and Voorhees 243–51).

When citing an entire work—whether a print source, a non-print source such as a film, a television program, or a Web source that has no pagination or any other reference numbers—MLA style recommends that you include in the text, rather than in a parenthetical reference, the name of the person or organization that begins the corresponding entry in the works-cited list.

Electronic Source With Author

William J. Kennedy's *Bits and Bytes* discusses new computer technologies in the context of the digital telecommunications revolution. (In the "Works Cited" list, the reader would find a complete reference under the author's name.)

Electronic Source Without Author

More companies today are using data mining to unlock hidden value in their data. The data mining program "TargetSource," described at the Tener Solutions Group Web site, helps organizations predict consumer behaviour. (In the "Works Cited" list, the reader would find a complete reference under "Tener Solutions Group," the organization that owns the Web site.)

Works Cited List

In-text citations lead the reader to complete bibliographical citations in the "Works Cited." This alphabetical listing may contain all works consulted or only those mentioned in the text. Check with your instructor or editor to learn what method is preferred. Below are selected guidelines summarizing important elements of the MLA format for "Works Cited," as shown in Figure C.2.

- **Medium of publication.** The seventh edition of the *MLA Handbook* mandates that every entry in the works-cited list indicate the medium of publication. For print periodicals (journals, newspapers, magazines), the medium appears after the page numbers. For non-periodical print publications (such as books and pamphlets), the medium appears after the date of publication; however, if the item being cited is only part of a larger work (e.g., an essay, poem, or short story in an anthology or an introduction, preface, foreword, or afterword in a book), give the inclusive page

FIGURE C.2 Model MLA Bibliography of Sample References

Works Cited

Air Canada. *2004 Annual Report.* Air Canada, Feb. 2005. Web. 26 May 2005. —— Online annual report

Beresford, Marcia. "The Shift in Profit." *Maclean's* 24 Oct. 2001: 25–26. Print. —— Magazine article

British Columbia Ministry of Education, Skills and Training, *The Impact of Demographic Change.* Victoria: Ministry of Education, Skills and Training, 2002. Print. —— Government publication

"Globalization Often Means That the Fast Track Leads Overseas." *Globe and Mail* 16 June 2002: A10. Print. —— Newspaper article, no author

Jahl, Andrew. "PowerPoint of No Return." *Canadian Business.* 24 Nov. 2003: 14–15. *CBCA Current Affairs.* George Brown College Library. Web. 27 May 2005. —— Online research database magazine article, where "CBCA Current Affairs" is the research database

Lancaster, Hal. "When Taking a Tip From a Job Network, Proceed With Caution." *Wall Street Journal* 7 Feb. 2002: B1. Print. —— Newspaper article, one author

Mark, John. "Feds Provide Summary of New Privacy Legislation for Internet Users." *globeandmail.com.* Globe and Mail, 5 June 2002. Web. 9 June 2009. —— Online newspaper article

"Message Treatment." *Communication, Culture and Media Studies.* N.p., n.d. Web. 23 May 2005 <http://www.cultsock.ndirect.co.uk/>. —— Web site, no author

Murdry, Henry. "Consumers Still Driving the Economy." *Marketing News Online.* Canadian Marketing Association, 31 Aug. 2001. Web. 1 Sept. 2005. —— Online magazine article

Pinnacle Security Services. *What Employers Should Know About Employees.* 2nd ed. Toronto: Pinnacle Information Centre, 2002. Print. —— Brochure

Rivers, John. Personal interview. 16 May 2005. —— Interview

Rose, Richard C., and Echo Montgomery Garrett. *How to Make a Buck and Still Be a Decent Human Being.* New York: HarperCollins, 1998. Print. —— Book, two authors

SPSS Inc. "Clementine@work." *SPSS.com.* 15 May 2005. Web. 7 Sept. 2009. <http://www.spss.com/customer/clem_stories/>. —— Company Web site, no author

Weathers, Nicholas. "Key Trends in Systems Development." *Journal of Information Management* 3.2 (2000): 5–20. Print. —— Journal article with volume and issue numbers

numbers of the piece you are citing after the publication date, then list the medium of publication. For Web publications, the medium appears between the date of publication and the date of access.

- **Hanging indented style.** Indent the second and succeeding line for each item. MLA format suggests double-spacing for the entire paper, including the works-cited list. However, Figure C.2 is single-spaced to represent preferred business usage.
- **Book and Web site titles.** Italicize the titles of books and use "headline style" for capitalization. This means that the initial letters of all main words are capitalized:

Lewe, Glenda, and Carol D. MacLeod. *Step Into the World of Workplace Learning: A Collection of Authentic Workplace Materials.* Scarborough, ON: Nelson Thomson Learning, 2001. Print.

"ACE Aviation to Take Minority Stake in Merged U.S. Airline." *CBC.ca*. 19 May 2005. Web. 23 May 2005.

- **Magazine titles.** For the titles of magazine articles, include the date of publication but omit volume and issue numbers:

  Lee, Mary M. "Investing in International Relationships." *Business Monthly* 18 Feb. 2000: 25–27. Print.

- **Journal articles.** For journal articles follow the same format as for magazine articles except include the volume number, issue number, and the year of publication inside parentheses:

  Collier, Roger. "Morals, Medicine, and Geography." *Canadian Medical Association Journal* 179.10 (2008): 996–98. Print. ["179.10" indicates volume 179, issue 10.]

- **Italics and underscoring.** MLA style now recommends italicizing book, magazine, and journal titles (instead of underscoring).

Electronic References

The objective in citing sources, whether print publications or electronic publications, is to provide enough information so that your reader can locate your sources. In addition to the information provided for all print sources (e.g., author's name if available, title, date of publication, medium of publication, etc.), a citation for an electronic source requires at least three other kinds of information. First, you must provide the publisher or sponsor of the site (if not available, use *N.p.*). Second, you must provide the date when you accessed the source. Finally, the medium of publication ("Web") must appear between the two dates (date of publication and date of access), reducing the potential for confusion.

The seventh edition of the MLA Handbook makes the following recommendations for citing Web publications:

- Give the same information for electronic sources as you would if you were citing a print publication (e.g., author name, title, page number).
- Give all relevant dates. Because electronic sources can change or move, cite the date the document was produced (if available; if not, use *n.d.*) as well as the date you accessed the information. The date of access is required because multiple versions of an electronic work may be available, and any version may vary from previous or future versions.
- Include the electronic address or universal resource locator (URL) only when requested by your instructor or if the reader could not locate your source without it. The MLA used to recommend the inclusion of URLs of Web sources in works-cited-list entries. However, URLs change frequently and may be of little value; readers are more likely to use a search engine to find titles and authors' names. If you insert a URL, it should appear immediately after the date of access, followed by a period and a space. It should be the complete address, if possible (include *http://*), and must be enclosed in angle brackets (<, >) and followed by a period. If the URL needs to be divided at the end of a line, do so only after the double slashes or a single slash. Never add a hyphen (or allow your word processor to add one) to mark a break in the address.
- Download or print (for future reference) any Web material you use, as online resources frequently move or even disappear.

Article in an Online Journal

Chrisman, Laura, and Laurence Phillips. "Postcolonial Studies and the British Academy." *Jouvert* 3.3 (1999). Web. 10 June 2009.

Brown, Ronnie R. "Photographs That Should Have Been Taken." *Room of One's Own* 18.2 (Summer 1995). Web. 26 May 2009.

Article in an Online Newspaper or on a Newswire

These sites change very frequently—in some cases daily—so it is a good idea to download or record citation information (and URL, if needed) immediately.

> Scarth, Deborah. "Many Top University Students Use Tutors to Keep an Edge." *globeandmail.com*. Globe and Mail, 4 June 2000. Web. 5 October 2009.

> "Canada's Unemployment Rate Dips." *CBCnews.ca*. Canadian Broadcasting Corporation, 4 June 2000. Web. 5 Aug. 2009.

Article in an Online Magazine

> Campbell, Colin. "Making Bad Times Good." *Macleans.ca*. Maclean's Magazine, 26 Feb. 2009. Web. 4 Mar. 2009.

Professional or Personal Web Site

List the publication information in the following order: the name of the creator of the site, the title of the site (italicized), a description (for example, *Home page*, neither italicized nor enclosed in quotation marks), publisher or sponsor of the site (if not available, use *N.p.*, the date of publication (day, month, year, as available; if no date is available, use *n.d.*), the medium of publication, the date you accessed the information, and the electronic address (if needed). If some of this information is unavailable, cite whatever is available.

> Canadian Tire Corporation Ltd. *Canadiantire.ca*. Investors page. N.d. Web. 28 May 2005.

> Ellison, Sara. *Sara's Home Page*. Home page. U of Victoria, n.d. Web. 29 July 2005. <http://orca.phys.uvic.ca/~sara/>.

Online Book

Many books are now available electronically, either independently or as part of a scholarly project. Some have appeared previously in print, while others exist only on the Web. Follow the general recommendations for citing books in print, but include the additional information required for electronic citations, as outlined below.

If a book that you are citing has appeared in print, it may be important to include the print version of the publication information (for example, if the book was scanned as part of an online database). In that case, give the name of the author first, if it is available; if not, give the name of the editor, translator, or compiler, followed by a comma and then the appropriate abbreviation *(ed., trans.,* or *comp.)*. Next give the title of the work (italicized if the work is independent; in quotation marks if the work is part of a larger work); the name of the editor, translator, or compiler (if relevant); and the edition or version used; followed by the publication information for the printed version (city of publication, name of the publisher, and year of publication). Then, instead of listing *Print* as the medium of publication at the end of the citation, add the following information: the title of the Web site or database (italicized), the medium of publication (*Web*), the date you accessed the information, and the URL (if needed).

If the book you are citing has not been previously published, follow the instructions above regarding the name of the author, editor, translator, or compiler, and the title of the work. Follow that information with the title of the Web site (italicized); the edition or version used; the publisher or sponsor of the Web site (if available; if not, use *N.p.*); the date of publication (day, month, year, if available; if not, use *n.d.*); the medium of publication *(Web)*; the date you accessed the information; and the URL (if needed).

> Montgomery, Lucy Maud. *Anne of Green Gables*. 1908. *The Literature Network*. Web. 30 May 2001.

> Dewey, John. *Democracy and Education*. London: Macmillan, 1916. *ILT Web*. Web. 22 Nov. 2009.

Scholarly Project or Information Services

Information on a wide variety of subjects is available through scholarly projects or in information services. If you are using information taken from these sources, use the instructions listed above for books that were not previously published. If you are citing an entire scholarly project, list the name of the editor first, if available (followed by a comma and *ed.*); then give the title of the overall Web site (italicized), and the rest of the information required for online-only books, as noted in the preceding section.

> "South Yorkshire." *Encyclopedia Britannica Online.* Encyclopedia Britannica, 2008. Web. 26 May 2009.

> *The Orlando Project: A History of Women's Writing in the British Isles.* Department of English and Film Studies, U of Alberta, 2000. Web. 25 April 2009.

Other Non-print Sources. The citations for other non-print sources will follow the recommendations for print versions, with some additional required information. Be sure to include the type of source you are citing (for example, *Transcript, Online posting,* or *E-mail*); this information will appear either before or after the date of publication/broadcast, depending on the type of source (see examples below). If you are citing an online posting, you may need to include the URL, as it could otherwise be difficult for your reader to find the posting.

Television/Radio

> "Sears Saga." Narr. Peter Mansbridge. *The National.* Canadian Broadcasting Corp. CBLT, Toronto, 4 June 2001. Television.

Transcript of Television/Radio Program

> "Sears Saga." Narr. Peter Mansbridge. *The National.* Canadian Broadcasting Corp. CBLT, Toronto, n.p., 4 June 2001. Transcript.

E-Mail Communication

> Pen Canada. "Your Inquiries to PEN." E-mail to author. 3 July 2009.

Online Posting

> Matus, Roger. "Another University Sends False Admission Emails." Online posting. *Robert Matus' Death By Email.* InBoxer Inc., 6 Apr. 2009. Web. 7 April 2009.

Material From an Online Research Database

Online services such as ProQuest and LexisNexis provide a variety of databases that your college library will have. Give the name of the service (in italics) before the medium of publication ("Web") and the date you accessed the information.

> Golden, Anne. "Do Our Foreign Investment Laws Still Have Legs?" *The Globe and Mail.* 1 Dec. 2004: A23. *CBCA Current Affairs.* Web. 2 March 2009.

APA Style—American Psychological Association

Popular in the social and physical sciences, the American Psychological Association (APA) documentation style uses parenthetic citations. That is, each author reference is shown in parentheses when cited in the text. Below are selected features of the APA style. For more information see the *Publication Manual of the American Psychological Association*, 6th Edition (Washington, DC: American Psychological Association, 2010).

In-Text Citation

In-text citations consist of the author's last name, year of publication, and pertinent page number(s). These items appear in parentheses, usually at the end of a clause or end of a sentence in which material is cited. This parenthetic citation, as shown in the following illustration, directs readers to a reference list at the end of the report where complete bibliographic information is recorded.

> The strategy of chicken king Don Tyson was to expand aggressively into other "center-of-the-plate" proteins, such as pork, fish, and turkey (Berss, 2000, p. 64).

Bibliography

All reference sources are alphabetized in a bibliography entitled "References." Below are selected guidelines summarizing important elements of the APA bibliographic format:

- Include authors' names with the last name first followed by initials, such as **Smith, M. A.** First and middle names are not used.
- Show the date of publication in parentheses, such as **Smith, M. A. (2001)**.
- Italicize the titles of books and use "sentence-style" (sometimes called *down style*) capitalization. This means that only the first word of a title, proper nouns, and the first word after an internal colon are capitalized. Book titles are followed by the place of publication and publisher's name, such as **Smith, M. A. (2001)**. *Communication for managers*. **Elmsford, NY: Pergamon Press.**
- Type the titles of magazine and journal articles without italics or quotation marks. Use sentence-style capitalization for article titles. However, italicize the names of magazines and journals and capitalize the initial letters of all important words. Also italicize the volume number, such as **Cheung, H. K., & Burn, J. M. (1994). Distributing global information systems resources in multinational companies—a contingency model.** *Journal of Global Information Management,* **2(3), 14–27.** ["2(3), 14–27" indicates volume 2, issue 3, pages 14 to 27.]
- Space only once following periods and colons.
- Do not include personal communications (such as interviews, telephone conversations, e-mail, and messages from non-archived discussion groups and online forums) in the reference list, since they are not retrievable.

Electronic References

When print information is available, APA suggests placing it first followed by online information. For example, a newspaper article: **Schellhardt, T. D. (1999, March 4). In a factory schedule, where does religion fit in?** *The Wall Street Journal,* **pp. B1, B12. Retrieved March 5, 1999, from http://interactive.wsj.com.** For additional discussion and examples, visit the APA Web site (**http://www.apastyle.org/elecref.html**).

Figure C.3 shows the format of an APA References List.

FIGURE C.3 Model APA Bibliography of Sample References

References

Online annual report

Air Canada. (2004). *2004 annual report*. Retrieved May 26, 2009, from http://www .aircanada.com/en/about/investor/index.html#reports

Magazine article

Berss, M. (2000, October 24). Protein man. *Forbes, 154,* 64–66.

Newspaper article, no author

Globalization often means that the fast track leads overseas. (2002, June 16). *The Financial Post,* p. A10.

Online research database magazine article

Jahl, A. (2003, November 24). PowerPoint of no return. *Canadian Business*, 14–15. Retrieved May 27, 2009, from CBCA Current Affairs, George Brown College Library.

Newspaper article, one author

Lancaster, H. (2002, February 7). When taking a tip from a job network, proceed with caution. *The Wall Street Journal,* p. B1.

Online newspaper article

Markoff, J. (1999, June 5). Voluntary rules proposed to help ensure privacy for Internet users. *The New York Times*. Retrieved June 9, 2009, from http://www.nytimes. com/library/cyber/week/y05dat.html

Online magazine article

Murphy, H. L. (1998, August 31). Saturn's orbit still high with consumers. *Marketing News Online*. Retrieved September 1, 2009, from http://www.ama.org/pubs/ mn/0818n1.htm

Brochure

Pinkerton Investigation Services. (1998). *The employer's guide to investigation services* (3rd ed.) [Brochure]. Atlanta, GA: Pinkerton Information Center.

Book, two authors

Rose, R. C., & Garrett, E. M. (1998). *How to make a buck and still be a decent human being*. New York: HarperCollins.

Government publication

Statistics Canada. (1995). *A portrait of persons with disabilities: Target groups project*. Ottawa, ON: Department of Industry, Science and Technology.

Web site, no author

Transmission models—criticism. (2005). *Communication, Culture and Media Studies*. Retrieved May 23, 2009, from http://www.cultshock.ndirect.co.uk/MUHome/cshtml/

Journal article with volume and issue numbers

Wetherbee, J. C., Vitalari, N. P., & Milner, A. (2000). Key trends in systems development in Europe and North America. *Journal of Global Information Management, 3*(2), 5–20.

Careful writers work hard over time to develop an effective style. While most writers can write simple declarative sentences (*The stock market is down today*) or even more complicated sentences (*The stock market is down today, despite the higher employment numbers*), more experienced writers recognize certain "tricks of the trade" that lend their writing a professional, persuasive tone. Some of these tricks are discussed below. Try incorporating them into your work as you progress through your course and your future career.

Emphasis

When you are talking with someone, you can emphasize your main ideas by saying them loudly or by repeating them slowly. You could pound the table if you wanted to show real emphasis. Another way you can signal the relative importance of an idea is by raising your eyebrows, shaking your head, or whispering. But when you write, you must rely on other means to tell your readers which ideas are more important than others. Emphasis in writing can be achieved in two ways: mechanically and stylistically.

Emphasis Through Mechanics

To emphasize an idea, a writer may use any of the following devices:

> You can emphasize an idea mechanically by using underlining, italics, boldface, font changes, all caps, dashes, and tabulation.

Underlining	<u>Underlining</u> draws the eye to a word.
Italics and boldface	Use *italics* or **boldface** for special meaning and emphasis.
Font changes	Changing from a large font to a smaller font or to a different font adds interest and emphasis.
All caps	Printing words in ALL CAPS is like shouting them.
Dashes	Dashes—if used sparingly—can be effective in capturing attention.
Tabulation	Listing items vertically makes them stand out: 1. First item 2. Second item 3. Third item

Other means of achieving mechanical emphasis include the arrangement of space, colour, lines, boxes, columns, titles, headings, and subheadings. Today's software and colour printers provide a wide choice of capabilities for emphasizing ideas.

Emphasis Through Style

> You can emphasize ideas stylistically by using vivid words, labelling the main idea, and positioning the main idea strategically.

Although mechanical means are occasionally appropriate, a good writer more often achieves emphasis stylistically. That is, the writer chooses words carefully and constructs sentences skillfully to emphasize main ideas and de-emphasize minor or negative ideas. Here are four suggestions for emphasizing ideas stylistically:

● **Use vivid words.** Vivid words are emphatic because the reader can picture ideas clearly.

> **General** One business uses personal selling techniques.

Vivid Avon uses face-to-face selling techniques.

General A customer said that he wanted the contract returned soon.

Vivid Mr. LeClerc insisted that the contract be returned by July 1.

- **Label the main idea.** If an idea is significant, tell the reader.

    Unlabelled Explore the possibility of leasing a site, but also hire a consultant.

    Labelled Explore the possibility of leasing a site, but most important, hire a consultant.

- **Place the important idea first or last in the sentence.** Ideas have less competition from surrounding words when they appear first or last in a sentence. Observe how the concept of productivity is emphasized in the first and second examples:

    Emphatic Productivity is more likely to be increased when profit-sharing plans are linked to individual performance rather than to group performance.

    Emphatic Profit-sharing plans linked to individual performance rather than to group performance are more effective in increasing productivity.

    Unemphatic Profit-sharing plans are more effective in increasing productivity when they are linked to individual performance rather than to group performance.

- **Place the important idea in a simple sentence or in an independent clause.** Don't dilute the effect of the idea by making it share the spotlight with other words and clauses.

    Emphatic You are the first trainee whom we have hired for this program. (Use a simple sentence for emphasis.)

    Emphatic Although we considered many candidates, you are the first trainee whom we have hired for this program. (Independent clause contains main idea.)

    Unemphatic Although you are the first trainee whom we have hired for this program, we had many candidates and expect to expand the program in the future. (Main idea is lost in a dependent clause.)

De-emphasize. To de-emphasize something such as bad news, try one of the following stylistic devices:

You can de-emphasize ideas through word choice and placement.

- **Use general words.**

    Vivid Our records indicate that you were recently fired.

    General Our records indicate that your employment status has changed recently.

- **Place the bad news in a dependent clause connected to an independent clause with something positive.** In sentences with dependent clauses, the main emphasis is always on the independent clause.

    Emphasizes bad news We cannot issue you credit at this time, but we do have a plan that will allow you to fill your immediate needs on a cash basis.

    De-emphasizes bad news We have a plan that will allow you to fill your immediate needs on a cash basis since we cannot issue credit at this time.

Active and Passive Voice

In sentences with active-voice verbs, the subject is the doer of the action. In passive-voice sentences, the subject is acted upon.

Active-voice sentences are direct and easy to understand.

Active verb Mr. Wong completed the tax return before the April 30 deadline. (The subject, *Mr. Wong*, is the doer of the action.)

Passive verb The tax return was completed before the April 30 deadline. (The subject, *tax return*, is acted upon.)

In the first sentence, the active-voice verb emphasizes Mr. Wong. In the second sentence, the passive-voice verb emphasizes the tax return. In sentences with passive-voice verbs, the doer of the action may be revealed or left unknown. In business writing, and in personal interactions, some situations demand tact and sensitivity. Instead of using a direct approach with active verbs, we may prefer the indirectness that passive verbs allow. Rather than making a blunt announcement with an active verb (*Gunnar made a major error in the estimate*), we can soften the sentence with a passive construction (*A major error was made in the estimate*).

Here's a summary of the best use of active- and passive-voice verbs:

- **Use the active voice for most business writing.** It clearly tells what the action is and who is performing that action.
- **Use the passive voice to emphasize an action or the recipient of the action.** *You have been selected to represent us.*
- **Use the passive voice to de-emphasize negative news.** *Your watch has not been repaired.*
- **Use the passive voice to conceal the doer of an action.** *A major error was made in the estimate.*

How can you tell if a verb is active or passive? Identify the subject of the sentence and decide whether the subject is doing the acting or being acted upon. For example, in the sentence *An appointment was made for January 1,* the subject is *appointment.* The subject is being acted upon; therefore, the verb (was made) is passive. Another clue in identifying passive-voice verbs is that they generally include a *to be* helping verb, such as *is, are, was, were, being,* or *been.*

Parallelism

Parallelism is a writing technique that creates balanced writing. Sentences written so that their parts are balanced or parallel are easy to read and understand. To achieve parallel construction, use similar structures to express similar ideas. For example, the words *computing, coding, recording,* and *storing* are parallel because they all end in *ing.* To express the list as *computing, coding, recording, and storage* is disturbing because the last item is not what the reader expects. Try to match nouns with nouns, verbs with verbs, and clauses with clauses. Avoid mixing active-voice verbs with passive-voice verbs. Your goal is to keep the wording balanced in expressing similar ideas.

Lacks parallelism The market for industrial goods includes manufacturers, contractors, wholesalers, and those concerned with the retail function.
Revision The market for industrial goods includes manufacturers, contractors, wholesalers, and retailers. (Parallel construction matches nouns.)

Lacks parallelism Our primary goals are to increase productivity, reduce costs, and the improvement of product quality.
Revision Our primary goals are to increase productivity, reduce costs, and improve product quality. (Parallel construction matches verbs.)

Lacks parallelism We are scheduled to meet in Toronto on January 5, we are meeting in Montreal on the 15th of March, and in Burlington on June 3.
Revision We are scheduled to meet in Toronto on January 5, in Montreal on March 15, and in Burlington on June 3. (Parallel construction matches phrases.)

Lacks parallelism Mrs. Chorney audits all accounts lettered A through L; accounts lettered M through Z are audited by Mr. Faheem.
Revision Mrs. Chorney audits all accounts lettered A through L; Mr. Faheem audits accounts lettered M through Z. (Parallel construction matches active-voice verbs in balanced clauses.)

In presenting lists of data, whether printed horizontally or tabulated vertically, be certain to express all the items in parallel form.

Parallelism in vertical list Three primary objectives of advertising are as follows:

1. Increase the frequency of product use.
2. Introduce complementary products.
3. Enhance the corporate image.

Unity

Unified sentences contain thoughts that are related to only one main idea. The following sentence lacks unity because the first clause has little or no relationship to the second clause:

Unified sentences contain only related ideas.

Lacks unity Our insurance plan is available in all provinces, and you may name anyone as a beneficiary for your coverage.
Revision Our insurance plan is available in all provinces. What's more, you may name anyone as a beneficiary for your coverage.

The ideas in a sentence are better expressed by separating the two dissimilar clauses and adding a connecting phrase. Three writing faults that destroy sentence unity are imprecise writing, mixed constructions, and misplaced modifiers.

Imprecise Writing

Sentences that twist or turn unexpectedly away from the main thought are examples of imprecise writing. Such confusing writing may result when too many thoughts are included in one sentence or when one thought does not relate to another. To rectify an imprecise sentence, revise it so that the reader understands the relationship between the thoughts. If that is impossible, move the unrelated thoughts to a new sentence.

Imprecise sentences often should be broken into two sentences.

Imprecise writing I appreciate the time you spent with me last week, and I have purchased a computer and software that generate graphics.
Revision I appreciate the time you spent with me last week. As a result of your advice, I have purchased a computer and software that generate graphics.

Imprecise writing The stockholders of a corporation elect a board of directors, although the chief executive officer is appointed by the board and the CEO is not directly responsible to the stockholders.
Revision The stockholders of a corporation elect a board of directors, who in turn appoint the chief executive officer. The CEO is not directly responsible to the stockholders.

Mixed Constructions

Writers who fuse two different grammatical constructions destroy sentence unity and meaning.

Mixed constructions confuse readers.

Mixed construction The reason I am late is because my car battery is dead.
Revision The reason I am late is that my car battery is dead. (The construction introduced by *the reason is* should be a noun clause beginning with *that*, not an adverbial clause beginning with *because*.)

Mixed construction When the stock market index rose five points was our signal to sell.
Revision When the stock market index rose five points, we were prepared to sell. OR Our signal to sell was an increase of five points in the stock market index.

Dangling and Misplaced Modifiers

Modifiers must be close to the words they describe or limit.

For clarity, modifiers must be close to the words they describe or limit. A modifier dangles when the word or phrase it describes is missing from its sentence. A modifier is misplaced when the word or phrase it describes is not close enough for the relationship to be clear. In both instances, the solution is to position the modifier closer to the word(s) it describes or limits. Introductory verbal phrases are particularly dangerous; be sure to follow them immediately with the words they logically describe or modify.

Dangling modifier To win the lottery, a ticket must be purchased. (Purchased by whom? The verbal phrase must be followed by a subject.)
Revision To win the lottery, you must purchase a ticket.

Dangling modifier Driving through Tetrahedron Plateau, the ocean suddenly came into view. (Is the ocean driving through Tetrahedron Plateau?)
Revision Driving through Tetrahedron Plateau, we saw the ocean suddenly come into view.

Try this trick for detecting and remedying dangling modifiers. Ask the question "Who or what?" after any introductory phrase. The words immediately following should tell the reader who or what is performing the action. Try the test on the previous danglers.

Misplaced modifier Seeing his error too late, the envelope was immediately re-sealed by Adrian. (Did the envelope see the error?)
Revision Seeing his error too late, Adrian immediately re-sealed the envelope.

Misplaced modifier A wart appeared on my left hand that I want removed. (Is the left hand to be removed?)
Revision I want to remove the wart that appeared on my left hand.

Misplaced modifier The busy human resources director interviewed only candidates who had excellent computer skills in the morning. (Were the candidates skilled only in the morning?)
Revision In the morning the busy human resources director interviewed only candidates who had excellent computer skills.

Paragraph Coherence

Three ways to create paragraph coherence are (1) repetition of key ideas, (2) use of pronouns, and (3) use of transitional expressions.

A paragraph is a group of sentences with a controlling idea, usually stated first. Paragraphs package similar ideas into meaningful groups for readers. Effective paragraphs are coherent; that is, they hold together. But coherence does not happen accidentally. It is achieved through effective organization and (1) repetition of key ideas, (2) use of pronouns, and (3) use of transitional expressions.

- **Repetition of key ideas or key words.** Repeating a word or key thought from a preceding sentence helps guide a reader from one thought to the next. This redundancy is necessary to build cohesiveness into writing.

    Effective repetition Quality problems in production are often the result of inferior raw materials. Some companies have strong programs for ensuring the quality of incoming production materials and supplies.

    The second sentence of the preceding paragraph repeats the key idea of quality. Moreover, the words *incoming production materials and supplies* refer to the raw materials mentioned in the preceding sentence. Good writers find similar words to describe the same idea, thus using repetition to clarify a topic for the reader.

- **Use of pronouns.** Pronouns such as *this, that, they, these,* and *those* promote coherence by connecting the thoughts in one sentence to the thoughts in a previous sentence. To make sure that the pronoun reference is clear, consider joining the pronoun with the word to which it refers, thus making the pronoun into an adjective.

Pronouns with clear antecedents can improve coherence.

Pronoun repetition Xerox has a four-point program to assist suppliers. This program includes written specifications for production materials and components.

Be very careful, though, in using pronouns. A pronoun without a clear antecedent can be annoying. That's because the reader doesn't know precisely to what the pronoun refers.

Faulty: When company profits increased, employees were given either a cash payment or company stock. *This* became a real incentive to employees. (Is *This* the cash or the stock or both?)

Revision: When company profits increased, employees were given either a cash payment or company stock. *This profit-sharing plan* became a real incentive to employees.

- **Use of transitional expressions.** One of the most effective ways to achieve paragraph coherence is through the use of transitional expressions. These expressions act as road signs: they indicate where the message is headed and they help the reader anticipate what is coming. Here are some of the most effective transitional expressions. They are grouped according to use.

Transitional expressions build paragraph coherence.

The most readable paragraphs contain eight or fewer printed lines.

Time Association	Contrast	Illustration
before, after	although	for example
first, second	but	in this way
meanwhile	however	
next	instead	
until	nevertheless	
when, whenever	on the other hand	

Cause, Effect	Additional Idea
consequently	furthermore
for this reason	in addition
hence	likewise
therefore	moreover

Paragraph Length

Although no rule regulates the length of paragraphs, business writers recognize the value of short paragraphs. Paragraphs with eight or fewer printed lines look inviting and readable. Long, solid chunks of print appear formidable. If a topic can't be covered in eight or fewer printed lines (not sentences), consider breaking it into smaller segments.

Writing Improvement Exercises

Emphasis. For each of the following sentences, circle (a) or (b). Be prepared to justify your choice.

1. Which is more emphatic?
   a. We need a faster, more efficient distribution system.
   b. We need a better distribution system.

2. Which is more emphatic?
   a. Increased advertising would improve sales.
   b. Adding $50,000 in advertising would double our sales.

3. Which is more emphatic?
   a. The committee was powerless to act.
   b. The committee was unable to take action.

4. Which sentence puts more emphasis on product loyalty?
   a. Product loyalty is the primary motivation for advertising.
   b. The primary motivation for advertising is loyalty to the product, although other purposes are also served.

5. Which sentence places more emphasis on the seminar?
   a. An executive training seminar that starts June 1 will include four candidates.
   b. Four candidates will be able to participate in an executive training seminar that we feel will provide a valuable learning experience.

6. Which sentence puts more emphasis on the date?
   a. The deadline is December 30 for applications for overseas jobs.
   b. December 30 is the deadline for applications for overseas jobs.

7. Which is less emphatic?
   a. Lily Takahashi said that her financial status had worsened.
   b. Lily Takahashi said that she had lost her job and owed $2,000.

8. Which sentence de-emphasizes the credit refusal?
   a. We are unable to grant you credit at this time, but we will reconsider your application later.
   b. Although we welcome your cash business, we are unable to offer you credit at this time; but we will be happy to reconsider your application later.

9. Which sentence gives more emphasis to judgment?
   a. He has many admirable qualities, but most important is his good judgment.
   b. He has many admirable qualities, including good judgment and patience.

10. Which is more emphatic?
    a. Three departments are involved: (1) Legal, (2) Accounting, and (3) Distribution.
    b. Three departments are involved:
       1. Legal
       2. Accounting
       3. Distribution

Active-Voice Verbs. Business writing is more forceful if it uses active-voice verbs. Revise the following sentences so that the verbs are in the active voice. Put the emphasis on the doer of the action. Add subjects if necessary.

Example The computers were powered up each day at 7 a.m.

Revision Kamal powered up the computers each day at 7 a.m.

1. Initial figures for the bid were submitted before the June 1 deadline.
2. New spices and cooking techniques were tried by Lick's to improve its hamburgers.

3. Substantial sums of money were earned by employees who enrolled early in our stock option plan.

4. A significant financial commitment has been made by us to ensure that our customers can take advantage of our discount pricing.

Passive-Voice Verbs. When indirectness or tact are required, use passive-voice verbs. Revise the following sentences so that they are in the passive voice.

Example Sade did not submit the accounting statement on time.

Revision The accounting statement was not submitted on time.

5. Andreas made a computational error in the report.

6. We cannot ship your order for 10 monitors until June 15.

7. The government first issued a warning regarding the use of this pesticide over 15 months ago.

8. We will notify you immediately if we make any changes in your travel arrangements.

9. We cannot allow a cash refund unless you provide a receipt.

Parallelism. Revise the following sentences so that their parts are balanced.

10. (Hint: Match verbs.) Some of our priorities include linking employee compensation to performance, keeping administrative costs down, the expansion of computer use, and the improvement of performance review skills of supervisors.

11. (Hint: Match active voice of verbs.) Yin Huang, of the Red River office, will now supervise our Western Division; and the Eastern Division will be supervised by our Ottawa office manager, David Ali.

12. (Hint: Match nouns.) Word processing software is used extensively in the fields of health care, by lawyers, by secretaries in insurance firms, for scripts in the entertainment industry, and in the banking field.

13. If you have decided to cancel our service, please cut your credit card in half, and the card pieces should be returned to us.

14. We need more laboratory space, additional personnel is required, and we also need much more capital.

15. The application for a grant asks for this information: funds required for employee salaries, how much we expect to spend on equipment, and what is the length of the project.

16. To lease a car is more expensive than buying one.

17. To use the copier, insert your account card, the paper trays must be loaded, indicate the number of copies needed, and your original sheet should be inserted through the feeder.

Sentence Unity. The following sentences lack unity. Rewrite, correcting the identified fault.

Example (Dangling modifier) By advertising extensively, all the open jobs were filled quickly.

Revision By advertising extensively, we were able to fill all the open jobs quickly.

18. (Dangling modifier) To open a money market account, a deposit of $3,000 is required.

19. (Mixed construction) The reason why Ms. Rutulis is unable to travel extensively is because she has family responsibilities.

20. (Misplaced modifier) Identification passes must be worn at all times in offices and production facilities showing the employee's picture.

21. (Misplaced modifier) The editor-in-chief's rules were to be observed by all staff members, no matter how silly they seemed.

22. (Imprecise sentence) The business was started by two engineers, and these owners worked in a garage, which eventually grew into a million-dollar operation.

Coherence. Revise the following paragraphs to improve coherence. Be aware that the transitional expressions and key words selected depend largely on the emphasis desired. Many possible revisions exist.

Appendix D: Style in Writing

Example Computer style checkers rank somewhere between artificial intelligence and artificial ignorance. Style checkers are like clever children: smart but not wise. Business writers should be cautious. They should be aware of the usefulness of style checkers. They should know their limitations.

Revision Computer style checkers rank somewhere between artificial intelligence and artificial ignorance. For example, they are like clever children: smart but not wise. For this reason, business writers should be cautious. Although they should be aware of the usefulness of these software programs, business writers should also know their limitations.

23. Our computerized file includes all customer data. It provides space for name, address, and other vital information. It has an area for comments. The area for comments comes in handy. It requires more time and careful keyboarding, though.

24. No one likes to turn out poor products. We began highlighting recurring problems. Employees make a special effort to be more careful in doing their work right the first time. It doesn't have to be returned to them for corrections.

25. Service was less than perfect for many months. We lacked certain intangibles. We didn't have the customer-specific data that we needed. We made the mistake of removing all localized, person-to-person coverage. We are returning to decentralized customer contacts.

Because many students need a review of basic grammar and mechanics, we provide a number of resources below. The Grammar/Mechanics Handbook, which offers you a rapid systematic review, consists of four parts:

- **Grammar/Mechanics Diagnostic Test.** This 65-point Grammar/Mechanics Diagnostic Test helps you assess your strengths and weaknesses in eight areas of grammar and mechanics.
- **Grammar/Mechanics Profile.** The G/M Profile enables you to pinpoint specific areas in which you need remedial instruction or review.
- **Grammar Review with Checkup and Editing Exercises.** A concise set of guidelines reviews basic principles of grammar, punctuation, capitalization, and number style. The review also provides checkup and quiz exercises that help you interact with the principles of grammar and test your comprehension. The guidelines not only provide a study guide for review but also serve as a reference manual throughout the writing course. The grammar review can be used for classroom-centred instruction or for self-guided learning.
- **Confusing Words and Frequently Misspelled Words.** A selected list of confusing words, along with a list of 160 frequently misspelled words, completes the Grammar/Mechanics Handbook.

The first step in your systematic review of grammar and mechanics involves completing a diagnostic test.

Grammar/Mechanics Diagnostic Test

Name _____

This diagnostic test is intended to reveal your strengths and weaknesses in using the following:

plural nouns	adjectives	punctuation
possessive nouns	adverbs	capitalization style
pronouns	prepositions	number style
verbs	conjunctions	

The test is organized into sections corresponding to these categories. In sections A–H, each sentence is either correct or has one error related to the category under which it is listed. If a sentence is correct, write C. If it has an error, underline the error and write the correct form in the space provided. Use ink to record your answers. When you finish, check your answers with your instructor and fill out the Grammar/Mechanics Profile at the end of the test.

A. Plural Nouns

<u>branches</u> **Example:** The newspaper named editors in chief for both <u>branchs</u>.

_____ 1. Three of the lawyers representing the defendants were from citys in other provinces.

_____ 2. Four students discussed the pros and cons of attending colleges or universities.

_____ 3. Since the 1990s, most companys have begun to send bills of lading with shipments.

_____ 4. Neither the Johnsons nor the Morris's knew about the changes in beneficiaries.

_____ 5. The manager asked all secretaries to work on the next four Saturday's.

B. Possessive Nouns

_____ 6. We sincerely hope that the jurys judgment reflects the stories of all the witnesses.

_____ 7. In a little over two months time, the analysts had finished three reports for the president.

_____ 8. Mr. Franklins staff is responsible for all accounts receivable contracted by customers purchasing electronics parts.

_____ 9. At the next shareholders meeting, we will discuss benefits for employees and dividends for shareholders.

_____ 10. Three months ago several employees in the sales department complained of Mrs. Kwons smoking.

C. Pronouns

me Example: Whom did you ask to replace Tom and <u>I</u>?

_____ 11. My manager and myself were willing to send the copies to whoever needed them.

_____ 12. Some of the work for Mr. Gagne and I had to be reassigned to Mark and him.

_____ 13. Although it's motor was damaged, the car started for the mechanic and me.

_____ 14. Just between you and me, only you and I know that she will be transferred.

_____ 15. My friend and I applied for employment at Reynolds, Inc., because of their excellent employee benefits.

D. Verb Agreement

has Example: The list of arrangements <u>have</u> to be approved by Tim and her.

_____ 16. The keyboard, printer, and monitor costs less than I expected.

_____ 17. A description of the property, together with several other legal documents, were submitted by my lawyer.

_____ 18. There was only two enclosures and the letter in the envelope.

_____ 19. Neither the manager nor the employees in the office think the solution is fair.

_____ 20. Because of the holiday, our committee prefer to delay its action.

E. Verb Mood, Voice, and Tense

_____ 21. If I was able to fill your order immediately, I certainly would.

_____ 22. To operate the machine, first open the CD caddy and then you insert the CD.

_____ 23. If I could chose any city, I would select Vancouver.

_____ 24. Those papers have laid on his desk for more than two weeks.

_____ 25. The auditors have went over these accounts carefully, and they have found no discrepancies.

F. Adjectives and Adverbs

_____ 26. Until we have a more clearer picture of the entire episode, we shall proceed cautiously.

_____ 27. For about a week their newly repaired copier worked just beautiful.

_____ 28. The recently elected prime minister benefited from his coast to coast campaign.

_____ 29. Mr. Snyder only has two days before he must complete the end-of-the-year report.

_____ 30. The architects submitted their drawings in a last minute attempt to beat the deadline.

G. Prepositions and Conjunctions

_____ 31. Can you tell me where the meeting is scheduled at?

_____ 32. It seems like we have been taking this test forever.

_____ 33. Our investigation shows that the distribution department is more efficient then the sales department.

_____ 34. My courses this semester are totally different than last semester's.

_____ 35. Do you know where this shipment is going to?

H. Commas

For each of the following sentences, insert any necessary commas. Count the number of commas that you added. Write that number in the space provided. All punctuation must be correct to receive credit for the sentence. If a sentence requires no punctuation, write C.

2 Example: However, because of developments in theory and computer applications, management is becoming more of a science.

_____ 36. For example management determines how orders assignments and responsibilities are delegated to employees.

_____ 37. Your order Mrs. Tahan will be sent from Toronto Ontario on July 10.

_____ 38. When you need service on any of your pieces of equipment we will be happy to help you Mr. Hamel.

_____ 39. Kevin Long who is the project manager at Techdata suggested that I call you.

_____ 40. You have purchased from us often and your payments in the past have always been prompt.

I. Commas and Semicolons 1

Add commas and semicolons to the following sentences. In the space provided, write the number of punctuation marks that you added.

_____ 41. The salesperson turned in her report however she did not indicate what time period it covered.

_____ 42. Some interest payments may be tax deductible dividend payments are not.

_____ 43. We are opening a branch office in Kelowna and hope to be able to serve all your needs from that office by the middle of January.

_____ 44. As suggested by the committee we must first secure adequate funding then we may consider expansion.

_____ 45. When you begin to conduct research for a report consider the many library sources available namely books periodicals government publications and databases.

J. Commas and Semicolons 2

_____ 46. After our office manager had the printer repaired it jammed again within the first week although we treated it carefully.

_____ 47. Our experienced courteous staff has been trained to anticipate your every need.

_____ 48. In view of the new law that went into effect April 1 our current liability insurance must be increased however we cannot immediately afford it.

_____ 49. As stipulated in our contract your agency will supervise our graphic arts and purchase our media time.

_____ 50. As you know Mrs. Laurendeau we aim for long-term business relationships not quick profits.

K. Other Punctuation

Each of the following sentences may require dashes, colons, question marks, quotation marks, periods, and underscores, as well as commas and semicolons. Add the appropriate punctuation to each sentence. Then, in the space provided, write the total number of marks that you added.

3 Example: Price˄service˄and reliability˄these are our prime considerations.

_____ 51. The following members of the department volunteered to help on Saturday Kim Carlos Dan and Sylvia.

_____ 52. Mr. Danner, Miss Reed, and Mrs. Rossi usually arrived at the office by 8 30 a.m.

_____ 53. Three of our top managers Tim, Marcy, and Asad received cash bonuses.

_____ 54. Did the vice president really say "All employees may take Friday off

_____ 55. We are trying to locate an edition of _Maclean's_ that carried an article entitled E-Mail Beats Office Politics

L. Capitalization

For each of the following sentences, circle any letter that should be capitalized. In the space provided, write the number of circles that you marked.

4 Example: Ⓥice Ⓟresident Ⓓaniels devised a procedure for expediting purchase orders from Ⓐrea 4 warehouses.

_____ 56. although english was his first language, he also spoke spanish and could read french.

_____ 57. on a trip to the east coast, uncle henry visited the bay of fundy.

_____ 58. karen enrolled in classes in history, german, and sociology.

_____ 59. the business manager and the vice president each received a new macintosh computer.

_____ 60. jane lee, the president of kendrick, inc., will speak to our conference in the spring.

M. Number Style

Decide whether the numbers in the following sentences should be written as words or as figures. Each sentence either is correct or has one error. If it is correct, write _C_. If it has an error, underline it and write the correct form in the space provided.

five Example: The bank had _5_ branches in three suburbs.

_____ 61. More than 2,000,000 people have visited the Parliament Buildings in the past five years.

_____ 62. Of the 35 letters sent out, only three were returned.

_____ 63. We set aside forty dollars for petty cash, but by December 1 our fund was depleted.

_____ 64. The meeting is scheduled for May 5th at 3 p.m.

_____ 65. In the past 20 years, nearly 15 percent of the population changed residences at least once.

Grammar/Mechanics Profile

In the spaces at the right, place a check mark to indicate the number of correct answers you had in each category of the Grammar/Mechanics Diagnostic Test.

		Number Correct*				
		5	4	3	2	1
1–5	Plural Nouns	___	___	___	___	___
6–10	Possessive Nouns	___	___	___	___	___
11–15	Pronouns	___	___	___	___	___
16–20	Verb Agreement	___	___	___	___	___
21–25	Verb Mood, Voice, and Tense	___	___	___	___	___
26–30	Adjectives and Adverbs	___	___	___	___	___
31–35	Prepositions and Conjunctions	___	___	___	___	___
36–40	Commas	___	___	___	___	___
41–45	Commas and Semicolons 1	___	___	___	___	___
46–50	Commas and Semicolons 2	___	___	___	___	___
51–55	Other Punctuation	___	___	___	___	___
56–60	Capitalization	___	___	___	___	___
61–65	Number Style	___	___	___	___	___

*Note: 5 = have excellent skills; 4 = need light review; 3 = need careful review; 2 = need to study rules; 1 = need serious study and follow-up reinforcement.

Grammar Review

Parts of Speech (1.01)

1.01 Functions. English has eight parts of speech. Knowing the functions of the parts of speech helps writers better understand how words are used and how sentences are formed.

a. **Nouns.** Name persons, places, things, qualities, concepts, and activities (for example, _Kevin, Montreal, computer, joy, work, banking_).

b. **Pronouns.** Substitute for nouns (for example, _he, she, it, they_).

c. **Verbs.** Show the action of a subject or join the subject to words that describe it (for example, _walk, heard, is, was jumping_).

d. **Adjectives.** Describe or limit nouns and pronouns and often answer the questions what kind? how many? and which one? (for example, _fast_ sale, _ten_ items, _good_ manager).

e. **Adverbs.** Describe or limit verbs, adjectives, or other adverbs and frequently answer the questions when? how? where? or to what extent? (for example, *tomorrow, rapidly, here, very*).

f. **Prepositions.** Join nouns or pronouns to other words in sentences (for example, desk *in* the office, ticket *for* me, letter *to* you).

g. **Conjunctions.** Connect words or groups of words (for example, you *and* I, Marc *or* Nikola).

h. **Interjections.** Express strong feelings (for example, *Wow! Oh!*).

Nouns (1.02–1.06)

Nouns name persons, places, things, qualities, concepts, and activities. Nouns may be classified into a number of categories.

1.02 Concrete and Abstract. Concrete nouns name specific objects that can be seen, heard, felt, tasted, or smelled. Examples of concrete nouns are *telephone, dollar, IBM,* and *grape*. Abstract nouns name generalized ideas such as qualities or concepts that are not easily pictured. *Emotion, power,* and *tension* are typical examples of abstract nouns.

Business writing is most effective when concrete words predominate. It's clearer to write *We need 16-pound bond paper* than to write *We need office supplies*. Chapter 3 provides practice in developing skill in the use of concrete words.

1.03 Proper and Common. Proper nouns name specific persons, places, or things and are always capitalized (*Nortel, Minnedosa, Dinah*). All other nouns are common nouns and begin with lowercase letters (*company, city, student*). Rules for capitalization are presented in Sections 3.01–3.16.

1.04 Singular and Plural. Singular nouns name one item; plural nouns name more than one. From a practical view, writers seldom have difficulty with singular nouns. They may need help, however, with the formation and spelling of plural nouns.

1.05 Guidelines for Forming Noun Plurals

a. Add *s* to most nouns (*chair, chairs; mortgage, mortgages; Monday, Mondays*).

b. Add *es* to nouns ending in *s, x, z, ch,* or *sh* (*bench, benches; boss, bosses; box, boxes;* Schultz, Schultzes).

c. Change the spelling in irregular noun plurals (*man, men; foot, feet; mouse, mice; child, children*).

d. Add *s* to nouns that end in *y* when *y* is preceded by a vowel (*jockey, jockeys; valley, valleys; journey, journeys*).

e. Drop the *y* and add *ies* to nouns ending in *y* when *y* is preceded by a consonant (*company, companies; city, cities; secretary, secretaries*).

f. Add *s* to the principal word in most compound expressions (*editors in chief, fathers-in-law, bills of lading, runners-up*).

g. Add *s* to most numerals, letters of the alphabet, words referred to as words, degrees, and abbreviations (*5s, 1990s, Bs, ands, CAs, yrs.*). Note that metric abbreviations take neither a period nor an *s* to make them plural.

h. Add *'s* only to clarify letters of the alphabet that might be misread, such as *A's, I's, M's,* and *U's* and *i's, p's,* and *q's*. An expression like *c.o.d.s* requires no apostrophe because it would not easily be misread.

1.06 Collective Nouns Nouns such as *staff, faculty, committee, group,* and *herd* refer to a collection of people, animals, or objects. Collective nouns may be considered singular or plural depending upon their action. See Section 1.10i for a discussion of collective nouns and their agreement with verbs.

Review Exercise A—Nouns

In the space provided for each item, write *a* or *b* to complete the following statements accurately. When you finish, compare your responses with those provided. Answers are provided for odd-numbered items. Your instructor has the remaining answers. For each item on which you need review, consult the numbered principle shown in parentheses.

1. Nearly all (a) editor in chiefs, (b) editors in chief demand observance of standard punctuation.

2. Several (a) jockeys, (b) jockies worked on the case together.

3. Please write to the (a) Davis's, (b) Davises about the missing contract.

4. The industrial complex has space for nine additional (a) companys, (b) companies.

5. That accounting firm employs two (a) secretaries, (b) secretarys for five CGAs.

6. Four of the wooden (a) benches, (b) benchs must be repaired.

7. The home was constructed with numerous (a) chimneys, (b) chimnies.

8. Tours of the production facility are made only on (a) Tuesdays, (b) Tuesday's.

9. We asked the (a) Jones's, (b) Joneses to contribute to the fundraising drive.

10. Both my (a) sister-in-laws, (b) sisters-in-law agreed to the settlement.

11. The stock market is experiencing abnormal (a) ups and downs, (b) up's and down's.

12. Three (a) mouses, (b) mice were seen near the garbage cans.

13. This office is unusually quiet on (a) Sundays, (b) Sunday's.

14. Several news (a) dispatchs, (b) dispatches were released during the strike.

15. Two major (a) countries, (b) countrys will participate in trade negotiations.

16. Some young children have difficulty writing their (a) bs and ds, (b) b's and d's.

17. The (a) board of directors, (b) boards of directors of all the major companies participated in the surveys.

18. In their letter the (a) Metzes, (b) Metzs said they intended to purchase the property.

19. In shipping we are careful to include all (a) bill of sales, (b) bills of sale.

20. Over the holidays many (a) turkies, (b) turkeys were consumed.

---

1. b (1.05f) 3. b (1.05b) 5. a (1.05e) 7. a (1.05d) 9. b (1.05b) 11. a (1.05g) 13. a (1.05a) 15. a (1.05e) 17. b (1.05f) 19. b (1.05f) (Only odd-numbered answers are provided. Consult your instructor for the others.)

Grammar/Mechanics Checkup—1

Nouns

Review Sections 1.01–1.06 above. Then study each of the following statements. Underline any mistakes and write a correction in the space provided. Record the appropriate Handbook section and letter that illustrates the principle involved. If a sentence is correct, write C. When you finish, compare your responses with those provided on page 508. If your answers differ, carefully study again the principles shown in parentheses.

Companies (1.05e) Example: Two surveys revealed that many <u>companys</u> will move to the new industrial park.

———— 1. Several attornies worked on the three cases simultaneously.

———— 2. Counter business is higher on Saturday's, but telephone business is greater on Sundays.

———— 3. Some of the citys in Kevin's report offer excellent opportunities.

_____ 4. Frozen chickens and turkies are kept in the company's lockers.

_____ 5. All secretaries were asked to check supplies and other inventorys.

_____ 6. Only the Nashs and the Lopezes brought their entire families.

_____ 7. In the 1980s profits grew rapidly; in the 1990's investments lagged.

_____ 8. Both editor in chiefs instituted strict proofreading policies.

_____ 9. Luxury residential complexes are part of the architect's plan.

_____ 10. Trustees in three municipalitys are likely to approve increased school taxes.

_____ 11. The instructor was surprised to find three Jennifer's in one class.

_____ 12. Andre sent descriptions of two valleys in France to us via the Internet.

_____ 13. How many copies of the statements showing your assets and liabilitys did you make?

_____ 14. My monitor makes it difficult to distinguish between *o*'s and *a*'s.

_____ 15. Both runner-ups complained about the winner's behaviour.

Pronouns (1.07–1.09)

Pronouns substitute for nouns. They are classified by case.

1.07 Case. Pronouns function in three cases, as shown in the following chart.

Nominative Case	Objective Case	Possessive Case
(Used for subjects of verbs and subject complements)	*(Used for objects of prepositions and objects of verbs)*	*(Used to show possession)*
I	me	my, mine
we	us	our, ours
you	you	your, yours
he	him	his
she	her	her, hers
it	it	its
they	them	their, theirs
who, whoever	whom, whomever	whose

1.08 Guidelines for Selecting Pronoun Case

a. Pronouns that serve as subjects of verbs must be in the nominative case:

> He and I (not *Him and me*) decided to apply for the jobs.

b. Pronouns that follow linking verbs (such as *am, is, are, was, were, be, being, been*) and rename the words to which they refer must be in the nominative case.

> It must have been she (not *her*) who placed the order. (The nominative-case pronoun *she* follows the linking verb *been* and renames *It*.)

> If it was he (not *him*) who called, I have his number. (The nominative-case pronoun *he* follows the linking verb *was* and renames *It*.)

c. Pronouns that serve as objects of verbs or objects of prepositions must be in the objective case:

> Mr. Laporte asked them to complete the proposal. (The pronoun *them* is the object of the verb *asked*.)

All computer printouts are sent to him. (The pronoun *him* is the object of the preposition *to*.)

Just between you and me, profits are falling. (The pronoun *me* is one of the objects of the preposition *between*.)

d. Pronouns that show ownership must be in the possessive case. Possessive pronouns (such as *hers*, *yours*, *ours*, *theirs*, and *its*) require no apostrophes:

We found my cell phone, but yours (not *your's*) may be lost.

All parts of the machine, including its (not *it's*) motor, were examined.

The house and its (not *it's*) contents will be auctioned.

Don't confuse possessive pronouns and contractions. In such cases as *it's* for *it is*, *there's* for *there is*, and *they're* for *they are*, contractions are shortened forms of subject–verb phrases.

e. When a pronoun appears in combination with a noun or another pronoun, ignore the extra noun or pronoun and its conjunction. In this way pronoun case becomes more obvious:

The manager promoted Jasper and me (not *I*). (Ignore *Jasper and*.)

f. In statements of comparison, mentally finish the comparative by adding the implied missing words:

Next year I hope to earn as much as she. (The verb *earns* is implied here: *as much as she earns*.)

g. Pronouns must be in the same case as the words they replace or rename. When pronouns are used with appositives, ignore the appositive:

A new contract was signed by us (not *we*) employees. (Temporarily ignore the appositive *employees* in selecting the pronoun.)

We (not *us*) citizens have formed our own organization. (Temporarily ignore the appositive *citizens* in selecting the pronoun.)

h. Pronouns ending in *self* should be used only when they refer to previously mentioned nouns or pronouns:

The CEO herself answered the telephone.

Robert and I (not *myself*) are in charge of the campaign.

i. Use objective-case pronouns as objects of the prepositions *between*, *but*, *like*, and *except*:

Everyone but John and him (not *he*) qualified for the bonus.

Employees like Miss Gallucci and her (not *she*) are hard to replace.

j. Use *who* or *whoever* for nominative-case constructions and *whom* or *whomever* for objective-case constructions. In making the correct choice, it's sometimes helpful to substitute *he* for *who* or *whoever* and *him* for *whom* or *whomever*:

For whom was this book ordered? (*This book was ordered for him/ whom?*)

Who did you say would drop by? (*Who/he . . . would drop by?*)

Deliver the package to whoever opens the door. (In this sentence the clause *whoever opens the door* functions as the object of the preposition *to*. Within the clause itself *whoever* is the subject of the verb *opens*. Again, substitution of *he* might be helpful: *He/Whoever opens the door*.)

1.09 Guidelines for Making Pronouns Agree With Their Antecedents.

Pronouns must agree with the words to which they refer (their antecedents) in gender and in number.

a. Use masculine pronouns to refer to masculine antecedents, feminine pronouns to refer to feminine antecedents, and neutral pronouns to refer to antecedents without gender:

> The woman opened her office door. (Feminine gender applies.)
>
> A man sat at his desk. (Masculine gender applies.)
>
> This computer and its programs fit our needs. (Neutral gender applies.)

b. Use singular pronouns to refer to singular antecedents.

Common-gender pronouns (such as *him* or *his*) traditionally have been used when the gender of the antecedent is unknown. Business writers construct sentences to avoid the need for common-gender pronouns. Study these examples for alternatives to the use of common-gender pronouns:*

> Each student must submit a report on Monday.
>
> All students must submit their reports on Monday.
>
> Each student must submit his or her report on Monday. (This alternative is least acceptable, since it is wordy and calls attention to itself.)

c. Use singular pronouns to refer to singular indefinite subjects and plural pronouns for plural indefinite subjects. Words such as *anyone*, *something*, and *anybody* are considered indefinite because they refer to no specific person or object. Some indefinite pronouns are always singular; others are always plural.

Always Singular			Always Plural
anybody	either	nobody	both
anyone	everyone	no one	few
anything	everything	somebody	many
each	neither	someone	several

> Somebody in the group of touring women left her (not *their*) purse in the museum.
>
> Either of the companies has the right to exercise its (not *their*) option to sell shares.

d. Use singular pronouns to refer to collective nouns and organization names:

> The engineering staff is moving its (not *their*) facilities on Friday. (The singular pronoun *its* agrees with the collective noun *staff* because the members of staff function as a single unit.)
>
> Jones, Cohen, & James, Inc., has (not *have*) cancelled its (not *their*) contract with us. (The singular pronoun *its* agrees with *Jones, Cohen, & James, Inc.,* because the members of the organization are operating as a single unit.)

e. Use a plural pronoun to refer to two antecedents joined by *and*, whether the antecedents are singular or plural:

> Our company president and our vice president will be submitting their expenses shortly.

---

*See Chapter 2 for additional discussion of common-gender pronouns and inclusive language.

f. Ignore intervening phrases—introduced by expressions such as *together with*, *as well as*, and *in addition to*—that separate a pronoun from its antecedent:

> One of our managers, along with several salespeople, is planning his retirement. (If you wish to emphasize both subjects equally, join them with *and*: *One of our managers and several salespeople are planning their retirements.*)

g. When antecedents are joined by *or* or *nor*, make the pronoun agree with the antecedent closest to it.

> Neither Jackie nor Kim wanted her (not *their*) desk moved.

Review Exercise B—Pronouns

In the space provided for each item, write *a*, *b*, or *c* to complete the statement accurately. When you finish, compare your responses with those provided. For each item on which you need review, consult the numbered principle shown in parentheses.

_____ 1. Mr. Behrens and (a) I, (b) myself will be visiting sales personnel in the New Brunswick district next week.

_____ 2. Joel promised that he would call; was it (a) him, (b) he who left the message?

_____ 3. Much preparation for the seminar was made by Mrs. Wiellmar and (a) I, (b) me before the brochures were sent out.

_____ 4. The Employee Benefits Committee can be justly proud of (a) its, (b) their achievements.

_____ 5. A number of inquiries were addressed to Jonelle and (a) I, (b) me, (c) myself.

_____ 6. (a) Who, (b) Whom did you say the letter was addressed to?

_____ 7. When you visit Mutual Trust, inquire about (a) its, (b) their certificates.

_____ 8. Copies of all reports are to be reviewed by Mr. Khan and (a) I, (b) me, (c) myself.

_____ 9. Apparently one of the female applicants forgot to sign (a) her, (b) their application.

_____ 10. Both the printer and (a) it's, (b) its cover are missing.

_____ 11. I've never known any man who could work as fast as (a) him, (b) he.

_____ 12. Just between you and (a) I, (b) me, the share price will fall by afternoon.

_____ 13. Give the supplies to (a) whoever, (b) whomever ordered them.

_____ 14. (a) Us, (b) We employees have been given an unusual voice in choosing benefits.

_____ 15. On her return from Mexico, Mrs. Lamas, along with many other passengers, had to open (a) her, (b) their luggage for inspection.

_____ 16. Either Jason or Raymond will have (a) his, (b) their work reviewed next week.

_____ 17. Any woman who becomes a charter member of this organization will be able to have (a) her, (b) their name inscribed on a commemorative plaque.

_____ 18. We are certain that (a) our's, (b) ours is the smallest wristwatch available.

_____ 19. Everyone has completed the reports except Danica and (a) he, (b) him.

_____ 20. Lack of work disturbs Mr. Jin as much as (a) I, (b) me.

---

1. a (1.08h)   3. b (1.08c)   5. b (1.08c, 1.08e)   7. a (1.09d)   9. a (1.09b)   11. b (1.08f)
13. a (1.08j)   15. a (1.09f)   17. a (1.09b)   19. b (1.08i)

Grammar/Mechanics Checkup—2

Pronouns

Review Sections 1.07–1.09 above. Then study each of the following statements. In the space provided, write the word that completes the statement correctly and the number of the Handbook principle illustrated. When you finish, compare your responses with those provided on page 508 again. If your responses differ, carefully study again the principles in parentheses.

__its (1.09d)__ **Example:** The Recreation and Benefits Committee will be submitting (its, their) report soon.

_____ 1. I was expecting the manager to call. Was it (he, him) who left the message?

_____ 2. Every one of the members of the men's soccer team had to move (his car, their cars) before the game could begin.

_____ 3. A serious disagreement between management and (he, him) caused his resignation.

_____ 4. Does anyone in the office know for (who, whom) this stationery was ordered?

_____ 5. It looks as if (her's, hers) is the only report that cites electronic sources.

_____ 6. Ms. Simmons asked my colleague and (I, me, myself) to help her complete the work.

_____ 7. My friend and (I, me, myself) were also asked to work on Saturday.

_____ 8. Both printers were sent for repairs, but (yours, your's) will be returned shortly.

_____ 9. Give the budget figures to (whoever, whomever) asked for them.

_____ 10. Everyone except the broker and (I, me, myself) claimed a share of the commission.

_____ 11. No one knows that problem better than (he, him, himself).

_____ 12. Investment brochures and information were sent to (we, us) shareholders.

_____ 13. If any one of the tourists has lost (their, her) scarf, she should see the driver.

_____ 14. Neither the glamour nor the excitement of the position had lost (its, it's, their) appeal.

_____ 15. Any new subscriber may cancel (their, his or her) subscription within the first month.

Cumulative Editing Quiz 1

Use proofreading marks (see Appendix B) to correct errors in the following sentences. All errors must be corrected to receive credit for the sentence. Check with your instructor for the answers.

Example: Nicholas and ~~him~~ he made all ~~there~~ their money in the 1990's.

1. Just between you and I, whom do you think would make the best manager?

2. Either Sari or me is responsible for correcting all errors in news dispatchs.

3. Several attornies asked that there cases be postponed.

4. One of the secretarys warned Sharif and I to get the name of whomever answered the phone.

5. The committee sent there decision to the president and I last week.

6. Who should Angela or me call to verify the three bill of sales received today?

7. Several of we employees complained that it's keyboard made the new computer difficult to use.

8. All the CEO's agreed that the low interest rates of the early 2000's could not continue.

9. Every customer has a right to expect there inquirys to be treated courteously.

10. You may send you're contribution to Eric or myself or to whomever is listed as your representative.

Verbs (1.10–1.15)
Verbs show the action of a subject or join the subject to words that describe it.

1.10 Guidelines for Agreement With Subjects.
One of the most troublesome areas in English is subject–verb agreement. Consider the following guidelines for making verbs agree with subjects.

a. A singular subject requires a singular verb:

> The stock market opens at 10 a.m. (The singular verb *opens* agrees with the singular subject *market*.)

> He doesn't (not *don't*) work on Saturday.

b. A plural subject requires a plural verb:

> On the packing slip several items seem (not *seems*) to be missing.

c. A verb agrees with its subject regardless of prepositional phrases that may intervene:

> This list of management objectives is extensive. (The singular verb *is* agrees with the singular subject *list*.)

> Every one of the letters shows (not *show*) proper form.

d. A verb agrees with its subject regardless of intervening phrases introduced by *as well as*, *in addition to*, *such as*, *including*, *together with*, and similar expressions:

> An important memo, together with several letters, was misplaced. (The singular verb *was* agrees with the singular subject *memo*.)

> The president as well as several other top-level executives approves of our proposal. (The singular verb *approves* agrees with the subject *president*.)

e. A verb agrees with its subject regardless of the location of the subject:

> Here is one of the letters about which you asked. (The verb *is* agrees with its subject *one*, even though it precedes *one*. The adverb *here* cannot function as a subject.)

> There are many problems yet to be resolved. (The verb *are* agrees with the subject *problems*. The adverb *there* cannot function as a subject.)

> In the next office are several printers. (In this inverted sentence the verb *are* must agree with the subject *printers*.)

f. Subjects joined by *and* require a plural verb:

> Analyzing the reader and organizing a strategy are the first steps in letter writing. (The plural verb *are* agrees with the two subjects, *analyzing* and *organizing*.)

> The tone and the wording of the letter were persuasive. (The plural verb *were* agrees with the two subjects, *tone* and *wording*.)

g. Subjects joined by *or* or *nor* may require singular or plural verbs. Make the verb agree with the closer subject:

> Neither the memos nor the report is ready. (The singular verb *is* agrees with *report*, the closer of the two subjects.)

h. The following indefinite pronouns are singular and require singular verbs: *anyone, anybody, anything, each, either, every, everyone, everybody, everything, many a, neither, nobody, nothing, someone, somebody,* and *something*:

> Either of the alternatives that you present is acceptable. (The verb *is* agrees with the singular subject *either*.)

i. Collective nouns may take singular or plural verbs, depending on whether the members of the group are operating as a unit or individually:

> Our management team is united in its goal.

> The faculty are sharply divided on the tuition issue. (Although acceptable, this sentence sounds better recast: *The faculty members are sharply divided on the tuition issue.*)

j. Organization names and titles of publications, although they may appear to be plural, are singular and require singular verbs.

> Deme, Sokolov, and Horne, Inc., has (not *have*) hired a marketing consultant.

> *Thousands of Investment Tips* is (not *are*) again on the bestseller list.

1.11 Voice. Voice is that property of verbs that shows whether the subject of the verb acts or is acted upon. Active-voice verbs direct action from the subject toward the object of the verb. Passive-voice verbs direct action toward the subject.

Active voice: Our employees write excellent letters.
Passive voice: Excellent letters are written by our employees.

Business writing that emphasizes active-voice verbs is generally preferred because it is specific and forceful. However, passive-voice constructions can help a writer be tactful. Strategies for effective use of active- and passive-voice verbs are presented in Chapter 7.

1.12 Mood. Three verb moods express the attitude or thought of the speaker or writer toward a subject: (1) the **indicative** mood expresses a fact; (2) the **imperative** mood expresses a command; and (3) the **subjunctive** mood expresses a doubt, a conjecture, or a suggestion.

Indicative: I am looking for a job.
Imperative: Begin your job search with the want ads.
Subjunctive: I wish I were working.

Only the subjunctive mood creates problems for most speakers and writers. The most common use of subjunctive mood occurs in clauses including *if* or *wish*. In such clauses substitute the subjunctive verb *were* for the indicative verb *was*:

> If he were (not *was*) in my position, he would understand.

> Mr. Dworski acts as if he were (not *was*) the boss.

> I wish I were (not *was*) able to ship your order.

The subjunctive mood may be used to maintain goodwill while conveying negative information. The sentence *I wish I were able to ship your order* sounds more pleasing to a customer than *I cannot ship your order*, although, for all practical purposes, the two sentences convey the same negative message.

1.13 Tense. Verbs show the time of an action by their tense. Speakers and writers can use six tenses to show the time of sentence action; for example:

Present tense:	I work; he works.
Past tense:	I worked; she worked.
Future tense:	I will work; he will work.
Present perfect tense:	I have worked; he has worked.
Past perfect tense:	I had worked; she had worked.
Future perfect tense:	I will have worked; he will have worked.

1.14 Guidelines for Verb Tense

a. Use present tense for statements that, although they may be introduced by past-tense verbs, continue to be true:

> What did you say his name is? (Use the present tense *is* if his name has not changed.)

b. Avoid unnecessary shifts in verb tenses:

> The manager saw (not *sees*) a great deal of work yet to be completed and remained to do it herself.

Although unnecessary shifts in verb tense are to be avoided, not all the verbs within one sentence have to be in the same tense; for example:

> She said (past tense) that she likes (present tense) to work late.

1.15 Irregular Verbs. Irregular verbs cause difficulty for some writers and speakers. Unlike regular verbs, irregular verbs do not form the past tense and past participle by adding *-ed* to the present form. Here is a partial list of selected troublesome irregular verbs. Consult a dictionary if you are in doubt about a verb form.

Troublesome Irregular Verbs

Present	Past	Past Participle *(always use helping verbs)*
begin	began	begun
break	broke	broken
choose	chose	chosen
come	came	come
drink	drank	drunk
go	went	gone
lay (to place)	laid	laid
lie (to rest)	lay	lain
ring	rang	rung
see	saw	seen
write	wrote	written

a. *Use only past-tense verbs to express past tense.* Notice that no helping verbs are used to indicate simple past tense:

> The auditors went (not *have went*) over our books carefully.

> He came (not *come*) to see us yesterday.

b. *Use past participle forms for actions completed before the present time.* Notice that past participle forms require helping verbs:

> Steve had gone (not *went*) before we called. (The past participle *gone* is used with the helping verb *had*.)

c. *Avoid inconsistent shifts in subject, voice, and mood.* Pay particular attention to this problem area, for undesirable shifts are often characteristic of student writing.

Inconsistent: When Mrs. Moscovitch read the report, the error was found. (The first clause is in the active voice; the second, passive.)

Improved: When Mrs. Moscovitch read the report, she found the error. (Both clauses are in the active voice.)

Inconsistent: The clerk should first conduct an inventory. Then supplies should be requisitioned. (The first sentence is in the active voice; the second, passive.)

Improved: The clerk should first conduct an inventory. Then he or she should requisition supplies. (Both sentences are in the active voice.)

Inconsistent: All workers must wear security badges, and you must also sign a daily time card. (This sentence contains an inconsistent shift in subject from *all workers* in first clause to *you* in second clause.)

Improved: All workers must wear security badges, and they must also sign a daily time card.

Inconsistent: Begin the transaction by opening an account; then you enter the customer's name. (This sentence contains an inconsistent shift from the imperative mood in first clause to the indicative mood in second clause.)

Improved: Begin the transaction by opening an account; then enter the customer's name. (Both clauses are now in the imperative mood.)

Review Exercise C—Verbs

In the space provided for each item, write *a* or *b* to complete the statement accurately. When you finish, compare your responses with those provided. For each item on which you need review, consult the numbered principle shown in parentheses.

_____ 1. A list of payroll deductions for our employees (a) was, (b) were sent to the personnel manager.

_____ 2. There (a) is, (b) are a customer service engineer and two salespeople waiting to see you.

_____ 3. Increased computer use and more complex automated systems (a) is, (b) are found in business today.

_____ 4. Crews, Meliotes, and Bauve, Inc., (a) has, (b) have opened an office in St. John's.

_____ 5. Yesterday Mrs. Phillips (a) choose, (b) chose a new office on the second floor.

_____ 6. The man who called said that his name (a) is, (b) was Johnson.

_____ 7. *Office Computing and Networks* (a) is, (b) are beginning a campaign to increase readership.

_____ 8. Either of the flight times (a) appears, (b) appear to fit my proposed itinerary.

_____ 9. If you had (a) saw, (b) seen the rough draft, you would better appreciate the final copy.

_____ 10. Across from our office (a) is, (b) are the parking structure and the information office.

_____ 11. Although we have (a) began, (b) begun to replace outmoded equipment, the pace is slow.

_____ 12. Specific training as well as ample experience (a) is, (b) are important for that position.

_____ 13. Inflation and increased job opportunities (a) is, (b) are resulting in increased numbers of working women.

_____ 14. Neither the organizing nor the staffing of the program (a) has been, (b) have been completed.

_____ 15. If I (a) was, (b) were you, I would ask for a raise.

_____ 16. If you had (a) wrote, (b) written last week, we could have sent a brochure.

_____ 17. The hydraulic equipment that you ordered (a) is, (b) are packed and will be shipped Friday.

_____ 18. One of the reasons that sales have declined in recent years (a) is, (b) are lack of effective advertising.

_____ 19. Either of the proposed laws (a) is, (b) are going to affect our business negatively.

_____ 20. Bankruptcy statutes (a) requires, (b) require that a failed company pay its debts to secured creditors first.

1. a (1.10c)   3. b (1.10f)   5. b (1.15a)   7. a (1.10j)   9. b (1.15b)   11. b (1.15b)   13. b (1.10f)
15. b (1.12)   17. a (1.10a)   19. a (1.10h)

Review Exercise D—Verbs

In the following sentence pairs, choose the one that illustrates consistency in use of subject, voice, and mood. Write _a_ or _b_ in the space provided. When you finish, compare your responses with those provided. For each item on which you need review, consult the numbered principle shown in parentheses.

_____ 1. (a) You need more than a knowledge of equipment; one also must be able to interact well with people.

(b) You need more than a knowledge of equipment; you also must be able to interact well with people.

_____ 2. (a) Maurice and Jon were eager to continue, but Bob wanted to quit.

(b) Maurice and Jon were eager to continue, but Bob wants to quit.

_____ 3. (a) The salesperson should consult the price list; then you can give an accurate quote to a customer.

(b) The salesperson should consult the price list; then he or she can give an accurate quote to a customer.

_____ 4. (a) Read all the instructions first; then you install the printer program.

(b) Read all the instructions first, and then install the printer program.

_____ 5. (a) She was an enthusiastic manager who always had a smile for everyone.

(b) She was an enthusiastic manager who always has a smile for everyone.

1. b (1.15c)   3. b (1.15c)   5. a (1.14b)

Grammar/Mechanics Checkup—3

Verbs

Review Sections 1.10–1.15 above. Then study each of the following statements. Underline any verbs that are used incorrectly. In the space provided, write the correct form (or C if correct) and the number of the Handbook principle illustrated. When you finish, compare your responses with those provided on page 508. If your responses differ, carefully study again the principles in parentheses.

was (1.10c) Example: Our inventory of raw materials were presented as collateral for a short-term loan.

_____ 1. Located across town is a research institute and our product-testing facility.

_____ 2. Can you tell me whether a current list with all customers' names and addresses have been sent to marketing?

_____ 3. The credit union, along with 20 other large national banks, offer a variety of savings plans.

_____ 4. Neither the plans that this bank offers nor the service just rendered by the teller are impressive.

_____ 5. Locating a bank and selecting a savings/chequing plan often require considerable research and study.

_____ 6. The budget analyst wants to know whether the Equipment Committee are ready to recommend a printer.

_____ 7. Either of the printers that the committee selects is acceptable to the budget analyst.

_____ 8. If Mr. Tutchone had chose the Maximizer Plus savings plan, his money would have earned maximum interest.

_____ 9. Although the applications have laid there for two weeks, they may still be submitted.

_____ 10. Nadia acts as if she was the manager.

_____ 11. One of the reasons that our Nunavut sales branches have been so costly are the high cost of living.

In the space provided, write the letter of the sentence that illustrates consistency in subject, voice, and mood.

_____ 12. (a) If you will read the instructions, the answer can be found.

(b) If you will read the instructions, you will find the answer.

_____ 13. (a) All employees must fill out application forms; only then will you be insured.

(b) All employees must fill out application forms; only then will they be insured.

_____ 14. (a) First, take an inventory of equipment; then, order supplies.

(b) First, take an inventory of equipment; then, supplies must be ordered.

_____ 15. (a) Select a savings plan that suits your needs; deposits may be made immediately.

(b) Select a savings plan that suits your needs; begin making deposits immediately.

Cumulative Editing Quiz 2

Use proofreading marks (see Appendix B) to correct errors in the following sentences. All errors must be corrected to receive credit for the sentence. Check with your instructor for the answers.

1. Assets and liabilitys is what my partner and myself must investigate.

2. If I was you, I would ask whomever is in charge for their opinion.

3. The faculty agree that it's first concern is educating students.

4. The book and it's cover was printed in Japan.

5. Waiting to see you is a sales representative and a job applicant who you told to drop by.

6. Every employee could have picked up his ballot if he had went to the cafeteria.

7. Your choice of mutual funds and bonds are reduced by this plan and it's restrictions.

8. My uncle and her come to visit my parents and myself last night.

9. According to both editor in chiefs, the tone and wording of all our letters needs revision.

10. The Davis'es, about who the article was written, said they were unconcerned with the up's and down's of the stock market.

Adjectives and Adverbs (1.16–1.17)

Adjectives describe or limit nouns and pronouns. They often answer the questions what kind? how many? or which one? (A special kind of adjective—an article—introduces nouns. *A* and *an* are indefinite articles; *the* is a definite article. Indefinite articles refer to non-specific nouns (e.g., Please call a caretaker to clean up that spill), while definite articles refer to specific nouns (e.g., Let's hire *the* candidate who talked about his time in Africa). Adverbs describe or limit verbs, adjectives, or other adverbs. They often answer the questions when? how? where? or to what extent?

1.16 Forms. Most adjectives and adverbs have three forms, or degrees: **positive**, **comparative**, and **superlative**.

	Positive	Comparative	Superlative
Adjective:	clear	clearer	clearest
Adverb:	clearly	more clearly	most clearly

Some adjectives and adverbs have irregular forms:

	Positive	Comparative	Superlative
Adjective:	good	better	best
	bad	worse	worst
Adverb:	well	better	best

Adverbs and some adjectives composed of two or more syllables are usually compared by the use of *more* and *most*; for example:

> The Payroll Department operates least efficiently when the manager is absent.

> The Payroll Department is more efficient than the Shipping Department.

1.17 Guidelines for Use

a. Use the comparative degree of the adjective or adverb to compare two persons or things; use the superlative degree to compare three or more:

> Of the two letters, which is better (not *best*)?

> Of all the plans, we like this one best (not *better*).

b. Do not create a double comparative or superlative by using -er with *more* or -est with *most*:

> His explanation couldn't have been clearer (not *more clearer*).

c. A linking verb (*is*, *are*, *look*, *seem*, *feel*, *sound*, *appear*, and so forth) may introduce a word that describes the verb's subject. In this case be certain to use an adjective, not an adverb:

> The characters on the monitor look bright (not *brightly*). (Use the adjective *bright* because it follows the linking verb *look* and modifies the noun *characters*. It answers the question *What kind of characters?*)

> The company's letter made the customer feel bad (not *badly*). (The adjective *bad* follows the linking verb *feel* and describes the noun *customer*.)

d. Use adverbs, not adjectives, to describe or limit the action of verbs:

> The business is running smoothly (not *smooth*). (Use the adverb *smoothly* to describe the action of the verb *is running*. *Smoothly* tells how the business is running.)

> Don't take his remark personally (not *personal*). (The adverb *personally* describes the action of the verb *take*.)

e. Two or more adjectives that are joined to create a compound modifier before a noun should be hyphenated:

> The four-year-old child was tired.

> Our agency is planning a coast-to-coast campaign.

Do not hyphenate a compound modifier if it appears after the noun it modifies.

> Our speaker is well known. (Omit the hyphen because the adjective appears after the noun.)

> She is a well-known speaker. (Include the hyphen because the adjective appears before the noun.)

f. Keep adjectives and adverbs close to the words that they modify:

> She asked for a cup of hot coffee (not a *hot cup of coffee*).

> Patty had only two days of vacation left (not *Patty only had two days*).

> Students may sit in the first five rows (not *in the five first rows*).

> He has saved almost enough money for the trip (not *He has almost saved*).

g. Don't confuse the adverb *there* with the possessive pronoun *their* or the contraction *they're*:

> Put the documents there. (The adverb *there* means "at that place or at that point.")

> There are two reasons for the change. (The adverb *there* is used as filler preceding a linking verb.)

> We already have their specifications. (The possessive pronoun *their* shows ownership.)

> They're coming to inspect today. (The contraction *they're* is a shortened form of *they are*.)

Review Exercise E—Adjectives and Adverbs

In the space provided for each item, write *a*, *b*, or *c* to complete the statement accurately. If two sentences are shown, select (a) or (b) to indicate the one expressed more effectively. When you finish, compare your responses with those provided. For each item on which you need review, consult the numbered principle shown in parentheses.

_____ 1. After the interview, Kyoko looked (a) calm, (b) calmly.

_____ 2. If you had been more (a) careful, (b) carefuler, the box might not have broken.

_____ 3. Because a new manager was appointed, the advertising campaign is running very (a) smooth, (b) smoothly.

_____ 4. To avoid a (a) face to face, (b) face-to-face confrontation, she wrote a letter.

_____ 5. Bayani completed the employment test (a) satisfactorily, (b) satisfactory.

_____ 6. I felt (a) bad, (b) badly that he was not promoted.

_____ 7. Which is the (a) more, (b) most dependable of the two models?

_____ 8. Can you determine exactly what (a) there, (b) their, (c) they're company wants us to do?

_____ 9. Of all the copiers we tested, this one is the (a) easier, (b) easiest to operate.

_____ 10. (a) Mr. Aldron almost was ready to accept the offer.

(b) Mr. Aldron was almost ready to accept the offer.

_____ 11. (a) We only thought that it would take two hours for the test.

(b) We thought that it would take only two hours for the test.

_____ 12. (a) Please bring me a glass of cold water.

(b) Please bring me a cold glass of water.

_____ 13. (a) The committee decided to retain the last ten tickets.

(b) The committee decided to retain the ten last tickets.

_____ 14. New owners will receive a (a) 60-day, (b) 60 day trial period.

_____ 15. The time passed (a) quicker, (b) more quickly than we expected.

_____ 16. We offer a (a) money back, (b) money-back guarantee.

_____ 17. Today the financial news is (a) worse, (b) worst than yesterday.

_____ 18. Please don't take his comments (a) personal, (b) personally.

_____ 19. You must check the document (a) page by page, (b) page-by-page.

_____ 20. (a) We try to file only necessary paperwork.

(b) We only try to file necessary paperwork.

---

1. a (1.17c) 3. b (1.17d) 5. a (1.17d) 7. a (1.17a) 9. b (1.17a) 11. b (1.17f) 13. a (1.17f)
15. b (1.17d) 17. a (1.17a) 19. a (1.17e)

Grammar/Mechanics Checkup—4

Adjectives and Adverbs

Review Sections 1.16 and 1.17 above. Then study each of the following statements. Underline any inappropriate forms. In the space provided, write the correct form (or C if correct) and the number of the Handbook principle illustrated. You may need to consult your dictionary for current practice regarding some compound adjectives. When you finish, compare your responses with those provided on page 508. If your answers differ, carefully study again the principles in parentheses.

<u>live-and-let-live (1.17e)</u> **Example:** He was one of those individuals with <u>a live and let live</u> attitude.

_____ 1. Most of our long time customers have credit card accounts.

_____ 2. Many subscribers considered the $50 per year charge to be a bargain.

_____ 3. Other subscribers complained that $50 per year was exorbitant.

_____ 4. The Internet supplied the answer so quick that we were all amazed.

_____ 5. He only had $5 in his pocket.

_____ 6. Some experts predict that double digit inflation may return.

_____ 7. Jeremy found a once in a lifetime opportunity.

_____ 8. Although the car was four years old, it was in good condition.

_____ 9. Of the two colours, which is best for a Web background?

_____ 10. Professor Candace Carbone is well known in her field.

_____ 11. Channel 12 presents up to the minute news broadcasts.

_____ 12. Lower tax brackets would lessen the after tax yield of some bonds.

_____ 13. The conclusion drawn from the statistics couldn't have been more clearer.

_____ 14. This new investment fund has a better than fifty fifty chance of outperforming the older fund.

_____ 15. If you feel badly about the transaction, contact your portfolio manager.

Prepositions (1.18)

Prepositions are connecting words that join nouns or pronouns to other words in a sentence. The words *about*, *at*, *from*, *in*, and *to* are examples of prepositions.

1.18 Guidelines for Use

a. Include necessary prepositions:

> What type of software do you need? (Not *What type software.*)

> I graduated from high school two years ago. (Not *I graduated high school.*)

b. Omit unnecessary prepositions:

> Where is the meeting? (Not *Where is the meeting at?*)

> Both printers work well. (Not *Both of the printers.*)

> Where are you going? (Not *Where are you going to?*)

c. Avoid the overuse of prepositional phrases:

> **Weak:** We have received your application for credit at our branch in the Halifax area.
>
> **Improved:** We have received your credit application at our Halifax office.

d. Repeat the preposition before the second of two related elements:

> Applicants use the résumé effectively by summarizing their most important experiences and by relating their education to the jobs sought.

e. Include the second preposition when two prepositions modify a single object:

> George's appreciation of and aptitude for computers led to a promising career.

Conjunctions (1.19)

Conjunctions connect words, phrases, and clauses. They act as signals, indicating when a thought is being added, contrasted, or altered. Coordinate conjunctions (such as *and*, *or*, *but*) and other words that act as connectors (such as *however*, *therefore*, *when*, *as*) tell the reader or listener in what direction a thought is heading. They're like road signs signalling what's ahead.

1.19 Guidelines for Use

a. Use coordinating conjunctions to connect only sentence elements that are parallel or balanced.

> **Weak:** His report was correct and written in a concise manner.
>
> **Improved:** His report was correct and concise.
>
> **Weak:** Management has the capacity to increase fraud, or reduction can be achieved through the policies it adopts.
>
> **Improved:** Management has the capacity to increase or reduce fraud through the policies it adopts.

b. Do not use the word *like* as a conjunction:

> It seems as if (not *like*) this day will never end.

c. Avoid using *when* or *where* inappropriately. A common writing fault occurs in sentences with clauses introduced by *is when* and *is where*. Written English ordinarily requires a noun (or a group of words functioning as a noun) following the linking verb *is*. Instead of acting as conjunctions in these constructions, the words *where* and *when* function as adverbs, creating faulty grammatical equations (adverbs cannot complete equations set up by linking verbs). To avoid the problem, revise the sentence, eliminating *is when* or *is where*.

Weak: A bullish market is when prices are rising in the stock market.
Improved: A bullish market is created when prices are rising in the stock market.

Weak: A flow chart is when you make a diagram showing the step-by-step progression of a procedure.
Improved: A flow chart is a diagram showing the step-by-step progression of a procedure.

Weak: Word processing is where you use a computer and software to write.
Improved: Word processing involves the use of a computer and software to write.

A similar faulty construction occurs in the expression *I hate when*. English requires nouns, noun clauses, or pronouns to act as objects of verbs, not adverbs.

Weak: I hate when we're asked to work overtime.
Improved: I hate it when we're asked to work overtime.
Improved: I hate being asked to work overtime.

d. Don't confuse the adverb *then* with the conjunction *than*. *Then* means "at that time"; *than* indicates the second element in a comparison:

We would rather remodel than (not *then*) move.

First, the equipment is turned on; then (not *than*) the program is loaded.

Review Exercise F—Prepositions and Conjunctions

In the space provided for each item, write a or b to indicate the sentence that is expressed more effectively. When you finish, compare your responses with those provided. For each item on which you need review, consult the numbered principle shown in parentheses.

_____ 1. (a) Do you know where this shipment is being sent?

(b) Do you know where this shipment is being sent to?

_____ 2. (a) She was not aware of nor interested in the company insurance plan.

(b) She was not aware nor interested in the company insurance plan.

_____ 3. (a) Mr. Samuels graduated college last June.

(b) Mr. Samuels graduated from college last June.

_____ 4. (a) "Flextime" is when employees arrive and depart at varying times.

(b) "Flextime" is a method of scheduling work time in which employees arrive and depart at varying times.

_____ 5. (a) Both employees enjoyed setting their own hours.

(b) Both of the employees enjoyed setting their own hours.

_____ 6. (a) I hate when the disc freezes in my DVD player.

(b) I hate it when the disc freezes in my DVD player.

_____ 7. (a) What style of font should we use?

(b) What style font should we use?

_____ 8. (a) Business letters should be concise, correct, and written clearly.

(b) Business letters should be concise, correct, and clear.

_____ 9. (a) Mediation in a labour dispute occurs when a neutral person helps union and management reach an agreement.

      (b) Mediation in a labour dispute is where a neutral person helps union and management reach an agreement.

_____ 10. (a) It looks as if the plant will open in early January.

      (b) It looks like the plant will open in early January.

_____ 11. (a) We expect to finish up the work soon.

      (b) We expect to finish the work soon.

_____ 12. (a) At the beginning of the program in the fall of the year at the central office, we experienced staffing difficulties.

      (b) When the program began last fall, the central office experienced staffing difficulties.

_____ 13. (a) Your client may respond by letter or a telephone call may be made.

      (b) Your client may respond by letter or by telephone.

_____ 14. (a) A résumé is when you make a written presentation of your education and experience for a prospective employer.

      (b) A résumé is a written presentation of your education and experience for a prospective employer.

_____ 15. (a) Stacy exhibited both an awareness of and talent for developing innovations.

      (b) Stacy exhibited both an awareness and talent for developing innovations.

_____ 16. (a) This course is harder then I expected.

      (b) This course is harder than I expected.

_____ 17. (a) An ombudsman is an individual hired by management to investigate and resolve employee complaints.

      (b) An ombudsman is when management hires an individual to investigate and resolve employee complaints.

_____ 18. (a) I'm uncertain where to take this document to.

      (b) I'm uncertain where to take this document.

_____ 19. (a) By including accurate data and by writing clearly, you will produce effective memos.

      (b) By including accurate data and writing clearly, you will produce effective memos.

_____ 20. (a) We need computer operators who can load software, monitor networks, and files must be duplicated.

      (b) We need computer operators who can load software, monitor networks, and duplicate files.

---

1. a (1.18b) 3. b (1.18a) 5. a (1.18b) 7. a (1.18a) 9. a (1.19c) 11. b (1.18b)
13. b (1.19a) 15. a (1.18e) 17. a (1.19c) 19. a (1.18d)

Grammar/Mechanics Checkup—5

Prepositions and Conjunctions

Review Sections 1.18 and 1.19 above. Then study each of the following statements. Write *a* or *b* to indicate the sentence in which the idea is expressed more effectively. Also record the number of the Handbook principle illustrated. When you finish, compare your responses with those provided on page 508. If your answers differ, carefully study again the principles shown in parentheses.

b (1.18a) **Example:** (a) Raoul will graduate college this spring.

                 (b) Raoul will graduate from college this spring.

_____ 1. (a) DataTech enjoyed greater profits this year then it expected.

      (b) DataTech enjoyed greater profits this year than it expected.

_____ 2. (a) I hate it when we have to work overtime.

      (b) I hate when we have to work overtime.

_____ 3. (a) Dr. Simon has a great interest and appreciation for the study of robotics.

      (b) Dr. Simon has a great interest in and appreciation for the study of robotics.

_____ 4. (a) Gross profit is where you compute the difference between total sales and the cost of goods sold.

      (b) Gross profit is computed by finding the difference between total sales and the cost of goods sold.

_____ 5. (a) We advertise to increase the frequency of product use, to introduce complementary products, and to enhance our corporate image.

      (b) We advertise to have our products used more often, when we have complementary products to introduce, and we are interested in making our corporation look better to the public.

_____ 6. (a) What type printer do you prefer?

      (b) What type of printer do you prefer?

_____ 7. (a) Where are you going to?

      (b) Where are you going?

_____ 8. (a) The sale of our Halifax office last year should improve this year's profits.

      (b) The sale of our office in Halifax during last year should improve the profits for this year.

_____ 9. (a) Do you know where the meeting is at?

      (b) Do you know where the meeting is?

_____ 10. (a) The cooling-off rule is a provincial government rule that protects consumers from making unwise purchases at home.

      (b) The cooling-off rule is where the provincial government has made a rule that protects consumers from making unwise purchases at home.

_____ 11. (a) Meetings can be more meaningful if the agenda is stuck to, the time frame is followed, and if someone keeps follow-up notes.

      (b) Meetings can be more meaningful if you stick to the agenda, follow the time frame, and keep follow-up notes.

_____ 12. (a) They printed the newsletter on yellow paper like we asked them to do.

      (b) They printed the newsletter on yellow paper as we asked them to do.

_____ 13. (a) A code of ethics is a set of rules indicating appropriate standards of behaviour.

      (b) A code of ethics is where a set of rules indicates appropriate standards of behaviour.

_____ 14. (a) We need an individual with an understanding and serious interest in black-and-white photography.

      (b) We need an individual with an understanding of and serious interest in black-and-white photography.

_____ 15. (a) The most dangerous situation is when employees ignore the safety rules.

(b) The most dangerous situation occurs when employees ignore the safety rules.

Cumulative Editing Quiz 3

Use proofreading marks (see Appendix B) to correct errors in the following sentences. All errors must be corrected to receive credit for the sentence. Check with your instructor for the answers.

1. If Treena types faster then her, shouldn't Treena be hired?
2. We felt badly that Mark's home was not chose for the tour.
3. Neither the company nor the workers is pleased at how slow the talks seems to be progressing.
4. Just between you and I, it's better not to take his remarks personal.
5. After completing there floor by floor inventory, managers will deliver there reports to Mr. Quinn and I.
6. If the telephone was working, Jean and myself could have completed our calls.
7. Powerful software and new hardware allows us to send the newsletter to whomever is currently listed in our database.
8. The thirteen year old girl and her mother was given hot cups of tea after there ordeal.
9. We begun the work two years ago, but personnel and equipment has been especially difficult to obtain.
10. Today's weather is worst then yesterday.

Punctuation Review

Commas 1 (2.01–2.04)

2.01 Series. Commas are used to separate three or more equal elements (words, phrases, or short clauses) in a series. To ensure separation of the last two elements, careful writers always use a comma before the conjunction in a series:

> Business letters usually contain a dateline, address, salutation, body, and closing. (This series contains words.)

> The job of an ombudsman is to examine employee complaints, resolve disagreements between management and employees, and ensure fair treatment. (This series contains phrases).

> Trainees complete basic keyboarding tasks, technicians revise complex documents, and editors proofread completed projects. (This series contains short clauses.)

2.02 Direct Address. Commas are used to set off the names of individuals being addressed:

> Your inquiry, Mrs. Johnson, has been referred to me.

> We genuinely hope that we may serve you, Mr. Lee.

2.03 Parenthetical Expressions. Skilled writers use parenthetical words, phrases, and clauses to guide the reader from one thought to the next. When these expressions interrupt the flow of a sentence and are unnecessary for its grammatical completeness, they should be set off with commas. Examples of commonly used parenthetical expressions follow:

all things considered	however	needless to say
as a matter of fact	in addition	nevertheless
as a result	incidentally	no doubt
as a rule	in fact	of course
at the same time	in my opinion	on the contrary
consequently	in the first place	on the other hand
for example	in the meantime	therefore
furthermore	moreover	under the circumstances

> As a matter of fact, I wrote to you just yesterday. (Phrase used at the beginning of a sentence.)

> We will, in the meantime, send you a replacement order. (Phrase used in the middle of a sentence.)

> Your satisfaction is our first concern, needless to say. (Phrase used at the end of a sentence.)

Do not use commas if the expression is necessary for the completeness of the sentence:

> Tamara had no doubt that she would finish the report. (Omit commas because the expression is necessary for the completeness of the sentence.)

2.04 Dates, Addresses, and Geographical Items. When dates, addresses, and geographical items contain more than one element, the second and succeeding elements are normally set off by commas.

a. Dates:

> The conference was held February 2 at our home office. (No comma is needed for one element.)

> The conference was held February 2, 2011, at our home office. (Two commas set off the second element.)

> The conference was held Wednesday, February 2, 2011, at our home office. (Commas set off the second and third elements.)

> In February 2011 the conference was held. (This alternate style omitting commas is acceptable if only the month and year are written.)

b. Addresses:

> The letter addressed to Mr. Jim W. Ellman, 600 Novella St., Red Deer, AB T0B 2P3, should be sent today. (Commas are used between all elements except the province and postal code, which in this special instance are considered a single unit.)

c. Geographical items:

> She moved from Windsor, Ontario, to Truro, Nova Scotia. (Commas set off the province—unless it appears at the end of the sentence, in which case only one comma is used.)

In separating cities from provinces or territories and days from years, many writers remember the initial comma but forget the final one, as in the examples that follow:

> The package from Edmonton, Alberta{,} was lost.

> We opened June 1, 1995{,} and have grown steadily since.

Review Exercise G—Commas 1

Insert necessary commas in the following sentences. In the space provided, write the number of commas that you add. Write C if no commas are needed. When you finish, compare your responses with those provided. For each item on which you need review, consult the numbered principle shown in parentheses.

_____ 1. As a rule we do not provide complimentary tickets.

_____ 2. You may be certain Mr. Kirchoff that your policy will be issued immediately.

_____ 3. I have no doubt that your calculations are correct.

_____ 4. The safety hazard on the contrary can be greatly reduced if workers wear rubber gloves.

_____ 5. Every accredited TV newscaster radio broadcaster and newspaper reporter had access to the media room.

_____ 6. Deltech's main offices are located in Vancouver British Columbia and Regina Saskatchewan.

_____ 7. The employees who are eligible for promotions are Terry Evelyn Maneesh Rosanna and Yves.

_____ 8. During the warranty period of course you are protected from any parts or service charges.

_____ 9. Many of our customers include architects engineers lawyers and others who are interested in database management programs.

_____ 10. I wonder Ms. Stevens if you would send my letter of recommendation as soon as possible.

_____ 11. The new book explains how to choose appropriate legal protection for ideas trade secrets copyrights patents and restrictive covenants.

_____ 12. The factory is scheduled to be moved to 2250 North Main Street Belleville Ontario L4A 1T2 within two years.

_____ 13. You may however prefer to correspond directly with the manufacturer in Hong Kong.

_____ 14. Are there any alternatives in addition to those that we have already considered?

_____ 15. The rally has been scheduled for Monday January 12 in the football stadium.

_____ 16. A cheque for the full amount will be sent directly to your home Mr. Ivanic.

_____ 17. Goodstone Tire & Rubber for example recalled 400,000 steel-belted radial tires because some tires failed their rigorous tests.

_____ 18. Alex agreed to unlock the office open the mail and check all the equipment in my absence.

_____ 19. In the meantime thank you for whatever assistance you are able to furnish.

_____ 20. Research facilities were moved from Montreal Quebec to Fredericton New Brunswick.

---

1. rule, (2.03)   3. C (2.03)   5. newscaster, radio broadcaster, (2.01)   7. Terry, Evelyn, Vicki, Rosanna, (2.01)   9. architects, engineers, lawyers, (2.01)   11. ideas, trade secrets, copyrights, patents, (2.01)   13. may, however, (2.03)   15. Monday, January 12, (2.04a)   17. Rubber, for example, (2.03)   19. meantime, (2.03)

Grammar/Mechanics Checkup—6

Commas 1

Review Sections 2.01–2.04 above. Then study each of the following statements and insert necessary commas. In the space provided, write the number of commas that you add; write 0 if no commas are needed. Also record the number of the Handbook principle illustrated. When you finish, compare your responses with those on page 508. If your answers differ, carefully study again the principles shown in parentheses.

2 (2.01) Example: In this class students learn to write clear and concise business letters, memos, and reports.

_____ 1. We do not as a rule allow employees to take time off for dental appointments.

_____ 2. You may be sure Ms. Schwartz that your car will be ready by 4 p.m.

_____ 3. Anyone who is reliable conscientious and honest should be very successful.

_____ 4. A conference on sales motivation is scheduled for May 5 at the Plainsview Hotel beginning at 2 p.m.

_____ 5. As a matter of fact I just called your office this morning.

_____ 6. We are relocating our distribution centre from Calgary Alberta to La Salle Quebec.

_____ 7. In the meantime please continue to send your orders to the regional office.

_____ 8. The last meeting recorded in the minutes was on February 4 2011 in Windsor.

_____ 9. Ms. Horne Mr. Hae Mrs. Andorra and Mr. Baker are our new representatives.

_____ 10. The package mailed to Ms. Leslie Holmes 3430 Larkspur Lane Regina Saskatchewan S5L 2E2 arrived three weeks after it was mailed.

_____ 11. The manager feels needless to say that the support of all employees is critical.

_____ 12. Eric was assigned three jobs: checking supplies replacing inventories and distributing delivered goods.

_____ 13. We will work diligently to retain your business Mr. Fuhai.

_____ 14. The vice president feels however that all sales representatives need training.

_____ 15. The name selected for a product should be right for that product and should emphasize its major attributes.

Commas 2 (2.05–2.09)

2.05 Independent Clauses. An independent clause is a group of words that has a subject and a verb and that could stand as a complete sentence. When two such clauses are joined by *and*, *or*, *nor*, or *but*, use a comma before the conjunction:

> We can ship your merchandise July 12, but we must have your payment first.

> Net income before taxes is calculated, and this total is then combined with income from operations.

Notice that each independent clause in the preceding two examples could stand alone as a complete sentence. Do not use a comma unless each group of words is a complete thought (that is, has its own subject and verb).

> Net income before taxes is calculated and is then combined with income from operations. (No comma is needed because no subject follows *and*.)

2.06 Dependent Clauses. Dependent clauses do not make sense by themselves; for their meaning they depend on independent clauses.

a. *Introductory clauses.* When a dependent clause precedes an independent clause, it is followed by a comma. Such clauses are often introduced by *when*, *if*, and *as*:

> When your request came, we responded immediately.

> As I mentioned earlier, Sandra James is the manager.

b. *Terminal clauses.* If a dependent clause falls at the end of a sentence, use a comma only if the dependent clause is an afterthought:

> The meeting has been rescheduled for October 23, if this date meets with your approval. (Comma used because dependent clause is an afterthought.)

> We responded immediately when we received your request. (No comma is needed.)

c. *Essential versus nonessential clauses.* If a dependent clause provides information that is unneeded for the grammatical completeness of a sentence, use commas to set it off. In determining whether such a clause is essential or nonessential, ask yourself whether the reader needs the information contained in the clause to identify the word it explains:

> Our district sales manager, who just returned from a trip to our Prairie region office, prepared this report. (This construction assumes that there is only one district sales manager. Since the sales manager is clearly identified, the dependent clause is not essential and requires commas.)

> The salesperson who just returned from a trip to our Prairie region office prepared this report. (The dependent clause in this sentence is necessary to identify which salesperson prepared the report. Therefore, use no commas.)

> The position of assistant sales manager, which we discussed with you last week, is still open. (Careful writers use *which* to introduce nonessential clauses. Commas are also necessary.)

> The position that we discussed with you last week is still open. (Careful writers use *that* to introduce essential clauses. No commas are used.)

2.07 Phrases. A phrase is a group of related words that lacks both a subject and a verb. A phrase that precedes a main clause is followed by a comma only if the phrase contains a verb form or has four or more words:

> Beginning November 1, Mutual Trust will offer two new combination chequing/savings plans. (A comma follows this introductory phrase because the phrase contains the verb form *Beginning*.)

> To promote their plan, we will conduct an extensive direct mail advertising campaign. (A comma follows this introductory phrase because the phrase contains the verb form *To promote*.)

> In a period of only one year, we were able to improve our market share by 30 percent. (A comma follows the introductory phrase—actually two prepositional phrases—because its total length exceeds four words.)

> In 1999 our organization installed a multi-user system that could transfer programs easily. (No comma needed after the short introductory phrase.)

2.08 Two or More Adjectives. Use a comma to separate two or more adjectives that equally describe a noun. A good way to test the need for a comma is this: mentally insert the word *and* between the adjectives. If the resulting phrase sounds natural, a comma is used to show the omission of *and*:

> We're looking for a versatile, bug-free operating system. (Use a comma to separate *versatile* and *bug-free* because they independently describe *operating system. And* has been omitted.)

> Our experienced, courteous staff is ready to serve you. (Use a comma to separate *experienced* and *courteous* because they independently describe *staff. And* has been omitted.)

> It was difficult to refuse the sincere young telephone caller. (No commas are needed between *sincere* and *young* because *and* has not been omitted.)

2.09 Appositives. Words that re-name or explain preceding nouns or pronouns are called appositives. An appositive that provides information not essential to the identification of the word it describes should be set off by commas:

> Rozmin Kamani, the project director for Sperling's, worked with our architect. (The appositive, *the project director for Sperling's*, adds nonessential information. Commas set it off.)

Review Exercise H—Commas 2

Insert only necessary commas in the following sentences. In the space provided, indicate the number of commas that you add for each sentence. If a sentence requires no commas, write C. When you finish, compare your responses with those provided. For each item on which you need review, consult the numbered principle shown in parentheses.

_____ 1. A corporation must be registered in the province in which it does business and it must operate within the laws of that province.

_____ 2. The manager made a point-by-point explanation of the distribution dilemma and then presented his plan to solve the problem.

_____ 3. If you will study the cost analysis you will see that our company offers the best system at the lowest price.

_____ 4. Molly Epperson who amassed the greatest number of sales points was awarded the bonus trip to Hawaii.

_____ 5. The salesperson who amasses the greatest number of sales points will be awarded the bonus trip to Hawaii.

_____ 6. To promote goodwill and to generate international trade we are opening offices in the Far East and in Europe.

_____ 7. On the basis of these findings I recommend that we retain Raine Jada as our counsel.

_____ 8. Mary Lam is a dedicated hard-working employee for our company.

_____ 9. The bright young student who worked for us last summer will be able to return this summer.

_____ 10. When you return the completed form we will be able to process your application.

_____ 11. We will be able to process your application when you return the completed form.

_____ 12. The employees who have been with us over ten years automatically receive additional insurance benefits.

_____ 13. Knowing that you wanted this merchandise immediately I took the liberty of sending it by Express Parcel Services.

_____ 14. The central processing unit requires no scheduled maintenance and has a self-test function for reliable performance.

_____ 15. International competition nearly ruined the Canadian shoe industry but the textile industry remains strong.

_____ 16. Joyce D'Agostino our newly promoted office manager has made a number of worthwhile suggestions.

_____ 17. For the benefit of employees recently hired we are offering a two-hour seminar regarding employee benefit programs.

_____ 18. Please bring your suggestions and those of Mr. Maisonneuve when you attend our meeting next month.

_____ 19. The meeting has been rescheduled for September 30 if this date meets with your approval.

_____ 20. Some of the problems that you outline in your recent memo could be rectified through more stringent purchasing procedures.

---

1. business, (2.05)   3. analysis, (2.06a)   5. C (2.06c)   7. findings, (2.07)   9. C (2.08)
11. C (2.06b)   13. immediately, (2.07)   15. industry, (2.05)   17. hired, (2.07)
19. September 30, (2.06b)

Grammar/Mechanics Checkup—7

Commas 2

Review Sections 2.05–2.09 above. Then study each of the following statements and insert necessary commas. In the space provided, write the number of commas that you add; write *0* if no commas are needed. Also record the number of the Handbook principle(s) illustrated. When you finish, compare your responses with those provided on page 508. If your answers differ, carefully study again the principles shown in parentheses.

1 (2.06a) Example: When businesses encounter financial problems‸they often reduce their administrative staffs.

_____ 1. As stated in the warranty this printer is guaranteed for one year.

_____ 2. Today's profits come from products currently on the market and tomorrow's profits come from products currently on the drawing boards.

_____ 3. Companies introduce new products in one part of the country and then watch how the product sells in that area.

_____ 4. One large automobile manufacturer which must remain nameless recognizes that buyer perception is behind the success of any new product.

_____ 5. The imaginative promising agency opened its offices April 22 in Cambridge.

_____ 6. The sales associate who earns the highest number of recognition points this year will be honoured with a bonus vacation trip.

_____ 7. Ian Sims our sales manager in the North Bay area will present the new sales campaign at the June meeting.

_____ 8. Our new product has many attributes that should make it appealing to buyers but it also has one significant drawback.

_____ 9. Although they have different technical characteristics and vary considerably in price and quality two or more of a firm's products may be perceived by shoppers as almost the same.

_____ 10. To motivate prospective buyers we are offering a cash rebate of $25.

_____ 11. When you receive the application please fill it out and return it before Monday January 3.

_____ 12. On the other hand we are very interested in hiring hard-working conscientious individuals.

_____ 13. In March we expect to open a new branch in Bragg Creek which is an area of considerable growth.

_____ 14. As we discussed on the telephone the ceremony is scheduled for Thursday June 9 at 3 p.m.

_____ 15. Dr. Adams teaches the morning classes and Ms. Miori is responsible for evening sections.

Commas 3 (2.10–2.15)

2.10 Degrees and Abbreviations. Degrees following individuals' names are set off by commas. Abbreviations such as *Jr.* and *Sr.* are also set off by commas unless the individual referred to prefers to omit the commas:

> Anne G. Turner, M.B.A., joined the firm.

> Michael Migliano, Jr., and Michael Migliano, Sr., work as a team.

> Anthony A. Gensler Jr. wrote the report. (The individual referred to prefers to omit commas.)

The abbreviations *Inc.* and *Ltd.* are set off by commas only if a company's legal name has a comma just before this kind of abbreviation. To determine a company's practice, consult its stationery or a directory listing:

> Firestone and Blythe, Inc., is based in Canada. (Notice that two commas are used.)

> Computers Inc. is extending its franchise system. (The company's legal name does not include a comma before Inc.)

2.11 Omitted Words. A comma is used to show the omission of words that are understood:

> On Monday we received 15 applications; on Friday, only 3. (Comma shows the omission of *we received*.)

2.12 Contrasting Statements. Commas are used to set off contrasting or opposing expressions. These expressions are often introduced by such words as *not*, *never*, *but*, and *yet*:

> The consultant recommended an FTP site, not an external memory drive, for our operations.

> Our budget for the year is reduced, yet adequate.

> The greater the effort, the greater the reward.

If increased emphasis is desired, use dashes instead of commas, as in *Only the sum of $100—not $1,000—was paid on this account.*

2.13 Clarity. Commas are used to separate words repeated for emphasis. Commas are also used to separate words that may be misread if not separated:

> The building is a long, long way from completion.

> Whatever is, is right.

> No matter what, you know we support you.

2.14 Quotations and Appended Questions

a. A comma is used to separate a short quotation from the rest of a sentence. If the quotation is divided into two parts, two commas are used:

> The manager asked, "Shouldn't the managers control the specialists?"

> "Not if the specialists," replied Xiang, "have unique information."

b. A comma is used to separate a question appended (added) to a statement:

> You will confirm the shipment, won't you?

2.15 Comma Overuse.

Do not use commas needlessly. For example, commas should not be inserted merely because you might drop your voice if you were speaking the sentence:

> One of the reasons for expanding our operations in the Atlantic region is{,} that we anticipate increased sales in that area. (Do not insert a needless comma before a clause.)

> I am looking for an article entitled{,} "State-of-the-Art Communications." (Do not insert a needless comma after the word *entitled*.)

> A number of food and nonfood items are carried in convenience stores such as{,} 7-Eleven and Stop-N-Go. (Do not insert a needless comma after *such as*.)

> We have{,} at this time{,} an adequate supply of parts. (Do not insert needless commas around prepositional phrases.)

Review Exercise I—Commas 3

Insert only necessary commas in the following sentences. Remove unnecessary commas with the delete sign (✐). In the space provided, indicate the number of commas inserted or deleted in each sentence. If a sentence requires no changes, write C. When you finish, compare your responses with those provided. For each item on which you need review, consult the numbered principle shown in parentheses.

_____ 1. We expected Charles Bedford not Krystina Rudko to conduct the audit.

_____ 2. Brian said "We simply must have a bigger budget to start this project."

_____ 3. "We simply must have" said Brian "a bigger budget to start this project."

_____ 4. In August customers opened at least 50 new accounts; in September, only about 20.

_____ 5. You returned the merchandise last month didn't you?

_____ 6. In short employees will now be expected to contribute more to their own retirement funds.

_____ 7. The better our advertising and recruiting the stronger our personnel pool will be.

_____ 8. Mrs. Delgado investigated selling her shares not her real estate to raise the necessary cash.

_____ 9. "On the contrary" said Ms. Mercer "we will continue our present marketing strategies."

_____ 10. Our company will expand into surprising new areas such as, women's apparel and fast foods.

_____ 11. What we need is more not fewer suggestions for improvement.

_____ 12. Randall Clark B. Comm. and Jonathon Georges M.B.A. joined the firm.

_____ 13. "Canada is now entering" said CEO Saunders "the Knowledge Age."

_____ 14. One of the reasons that we are inquiring about the publisher of the software is, that we are concerned about whether that publisher will be in the market five years from now.

_____ 15. The talk by D. A. Spindler Ph.D. was particularly difficult to follow because of his technical and abstract vocabulary.

_____ 16. The month before a similar disruption occurred in distribution.

_____ 17. We are very fortunate to have, at our disposal, the services of excellent professionals.

_____ 18. No matter what you can count on us for support.

_____ 19. Mary Sandoval was named legislative counsel; Jacy Freeman executive adviser.

_____ 20. The data you are seeking can be found in an article entitled, "The Fastest Growing Game in Computers."

1. Bedford, Rudko, (2.12)   3. have," said Brian, (2.14a)   5. month, (2.14b)   7. recruiting, (2.12)
9. contrary," Mercer, (2.14a)   11. more, not fewer, (2.12)   13. entering," Saunders, (2.14a)
15. Spindler, Ph.D., (2.10)   17. have at our disposal (2.15)   19. Freeman, (2.11)

Grammar/Mechanics Checkup—8

Commas 3

Review Sections 2.10–2.15 above. Then study each of the following statements and insert necessary commas. In the space provided, write the number of commas that you add; write *0* if no commas are needed. Also record the number of the Handbook principle(s) illustrated. When you finish, compare your responses with those provided on page 508. If your answers differ, carefully study again the principles shown in parentheses.

2(2.12) Example: It was Lucia Bosano‸not Melinda Ho‸who was given the Kirkland account.

_____ 1. "The choice of a good name" said President Etienne "cannot be overestimated."

_____ 2. Hanna H. Cox Ph.D. and Katherine Meridian M.B.A. were hired as consultants.

_____ 3. Their August 15 order was shipped on Monday wasn't it?

_____ 4. The Web is most useful in providing customer service such as online catalogue information and verification of shipping dates.

_____ 5. The bigger the investment the greater the profit.

Review Commas 1, 2, 3

_____ 6. As you requested your order for cartridges file folders and copy paper will be sent immediately.

_____ 7. We think however that you should reexamine your Web site and that you should consider redesigning its navigation system.

_____ 8. Within the next eight-week period we hope to hire Mina Vidal who is currently CEO of a small consulting firm.

_____ 9. Our convention will attract more participants if it is held in a resort location such as Collingwood the Laurentians or Banff.

_____ 10. If everyone who applied for the position were interviewed we would be overwhelmed.

_____ 11. In the past ten years we have employed over 30 well-qualified individuals many of whom have selected banking as their career.

_____ 12. Kimberly Johansson who spoke to our class last week is the author of a book entitled *Writing Winning Résumés.*

_____ 13. A recent study of productivity that was conducted by authoritative researchers revealed that Canadian workers are more productive than workers in Europe or Japan.

_____ 14. The report concluded that Canada's secret productivity weapon was not bigger companies more robots or even brainier managers.

_____ 15. As a matter of fact the report said that Canada's productivity resulted from the rigours of unprotected hands-off competition.

Cumulative Editing Quiz 4

Use proofreading marks (see Appendix B) to correct errors and omissions in the following sentences. All errors must be corrected to receive credit for the sentence. Check with your instructor for the answers.

1. Business documents must be written clear, to ensure that readers comprehend the message quick.

2. Needless to say the safety of our employees have always been most important to the president and I.

3. Agriculture and Agri-Food Canada which provide disaster loans are setting up an office in Brandon Manitoba.

4. Many entrepreneurs who want to expand there markets, have choosen to advertise heavy.

5. Our arbitration committee have unanimously agreed on a compromise package but management have been slow to respond.

6. Although the business was founded in the 1970's its real expansion took place in the 1990s.

7. According to the contract either the dealer or the distributor are responsible for repair of the product.

8. Next June, Lamont and Jones, Inc., are moving their headquarters to Calgary Alberta.

9. Our company is looking for intelligent, articulate, young, people who has a desire to grow with an expanding organization.

10. As you are aware each member of the jury were asked to avoid talking about the case.

Semicolons (2.16)

2.16 Independent Clauses, Series, and Introductory Expressions

Notice that the word following a semicolon is not capitalized (unless, of course, that word is a proper noun).

a. *Independent clauses with conjunctive adverbs.* Use a semicolon before a conjunctive adverb that separates two independent clauses. Some of the most common conjunctive adverbs are *therefore, consequently, however,* and *moreover*:

> Business letters should sound conversational; therefore, familiar words and contractions are often used.

> The bank closes its doors at 3 p.m.; however, the ABM is open 24 hours a day.

b. *Independent clauses without conjunctive adverbs.* Use a semicolon to separate closely related independent clauses when no conjunctive adverb is used:

> Some interest payments are tax deductible; dividend payments are not.

> Ambient lighting fills the room; task lighting illuminates each workstation.

Use a semicolon in compound sentences, not in complex sentences:

> After one week the paper feeder jammed; we tried different kinds of paper. (Use a semicolon in a compound sentence.)

> After one week the paper feeder jammed, although we tried different kinds of paper. (Use a comma in a complex sentence. Do not use a semicolon after *jammed*.)

The semicolon is very effective for joining two closely related thoughts. Don't use it, however, unless the ideas are truly related.

c. *Independent clauses with other commas.* Normally, a comma precedes *and*, *or*, and *but* when those conjunctions join independent clauses. However, if either clause contains commas, change the comma preceding the conjunction to a semicolon to ensure correct reading:

> If you arrive in time, you may be able to purchase a ticket; but ticket sales close promptly at 8 p.m.

> Our primary concern is financing; and we have discovered, as you warned us, that money sources are quite scarce.

d. *Series with internal commas.* Use semicolons to separate items in a series when one or more of the items contains internal commas:

> Delegates from Brandon, Manitoba; Lethbridge, Alberta; and North Bay, Ontario, attended the conference.

> The speakers were Katrina Lang, manager, Riko Enterprises; Henry Holtz, vice president, Trendex, Inc.; and Margaret Slater, personnel director, West Coast Productions.

e. *Introductory expressions.* Use a semicolon when an introductory expression such as *namely*, *for instance*, *that is*, or *for example* introduces a list following an independent clause:

> Switching to computerized billing are several local companies; namely, Ryson Electronics, Miller Vending Services, and Blaque Advertising.

> The author of a report should consider many sources; for example, books, periodicals, databases, and newspapers.

Colons (2.17–2.19)

2.17 Listed Items

a. *With colon.* Use a colon after a complete thought that introduces a formal list of items. A formal list is often preceded by such words and phrases as *these*, *thus*, *the following*, and *as follows*. A colon is also used when words and phrases like these are implied but not stated:

> Additional costs in selling a house involve the following: title examination fee, title insurance costs, and closing fee. (Use a colon when a complete thought introduces a formal list.)

> Collective bargaining focuses on several key issues: cost-of-living adjustments, fringe benefits, job security, and hours of work. (The introduction of the list is implied in the preceding clause.)

b. *Without colons.* Do not use a colon when the list immediately follows a *to be* verb or a preposition:

> The employees who should receive the preliminary plan are James Sachi, Ramona Speers, and Rose Paquet. (No colon is used after the verb *are*.)

> We expect to consider equipment for Accounting, Legal Services, and Payroll. (No colon is used after the preposition *for*.)

2.18 Quotations. Use a colon to introduce long one-sentence quotations and quotations of two or more sentences:

> Our consultant said: "This system can support up to 32 users. It can be used for decision support, computer-aided design, and software development operations at the same time."

2.19 Salutations. Use a colon after the salutation of a business letter:

> Gentlemen:

> Dear Ms. Tsang:

> Dear Odin:

Review Exercise J—Semicolons, Colons

In the following sentences, add semicolons, colons, and necessary commas. For each sentence indicate the number of punctuation marks that you add. If a sentence requires no punctuation, write C. When you finish, compare your responses with those provided. For each item on which you need review, consult the numbered principle shown in parentheses.

_____ 1. A strike in Montreal has delayed shipments of parts consequently our production has fallen behind schedule.

_____ 2. Our branch in Burnaby specializes in industrial real estate our branch in Island Lakes concentrates on residential real estate.

_____ 3. The sedan version of the automobile is available in these colours Olympic red metallic silver and Aztec gold.

_____ 4. If I can assist the new manager please call me however I will be gone from June 10 through June 15.

_____ 5. The individuals who should receive copies of this announcement are Jeff Doogan Alicia Green and Kim Wong.

_____ 6. We would hope of course to send personal letters to all prospective buyers but we have not yet decided just how to do this.

_____ 7. Many of our potential customers are in southern British Columbia therefore our promotional effort will be strongest in that area.

_____ 8. Since the first of the year we have received inquiries from one lawyer two accountants and one information systems analyst.

_____ 9. Three dates have been reserved for initial interviews January 15 February 1 and February 12.

_____ 10. Several staff members are near the top of their salary ranges and we must re-classify their jobs.

_____ 11. Several staff members are near the top of their salary ranges we must re-classify their jobs.

_____ 12. Several staff members are near the top of their salary ranges therefore we must re-classify their jobs.

_____ 13. If you open an account within two weeks you will receive a free cookbook moreover your first 500 cheques will be printed at no cost to you.

_____ 14. Monthly reports from the following departments are missing Legal Department Human Resources Department and Engineering Department.

_____ 15. Monthly reports are missing from the Legal Department Human Resources Department and Engineering Department.

_____ 16. Since you became director of that division sales have tripled therefore I am recommending you for a bonus.

_____ 17. The convention committee is considering Dartmouth Nova Scotia Moncton New Brunswick and Charlottetown Prince Edward Island.

_____ 18. Several large companies allow employees access to their personnel files namely Nortel Corel Corp. and Ford Canada.

_____ 19. Sylvie first asked about salary next she inquired about benefits.

_____ 20. Sylvie first asked about the salary and she next inquired about benefits.

---

1. parts; consequently, (2.16a)   3. colours: Olympic red, metallic silver, (2.01, 2.17a) 5. Doogan, Alicia Green, (2.01, 2.17b)   7. British Columbia; therefore, (2.16a)   9. interviews: January 15, February 1, (2.01, 2.17a)   11. ranges; (2.16b)   13. weeks, cookbook; moreover, (2.06a, 2.16a)   15. Department, Human Resources Department, (2.01, 2.17b)   17. Dartmouth, Nova Scotia; Moncton, New Brunswick; Charlottetown, (2.16d)   19. salary; (2.16b)

Grammar/Mechanics Checkup—9

Semicolons and Colons

Review Sections 2.16–2.19 above. Then study each of the following statements. Insert any necessary punctuation. Use the delete symbol to omit unnecessary punctuation. In the space provided, indicate the number of changes you made and record the number of the Handbook principle(s) illustrated. (When you replace one punctuation mark with another, count it as one change.) If you make no changes, write *0*. This exercise concentrates on semicolon and colon use, but you will also be responsible for correct comma use. When you finish, compare your responses with those shown on page 508. If your responses differ, carefully study again the specific principles shown in parentheses.

<u>2(2.16a)</u> **Example:** The job of Mr. Wellworth is to make sure that his company has enough cash to meet its obligations moreover he is responsible for locating credit when needed.

_____ 1. Short-term financing refers to a period of under one year long-term financing on the other hand refers to a period of ten years or more.

_____ 2. Cash resulting from product sales does not arrive until December therefore our cash flow becomes critical in October and November.

_____ 3. We must negotiate short-term financing during the following months September October and November.

_____ 4. Large corporations that offer huge amounts of trade credit are, automobile dealers, utility companys, oil companys, and computer hardware manufacturers.

_____ 5. Although some firms rarely, if ever, need to borrow short-term money many businesses find that they require significant credit to pay for current production and sales costs.

_____ 6. A grocery store probably requires no short-term credit, a greeting card manufacturer however typically would need considerable short-term credit.

_____ 7. We offer three basic types of credit loans promissory notes and floating lines of credit.

_____ 8. Speakers at the conference on credit include the following business-people Mary Ann Mahan financial manager Ritchie Industries Terry L. Buchanan comptroller International Bank and Edmée Cavalier operations Business Bank of Canada.

_____ 9. The prime interest rate is set by the Bank of Canada and this rate goes up or down as the cost of money to the bank itself fluctuates.

_____ 10. Most banks are in business to lend money to commercial customers for example retailers service companies manufacturers and construction firms.

_____ 11. Avionics, Inc. which is a small electronics firm with a solid credit rating recently applied for a loan but the Federal Business Development Bank refused the loan application because the risk was too great.

_____ 12. When Avionics, Inc., was refused by Federal Business Development Bank its financial managers submitted applications to the following Worldwide Investments, Dominion Securities, and Mid Mountain Group.

_____ 13. The cost of financing capital investments at the present time is very high therefore Avionics' managers may elect to postpone certain expansion projects.

_____ 14. If interest rates reach as high as 18 percent the cost of borrowing becomes prohibitive and many businesses are forced to reconsider or abandon projects that require financing.

_____ 15. Several investors decided to pool their resources then they could find attractive investments.

Apostrophes (2.20–2.22)

2.20 Basic Rule. The apostrophe is used to show ownership, origin, authorship, or measurement.

Ownership:	We are looking for Dmitri's keys.
Origin:	At the president's suggestion, we doubled the order.
Authorship:	The accountant's annual report was questioned.
Measurement:	In two years' time we expect to reach our goal.

a. *Ownership words not ending in* s. To place the apostrophe correctly, you must first determine whether the ownership word ends in an s sound. If it does not, add an apostrophe and an s to the ownership word. The following examples show ownership words that do not end in an s sound:

the employee's file	(the file of a single employee)
a member's address	(the address of a single member)
a year's time	(the time of a single year)
a month's notice	(notice of a single month)
the company's building	(the building of a single company)

b. *Ownership words ending in* s. If the ownership word does end in an s sound, usually add only an apostrophe:

several employees' files	(files of several employees)
ten members' addresses	(addresses of ten members)
five years' time	(time of five years)
several months' notice	(notice of several months)
many companies' buildings	(buildings of many companies)

A few singular nouns that end in *s* are pronounced with an extra syllable when they become possessive. To these words, add *'s*.

my boss's desk   the waitress's table   the actress's costume

Use no apostrophe if a noun is merely plural, not possessive:

> All the sales representatives, as well as the secretaries and managers, had their names and telephone numbers listed in the directory.

2.21 Names. The writer may choose either traditional or popular style in making singular names that end in an *s* sound possessive. The traditional style uses the apostrophe plus an *s*, while the popular style uses just the apostrophe. Note that only with singular names ending in an *s* sound does this option exist.

Traditional style	Popular style
Russ's computer	Russ' computer
Mr. Jones's car	Mr. Jones' car
Mrs. Morris's desk	Mrs. Morris' desk
Ms. Horowitz's job	Ms. Horowitz' job

The possessive form of plural names is consistent: the *Joneses'* car, the *Horowitzes'* home, the *Morrises'* daughter.

2.22 Gerunds. Use *'s* to make a noun possessive when it precedes a gerund, a verb form used as a noun:

> Mr. Smith's smoking prompted a new office policy. (*Mr. Smith* is possessive because it modifies the gerund *smoking*.)

> It was Britta's careful proofreading that revealed the discrepancy.

Review Exercise K—Apostrophes

Insert necessary apostrophes in the following sentences. In the space provided for each sentence, indicate the number of apostrophes that you added. If none were added, write C. When you finish, compare your responses with those provided. For each item on which you need review, consult the numbered principle shown in parentheses.

_____ 1. Your account should have been credited with six months interest.

_____ 2. If you go to the third floor, you will find Mr. Londons office.

_____ 3. All the employees personnel folders must be updated.

_____ 4. In a little over a year's time, that firm was able to double its sales.

_____ 5. The Harrises daughter lived in Whitehorse for two years.

_____ 6. An inventors patent protects his or her patent for several years.

_____ 7. Both companies headquarters will be moved within the next six months.

_____ 8. That position requires at least two years experience.

_____ 9. Some of their assets could be liquidated; therefore, a few of the creditors were satisfied.

_____ 10. All secretaries workstations were equipped with terminals.

_____ 11. The package of electronics parts arrived safely despite two weeks delay.

_____ 12. Many nurses believe that nurses notes are not admissible evidence.

_____ 13. According to Mr. Cortez latest proposal, all employees would receive an additional holiday.

_____ 14. Many of our members names and addresses must be checked.

_____ 15. His supervisor frequently had to correct Jacks financial reports.

_____ 16. We believe that this firms service is much better than that firms.

_____ 17. Mr. Schur estimated that he spent a years profits in reorganizing his staff.

_____ 18. After paying six months rent, we were given a receipt.

_____ 19. The contract is not valid without Ms. Harris signature.

_____ 20. It was Mr. Smiths signing of the contract that made us happy.

1. months' (2.20b)   3. employees' (2.20b)   5. Harrises' (2.21)   7. companies' (2.20b)
9. C (2.20b)   11. weeks' (2.20b)   13. Cortez' [or Cortez's] (2.21)   15. Jack's (2.21)
17. year's (2.20a)   19. Harris' [or Harris's] (2.21)

Grammar/Mechanics Checkup—10

Possessives

Review Sections 2.20–2.22 above. Then study each of the following statements. Underline any inappropriate form. Write a correction in the space provided, and record the number of the Handbook principle(s) illustrated. If a sentence is correct, write C. When you finish, compare your responses with those on page 508. If your answers differ, carefully study again the principles shown in parentheses.

__years' (2.20b)__ **Example:** In just two <u>years</u> time, the accountants and managers devised an entirely new system.

_____ 1. Two supervisors said that Mr. Ruskins work was excellent.

_____ 2. In less than a years time, the offices of both lawyers were moved.

_____ 3. None of the employees in our Electronics Department had taken more than two weeks vacation.

_____ 4. All the secretaries agreed that Ms. Lanhams suggestions were practical.

_____ 5. After you obtain your boss approval, send the application to Human Resources.

_____ 6. We tried to sit in our favourite server section, but all her tables were filled.

_____ 7. Despite Kaspar grumbling, his wife selected two bonds and three stocks for her investments.

_____ 8. The apartment owner requires two months rent in advance from all applicants.

_____ 9. Four companies buildings were damaged in the fire.

_____ 10. In one months time we hope to be able to complete all the address files.

_____ 11. One secretaries desk will have to be moved to make way for the computer.

_____ 12. Several sellers permits were issued for two years.

_____ 13. Marks salary was somewhat higher than David.

_____ 14. Latikas job in accounts receivable ends in two months.

Cumulative Editing Quiz 5

Use proofreading marks (see Appendix B) to correct errors and omissions in the following sentences. All errors must be corrected to receive credit for the sentence. Check with your instructor for the answers.

1. The three C's of credit are the following character capacity and capital.

2. We hope that we will not have to sell the property however that may be our only option.

3. As soon as the supervisor and her can check this weeks sales they will place an order.

4. Any of the auditors are authorized to proceed with an independent action however only the CEO can alter the councils directives.

5. Although reluctant technicians sometimes must demonstrate there computer software skills.

6. On April 6 1998 we opened an innovative fully-equipped employee computer centre.

7. A list of maintenance procedures and recommendations are in the owners manual.

8. The Morrises son lived in London Ontario however there daughter lived in Saint John New Brunswick.

9. Employment interviews were held in Winnipeg Manitoba Calgary Alberta and Victoria British Columbia.

10. Mr. Lees determination courage and sincerity could not be denied however his methods was often questioned.

Other Punctuation (2.23–2.29)

2.23 Periods

a. *Ends of sentences.* Use a period at the end of a statement, command, indirect question, or polite request. Although a polite request may have the same structure as a question, it ends with a period:

> Corporate legal departments demand precise skills from their workforce. (End a statement with a period.)

> Get the latest data by reading current periodicals. (End a command with a period.)

> Mr. Rand wondered whether we had sent any follow-up literature. (End an indirect question with a period.)

> Would you please reexamine my account and determine the current balance. (A polite request suggests an action rather than a verbal response.)

b. *Abbreviations and initials.* Use periods after initials and after many abbreviations.

R. M. Johnson	c.o.d.	Ms.
M.D.	a.m.	Mr.
Inc.	i.e.	Mrs.

Use just one period when an abbreviation falls at the end of a sentence:

> Guests began arriving at 5:30 p.m.

2.24 Question Marks. Direct questions are followed by question marks:

> Did you send your proposal to Datatronix, Inc.?

Statements with questions added are punctuated with question marks:

> We have completed the proposal, haven't we?

2.25 Exclamation Points. Use an exclamation point after a word, phrase, or clause expressing strong emotion. In business writing, however, exclamation points should be used sparingly:

> Incredible! The entire network is down.

2.26 Dashes. The dash (constructed at a keyboard by striking the hyphen key twice in succession) is a legitimate and effective mark of punctuation when used according to accepted conventions. As an emphatic punctuation mark, however, the dash loses effectiveness when overused.

a. *Parenthetical elements.* Within a sentence a parenthetical element is usually set off by commas. If, however, the parenthetical element itself contains internal commas, use dashes (or parentheses) to set it off:

> Three top salespeople—Tom Judkins, Morgan Templeton, and Mary Yashimoto—received bonuses.

b. *Sentence interruptions.* Use a dash to show an interruption or abrupt change of thought:

> News of the dramatic merger—no one believed it at first—shook the financial world.

> Ship the materials Monday—no, we must have them sooner.

Sentences with abrupt changes of thought or with appended afterthoughts can usually be improved through rewriting.

c. *Summarizing statements.* Use a dash (not a colon) to separate an introductory list from a summarizing statement:

> Sorting, merging, and computing—these are tasks that our data processing programs must perform.

2.27 Parentheses. One means of setting off nonessential sentence elements involves the use of parentheses. Nonessential sentence elements may be punctuated in one of three ways: (1) with commas, to make the lightest possible break in the normal flow of a sentence; (2) with dashes, to emphasize the enclosed material; and (3) with parentheses, to de-emphasize the enclosed material. Parentheses are frequently used to punctuate sentences with interpolated directions, explanations, questions, and references:

> The cost analysis (which appears on page 8 of the report) indicates that the copy machine should be leased.

> Units are lightweight (approximately 500 g) and come with a leather case and operating instructions.

> The new IBM laser printer (have you heard about it?) will be demonstrated for us next week.

A parenthetical sentence that is not embedded within another sentence should be capitalized and end-punctuated:

> The Model 20 has stronger construction. (You may order a Model 20 brochure by circling 304 on the reader service card.)

2.28 Quotation Marks

a. *Direct quotations.* Use double quotation marks to enclose the exact words of a speaker or writer:

> "Keep in mind," Mrs. Fontaine said, "that you'll have to justify the cost of automating our office."

> The boss said that automation was inevitable. (No quotation marks are needed because the exact words are not quoted.)

b. ***Quotations within quotations.*** Use single quotation marks (apostrophes on the keyboard) to enclose quoted passages within quoted passages:

> In her speech, Ms. Deckman remarked, "I believe it was the poet Robert Frost who said, 'All the fun's in how you say a thing.'"

c. ***Short expressions.*** Slang, words used in a special sense, and words following *stamped* or *marked* are often enclosed within quotation marks:

> Rafael described the damaged shipment as "gross." (Quotation marks enclose slang.)

> Students often have trouble spelling the word "separate." (Quotation marks enclose words used in a special sense.)

> Jobs were divided into two categories: most stressful and least stressful. The jobs in the "most stressful" list involved high risk or responsibility. (Quotation marks enclose words used in a special sense.)

> The envelope marked "Confidential" was put aside. (Quotation marks enclose words following *marked*.)

In the four preceding sentences, the words enclosed within quotation marks could instead be set in italics, if italics are available.

d. ***Definitions.*** Double quotation marks are used to enclose definitions. The word or expression being defined should be underscored or set in italics:

> The term *penetration pricing* is defined as "the practice of introducing a product to the market at a low price."

e. ***Titles.*** Use double quotation marks to enclose titles of some literary and artistic works, such as magazine and newspaper articles, chapters of books, poems, lectures, and songs. Names of major publications (e.g., books, magazines, pamphlets, and newspapers) and other works such as movies, plays, and television shows are set in italics (or underscored) or typed in capital letters.

> Particularly helpful was the chapter in Smith's EFFECTIVE WRITING TECHNIQUES entitled "Right Brain, Write Well!"

> John's article, "E-Mail Blunders," appeared in *The Toronto Star*; however, we could not locate it in a local library.

f. ***Additional considerations.*** Periods and commas are always placed inside closing quotation marks. Semicolons and colons, on the other hand, are always placed outside quotation marks:

> Mrs. Levesque said, "I could not find the article entitled 'Cell Phone Etiquette.'"

> The president asked for "absolute security": all written messages were to be destroyed.

Question marks and exclamation points may go inside or outside closing quotation marks, as determined by the form of the quotation:

> Sales Manager Motega said, "Who placed the order?" (The quotation is a question.)

> When did the sales manager say, "Who placed the order?" (Both the incorporating sentence and the quotation are questions.)

> Did the sales manager say, "Narwinder placed the order"? (The incorporating sentence asks question; the quotation does not.)

> "In the future," shouted Bob, "ask me first!" (The quotation is an exclamation.)

2.29 Brackets. Within quotations, square brackets are used by the quoting writer to enclose his or her own inserted remarks. Such remarks may be corrective, illustrative, or explanatory:

> June Cardillo said, "CRTC [Canadian Radio-television and Telecommunications Commission] has been one of the most widely criticized agencies of the federal government."

Review Exercise L—Other Punctuation

Insert necessary punctuation in the following sentences. In the space provided for each item, indicate the number of punctuation marks that you added. Count sets of parentheses and dashes as two marks. Emphasis or de-emphasis will be indicated for some parenthetical elements. When you finish, compare your responses with those provided. For each item on which you need review, consult the numbered principle shown in parentheses.

_____ 1. Will you please stop payment on my Cheque No. 233

_____ 2. (Emphasize.) Your order of October 16 will be on its way you have my word by October 20.

_____ 3. Mr Sirakides, Mrs Sylvester, and Miss Sidhu have not yet responded

_____ 4. Wanda Penner asked if the order had been sent cod

_____ 5. Interviews have been scheduled for 3:15 pm, 4 pm, and 4:45 pm

_____ 6. (De-emphasize.) Three knowledgeable individuals the plant manager, the construction engineer, and the construction supervisor all expressed concern about soil settlement.

_____ 7. Fantastic The value of our shares just rose 10 points on the stock market exchange

_____ 8. The word de facto means existing in fact regardless of the legal situation.

_____ 9. (De-emphasize.) Although the appliance now comes in limited colours brown, beige, and ivory, we expect to see new colours available in the next production run.

_____ 10. Was it the manager who said "What can't be altered must be endured

_____ 11. The stock market went ballistic over the news of the takeover.

_____ 12. Because the envelope was marked Personal, we did not open it.

_____ 13. Price, service, and reliability these are our prime considerations in equipment selection.

_____ 14. The letter carrier said Would you believe that this package was marked Fragile

_____ 15. (Emphasize.) Three branch managers Kelly Cardinal, Stan Meyers, and Ivan Sergo will be promoted.

_____ 16. (De-emphasize.) The difference between portable and transportable computers see Figure 4 for weight comparisons may be considerable.

_____ 17. All the folders marked Current Files should be sent to Human Resources.

_____ 18. I am trying to find the edition of Canadian Business that carried an article entitled The Future Without Shock.

_____ 19. Martha Simon MD and Gail Nemire RN were hired by Healthnet, Inc

_____ 20. The computer salesperson said This innovative, state-of-the-art laptop sells for a fraction of the cost of big-name computers.

---

1. 233. (2.23a)   3. Mr. Ms. responded. (2.23a, 2.23b)   5. p.m. p.m. p.m. (2.23b)   7. Fantastic! exchange! (2.25)   9. (brown ivory) (2.27)   11. "ballistic" (2.28c)   13. reliability—(2.26c) 15. managers—Sergo—(2.26a)   17. "Current Files" (2.28c)   19. Simon, M.D., Nemire, R.N., Inc. (2.23b)

Grammar/Mechanics Checkup—11

Other Punctuation

Although this checkup concentrates on Sections 2.23–2.29 above, you may also refer to other punctuation principles. Insert any necessary punctuation. In the space provided, indicate the number of changes you make and record the number of the Handbook principle(s) illustrated. Count each mark separately; for example, a set of parentheses counts as 2. If you make no changes, write *0*. When you finish, compare your responses with those provided on page 508. If your responses differ, carefully study again the specific principles shown in parentheses.

<u>2 (2.27)</u> **Example:** (De-emphasize.) The consumption of cereal products is highest in certain provinces (Manitoba, Saskatchewan, Alberta, and Newfoundland), but this food trend is spreading to other parts of the country.

_____ 1. (Emphasize.) The convention planning committee has invited three managers Yu Wong, Frank Behr, and Yvette Sosa to make presentations.

_____ 2. Would you please Miss Fundy use your computer to recalculate these totals.

_____ 3. (De-emphasize.) A second set of demographic variables see Figure 13 on page 432 includes nationality, religion, and race.

_____ 4. Because the word recommendation is frequently misspelled we are adding it to our company style book.

_____ 5. Recruiting, hiring, and training these are three important functions of a human resources officer.

_____ 6. The office manager said, Who placed an order for two dozen printer cartridges

_____ 7. Have any of the research assistants been able to locate the article entitled How Tax Reform Will Affect You

_____ 8. (Emphasize.) The biggest oil-producing provinces Alberta, Newfoundland, and Ontario are experiencing significant tax cuts.

_____ 9. Have you sent invitations to Mr Kieran E Manning, Miss Kathy Tanguay, and Ms Petra Bonaventura?

_____ 10. Dr. Y. W. Yellin wrote the chapter entitled Trading on the Options Market that appeared in a book called Securities Markets.

_____ 11. James said, "I'll be right over" however he has not appeared yet.

_____ 12. In business the word liability may be defined as any legal obligation requiring payment in the future.

_____ 13. Because the work was scheduled to be completed June 10 we found it necessary to hire temporary workers to work June 8 and 9.

_____ 14. Did any c o d shipments arrive today

_____ 15. Hooray I have finished this checkup haven't I

Grammar/Mechanics Checkup—12

Punctuation Review

Review Sections 1.19 and 2.01–2.29. Study the groups of sentences below. In the space provided write the letter of the one that is correctly punctuated. When you finish, compare your responses with those on page 509. If your responses differ, carefully study again the principles in parentheses.

_____ 1. a. Our accounting team makes a point of analyzing your business operations, and getting to know what's working for you and what's not.

       b. We are dedicated to understanding your business needs over the long term, and taking an active role when it comes to creating solutions.

       c. We understand that you may be downsizing or moving into new markets, and we want to help you make a seamless transition.

_____ 2. a. If you are growing, or connecting to new markets, our team will help you accomplish your goals with minimal interruptions.

       b. When you look at our organization chart, you will find the customer at the top.

       c. Although we offer each customer a dedicated customer account team we also provide professional general services.

_____ 3. a. The competition is changing; therefore, we have to deliver our products and services more efficiently.

       b. Although delivery systems are changing; the essence of banking remains the same.

       c. Banks will continue to be available around the corner, and also with the click of a mouse.

_____ 4. a. One of the reasons we are decreasing the number of our ABMs, is that two thirds of the bank's customers depend on customer care representatives for transactions.

       b. We are looking for an article entitled, "Online Banking."

       c. Banks are at this time competing with non-traditional rivals that can provide extensive financial services.

_____ 5. a. We care deeply about the environment; but we also care about safety and good customer service.

       b. The president worked with environmental concerns; the vice president focused on customer support.

       c. Our Web site increases our productivity, it also improves customer service.

_____ 6. a. Employees who will be receiving salary increases are: Terri, Mark, Rob, and Géza.

       b. The following employees are eligible for bonuses: Robin, Olivia, Bill, and Jorge.

       c. Our consulting firm is proud to offer Web services for: site design, market analysis, e-commerce, and hosting.

_____ 7. a. All secretaries' computers were equipped with Excel.

       b. Both lawyers statements confused the judge.

       c. Some members names and addresses must be re-keyed.

_____ 8. a. Our committee considered convention sites in Regina, Saskatchewan, Charlottetown, Prince Edward Island; and Banff, Alberta.

       b. Alizar was from Humbolt, Saskatchewan; Josh was from The Pas, Manitoba, and Rachel was from Whitehorse, Yukon.

       c. The following engineers were approved: J. W. Ellis, civil; Dr. Thomas Lu, structural; and W. R. Proudlove, mechanical.

_____ 9. a. The package from Albany, New York was never delivered.

       b. We have scheduled an inspection tour on Tuesday, March 5, at 4 p.m.

       c. Send the check to M. E. Williams, 320 Summit Ridge, Elizabethtown, Ontario K6T 1A9 before the last mail pickup.

_____ 10. a. The best plan of action in my opinion, is a straightforward approach.

        b. Under the circumstances we could not have hoped for better results.

        c. Our department will, in the meantime, reduce its services.

_____ 11. a. If you demand reliable, competent service, you should come to us.

        b. We could not resist buying cookies from the enthusiastic, young Girl Guide.

        c. Our highly trained technicians, with years of experience are always available to evaluate and improve your network environment.

_____ 12. a. We guarantee same-day, not next-day, service.

        b. Our departmental budget requests are considerably reduced yet adequate.

        c. The nominating committee selected Todd Shimoyama, not Suzette Chase as its representative.

_____ 13. a. Their wealthy uncle left $1 million to be distributed to Hayden, Carlotta, and Susanna.

        b. Their wealthy uncle left $1 million to be distributed to Hayden, Carlotta and Susanna.

        c. Our agency will maintain and upgrade your computers, printers, copiers and fax machines.

_____ 14. a. Beginning June 1, we will service many top vendors, including: Compaq, Hewlett Packard, IBM, Dell and Mita.

        b. To promote our new business we are offering a 10 percent discount.

        c. In a period of only one month, we gained 150 new customers.

_____ 15. a. We specialize in network design, however we also offer troubleshooting and consulting.

        b. We realize that downtime is not an option; therefore, you can count on us for reliable, competent service.

        c. Our factory-trained and certified technicians perform repair at your location, or in our own repair depot for products under warranty and out of warranty.

Cumulative Editing Quiz 6

Use proofreading marks (see Appendix B) to correct errors and omissions in the following sentences. All errors must be corrected to receive credit for the sentence. Check with your instructor for the answers.

1. Although the envelope was marked Confidential the vice presidents assistant thought it should be opened.
2. Would you please send my order c.o.d?
3. To be eligible for an apartment you must pay two months rent in advance.
4. We wanted to use Russ computer, but forgot to ask for permission.
5. Wasnt it Jeff Singh not Eileen Lee who requested a 14 day leave.
6. Miss. Judith L. Beam is the employee who the employees council elected as their representative.
7. The Leader Post our local newspaper featured an article entitled The Worlds Most Expensive Memo.
8. As soon as my manager or myself can verify Ricks totals we will call you, in the meantime you must continue to disburse funds.

9. Just inside the entrance, is the receptionists desk and a complete directory of all departments'.

10. Exports from small companys has increased thereby affecting this countrys trade balance positively.

Style and Usage

Capitalization (3.01–3.16)

Capitalization is used to distinguish important words. However, writers are not free to capitalize all words they consider important. Rules or guidelines governing capitalization style have been established through custom and use. Mastering these guidelines will make your writing more readable and more comprehensible.

3.01 Proper Nouns. Capitalize proper nouns, including the specific names of persons, places, schools, streets, parks, buildings, religions, holidays, months, agreements, programs, services, and so forth. Do not capitalize common nouns that make only general references.

Proper Nouns	Common Nouns
Michael DeNiro	a salesperson in electronics
Germany, Japan	major trading partners of Canada
George Brown College	a community college
Assiniboine Park	a park in the city
Phoenix Room, Delta Inn	a meeting room in the hotel
Catholicism, Buddhism	two religions
Canada Day, New Year's Day	two holidays
Priority Post	a special package delivery service
Lions Gate Bridge	a bridge
Consumer Protection Act	a law to protect consumers
Winnipeg Chamber of Commerce	a chamber of commerce
Digby Municipal Airport	a municipal airport

3.02 Proper Adjectives. Capitalize most adjectives that are derived from proper nouns:

Greek symbol	British thermal unit
Roman numeral	Norwegian ship
Xerox copy	Inuit land claims

Do not capitalize the few adjectives that, although originally derived from proper nouns, have become common adjectives through usage. Consult your dictionary when in doubt:

manila folder	diesel engine
india ink	french fries

3.03 Geographic Locations. Capitalize the names of specific places such as cities, states, mountains, valleys, lakes, rivers, oceans, and geographic regions:

Iqualuit	Lake Ontario
Rocky Mountains	Arctic Ocean
Cape Breton Island	James Bay
the East Coast	the Pacific Northwest

3.04 Organization Names. Capitalize the principal words in the names of all business, civic, educational, governmental, labour, military, philanthropic, political, professional, religious, and social organizations:

Inland Steel Company	Board of Directors, Teachers' Credit Union
The Globe and Mail*	The Rainbow Society
Toronto Stock Exchange Commission	Securities and Exchange
United Way	Psychological Association of Manitoba
Child and Family Services	Mennonite Brethren Bible College

3.05 Academic Courses and Degrees. Capitalize particular academic degrees and course titles. Do not capitalize references to general academic degrees and subject areas:

Professor Bernadette Ordian, Ph.D., will teach Accounting 221 next fall.

Beth Snyder, who holds bachelor's and master's degrees, teaches marketing classes.

René enrolled in classes in history, business English, and management.

3.06 Personal and Business Titles

a. Capitalize personal and business titles when they precede names:

Vice President Ames	Uncle Edward
Board Chairman Frazier	Councillor Hebert
Member of Parliament Ronald Fontaine	Sales Manager Klein
Professor McLean	Dr. Myra Rosner

b. Capitalize titles in addresses, salutations, and closing lines:

Mr. Juan deSanto	Very truly yours,
Director of Purchasing	
Space Systems, Inc.	Clara J. Smith
Richmond, BC V3L 4A6	Supervisor, Marketing

c. Capitalize titles of high government rank or religious office, whether they precede a name, follow a name, or replace a name:

the Prime Minister of Canada	Gaston Pelletier, Senator
the Premier's office	the Speaker of the House of Commons
the Lieutenant-Governor of British Columbia	an audience with the Pope
J. W. Ross, Minister of Finance	

d. Do not capitalize most common titles following names:

The speech was delivered by Wayne Hsu, president, Inter-Tel Canada.

Lois Herndon, chief executive officer, signed the order.

e. Do not capitalize common titles appearing alone:

Please speak to the supervisor or to the office manager.

Neither the president nor the vice president was asked.

---

*Capitalize *the* only when it is part of the official name of an organization, as printed on the organization's stationery.

However, when the title of an official appears in that organization's minutes, bylaws, or other official document, it may be capitalized.

f. Do not capitalize titles when they are followed by appositives naming specific individuals:

> We must consult our director of research, Ronald E. Weston, before responding.

g. Do not capitalize family titles used with possessive pronouns:

> my mother   our aunt   your father   his cousin

h. Capitalize titles of close relatives used without pronouns:

> Both Mother and Father must sign the contract.

3.07 Numbered and Lettered Items.

Capitalize nouns followed by numbers or letters (except in page, paragraph, line, and verse references):

Flight 34, Gate 12	Plan No. 2
Volume I, Part 3	Warehouse 33-A
Invoice No. 55489	Figure 8.3
Model A5673	Serial No. C22865404-2
Rural Route 10	page 6, line 5

3.08 Points of the Compass.

Capitalize *north*, *south*, *east*, *west*, and their derivatives when they represent specific geographical regions. Do not capitalize the points of the compass when they are used in directions or in general references.

Specific Regions	General References
from the South	heading north on the highway
living in the North	west of the city
Easterners, Westerners	western Ontario, southern Saskatchewan
going to the Middle East	the northern part of Canada
from the East Coast	the east side of the street

3.09 Departments, Divisions, and Committees.

Capitalize the names of departments, divisions, or committees within your own organization. Outside your organization capitalize only specific department, division, or committee names:

> The inquiry was addressed to the Legal Department in our Consumer Products Division.

> John was appointed to the Employee Benefits Committee.

> Send your résumé to their human resources division.

> A planning committee will be named shortly.

3.10 Governmental Terms.

Do not capitalize the words *federal*, *government*, *nation*, or *province* unless they are part of a specific title:

> Unless federal support can be secured, the state project will be abandoned.

> The Provincial Employees' Pension Fund is looking for secure investments.

3.11 Product Names. Capitalize product names only when they refer to trademarked items. Except in advertising, common nouns following manufacturers' names are not capitalized:

Magic Marker	Apple computer
Kleenex tissues	Swingline stapler
Q-tips	SanDisk flash drive
Levi's 501 jeans	Sony dictation machine
DuPont Teflon	Canon camera

3.12 Literary Titles. Capitalize the principal words in the titles of books, magazines, newspapers, articles, movies, plays, songs, poems, and reports. Do not capitalize articles (*a, an, the*), short conjunctions (*and, but, or, nor*), and prepositions of fewer than five (some say four) letters (*in, to, by, for,* etc.) unless they begin or end the title:

Jackson's *What Job Is for You?* (Capitalize book titles.)

Gant's "Software for the Executive Suite" (Capitalize principal words in article titles.)

TVO's *The Agenda* (Capitalize TV show titles; capitalize an article that begins a title.)

"The Improvement of Fuel Economy with Alternative Motors" (Capitalize report titles.)

3.13 Beginning Words. In addition to capitalizing the first word of a complete sentence, capitalize the first word in a quoted sentence, independent phrase, item in an enumerated list, and formal rule or principle following a colon:

The business manager said, "All purchases must have requisitions." (Capitalize first word in a quoted sentence.)

Yes, if you agree. (Capitalize an independent phrase.)

Some of the duties of the position are as follows:

1. Editing and formatting Word files

2. Receiving and routing telephone calls

3. Verifying records, reports, and applications (Capitalize items in an enumerated list.)

One rule has been established through the company: No smoking is allowed in open offices. (Capitalize a rule following a colon.)

3.14 Celestial Bodies. Capitalize the names of celestial bodies such as Mars, Saturn, and Neptune. Do not capitalize the terms *earth*, *sun*, or *moon* unless they appear in a context with other celestial bodies:

Where on earth did you find that manual typewriter?

Venus and Mars are the closest planets to Earth.

3.15 Ethnic References. Capitalize terms that refer to a particular culture, language, or race:

Asian	Hebrew	Latino	Japanese
Caucasian	Indian	Persian	Judeo-Christian

3.16 Seasons. Do not capitalize seasons:

> In the fall it appeared that winter and spring sales would increase.

Review Exercise M—Capitalization

In the following sentences, correct any errors that you find in capitalization. Circle any lowercase letter that should be changed to a capital letter. Draw a slash (/) through a capital letter that you wish to change to a lowercase letter. In the space provided, indicate the total number of changes you have made in each sentence. If you make no changes, write *0*. When you finish, compare your responses with those provided. For each item on which you need review, consult the numbered principle shown in parentheses.

5 Example: Bill McAdams, currently Assistant Manager in our Personnel department, will be promoted to Manager of the Employee Services division.

_____ 1. The pensions act, passed in 1949, established the present system of social security.

_____ 2. Our company will soon be moving its operations to the west coast.

_____ 3. Marilyn Hunter, m.b.a., received her bachelor's degree from McGill university in montreal.

_____ 4. The President of Datatronics, Inc., delivered a speech entitled "Taking off into the future."

_____ 5. Please ask your Aunt and your Uncle if they will come to the Lawyer's office at 5 p.m.

_____ 6. Your reservations are for flight 32 on air canada leaving from gate 14 at 2:35 p.m.

_____ 7. Once we establish an organizing committee, arrangements can be made to rent holmby hall.

_____ 8. Bob was enrolled in history, spanish, business communications, and physical education courses.

_____ 9. Either the President or the Vice President of the company will make the decision about purchasing xerox copiers.

_____ 10. Rules for hiring and firing Employees are given on page 7, line 24, of the Contract.

_____ 11. Some individuals feel that canadian management does not have the sense of loyalty to their employees that japanese management has.

_____ 12. Where on Earth can we find better workers than Robots?

_____ 13. The minister of finance said, "we must encourage our domestic producers to compete internationally."

_____ 14. After crossing the lions gate bridge, we drove to Southern British Columbia for our vacation.

_____ 15. All marketing representatives of our company will meet in the empire room of the red lion motor inn.

_____ 16. Richard Elkins, ph.d., has been named director of research for spaceage strategies, inc.

_____ 17. The special keyboard for the IBM Computer must contain greek symbols for Engineering equations.

_____ 18. After she received a master's degree in electrical engineering, Joanne Dudley was hired to work in our product development department.

_____ 19. In the Fall our organization will move its corporate headquarters to the franklin building in downtown vancouver.

_____ 20. Dean Amador has one cardinal rule: always be punctual.

1. Pensions Act (3.01)   3. M.B.A. University Montreal (3.01, 3.05)   5. aunt uncle lawyer's (3.06e, 3.06g)   7. Holmby Hall (3.01)   9. president vice president Xerox (3.06e, 3.11) 11. Canadian Japanese (3.02)   13. We foreign (3.10, 3.13)   15. Empire Room Red Lion Motor Inn (3.01)   17. computer Greek engineering (3.01, 3.02, 3.11)   19. fall Franklin Building Vancouver (3.01, 3.03, 3.16)

Grammar/Mechanics Checkup—13

Capitalization

Review Sections 3.01–3.16 above. Then study each of the following statements. Circle any lowercase letter that should be capitalized. Draw a slash (/) through any capital letter that you wish to change to lowercase. Indicate in the space provided the number of changes you made in each sentence and record the number of the Handbook principle(s) illustrated. If you made no changes, write 0. When you finish, compare your responses with those provided on page 509. If your responses differ, carefully study again the principles in parentheses.

4 (3.01, 3.06a) Example: After consulting our ~~A~~ttorneys for ~~L~~egal advice, Vice ~~p~~resident Fontaine signed the ~~C~~ontract.

_____ 1. All canadian passengers from Flight 402 must pass through Customs Inspection at Gate 17 upon arrival at Pearson international airport.

_____ 2. Personal tax rates for japanese citizens are low by International standards; rates for japanese corporations are high, according to Iwao Nakatani, an Economics Professor at Osaka university.

_____ 3. In the end, Business passes on most of the burden to the Consumer: What looks like a tax on Business is really a tax on Consumption.

_____ 4. Abel enrolled in courses in History, Sociology, Spanish, and Computer Science.

_____ 5. Did you see the *Maclean's* article entitled "Careers in horticulture are nothing to sneeze at"?

_____ 6. Although I recommend Minex Printers sold under the brandname MPLazerJet, you may purchase any Printers you choose.

_____ 7. According to a Federal Government report, any development of Provincial waterways must receive an environmental assessment.

_____ 8. The deputy prime minister of canada said, "this country continues to encourage Foreign investment."

_____ 9. The Comptroller of Ramjet International reported to the President and the Board of Directors that canada revenue agency was beginning an investigation of their Company.

_____ 10. My Mother, who lives near Plum Coulee, reports that protection from the Sun's rays is particularly important when travelling to the South.

_____ 11. Our Managing Editor met with Leslie Hawkins, Manager of the Advertising Sales Department, to plan an Ad Campaign for our special issue.

_____ 12. Next week, Editor in Chief Mercredi plans an article detailing the astounding performance of the euro.

_____ 13. To reach Terrasee Vaudreuil park, which is located on an Island in the St. Lawrence river, tourists pass over the vanier bridge.

_____ 14. On page 6 of the catalogue you will see that the computer science department is offering a number of courses in programming.

_____ 15. Please consult figure 3.2 in chapter 5 for statistics Canada figures regarding non-english-speaking residents.

Cumulative Editing Quiz 7

Use proofreading marks (see Appendix B) to correct errors and omissions in the following sentences. All errors must be corrected to receive credit for the sentence. Check with your instructor for the answers.

1. The Manager thinks that you attending the three day seminar is a good idea, however we must find a replacement.

2. We heard that professor watson invited edward peters, president of micropro, inc. to speak to our business law class.

3. Carla Jones a new systems programmer in our accounting department will start monday.

4. After year's of downsizing and restructuring canada has now become one of the worlds most efficient manufacturers.

5. When our company specialized in asian imports our main office was on the west coast.

6. Company's like amway discovered that there unique door to door selling methods was very successful in japan.

7. If you had given your sony camera to she or I before you got on the roller coaster it might have stayed dry.

8. Tracy recently finished a bachelors degree in accounting, consequently she is submitting many résumé's to companys across the country.

9. The Lopezs moved from Edmonton Alberta to Vancouver British Columbia when mr lopez enrolled at the university of british columbia.

10. When we open our office in montreal we will need employees whom are fluent in english and french.

Number Style (4.01–4.13)

Usage and custom determine whether numbers are expressed in the form of figures (for example, 5, 9) or in the form of words (for example, *five*, *nine*). Numbers expressed as figures are shorter and more easily understood, yet numbers expressed as words are necessary in certain instances. The following guidelines are observed in expressing numbers in written sentences. Numbers that appear on business forms—such as invoices, monthly statements, and purchase orders—are always expressed as figures.

4.01 General Rules

a. The numbers one through ten are generally written as words. Numbers above ten are written as figures:

> The bank had a total of nine branch offices in three suburbs.

> All 58 employees received benefits in the three categories shown.

> A shipment of 45,000 light bulbs was sent from two warehouses.

b. Numbers that begin sentences are written as words. If a number beginning a sentence involves more than two words, however, the sentence should be written so that the number does not fall at the beginning.

> Fifteen different options were available in the annuity programs.

> A total of 156 companies participated in the promotion (not *One hundred fifty-six companies participated in the promotion*).

4.02 Money. Sums of money $1 or greater are expressed as figures. If a sum is a whole dollar amount, omit the decimal and zeros (whether or not the amount appears in a sentence with additional fractional dollar amounts):

> We budgeted $30 for blank CDs, but the actual cost was $37.96.

> On the invoice were items for $6.10, $8, $33.95, and $75.

Sums less than $1 are written as figures that are followed by the word *cents*.

> By shopping carefully, we can save 15 cents per blank CD.

4.03 Dates. In dates, numbers that appear after the name of the month are written as cardinal figures (*1, 2, 3,* etc.). Those that stand alone or appear before the name of a month are written as ordinal figures (*1st, 2nd, 3rd,** etc.):

> The Personnel Practices Committee will meet May 7.

> On the 5th day of February and again on the 25th, we placed orders.

In domestic business documents, dates generally take the following form: *January 4, 2010.* An alternative form, used primarily in military and foreign correspondence, begins with the day of the month and omits the comma: *4 January 2010.*

4.04 Clock Time. Figures are used when clock time is expressed with *a.m.* or *p.m.* Omit the colon and zeros in referring to whole hours. When exact clock time is expressed with the contraction *o'clock*, either figures or words may be used:

> Mail deliveries are made at 11 a.m. and 3:30 p.m.

> At four (or 4) o'clock employees begin to leave.

4.05 Addresses and Telephone Numbers

a. Except for the number *one*, house numbers are expressed in figures:

540 Elm Street	17802 Parliament Avenue
One Desmeurons Boulevard	2 Highland Street

b. Street names containing numbers ten or lower are written entirely as words. For street names involving numbers greater than ten, figures are used:

330 Third Street	3440 Seventh Avenue
6945 East 32 Avenue	4903 West 103 Street

If no compass direction (*North, South, East, West*) separates a house number from a street number, the street number is expressed in ordinal form (*-st, -nd, -rd, -th*):

256 42nd Street	1390 11th Avenue

c. Telephone numbers are expressed with figures. When used, the area code is placed in parentheses preceding the telephone number:

> Please call us at (818) 347-0551 to place an order.

> Mr. Sui asked you to call (619) 554-8923, Ext. 245, after 10 a.m.

4.06 Related Numbers. Numbers are related when they refer to similar items in a category within the same reference. All related numbers should be expressed as

---

*Some writers today are using the more efficient *2d* and *3d* instead of *2nd* and *3rd*.

the largest number is expressed. Thus if the largest number is greater than ten, all the numbers should be expressed in figures:

> Only 5 of the original 25 applicants completed the processing. (Related numbers require figures.)

> The two plans affected 34 employees working in three sites. (Unrelated numbers use figures and words.)

> Petro-Canada operated 86 rigs, of which 6 were rented. (Related numbers require figures.)

> The company hired three accountants, one customer service representative, and nine sales representatives. (Related numbers under ten use words.)

4.07 Consecutive Numbers. When two numbers appear consecutively and both modify a following noun, generally express the first number in words and the second in figures. If, however, the first number cannot be expressed in one or two words, put it in figures also (*120 34-cent stamps*). Do not use commas to separate the figures.

> Historians divided the era into four 25-year periods. (Use word form for the first number and figure form for the second.)

> We ordered fifteen 30-page colour brochures. (Use word form for the first number and figure form for the second.)

> Did the manager request 150 100-watt bulbs? (Use figure form for the first number since it would require more than two words.)

4.08 Periods of Time. Periods of time are generally expressed in word form. However, figures may be used to emphasize business concepts such as discount rates, interest rates, warranty periods, credit terms, loan or contract periods, and payment terms:

> This business was incorporated over fifty years ago. (Use words for a period of time.)

> Any purchaser may cancel a contract within 72 hours. (Use figures to explain a business concept.)

> The warranty period is 5 years. (Use figures for a business concept.)

> Cash discounts are given for payment within 30 days. (Use figures for a business concept.)

4.09 Ages. Ages are generally expressed in word form unless the age appears immediately after a name or is expressed in exact years and months:

> At the age of twenty-one, Elizabeth inherited the business.

> Wanda Unger, 37, was named acting president.

> At the age of 4 years and 7 months, the child was adopted.

4.10 Round Numbers. Round numbers are approximations. They may be expressed in word or figure form, although figure form is shorter and easier to comprehend:

> About 600 (or *six hundred*) stock options were sold.

> It is estimated that 1,000 (or *one thousand*) people will attend.

For ease of reading, round numbers in the millions or billions should be expressed with a combination of figures and words:

> At least 1.5 million readers subscribe to the ten top magazines.

> Deposits in money market accounts totalled more than $115 billion.

4.11 Weights and Measurements. Weights and measurements are expressed with figures:

> The new deposit slip measures 5 by 15 cm.

> Her new suitcase weighed only 1.2 kg.

> Regina is 750 kilometres from Calgary.

4.12 Fractions. Simple fractions are expressed as words. Complex fractions may be written either as figures or as a combination of figures and words:

> Over two thirds of the shareholders voted.

> This microcomputer will execute the command in 1 millionth of a second. (Combination of words and numbers is easier to comprehend.)

> She purchased a one-fifth share in the business. *

4.13 Percentages and Decimals. Percentages are expressed with figures that are followed by the word *percent*. The percent sign (%) is used only on business forms or in statistical presentations:

> We had hoped for a 7 percent interest rate, but we received a loan at 8 percent.

> Over 50 percent of the residents supported the plan.

Decimals are expressed with figures. If a decimal expression does not contain a whole number (an integer) and does not begin with a zero, a zero should be placed before the decimal point:

> The actuarial charts show that 1.74 out of 1,000 people will die in any given year.

> Inspector Norris found the setting to be .005 centimetres off. (Decimal begins with a zero and does not require a zero before the decimal point.)

> Considerable savings will accrue if the unit production cost is reduced by 0.1 percent. (A zero is placed before a decimal that neither contains a whole number nor begins with a zero).

Quick Chart—Expression of Numbers

Use Words	Use Figures
Numbers ten and under	Numbers 11 and over
Numbers at beginning of sentence	Money
Periods of time	Dates
Ages	Addresses and telephone numbers
Fractions	Weights and measurements
	Percentages and decimals

*Fractions used as adjectives require hyphens.

Review Exercise N—Number Style

Circle *a* or *b* to indicate the preferred number style. Assume that these numbers appear in business correspondence. When you finish, compare your responses with those provided. For each item on which you need review, consult the numbered principle shown in parentheses.

_____	1. (a) 2 alternatives	(b) two alternatives
_____	2. (a) Seventh Avenue	(b) 7th Avenue
_____	3. (a) sixty sales reps	(b) 60 sales reps
_____	4. (a) November ninth	(b) November 9
_____	5. (a) forty dollars	(b) $40
_____	6. (a) on the 23d of May	(b) the twenty-third of May
_____	7. (a) at 2:00 p.m.	(b) at 2 p.m.
_____	8. (a) 4 two-hundred-page books	(b) four 200-page books
_____	9. (a) at least 15 years ago	(b) at least fifteen years ago
_____	10. (a) 1,000,000 viewers	(b) 1 million viewers
_____	11. (a) twelve cents	(b) 12 cents
_____	12. (a) a sixty-day warranty	(b) a 60-day warranty
_____	13. (a) ten percent interest rate	(b) 10 percent interest rate
_____	14. (a) 4/5 of the voters	(b) four fifths of the voters
_____	15. (a) the rug measures two by four metres	(b) the rug measures 2 by 4 metres
_____	16. (a) about five hundred people attended	(b) about 500 people attended
_____	17. (a) at eight o'clock	(b) at 8 o'clock
_____	18. (a) located at 1 Broadway Boulevard	(b) located at One Broadway Boulevard
_____	19. (a) three computers for twelve people	(b) three computers for 12 people
_____	20. (a) 4 out of every 100 licences	(b) four out of every 100 licences

1. b (4.01a)   3. b (4.01a)   5. b (4.02)   7. b (4.04)   9. b (4.08)   11. b (4.02)   13. b (4.13)
15. b (4.11)   17. a or b (4.04)   19. b (4.06)

Grammar/Mechanics Checkup—14

Number Style

Review Sections 4.01–4.13 above. Then study each of the following pairs. Assume that these expressions appear in the context of letters, reports, or e-mails. Write *a* or *b* in the space provided to indicate the preferred number style and record the number of the Handbook principle illustrated. When you finish, compare your responses with those on page 509. If your responses differ, carefully study again the principles in parentheses.

a (4.01) Example: (a) six investments (b) 6 investments

_____	1. (a) sixteen credit cards	(b) 16 credit cards
_____	2. (a) Fifth Avenue	(b) 5th Avenue
_____	3. (a) 34 newspapers	(b) thirty-four newspapers

	4. (a) July eighth	(b) July 8
——————	5. (a) twenty dollars	(b) $20
——————	6. (a) on the 15th of June	(b) on the fifteenth of June
——————	7. (a) at 4:00 p.m.	(b) at 4 p.m.
——————	8. (a) 3 200-page reports	(b) three 200-page reports
——————	9. (a) over 18 years ago	(b) over eighteen years ago
——————	10. (a) 2,000,000 people	(b) 2 million people
——————	11. (a) fifteen cents	(b) 15 cents
——————	12. (a) a thirty-day warranty	(b) a 30-day warranty
——————	13. (a) 2/3 of the e-mails	(b) two thirds of the e-mails
——————	14. (a) two telephones for 15 employees	(b) 2 telephones for 15 employees
——————	15. (a) 6 of the 130 letters	(b) six of the 130 letters

Cumulative Editing Quiz 8

Use proofreading marks (see Appendix B) to correct errors and omissions in the following sentences. All errors must be corrected to receive credit for the sentence. Check with your instructor for the answers.

1. The prime minister of Canada recommended a 30 day cooling off period in the united nations peace negotiations.

2. Please meet at my lawyers office at four p.m. on May 10th to sign our papers of incorporation.

3. A Retail Store at 405 7th avenue had sales of over one million dollars last year.

4. Every new employee must receive their permit to park in lot 5-A or there car will be towed.

5. Mr thompson left three million dollars to be divided among his 4 children rachel, timothy, rebecca and kevin.

6. Most companys can boost profits almost one hundred percent by retaining only 5% more of there current customers.

7. Although the bill for coffee and doughnuts were only three dollars and forty cents Pavel and myself had trouble paying it.

8. Only six of the 19 employees, who filled out survey forms, would have went to hawaii as their vacation choice.

9. Danielles report is more easier to read then david because her's was better organized and had good headings.

10. At mcdonald's we devoured 4 big macs 3 orders of french fries and 5 coca colas for lunch.

Confusing Words

accede:	to agree or consent	*advise:*	to counsel or recommend
exceed:	over a limit		
accept:	to receive	*affect:*	to influence
except:	to exclude; (*prep.*) but	*effect:*	(*n.*) outcome, result; (*v.*) to bring about, to create
advice:	suggestion, opinion		

all ready:	prepared	*hole:*	an opening
already:	by this time	*whole:*	complete
all right:	satisfactory	*imply:*	to suggest indirectly
alright:	unacceptable variant spelling	*infer:*	to reach a conclusion
altar:	structure for worship	*liable:*	legally responsible
alter:	to change	*libel:*	damaging written statement
appraise:	to estimate	*loose:*	not fastened
apprise:	to inform	*lose:*	to misplace
assure:	to promise	*miner:*	person working in a mine
ensure:	to make certain	*minor:*	a lesser item; person under age
insure:	to protect from loss		
capital:	(*n.*) city that is seat of government; wealth of an individual; (*adj.*) chief	*patience:*	calm perseverance
		patients:	people receiving medical treatment
capitol:	building that houses state or national lawmakers	*personal:*	private, individual
		personnel:	employees
cereal:	breakfast food	*precede:*	to go before
serial:	arranged in sequence	*proceed:*	to continue
cite:	to quote; to summon	*precedence:*	priority
site:	location	*precedents:*	events used as an example
sight:	a view; to see	*principal:*	(*n.*) capital sum; school official; (*adj.*) chief
complement:	that which completes		
compliment:	to praise or flatter	*principle:*	rule of action
conscience:	regard for fairness	*stationary:*	immovable
conscious:	aware	*stationery:*	writing material
council:	governing body	*than:*	conjunction showing comparison
counsel:	to give advice; advice	*then:*	adverb meaning "at that time"
desert:	arid land; to abandon		
dessert:	sweet food	*their:*	possessive form of they
device:	invention or mechanism	*there:*	at that place or point
devise:	to design or arrange	*they're:*	contraction of "they are"
disburse:	to pay out		
disperse:	to scatter widely	*to:*	a preposition; the sign of the infinitive
elicit:	to draw out		
illicit:	unlawful	*too:*	adverb meaning "also" or "to an excessive extent"
every day:	each single day		
everyday:	ordinary		
farther:	a greater distance	*two:*	a number
further:	additional	*waiver:*	abandonment of a claim
formally:	in a formal manner	*waver:*	to shake or fluctuate
formerly:	in the past		

Frequently Misspelled Words

absence	desirable	independent	prominent
accommodate	destroy	indispensable	qualify
achieve	development	interrupt	quantity
acknowledgment	disappoint	irrelevant	questionnaire
across	dissatisfied	itinerary	receipt
adequate	division	judgment	receive
advisable	efficient	knowledge	recognize
analyze	embarrass	legitimate	recommendation
annually	emphasis	licence (*n.*)	referred
appointment	emphasize	license (*v.*)	regarding
argument	employee	maintenance	remittance
automatically	envelope	manageable	representative
bankruptcy	equipped	manufacturer	restaurant
becoming	especially	mileage	schedule
beneficial	evidently	miscellaneous	secretary
budget	fiscal	mortgage	separate
business	exaggerate	necessary	similar
calendar	excellent	nevertheless	sincerely
cancelled	exempt	ninety	software
catalogue	existence	ninth	succeed
changeable	extraordinary	noticeable	sufficient
column	familiar	occasionally	supervisor
committee	fascinate	occurred	surprise
congratulate	feasible	offered	tenant
conscience	February	omission	therefore
conscious	foreign	omitted	thorough
consecutive	forty	opportunity	though
consensus	fourth	opposite	through
consistent	friend	ordinarily	truly
control	genuine	paid	undoubtedly
convenient	government	pamphlet	unnecessarily
correspondence	grammar	permanent	usable
courteous	grateful	permitted	usage
criticize	guarantee	pleasant	using
decision	harass	practical	usually
deductible	height	prevalent	valuable
defendant	hoping	privilege	volume
definitely	immediate	probably	weekday
dependent	incidentally	procedure	writing
describe	incredible	profited	yield

Key to Grammar/Mechanics Checkups

Checkup 1

1. attorneys (1.05d) **2.** Saturdays (1.05a) **3.** cities (1.05e)
4. turkeys (1.05d) **5.** inventories (1.05e) **6.** Nashes (1.05b)
7. 1990s (1.05g) **8.** editors in chief (1.05f) **9.** complexes (1.05b)
10. counties (1.05e) **11.** Jennifers (1.05a) **12.** C (1.05d)
13. liabilities (1.05e) **14.** C (1.05h) **15.** runners-up (1.05f)

Checkup 2

1. he (1.08b) **2.** his car (1.09b) **3.** him (1.08c) **4.** whom (1.08j)
5. hers (1.08d) **6.** me (1.08c) **7.** I (1.08a) **8.** yours (1.08d)
9. whoever (1.08j) **10.** me (1.08i) **11.** he (1.08f) **12.** us (1.08g)
13. her (1.09c) **14.** its (1.09g) **15.** his or her (1.09b)

Checkup 3

1. *are* for *is* (1.10e) **2.** *has* for *have* (1.10c) **3.** *offers* for *offer*
(1.10d) **4.** *is* for *are* (1.10g) **5.** C (1.10f) **6.** *is* for *are* (1.10i)
7. C (1.10h) **8.** chosen (1.15) **9.** *lain* for *laid* (1.15) **10.** *were* for
was (1.12) **11.** *is* for *are* (1.10c) **12.** b (1.15c) **13.** b (1.15c)
14. a (1.15c) **15.** b (1.15c)

Checkup 4

1. long-time (1.17e) **2.** $50-per-year (1.17e) **3.** C (1.17e)
4. quickly (1.17d) **5.** had only (1.17f) **6.** double-digit (1.17e)
7. once-in-a-lifetime (1.17e) **8.** C (1.17e) **9.** better (1.17a)
10. well-known (1.17e) **11.** up-to-the-minute (1.17e) **12.** after-
tax (1.17e) **13.** couldn't have been clearer (1.17b) **14.** fifty-fifty
(1.17e) **15.** feel bad (1.17c)

Checkup 5

1. b (1.19d) **2.** a (1.19d) **3.** b (1.18e) **4.** b (1.19c) **5.** a (1.19a)
6. b (1.18a) **7.** b (1.19d) **8.** a (1.18c) **9.** b (1.18b) **10.** a (1.19c)
11. b (1.19a) **12.** b (1.19b) **13.** a (1.19c) **14.** b (1.18c)
15. b (1.19c)

Checkup 6

1. (2) not, as a rule, (2.03) **2.** (2) sure, Mrs. Schwartz, (2.02)
3. (2) reliable, conscientious, (2.01) **4.** (0) **5.** (1) fact, (2.03)
6. (3) Calgary, Alberta, La Salle, (2.04c) **7.** (1) meantime, (2.03)
8. (2) February 4, 2011, (2.04a) **9.** (2) Ms. Horne, Mr. Hae,
(2.01) **10.** (4) Holmes, Lane, Regina, Saskatchewan S5L 2E2,
(2.04b) **11.** (2) feels, needless to say, (2.03) **12.** (2) supplies,
replacing inventories, (2.01) **13.** (1) business, (2.02) **14.** (2) feels,
however, (2.03) **15.** 0

Checkup 7

1. (1) warranty, (2.06a) **2.** (1) market, (2.05) **3.** (0) (2.05)
4. (2) manufacturer, nameless, (2.06c) **5.** (1) imaginative, (2.08)
6. (0) (2.06c) **7.** (2) Sims, area, (2.09) **8.** (1) buyers, (2.05)
9. (1) quality, (2.06a) **10.** (1) buyers, (2.07) **11.** (2) application,

Monday, (2.06a, 2.04a) **12.** (2) hand, hard-working, (2.03, 2.08)
13. (1) Bragg Creek, (2.06c) **14.** (3) telephone, Thursday, June 9,
(2.06a, 2.04a) **15.** (1) classes, (2.05)

Checkup 8

1. (2) name," Etienne, (2.14a) **2.** (4) Cox, Ph.D., Meridian,
M.B.A., (2.10) **3.** (1) Monday, (2.14b) **4.** (0) (2.15)
5. (1) investment, (2.12) **6.** (3) requested, cartridges, folders,
(2.06a, 2.01) **7.** (2) think, however, (2.03) **8.** (2) period,
Vidal, (2.07, 2.06c) **9.** (2) Collingwood, Laurentians, (2.01,
2.15) **10.** (1) interviewed, (2.06a, 2.06c) **11.** (2) years, individuals, (2.07, 2.09) **12.** (2) Johansson, week, (2.05c, 2.15)
13. (0) (2.06c) **14.** (2) companies, robots, (2.01) **15.** (2) act,
unprotected, (2.03, 2.08)

Checkup 9

1. (3) one year; long-term financing, hand, (2.03, 2.16b)
2. (2) December; therefore, (2.16a) **3.** (3) months: September,
October, (2.01, 2.17a) **4.** (1) are [omit comma] (2.17b)
5. (1) money, (2.06a, 2.16b) **6.** (3) short-term credit; manufacturer, however, (2.03, 2.16a) **7.** (3) credit: loans, promissory
notes, (2.03, 2.16a) **8.** (8) businesspeople: Mary Ann Mahan,
financial manager, Ritchie Industries; Buchanan, comptroller,
Edmée Cavalier, operations, (2.16d, 2.17) **9.** (1) Canada, (2.05)
10. (5) customers; for example, retailers, service companies,
manufacturers, (2.16e) **11.** (2) Inc., rating, (2.06c, 2.16c)
12. (2) Bank, applications to the following: (2.06a, 2.17a)
13. (2) high; therefore, (2.16) **14.** (2) 18 percent, prohibitive;
(2.06a, 2.16c) **15.** (1) resources; (2.16b)

Checkup 10

1. Mr. Ruskin's (2.20a, 2.21) **2.** year's (2.20a) **3.** weeks' (2.20b)
4. Ms. Lanham's (2.21) **5.** boss's (2.20b) **6.** server's (2.20b)
7. Kaspar's (2.22) **8.** months' (2.20b) **9.** companies' (2.20b)
10. month's (2.20a) **11.** secretary's (2.20b) **12.** sellers' (2.20b)
13. Mark's, David's (2.20a) **14.** Latika's (2.20a)

Checkup 11

1. (2) managers—Yu Sosa—(2.26a, 2.27) **2.** (3) please, Miss
Fundy, totals? (2.20, 2.23a) **3.** (2) variables (see Figure 13 on
page 432) (2.27) **4.** (3) "recommendation" misspelled, (2.06a,
2.28c) **5.** (1) training— (2.26c) **6.** (2) said, "Who cartridges?"
(2.28f) **7.** (3) "How You"? (2.28e, 2.28f) **8.** (2) provinces—
Alberta, Newfoundland, and Ontario— (2.26a) **9.** (4) Mr. Kieran
E. Manning, Miss Kathy Tanguay, and Ms. Petra (2.23b, 2.24)
10. (3) "Trading Market" <u>Securities Markets</u> (2.28e)
11. (2) over"; however, (2.16, 2.28f) **12.** (3) <u>liability</u> defined as
"any future." (2.28d) **13.** (1) June 10; (2.06) **14.** (4) c.o.d. today?
(2.23b, 2.24) **15.** (3) Hooray! checkup, haven't I? (2.24, 2.25)

Checkup 12

1. c (2.05) **2.** b (2.06) **3.** a (2.16a) **4.** c (2.15) **5.** b (2.16b)
6. b (2.17a) **7.** a (2.20) **8.** c (2.16d) **9.** b (2.04a) **10.** c (2.03)
11. a (2.08) **12.** a (2.12) **13.** a (2.01) **14.** c (2.07) **15.** b (2.16)

Checkup 13

1. (5) Canadian customs inspection International Airport (3.01,
3.02, 3.07) **2.** (6) Japanese international Japanese economics
professor University (3.01, 3.02, 3.04, 3.06d) **3.** (4) business
consumer business consumption (3.01, 3.13) **4.** (4) history
sociology computer science (3.05) **5.** (5) Horticulture Are
Nothing Sneeze At (3.12) **6.** (2) printers printers (3.11)
7. (3) federal government provincial (3.10)

8. (3) Canada This foreign (3.01, 3.06c, 3.13) **9.** (8) comptroller
president board directors Canada Revenue Agency company
(3.01, 3.04, 3.06c) **10.** (2) mother sun's (3.03, 3.06g, 3.08, 3.14)
11. (5) managing editor manager ad campaign (3.01, 3.06d,
3.06e, 3.09) **12.** (3) Austrian German Italian (3.02, 3.06a, 3.16)
13. (4) Park island Vanier Bridge (3.01, 3.03) **14.** (3) Computer
Science Department (3.05, 3.07, 3.09) **15.** (4) Figure Chapter
Statistics English (3.02, 3.04, 3.07)

Checkup 14

1. b (4.01a) **2.** a (4.05b) **3.** a (4.01a) **4.** b (4.03) **5.** b (4.02)
6. a (4.03) **7.** b (4.04) **8.** b (4.07) **9.** b (4.08) **10.** b (4.10)
11. b (4.02) **12.** b (4.08) **13.** b (4.12) **14.** a (4.06) **15.** a (4.06)

Notes

Chapter 1

1 Don Tapscott, *Grown Up Digital: How the Net Generation Is Changing the World* (Toronto: McGraw Hill, 2009), 150.

2 Backdraft Corporation, "History & Clients," accessed April 26, 2005, http://www.backdraft.org/history.htm.

3 Statistics Canada predicts that by 2017, visible minorities will in fact be the majority of the population in major centres like Toronto, Vancouver, and Montreal. See Statistics Canada, *The Daily*, March 22, 2005, http://www.statcan.ca/Daily/English/050322/d050322b.htm.

4 Anne Papmehl, "Remote Access," *CMA Management* 75, no. 3 (May 2001): 11.

5 Desmond Beckstead and Tara Vinodrai, "Dimensions of Occupational Changes in Canada's Knowledge Economy, 1971–1996," The Canadian Economy in Transition Series, Catalogue no. 11-622-MIE—No. 004, Statistics Canada, 2003, accessed April 26, 2005, http://www.statcan.ca/cgi-bin/downpub/listpub.cgi?catno=11-622-MIE2003004.

6 James Adams, "*Post* Drops Columnist for Alleged Plagiarism," *The Globe and Mail*, November 6, 2004, A12.

7 Sandra Gabriele and JoAnn Stober, "Old Messengers, New Media: The Legacy of Innis and McLuhan," accessed May 26, 2008, http://www.collectionscanada.gc.ca/innis-mcluhan/index-e.html.

8 J. Burgoon, D. Coker, and R. Coker, "Communicative Explanations," *Human Communication Research*, 12 (1986): 463–94.

9 Ray Birdwhistell, *Kinesics and Context* (Philadelphia: University of Pennsylvania Press, 1970).

10 Edward T. Hall, *The Hidden Dimension* (Garden City, NY: Doubleday, 1966), 107–22.

11 Catherine Bell, "Prime Impressions Corporate Training," "Prime Impressions Telecoaching," accessed April 26, 2005, http://www.prime-impressions.com.

12 Anthony Wilson-Smith, "A Quiet Passion," *Maclean's*, July 1, 1995, 8–12.

13 Jon P. Alston and Theresa M. Morris, "Comparing Canadian and American Values: New Evidence from National Surveys," *Canadian Review of American Studies* 26, no. 3 (Autumn 1996): 301–15.

14 Seymour Martin Lipset, *Continental Divide: The Values and Institutions of the United States and Canada* (New York: Routledge, 1991).

15 Ian Austin, "Canucks Polite, Vancouverites More So, Readers Digest Finds," accessed May 28, 2008, http://www.canada.com/theprovince/news/story.html?id=b3610ee8-156f-4d46-aa69-d53c89bdc740.

16 Norman McGuinness and Nigel Campbell, "Selling Machinery to China: Chinese Perceptions of Strategies and Relationships," *Journal of International Business Studies* 22, no. 3 (1991): 187.

17 "Labour Force Characteristics by Age and Sex," accessed November 8, 2010, http://www40.statcan.ca/l01/cst01/labor20a-eng.htm.

18 Ibid.

19 Virginia Galt, "Western Union Remakes Canadian Image: Profits from Overseas Hiring, Staff Diversity," *The Globe and Mail*, November 23, 2004, B1.

20 Lee Gardenswartz and Anita Rowe, *Managing Diversity: A Complete Desk Reference and Planning Guide*. New York: McGraw-Hill, 1998, 124.

21 Joel Makower, "Managing Diversity in the Workplace," *Business & Society Review* 92 (Winter 1995): 48–54, accessed February 2, 2008, Business Source Premier database.

Chapter 2

1 John DeGoey, personal interview, January 18, 2011.

2 Editorial Staff, "Canadian CEOs Are Big on Communication," *CMA Management* 74, no. 9 (November 2000): 8.

3 Don Tapscott, "R U N2 It?" *enRoute*, October 2003, 35–36.

4 Kevin Marron, "Instant Messaging Comes of Age," *The Globe and Mail*, November 1, 2001, B30.

5 Earl N. Harbert, "Knowing Your Audience," *The Handbook of Executive Communication*, ed. John L. Digaetani (Homewood, IL: Dow Jones/Irwin, 1986), 17.

Chapter 3

1 Shelley Datseris, personal interview, March 3, 2011.

2 The UVic Writer's Guide, "The First Draft," *UVic English*, accessed May 25, 2011, http://web.uvic.ca/wguide/Pages/EssayWritingFirstDraft.html.

3 Maryann V. Piotrowski, *Effective Business Writing* (New York: Harper Perennial, 1996), 12.

4 Daniel Kies, "Evaluating Grammar Checkers: A Comparative Ten-Year Study," accessed January 10, 2011, http://papyr.com/hypertextbooks/grammar/gramchek.htm.

Chapter 4

1 Peter Schneider, personal interview, March 20, 2011.

2 "Emails Reach 210 Billion per Day," accessed January 24, 2011, http://www.techwatch.co.uk/2009/01/26/emails-reach-210-billion-per-day.

3 "Business and Government Use of Information Communication Technologies," accessed January 24, 2011, http://www40.statcan.ca/l01/cst01/econ146a-eng.htm.

4 Sinclair Stewart, "CIBC Turns Up Heat as Fight With Genuity Hits Home," *The Globe and Mail*, February 17, 2005, B4.

5 Paul B. Brown, "Same Office, Different Planets," *New York Times*, January 26, 2008, B5.

6 Nova Scotia Human Rights Commission, "Rights on Religion or Creed," accessed April 27, 2005, http://www.gov.ns.ca/humanrights/human-rights-act.asp.

7 Editors, "'Surfeillance' in the Workplace," *Worklife Report*, 12, no. 4 (2000): 13.

8 Ibid.

9 Ibid.

[10] Chris Wood and Brenda Branswell, "Do You Know Who's Watching You?" *Maclean's*, February 19, 2001.

[11] Ibid.

Chapter 5

[1] Reg Pirie, "The Lost Art of Business Letter Writing," *CanadaOne Magazine*, June 1999, accessed April 29, 2005, http://www.canadaone.com/ezine/june99/letters.html.

[2] Judith Colbert, Helene Carty, and Paul Beam, "Practice: Assessing Financial Documents for Readability," Task Force on the Future of the Canadian Financial Services Sector, accessed July 28, 2011, http://dsp-psd.pwgsc.gc.ca/Collection/F21-6-1998-8-1E.pdf, pp. 31–41.

[3] James Fallows, "Enough Keyword Searches. Just Answer My Question," *New York Times*, June 12, 2005, BU3.

[4] Marcia Mascolini, "Another Look at Teaching the External Negative Message," *The Bulletin of the Association of Business Communication*, June 1994, 46.

[5] Pamela Gilbert, "Two Words That Can Help a Business Thrive," *Wall Street Journal*, December 30, 1996, A12.

[6] "CSR Governance Guidelines," Canadian Business for Social Responsibility, accessed May 26, 2011, http://www.cbsr.ca/resources/cbsr-publications.

Chapter 6

[1] Jose Ribau, personal interview, April 29, 2005.

[2] "How to Ask For—and Get—What You Want!" *Supervision*, 1 February 1990, 11, accessed March 2, 2008, http://www.allbusiness.com/human-resources/workforce-management/117804-1.html.

[3] Dean Rieck, "Great Letters and Why They Work," *Direct Marketing*, June 1998, 20–24, accessed March 2, 2008, Academic Search Premier (EBSCO).

[4] Ernest Nicastro, "Five Deadly Sales Letter Mistakes," accessed July 28, 2011, http://ezinearticles.com/?Five-Deadly-Sales-Letter-Mistakes&id=18597.

[5] Dennis Chambers, *The Agile Manager's Guide to Writing to Get Action* (Bristol, VT: Velocity Press, 1998), 86.

[6] Michael Lowenstein, "Make Both an Emotional and Rational Appeal to Your Customers: Inside-Out and Outside-In Commitment and Advocacy," *Digital Marketing*, accessed July 28, 2011, http://www.digitalmarketingone.com/article/make_emotional_rational_appeal_customers.

[7] To learn more about this tool, visit http://www.hp.com/hpinfo/blogs/codeofconduct.html.

[8] *PR Week* and Burston Marsteller study cited in S. Rubel, "Study: 47% of CEOs Say Blogs Useful for PR," *WebPro News*, November 7, 2005, accessed July 28, 2011, http://www.webpronews.com/study-of-ceos-say-blogs-useful-for-pr-2005-11.

[9] Deborah Asbrand, "Designing a New Way to Connect," *Microsoft Business & Industry*, August 30, 2007, accessed July 28, 2011, http://www.microsoft.com/canada/business/peopleready/business/operations/insight/portals.mspx.

[10] Mark Pilgrim, "What is RSS?" *O'Reilly About*, accessed July 28, 2011, http://oreilly.com/feeds/.

[11] Tamar Weinberg. *The New Community Rules: Marketing on the Social Web* (Sebastopol, CA: O'Reilly Media, 2009), 127, 128–29.

[12] See note 8 above.

[13] Canadian Fitness and Lifestyle Research Institute, "2002 Physical Activity Monitor," accessed July 28, 2011, http://72.10.49.94/node/595.

[14] Government of Canada, Public Service Commission, Recourse Branch, "Workplace Conflict? Making the Right Choice," July 2000.

[15] Statistics Canada, "Sources of Workplace Stress," *The Daily*, June 25, 2003, accessed July 1, 2011, http://www.statcan.gc.ca/pub/75-001-x/00603/6533-eng.html.

[16] Bernard Morrow and Lauren M. Bernardi, "Resolving Workplace Disputes," *Canadian Manager* 24, no. 1 (Spring 1999): 17.

[17] Nora Wood, "Singled Out," *Incentive*, July 1998, 20–23.

Chapter 7

[1] Maria Duncan, personal interview, April 28, 2005.

[2] Mohan R. Limaye, "Further Conceptualization of Explanations in Negative Messages," *Business Communication Quarterly*, June 1997, 46.

[3] Elizabeth M. Dorn, "Case Method Instruction in the Business Writing Classroom," *Business Communication Quarterly*, March 1999, 51–52.

[4] Marcia Mascolini, "Another Look at Teaching the External Negative Message," *Bulletin of the Association for Business Communication*, June 1994, 47.

[5] "Collection Letters," *CreditGuru.com*, accessed April 30, 2005, http://www.creditguru.com/collection.htm.

[6] Michael Granberry, "Lingerie Chain Fined $100,000 for Gift Certificates," *Los Angeles Times*, November 14, 1992, D3.

[7] See note 3 above.

[8] Based on "SUV Surprise," *Wall Street Journal*, June 15, 2004, W7.

Chapter 8

[1] Heather Jack, personal interview, May 12, 2005.

[2] S. Klie, "LGBT Employees Still Face Barriers," *Canadian HR Reporter*, 13 July 2009, 8, accessed February 4, 2011, CBCA Business (Proquest).

[3] M. Theodore Farries II, Jeanne D. Maes, and Ulla K. Bunz, "References and Bibliography: Citing the Internet," *Journal of Applied Business Research*, Summer 1998, 33–36.

Chapter 9

[1] Len Willschick, personal interview, May 24, 2005.

[2] Herman Holtz, *The Consultant's Guide to Proposal Writing* (New York: John Wiley, 1990), 188.

[3] Joel Deane, "Why is the Web Like an Iceberg?" accessed July 28, 2011, http://www.zdnet.com/news/why-is-the-web-like-an-iceberg/102729; and Kimberly A. Killmer and Nicole B. Koppel, "So Much Information, So Little Time: Evaluating Web Resources With Search Engines," *THE Journal*, accessed June 6, 2008, http://www.thejournal.com/articles/16051.

[4] Leslie Brooks Suzukamo, "Search Engines Become Popular for Fact-Finding, Game Playing," July 3, 2002, *Knight-Ridder/Tribune News Service*, K6110.

[5] "Integrated Web Services: Technologies and Definitions," Cornell University, 2008, accessed June 6, 2008, http://iws.cit.cornell.edu/iws2/technology/techinfo.crm.

[6] William M. Bulkeley, "Marketers Scan Blogs for Brand Insights," *Wall Street Journal*, June 23, 2005, B1, accessed June 6, 2008, http://online.wsj.com.

[7] Benjamin Pimentel, "Writing the Codes on Blogs: Companies Figure Out What's OK, What's Not in Online Realm," *San Francisco Chronicle*, June 13, 2001, E1, accessed June 6, 2008, http://www.sfgate.com/cgi-bin/article.cgi?file=/c/a/2005/06/13/BLOG.TMP.

8 William Beutler, "Yes, but How Many Blogs Are There Really?" *Blog, P.I.*, April 10, 2007, accessed June 6, 2008, http://www.blogpi.net/yes-but-how-many-blogs-are-there-really.

9 Stephen Baker and Heather Green, "Beyond Blogs: What Business Needs to Know," *BusinessWeek Online*, May 22, 2008, accessed June 6, 2008, http://www.businessweek.com/magazine/content/08_22/b4086044617865.htm?chan=search.

10 See note 9 above.

11 Sarah Schmidt, "Older Profs More Worried About Net-Savvy Cheaters," *Ottawa Citizen*, October 21, 2006, accessed July 3, 2008, http://www.canada.com/ottawacitizen/story.html?id=030b0bdb-2b0d-4ccd-9260-f4b7ce328f93&k=83050.

12 Based on Karen S. Sterkel, "Integrating Intercultural Communication and Report Writing in the Communication Class," *The Bulletin of the Association for Business Communication*, 1988, 14–16.

13 Based on Sarah Skidmore, "Some Retailers Give Vinyl Records a Spin," *Los Angeles Times*, June 10, 2008, C6.

14 Don Tapscott, and Anthony D. Williams, "The Wiki Workplace," *Business Week Online*, March 26, 2007, accessed June 10, 2008, http://www.businessweek.com/innovate/content/mar2007/id20070326_237620.htm.

Chapter 10

1 Orna Spira, personal interview, March 2, 2011.

2 Patricia M. Buhler, "Workplace Civility: Has It Fallen by the Wayside?" *SuperVision*, April 2003, 20, accessed June 24, 2008, ProQuest database.

3 "Civility," Wikipedia, accessed June 20, 2008, http://en.wikipedia.org/wiki/Wikipedia:CIV.

4 Dorothea Johnson, "Dine Like a Diplomat," Seminar Script, The Protocol School of Washington, 1998–2006.

5 Karl Albrecht, *Social Intelligence: The New Science of Success* (San Francisco: Pfeiffer, 2005), 3.

6 John T. Molloy, *New Dress for Success* (New York: Warner Books, 1988), 13–14.

7 Douglas Chismar, "Vice and Virtue in Everyday (Business) Life," *Journal of Business Ethics* 29 (2001): 169–76.

8 Tash Hughes, "Being a Professional," *Wordconstructions.com*, accessed June 16, 2008, http://www.wordconstructions.com/articles/business/professional.html; and Cornelius Grove and Willa Hallowell, "The Seven Balancing Acts of Professional Behavior in the United States: A Cultural Values Perspective," *Grovewell.com*, accessed July 18, 2008, http://www.grovewell.com/pub-usa-professional.html.

9 Paul Brent, "Soft Skills Speak Volumes," *CA Magazine* 139 (November 2006): 112, accessed June 16, 2008, ProQuest database.

10 Michael Laff, "Wanted: CFOs With Communications Skills," *T+D* 60, no. 12 (December 2006): 20, accessed July 28, 2011, http://www.pecktraining.com/articles.html.

11 Shearlean Duke, "E-Mail: Essential in Media Relations, But No Replacement for Face-to-Face Communication," *Public Relations Quarterly*, Winter 2001, 19; Lisa M. Flaherty, Kevin J. Pearce, and Rebecca B. Rubin, "Internet and Face-to-Face Communication: Not Functional Alternatives," *Communication Quarterly*, Summer 1998, 250.

12 Aimee L. Drolet and Michael W. Morris, "Rapport in Conflict Resolution: Accounting for How Face-to-Face Contact Fosters Mutual Cooperation in Mixed-Motive Conflicts," *Journal of Experimental Social Psychology*, January 2000, 26.

13 Jean Miculka, *Speaking for Success* (Cincinnati: South-Western, 1999), 19.

14 Cheryl Hamilton with Cordell Parker, *Communicating for Success*, 6th ed. (Belmont, CA: Wadsworth, 2001), 100–104.

15 Miculka, *Speaking*, 127.

16 "Fire Up Your Phone Skills," *Successful Meetings*, November 2000, 30.

17 Winston Fletcher, "How to Make Sure It's a Good Call," *Management Today*, February 2000, 34.

18 "Did You Know That . . . ," *Boardroom Reports*, August 15, 1992.

19 Elizabeth Guilday, "Voicemail Like a Pro," *Training & Development*, October 2000, 68.

20 Gail Edmondson, "BMW's Dream Factory," *Business Week*, October 16, 2006, 80, accessed June 17, 2008, http://www.businessweek.com/magazine/content/06_42/b4005072.htm.

21 M. Katherine Brown, Brenda Huettner, and Charlene James-Tanny, *Managing Virtual Teams: Getting the Most of Wikis, Blogs, and Other Collaborative Tools* (Plano, TX: Wordware Publishing, 2007); and Jessica Lipnack and Jeffrey Stamps, *Virtual Teams: People Working Across Boundaries With Technology*, 2nd ed. (New York: Wiley, 2000), 18.

22 Gale Cutler, "Mike Leads His First Virtual Team," *Research-Technology Management* 50, no. 1 (January–February 2007): 66, accessed June 17, 2008, ABI/INFORM database.

23 A. C. Amason, W. A. Hochwarter, K. R. Thompson, and A. W. Harrison, "Conflict: An Important Dimension in Successful Management Teams," *Organizational Dynamics* 24, no. 2 (Autumn 1995): 1, accessed June 17, 2008, EBSCO database; and Richard Romando, "Advantages of Corporate Team Building," *Ezine Articles* (November 9, 2006), accessed June 17, 2008, http://ezinearticles.com/?Advantages-of-Corporate-Team-Building&id=352961.

24 Betsy Ruffin, "T.E.A.M. Work: Technologists, Educators, and Media Specialists Collaborating," *Library Media Connection* 24, no. 4 (January 2006): 49, accessed June 20, 2008, EBSCO database.

25 Jon R. Katzenbach and Douglas K. Smith, *The Wisdom of Teams* (New York: HarperBusiness, 1994), 45.

26 Sarah Fister Gale, "Common Ground," *PM Network*, July 2006, 48, accessed June 17, 2008, EBSCO database.

27 Hal Lancaster, "Learning Some Ways to Make Meetings Slightly Less Awful," *Wall Street Journal*, May 26, 1998, B1.

28 Tom McDonald, "Minimizing Meetings," *Successful Meetings*, June 1996, 24.

29 "I've Got to Go to Another . . . Meeting," *Interventions: The EFAP Journal of CMR Canada*, November 2000, accessed May 25, 2005, http://www.cmrcanada.ca/InterventionsNov2000.html.

30 John C. Bruening, "There's Good News About Meetings," *Managing Office Technology*, July 1996, 24–25.

31 Kirsten Schabacker, "A Short, Snappy Guide to Meaningful Meetings," *Working Women*, June 1991, 73.

32 J. Keith Cook, "Try These Eight Guidelines for More Effective Meetings," *Communication Briefings* Bonus Item, April 1995, 8a. See also Morey Stettner, "How to Manage a Corporate Motormouth," *Investor's Business Daily*, October 8, 1998, A1.

33 Hamilton and Parker, *Communicating*, 311–12.

Chapter 11

1 Lee Jacobson, personal interview, March 3, 2011.

2 Bob Hooey, "Speaking for Success!" *Speaking success*, Toastmasters International Web site, accessed June 24, 2008, http://members.shaw.ca/toasted/speaking_succes.htm.

3 Linda Barrington and Jill Casner-Lotto, "Are They Really Ready to Work?" *The Conference Board*, May 2008, accessed June 26, 2008, http://www.conference-board.org/pdf_free/BED-06-Workforce.pdf.

4 Dianna Booher, *Executive's Portfolio of Model Speeches for All Occasions* (Upper Saddle River, NJ: Prentice Hall, 1991), 260.

5 Wharton Applied Research Center, "A Study of the Effects of the Use of Overhead Transparencies on Business Meetings, Final Report" cited in "Short, Snappy Guide to Meaningful Presentations," *Working Woman*, June 1991, 73.

6 Justin Pope, "Business School Requires PowerPoint," *Oakland Tribune*, 5 August 2007, 1, accessed July 1, 2008, ProQuest database.

7 C. Nass, quoted in Tad Simons, "When Was the Last Time PowerPoint Made You Sing?" *Presentations*, July 2001, 6. See also Edward R. Tufte, *The Cognitive Style of PowerPoint: Pitching Out Corrupts Within* (Cheshire, CT: Graphics Press, 2006).

8 Andrew Wahl, "PowerPoint of No Return," *Canadian Business*, November 2003, accessed July 28, 2011, www.sociablemedia .com/PDF/press_canadian_business_11_11_03.pdf.

9 Dianna Booher, *Speak With Confidence: Powerful Presentations That Inform, Inspire, and Persuade* (New York: McGraw-Hill Professional, 2003), 126. See also http://www.indezine.com/ ideas/prescolors.html.

10 Suzanne Bates, *Speak Like a CEO: Secrets for Commanding Attention and Getting Results* (New York: McGraw-Hill Professional, 2005), 113.

11 Joseph Sommerville, "The Seven Deadly Sins of PowerPoint Presentations," *About.com: Entrepreneurs*, accessed June 26, 2008, http://entrepreneurs.about.com/cs/marketing/ a/7sinsofppt.htm.

12 Peter Burrows and Ronald Grover, "Steve Jobs' Magic Kingdom," *BusinessWeek*, February 6, 2006, accessed June 26, 2008, http://www.businessweek.com; see also Carmine Gallo, "How to Wow 'em Like Steve Jobs," *BusinessWeek*, April 6, 2006, accessed June 26, 2008, http://www.businessweek.com.

13 See http://www.tlccreative.com/images/tutorials/ PreShowChecklist.pdf.

14 John Ellwood, "Less PowerPoint, More Powerful Points," *Times* (London) August 4, 2004, 6.

15 See more information at http://www.stthomas.edu/irt/support/ adobeconnect/presenter.html.

16 Robert J. Boeri, "Fear of Flying? Or the Mail? Try the Web Conferencing Cure," *Emedia Magazine*, March 2002, 49.

17 Booher, *Executive's Portfolio*, 259.

18 Michael Jackson, quoted in "Garbage In, Garbage Out," *Consumer Reports*, December 1992, 755.

Chapter 12

1 "Will Facebook kill the resume? Social networking catching up fast, managers' poll finds," *Victoria Times Colonist*, February 18, 2011, B6, accessed July 28, 2011, Canadian Newsstand Database.

2 Gordon Betcherman, *The Canadian Workplace in Transition* (Kingston, ON: IRC Press, 1994).

3 Ibid., 11.

4 Olga Kharif, "Online Job Sites Battle for Share," *BusinessWeek*, January 3, 2007, accessed July 8, 2008, http://www.businessweek.com/technology/content/jan2007/ tc20070103_369308.htm.

5 Phyllis Korkki, "So Easy to Apply, So Hard to Be Noticed," *New York Times*, July 1, 2007, accessed July 8, 2008, LexisNexis database.

6 Katy Marquardt, "5 Tips on Finding a New Job," *U.S. News & World Report*, February 21, 2008, accessed July 6, 2008, http://www.usnews.com/articles/business/ careers/2008/02/21/5-tips-on-finding-a-new-job.html.

7 Gerry Crispin and Mark Mehler, "Impact of the Internet on Source of Hires—2002," *CareerXroads.com*, January 2003,

accessed July 6, 2008, http://www.careerxroads.com/ news/03sourceofhire.html.

8 Liz Ryan, "Online Job Searching," *BusinessWeek*, video interview, accessed July 21, 2011, http://www.businessweek .com/mediacenter/video/managing/5e1ec1bacf73ae689d381f30e 80dfea30cd52108.html.

9 Lorraine Farquharson, "Technology Special Report: The Best Way to Find a Job," *Wall Street Journal*, September 15, 2003, R8, accessed July 28, 2011, http://articles.chicagotribune .com/2003-09-24/business/0309240303_1_sites-focus-on -particular-industries-job-boards.

10 Aili McConnon, "Social Networking Graduates and Hits the Job Market," *BusinessWeek*, August 30, 2007, accessed July 8, 2008, http://www.businessweek.com/innovate/content/ aug2007/id20070830_886412.htm?chan=search.

11 Ibid.

12 Joel Cheesman, quoted in Liz Wolgemuth, "Using the Web to Search for a Job," *U.S. News & World Report*, February 25, 2008, accessed July 28, 2011, http://money.usnews.com/ money/careers/articles/2008/02/25/using-the-web-to-search -for-a-job.

13 Debra Feldman, quoted in Marquardt, "5 Tips."

14 Dan Black, quoted in Emily Brandon, "Tips for Getting That First Job," *U.S. News & World Report*, January 31, 2007, accessed July 8, 2008, http://www.usnews.com/usnews/ biztech/articles/070131/31firstjob.htm.

15 Christopher Jones, "What Do Recruiters Want Anyway?" *Yahoo HotJobs Exclusive* (2007), accessed July 8, 2008, http:// hotjobs.yahoo.com/jobseeker/tools/article_print.html?id=What_ Do_Recruiters_Want_Anyway__20021114–1412.xml.

16 Elizabeth Blackburn-Brockman and Kelly Belanger, "One Page or Two? A National Study of CPA Recruiters' Preferences for Résumé Length," *The Journal of Business Communication*, January 2001, 29–57, accessed July 8, 2008, Sage Journals Online.

17 Kim Isaacs, "How to Decide on Résumé Length," *Monster Career Advice*, accessed July 8, 2008, http://career-advice .monster.com/resumes-cover-letters/resume-writing-tips/how -to-decide-on-resume-length/article.aspx.

18 Anne Fisher, "Does a Resume Have to Be One Page Long?" *CNNMoney.com*, March 29, 2007, accessed July 8, 2008, http://money.cnn.com/2007/03/28/news/economy/resume .fortune/index.htm.

19 Katharine Hansen, "Should You Use a Career Objective on Your Résumé?" *Quintessential Careers*, accessed July 8, 2008, http://www.quintcareers.com/resume_objectives.html.

20 Korkki, "So Easy."

21 David Koeppel, "Those Low Grades in College May Haunt Your Job Search," *New York Times*, December 31, 2006, 1, accessed July 8, 2008, Academic Search Premier (EBSCO) database.

22 Abby Locke, "Is Your Resume Telling the Wrong Story?" accessed July 28, 2011, http://www.bryantassociates.com/ candidates/career_resources/articles/resume_considerations.html.

23 Tom Washington, "Effective Resumes Bring Results to Life," *HM Price*, accessed July 9, 2008, http://www.hmprice.com/ resume.html#3.

24 "The Video Resume Technique," accessed July 9, 2008, http:// www.collegegrad.com/jobsearch/guerrilla-insider-techniques/ the-video-resume-technique/.

25 Tom A. Peter, "Résumés Get a Technology Makeover," *Christian Science Monitor*, March 26, 2007, 13, accessed July 8, 2008, LexisNexis database.

26 Roland E. Kidwell Jr., "'Small' Lies, Big Trouble: The Unfortunate Consequences of Résumé Padding from Janet Cooke to George O'Leary," *Journal of Business Ethics*, May 2004, 175.

27 Clinton D. Korver, "The Ethics of Resume Writing," *BusinessWeek/Harvard Business Online*, May 19, 2008, accessed July 9, 2008, http://www.businessweek.com/print/managing/content/may2008/ca20080527_367723.htm.

28 Sarah E. Needleman, "Why Sneaky Tactics May Not Help Résumé," *Wall Street Journal*, March 6, 2007, B8.

29 Harriet Augustin, "The Written Job Search: A Comparison of the Traditional and a Nontraditional Approach," *The Bulletin of the Association for Business Communication*, September 1991, 13.

30 Korkki, "So Easy."

31 Judith Schroer, "Seek a Job With a Little Help From Your Friends," *USA Today*, November 19, 1990, B1.

Chapter 13

1 Michael Stern, "Dear Sir: You Are an Oaf . . . ," *Canadian Business*, April 1998, 38.

2 "Panel Interview," *Job-Employment-Guide.com*, accessed July 11, 2008, http://www.job-employment-guide.com/panel-interview.html.

3 J. Steven Niznik, "What's a Group Interview?" *About.com: Tech Careers*, accessed July 11, 2008, http://jobsearchtech.about.com/od/interview/l/aa121602.htm.

4 Marc Dorio, *The Complete Idiot's Guide to the Perfect Interview*, 2nd ed. (Indianapolis, IN: Alpha Books, 2000), 217–18.

5 Liz Ryan, "Job Seekers: Prepare Your Stories," *EzineArticles.com*, February 9, 2006, accessed July 19, 2008, http://ezinearticles.com/?Job-Seekers:-Prepare-Your-Stories&id=142327.

6 Alan Finder, "For Some, Online Persona Undermines a Résumé," *New York Times*, June 11, 2006, accessed July 19, 2008, http://www.nytimes.com/2006/06/11/us/11recruit.html?_r=1&scp=1&sq=For%20some,%20online%20persona%20undermines&st=cse&oref=slogin.

7 Sarah E. Needleman, "Need a New Situation? Check the Internet: Recruiters and Job Seekers Find Each Other Through Facebook, 'Fan' Pages, Videos," *Wall Street Journal*, February 12, 2007, B6, accessed July 20, 2008, ProQuest database.

8 Caryl Rae Krannich and Ronald L. Krannich, *Dynamite Answers to Interview Questions* (Manassas Park, VA: Impact Publications, 1994), 46.

9 "Situational Interview," *Money-Zine.com*, accessed July 19, 2008, http://www.money-zine.com/Definitions/Career-Dictionary/Situational-Interview.

10 Daisy Wright, "Tell Stories, Get Hired," *OfficePro* 64, no. 6 (August/September 2004): 32–33, accessed July 19, 2008, Business Source Premier (EBSCO).

11 Joann Lublin, "Notes to Interviewers Should Go Beyond a Simple Thank You," *Wall Street Journal*, February 5, 2008, B1, accessed July 19, 2008, ProQuest database.

12 Ibid.

13 Sarah E. Needleman, "Be Prepared When Opportunity Calls," *Wall Street Journal*, February 7, 2006, B4.

14 Kathryn Lee Bazen, "The Art of the Follow-Up After Job Interviews," *QuintCareers.com*, accessed July 19, 2008, http://www.quintcareers.com/job_interview_follow-up.html.

Index

Voice mail
    best practices for, 289–290
    as communication channel, 37f
    etiquette, 286–290
    outgoing message, 386
Voice over Internet Protocol
    (VoIP), 8f
Voice recognition, 8f
VoIP (Voice over Internet Protocol), 8f
Volin, Kathryn J., 277
Volume, 282, 289
Volunteer work, 346

W

Wahl, Andrew, 318
Ward, Toby, 32
Warranties, 155
"Watch your (digital) mouth"
    (MacArthur), 83
Wealink (networking site), 349
Weaver, Warren, 10, 11
Web
    browsers, 238
    evaluation of resources, 206,
        228, 238
    introduction to, 237–238
    job searching on, 346
    searching tips and techniques,
        238–239
Web 2.0, 31–32
Web conferencing, 9f
Web pages, designing and
    producing, 6
Web presentations, 327

Web seminars, 319
Web sites
    of associations, 348–349
    citing, 430–431, 432
    corporate, 348
    job search, 346–349, 347f
WebEx, 9f
Weblogs, 9f, 37f, 85–86, 159,
    239–240
Weights and measurements, 503
Weinberg, Tamar, 160
Wempen, Faithe, 318
Western culture, characteristics of,
    17–19
White space, 68–69, 87, 363
Whiteboards, 317, 317f
Wikipedia, 31, 159, 239, 277
Wikis, 9f, 37f, 86, 159–160,
    239–240, 271
Willschick, Len, 230
Windows 7 phone, 34
Wipe down transition effect, 326
Wireless devices, 8f
Women, in the workforce, 21
Wong, Tony, 221
Word processing programs, 6–7, 71
WordPress, 241
Wording, appropriate, 65–68
Work environments, changing, 5
Work experiences, in résumés,
    352–354
Workforce diversity, 21–22
Workopolis, 346, 347, 348
Workplace conflict
    confronting, 292–293

    in meetings, 296
    resolving, 171, 285–286
    six-step procedures of dealing
        with, 286
    value of, 271
Workplace language, 2
Works cited list, 242, 252, 261f, 428,
    429–431
World of work, changes in, 5
World Wide Web. See Web
Worst-case/best-case scenarios, 315
Writing
    data organization, 56–59
    effective sentences, 59–61
    first draft, 61
    informal reports, 204–208
    as phase of writing process, 35
    research, 55–56
    technology and, 5–7, 10
Writing plan
    announcing bad news to
        customers and
        employees, 183
    claims, 121
    for e-mail and memo replies, 104
    for information and procedures
        e-mails and memos, 101
    for information or action
        request, 119
    for letter of recommendation, 128
    negative messages, 175
    persuasive claim or complaint, 149
    persuasive requests, 147
    refusing requests or claims, 179
    for replying to claims, 125

    replying to claims, 125
    for request e-mails and
        memos, 103
    sales message, 153
Writing process
    for business messages and oral
        presentations, 34–36
    effective internal messages, 93–94
    for letter of recommendation, 128
    overview of, 34f, 55f, 61f
    replying to requests, 122
    schedule for, 35–36
Writing style for reports,
    206–207, 207f
Written communication, cross-cultural
    audiences, 20

X

Xing (networking site), 349

Y

Yahoo, 238
Yahoo! Messenger, 99
"You," use of, 40–41

Z

Ziba Design, 159–160
Zones of social interaction, 15, 15f